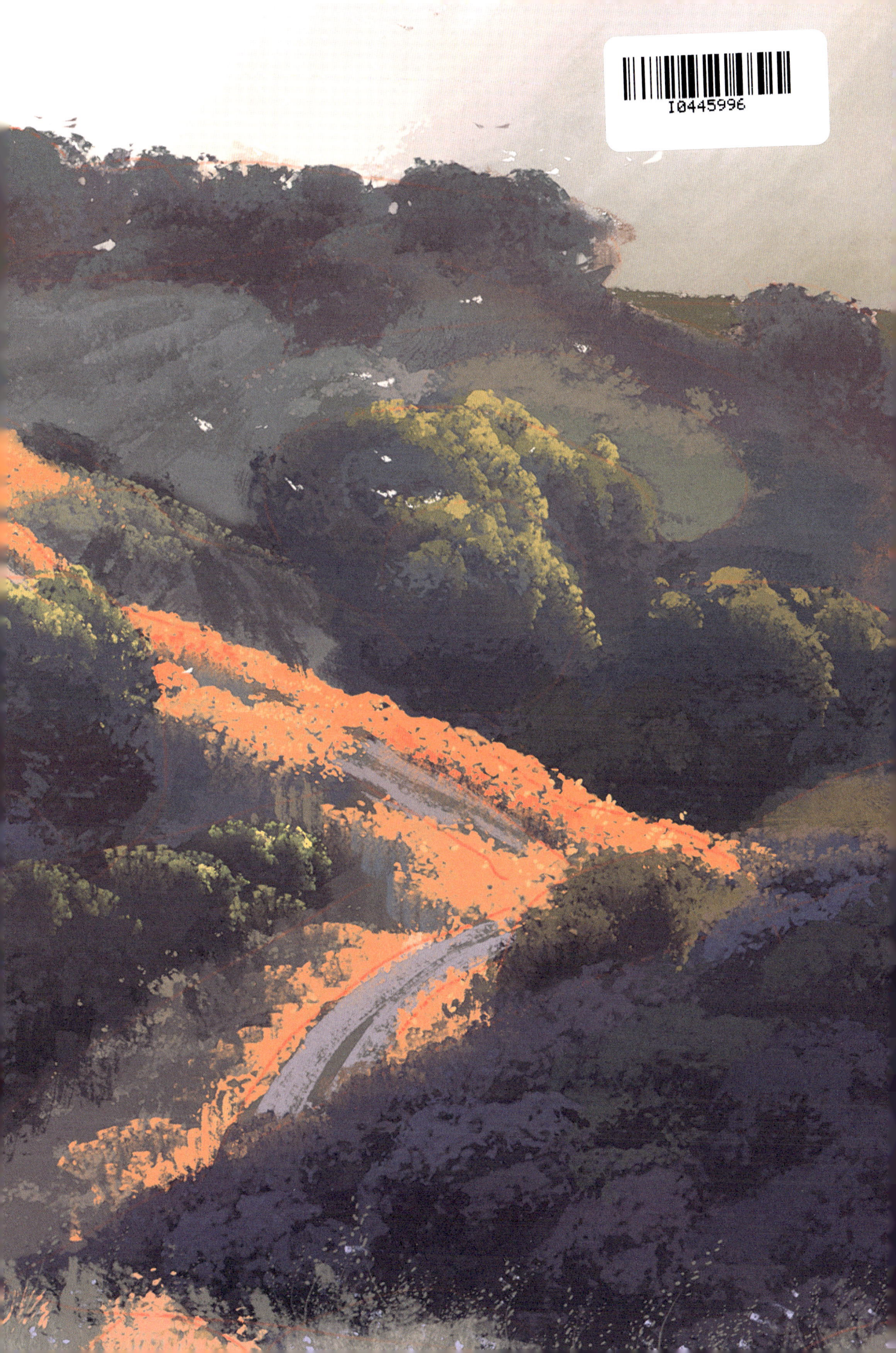

DESIGNING
IMAGINATIVE
ENVIRONMENTS

CREATING LOCATIONS & LANDSCAPES
FOR CONCEPT ART & ILLUSTRATION

NATHAN FOWKES

3dtotalPublishing

Correspondence: publishing@3dtotal.com
Website: store.3dtotal.com

First published in the United Kingdom, 2026, by 3dtotal Publishing.

Address: 3dtotal.com Ltd,
6 Sansome Street, Worcester,
WR1 1UH, United Kingdom.

Hard cover ISBN: 978-1-915992-28-4
Printed and bound in China
by C&C Offset Printing Co., Ltd

Visit **store.3dtotal.com** for a complete list of available book titles.

Editor: Marisa Lewis
Designer: Matthew Lewis
Lead Editor: Samantha Rigby
Lead Designer: Joseph Cartwright
Studio Manager: Simon Morse
Managing Director: Tom Greenway

Cover images © Nathan Fowkes

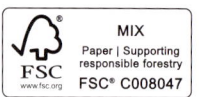

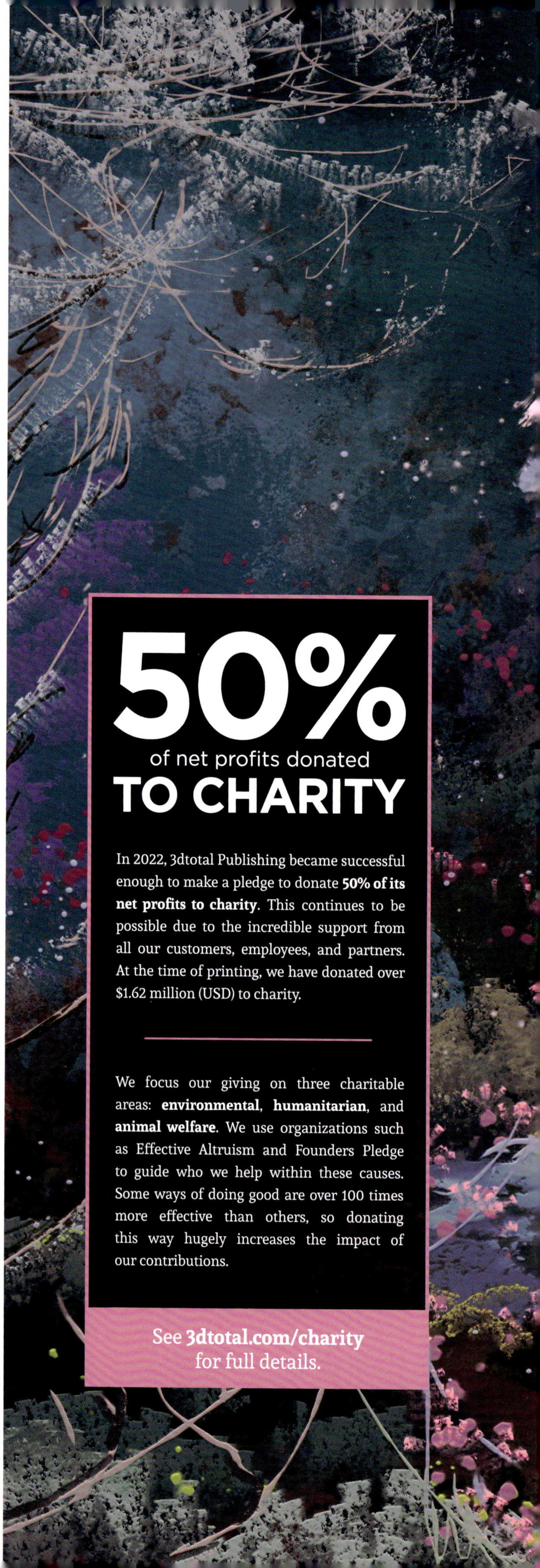

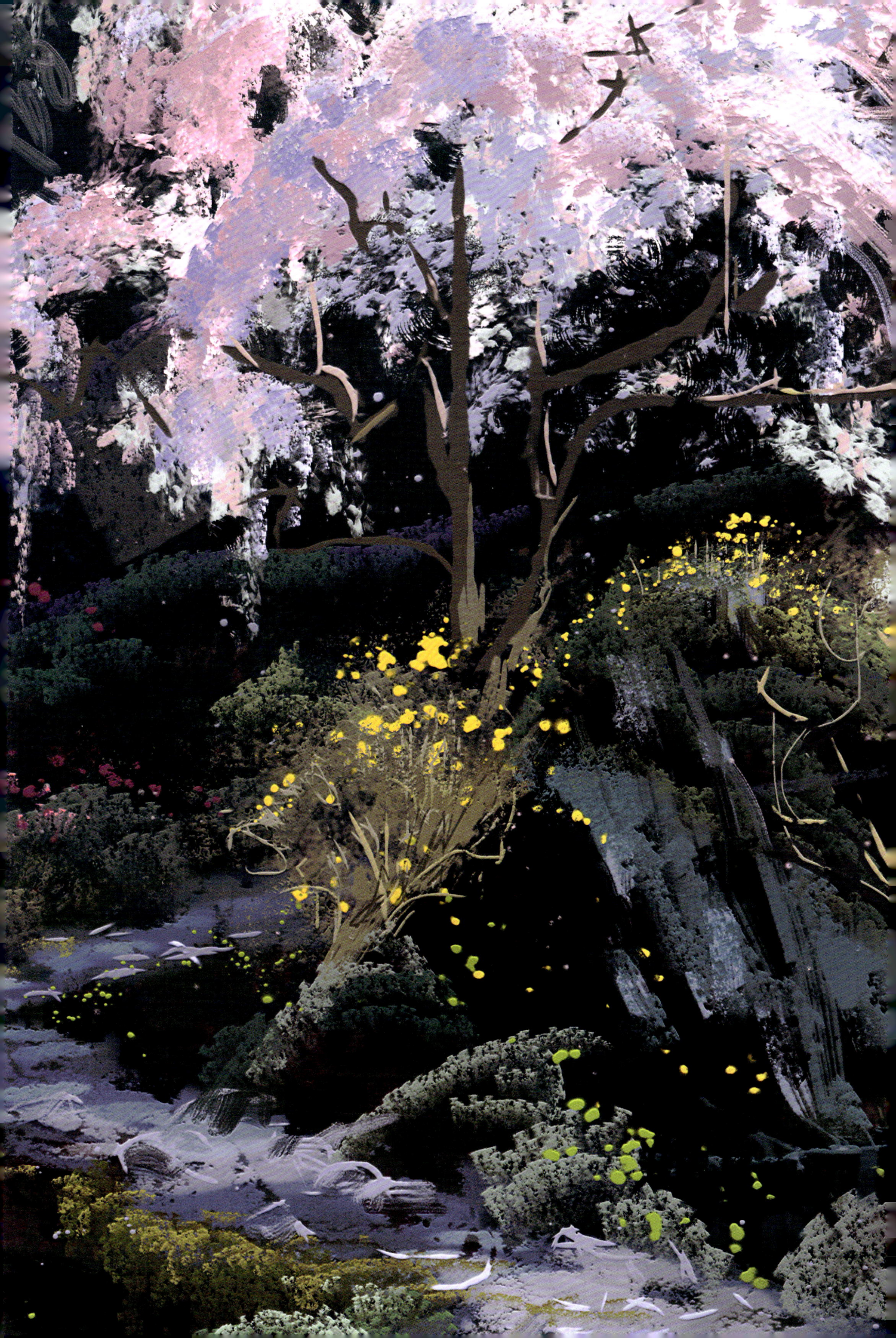

CONTENTS

INTRODUCTION

I've done my best to spend my entire career
with an inquisitive attitude, working on
all these different environments, and it's
my turn to pass it all along to you.

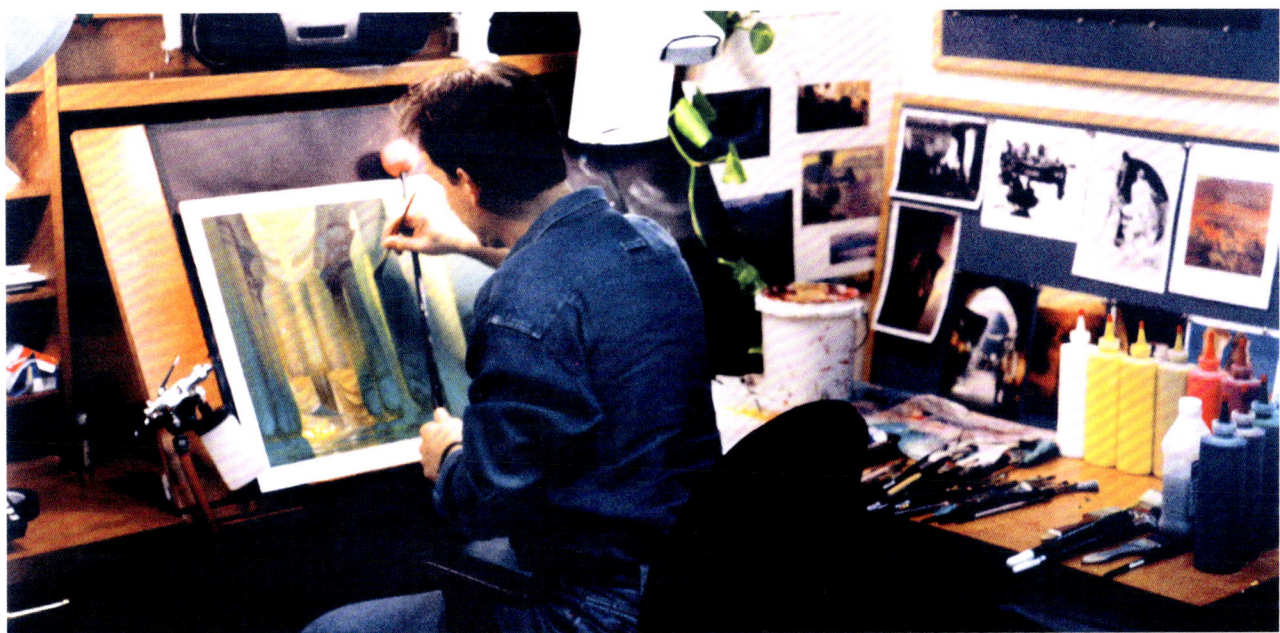

I'm excited to be here with you, because environment design is where we prove our chops as artists. I mean, how do you take a tree or a rock or a mountain or a building and imbue it with purpose and emotion? How do you do that? Emotion is a primary subject of this book because if you can convey emotions visually, you can create extraordinary places, places that your audience can only experience by coming to you, which gives you great value as an artist. So let's figure out how to get good at this. Please allow me to share some thoughts with you to set the stage, and then I'll circle back and dive into the principles of how to create meaningful environments.

I went to art school back in the nineties, and while I was there something happened that changed everything for me. Let me explain. The nineties were a strange time to go to art school, though it's always a strange time to go to art school – art schools are strange places! But back in the nineties, there was a particular trend going on in editorial illustration. For decades, the area where artists could make a living at art commercially was editorial illustration – illustration for magazines, book covers, posters, and so on. This genre had been evolving for decades, with each new generation of artists wanting to bring a new style and a new look, and that's a good thing. Art movements often analyze what's been done before and push away into something new, but they can get kind of weird. As each new style removes itself further from the previous, it's like they end up analyzing themselves out of existence. The editorial illustration that was being done and taught at the time had taken on a very narrow bandwidth. Much of it had deteriorated into a mash-up of dark, brooding imagery. Don't get me wrong, I like dark, brooding artwork, but not all the time – I'm not a dark, brooding kind of guy!

The year was 1993, and I had been in art school for a year and a half doing foundational studies – how to draw, how to paint, how to make pictures – and I loved it! But then I started to get funneled into the editorial-illustration driven classes, because that's what the instructors did for a living. And luckily for me, that's the moment when the big game-changer arrived: the movie *Jurassic Park*!

Maybe it seems quaint now, but at the time we had never seen anything like it. It was big, adventurous, shocking, entertaining; the emotional rollercoaster ride that blockbuster movies are meant to be. Real dinosaurs smashing through real environments – or at least the believable illusion of those things, but, as with every good movie, the experience felt emotionally real. I loved it. I watched it three times in movie theaters, and every time I came home, I felt about two inches tall. I looked at my desk, at the artwork I was doing, and it was kind of pathetic. I had to take my work up to another level, and then a level above that, or I would spend my career feeling small and insignificant.

So after spending a week depressed, I pulled myself out of bed, dusted myself off, and went to my instructors. I told them that I wasn't going to do any more editorial illustration work. I was going to do imaginative events in imaginative environments and that was that. Some were supportive and some were not, but it didn't matter. Something new was on the horizon and I was going to be a part of it or die.

The year was 1995, and I was graduating from art school at the same time that Steven Spielberg (the director of *Jurassic Park*) and Jeffrey Katzenberg (from Disney Animation) launched DreamWorks Animation. They were looking for painters to work on their first animated epic, *The Prince of Egypt*, and I got hired! But it was a close thing. I didn't know at the time, but I found out later that the hiring committee couldn't agree on bringing me on board, as I was a very good painter but without animation experience. I will forever be grateful to the artistic supervisor, Paul Lasaine, who liked my approach to painting, believed in me, and insisted that he wanted me in his department.

I got a three-year contract with the studio, which was amazing, except that it had a six-month provision that if for some reason things didn't work out, and I didn't live up to their expectations, they could let me go. Knowing this, I worked day and night. I worked all day at the studio and then I went home and kept practicing. This project was everything that I had hoped to be a part of: painterly, atmospheric, epic, historic. It was the moment I had trained for my whole life. And my job was ... environment design!

Every scene in the movie was a combination of painted environment and animated characters. I'm not an animator but I painted the scenes by the dozens. The first step was to do what we called 'color keys' – small sketches that worked out the design of a scene, including characters. Though small and loose, they had to have the color, lighting, mood, and atmosphere that were appropriate for each moment in the movie. These color keys would hopefully be approved by the director and then we would paint the finished scene that appeared in the movie. Any animation would be composited on top, plus any visual effects needed to create the final scene.

Professionally it was one of the greatest times of my life. I was in Los Angeles at DreamWorks, surrounded by some of the greatest artists in the world, and that was my real art school. I went to every guest lecture, every life-drawing session. I talked to everybody, gleaning as much knowledge as I could – and there was a lot to glean.

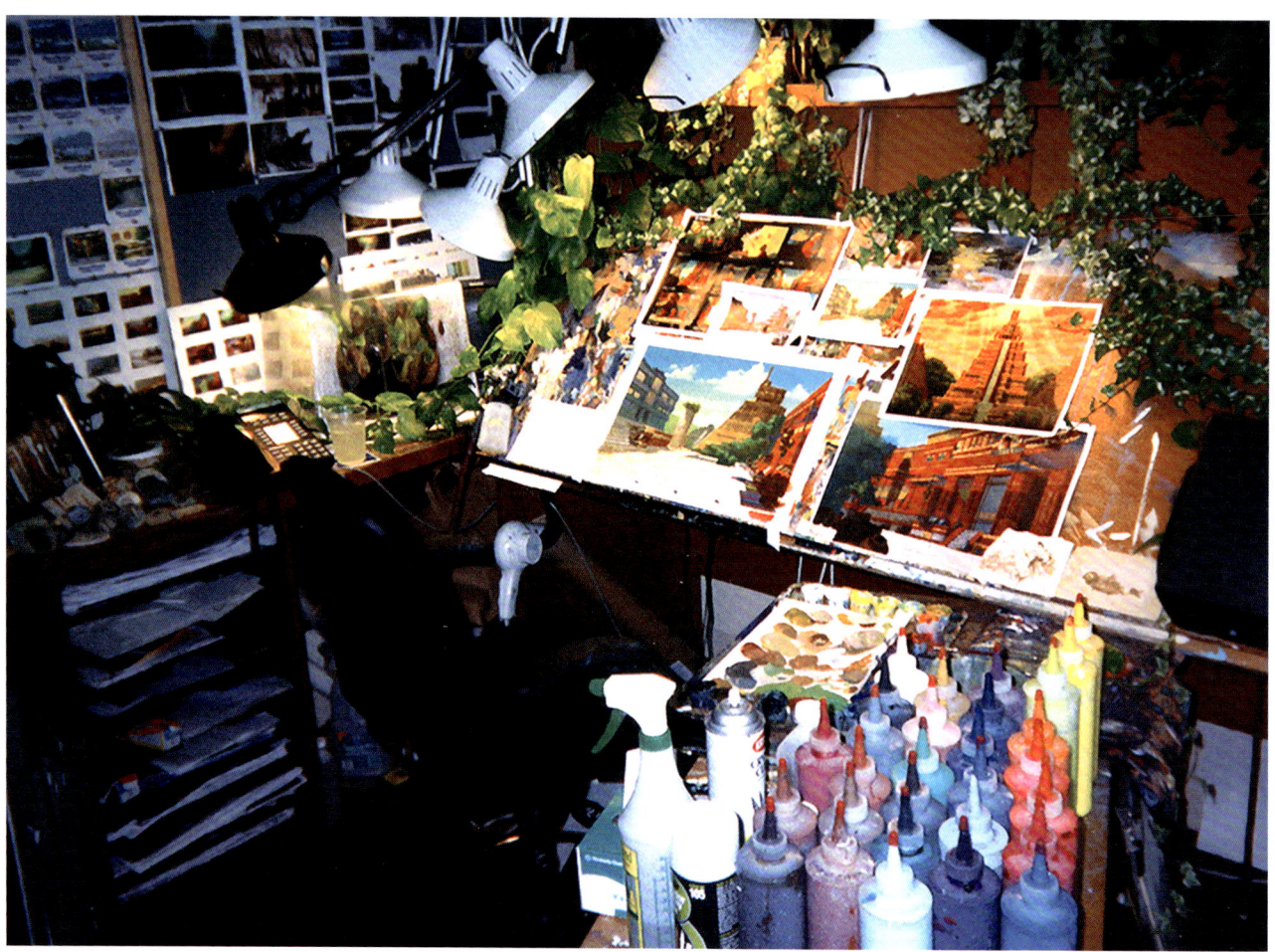

The moment you have the ability to reach out and engage your audience on that gut emotional level where art and storytelling live, you are a real artist.

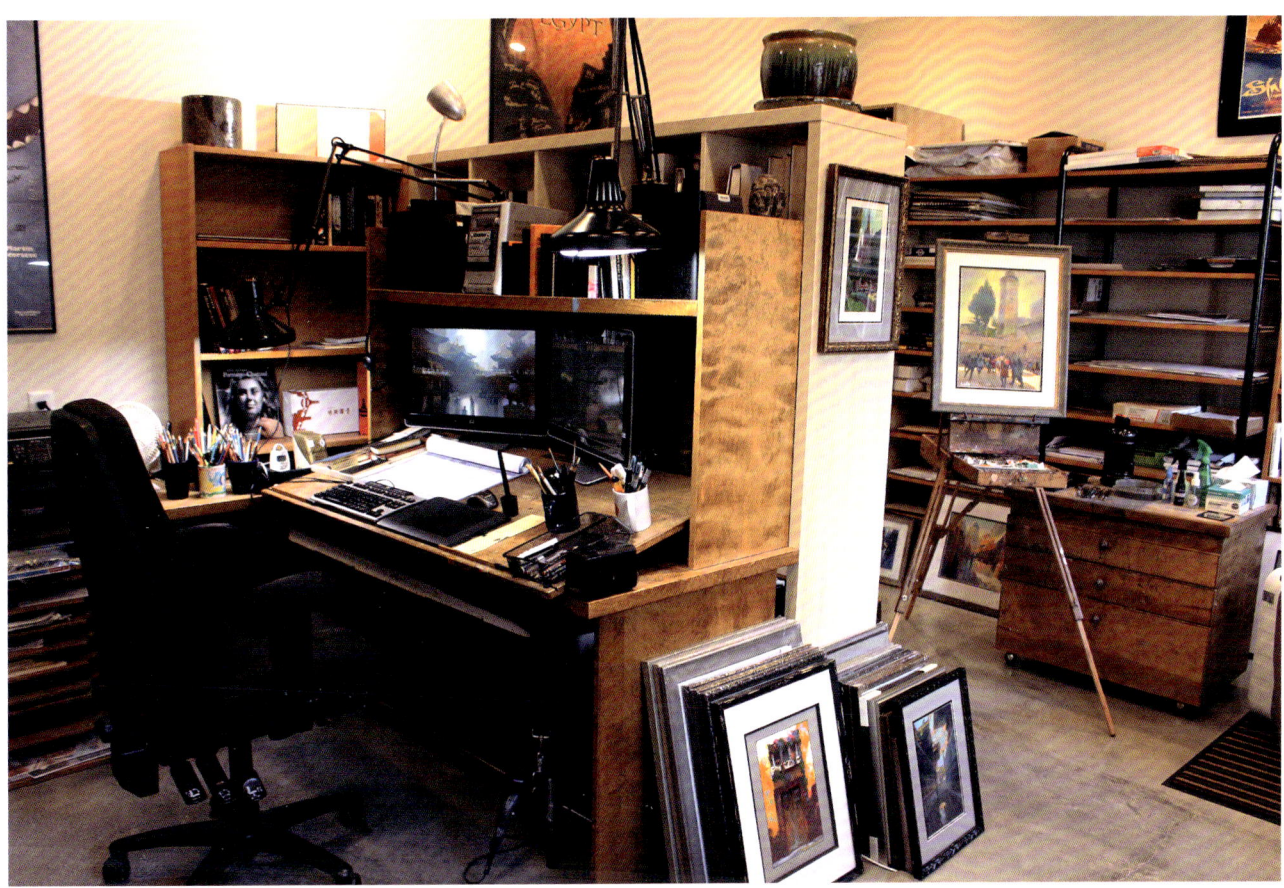

We designed and worked on so many environments over the years. The next movie, *The Road to El Dorado*, was set in sixteenth-century Central America. Then we painted the vast expanses of the American West in *Spirit: Stallion of the Cimarron*, the voyages of *Sinbad: Legend of the Seven Seas*, and under the ocean in *Shark Tale*. We painted the sewers of London in *Flushed Away*, a fairy-tale version of Europe for the *Shrek* and *Puss in Boots* projects, the imagined Nordic fjords of *How to Train Your Dragon*, the Brazilian rainforest of the *Rio* movies, the Spanish bullring of *Ferdinand*, the vast expanse of a fictional Southeast-Asian empire for *Raya and the Last Dragon*, and more!

And so here I am now, decades later. I've done my best to spend my entire career with an inquisitive attitude, working on all these different environments, and it's my turn to pass it all along to you here in this book.

If it seems like I'm going on about all my experience, well, it was often learned the hard way. It took me way too long to understand all I needed to about great storytelling and great environment design. And that's the purpose of this book – saving you from going down all the blind alleys that I did. The best information is condensed into this book, helping you jump to the front of the line with artwork that has a great quality of engagement. No matter how much you might still have to learn, the moment you have the ability to reach out and engage your audience on that gut emotional level where art and storytelling live, you are a real artist.

MAKING REAL IMPROVEMENT

Let's begin your learning process with some daily exercises that can be tremendously helpful. I've mentioned all the extra practice I did while I was starting out at DreamWorks in the nineties, but it didn't end there. At that time, I committed to doing at least one extra practice sketch every day, and I've kept that habit consistently to this day. It's made all the difference as I've weathered layoffs, major periods of change, and other challenges. So I strongly recommend that you commit to the idea of daily practice as well, in these three areas:

• **Master-copy sketches.** I suggest you begin with master studies. We call this 'standing on the shoulders of giants' because you learn by studying great artists and image-makers, and then bring that skill set to your own ideas and the ideas of your clients. I'll give a step-by-step demonstration of this shortly.

• **Sketches from life.** These are critical because the awe-inspiring qualities of nature and the natural environment will inform your work in the best way possible. Life sketching is not the specific focus of this book, but 3dtotal Publishing and I have many other resources available.

• **Sketches from imagination.** If you're an imaginative artist, dreaming up places that don't exist in reality, then you've got to practice sketching from imagination. You've got to make sure that you're able to bring all the knowledge of your master studies and life studies to bear in your imagined work. This book will cover sketching environments from imagination in detail.

RECOMMENDED EXERCISE: MASTER STUDIES

In this exercise, we will be working with a beautifully epic environment: *Buffalo Trail: The Impending Storm*, shown below, by the American artist Albert Bierstadt (1830–1902). I recommend spending one hour or less on a study like this. The limited time helps our practice fit into our busy schedules, but more importantly it forces us to carefully analyze the subject to learn why the image works so well. I like to think through a hierarchy of what might be most important in an image to help me break it down.

It feels as though the primary purpose of this image is to convey the epic authority and majesty of this environment through light, wind, and storm. Note how the force of the wind is conveyed throughout, even in the direction of the moving buffalo herd. I'll focus my efforts on these ideas and leave out less significant details. To keep things simple, I tend to concentrate on only five things – value (the lights and darks), shape, edge, color, and texture – pushing each of these toward the purpose of the painting.

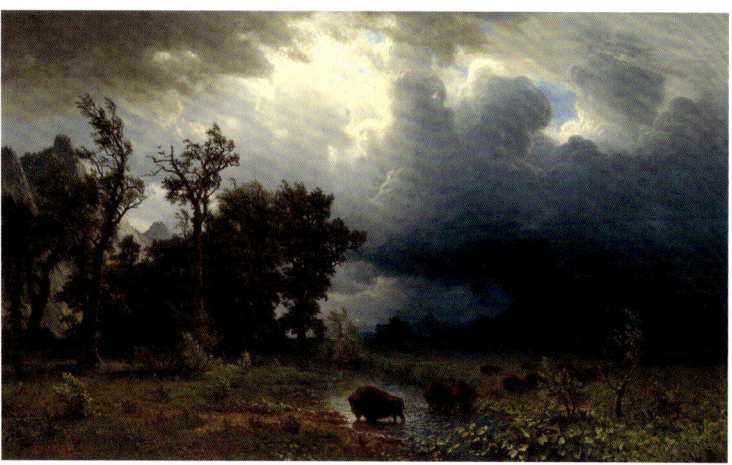
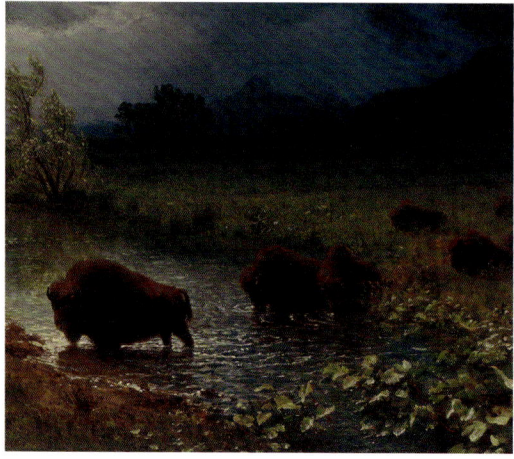

PAINTING TOOLS

For concept and production art, my painting tools are digital. I'm specifically using Adobe Photoshop, which at the time of writing is the industry standard for digital painting. But, frankly, nobody cares what you use as long as you achieve the desired results.

So here's my workspace and some examples of my basic brushes, but this book is not about specific techniques or brushes. You can get all of that for free on the internet and those things change over time. Good principles, however, do not change, and this is a principles-driven book.

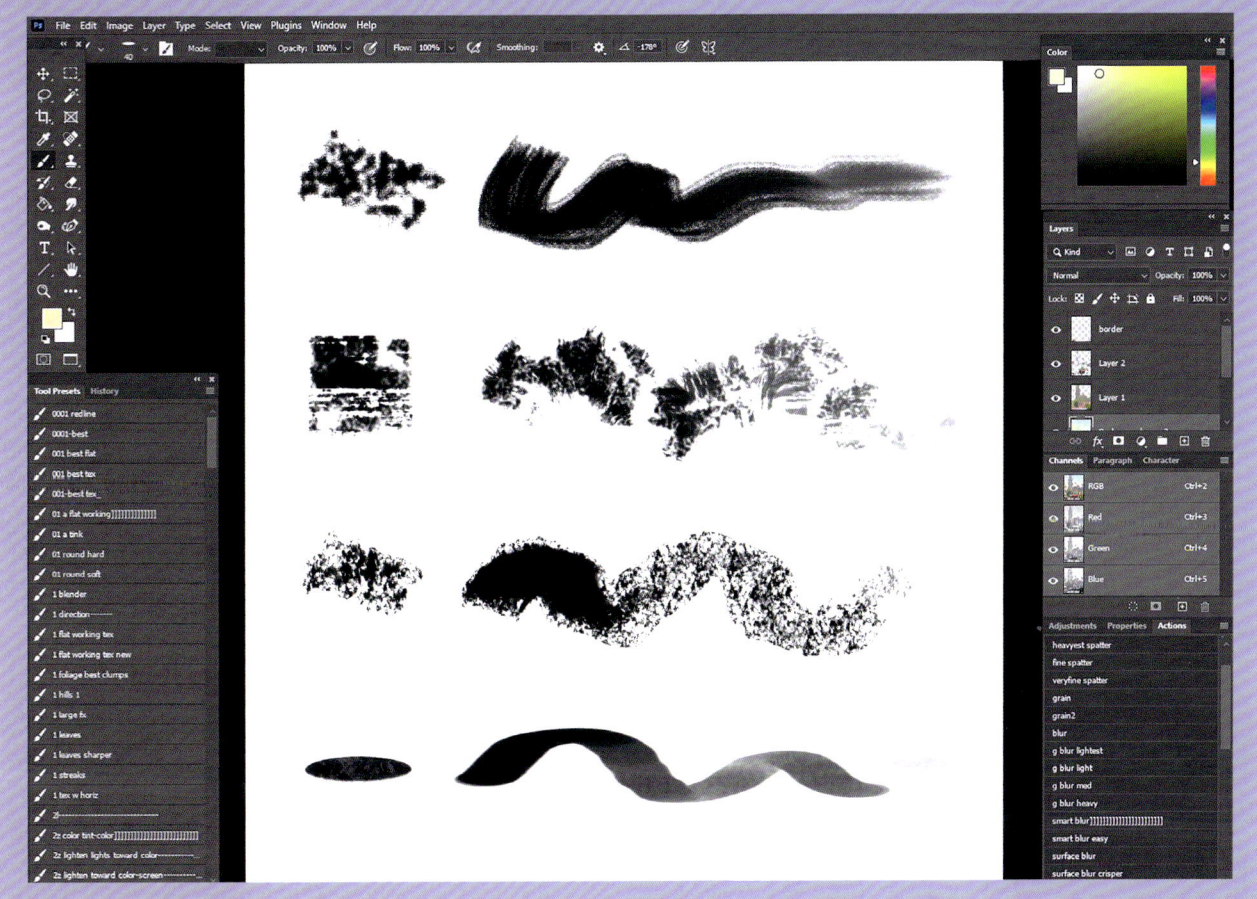

01. SIMPLE SHAPES

Based on Bierstadt's painting, I draw very simple lines to define the big shapes of the environment. I'm not looking for individual elements but how the individual elements form groups and masses.

01. Make a basic sketch of the key elements

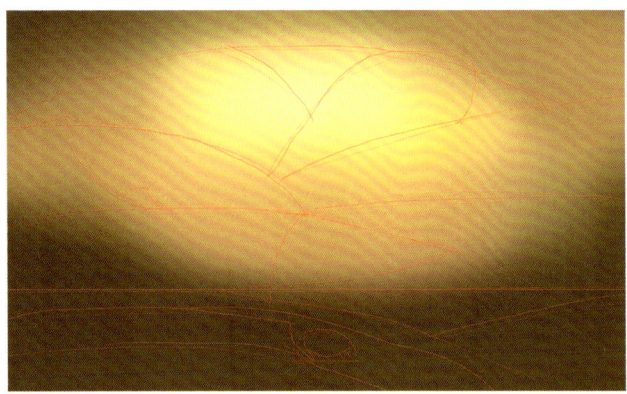

02. Add a rough gradient as a base for the painting

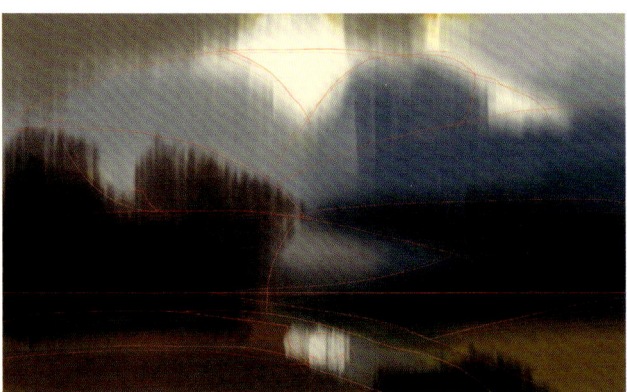

03. Fill out the biggest masses of the scene with color

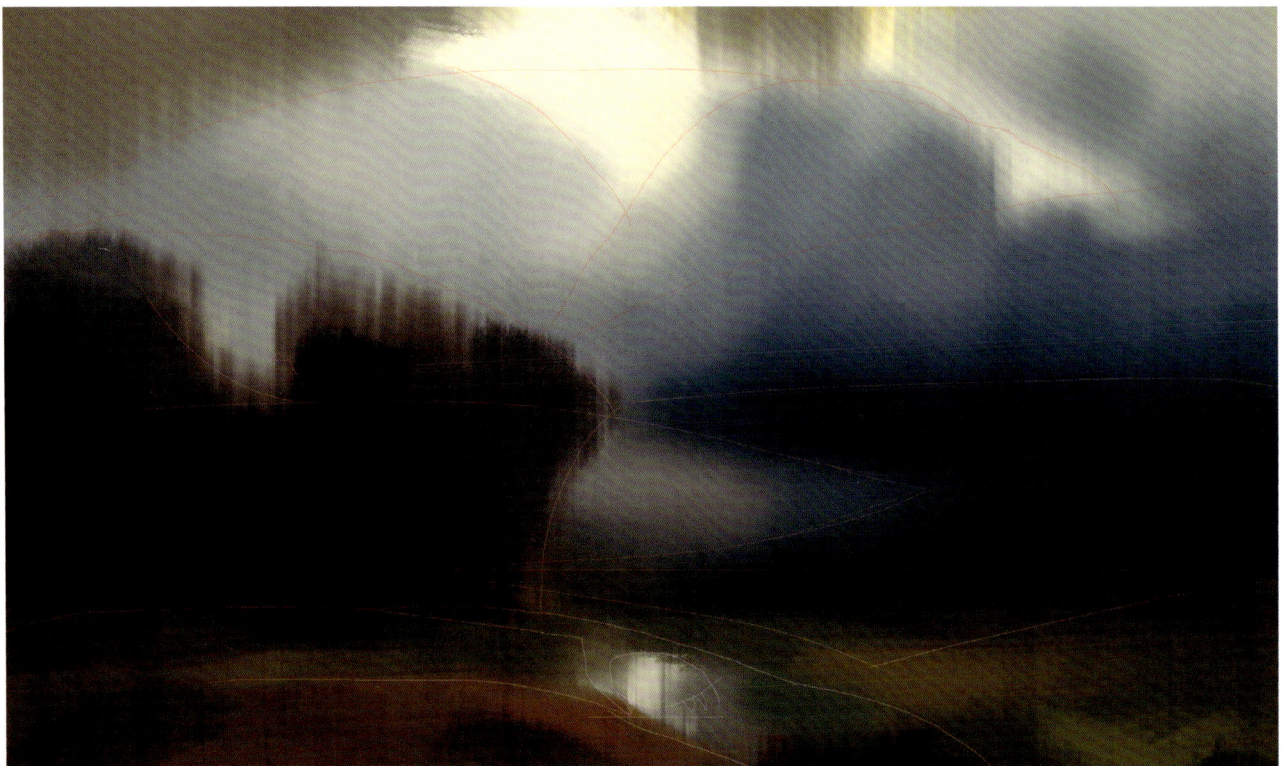

04. Begin clarifying the scene's hard and soft edges

02. BASE GRADIENT

The warm glow of the light and the warm underlying colors of the earth are central to the impact of this painting, so I create a simple gradation beneath the sketch to get the painting process started.

03. MAJOR MASSES

I now create an overall underpainting by searching for the biggest, simplest masses of the environment. You can see here how the line drawing was helpful to get to this very important point.

04. ADD EDGES

Now I think more about the edges of the masses: where they are atmospheric and soft or where they are firmer, especially in the mid-ground and foreground. I also start to add local colors over the top of my brown underpainting – for example, the greens of the prairie grasses.

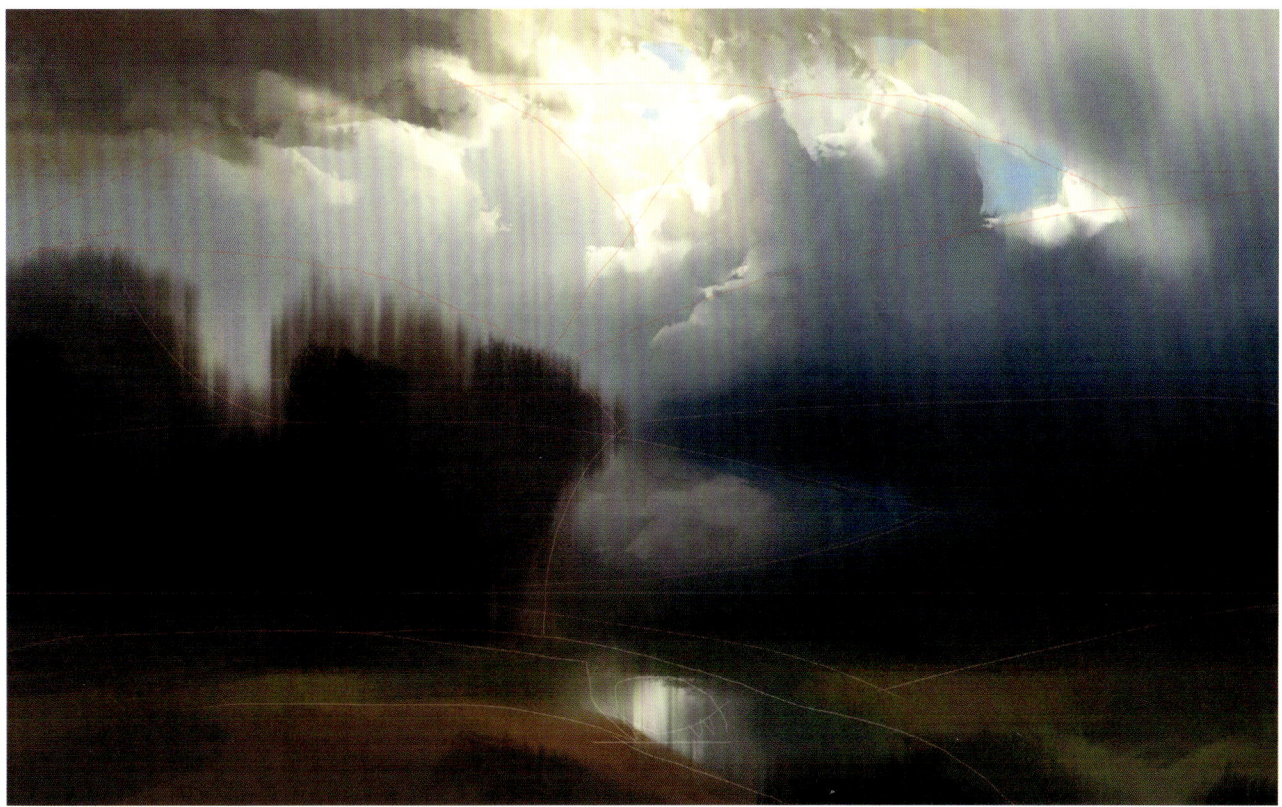

05. The Smudge tool helps give depth to the clouds

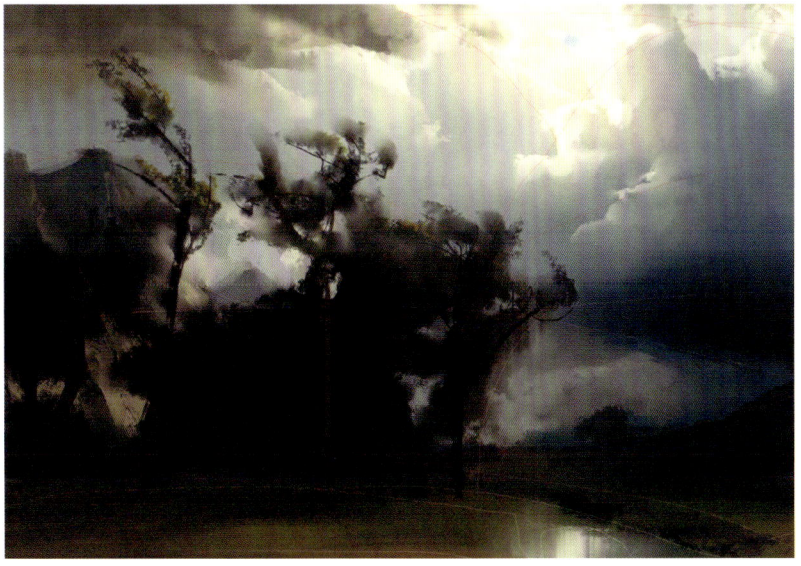

06. Use a textured brush to add definition to the trees

05. SKY LIGHTING

It's time to get specific lighting into the sky. I brush in the lights, making sure my strokes wrap around the forms of the clouds. Then I use Photoshop's Smudge tool to soften appropriate edges to emphasize the lighting's 'wrap-around' effect.

06. TREES

Let's get into the mid-ground now. For the trees, I mass in their shape with a textured brush, as shown in the palette on page 11, then use the Smudge tool to soften the edges and pull the shapes with the flow of the wind. Be sure that every mark you make serves the central purpose of every environment you paint.

> Be sure that every mark you make serves the central purpose of every environment you paint.

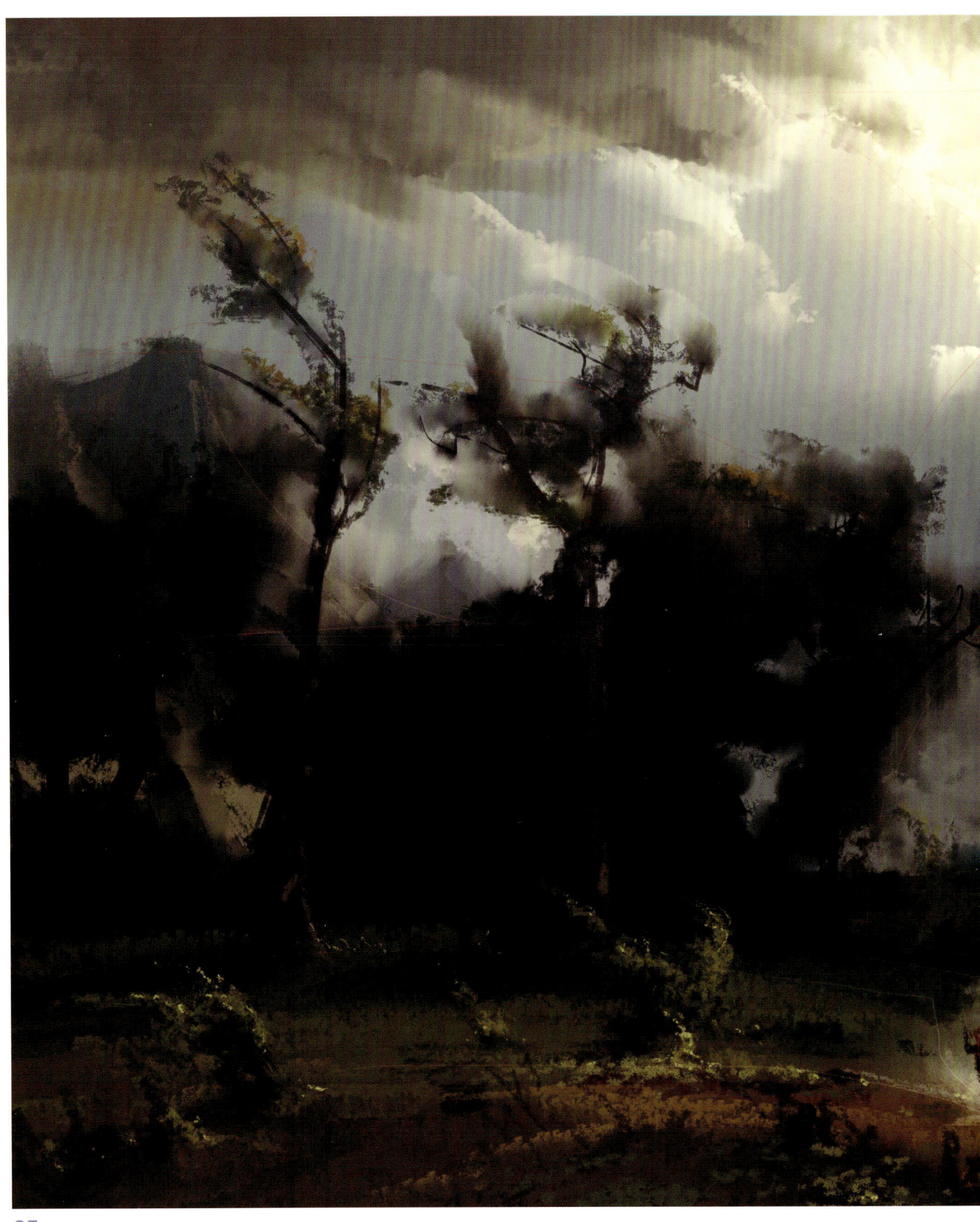

07. The finished 30-minute study

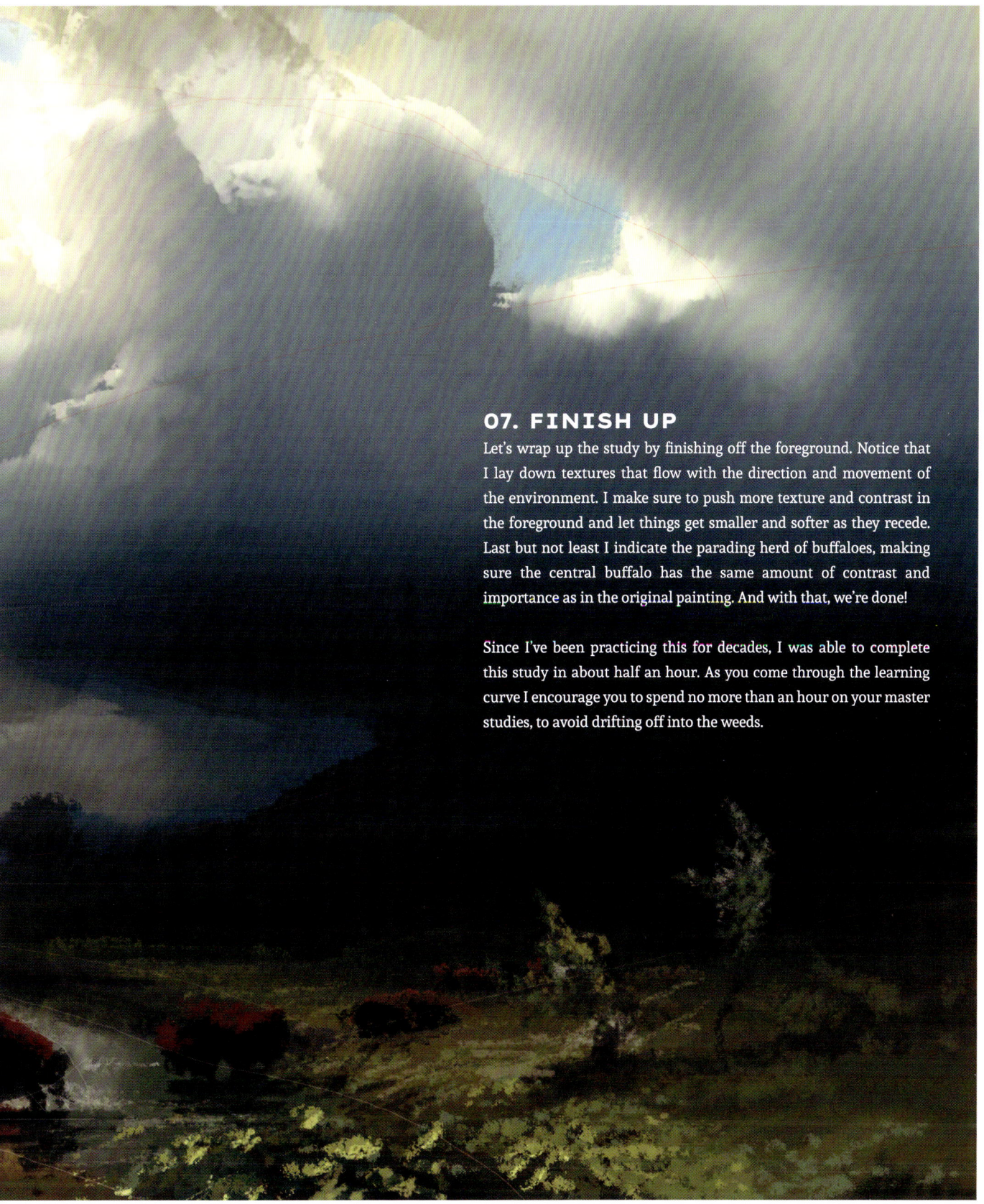

07. FINISH UP

Let's wrap up the study by finishing off the foreground. Notice that I lay down textures that flow with the direction and movement of the environment. I make sure to push more texture and contrast in the foreground and let things get smaller and softer as they recede. Last but not least I indicate the parading herd of buffaloes, making sure the central buffalo has the same amount of contrast and importance as in the original painting. And with that, we're done!

Since I've been practicing this for decades, I was able to complete this study in about half an hour. As you come through the learning curve I encourage you to spend no more than an hour on your master studies, to avoid drifting off into the weeds.

DESIGN &
DEVELOPMENT
PROCESS

If it looks right it is right, and if it
feels right it's even more right.

Let's talk process now, so that as we study principles together you'll understand the context in which they'll be used. Let me share a particular experience with you that will stress how very difficult design and development can be, and why we need clearly defined goals.

FILM PRODUCTION IS LIKE A HORROR MOVIE

The *Shrek* franchise from DreamWorks Animation was something I had a great time working on back in the day. The one spin-off that was a particular adventure was *Puss in Boots*. If you haven't seen those movies, they chronicle an extraordinary little cat's larger-than-life adventures against the backdrop of a magical medieval setting.

An especially difficult environment to design was the cat cantina, a central lair where the cat characters hung out. The difficult question for us was, 'Who built the cantina?' Was it built by cats, or was it built by humans and taken over by cats? We tried roughing out both versions, doing dozens and dozens of sketches, and in the end ... we threw them all out! The cat-built version just didn't feel believable, but the human-built version dwarfed our very small main characters, the cats. In the end we simply went with what felt right: we split the difference but leaned toward a human scale. This led to a maxim of mine: 'If it looks right it is right, and if it feels right it's even more right.'

As movies are developed, a lot of different artists and designers are brought on to solve problems, but not all the solutions take and not all the artists are kept. In fact, it starts feeling like a horror movie, you know, where someone disappears and the others go out the door looking for them but never return. You're left in the dead quiet, whispering to no one, 'Guys, are you there? What happened to everybody?' And there's no answer and never will be. I was once on a production where I came in one day to an entire empty floor. Everyone had been let go from the production except me and I was left to carry on alone, trying to solve these problems, proud that I had survived but fearful that I might be next!

So it's how things look and feel that matters to our audience, or better said, it's the *purpose and emotion* that we generally focus on first. More than anything else, our audience responds to how things feel. I've learned to make that a major consideration in my work and it's a major consideration in what follows here.

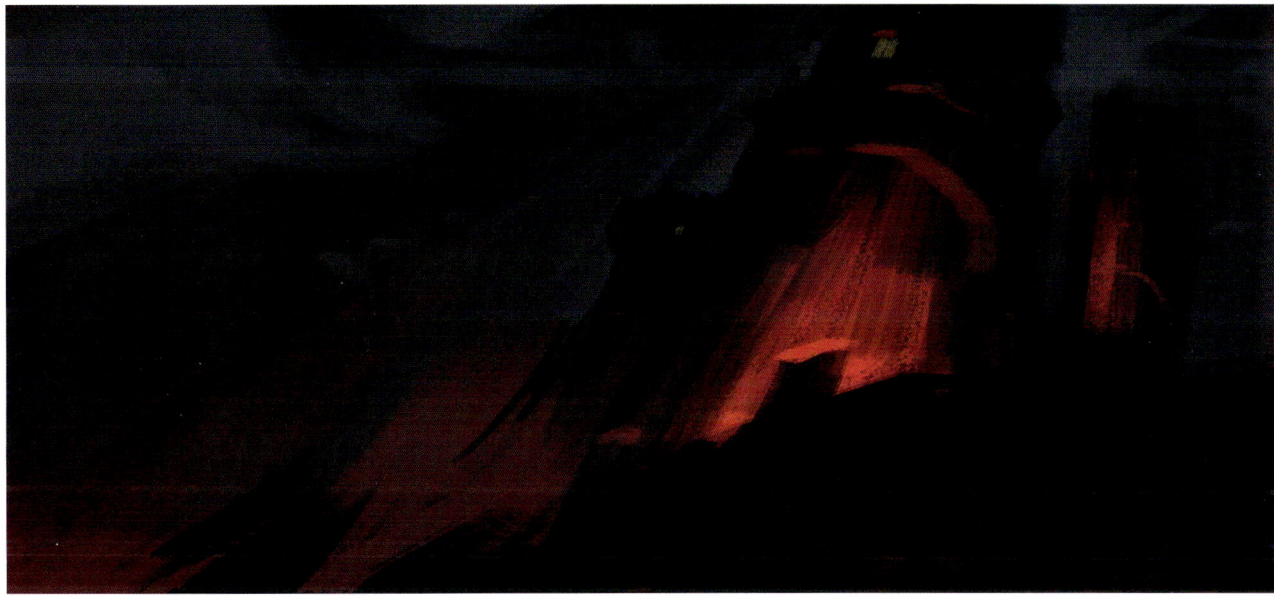

△ Feeling and emotion are essential for connecting with our audience

ENVIRONMENT DESIGN CHECKLIST

Let me give you an environment design checklist to start with. This is a series of questions to help narrow your focus, getting straight to the right quality of environment design for your concept or story. Each of these concepts will be thoroughly addressed as we proceed through the chapters of this book, so don't worry if they seem to require more information. This checklist will be here for you to come back to later.

STORYTELLING BASICS

- What purpose does the environment serve in this story or concept?
- What is the overall emotional quality of the environment?
- What is the point of view? *(The eye level and perspective.)*
- Does the story require an indoor or an outdoor scenario?
- What is the scale of the environment? *(Epic and grand, close and intimate, or anywhere in between.)*

LOCATION & NATURE

- What is the biome of the environment? *(Desert, woods, jungle, swamp, mountains, forest, etc.)*
- What parts of the foliage are alive and new, and what parts are dead or old?
- What is the weather and atmosphere of the environment?
- Are there animals in the environment or birds in the sky?
- Should there be water in the environment? *(Ocean, lake, pond, puddle, river, etc.)*
- What is the age and history of the place?
- What quality of architecture will inform us about the people who live in the environment?

SHAPE, TEXTURE & MOOD

- What objects need to be in the environment and which are most important?
- What quality of shape do the objects have? *(Sharp or smooth, round or angular, etc.)*
- How active or passive is the environment?
- How empty or cluttered is the environment?
- What angles are the objects in the environment? *(Horizontal, vertical, or diagonal.)*
- What is the lighting and time of day (or night)?
- What are the local colors of objects that make up the environment?
- What are the important textures in the environment?

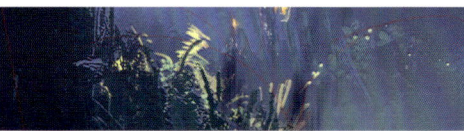

REMINDERS

- What is the most important aspect of the place? Have I focused proper attention on that?
- Have I allowed less-important elements of the environment to become too contrasty, important, and distracting?

PRODUCTION PIPELINE

So let's take a look at the design and development process from the standpoint of animation and video-game projects. We're doing this because, at the time of writing, the vast majority of opportunities as a professional artist are in these and related fields. You might be saying, 'Wait a minute, Nathan. Just like you didn't want to be an editorial artist in the nineties, I don't want to be an animation artist now!' No worries. No matter what kind of artistic work you're headed toward, if it takes place in an environment, it needs design and development, which means you've come to the right place and you're reading the right book! We'll get to that shortly.

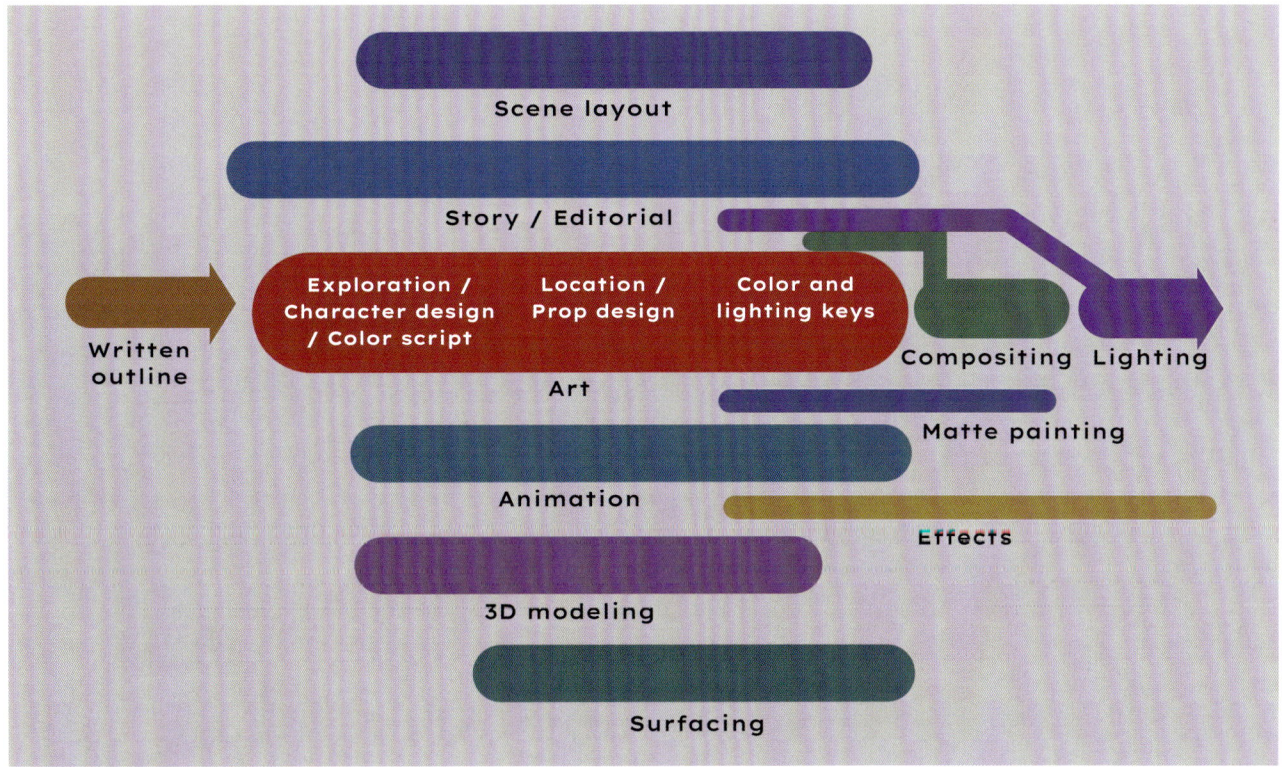

△ A typical design and development pipeline for an animation or game

The great thing about animation and video-game design is that it's an incredibly collaborative process. Everyone is really good at their particular discipline and you can see above how many different disciplines come together to create a project. If you're not 100% sure you want to be a painter or an illustrator, some of the other parts of the pipeline might just be for you. These are skills like 3D modeling, 3D texturing, 3D lighting, matte painting, and so on – all of which are done most successfully with a good knowledge of environment design. Let's focus now on the art department, the section in red.

The process begins with a written outline. We, the art department, review the outline and identify who the characters are, what the environments are, and the key story moments. Then we do exploratory sketches, seeking approval from the director, and refining our work until we get to a final 'look of picture' that is approved by the director and studio. Next we work toward 'final design', the process of identifying every single object that will appear on screen and rendering what their final look will be. These drawings and draftings are passed along to the 3D-modeling department and scene-layout department, where 3D sets are created and camera POVs are set up. At this point we can use these layouts as a basis to paint what we call 'color keys' – paintings that establish the final color, lighting, and look of key scenes in the project.

It's a huge undertaking and can take many years, but it doesn't have to. You might be working on a children's book or a graphic novel, a one-off illustration or personal work. What's the process for those? It's almost the same, so let's take a look at another chart on the next page to illustrate. Then I'll demonstrate for you how to go through the entire process very quickly.

'Wait a minute, Nathan. Just like you didn't want to be an editorial artist in the nineties, I don't want to be an animation artist now!' No worries. No matter what kind of artistic work you're headed toward, if it takes place in an environment, it needs design and development.

CREATIVE PIPELINE FOR ENVIRONMENTS

Our process is to first identify what environment is needed, then identify its story-driven purpose, identify its story-driven emotion, rough out many quick sketches to find the right look, create final roughs to firm up our ideas, and then develop the roughs into final concept paintings.

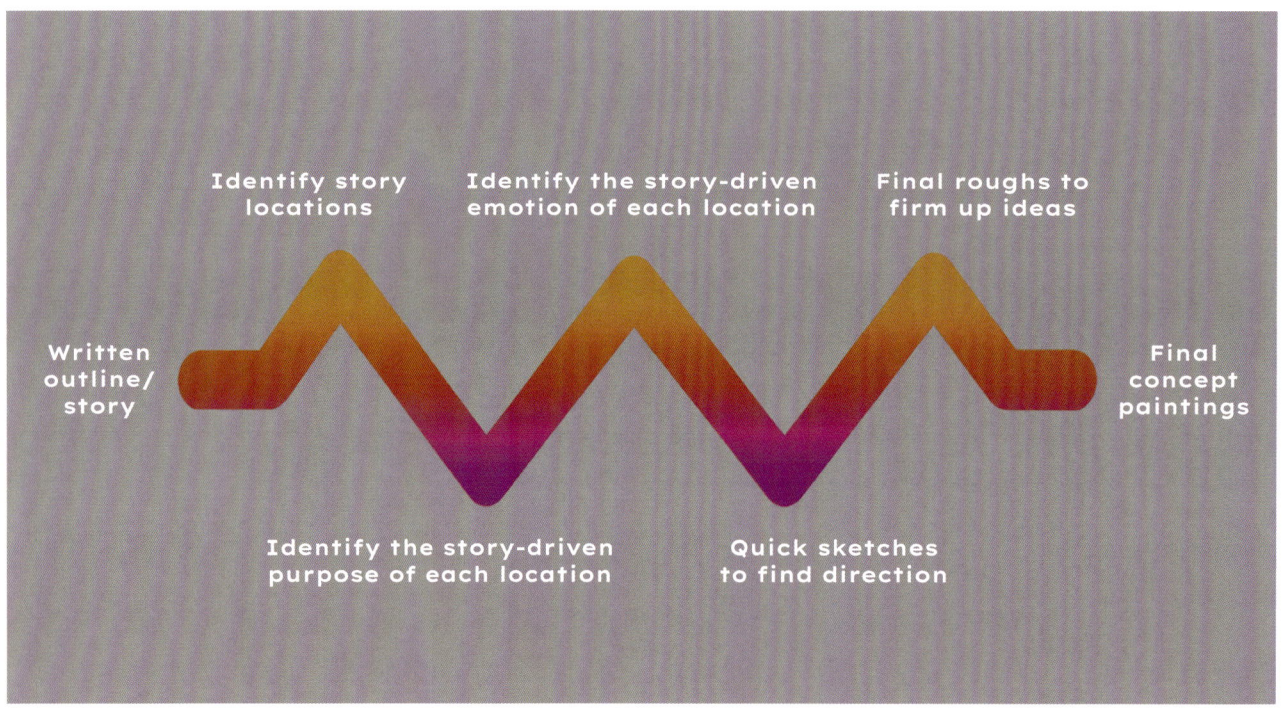

△ This pipeline can apply to a major professional project or a small personal one

This is all easy to say, but now let's do the hard part. I'll demonstrate each step of the process. For starters, we'll keep things very straightforward. Imagine a story where the good guys live in a mighty castle, and the villain also lives in a castle, but that castle looks, well, full of villainy. This will allow us to take the same kind of subjects but treat them completely differently because they serve different purposes in the story.

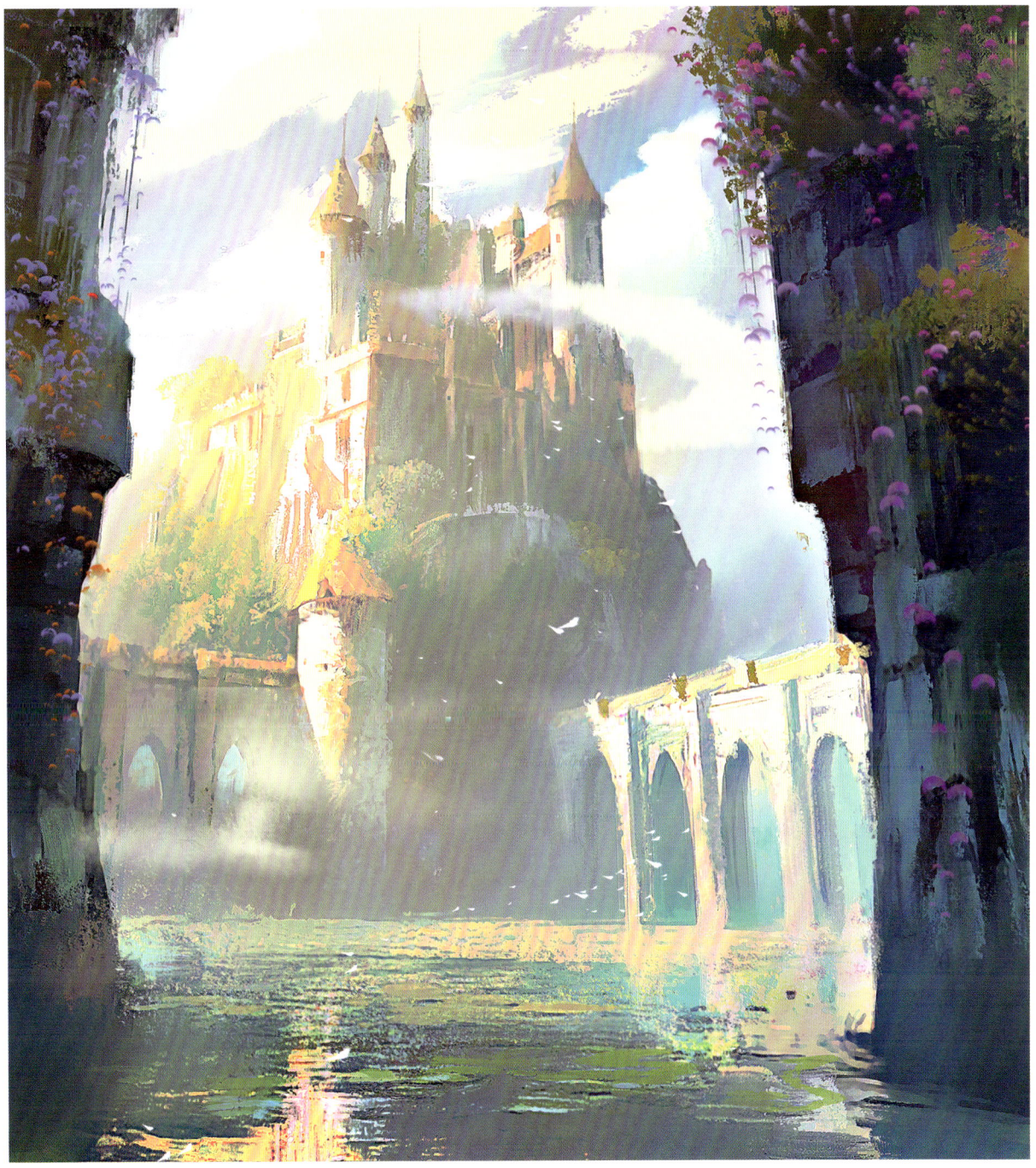

01. Every aspect of this environment emphasizes a quality of goodness and might

01. 'GOOD GUY' CASTLE

The 'good guy' castle must look as such, and so we employ visual elements
that suggest goodness and might. The castle and its environment are:

- tall and proud
- warm
- colorful
- lit by glowing, luminous, late-afternoon backlighting
- surrounded by sweeping clouds
- lush with flowers and birds

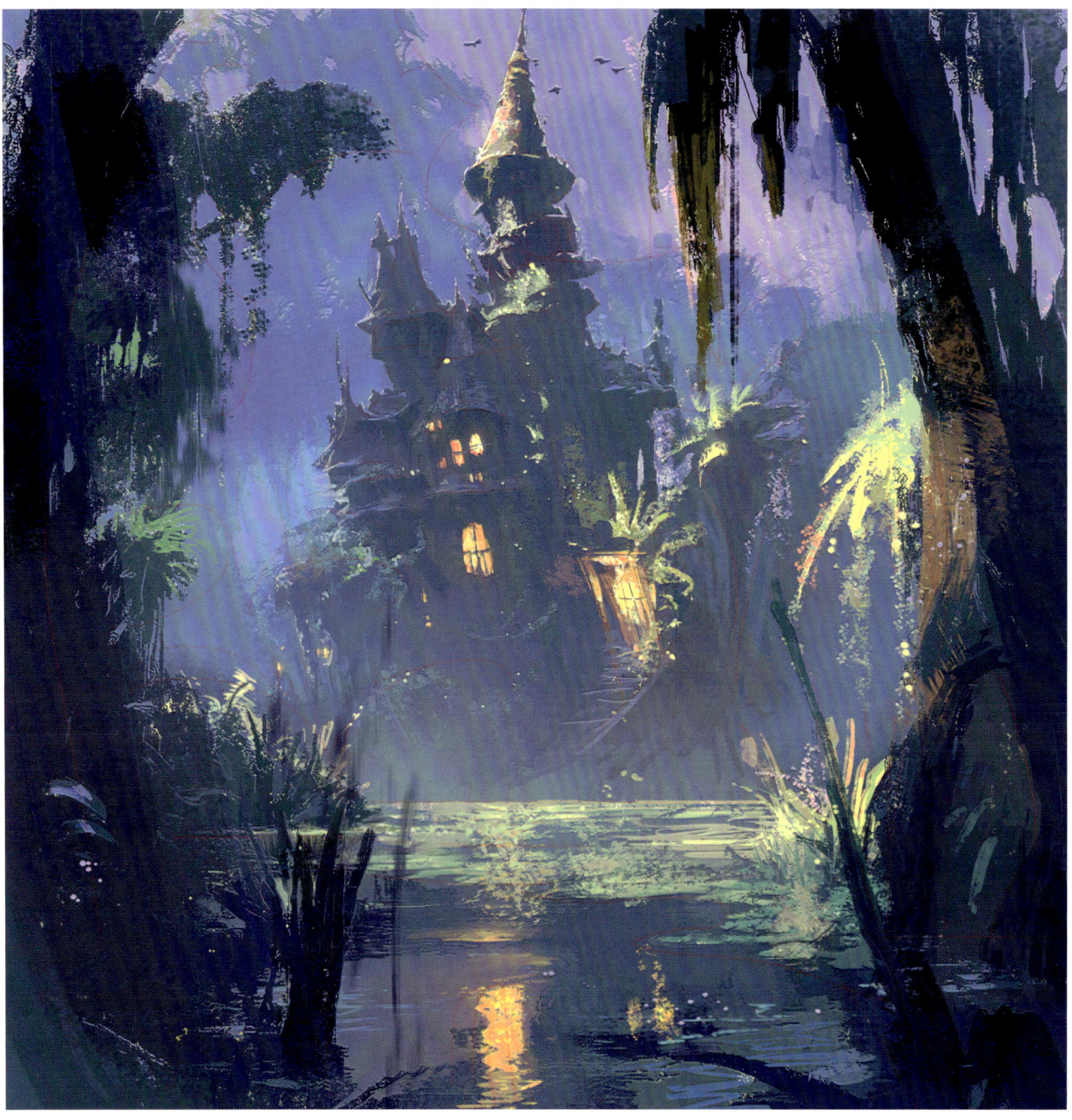

02. This environment is tailored to convey threat and villainy

02. 'BAD GUY' CASTLE

The 'bad guy castle' and environment must look very different, and need to immediately have the character of 'badness'. Therefore, they are:

• chaotic and unbalanced
• swampy
• darkly silhouetted with spotty lighting
• lit by glowing windows
• full of moss and foliage
• shaped with tipping diagonals
• surrounded by bats

You can see how both of these castles employ a very different visual language to communicate their emotional quality. That's exactly what good environment design is: clear visual communication.

03. FULL PROCESS MAP

And now let's review the process by which one of these images (the villain's castle) was created, including the initial rough, final rough, and completed illustration. You see here a flow chart of how the process fits into the design and development process as outlined so far. Next we'll get into specific details on each step of the process.

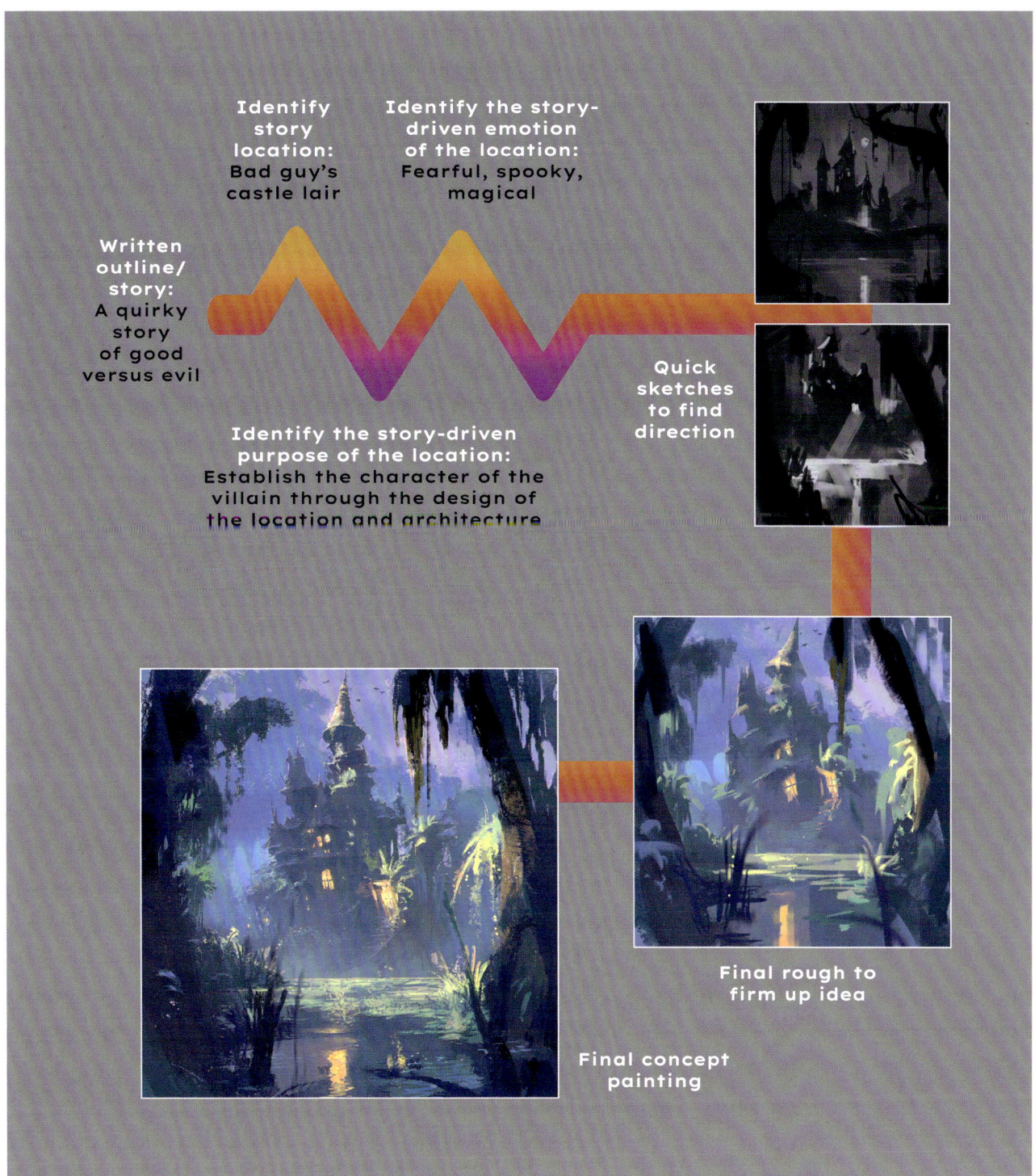

Written outline/story: A quirky story of good versus evil

Identify story location: Bad guy's castle lair

Identify the story-driven emotion of the location: Fearful, spooky, magical

Identify the story-driven purpose of the location: Establish the character of the villain through the design of the location and architecture

Quick sketches to find direction

Final rough to firm up idea

Final concept painting

03. An overview of the process for designing the villain's castle

TONAL ROUGHS

01. FIRST VERSION

I begin the process by roughing out some quick ideas in black and white, based on the brainstorming described previously. I don't want to worry about color yet because that quickly gets complicated. I just want to bang out quick ideas so that I avoid becoming too invested too early – we need to easily throw out ideas that don't serve our purpose, even if they look good. So I start by roughing out a vertical castle that shows the villain's authority, set within the confines of a chaotic swamp. I immediately realize this is wrong, though – the castle's vertical shapes make it too similar to the good castle. I need to make the architecture itself chaotic and unbalanced. I need to do another rough.

02. SECOND VERSION

This sketch is quick and dirty but does the trick. I rough out a leaning castle in a spooky swamp, with rim lighting on the castle and light on the water to emphasize the darkness of this silhouette. The swamp environment is characterized by tipping diagonals for an unsettled quality. And, of course, there are the bats.

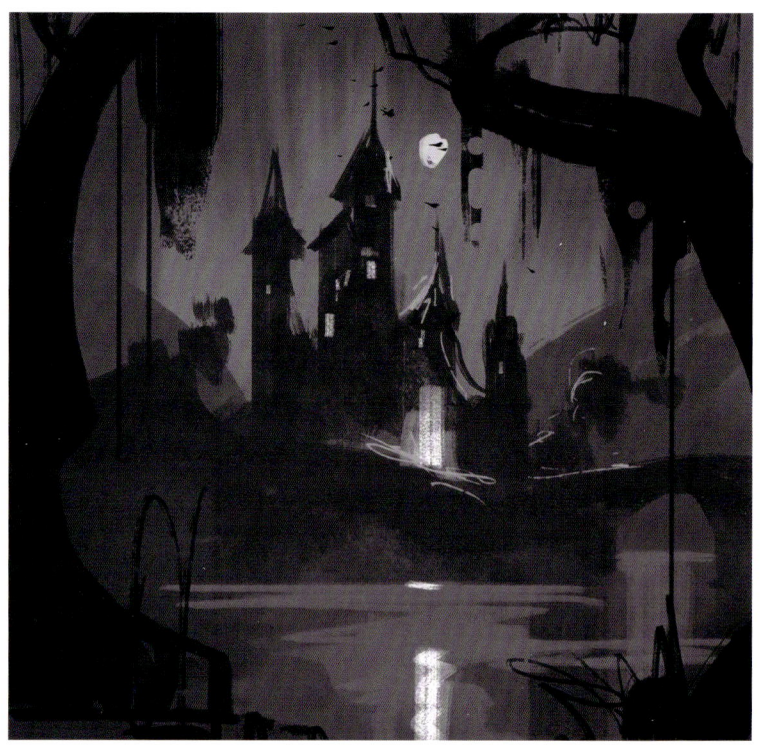

01. Plan out the scene in black and white

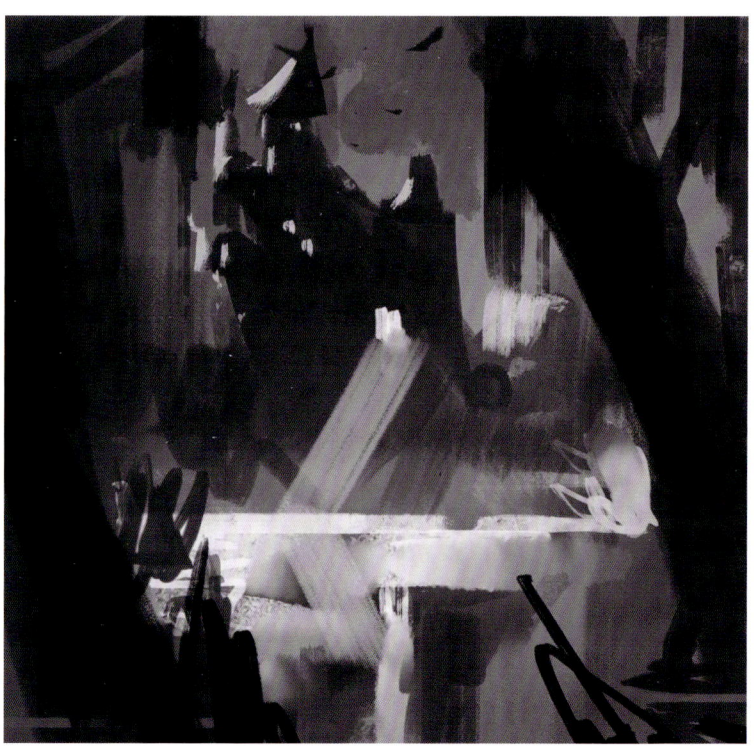

02. Diagonals and irregular shapes are more fitting

COLOR ROUGH

03. BASE SKETCH

The story I'm pursuing here is not a horror movie. I think the environment should remain playful despite being spooky and mysterious, so beginning with a playful color will help me do that. A gray magenta should do the trick, and will also help me infuse warmth into the many atmospheric cools that will follow. I then do a very simple line drawing to help with the placement of big objects. I begin with the line where the castle meets the water and work up from there, just thinking about the simple tube of the castle and the simple diagonals that surround it.

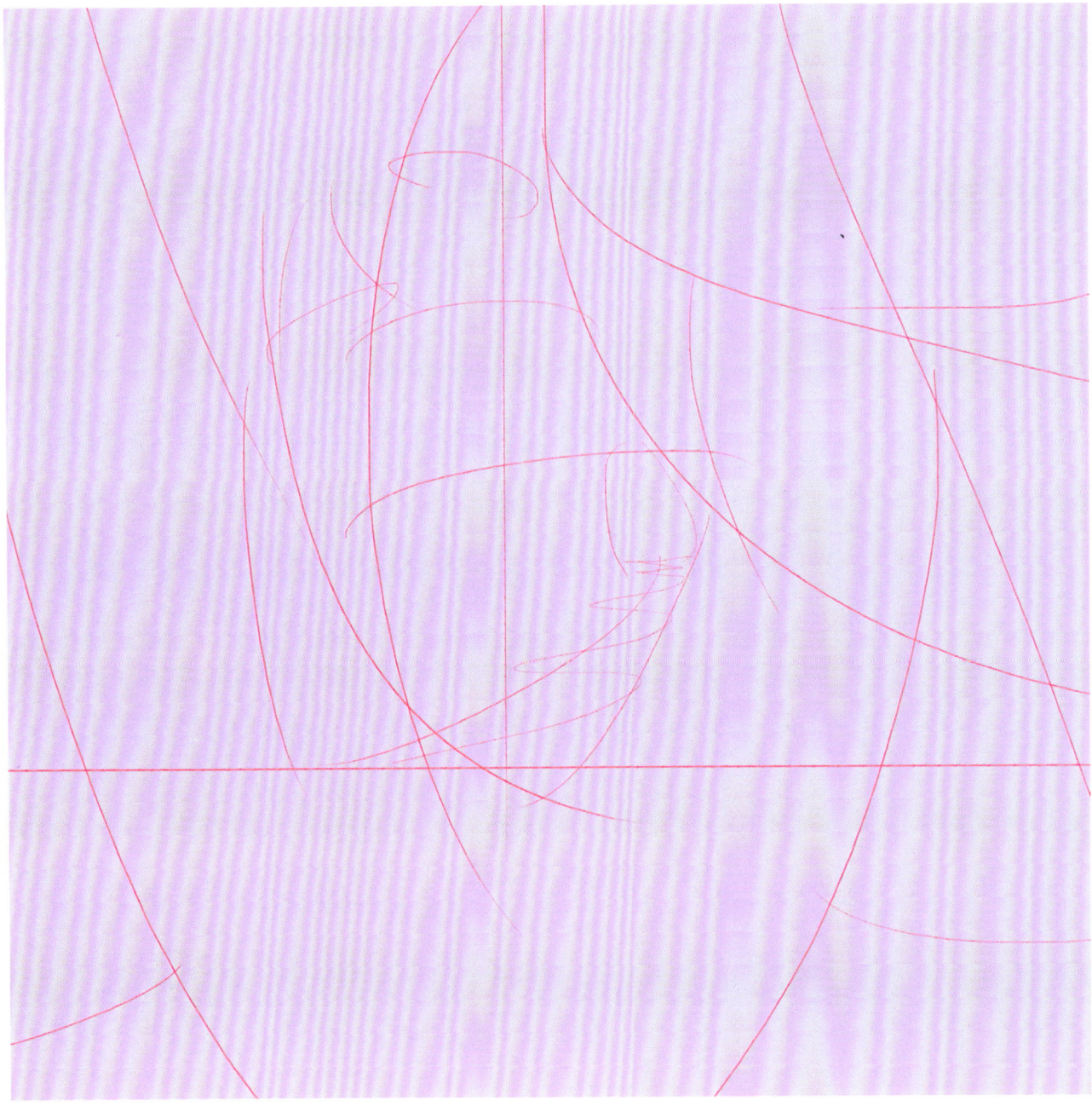

03. Start the next rough from a colored base

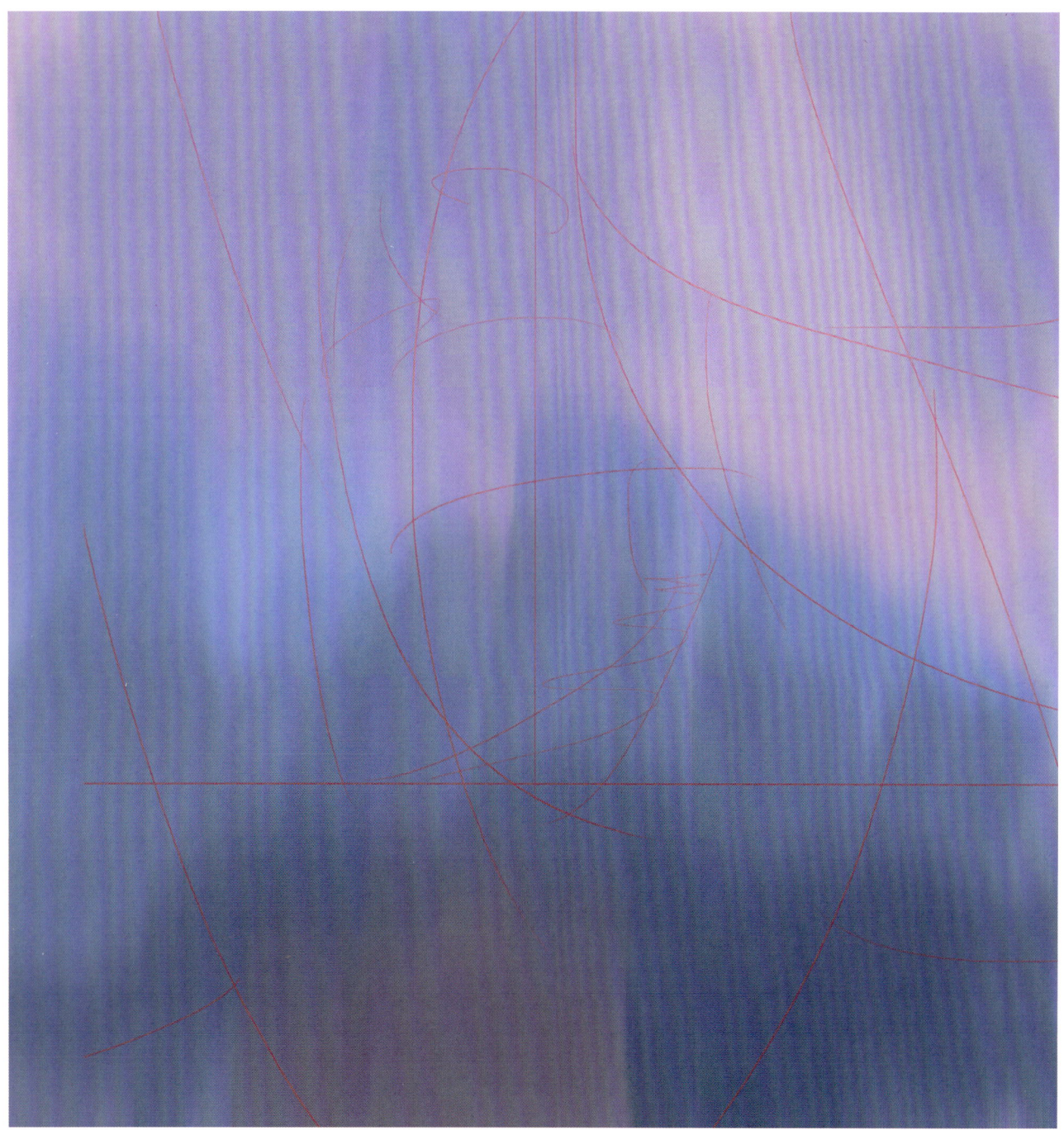

04. Paint a rough color base for the environment

04. BASE COLORS

To get the feeling that this castle lair is deep in a swamp, I start layering masses that will eventually become groves of trees, going from a background mass of ultramarine blue to a cool gray-green in the mid-ground. From there I lay down some warms in the foreground and apply a motion blur on everything to keep it soft and atmospheric.

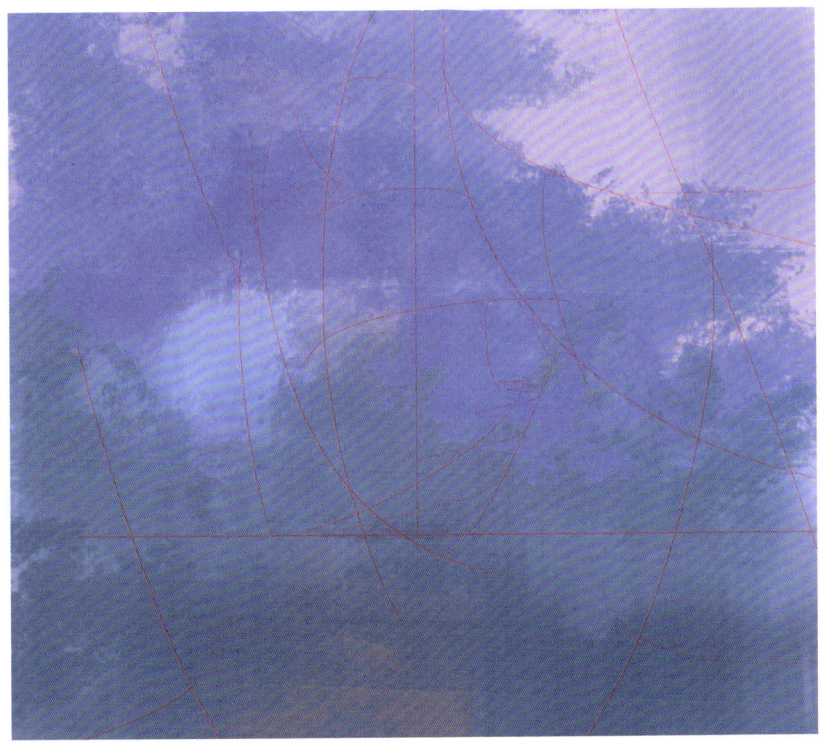

05. BASE TEXTURES

I'm now getting more specific with my atmospheric shapes of trees and getting a little bit more texture there. My target is creating colors and textures that will sit nicely behind the castle lair.

06. CASTLE SHAPE

I rough in the overall shape of the castle, concentrating on its curving and tipping quality. I'm also going from darker on top to more neutral below to get the misty, swampy quality I'm looking for.

05. Add more definition to the shapes and textures

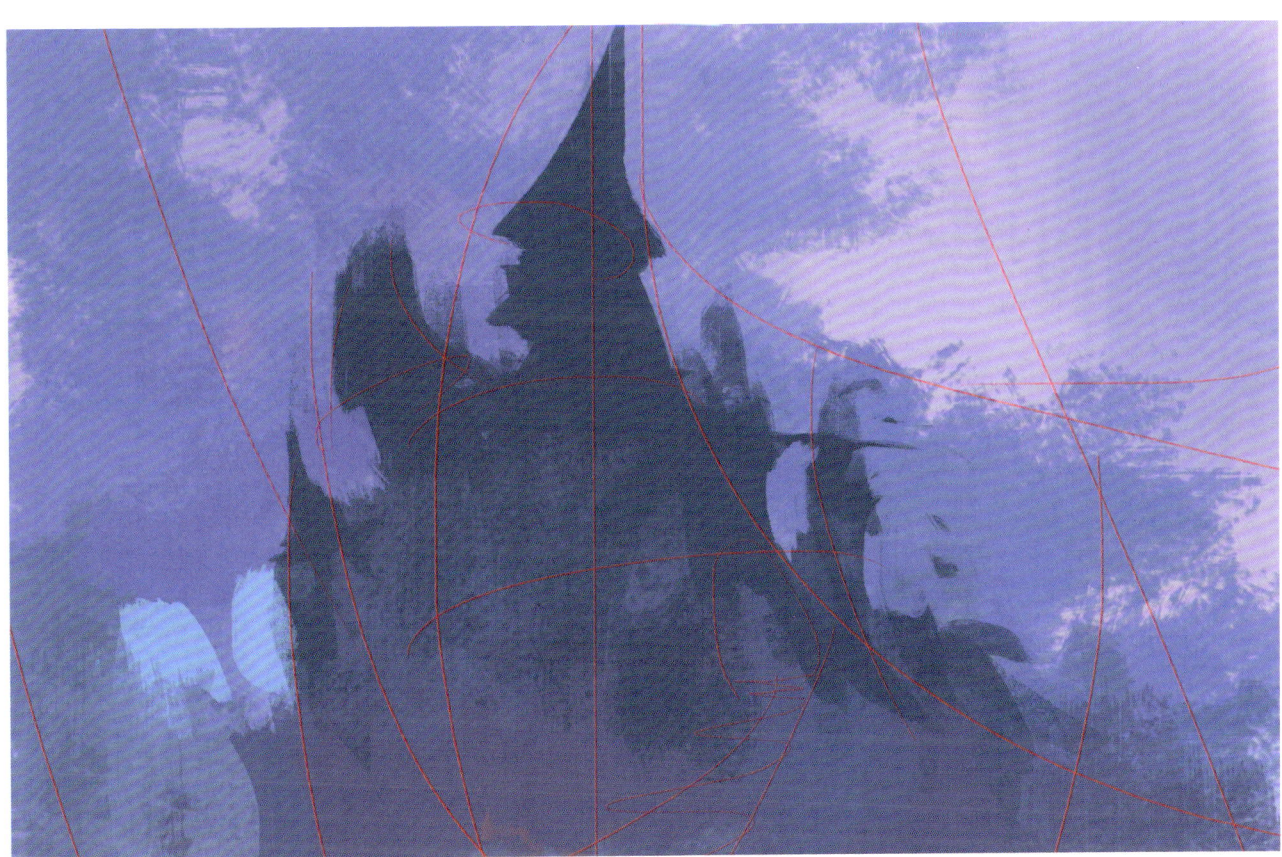

06. Add in the castle's rough silhouette

07. FOREGROUND

Just a few strokes are needed to get the big framing diagonals of the foreground trees. I'm using a darker and more saturated green here to establish the depth and atmosphere of the environment.

08. LIGHTING

The scene is ready for some lighting now and I need to be very selective with where I put it. I use simple strokes to put a few warm lights at the top of the castle, especially the primary turret. Next are the illuminated windows and doorway; I add hot, glowing lights there, so we know that dirty work must be afoot inside. Finally, I add a layer of light across the distant water and reflections in the foreground. This gives something for the castle to play against – something to help it feel dark and silhouetted.

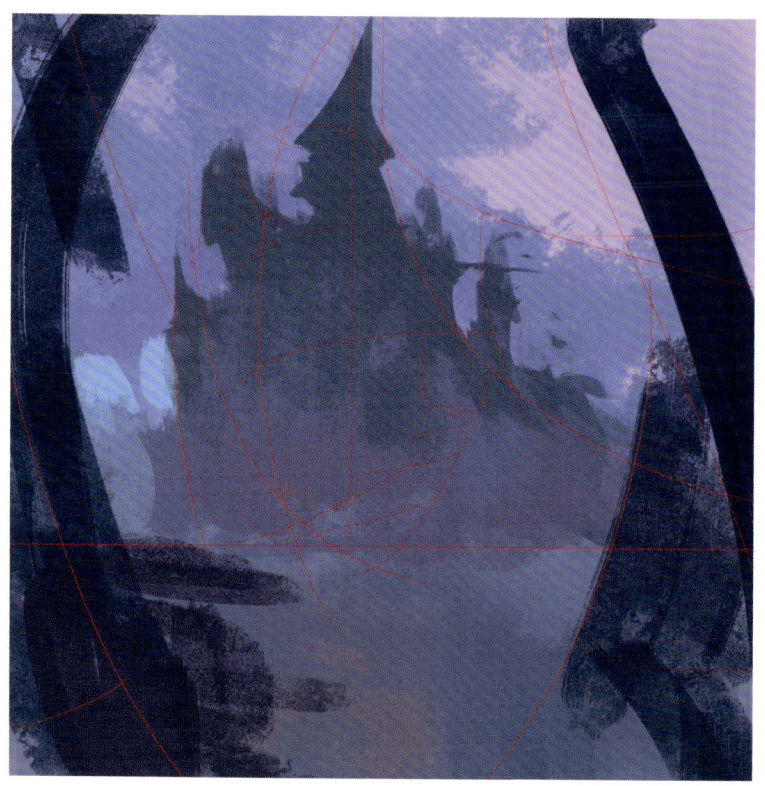

07. Sketch in the foreground tree trunks

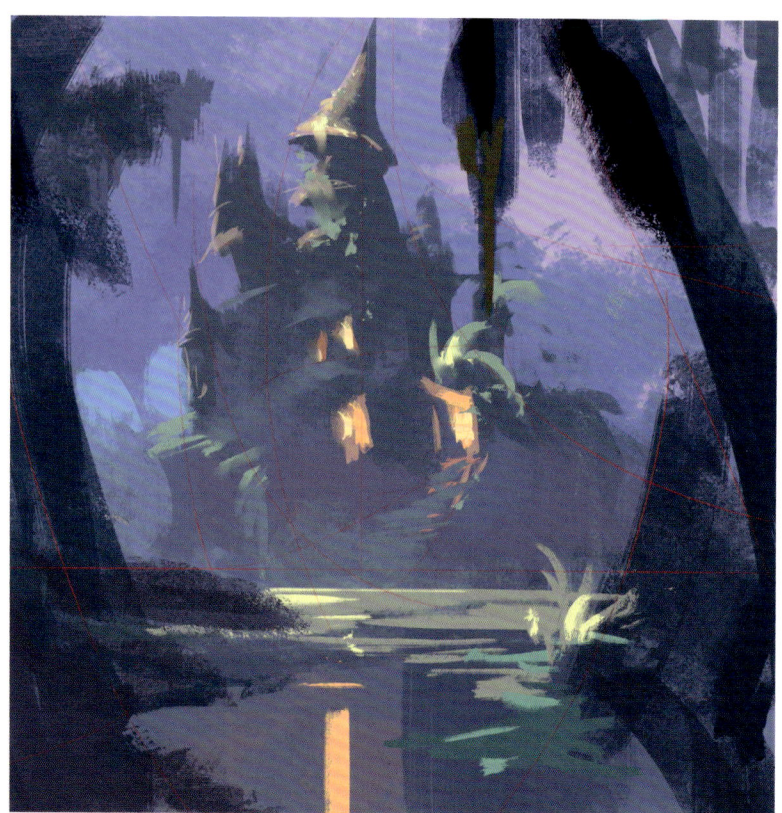

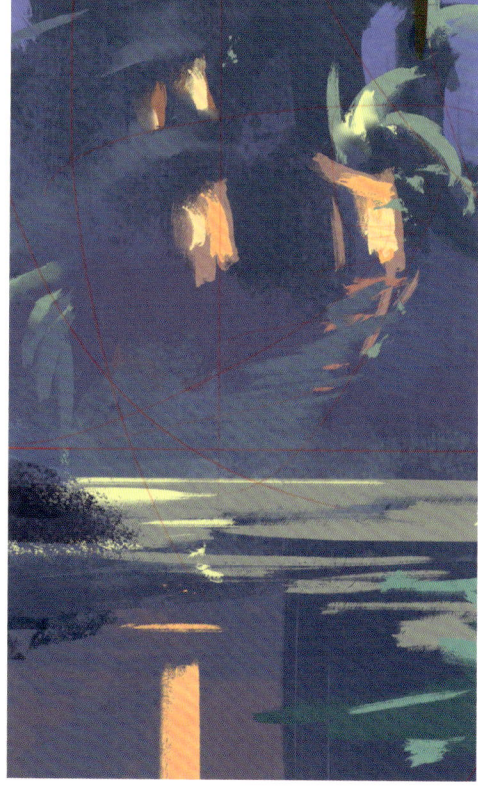

08. Light the castle and add reflections

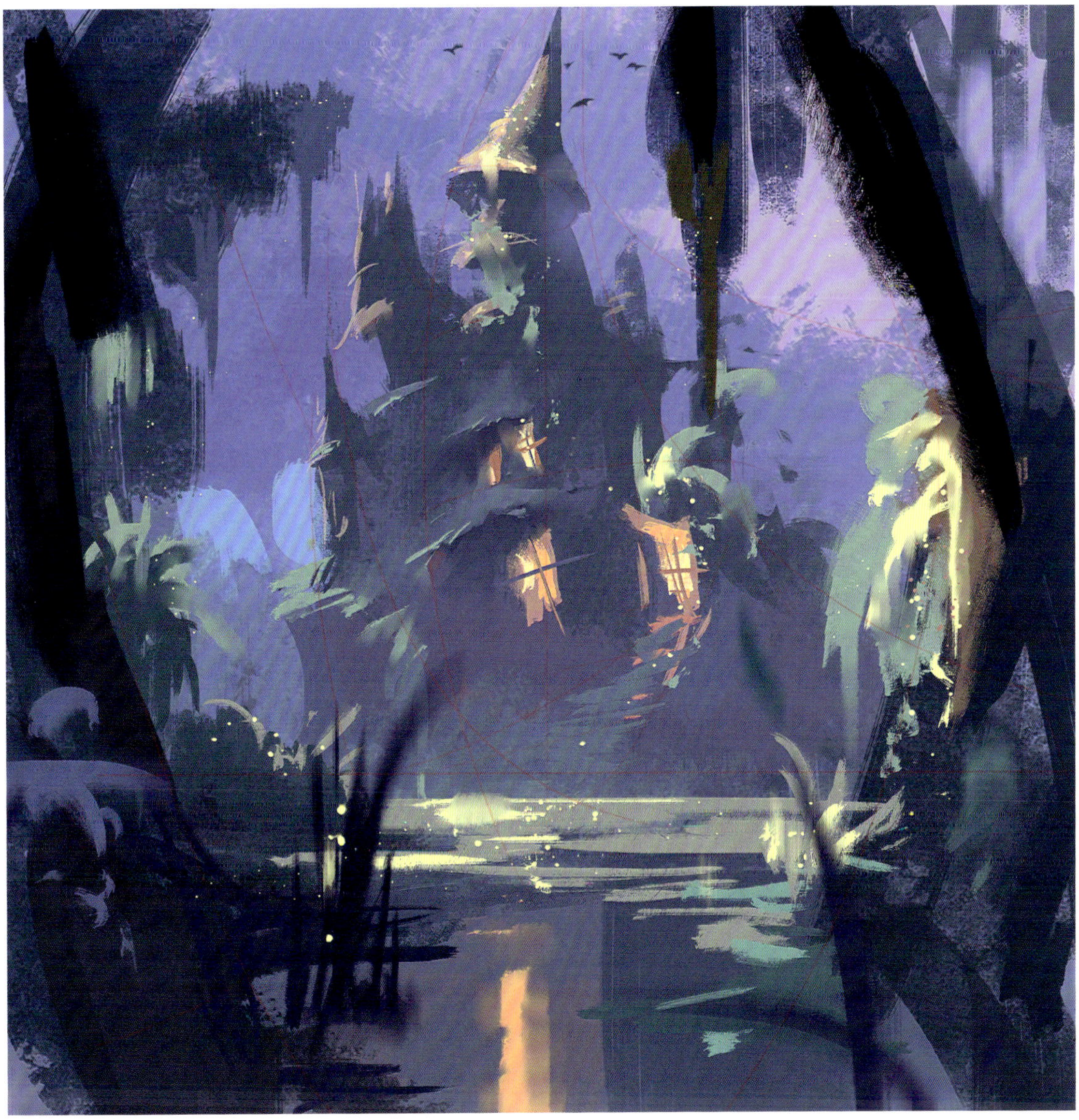

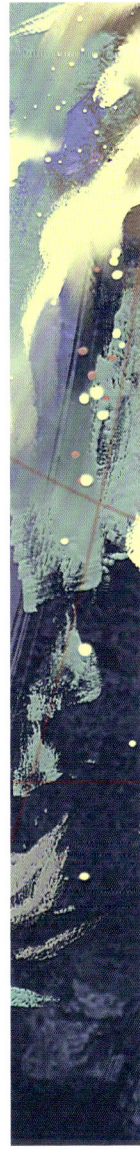

09. The finished color rough

I have to make sure that I'm not creating distractions, so I try and arrange every accent in a way that serves the purpose of the castle subject.

09. ROUGH DETAILS

I add the suggestion of more foliage, especially in the foreground. Notice that these new dark strokes tip inward, leading our eye up into the castle. I add a little more light hitting the mid-ground, but very cautiously. I have to make sure that I'm not creating distractions, so I try and arrange every accent in a way that serves the purpose of the castle subject. Finally, I throw in the promised bats up above, because everyone knows that bats are attracted to bad castles. And I've completed my color rough! It's now time to show it to the project director or client to get their approval.

FINAL CONCEPT PROCESS

10. INITIAL LINEWORK

Having a strong color rough is a great confidence-builder – I'm excited to move forward knowing that there's a good solution at hand. I like the pinkish starting point I used in the rough, but I don't want my approach to be too sugary, so this time I'll start with the very opposite color: a light, warm green. The gray-pink will still be in the picture but established in a later step. For the line drawing, I use the rough sketch as a template, drawing basic lines over the top of it and then transferring the drawing to this file. I'm only indicating key objects and key placements here, so the crest of the castle is clearly defined, as well as its overall shape and the position of the windows and doorway. A few lines position the framing trees and masses of foliage.

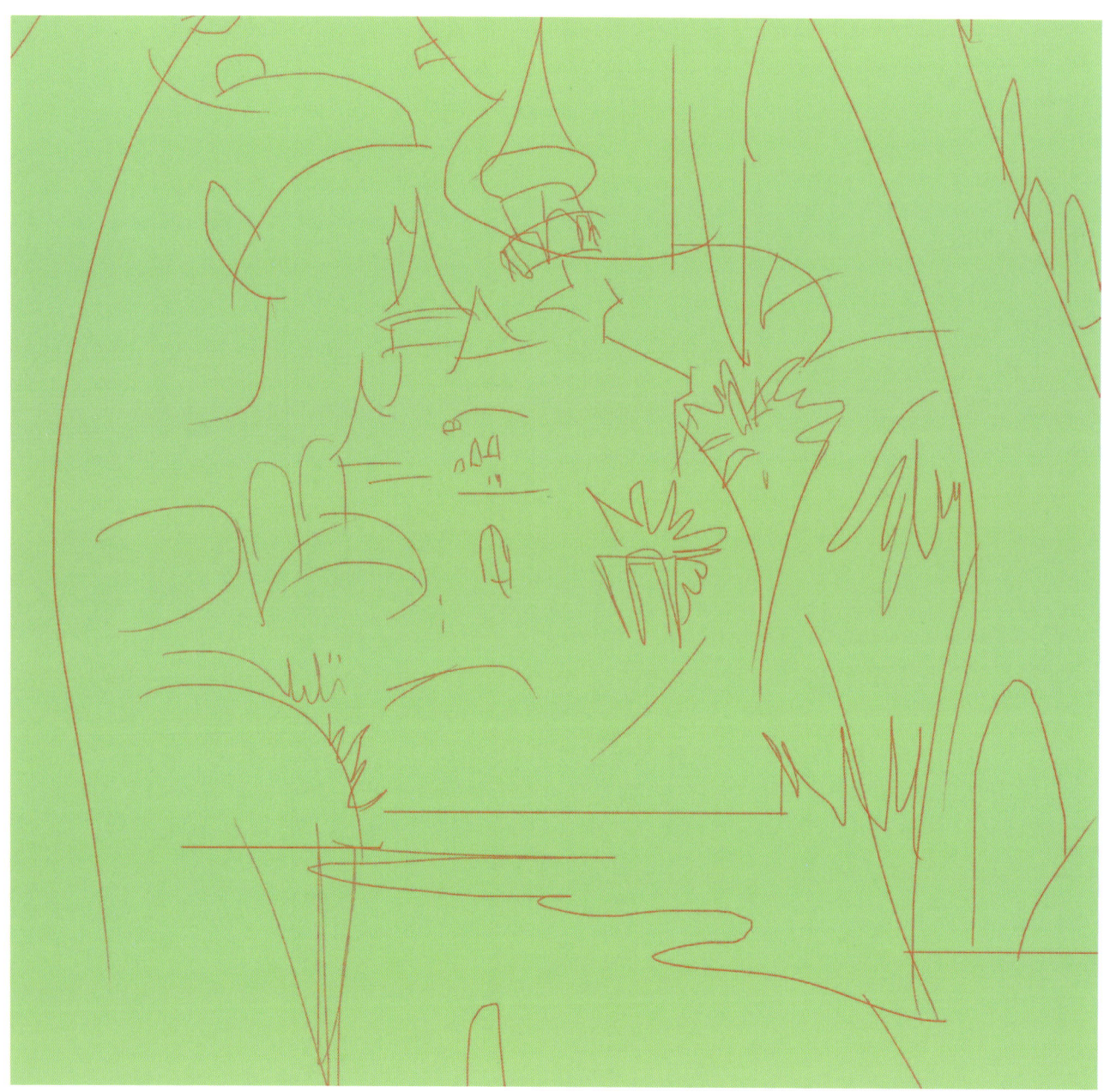

10. Use a green base for the final painting

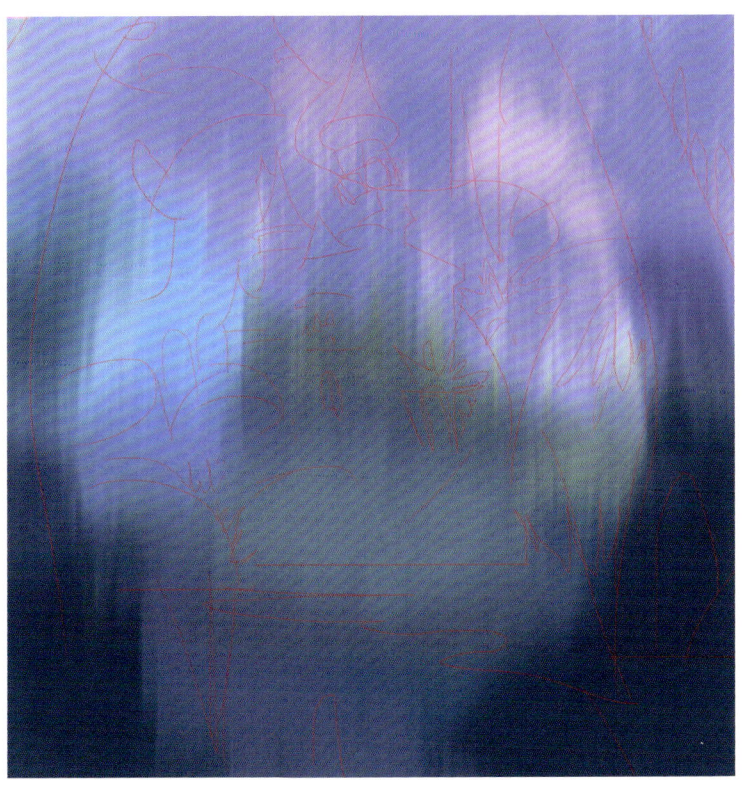

11. Eyedropper and motion blur create a quick base

11. BLURRED COLORS

I am happy with the colors from the rough and simply use the Photoshop's Eyedropper tool to borrow colors right out of it. That's one of the uses of a good color rough – you can rely on it for your color choices in the final. So I get the same layering of colors and masses that I used previously, and apply a motion blur to create the misty, atmospheric quality that I'm looking for.

12. BACKGROUND TREES

For the background masses of trees, I continue matching the color palette from the rough version and apply a brush with an organic-looking texture. I'm very specific about the shape and positioning of this background mass of foliage since I want it to frame the castle roof. I constantly remind myself of the hierarchy of purpose in my painting, carefully preparing each layer for what will follow. The entryway to the castle should upstage everything else in importance, so I'm preparing my background design to serve that purpose.

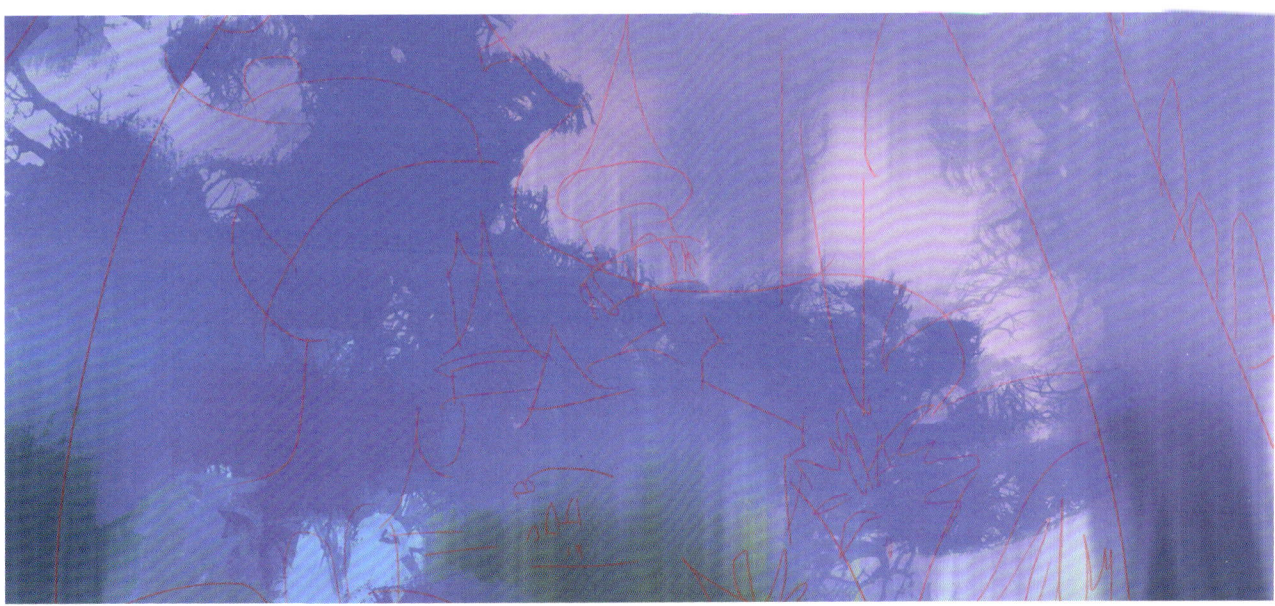

12. Add a background layer of foliage

I constantly remind myself of the hierarchy of purpose in my painting, carefully preparing each layer for what will follow.

31

13. CASTLE SHAPE

I work out the castle shape with a color that's darker and warmer than the background trees. This color choice helps it emerge from the atmosphere. I use only one color initially to keep things simple, but then add some variety – gray-greens, browns, and neutral violets that create an overall mossy, organic color palette. I keep the general silhouette big and simple but give the edges a very bumpy, active quality, as if the architecture is very much at one with the swamp.

14. FOREGROUND

My first strokes here are the big tree trunks. I keep them strong and graphic, since they're the simple 'architecture' that all of the foliage hangs from. I add in patches of foliage and hanging fronds of moss. To make a location feel creepy and swampy, hanging moss really does the trick! I avoid getting too colorful but make sure that there are some color variations in the foliage, going from neutral blues and browns to neutral greens. The greens are a little more distinctive and I concentrate them on the edges that point in toward the center.

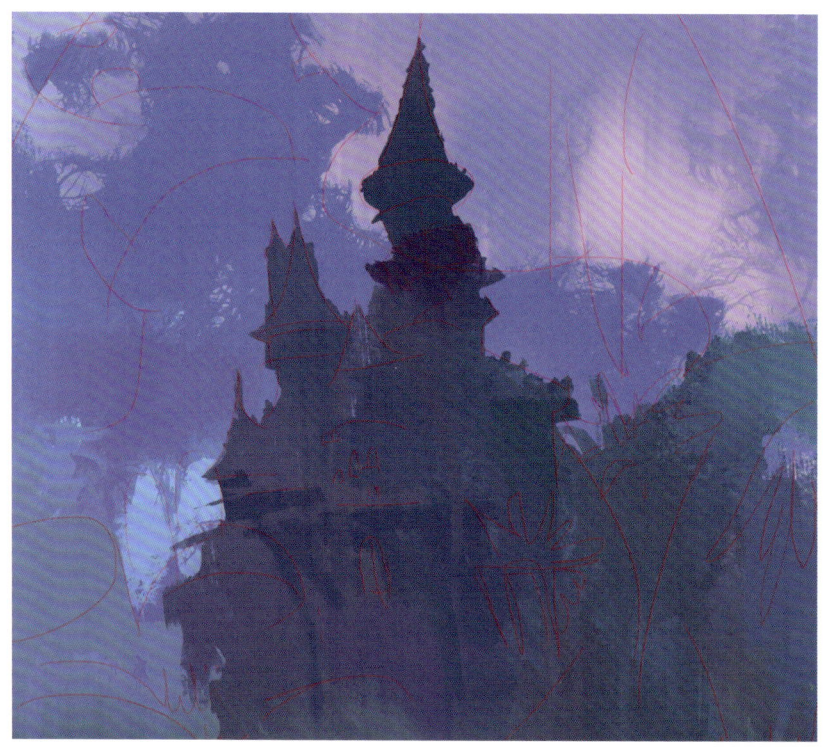

13. Add the silhouette of the castle

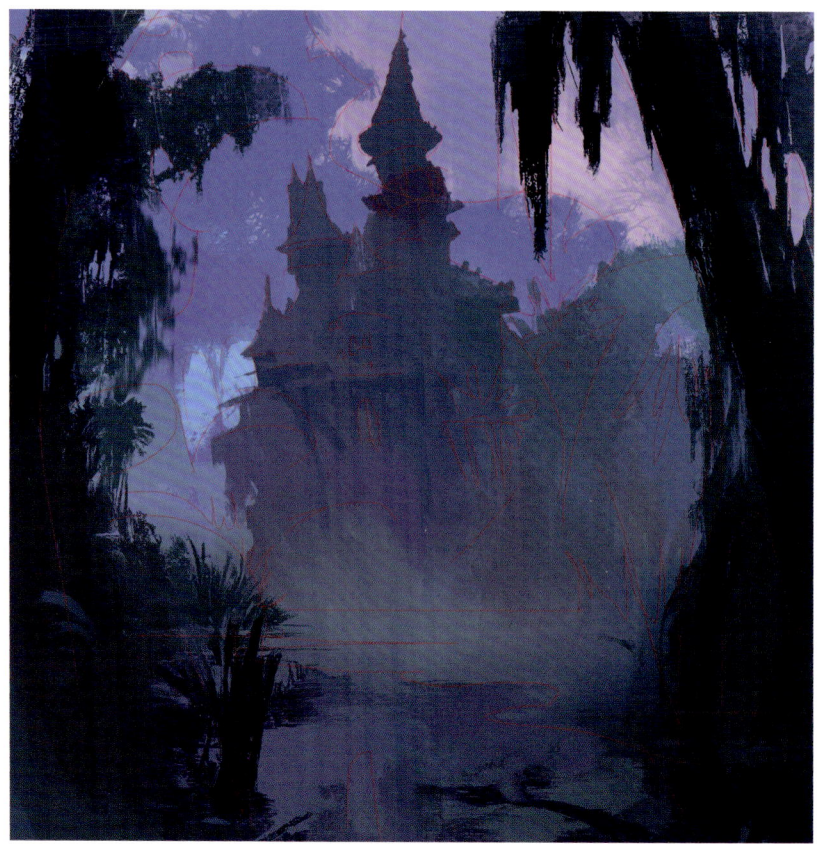

14. Paint trees and foliage in the foreground

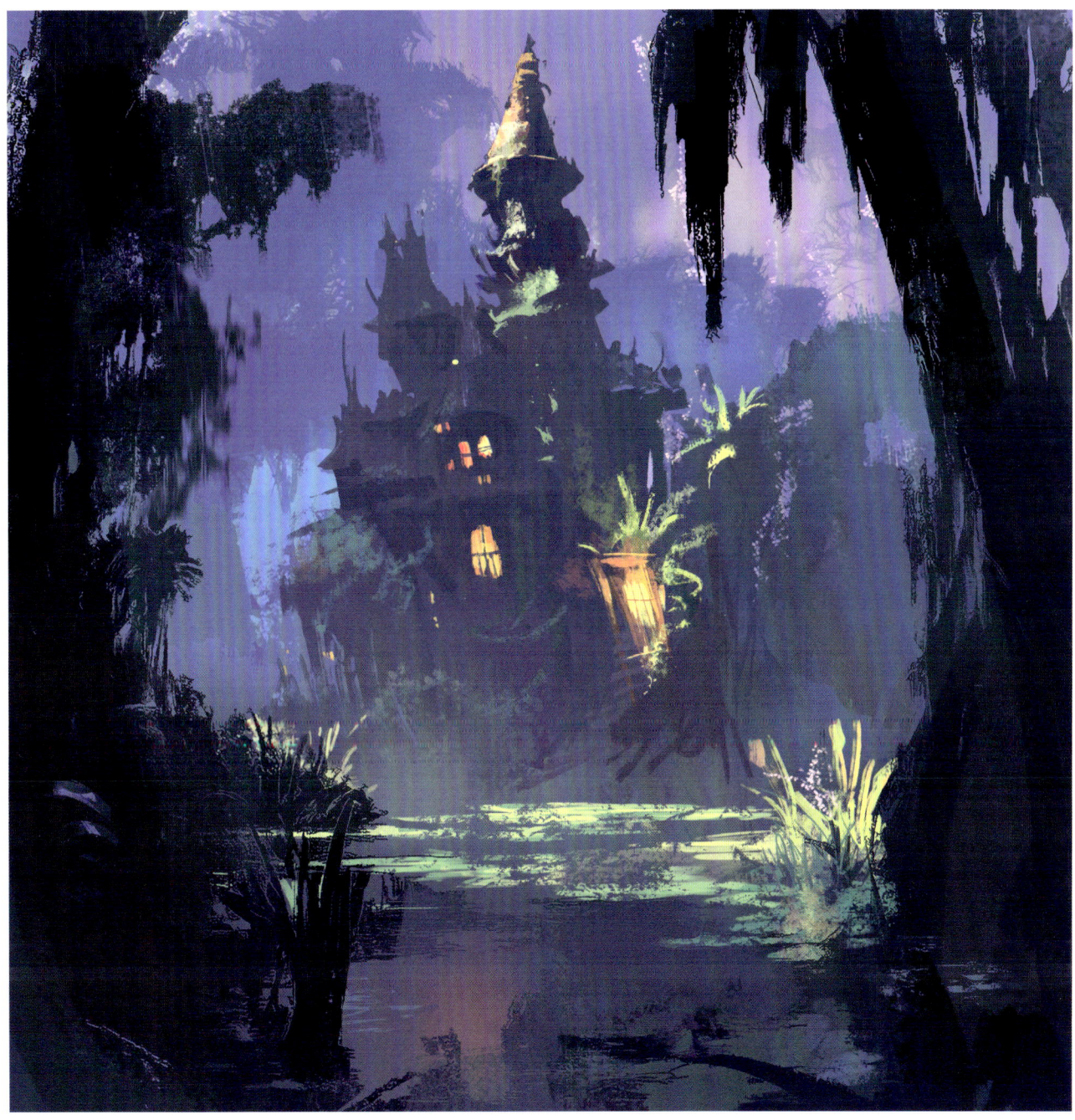

15. Add warm lighting and reflections

15. LIGHTING

For the lighting, it's very important that I keep to my concept and put the light only where it helps. The light creates contrast, contrast is what we pay attention to, and what we pay attention to must serve the purpose of the image. If I put patches of light anywhere and everywhere, the image would be a disaster, even if the quality of the rendering was good. Remember: purpose, purpose, purpose. So my lighting hits the crest of the tower and the mid-ground right in front of the castle. For the illuminated windows, I apply strong golds and oranges, as well as the criss-cross bars that everyone knows windows have.

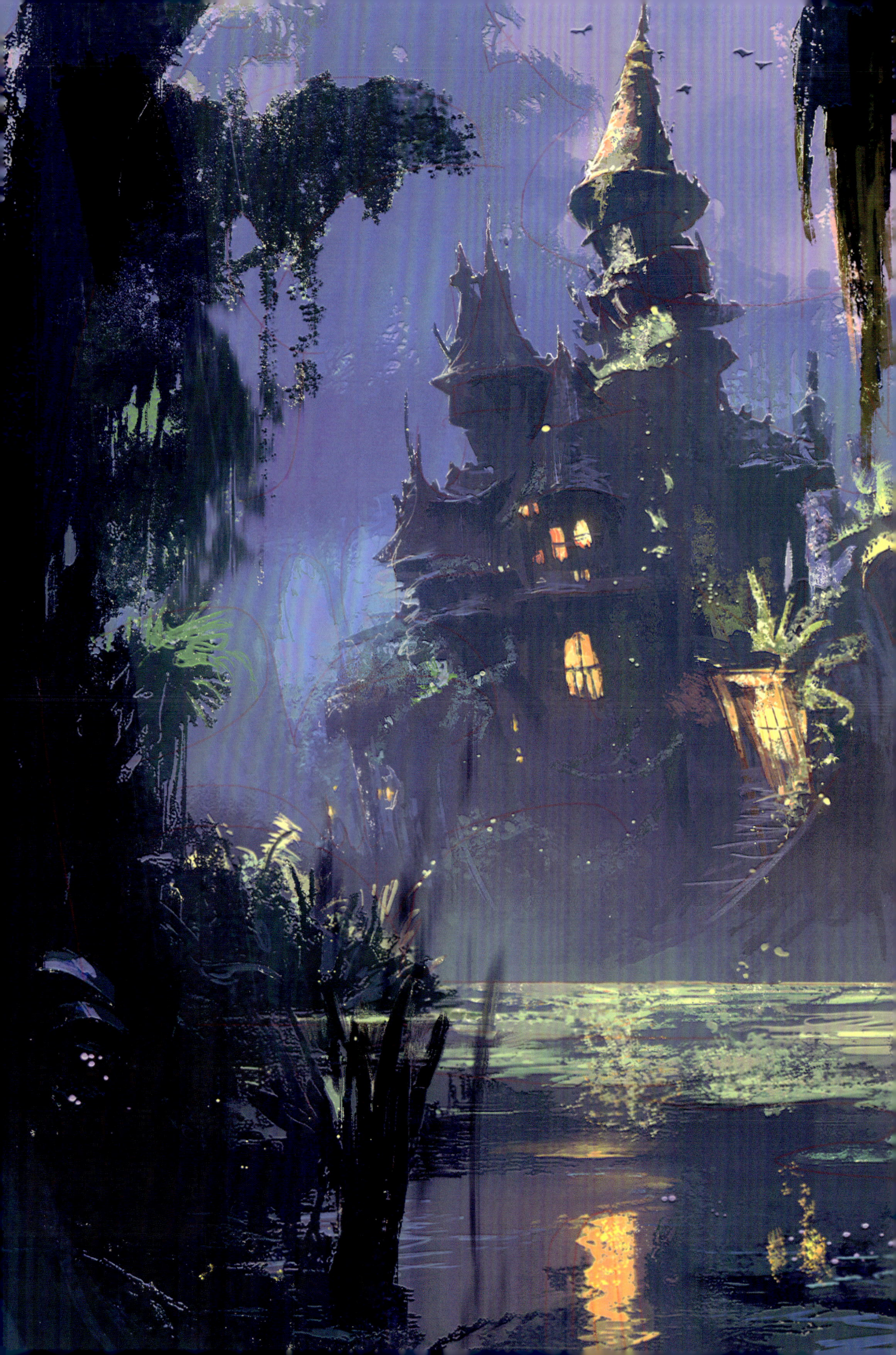

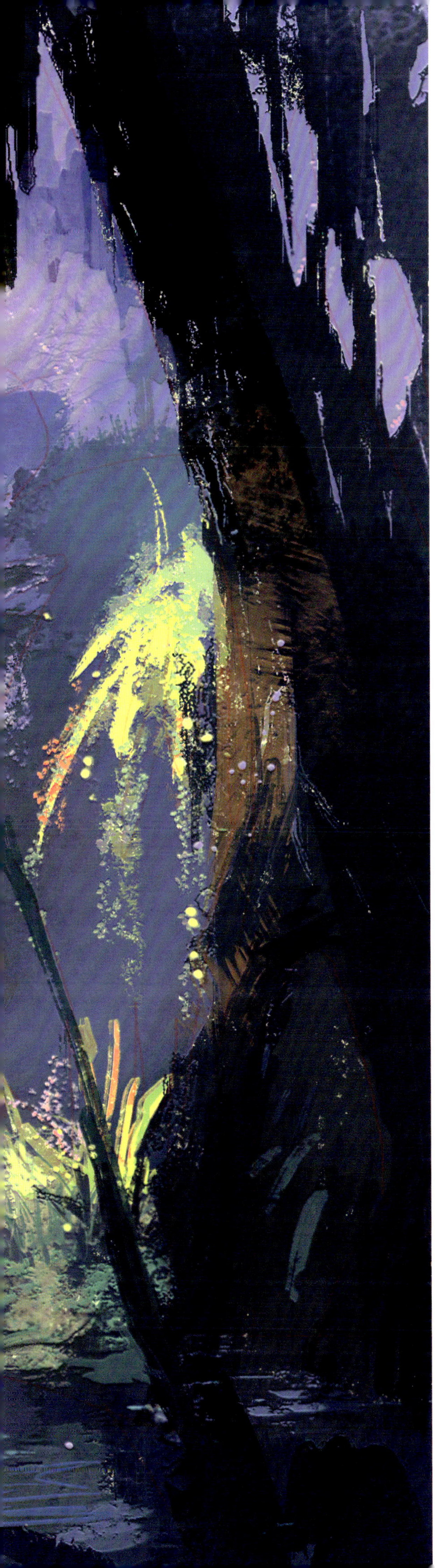

16. FINAL DETAILS

And now for the grand finale! This step is about giving a quality of finish to the image. I apply a little bit more lighting to key areas as well as adding reflections to the water. I add a tiny bit of rim light to other parts of the castle to strengthen its overall silhouette. The primary light source is the sun, of course, but I don't forget the skylight coming down from above and giving a bit of cool illumination and shadows. I avoid adding too much detail but make sure this cool illumination makes it onto any roofs and overhangs. And with the addition of some bats, the villain's lair is complete!

DETAIL CLOSE-UP

Here's a closer crop of the image so you can see it in greater detail. You'll see that the detail is not much more than dots and dashes strategically placed. And I did use a slight embossed effect, created from the filter gallery in Photoshop, that gives the illusion of a textural surface. This is easy to overdo, so if you choose to use this approach, easy does it!

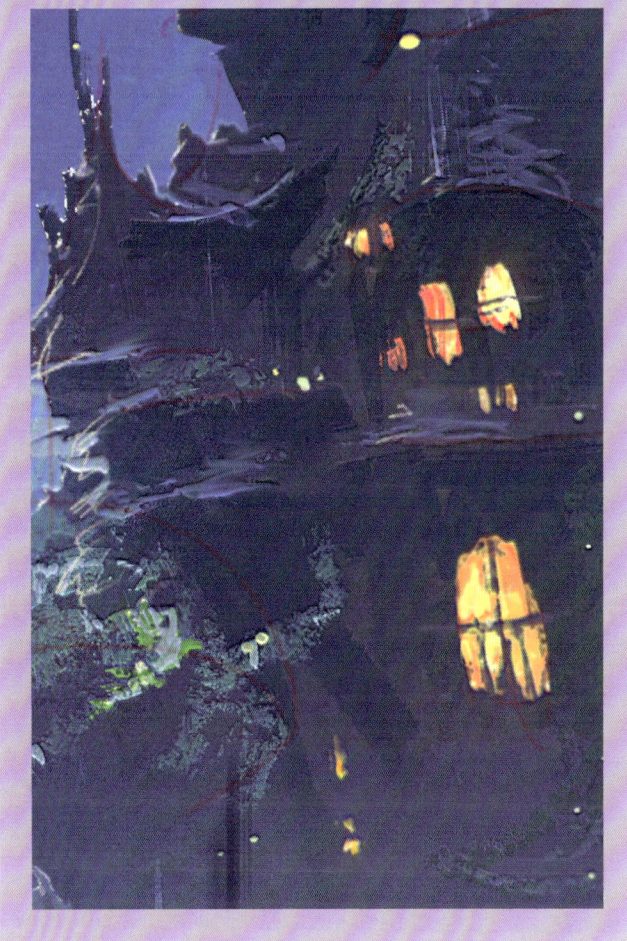

RECOMMENDED EXERCISE:
EXTREME SIMPLIFICATION

Here's an exercise that's simple in principle but very difficult in practice. It's one of the most valuable exercises that I'm aware of. Take some of your favorite artwork from other artists and simplify them into three tones of light and dark (we refer to these tones as 'values') with only hard edges. There should be no rendering, no linework, no cross-hatching – only the three values. They can be any three values, whichever ones convey the purpose of the original best.

The reason for this approach is that you cannot mindlessly render or get caught up in distractions and unnecessary contrasts. You must very carefully think through the purpose of the original image, and then put in only the elements that clearly convey that purpose. With only three values, it simply won't be possible to render further than that. This exercise forces you to think about clear visual communication. I recommend you do this daily – you might be surprised how your own artwork starts to click into place.

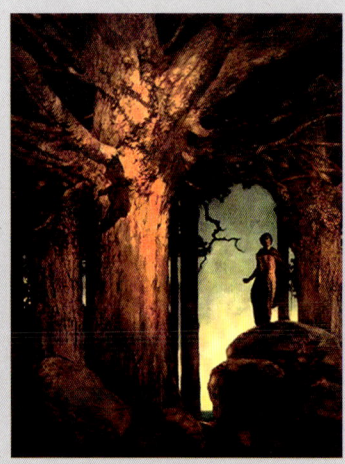

Original

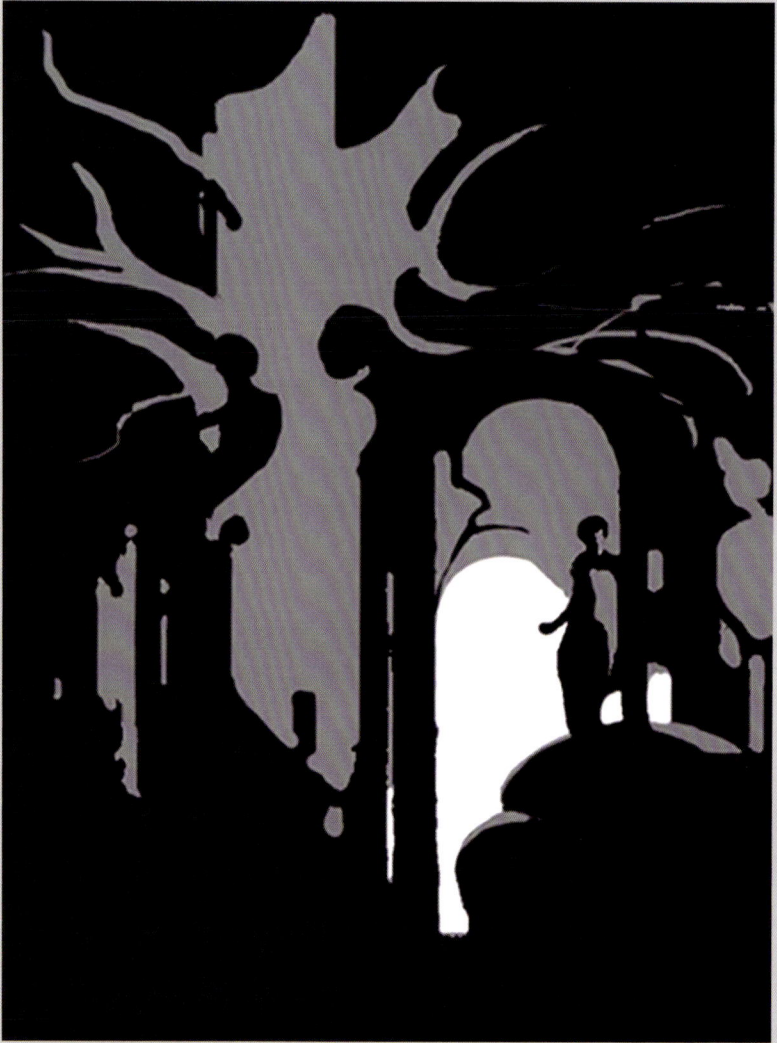

Three-value study
with only hard edges

△ Simplified studies based on master paintings

Image: *Jason and the Talking Oak* by Maxfield Parrish

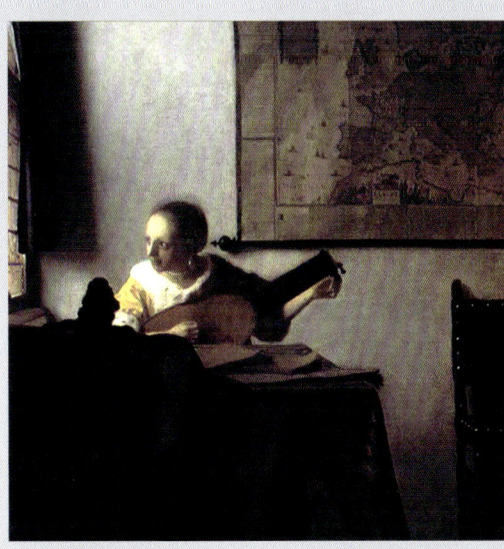

Original

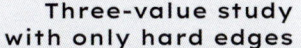

Three-value study
with only hard edges

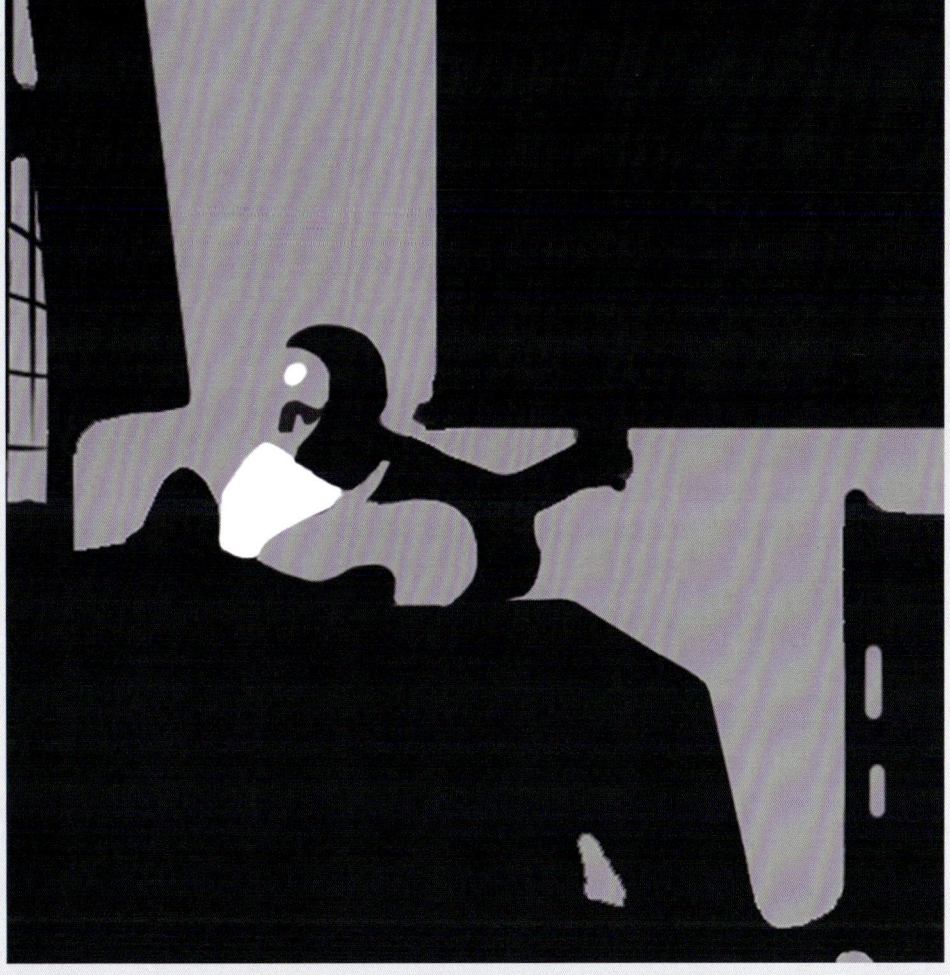

△ Simplified studies based on master paintings

Image: *Woman with a Lute* by Johannes Vermeer

THE MIGHTY IMPACT OF ENVIRONMENT

We cannot think of the environment as a mere place. It's not. It's filled with so much awe-striking power that our ancient ancestors sincerely believed that gods and giants were striding through the mountains and skies.

EARTHQUAKE!

Way back in 1983, I found myself at the epicenter of a devastating earthquake in my hometown of Coalinga, California. It's a small town located halfway between Los Angeles and San Francisco in the middle of the San Joaquin Valley.

On this particular afternoon, I was reading in the city library when all of a sudden the ground jumped ferociously. A dead second of silence followed and then the ground moved in a way that I couldn't have imagined. We'd had small temblors before and I knew what those felt like, but this was something different. I knew to duck and cover under the table, and did so immediately, but the ground shook so hard that it kept tossing me out, despite my efforts to stay in place. I watched the bookshelves fall one by one, just like dominoes, leaving piles of books a meter high in between them. When it was all over, I stumbled outside to a layer of dust hanging over the town. I was met by the sight of the brick buildings of our downtown all crumbled to the ground.

This was an absolutely shocking experience to go through and it wasn't just the shaking and the devastation that I can never forget – it was also the sound. Imagine being in between two trains roaring in opposite directions. That's the closest comparison I can think of.

My point in telling you this story is as a reminder that we cannot think of the environment as a mere place. It's not. It's filled with so much awe-striking power that our ancient ancestors sincerely believed that gods and giants were striding through the mountains and skies. I think it serves us best to think of the environment as an experience; an especially emotional experience. The environment that surrounds us can be filled with bliss and happiness, and it can be so shocking as to defy description. It's with this potency in mind that we will work out how to visually convey the mighty impact of environment in this chapter.

△ I kept this newspaper clipping about the incident

THE IMPORTANCE OF EMPHASIS

If we're going to give our environments authority and power, we must give a strong emphasis to the environmental elements that create these effects. Let me take you through a tutorial here on creating emphasis.

The foundational building blocks of any picture are value, shape, edge, hue, saturation, and texture. There are many components to environments and art, so why do I consider these in particular to be primary building blocks? It's because they are the most basic ways to create contrast, and so much of what we do as artists is about the design of contrast. Why is contrast so important? Because it's what people pay attention to! People are hardwired to look at areas of highest contrast first. We do it automatically, without even thinking about it, because our eyes and our brain want to take in as much information as possible as quickly as possible. It's a survival trait. Highest contrast equals highest amount of information. There's so much we can do by applying these contrasts to an environment. The following is a series of variations to demonstrate creating emphasis through environmental contrasts.

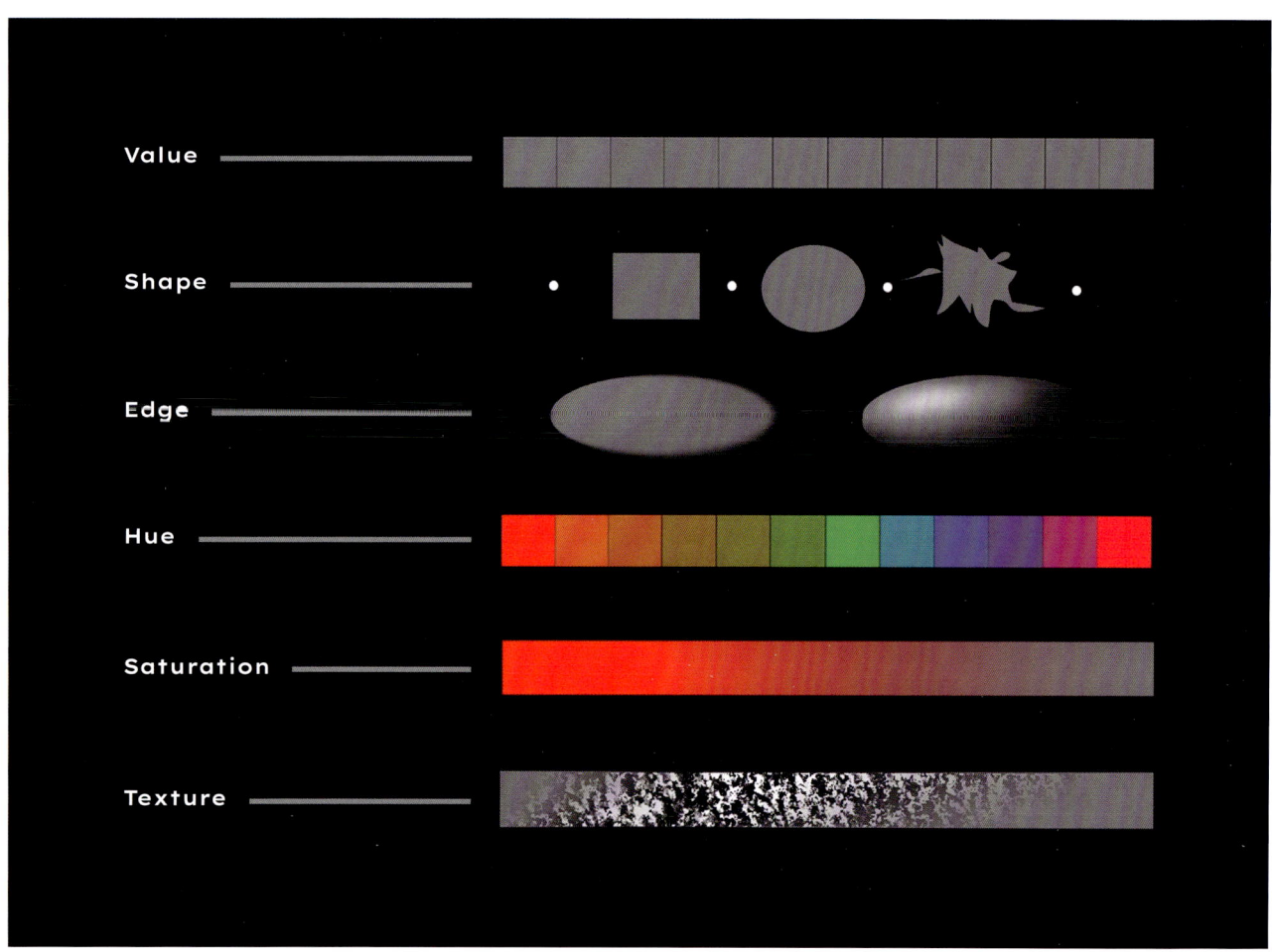

△ We can create contrast with these components

People are hardwired to look at areas of highest contrast first, to take in as much information as possible as quickly as possible. It's a survival trait.

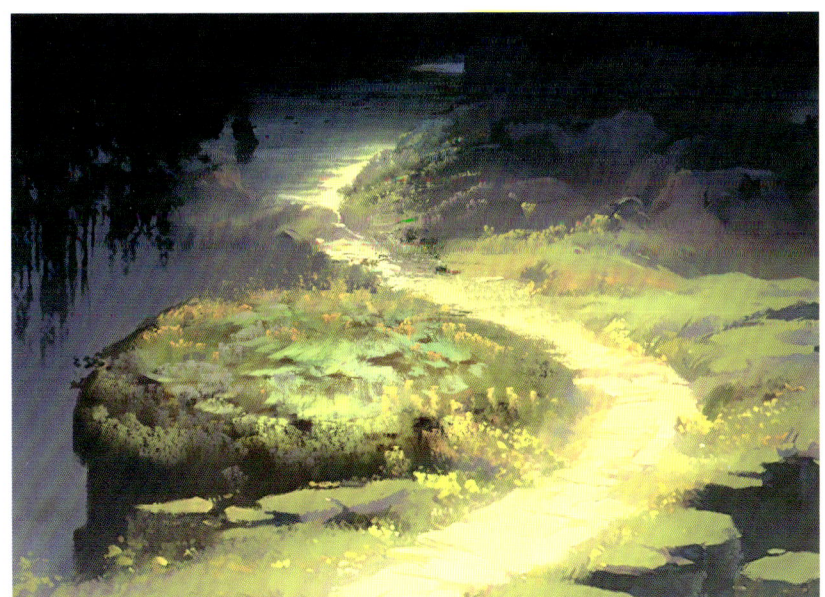

01. This simple scene will be the basis for my experiment

01. STARTING SCENE

Here's a pleasant pathway taking you from one place to another without significant distractions along the way. There's a strange, rounded area just to the left of the path, but it's probably not noticeable enough to cause you to stop on your journey. So in the upcoming images, let's add elements that have enough visual emphasis to get you to stop and investigate.

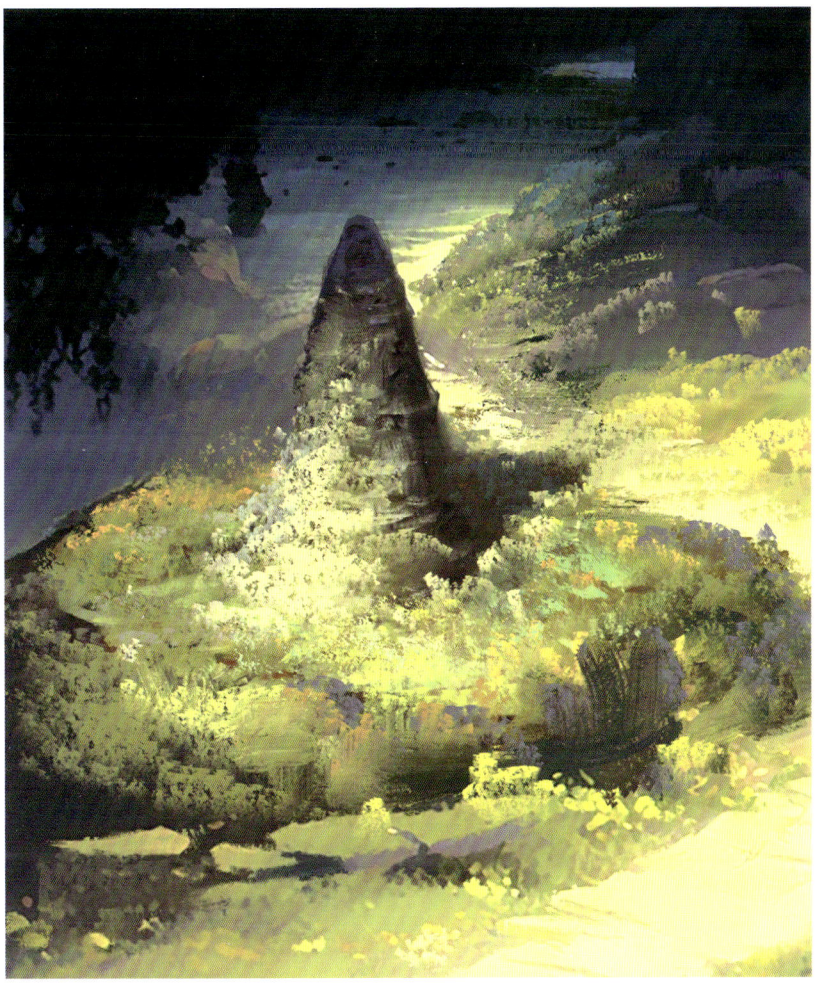

02. A mysterious obelisk-like object raises questions immediately

02. ADDING A THING

We've added a random thing sticking up out of the ground here. Travelers would just *have* to stop to try and figure out what in the world is going on. Was it carved by people? Is it natural? What's its purpose? We've designed an element that gets people to stop and look, and getting people to stop and look is what artists do.

> We've designed an element that gets people to stop and look, and getting people to stop and look is what artists do.

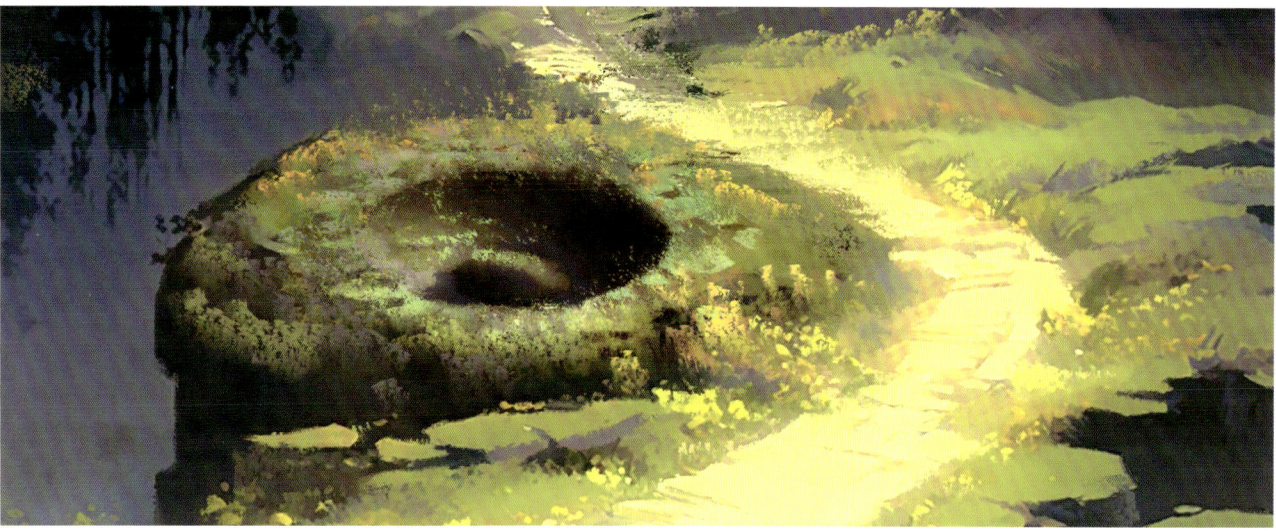

03. Taking something away can be just as effective

03. UNEXPECTED HOLE

In my experience, our instinct is to add things to create visual interest, so to change things up, let's take something away. Now there's a big hole in the ground! Our travelers will just have to stop and investigate. Is it a crater? Is it human-made? Why is it there? Something as simple as an unexpected hole in the ground creates an emphasis in the environment, something that must be investigated.

04. THE BIRDS

Let's go back to our protuberance sticking out of the ground and give it even more emphasis. Now it has an interesting rocky texture and has become a nesting place for local birds. They're flocking like in an Alfred Hitchcock horror movie! Not to mention all the white guano they deposit on the precipice. We've created some serious visual interest in the environment. Mission accomplished!

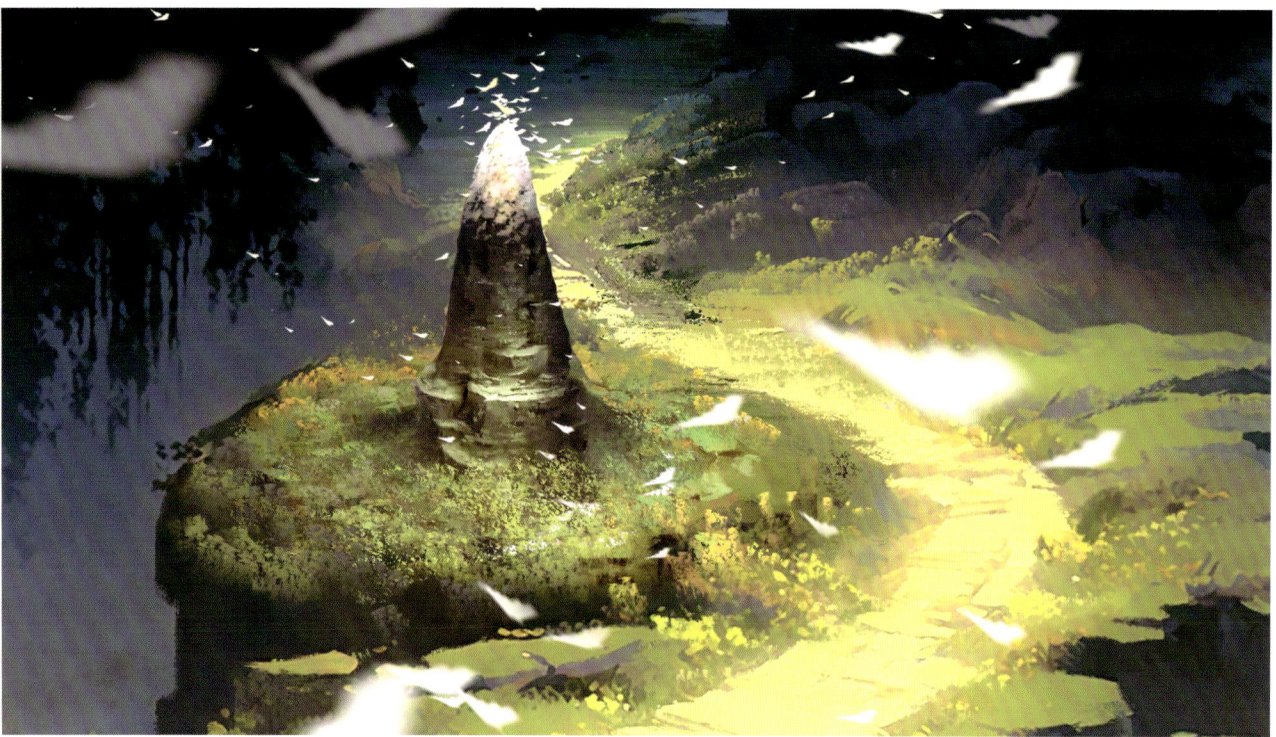

04. A lively flock of birds gives the object even more emphasis

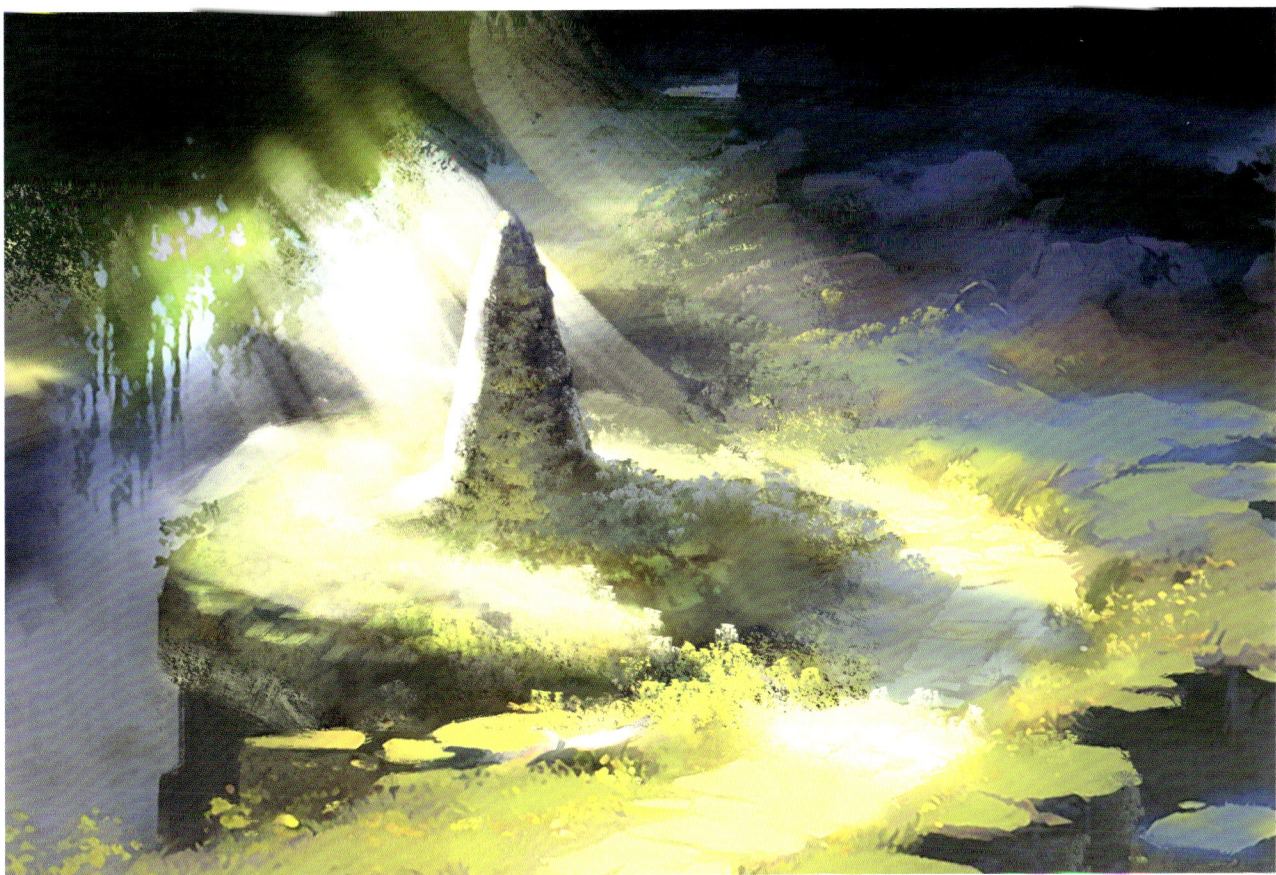

05. A beam of light can be used to highlight areas of importance

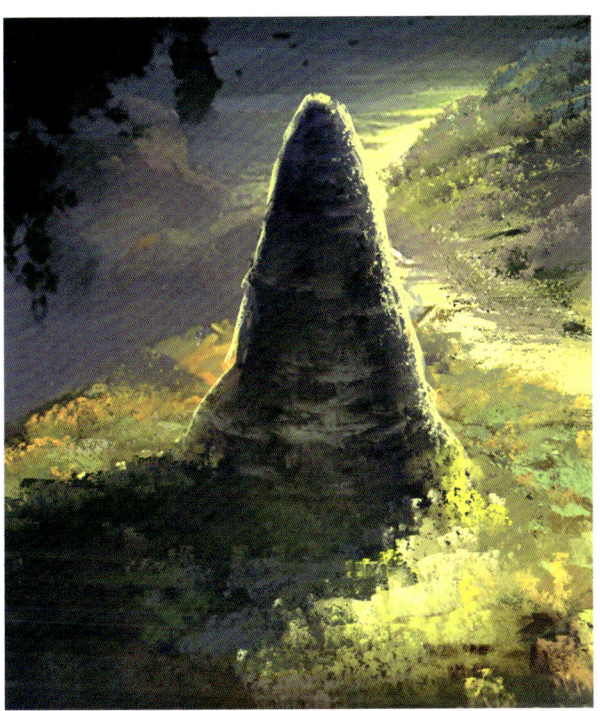

06. A backlit silhouette creates subtler drama

05. IN THE SPOTLIGHT

For a simpler way to add visual interest to this image, we can use light. Sending a beam of light right onto our subject tells our audience that this environmental element must be very important. Also, as we just spoke about adding elements and taking elements away, notice that the background is plunged into murky shadow. Lighting (and lack of) is a potent tool to create visual interest and purpose. We'll devote an entire chapter to this subject later.

06. IN SILHOUETTE

Let's keep going with our light and shadow idea to bring importance to the subject of our environment. This time we'll use simple backlighting. Allowing the subject to fall into dark shadow and be surrounded by a sharp sliver of light gives it all the attention it needs. Note how I've carefully surrounded it with a nice pool of light and kept the far background in simple shadow. The mighty god rays of the previous image were exciting and effective, but we can be much more subtle and get all the contrast we need.

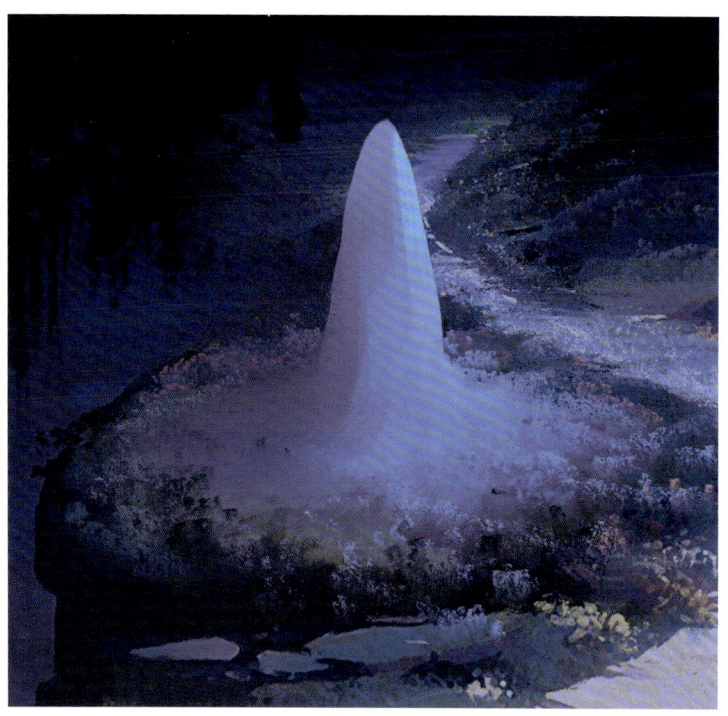

07. LOCAL COLOR & VALUE

We've been focusing on adding light to our subject, but now let's take most of the light away and plunge the scene into night, leaving just a little cool moonlight. How do we bring importance to our subject now? We can simply change its local color and value. In this case, let's make it a clean white, like it's made of chalk or marble. Carefully designed local colors and local values are an important consideration when designing the elements that make up our environments.

08. LIGHT IN THE DARK

Now let's say that we really need to bring a more powerful attention to our subject. We'll keep what we have but add warm direct lighting back in. Now our subject is inescapable in its demand for our attention. It has light and shadow, warm and cool colors, and a local value contrast from its environment. Not to mention that it's still some weird icon protruding from the environment!

07. A lighter object stands out better against a nocturnal palette

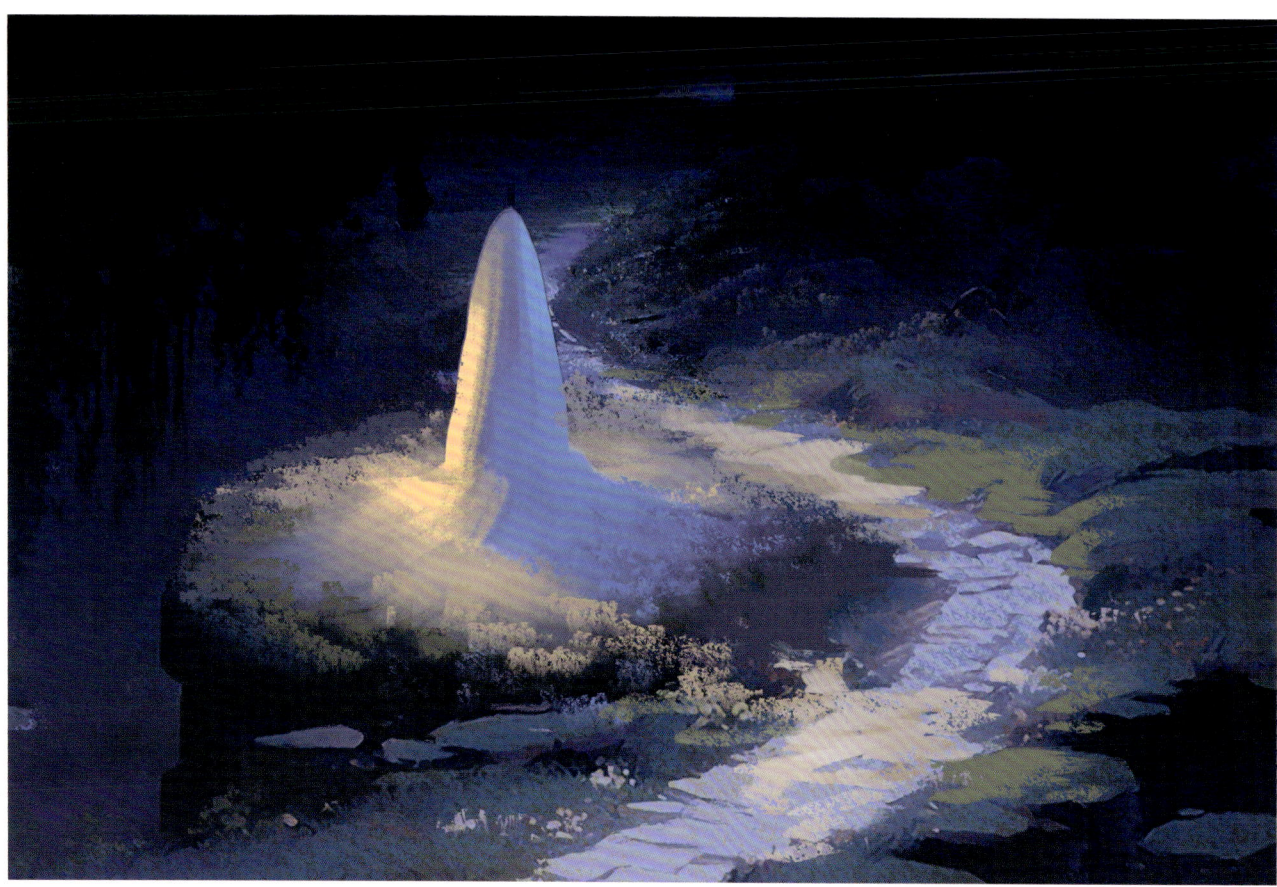

08. Warm lighting creates contrast with the cool surroundings

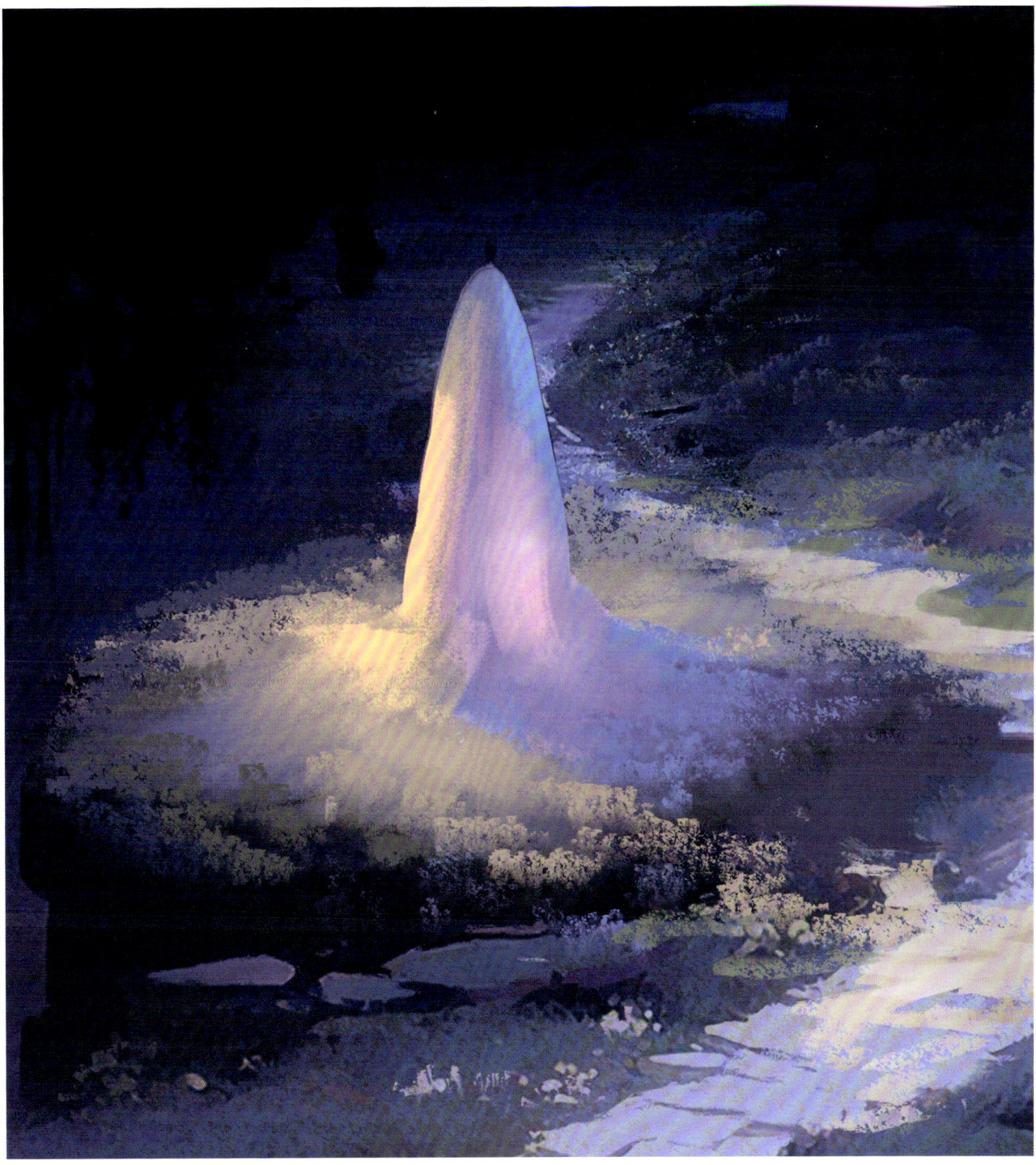

09. A pinkish inner light makes the object feel translucent

09. MATERIAL CHANGE

If we need to bring even more attention to our icon, we can change its material. Let's have it be made of translucent crystal! Now we get a lensing effect that puts a beautiful droplet of light into the shadow area. I make sure it has a little extra color, which does the trick.

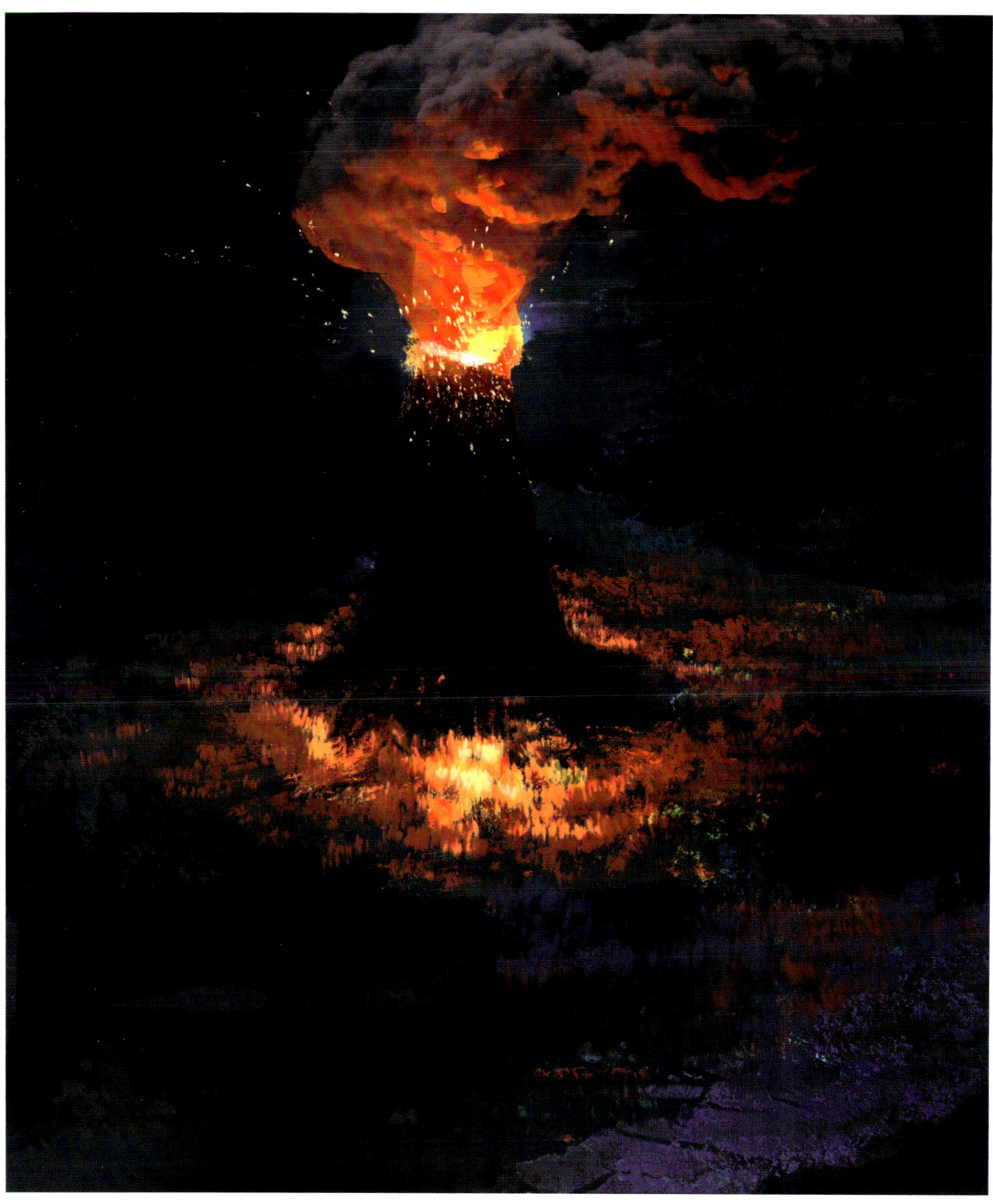

10. How about a fiery volcano...

10. NOW IT'S ERUPTING!

Need I say more?

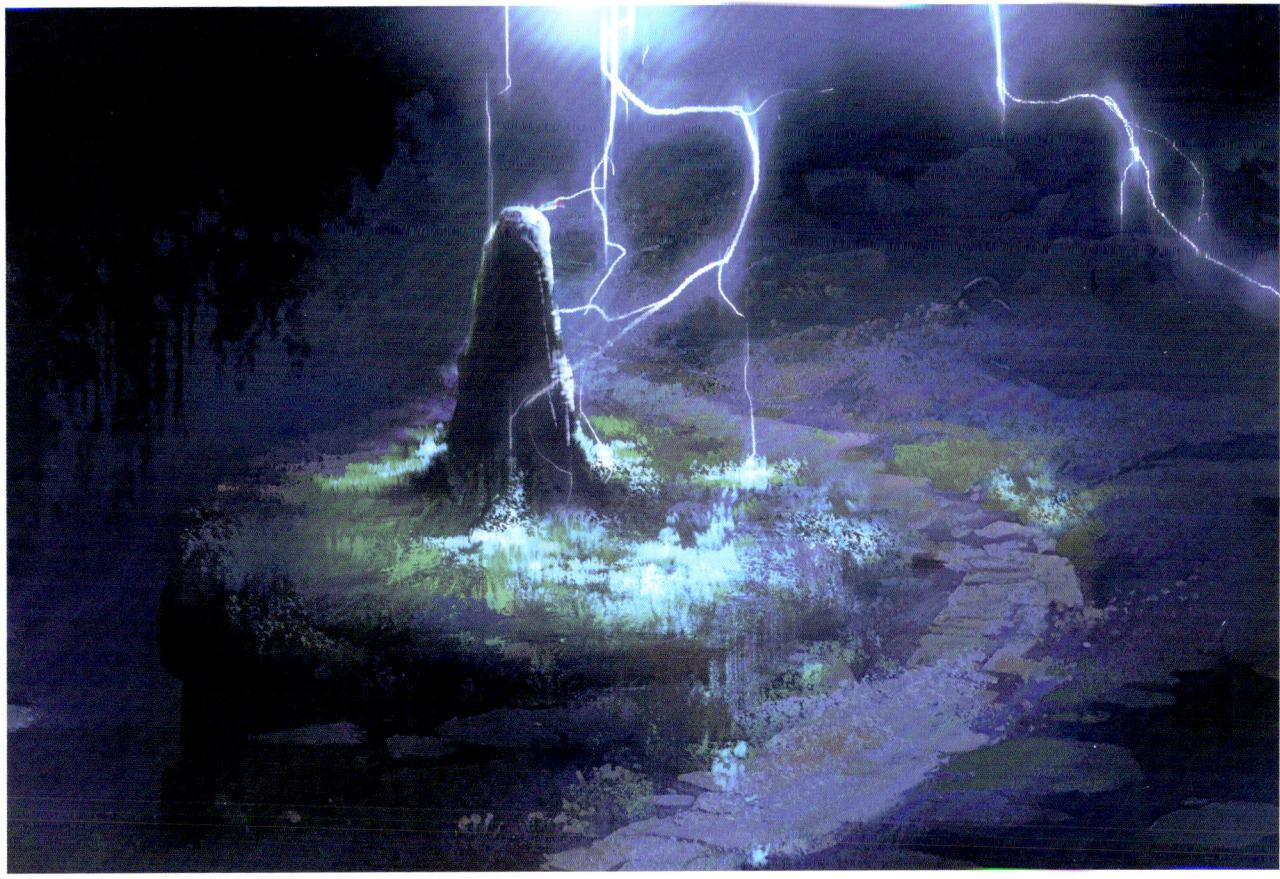

11. ...or the stark flash of a lightning strike?

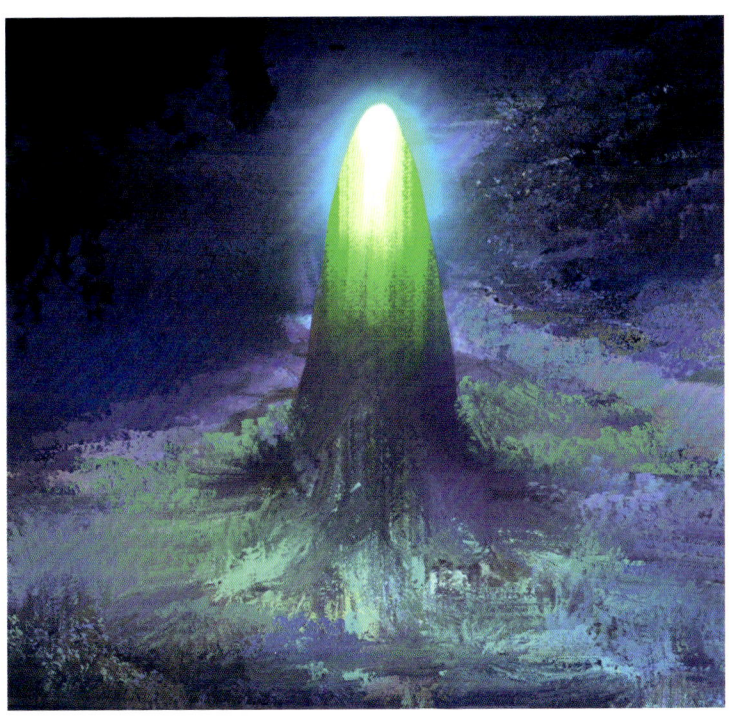

12. A magical green glow creates irresistible mystery!

11. LIGHTNING STRIKE

We'll stay all-natural but let's really design the *kaboom of doom* into this thing. Let's have a blast of lightning come flashing in, in a way that gives an extraordinary and inescapable emphasis.

12. MAGIC GLOW

And now for the grand finale – let's lay some serious magic into our object. It's got magic, it's got power, it has an inner glow, a vivid green light! Now it's an absolutely inescapable subject and has far more visual contrast than anything else in the environment. Now we've completely forgotten our journey down the path and we simply must investigate.

All these ideas are just a taste of further discussions in the book. They set the stage for powerful environment design and all the potent solutions that are at our fingertips.

DEMONSTRATION: MAKING A MIGHTY IMPACT

Let me do a demonstration for you to illustrate how to roll together all the ideas we've just been discussing to give a mighty impact to our environments. I'm going to use lighting, local color, weather, atmosphere, lightning, hot lava, crashing waves – everything I can think of to get the environment to cry out for our attention.

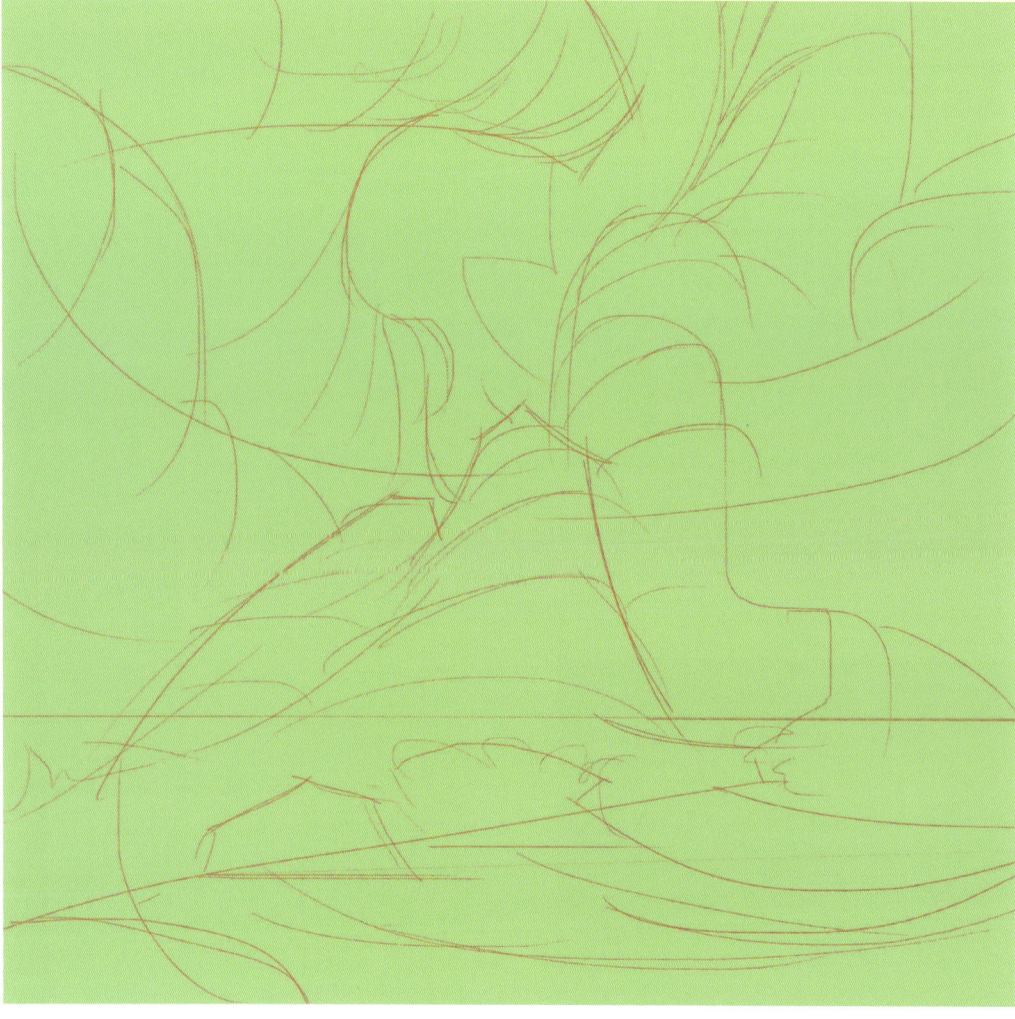

01. Start with a simple construction drawing and color base

01. INITIAL LINEWORK

I'd like this environment to have a surreal and unsettling quality, so I start with an underlying green color, something that really lets you know that all is not well. My line drawing is very simple but carefully crafted in terms of composition and form. I'm purposely making an 'eye of the storm' effect that's opening up above an island, filling the sky with crackling lightning. I begin by placing the horizon/eye-level line in the scene, which is usually my first step in the process. I'll give you a complete discussion on where and why you'll place horizon lines in a later chapter (page 110). In this case I place it so I have room for a full and active sky as well as a breadth of sea full of crashing waves. Notice that I've placed lines that give three-dimensional form to objects in the environment. The island and the clouds are treated like cylinders, twisting and moving through the scene, and I've suggested a few rocks in the bottom foreground to help create depth.

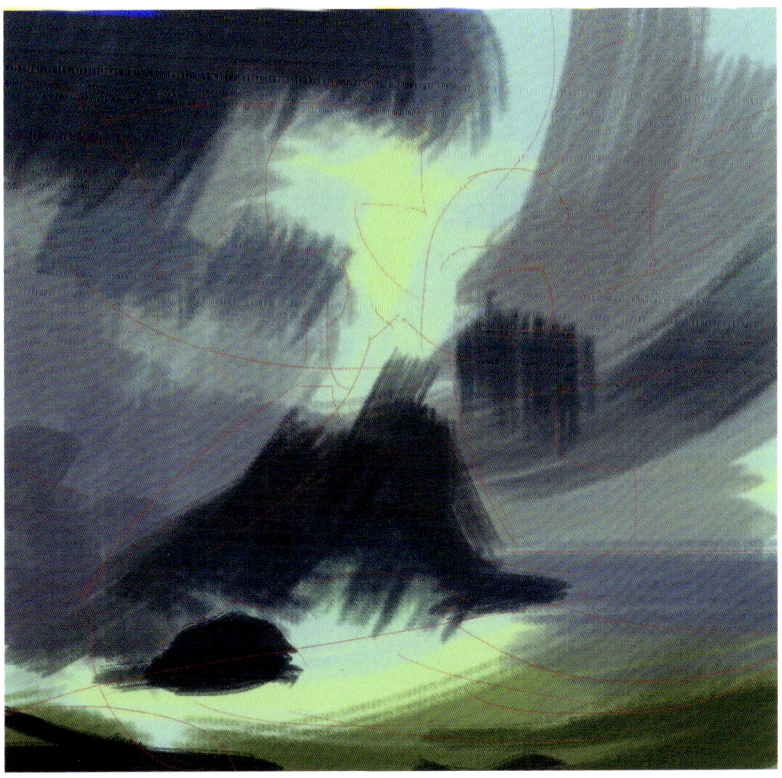

02. Block out the large, simple elements of the scene

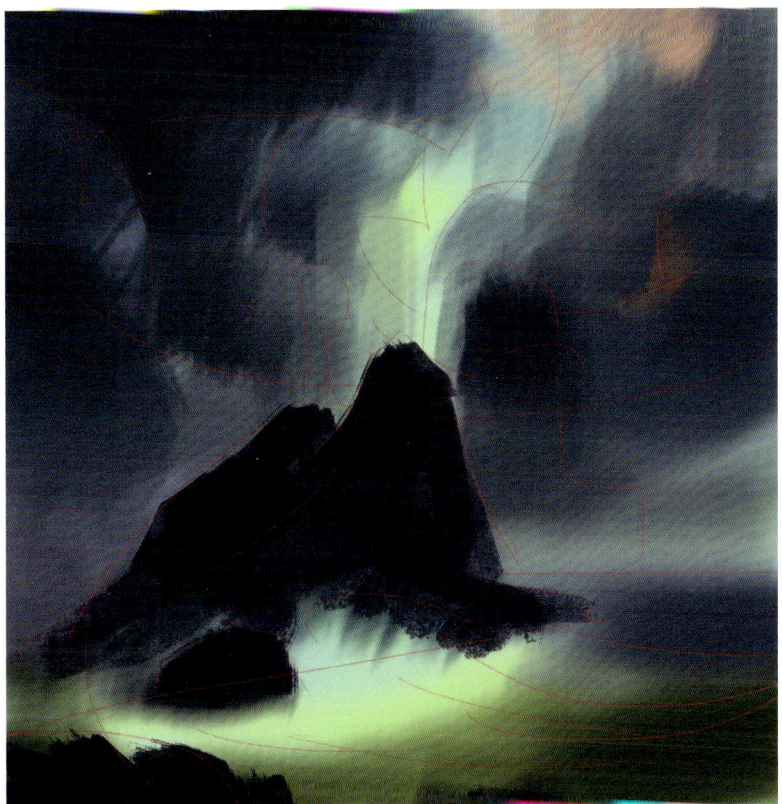

03. Build up the shapes and values of the island and clouds

If you want
to give an
environment
absolute
authority, have
very different
elements all
doing the
same thing.

02. BLOCKING IN

It looks like I've done a lot in this step, but I want you to notice how simple it is. I've arranged the elements so that the hierarchy of importance starts with the green glow below the island, which leads to the island itself, then up into the open part of the sky. The surrounding darkness acts as a frame for this central area. Notice that everything is unified in direction: the island itself tips to the right, the wind is blowing to the right, and the clouds all tip to the right. If you want to give an environment absolute authority, have very different elements all doing the same thing.

03. SHAPE & VALUE

It's time to start getting committed now, so I give the island its proper shape and dark value. I do the same with the clouds. Also important is the orange up at the top of the sky, which serves two purposes: it completes the diagonal composition and is a counterpoint to the greens in the rest of the environment.

04. CLOUD FORMATIONS

And now for the clouds. They have two light sources for us to deal with: a cool ambient light coming from above and the brighter greenish light coming from the lightning. I begin with a textured brush that has harder edges on the top and softer edges on the bottom to help suggest the broken forms of the clouds. I simply wrap these lights around the cloud shapes as laid out in the line drawing. The brighter green light is coming from the center area of the clouds, so I add it only in the areas of cloud that face that direction.

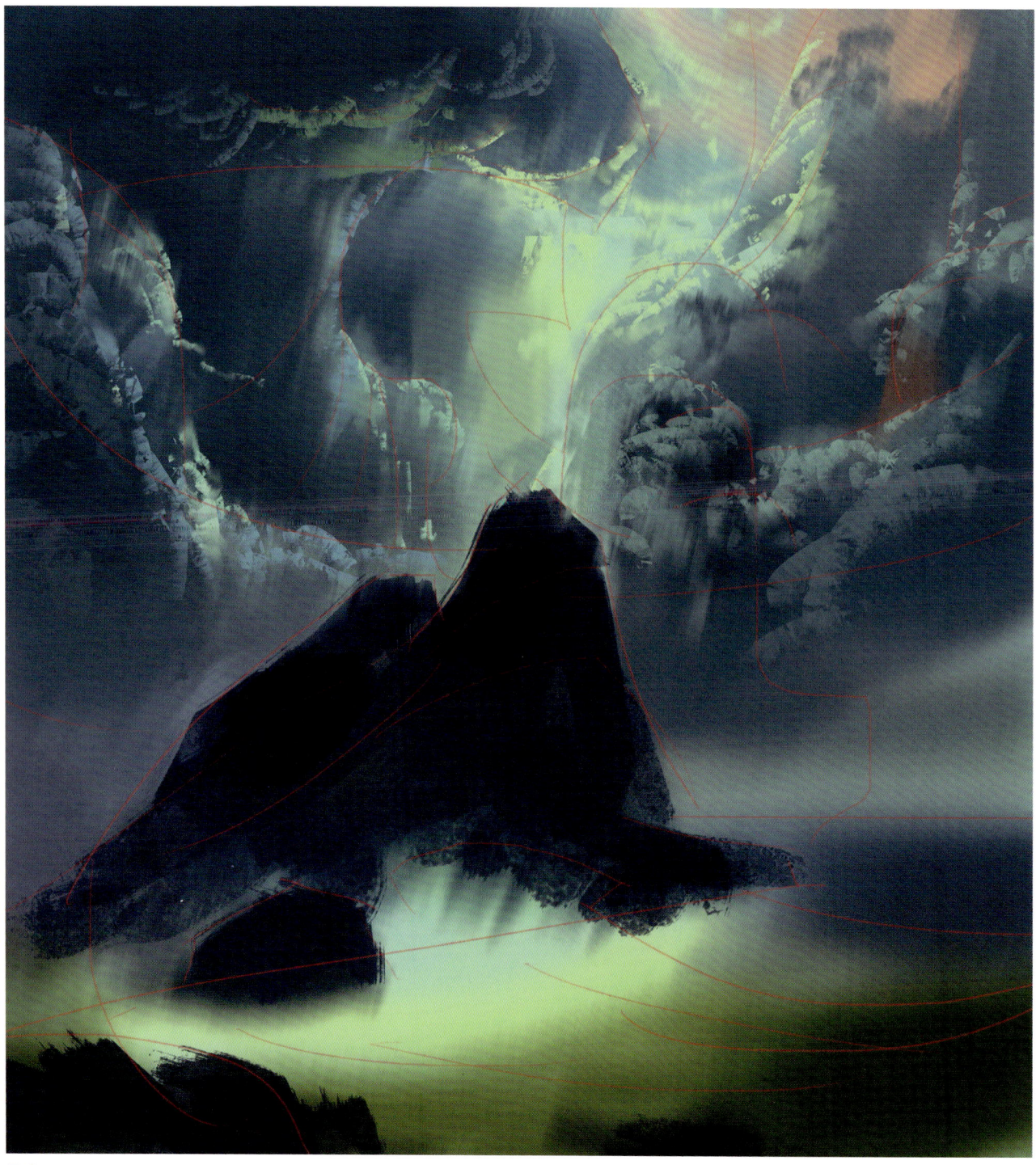

04. Two light sources give the clouds their dramatic form

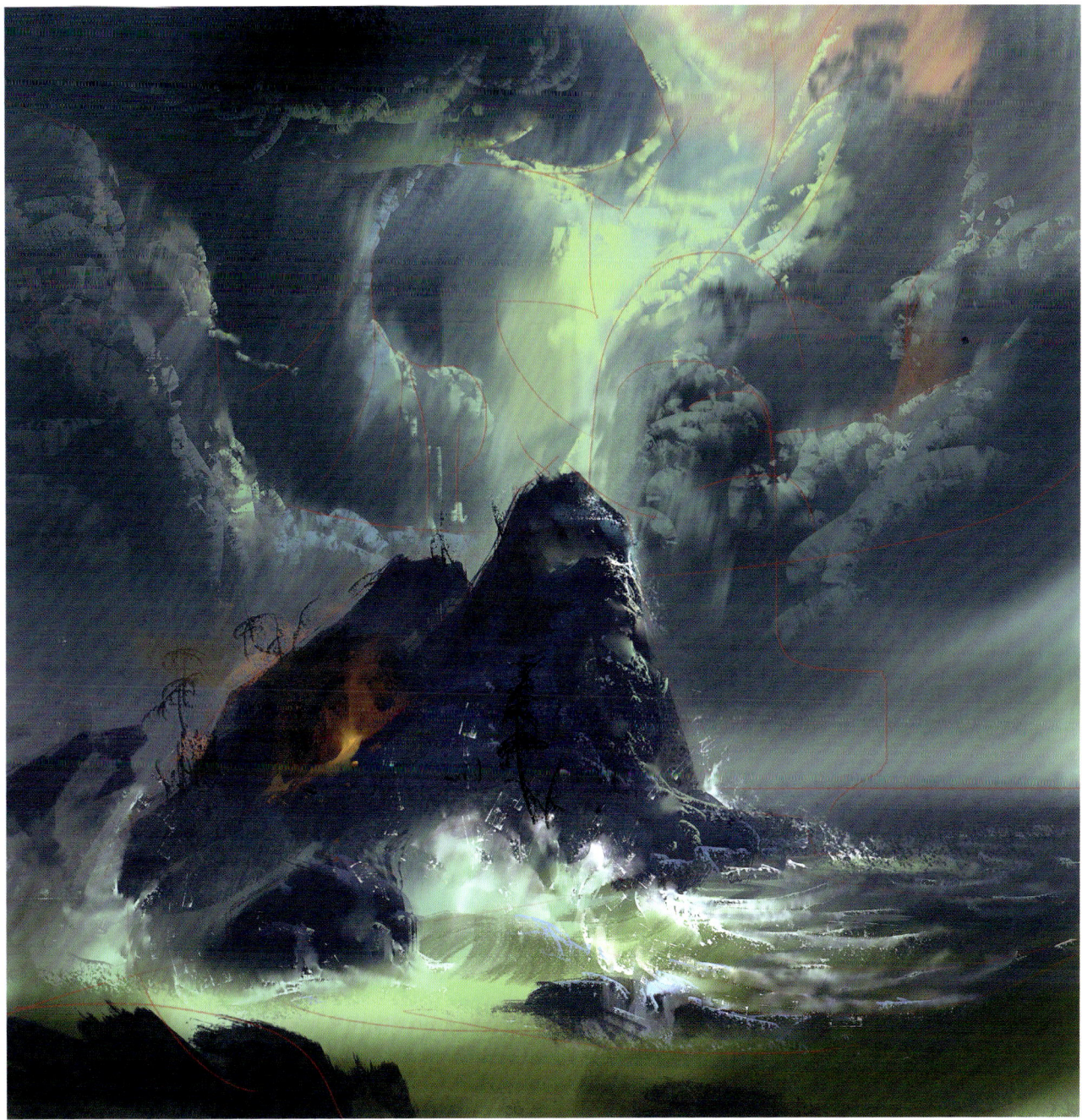

05. Add light and texture to the island and water

05. ISLAND TEXTURES

I've been saving the lightning until last so I can design its intensity based on the rest of the scene. Let's bring everything else to a finish first. I treat the island in exactly the same way as I did the clouds, with cool atmospheric light wrapping around the cylindrical shapes, then a brighter rim lighting along its right side. Getting some hot lava in there is completely irresistible and adds a nice hot contrast to the environmental green, so I find a spot for that on the island. I also add in the suggestion of a few trees on the island to help the audience understand its scale. The crashing waves are critical to this scene, so I carefully work them up around the island, especially concentrating them in the lower center and left of the image to assist in the diagonal composition.

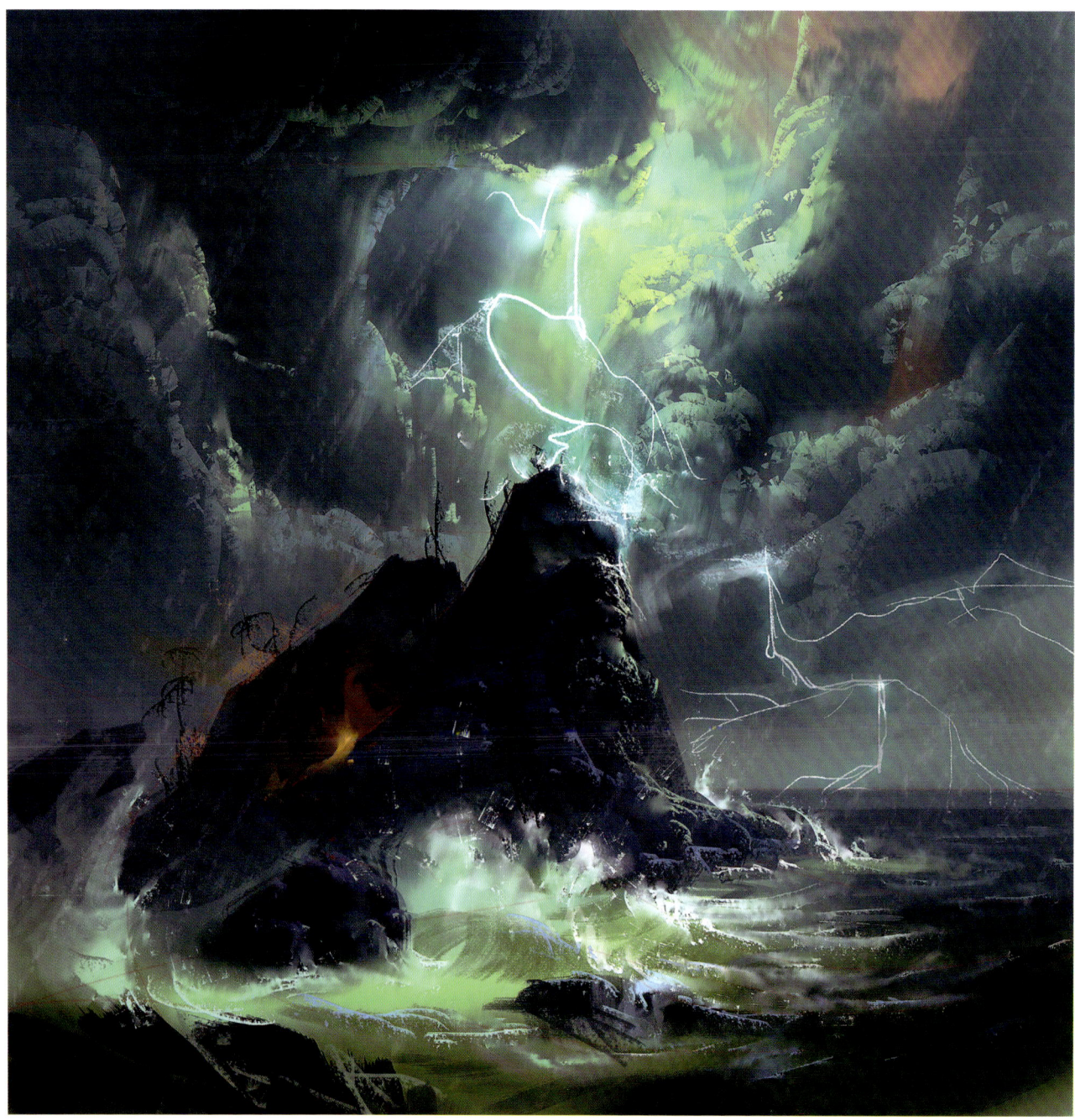

06. Finish off the scene with weather effects

06. WEATHER EFFECTS

It's time for the lightning. I work out some shapes that give
action and movement to the scene, surrounding the streaks
of lightning with a crackling ozone-blue glow. I also complete
the foreground area, giving it some simple rim lighting along
its forms. Now I've thrown everything I can think of at this
scene and, if you don't mind me saying so, I'm very happy
with the result!

RECOMMENDED EXERCISE:
STUDIES FROM IMAGINATION

Throughout this chapter I've been pushing the idea of creating purposeful images, images that are designed to tell the story of an environment. I have a panel of such studies for you here that I've done as part of my daily practice. Each one is kept simple by imagining a quality of environment and then undertaking to convey it as simply as possible.

For instance, if you envision an environment that has an important precipice, as shown in the first sketch, you might have the entirety of the environment follow the thrust of that precipice. If you envision a moody but hopeful environment, you might rough out a place with cool mist that has a warm sun emerging into it, as shown in the middle-left environment. And if you want to create the same effect but at night, you might go with dark and spooky colors but have the environment lift into a luminous starlit sky.

Throw everything you can think of at this exercise to begin expanding the limits of your capabilities. I'll share with you more and more ideas and approaches to get effective at this process, but I encourage you to start now.

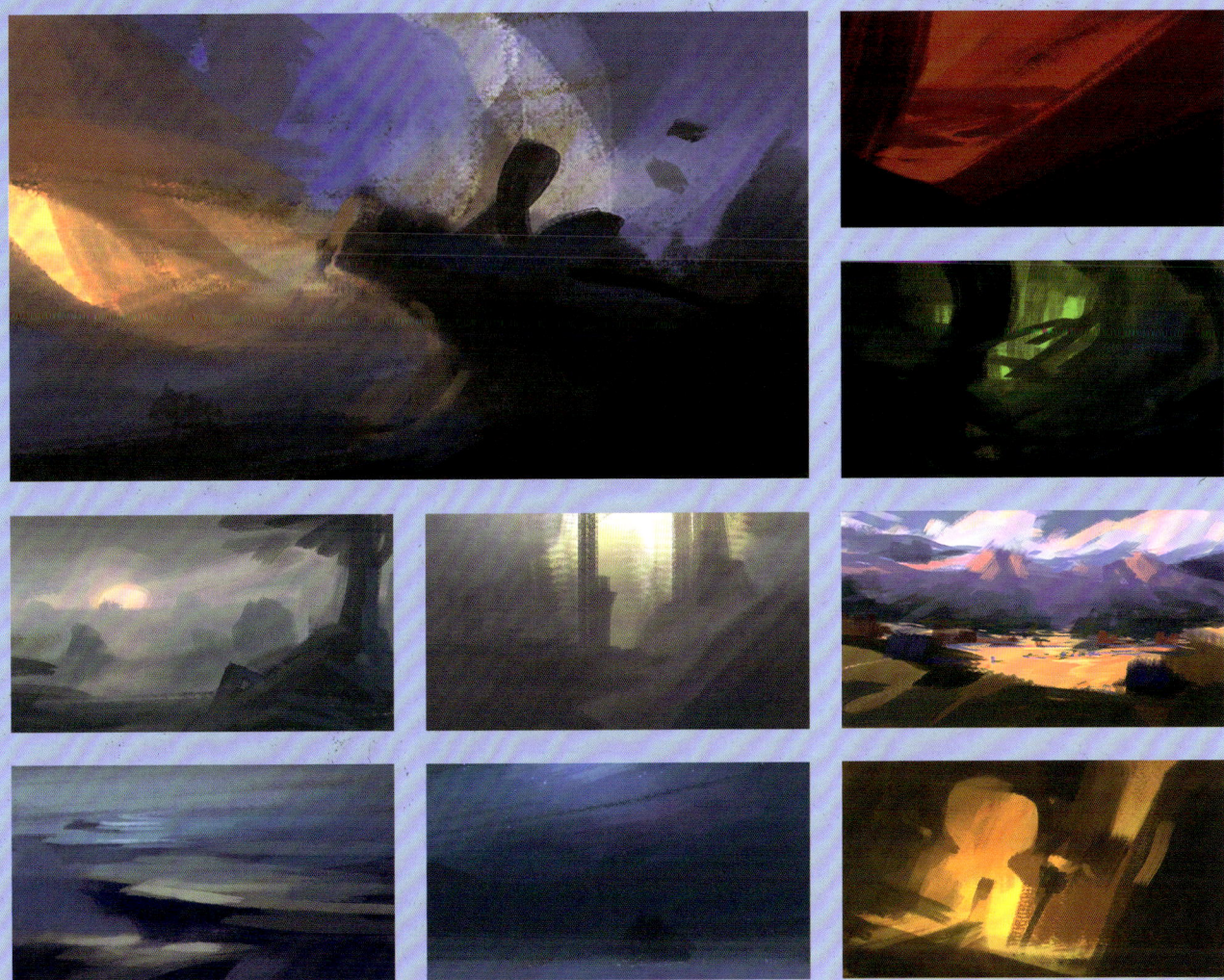

△ Examples of my daily environment sketches

THE DESIGN OF VALUE

I like to refer to what we do as artists as *clarity with artistry*, making our subject clear and giving it visual interest and meaning.

In this chapter we'll dig into clarity through the design of value, then in the next chapter we'll advance into artistry and how to bring a deep emotion into our environments. And a reminder, *value* is the term artists use to describe the range of tone from white to black and everything in between.

THE PHONE CALL OF A LIFETIME

First let me tell you about an interesting phone call I received some time back in my career. I was working full time at DreamWorks as a concept artist for animation and I was teaching a few life-drawing classes on the side.

By this time in my career I was fairly well known in animation, as well as in the life-drawing classroom. While in my office at DreamWorks, I got a call, and I immediately had to lower my voice because the call was from Disney! They were looking for a life-drawing instructor to work with their artists once a week after hours. I looked over my contract and there was no conflict of interest, since I would not be discussing animation design with my Disney students. It was strictly about figurative drawing in charcoal.

Way back in art school, I had hoped that somehow my work would get some traction and I might be able to someday work with a notable studio or two. And now I found myself working at Disney and DreamWorks ... at the same time!

You may not be aware that one of the Disney campuses is literally across the street from DreamWorks Animation. The companies are not in any way related to each other but they are within throwing distance. So every Wednesday I would walk across the street to teach my class and let myself in with my Disney key card. Then I would wrap up by going to the Disney kitchenette and rifling through their snacks. And if they didn't have anything good, I would walk back across the street, around 10 pm, and let myself into DreamWorks to see if they had better snacks. Frankly I couldn't believe it. I could let myself into both Disney and DreamWorks at any time I wanted, day or night! (And if you need to know, DreamWorks usually had better snacks than Disney.)

But my point is that this opportunity came my way because I had been working tirelessly to gain a skill set that had real value to people. I had spent thousands of hours not just studying animation art but backing it up with analytical life drawing. This is something that gave me the ability to give form and clarity to my work. It trained me in how to take a two-dimensional surface and give it the appearance of form and substance with nothing but light and dark.

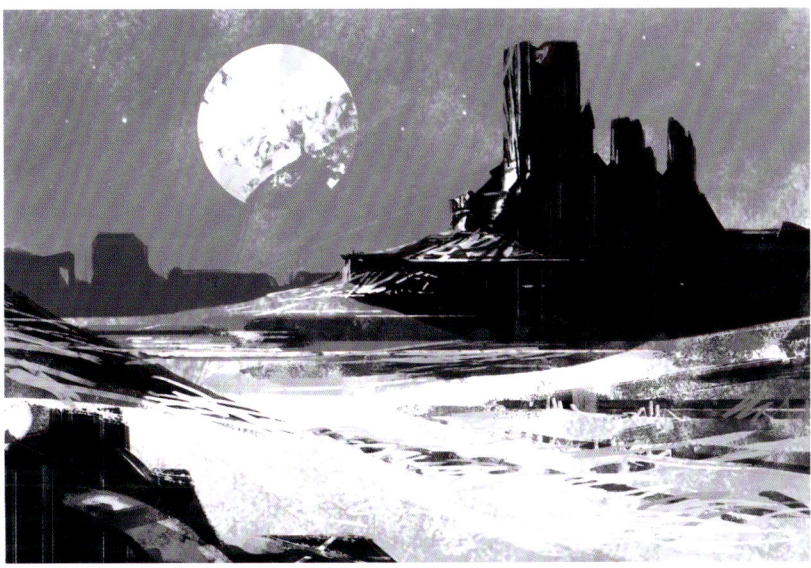
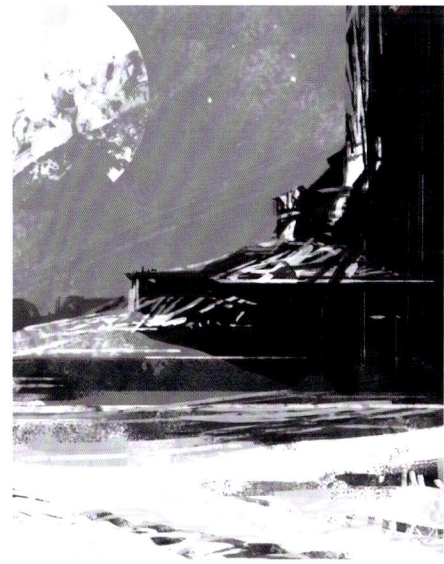

△ Light and dark values are what give an image depth and form

THE SIMPLE VALUE STATEMENT

Let's begin with the painting shown below, *The Teton Range*, by the great American landscape painter Thomas Moran (1837–1926).

It's a gorgeous oil painting filled with lavish textures and fine detail; a painting so skillfully done that it would be a challenge for the best of us to match. So if most of us just can't paint as well as Thomas Moran did, what's the point? Well, how about we do a little breakdown of the painting and see if it's really so far out of reach.

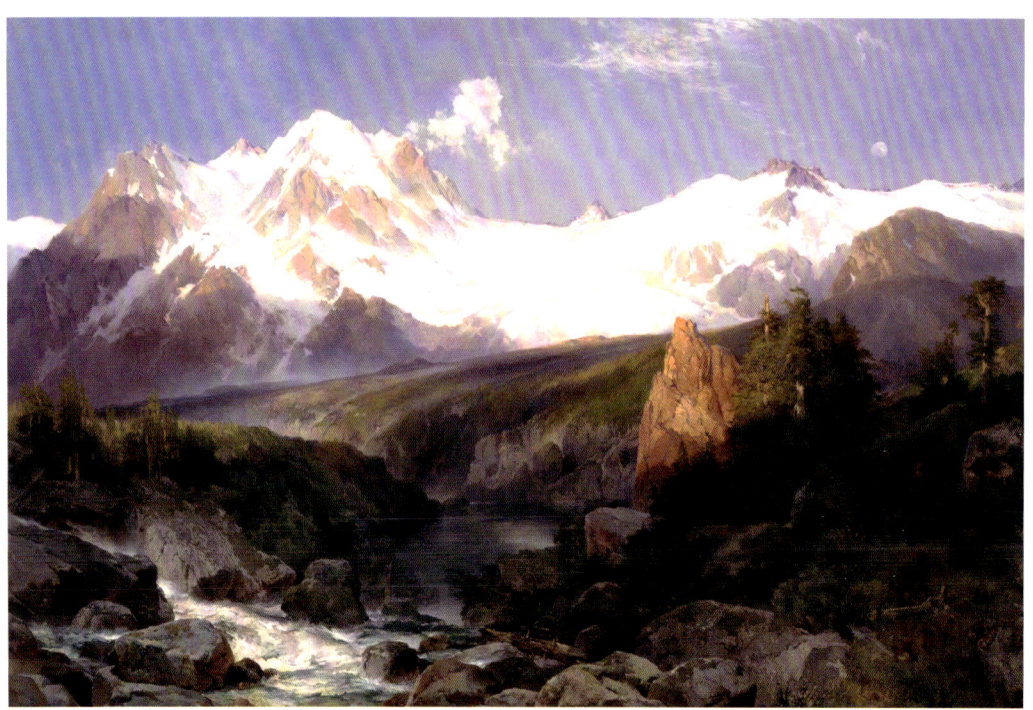

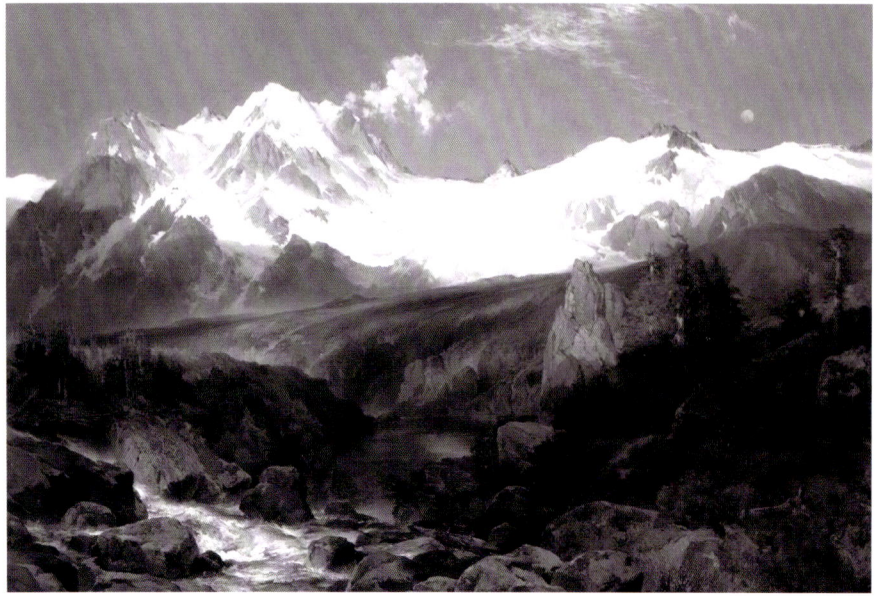

01. GRAYSCALE REFERENCE

First I shift the original painting (above) to a value-only version (left). All the beautiful detail work is still there, but you might notice that the values are very simply organized.

01. A grayscale version of *The Teton Range*

The Teton Range (1897) by Thomas Moran

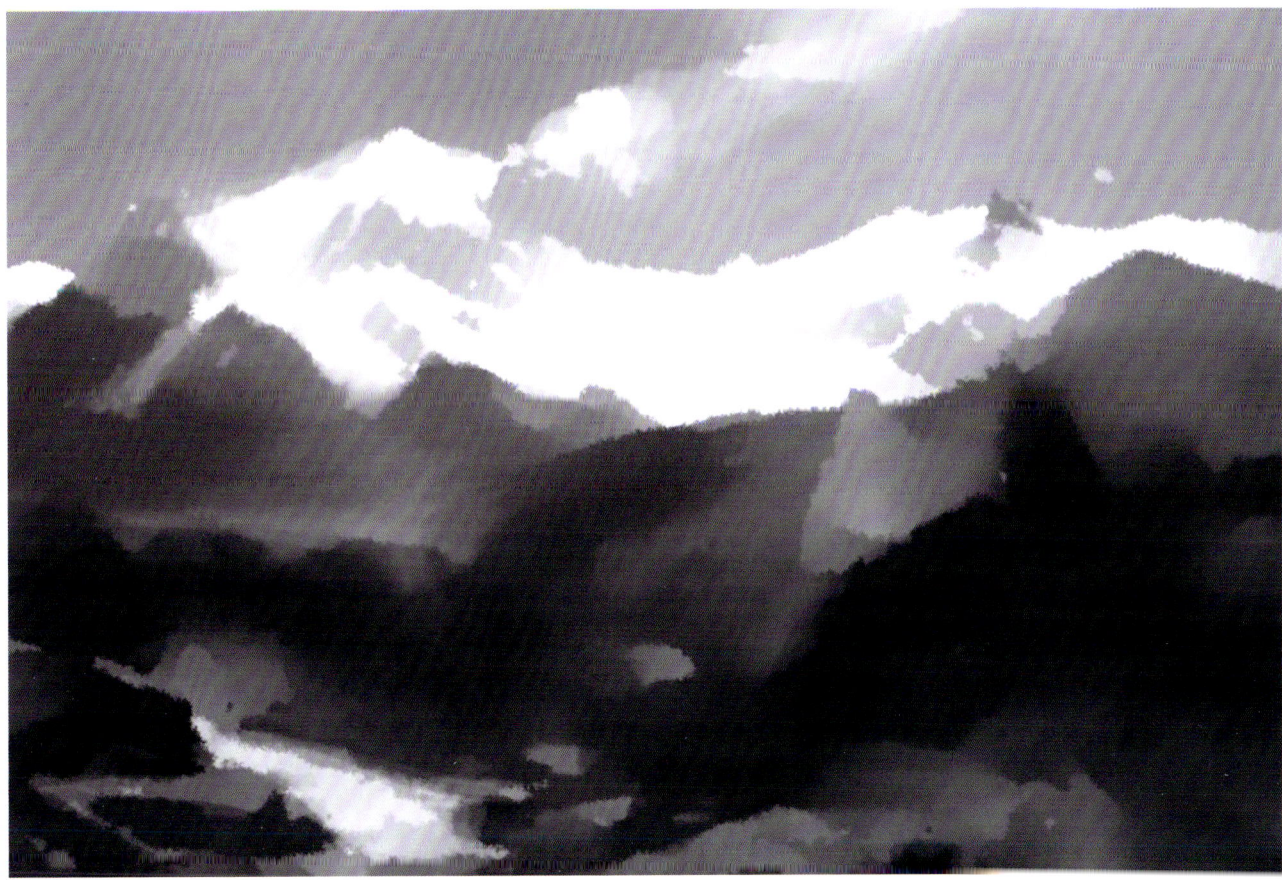

02. A simplified version with no details

02. SIMPLIFICATION

Next, I create a simplified version of the image – blending away all of the texture and small detail so we can see the simple statement of value that lies underneath. But to me, the big reveal is the next step, so let's jump to the next image!

03. MORE SIMPLIFICATION

I've now created an extreme simplification of the image, and what do you know? Beneath all that wonderful rendering is an ultra-simple and powerful value statement. You and I might not yet have the capabilities of Thomas Moran, but we have the capability to understand and use the simple value structures that make his paintings powerful. So next let's take a stab at creating our own epic environment with carefully designed values.

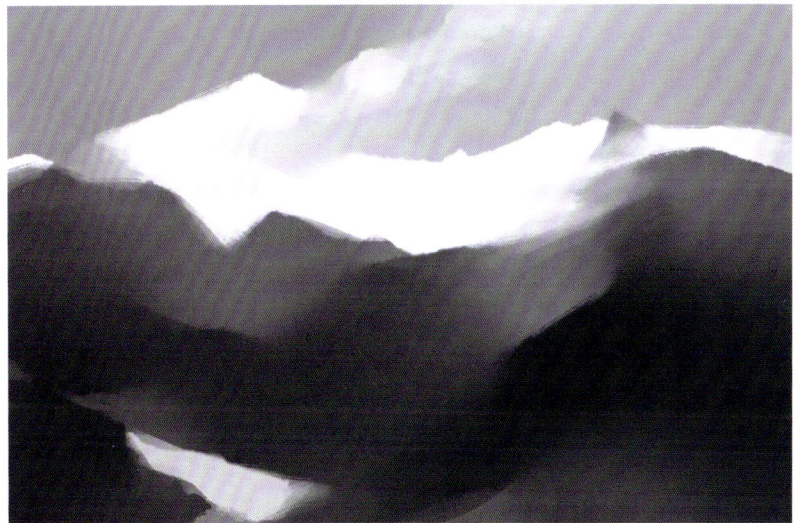

03. The simplest possible version of the painting

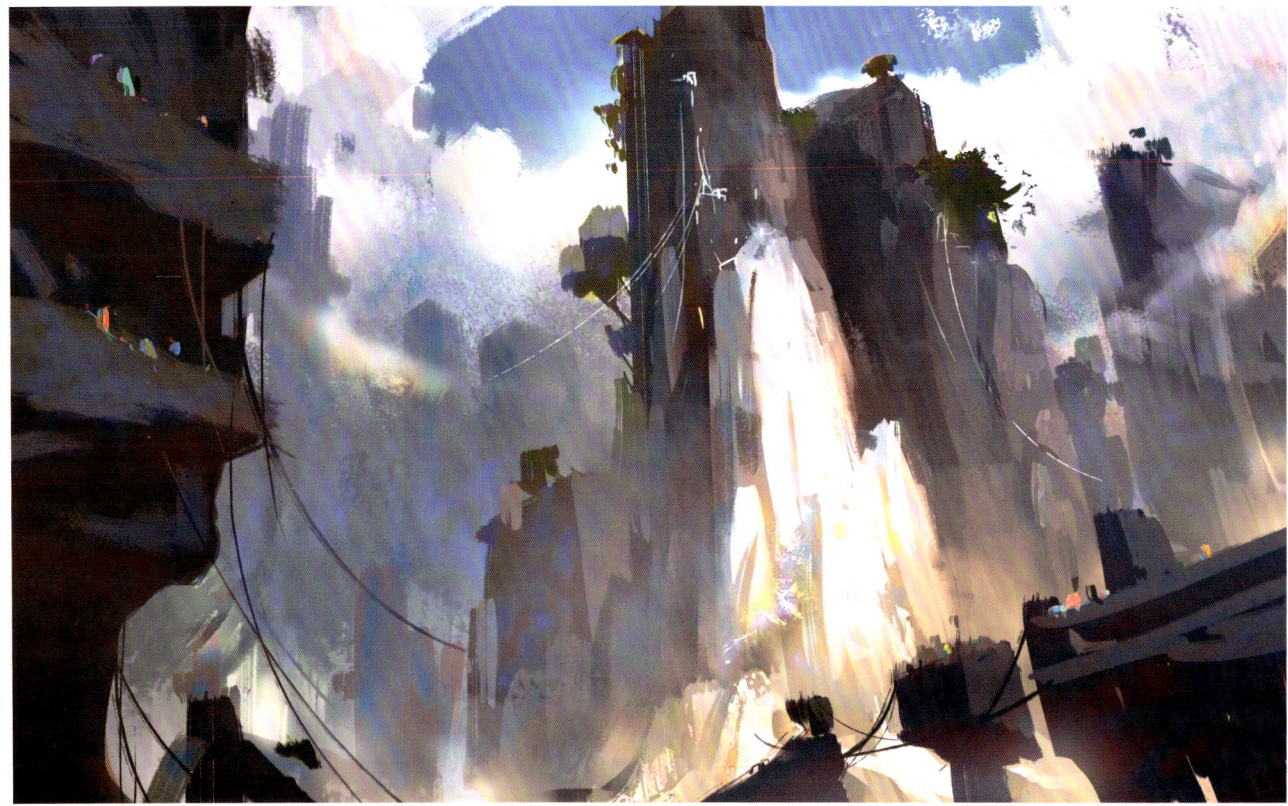

04. A color painting inspired by Moran's use of value

04. QUICK PAINTING

OK, this painting is no Thomas Moran, but I spent a few hours on mine and Moran must have spent weeks on his. Many of us have tough deadlines where we need to complete environments quickly while making sure they have both clarity and artistry. Let's look at this one in black and white and see how I did.

05. VALUES ONLY

My goals for this study were as follows: to set up a good quality of depth using a dark foreground with some dusty atmosphere behind it, then grab the eye with the light rock face in the center and lift us up into the picture. I intentionally surrounded that area with darker mountains for contrast, then shifted values again to bright white clouds at the top. I then opened a big circle in the clouds around the spire to grant the scene a quality of purpose.

06. SIMPLE VERSION

And here's the simplified version of the image. How did I do in terms of getting a simple and purposeful value statement that has clarity and artistry?

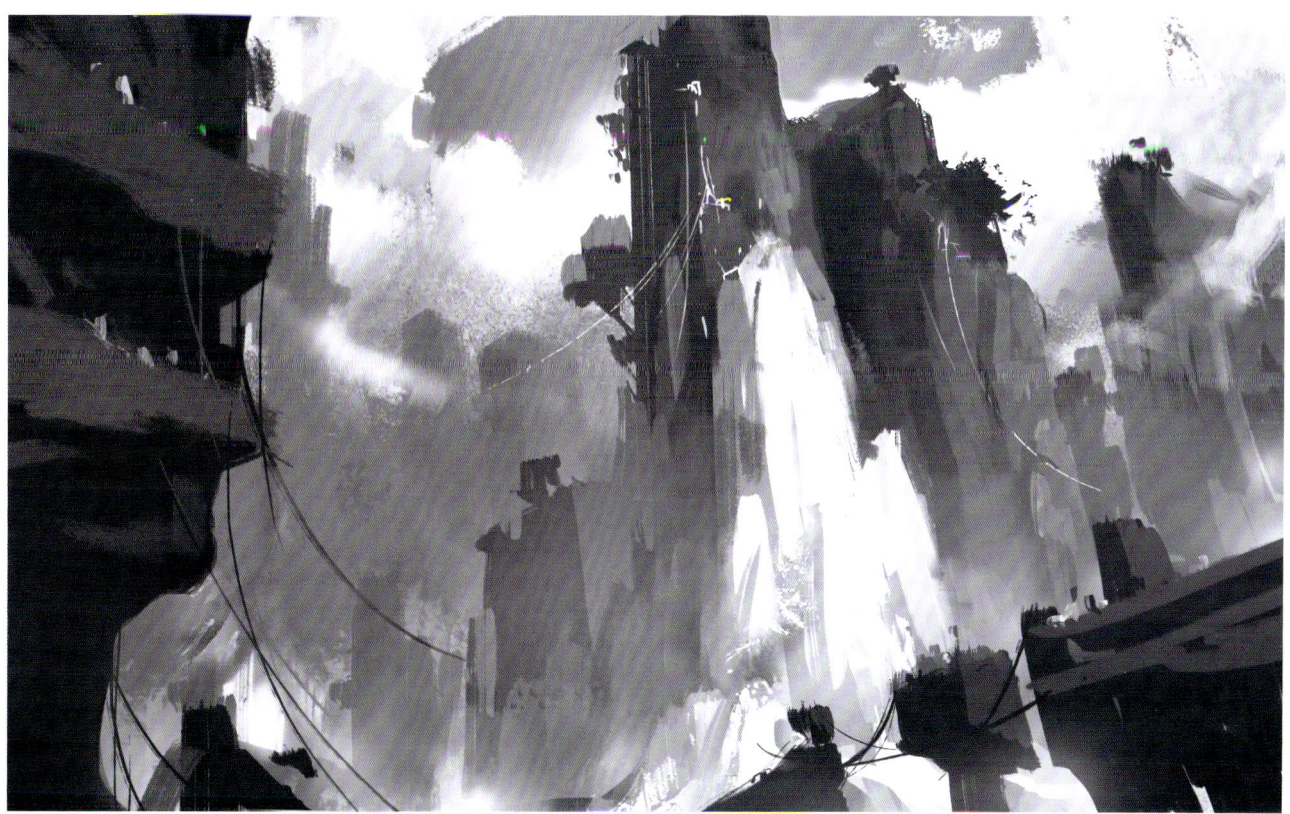

05. The painting holds up well viewed in grayscale

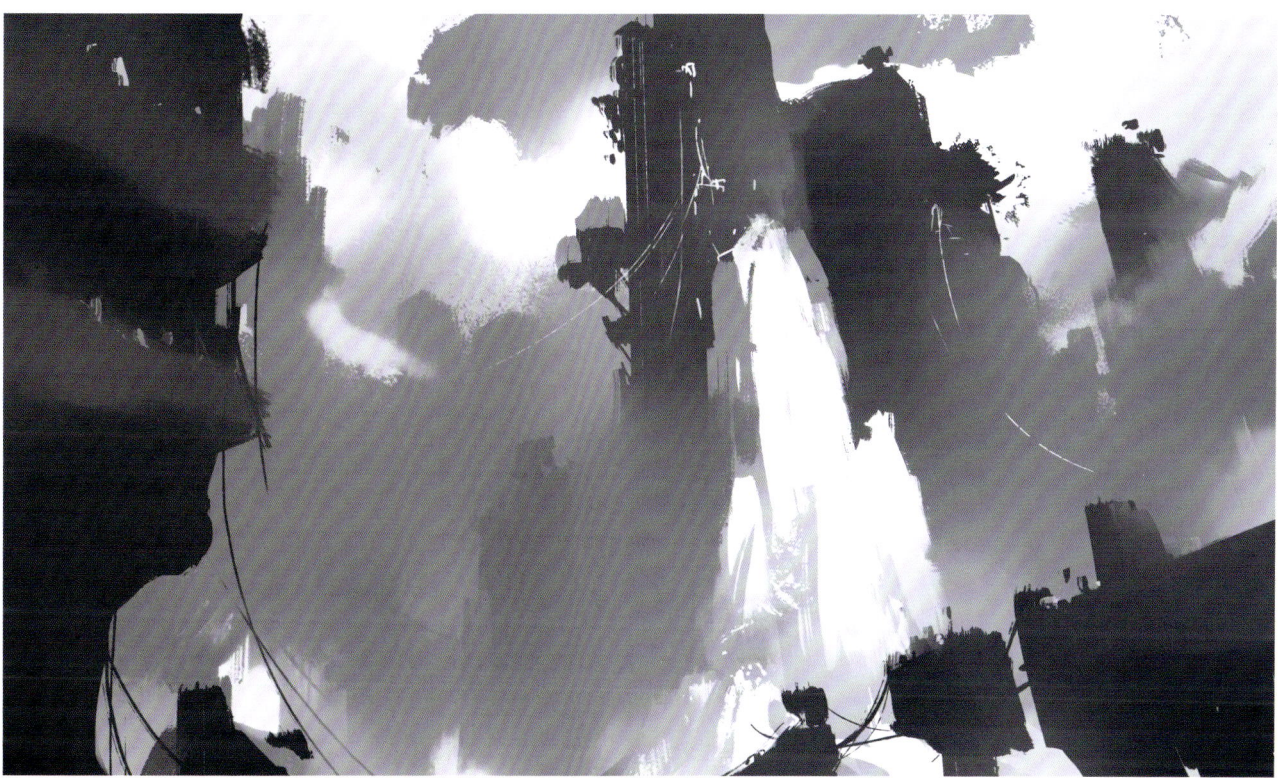

06. The super-simplified version

THE THREE CONSIDERATIONS OF VALUE

Now let's break things down to be sure we understand the basic ways in which value is used. Value has only these three considerations: silhouette, local values, and light and shadow.

This is great for us! Keeping things simple gives us the ability to manage complicated subjects.

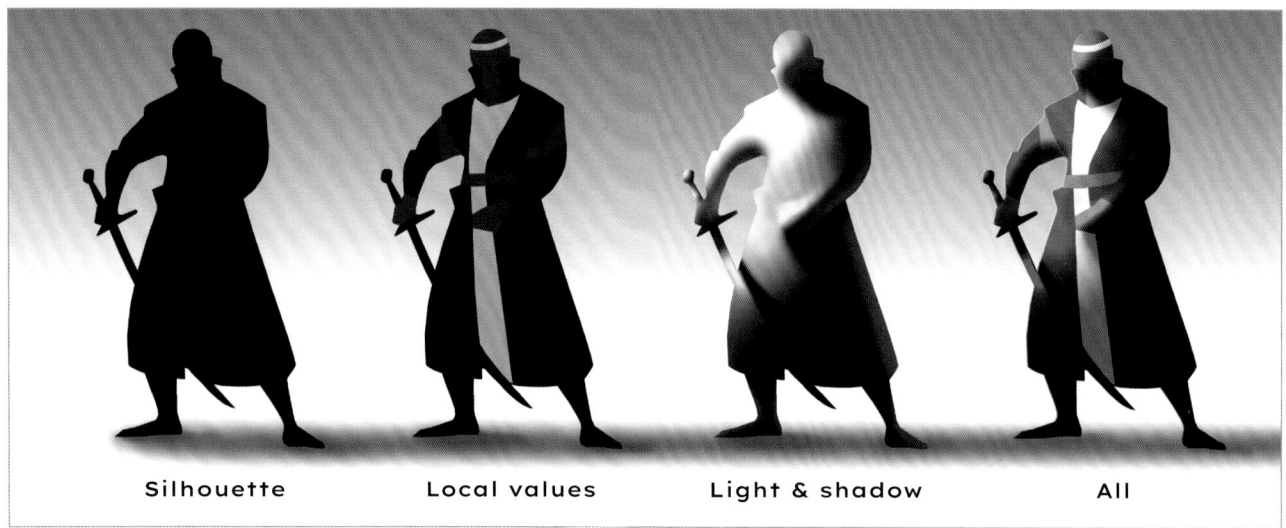

| Silhouette | Local values | Light & shadow | All |

01. The basics of value demonstrated on a character

01. CHARACTER VALUES

Let's start with a familiar subject, such as a character, and show the shape or silhouette, the local values, and the light and shadow. In case the term 'local value' creates any confusion, it refers to the value of the object independent of the lighting. For example, the local values of this character's jacket and shirt are dark and light, respectively.

02. ENVIRONMENT VALUES

Now we'll take the same idea into the realm of environments. We'll take a generic haunted-house idea and break it down into the same simple considerations as before: silhouette, local value, and light and shadow.

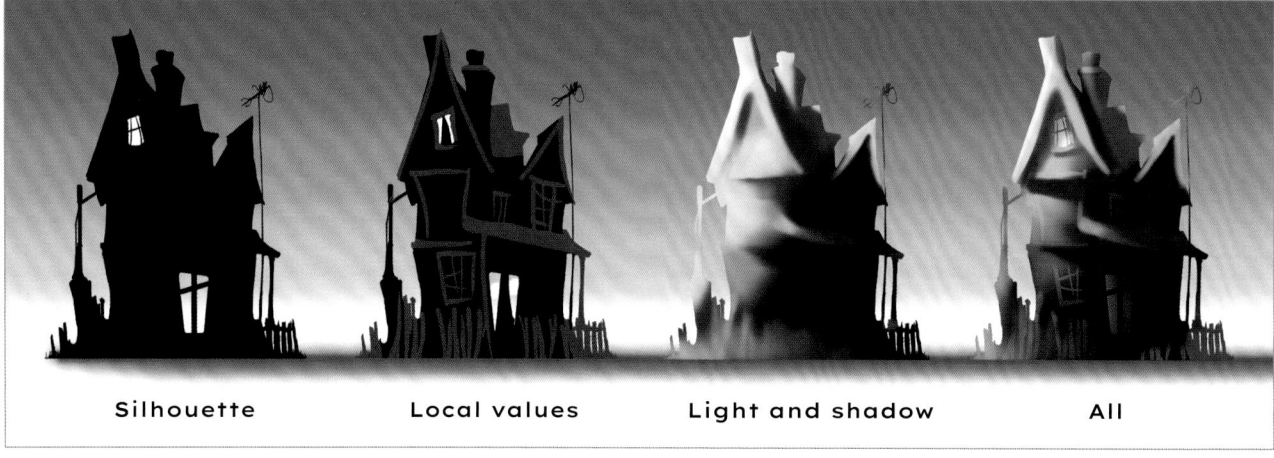

| Silhouette | Local values | Light and shadow | All |

02. The basics of value applied to an environmental subject

03. FULL-SCENE VALUES

Now let's bring these ideas to an entire environment. Let's take this spooky tree with its surroundings and break it down into the same three considerations. In version two, on the bottom left, I've simplified it into its most basic silhouette. In version three, on the bottom right, we can see the simple silhouettes, local values, and lighting. This particular painting was tricky for me to do, but keeping a careful eye on these three considerations of value made it manageable.

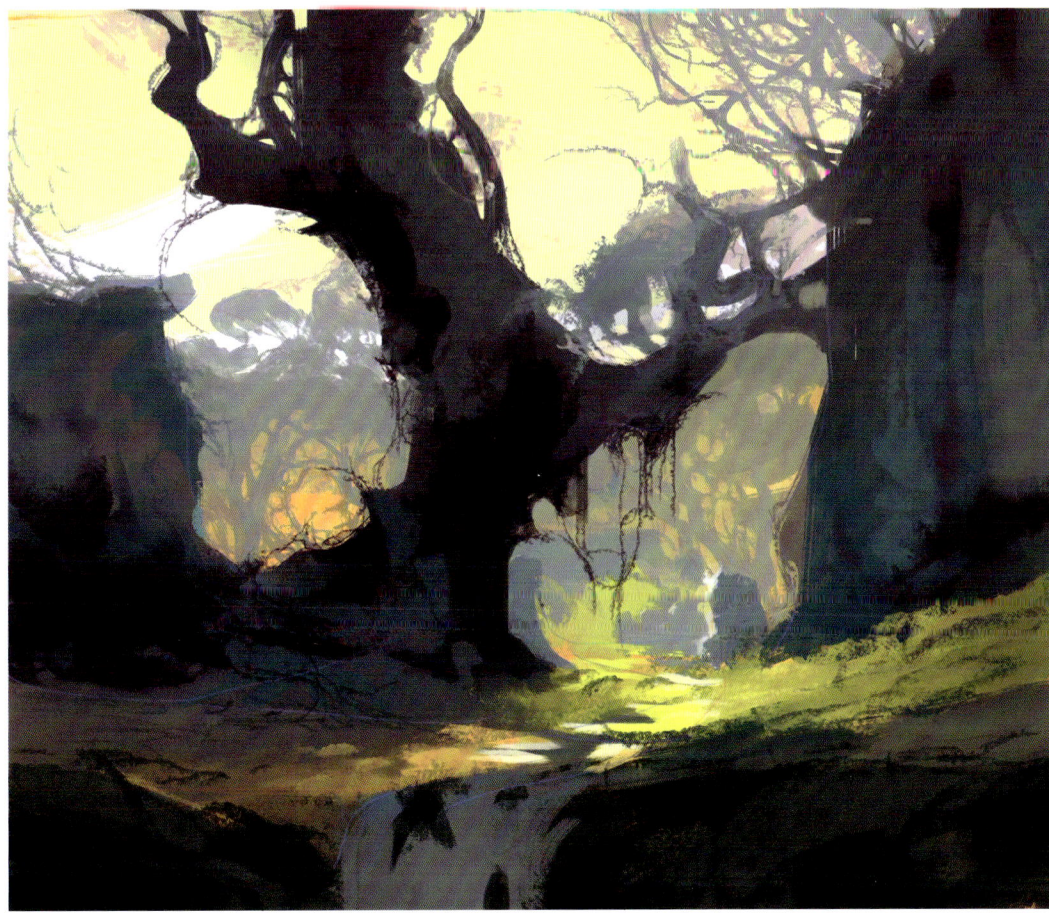

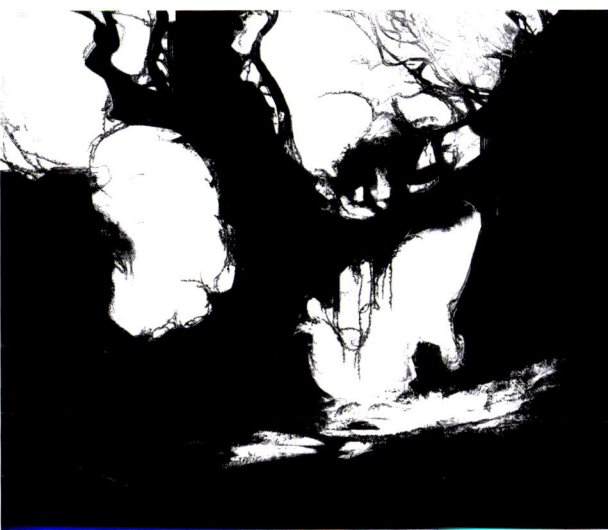

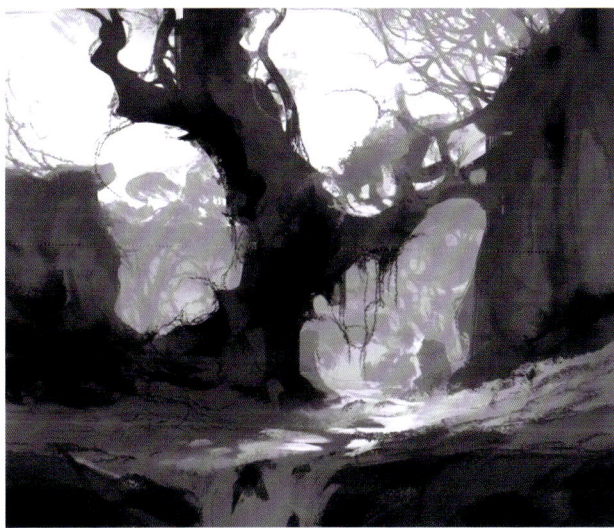

03. An entire environment painting broken down into its component values

VALUE KEY

Our next concept to review is something many artists and photographers refer to as 'key'. Let's use another imaginary scene as an example.

I've shifted the original scene in three ways: the dark and brooding low-key version, the bright and atmospheric high-key version, and the higher-contrast mid-key version.

Most of us are used to thinking about designing our color palettes, but we often forget to do the same with value. For instance, everyone understands that an image that has an overall blue color palette will carry a specific mood with it; at the same time, we could design such a scene with a low-key, brooding value palette as well. Designing value palettes is often as important as designing color palettes.

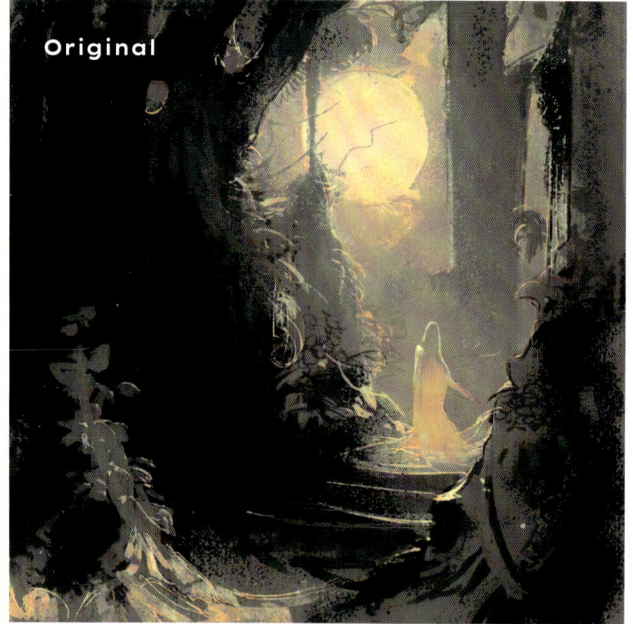

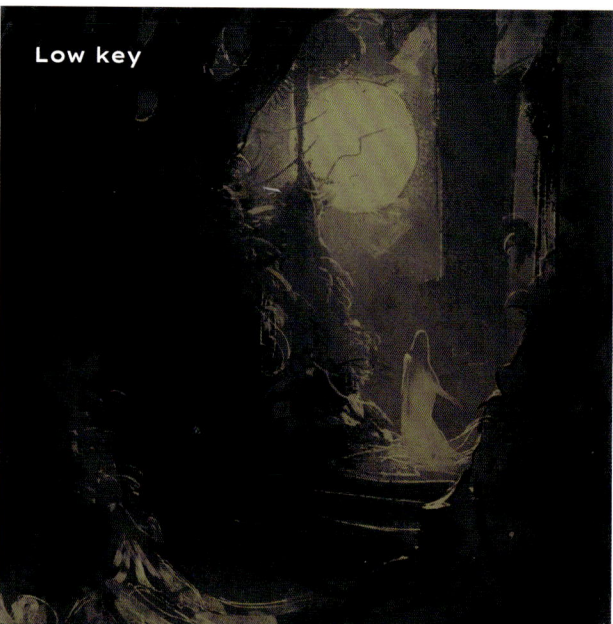

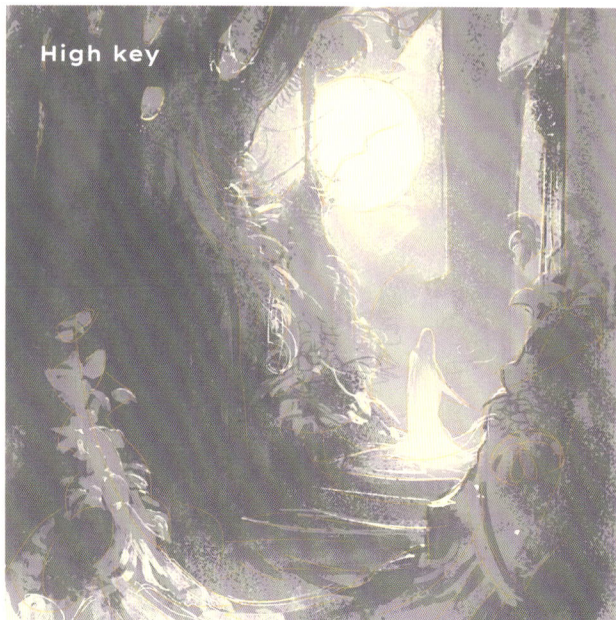

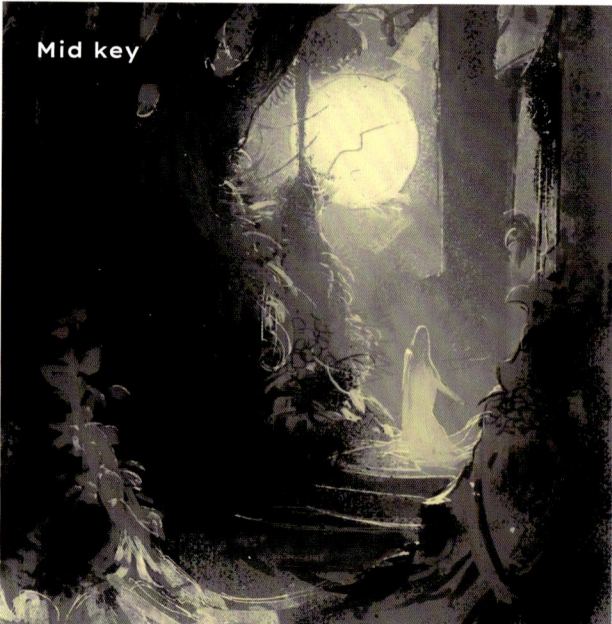

△ Choosing a suitable value key for an environment is as vital as choosing colors

PURPOSE THROUGH VALUE DESIGN

Let's get back to the critically important topic of purpose. We've discussed at length the idea that every environment has a purpose and that it must be carefully designed to fulfill that purpose, so let's apply that idea to value. I'm going to take you through several examples now, so hold on to your seat!

01. KNOW THE PURPOSE

For this image, I had the idea of a mysterious person out in a mysterious nighttime environment. I made up a light source coming in from the right. It could be the last light of the sun or a nearby bright city light, but being literal doesn't matter so much here; what matters is illuminating the purpose of the image. So I placed the character near the center, then reinforced it with a dark architectural icon directly above, and then placed the moon above that. These elements are all aligned to suggest a quality of purpose, and I used value to create a visually engaging contrast between them.

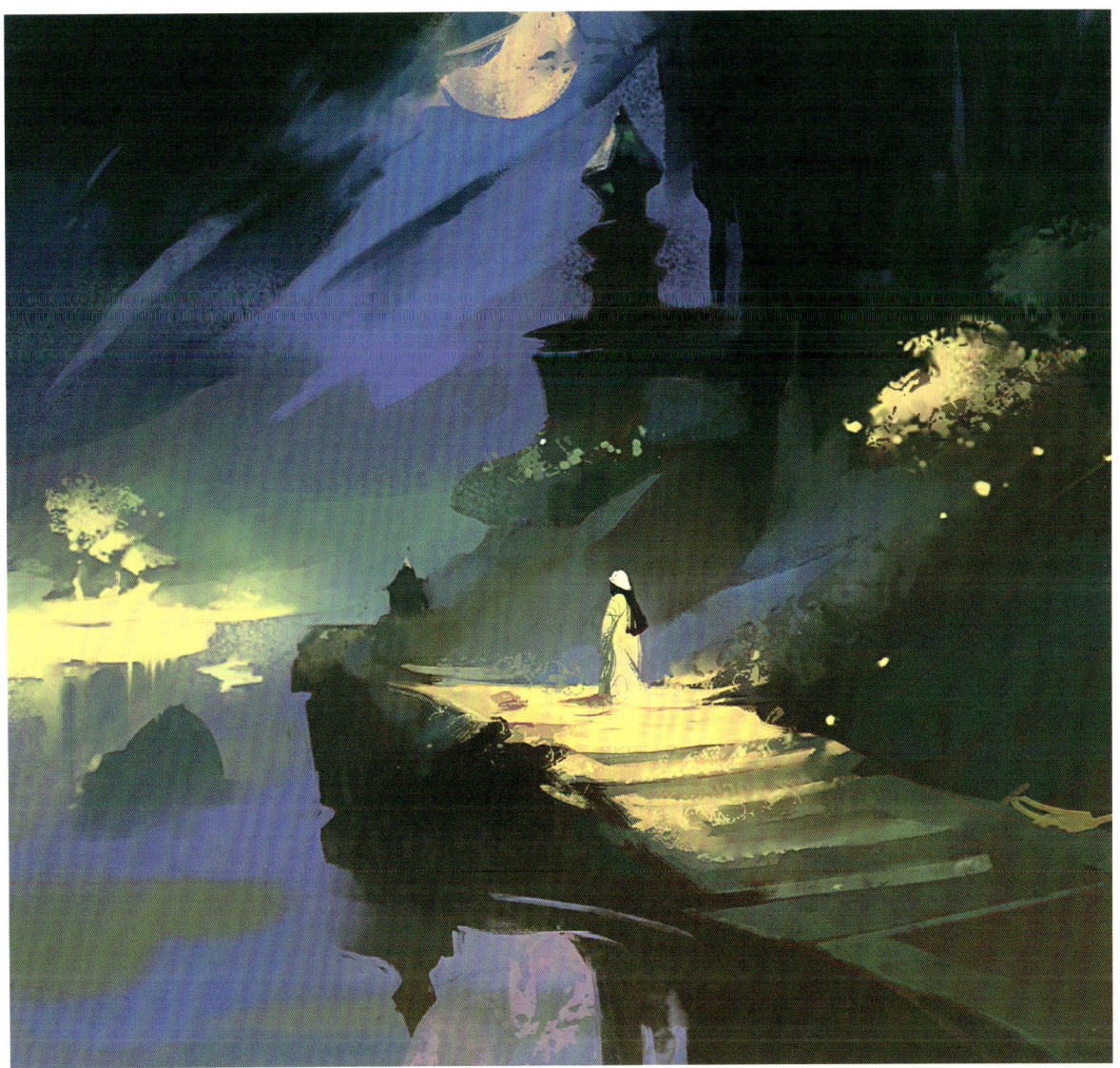

01. This image's goal is to convey an enigmatic nighttime atmosphere

02. REINFORCE WITH VALUE

Take a look at the black-and-white version to the right and you'll notice how the massings of light and dark are carefully grouped to reinforce the quality of purpose.

Now let's compare that with my simplified breakdown below. I've used silhouette, local value, and light and shadow to carefully organize the purpose of this environment. Notice how this simplification is not so very different in concept from the Thomas Moran image we reviewed on page 56.

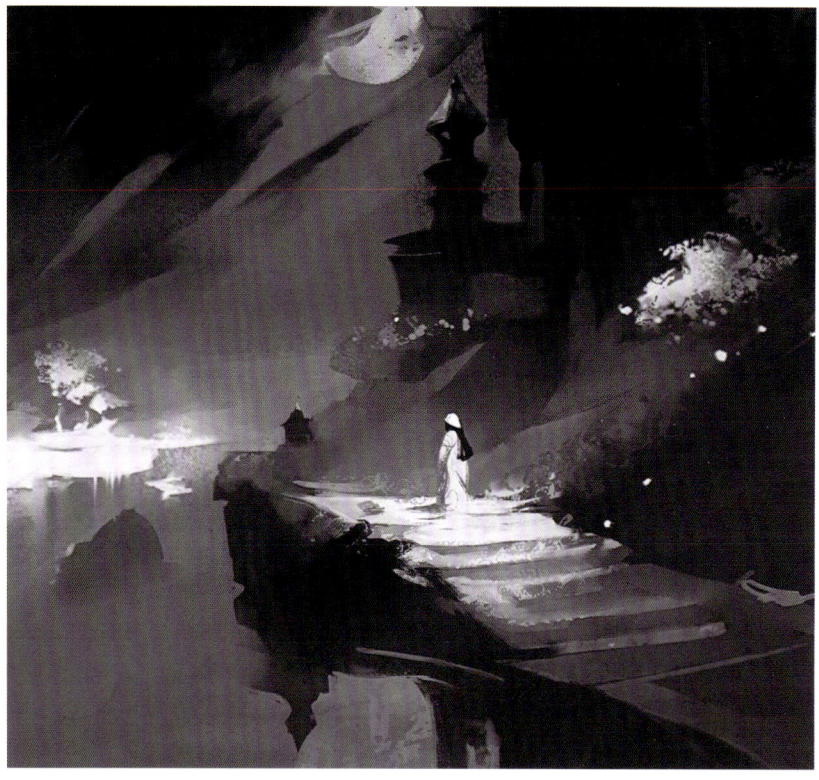

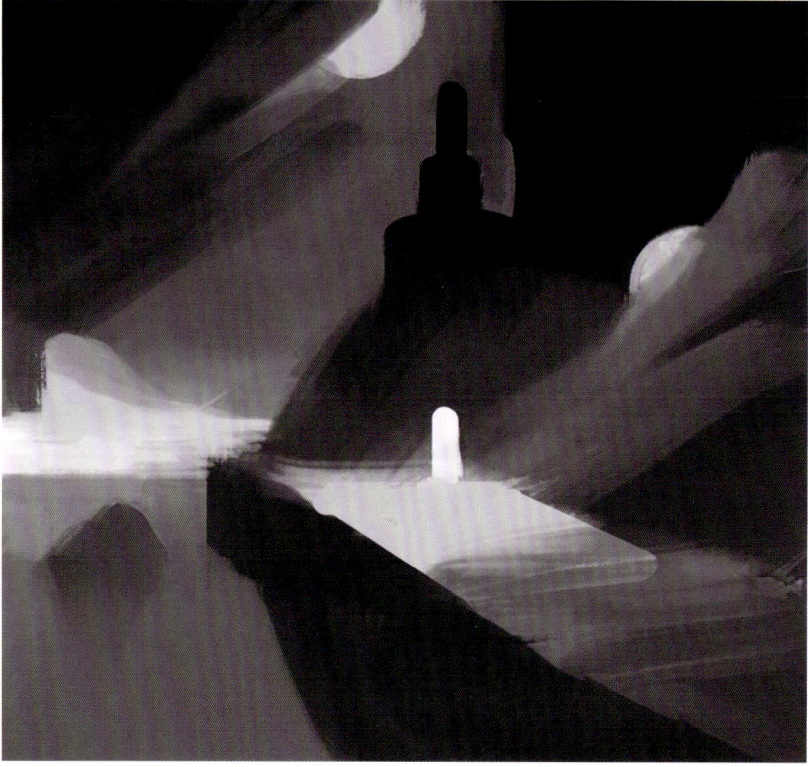

02. All value choices are made to support the image's purpose

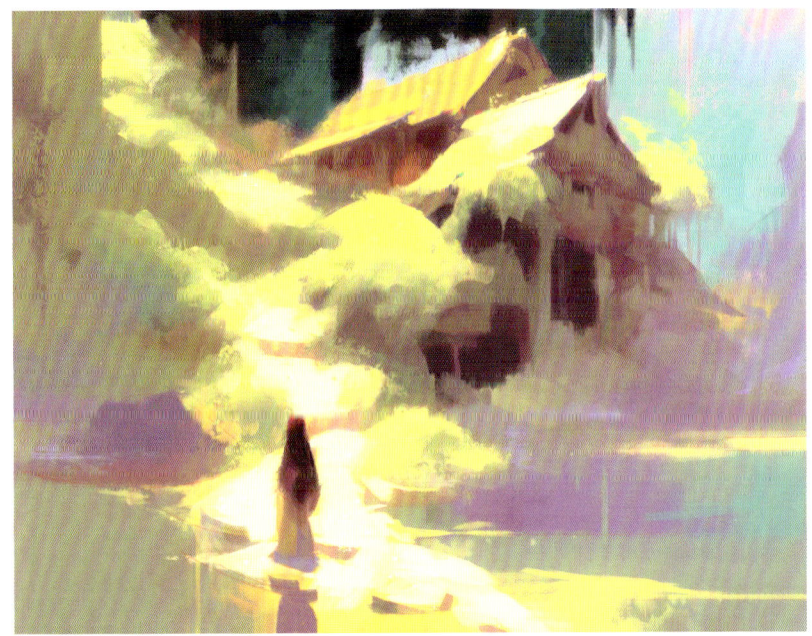

03. TROPICAL BEACH SCENE

In this lush tropical scene of beach huts on the seashore, there are potentially many elements that could demand our attention. I could have put tons of value contrast into the light and shadow and local values of the foliage and shoreline, but I didn't, because those don't serve my purpose for this image. This is an image where I'd like the viewer to pay careful attention to the beach huts and the character, with everything else being secondary. Take a look at my value simplification and see how very carefully I controlled where I placed the value contrast.

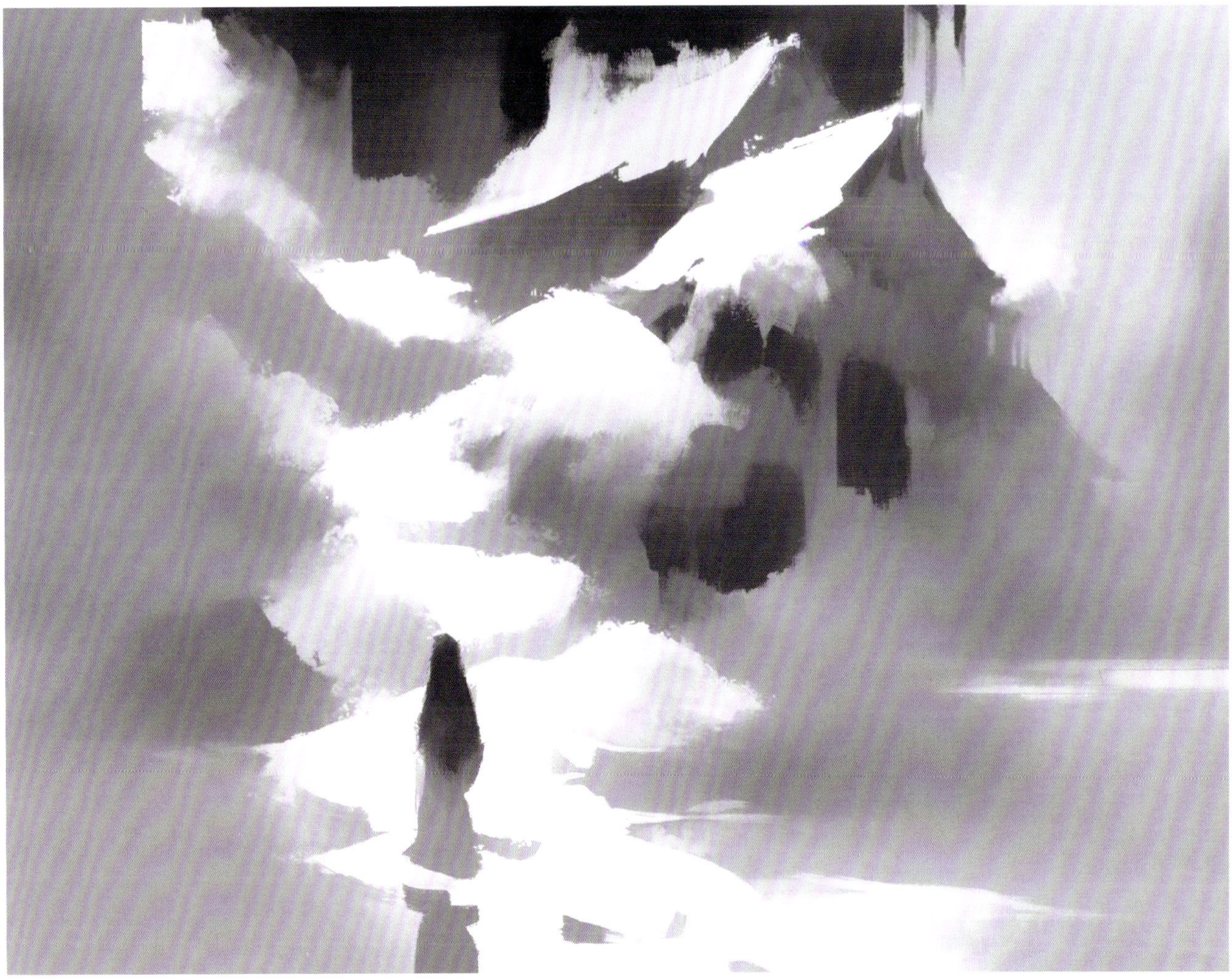

03. In contrast, the goal here is a daytime scene that feels bright and open

CHARACTER & ENVIRONMENT

Let's continue with a few more images to really clinch this idea of creating clarity and artistry of purpose through value design. For this first example, I intentionally used vivid colors to show how value design is still critically important in most images. We have two mysterious characters who are meeting in a rocky canyon environment, and I've very carefully staged the values to focus on that purpose.

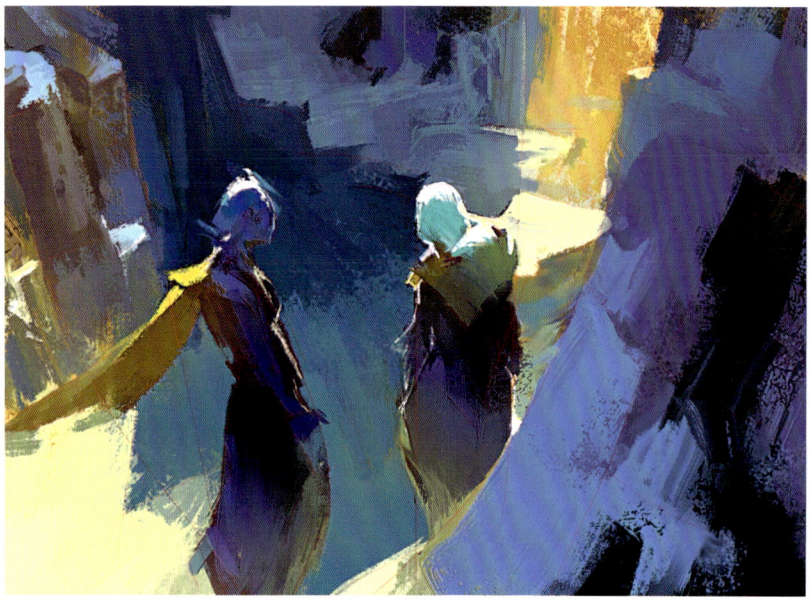

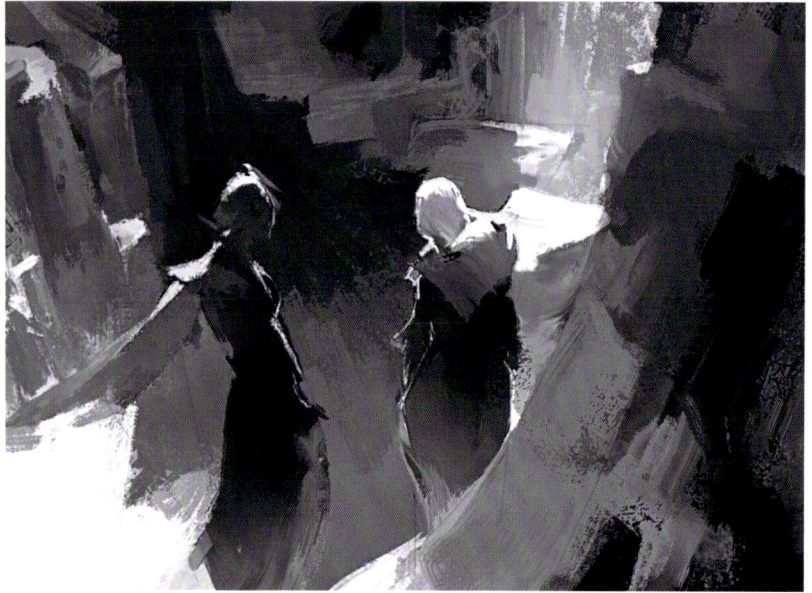

01. CHARACTER-FOCUSED SCENE

Take a look at the value-only version of the image and follow along with me as I describe the thought process. I've given the characters dark overall silhouettes and a strong rim light to reinforce their importance through contrast. In terms of local value, I've given a little variety to their outfits with lighter capes, and one of their heads has a very light value. Especially notice how I've staged the environment: the dark mass in the background emphasizes their heads, the most important part of this painting. Then that dark fades outward into carefully crafted lighter areas. Part of this effect is created by having a harsh light hitting the ground on the lower left with dusty bounce light illuminating its surroundings.

I've suggested some snow on the cliff in the right foreground, so that I didn't fall back on the cliché of always having a dark foreground element. Also, notice the lights filtering down from the upper left and right corners, guiding us to the characters and reinforcing their importance. This is environment design through value!

01. The value choices here emphasize the two characters

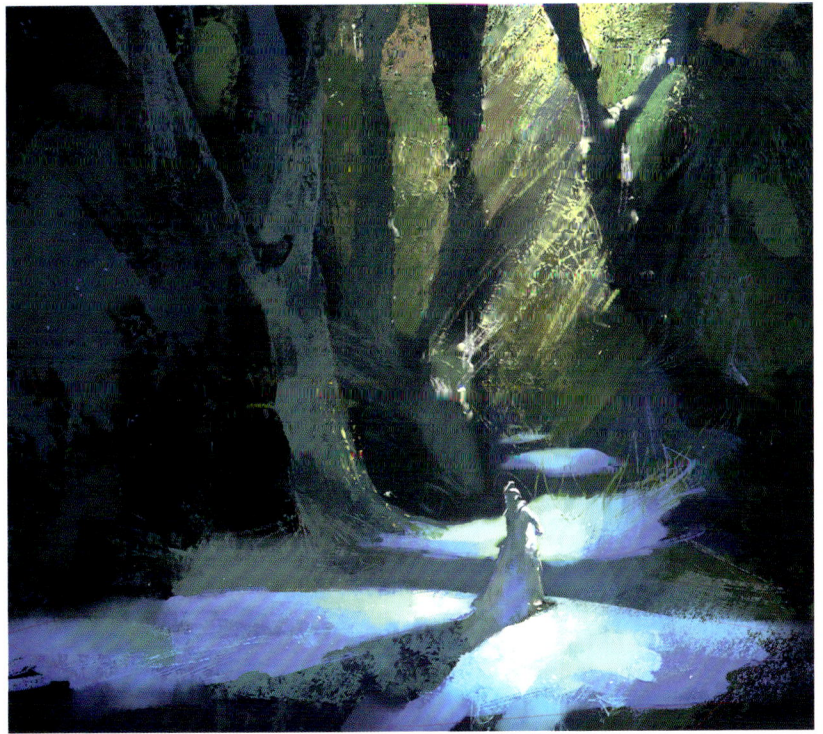

02. ANOTHER EXAMPLE

Let's wrap up our value-driven concept paintings with this very abstract offering. I'll let you make your own judgments about this one. What is designed to be most important here? How was value used to do that?

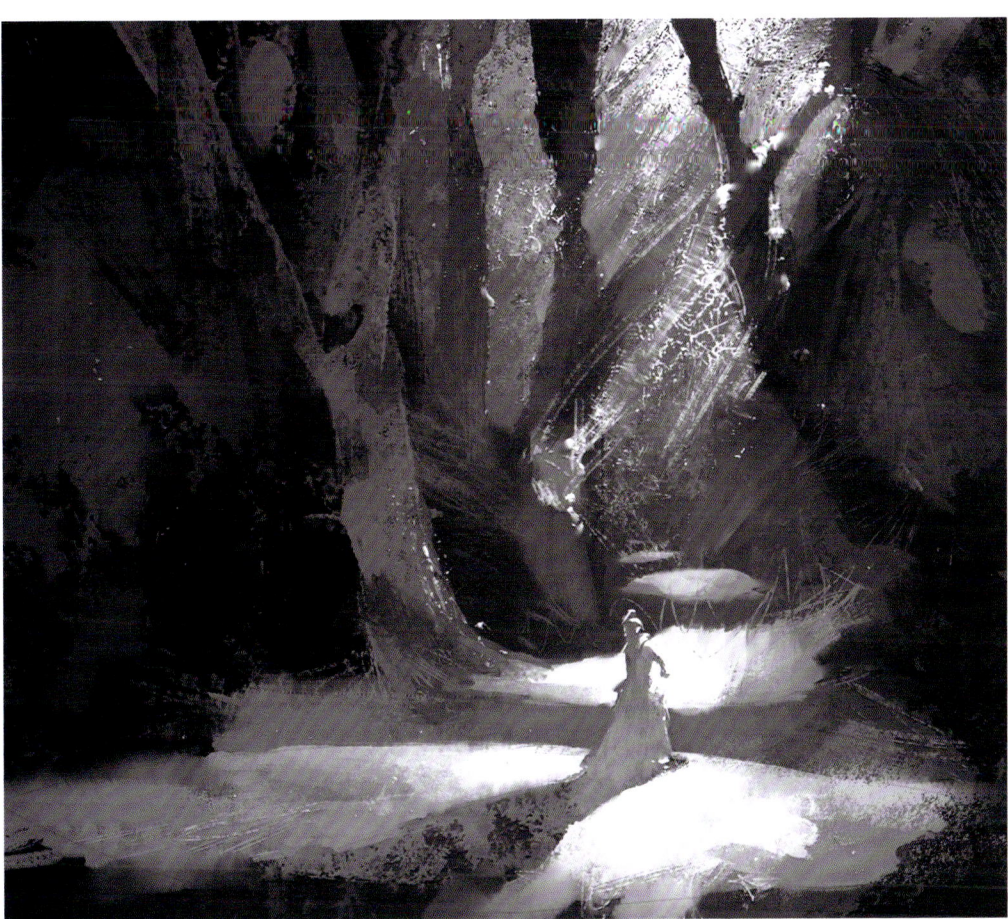
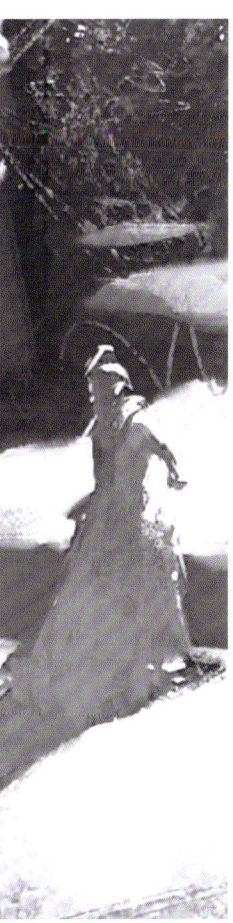

02. What do these striking values do for this character scene?

VALUE DESIGN DEMONSTRATION: SUBTLE GRADATION

For our demonstration, let's really put value design to the test, using some vivid warm and cool colors while carefully controlling our value organization. I'd like to review the value structure of the image first, so you thoroughly understand our goals as we move through this step by step.

Here's the painting in color, in black and white, and in an extremely simplified form. My goals were as follows: a dark foreground that gradually and softly transitions into a sunny background glow, with enough of a value shift that the character will read as dark against light. The light on the ground is meant to give a luminous sparkly effect to the painting and give contrast to the darker figure.

This painting could have easily become a mess of branches, leaves, and rocks, but that wasn't the purpose. The challenge was to carefully control both color and value at the same time to achieve my stated goals. One of my favorite artists, Herb Ryman, who was Walt Disney's right-hand man, once said, 'The hardest thing to achieve is a simple statement.' And it's true – this simple painting was very difficult! Let's go through it step by step.

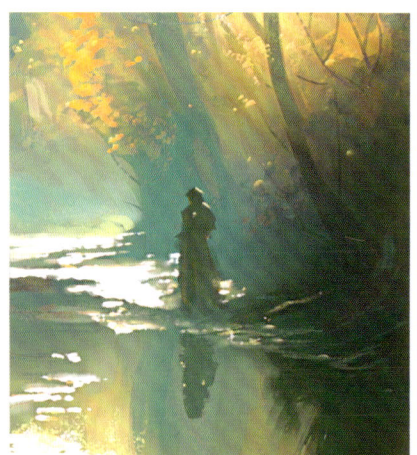
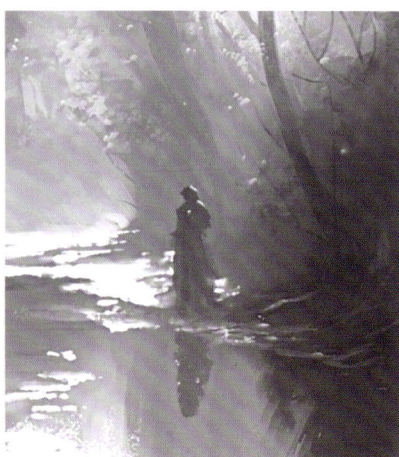
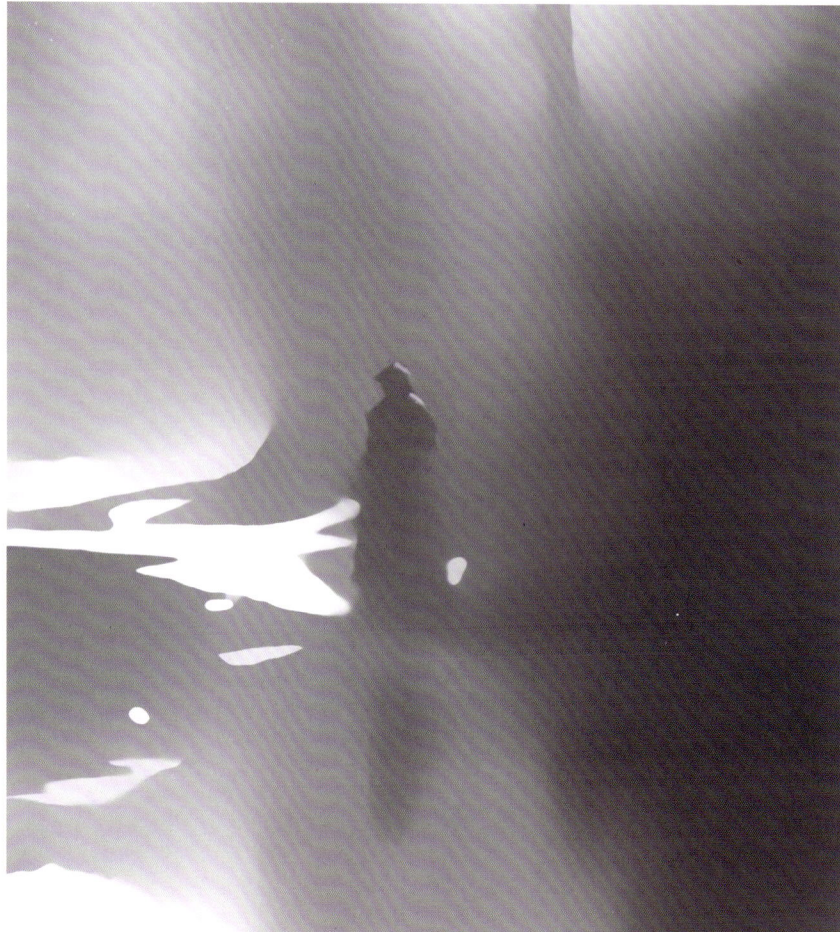

△ The finished painting, value-only version, and simplified values

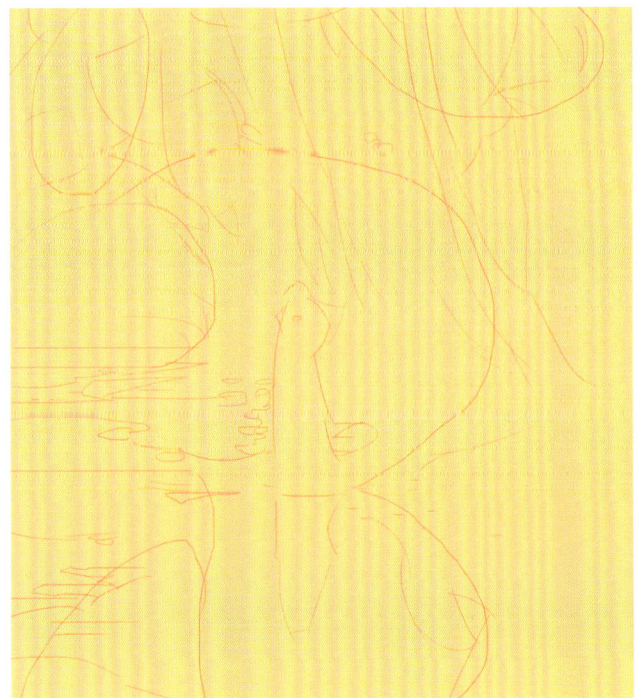

01. The background color and linework

02. Rough colors for the shadow masses

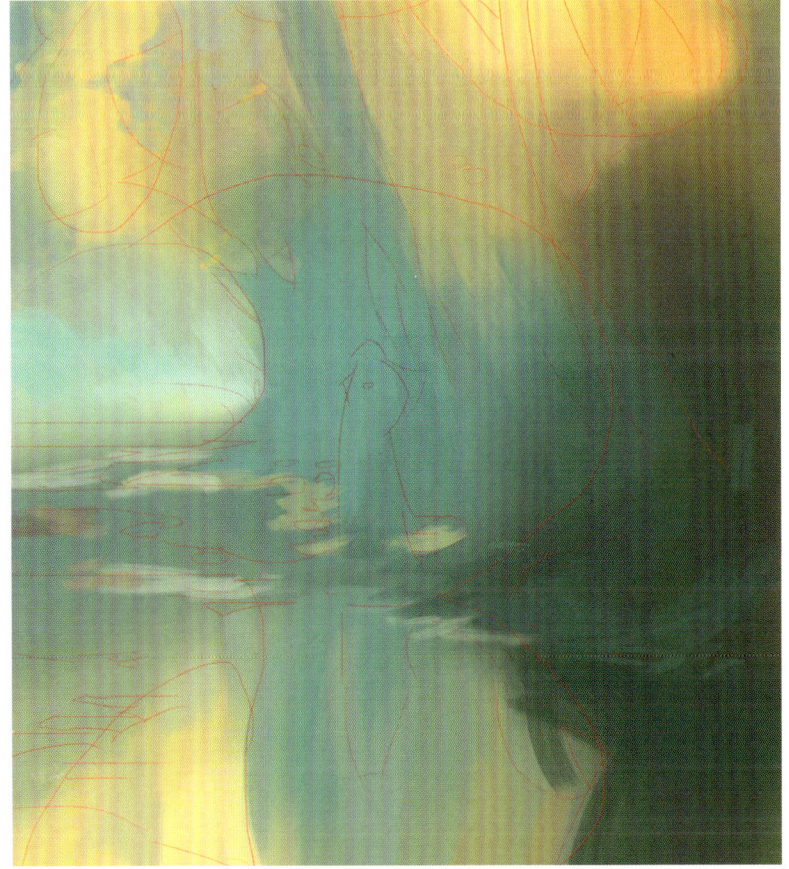

03. Begin to simply render the scene

01. YELLOW BASE

I begin with a calm yellow background, to assist with the overall warmth of sunshine, and a carefully worked-out drawing so that I'm ready to place all the elements properly.

02. COLOR MASSES

Next is a very simple massing of shadow colors: the light cyan that will be behind the character, the dark foreground, and the reflections into the water.

03. SIMPLE SHAPES

I begin to get a bit more specific now. I suggest clumps of trees and add a little definition to the rocky shoreline, but you'll notice how my values remain extremely simple.

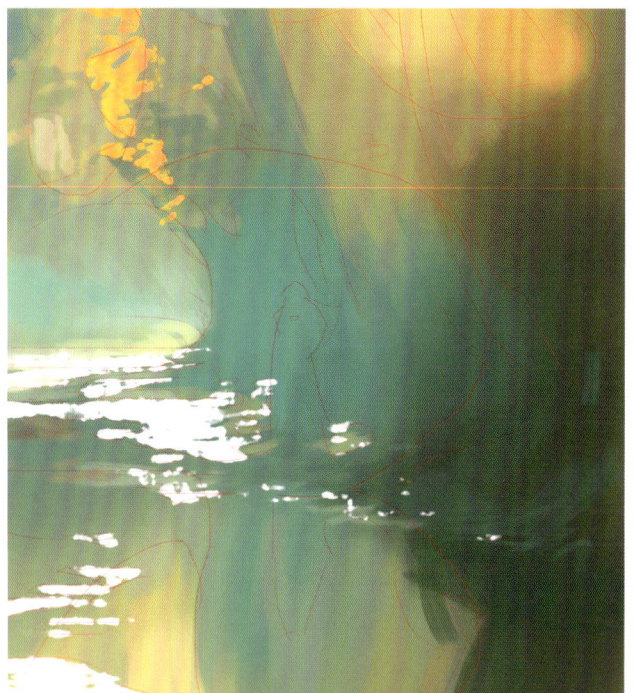

04. Add bright water reflections and sunlit leaves

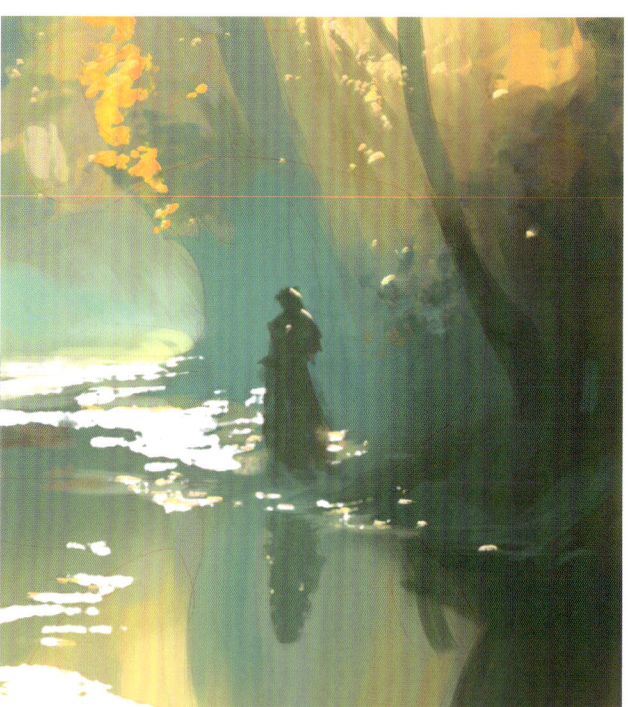

05. Add a figure in simple values

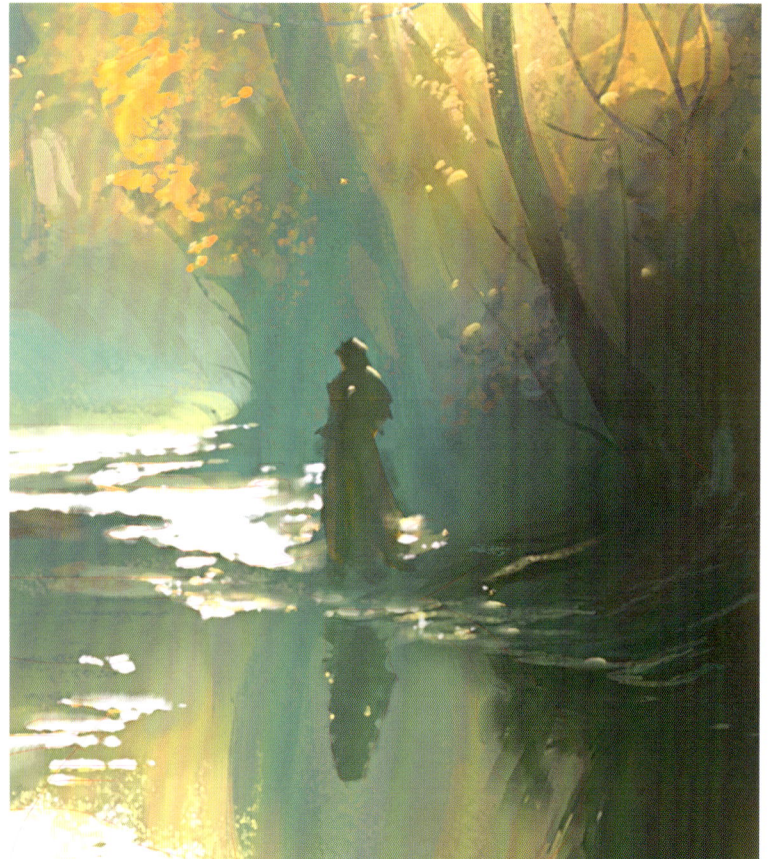

06. Refine the scene with more detail and texture

04. DETAILS

Now it's time for rocks, leaves, and water. I use a brilliant white to show the sun reflecting off of the light rocks on the shoreline, and I have sunlight falling across leaves in the upper left, leading our eye down to where the character will be.

05. CHARACTER

Next I work out a mysterious-looking figure, keeping their values grouped, with a hint of rim light making it through the trees onto the character. I drop in a few tree trunks and branches and work further on the leaves.

06. FINAL SCENE

And now it's just a matter of refining. I need to carefully decide how many branches, rocks, and leaves would be too few or too much. My thinking is to keep the top area more active and the area around the figure's head much more passive and non-distracting. I also hold on to the visual interest surrounding the bottom of the figure and add a bit more detail in the foreground. And voilà, it's a wrap!

STUDY RECOMMENDATION: FIELD STUDIES

Want to get out your sketchbook and have a great time? Here's my suggestion: get a hold of a small watercolor sketchbook, a water-soluble black ink pen (mine is a Pentel Color Brush pen), a refillable water brush, and an orange colored pencil (mine is a Prismacolor Verithin). Or experiment with your own favorite black-and-white medium. I love taking this sketchbook out and about. Making these sketches is a great exercise that doesn't require the length of time or frustration of complex full-color images.

I painted this first one (*Mineral Springs Road*) many years ago, but I still remember the challenge of it. I could see details by the billions, but all I had was this simple black-and-white medium and the tight deadline created by the setting sun. So I made a sketch about the road and let everything else drift off to simplicity. I caught the contrasting illumination on the road, the surrounding dark contrasts of the fence, and a suggestion of the mountain directly beyond. And *boom*, time was up! It was too dark to paint any further. Frankly, the limitations made this a much better study. Why? Because they forced me to give the sketch an immediate sense of purpose.

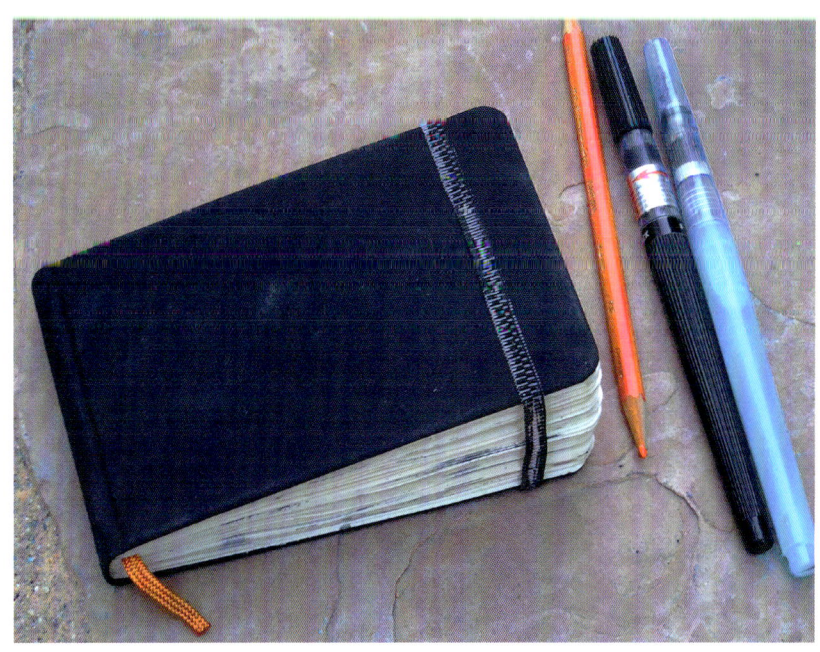

△ My tools of choice for sketching quick studies on the go

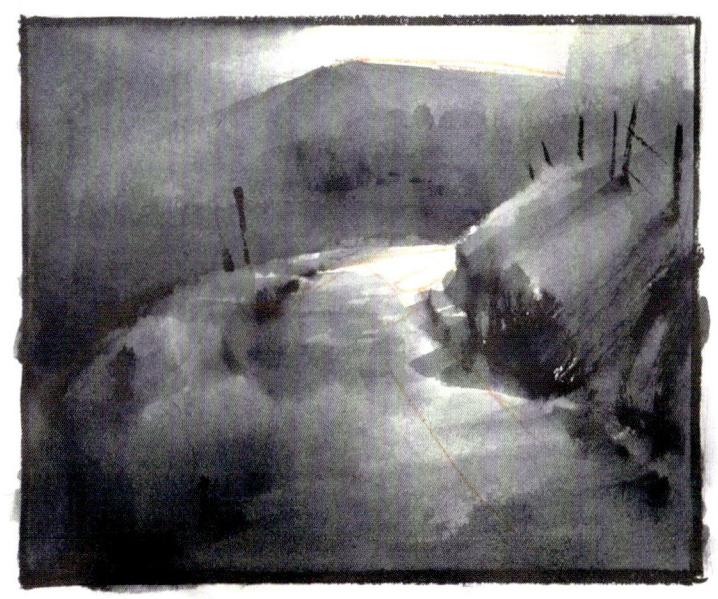

Mineral Springs Road

△ This sketch was a race against time!

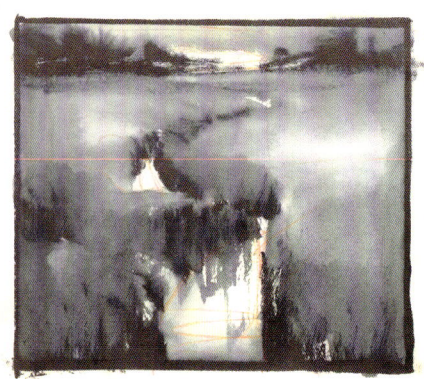

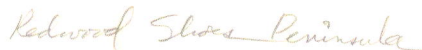

Redwood Shores Peninsula

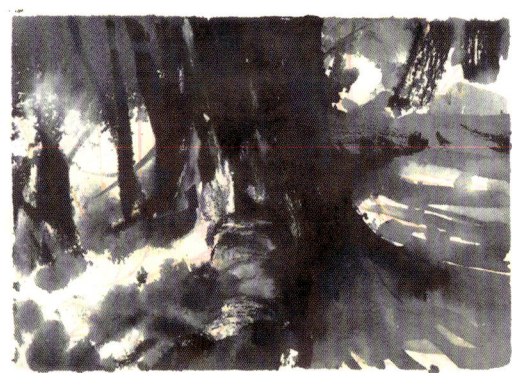

Cedar Creek Woods

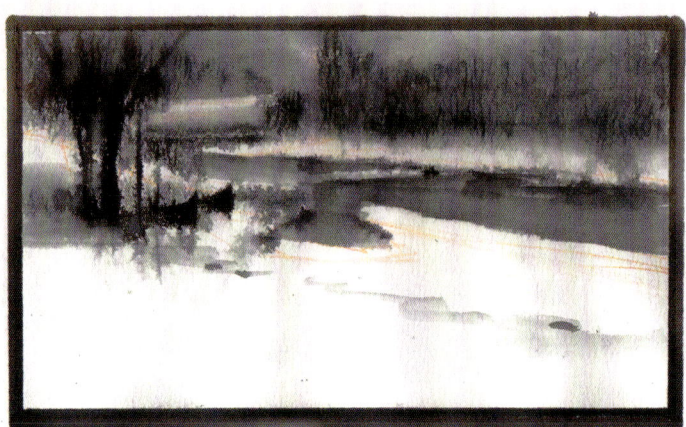

Snake River Idaho

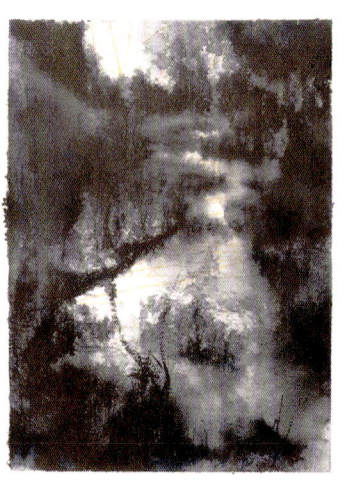

Placerita Canyon Creek

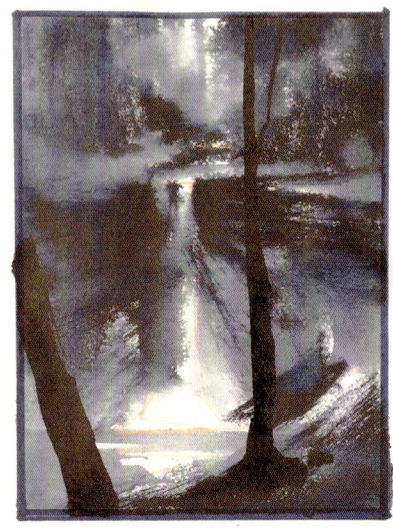

Woodland Falls

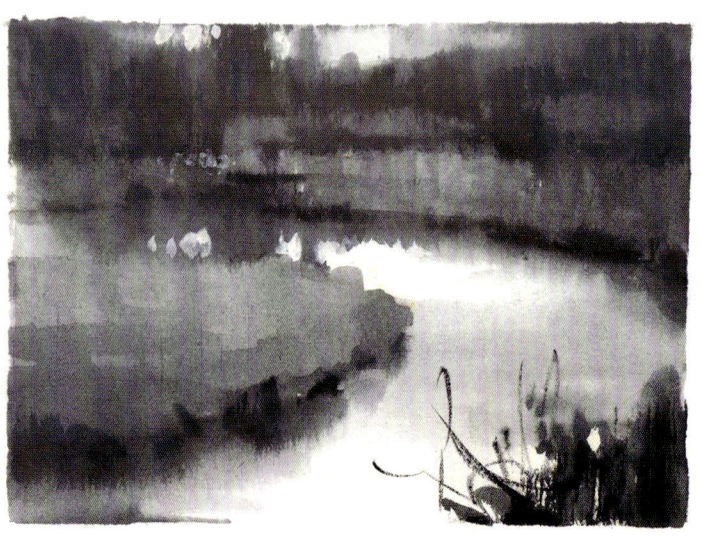

△ More sketches approached in the same way but at different times and in very different environments

RECOMMENDED EXERCISE:
MASTER STUDIES IN VALUE

For the recommended exercise, let's take a look at two images and do some straightforward black-and-white studies. This is an exercise about clarity and purpose, so the goal is to render the bare minimum of information without losing the clear purpose of the original image.

I recommend that you collect some of your own favorite images and make simplified but purposeful black-and-white copies of them.

Be sure to do these studies in less than an hour, as that will force you to think carefully through the purpose of the image rather than getting mindlessly caught up in secondary details. Remember: extra daily practice trains your eyes, your mind, and your hand in the 'muscle memory' of making strong artwork. Don't worry about if you have enough talent – worry about if you're doing enough practice! If you practice daily and without fail, your growth will be significant over time.

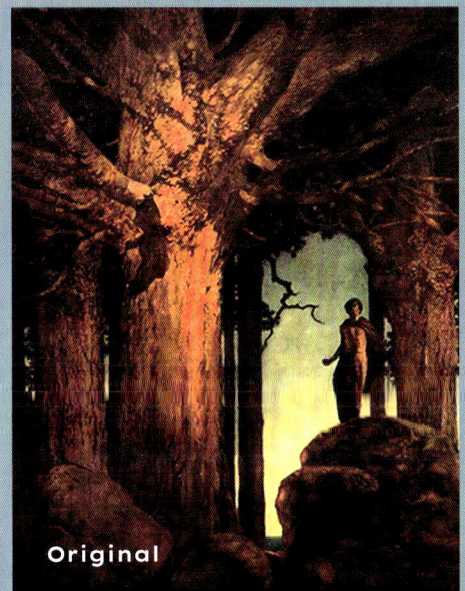
Original

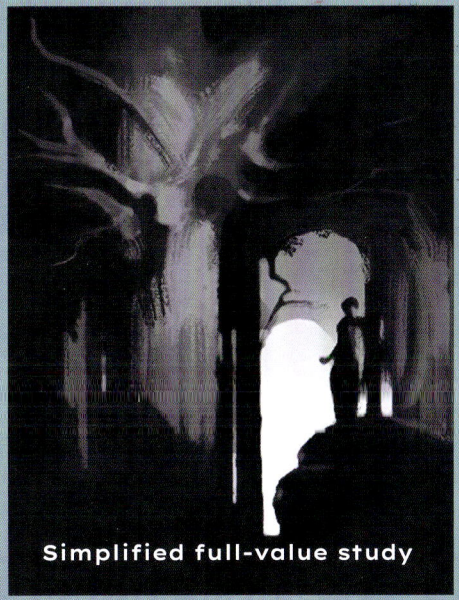
Simplified full-value study

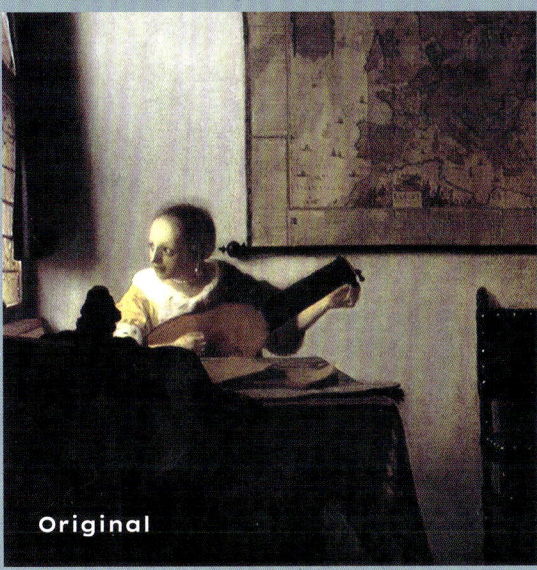
Original

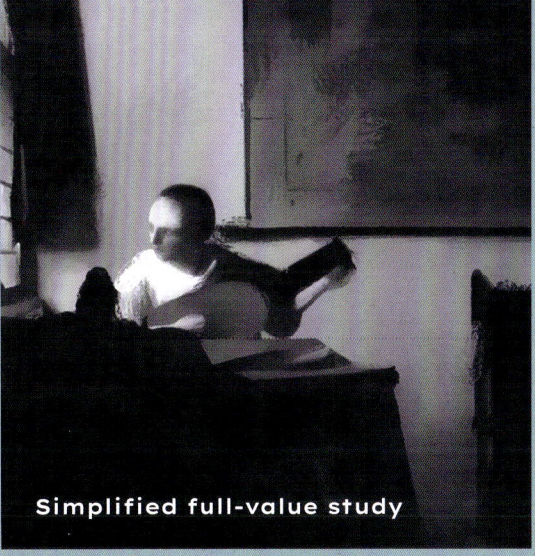
Simplified full-value study

△ Spend less than one hour painting a simple value-only study of your favorite painting

EMOTIONAL LANGUAGE: THE DESIGN OF SHAPE & LINE

How do we give completely inanimate objects
a sense of character and emotion?

ME VS THE CHARACTER DESIGNERS

Let me describe something that happened all the time early on in my career. At the beginning of a movie project, we'd spend about six months preparing a 'look of picture' presentation: a presentation where the character designers and concept artists propose their vision of what the movie will look like. These presentations were serious do-or-die situations because a movie would only be fully funded if the studio executives were satisfied that the project would have real value to the audience. They were so serious that we'd do a full rehearsal and run-through of our presentation the night before the meeting.

Imagine the head studio executive is a Roman emperor, wearing a toga and laurels, at the gladiators' stadium. You give your presentation and, at the very end, with bated breath, everyone quakes in fear as the executive reaches out their arm and gives the thumbs-up or the thumbs-down. If it's the thumbs-up, you get to spend the next several years making a movie. But if they give the thumbs-down, the trapdoor opens beneath your feet and you all end up out in the Mojave Desert – you know, where the bodies are buried. That's what those green-light meetings felt like.

Let's say that I've spent a full week on one of my paintings and I'm feeling really good about it. That it's going to be great, it's going to be big, it's going to be epic and commanding. It's going to give the scope and the scale of our whole movie. I've put in the color, the light, the design. I've got god rays streaming into that baby. I've got those little white birds – the ones that give it scale and life. I think, 'Man, I'm at the top of my game and I'm gonna show them single-handedly that we have a movie!'

Then we go into the presentation and go through the artwork. My turn comes and I bring up my image. I just know they're going to gasp with delight. They're going to say, 'Nathan, we see this image and we now know that we have a movie. Nathan, we know you've been working really hard on this. Take the rest of the week off. You've earned it.'

That's my fantasy. Now for the reality.

I bring up the image and the studio executive, the person running the show, looks at it. There's a dead pause, and then they say, 'Oh, wow, huh. That's, uh, really great. You know, I always envisioned our world being warmer than that. Make it 15% warmer, then I think we have something we can work with. OK, next.'

Well, that's disappointing! But I'll be honest with you – if the only note I get is 'make it a little bit warmer', then I'm actually doing OK. I can live with that.

But here's where the humiliation comes in. Next up is a character designer. They bring up some sketches where they maybe put two characters together in a comical way – something that they just threw together on a napkin. And guess what? Everyone instantly erupts into appreciative laughter. They clap, they cry. They say, 'We weren't sure if we had a movie, but we do! You've given us characters that we've instantly fallen in love with, and our audience will fall in love with them, too. Thumbs-up, green light! We know you've been working really hard on these 15-minute sketches. Take the rest of the week off. You're beautiful. Can we get you something on your way out? Hey, Nathan! You aren't doing anything over there – get this artist a cup of coffee!'

And that's what happens. No respect, right? But I've learned my lesson. I've had to learn to beat the character designers at their own game. I've learned that the qualities of character that connect with an audience can also be brought to environment design.

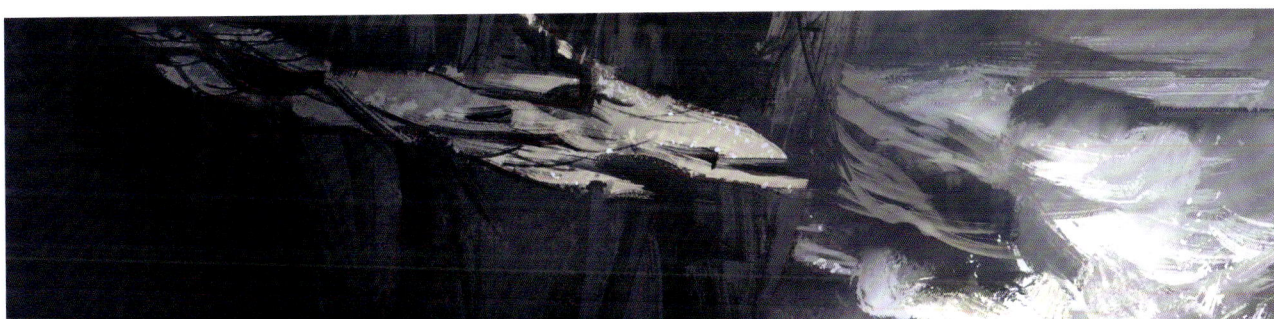

△ Our environments need to have as much character as characters!

ENVIRONMENT AS CHARACTER

Let me give you a specific example. Below is a page out of my DreamWorks production notebook, from my very first day on the animated movie *How to Train Your Dragon.* You'll notice the very first thing I wrote was 'rock language'. You see, this is where I put the idea of 'environment as character' to the test. At the same time as the actual characters were being designed, I was designing ... *rocks.* But they were darn good rocks. They were good because they weren't just

rocks – they were crafted to feel like dragon characters, to have the fierce quality of tooth and claw in their 'language'. I was specifically working on the design of Dragon Island, where the dragons reside. As the human characters make their way to Dragon Island, they are filled with fear and dread as they see the volcanic dragon-like shapes of towering rocks emerge out of the mist. How well did I do? Watch the movie and see!

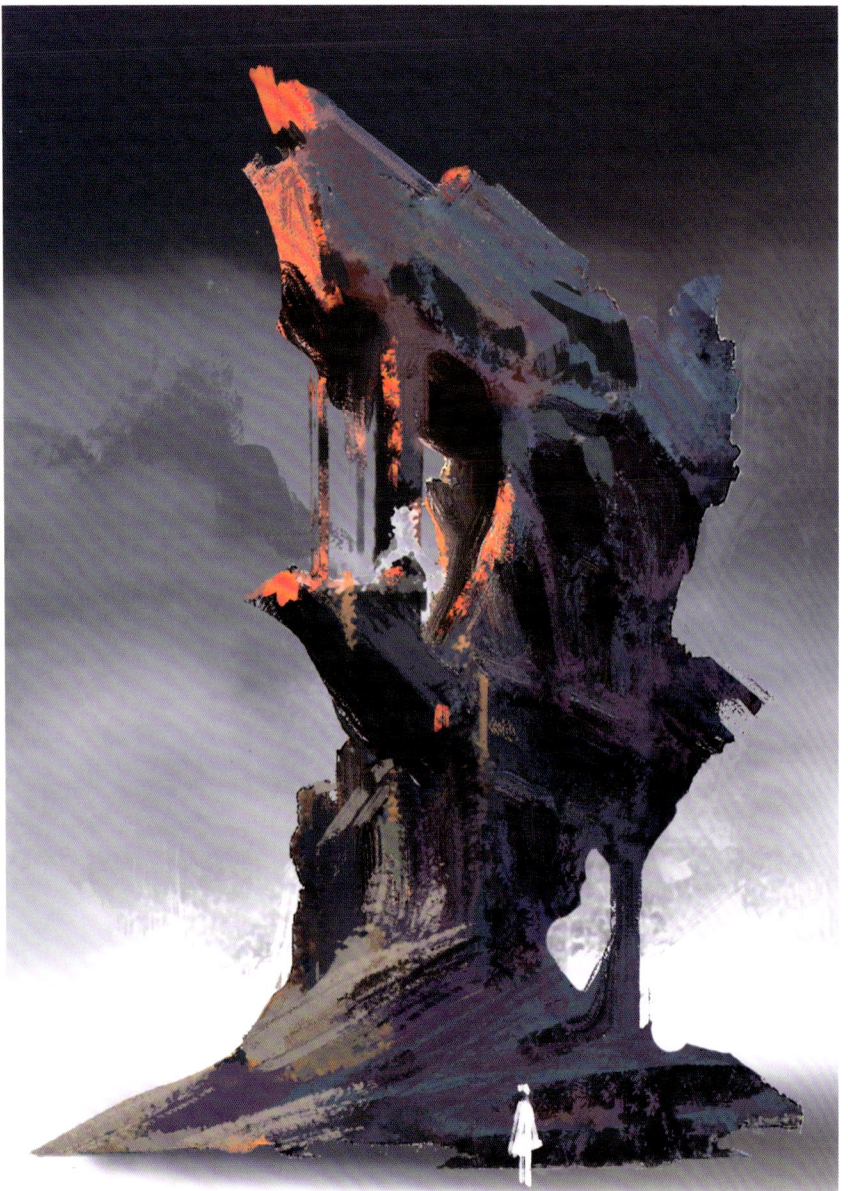

△ This rock design is imbued with character!

△ Written notes from my *How to Train Your Dragon* notebook

On the left I've roughed out an example to convey the idea that a rock can be so much more than a rock. In fact, every inanimate object in an environment can be crafted with character, purpose, and emotion. This chapter will show you some simple but powerful ways to do this.

THE DESIGN OF SHAPE

The concept of shape design is simplicity itself. Round-shaped things don't tend to hurt you, they feel friendly and unobtrusive. In contrast, we unconsciously guard against sharp objects as we make our way through the world, so sharp, triangular objects are perceived to be very dangerous. Designs based on squares tend to feel inherently stable and immovable.

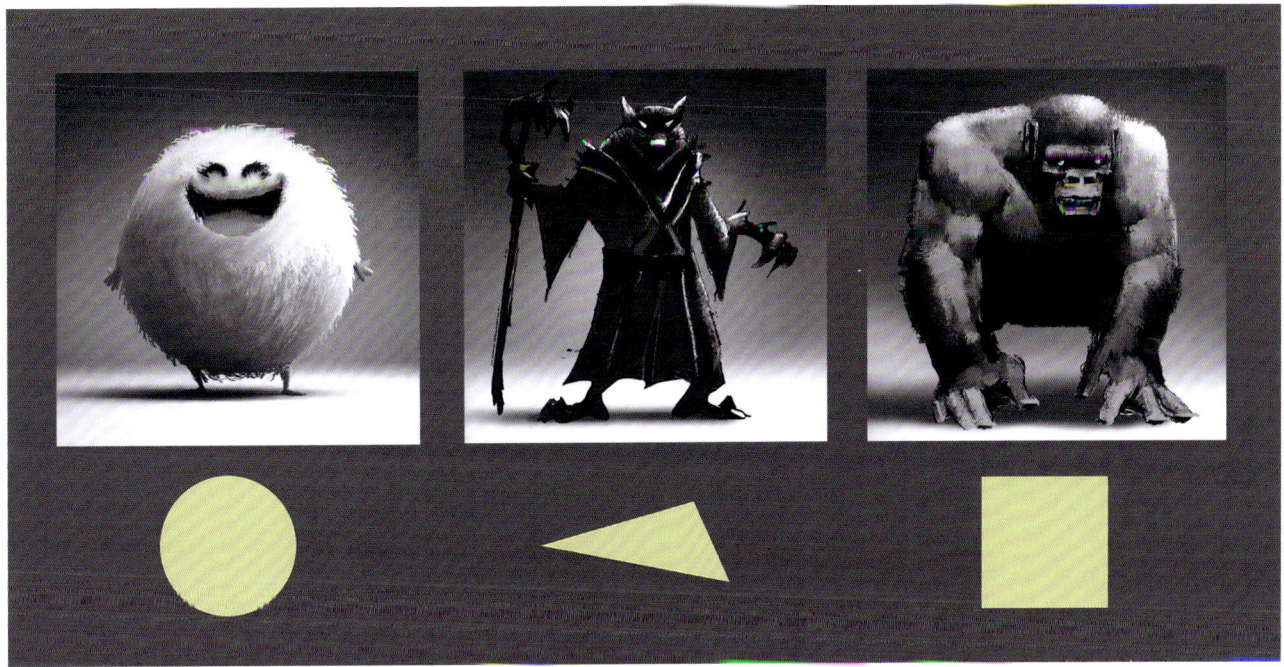

01. Characters feel very different depending on their shape design

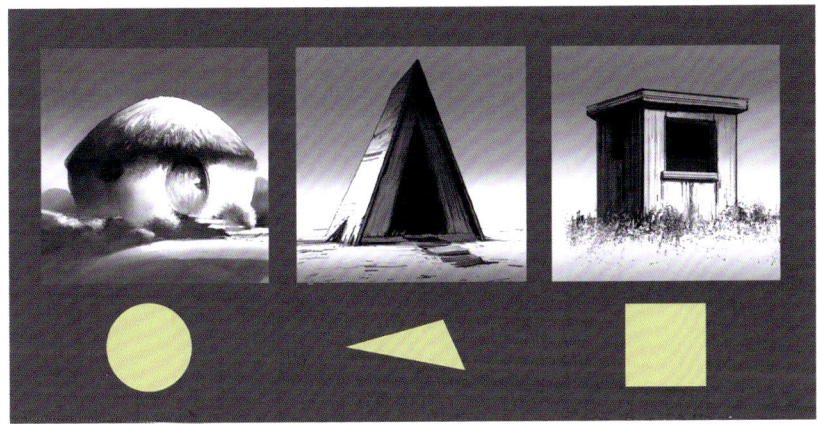

02. The same shape theory applies to non-character subjects

01. CHARACTERS

Since we've been comparing character design to environment design, here are three characters that have very different qualities. The round character is a friendly delight based on nothing more than a circle. In comparison, the character based on sharp triangles feels inherently dangerous. And don't try to make the strong, square character get out of your way – it's not going anywhere.

02. OBJECTS

Now let's look at inanimate environmental subjects that are given the same treatment. The circular hut feels friendly and inviting, the triangular hut suggests caution, and the square hut is passive and stable.

03. LOCATIONS

Let's bring the same effect into an overall environment.
What would your reaction be to these three different villages?
As you came over the rise, what would your immediate
response be to each one?

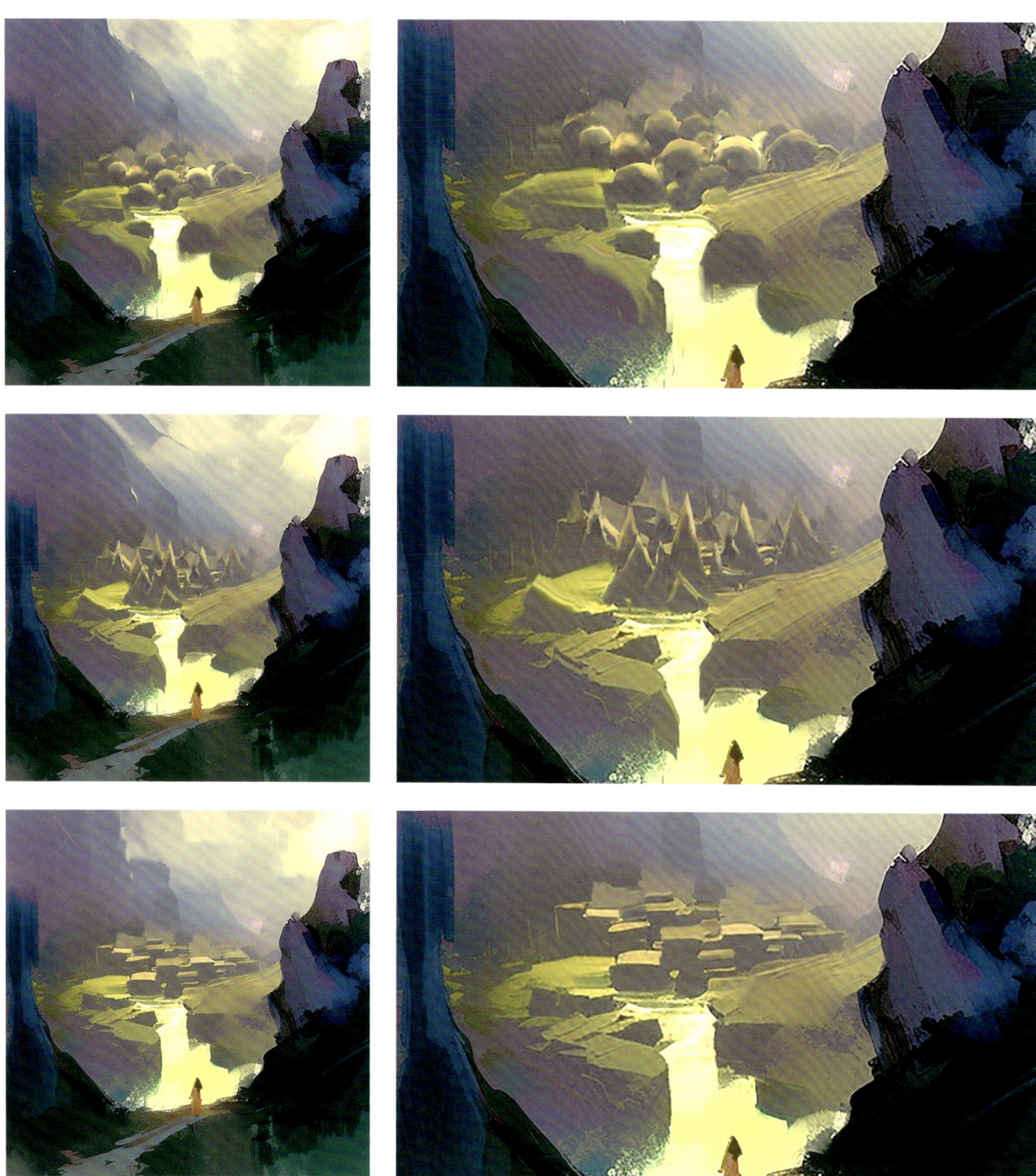

03. Shape changes our impression of a place

04. SETTING THE SCENE WITH SHAPE

Here are some individual examples. The first scene has soft, rounded shapes repeated everywhere, which give it an inviting quality. It's a mysterious place, but the kind of mystery that invites you to come in and explore. It doesn't feel like anything here is about to kill you – unlike the next example. Those sharp triangle mountains definitely do feel like they're trying to kill you. If you're determined to travel here, be sure to bring plenty of water and heavy protective clothing – or better yet, leave it alone, because you might not come back! And then, in the third scene, let's join our square gorilla friend in a very stable environment. The environment itself is neither friendly nor dangerous, but it's there to last. The fourth image in this group is quite different – it's absolutely action packed and is a good introduction to movement and line, which is our next topic.

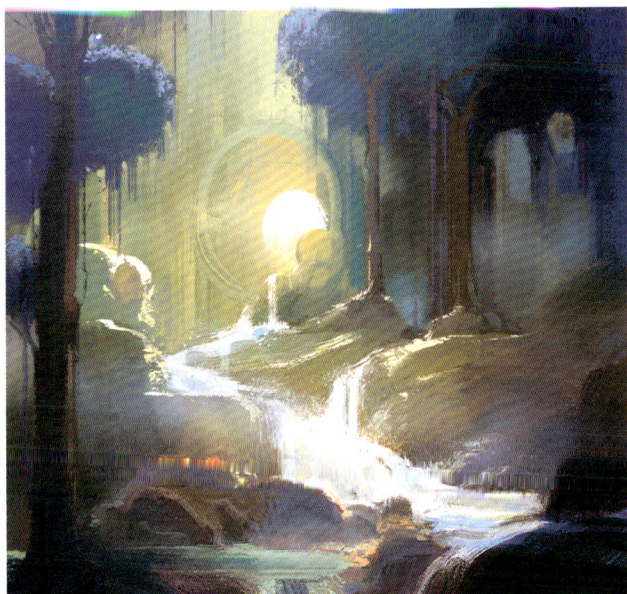

04a. Soft, rounded, and peaceful

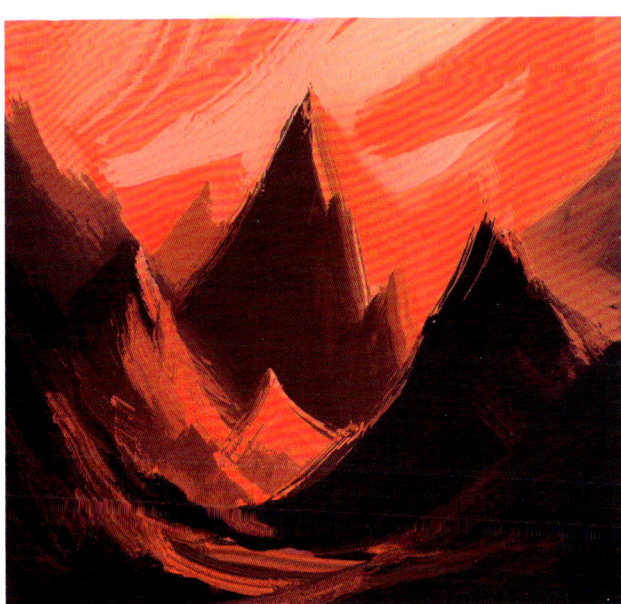

04b. Angular, sharp, and threatening

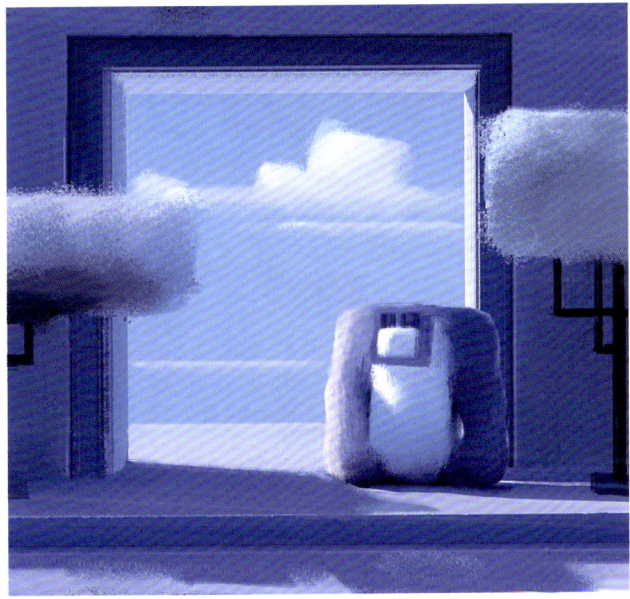

04c. Calm, solid, and strong

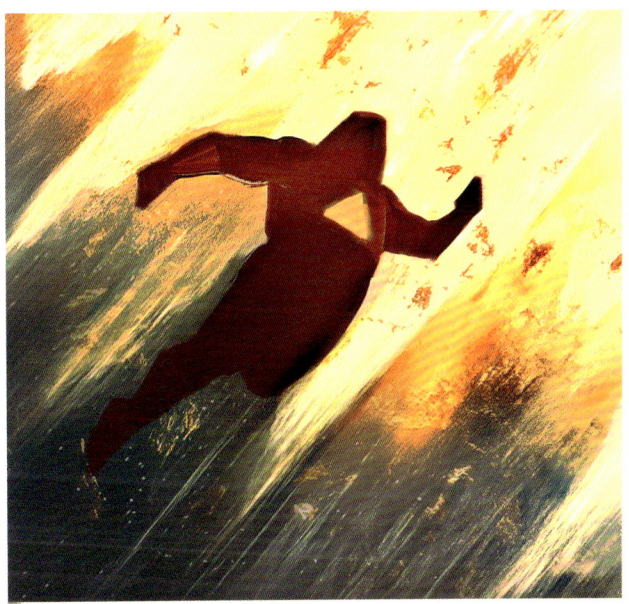

04d. Dynamic, diagonal, and active

THE DESIGN OF LINE

It's fascinating how potent simple line design can be, and it all has to do with the force of gravity. Gravity is something that our muscles work against every moment of every day, but in a deeply unconscious way. And so we tend to anthropomorphize lines. Take a look at the second image below, which turns three lines into simple characters. A horizontal line tends to feel at rest, a vertical line feels stable and alert, and a diagonal line immediately suggests motion. It's the diagonal line that fascinates me the most – it so profoundly feels like it's in motion, or at least potentially in motion. It reminds me of an archer pulling back on their bow, with all that energy poised to spring into action, to project that arrow with devastating force. On the next pages, let's review some examples I've created for you.

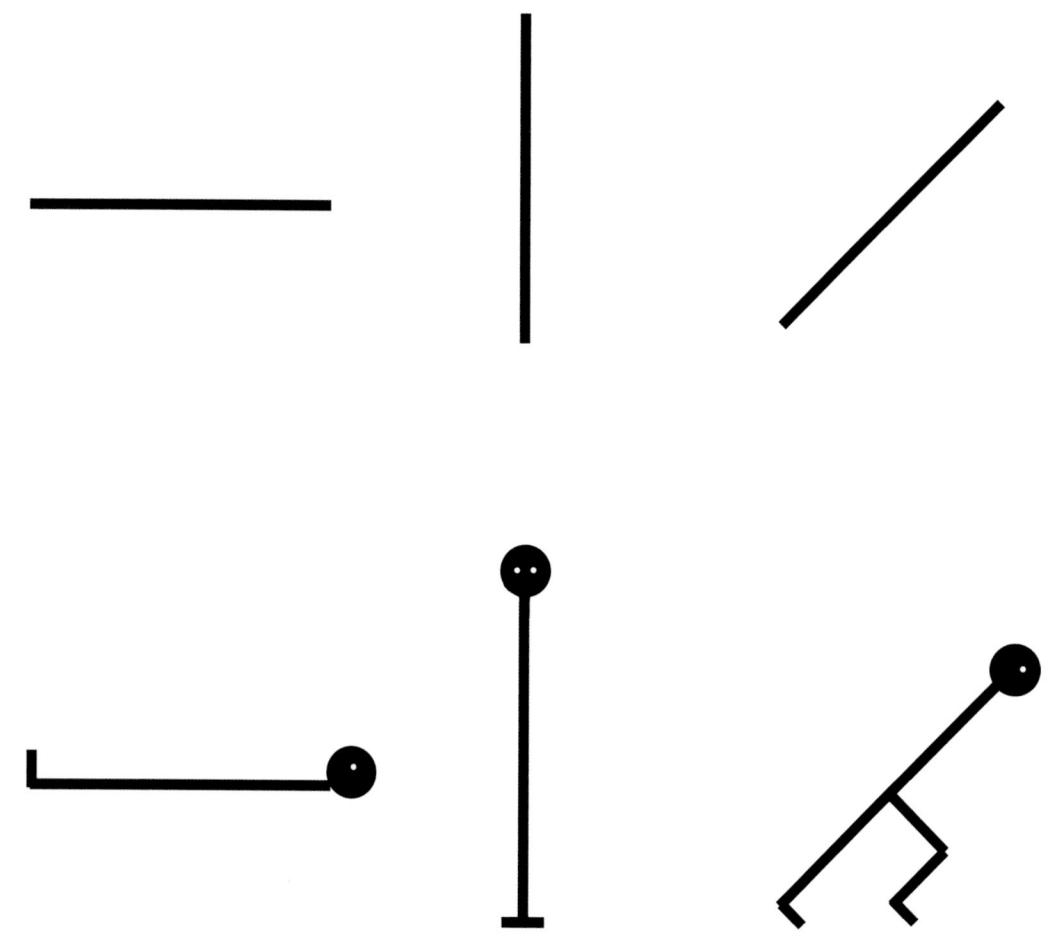

△ We tend to ascribe anthropomorphic qualities to lines

A horizontal line tends to feel at rest, a vertical line feels stable and alert, and a diagonal line immediately suggests motion.

01. HORIZONTAL

This is meant to be a very simple, very passive scene (but with a little variety going on, so it doesn't bore everyone to death). The horizontal is strongly emphasized to create a sense of calm, as seen in the 'at rest' diagram on the previous page.

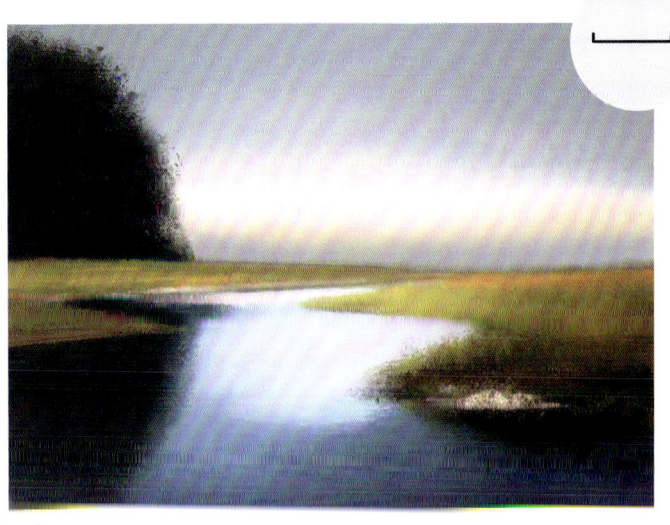

01. A strong horizontal quality creates a calm, restful image

02. VERTICAL

For the vertical example, here's a palace built into a cliffside. The makers of such a palace want you to know that they are deeply serious and not kidding around. Don't try to storm this castle, as these people have committed such vast resources that they've undoubtedly devised lethal protections. They've clearly made a statement that they are a steadfast people who will stand the test of time. Come back in a thousand years and they will still be here.

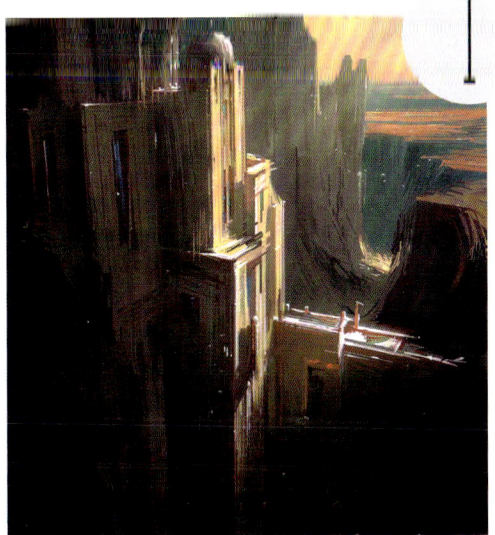

02. This deep vertical scene feels vast, powerful, and permanent

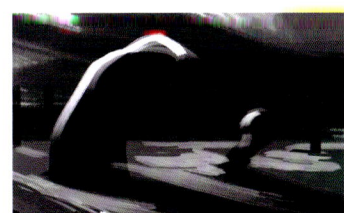

03. DIAGONAL

For the diagonal, first let me show you a little character sketch. It's a big scary thing leaning in diagonally to threaten a little thing. Compare that to this dark cliffside painting, where the rock walls and the rock surfaces are pitched at a diagonal, leaning in threateningly just like the character sketch. Imagine this is a mysterious island with rumors that strange creatures abide here and that no explorer before you has ever returned. Walking through a tipping environment makes it feel like something is always about to happen. It creates a great tension for your audience and really puts them on the edge of their seat. It's 'rock language' again.

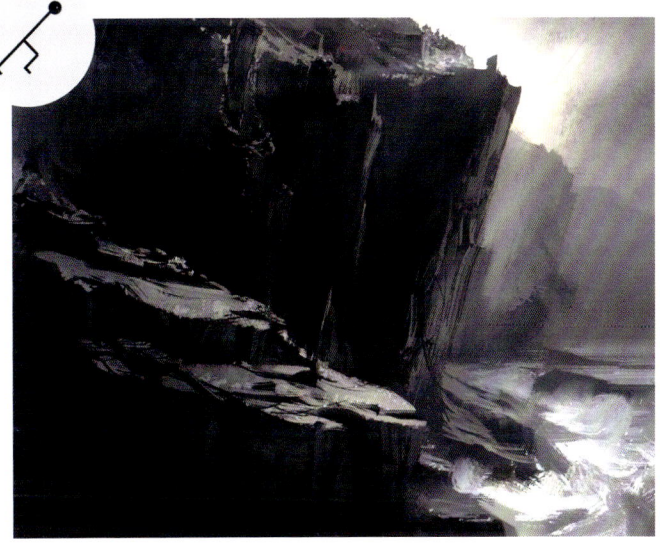

03. Diagonals create a feeling of tension

04. HORIZON ANGLE

You can also achieve diagonal drama by simply tipping the horizon or eye-level line. You'll see this done often in film, where a dramatic action scene has the camera tipped at a diagonal so that everything happens off-kilter. Doing this increases the emotional impact of a scene. In this case we have a simple grove of trees pitched diagonally, but the trees aren't growing that way – it's a product of the point of view being tipped. Notice that the ground plane tips perpendicular to the vertical trees. This helps give an otherwise passive grove of trees a sense of foreboding, as if things are likely to go awry should you enter here.

05. PERSPECTIVE

Another way to create active and bold diagonals is with perspective. This sketch uses a three-point perspective where everything is tipping upward toward a vanishing point that's set to the far right and off-screen. This helps create the effect of certain peril should you ever visit a place such as this.

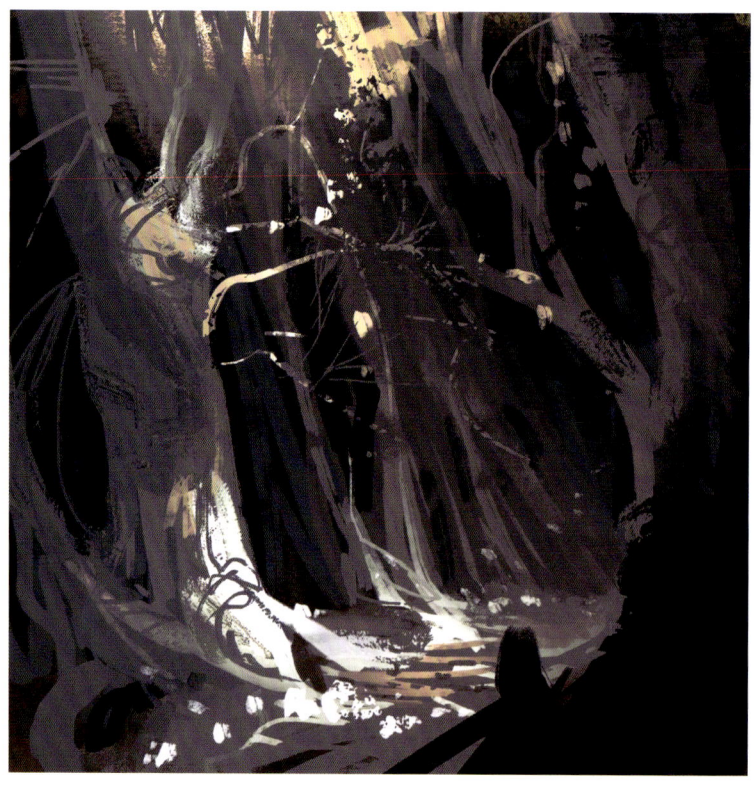

04. An off-kilter angle makes this scene more tense and intriguing

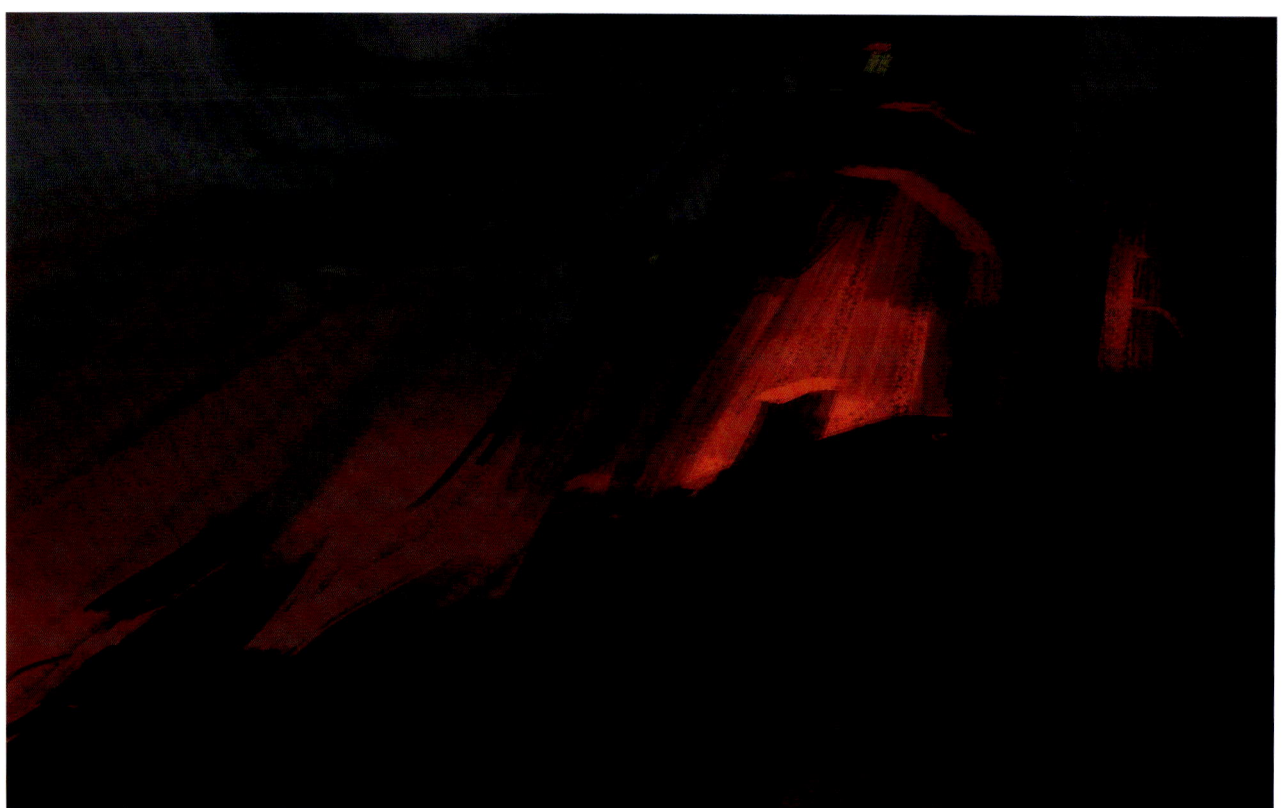

05. The perspective gives this scene a steep, dramatic angle

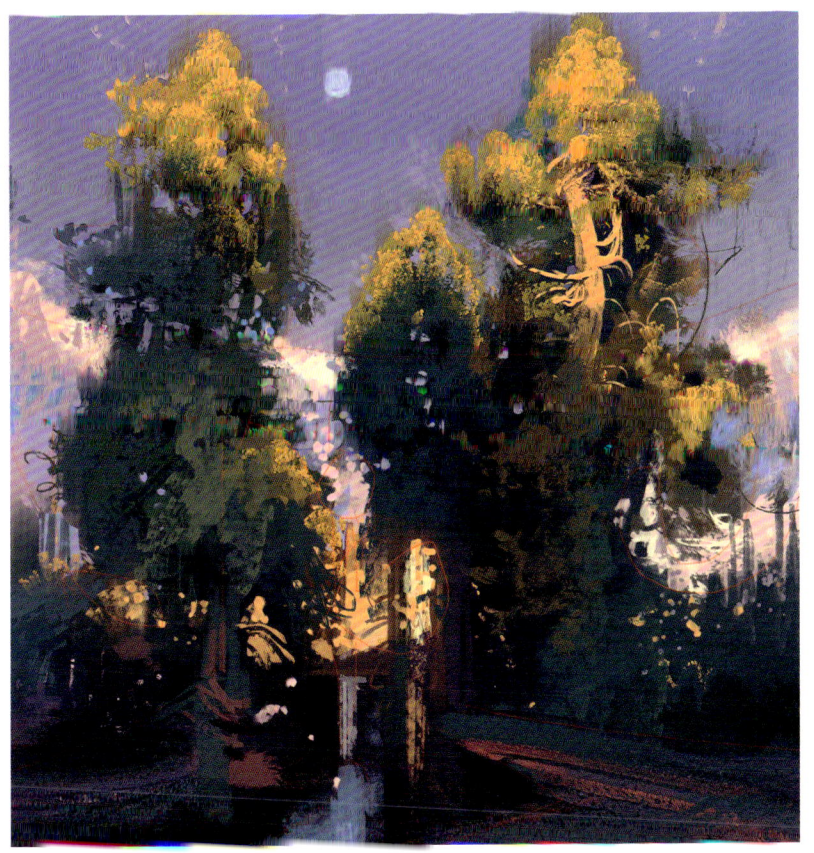

06. COMPARING LINE DESIGN

Here are two paintings of trees I did on a trip to Zion National Park in Utah. They're very similar in color palette and subject, but quite different in mood. The difference, of course, is line design. In the first, the trees are tall, proud, and vertical. In the second, there's a different group of trees framed more closely than the first. This group had a wind-swept quality that I really loved and chose to emphasize. The trees were already tipping due to constant winds rushing through the canyon and I chose to exaggerate that effect for more action and drama.

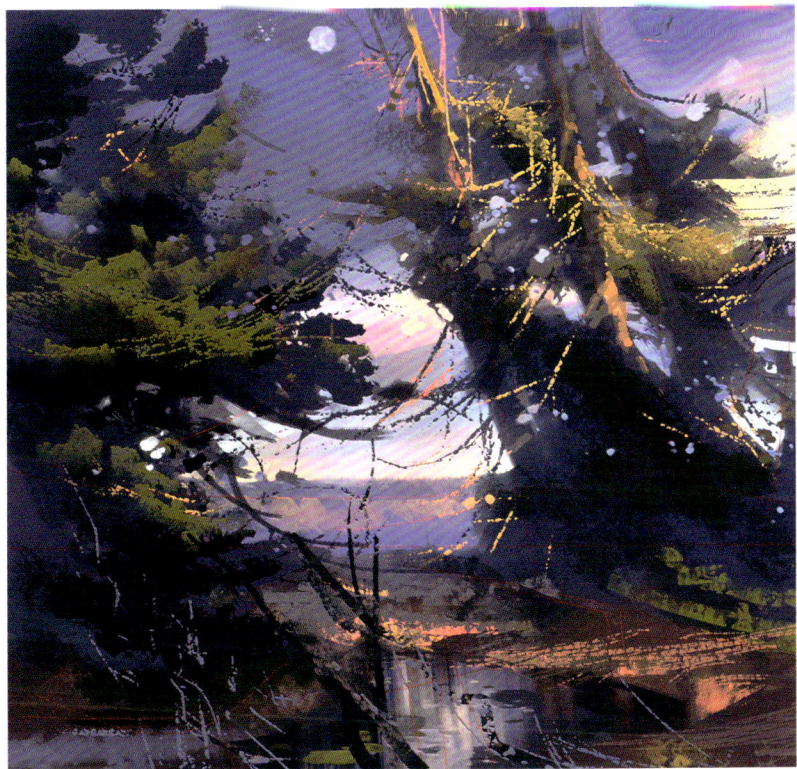

06. Line design makes these two scenes feel very different, despite being otherwise similar

07. ATMOSPHERE

These three images are targeting different kinds of spooky emotions. The image on the left is an invented scene inspired by gothic novel covers from the 1960s and 1970s. At that time, tales of women in peril under the ominous eye of a fearful mansion were in fashion, and I attempted to recreate that spookiness here. There was a whole section of these novels at the local library when I was a kid, and I was quite fascinated by the spookiness of them. In fact, when I started college in the late 1980s, animation was nothing like the powerhouse industry it is today, and I actually thought I wanted to be a book-cover artist – such was the influence of emotional book covers on me.

The top-right image takes us out of the warmth and into an ice-cold environment full of sharp and angular shapes. Are they icicles, stalactites, or roots? All of those elements can be quite eerie, so for me, it doesn't matter in a somewhat abstract sketch like this. If it feels right, it *is* right.

The bottom-right image is that age-old juxtaposition of youth and innocence with fear and decay. Our images are not always about one thing; they commonly have complex layers of emotion to create extremes of contrast, subtlety, and irony.

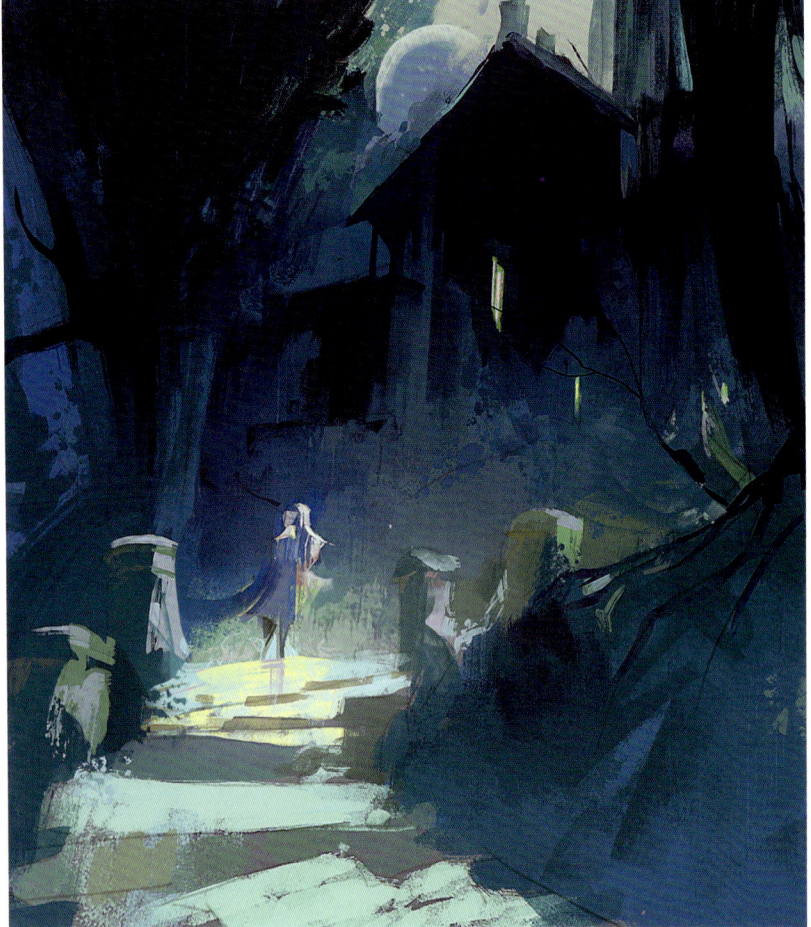

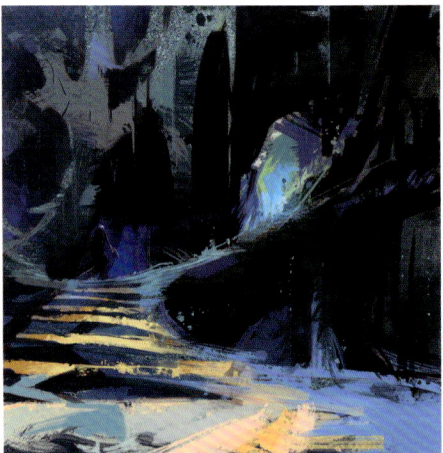

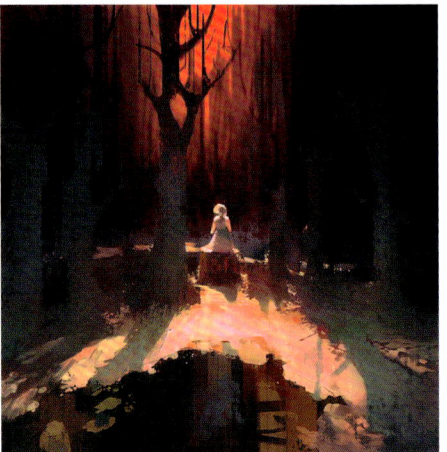

07. The use of shape and line design is essential to creating drama in these scenes

Our images are not always about one thing; they commonly have complex layers of emotion to create extremes of contrast, subtlety, and irony.

DEMONSTRATION: MOUNTAINSIDE PALACE

I'd like to show you the step-by-step process of the image shown on page 81 to demonstrate the emotional use of vertical line. This is a great opportunity to review the ideas that I've been advising you to keep at the top of your list: 'What is the purpose of the image?' and 'What is the appropriate emotion associated with it?' Here I'm creating stone structures that have an immense sense of security, stability, and authority, as we've discussed.

Let me first define my terms here. I tend to think in three stages: rough, comp, and finish. A rough tends to be a starting point that's for my eyes only, not something that's ready for the client to review. 'Comp' is short for 'comprehensive sketch', which is an old-school term from publishing that nobody says anymore. A comp is still rough, but it's worked out well enough to show the client for approval to move forward to the finish. For this image, I'll skip straight to the comp stage, since I already have the idea firmly in mind.

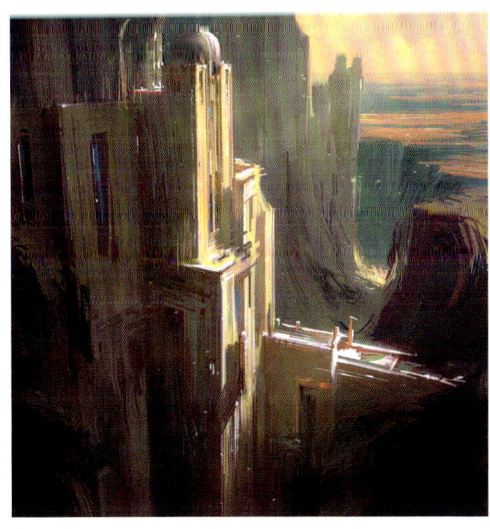

△ The dramatic mountain fortification shown as a 'vertical' example on page 81

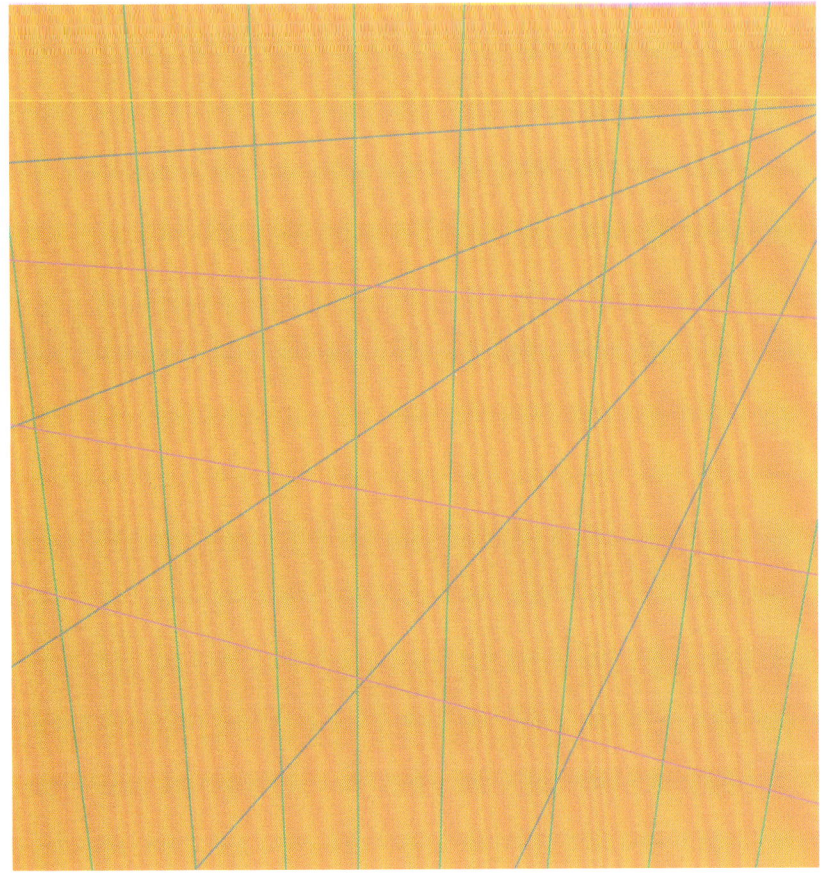

01. Start with a warm base and perspective grid

01. BASE TONE & GRID

First we'll work out the comp, to be sure we have a solid working idea, and then we'll take that to a finish. I begin here with a warm tone and a three-point perspective grid. I believe this view will work well for this subject as it rises powerfully from the earth, and it allows us to see a full expanse of the environment the fortress is in.

The first step in a perspective grid is almost always placing the horizon line where it will serve the environment best; then you can work out your grid from there. If you need a hand with this subject, please see the excellent book *Artists' Master Series: Perspective & Depth*, in which I also discuss this subject.

02. CONSTRUCTION LINES

Next I work out some lines to construct the cliffs and buildings. Everything is made from simple block shapes – I only need to consider front planes, side planes, and top planes for my linework. I follow the logic of gravity by having bigger blocks below, making the building smaller at the top. Then I cap it with a dome for a feeling of purpose and completion.

Every building needs windows, and since this concept is all about long, sturdy verticals, I make sure the windows are elongated as well. The buildings are built right into the cliffside, so I work out a few lines for the transition where wall meets cliff. I add a few canyon shapes in the far background; notice how I'm carefully following my perspective grid even there.

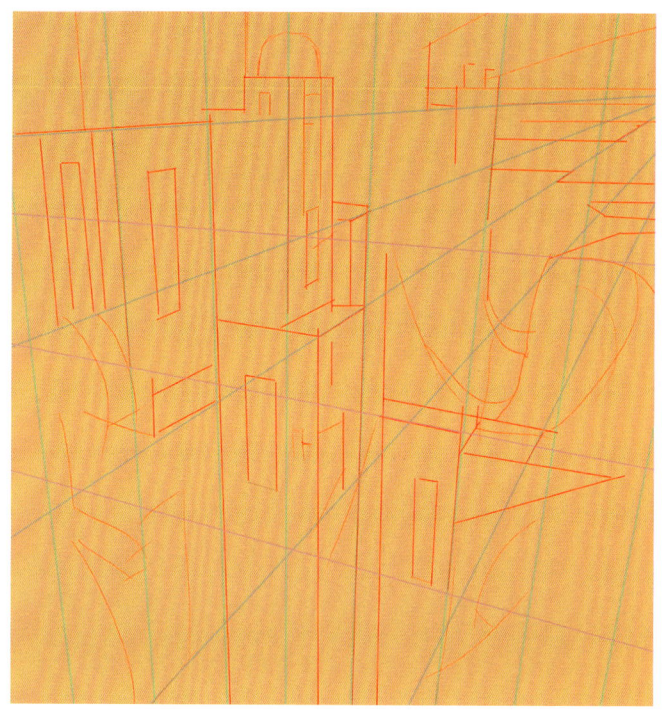

02. Sketch out the planes of the scene

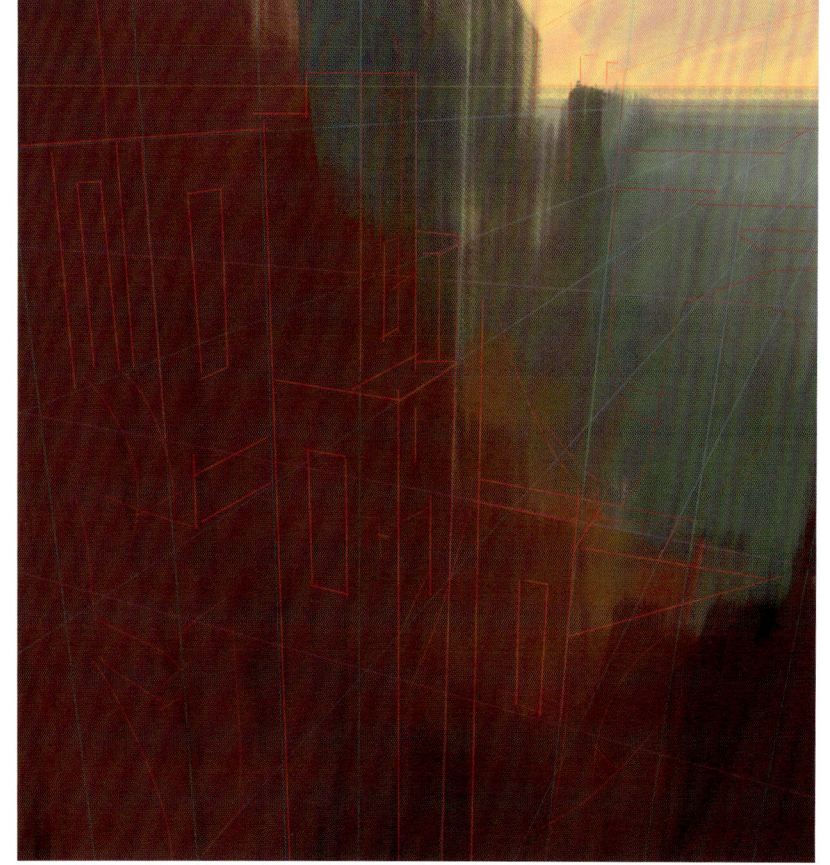

03. Roughly lay down contrasting red and cyan hues

03. COLOR PALETTE

This will be an environment that has very little local color in it, but I still want it to be rich and visually interesting. My idea is that the stone here has a strong red hue but takes on a contrasting cyan as the distant shadows cool down in the atmosphere. In the very late afternoon, it's common for the sky to have lots of warmth very low near the horizon. That's another way I can create some interesting color contrast.

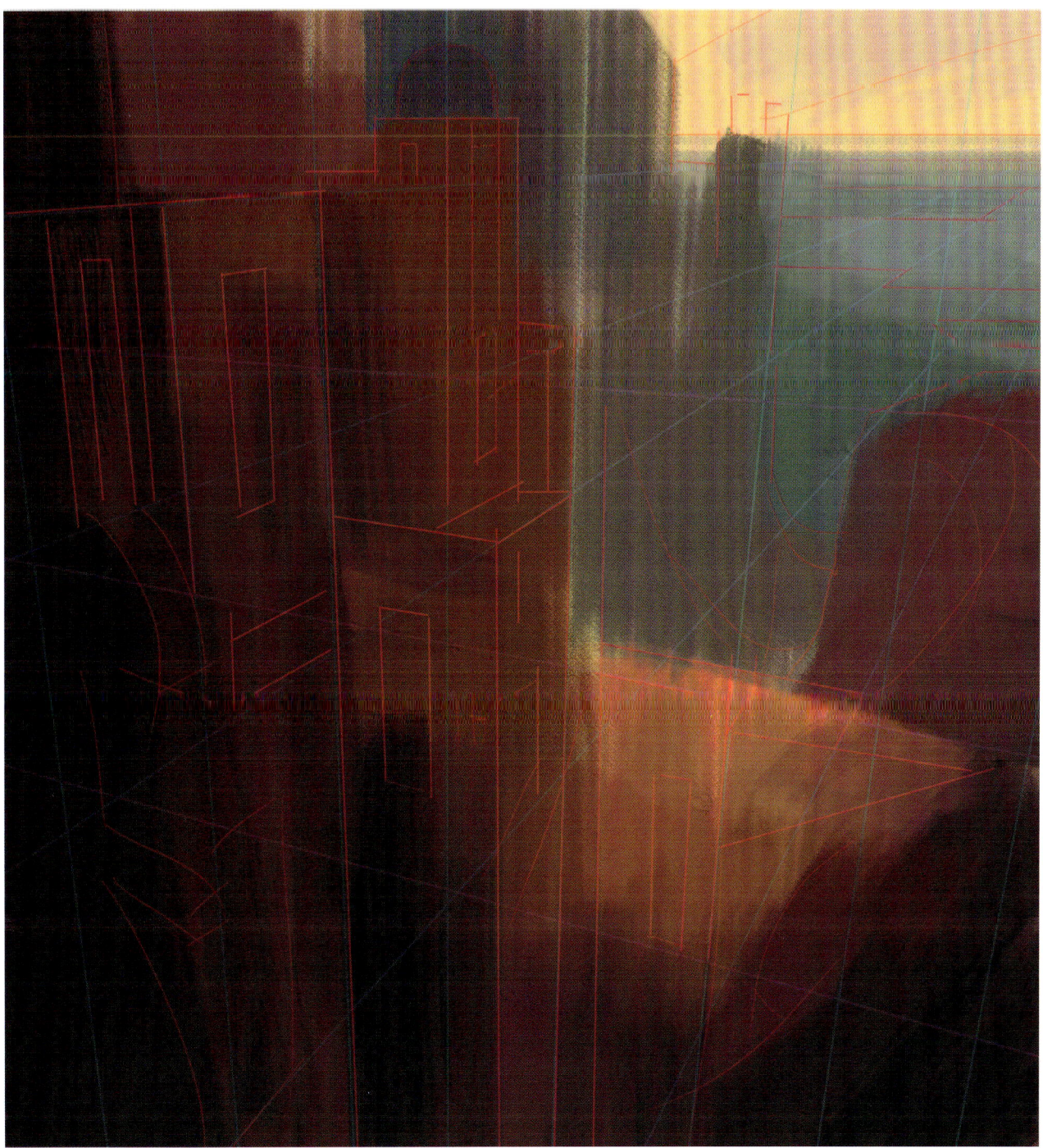

04. Begin adding form with darker values

04. ROUGH SHADOWS

Now I start indicating the realities of form in the shadow, making the scene deeper and darker in value as it disappears into the canyon below. I establish the idea that the planes facing us will be darkest, the side planes will be lighter, and the top planes will be lighter yet. These are all considerations of what's happening in shadow; we'll be ready to consider the direct light shortly.

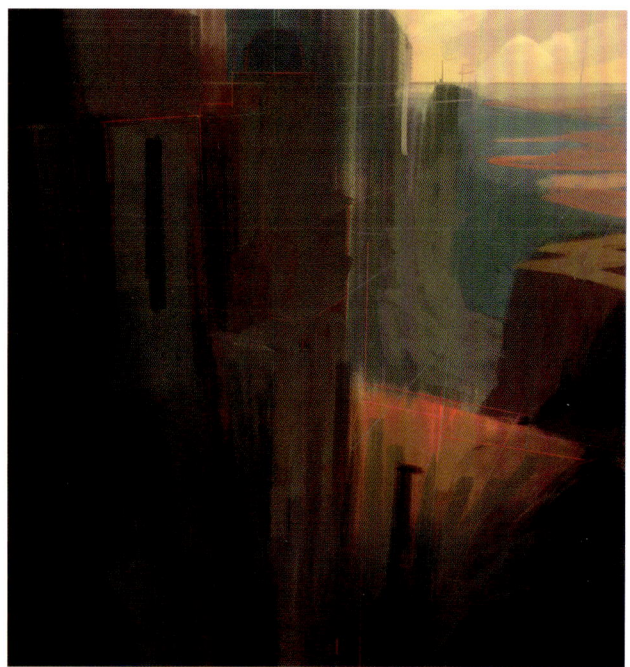

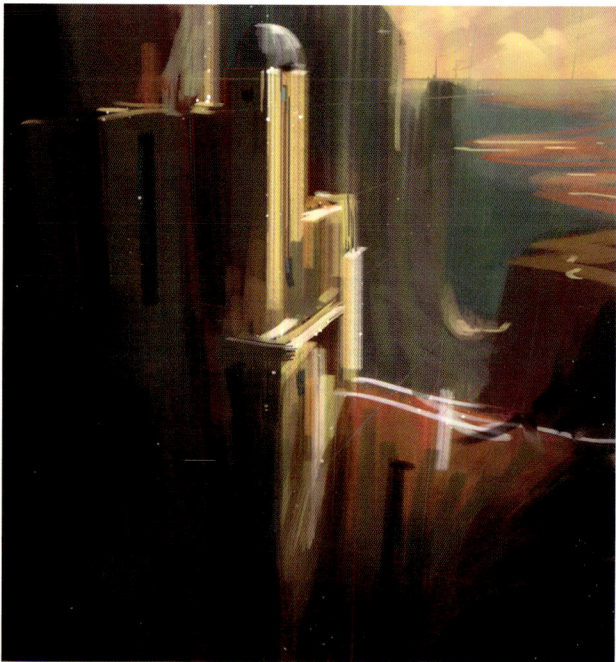

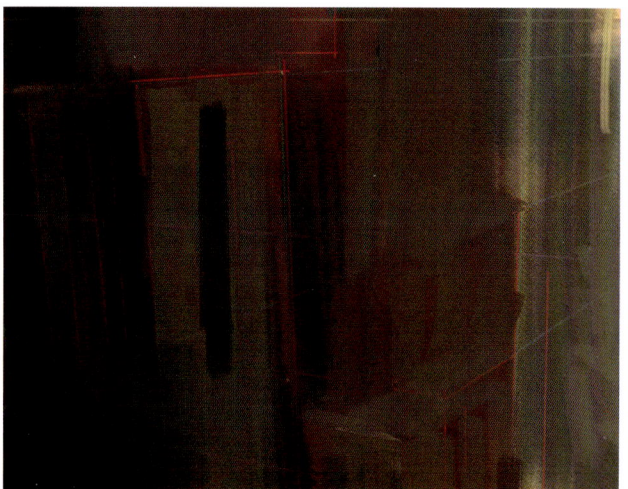

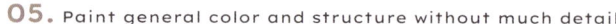

05. Paint general color and structure without much detail

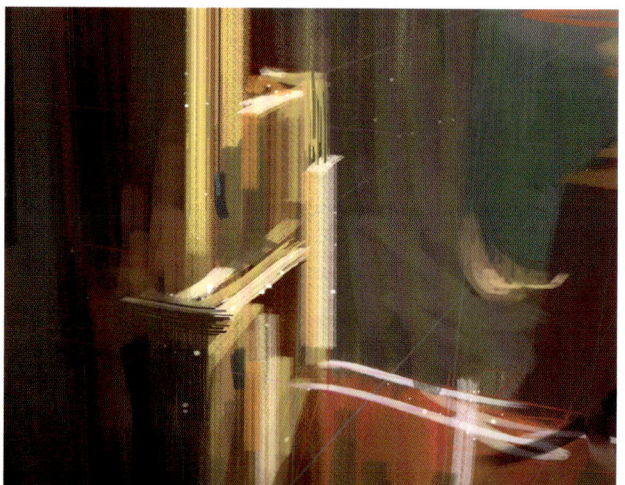

06. Finish off the comp stage by adding light

05. LOOSE RENDERING

Since this is a rough idea I'm working on and not the finish, I don't worry about being precise. I don't want to take too long. This stage needs to remain about generalities rather than getting bogged down in detail. So I scribble in colors that are created by cooler light coming down from above and influencing the planes of the building. Remember, we see a yellow sky in the distance, but that's just a narrow band of the overall sky dome; if we were there and looking straight up, we'd see blues. Remember that the sky is a light source that greatly influences shadow.

06. SUNLIGHT

And now everything is in place for us to lay in the direct sunlight. This is warm late-afternoon light, coming in from the right at an angle of around 30 degrees. It will illuminate side planes and top planes where it hits surfaces. However, remember that this is meant to be a highly purposeful and emotionally strong image, and the light must be carefully designed to serve that purpose. So it makes sense that it hits the main building and the bridge leading to it, and drops out almost everywhere else. This is legit because who's to say there's not a cliffside out of frame, blocking the light from hitting the areas we want to keep in shadow? Our comp is now complete!

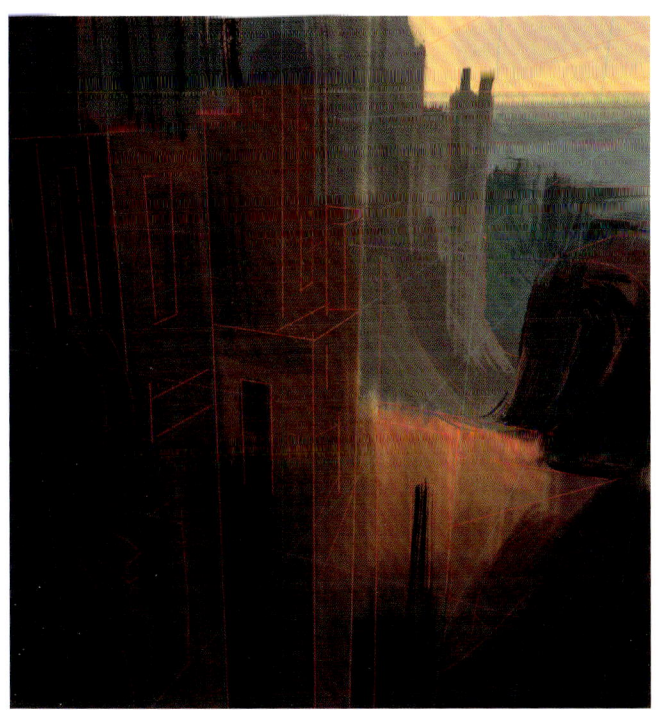

07. Scale up the color rough and continue painting

07. STARTING THE FINAL

From the comp, we can move on to the finished version. My initial rough in, step 04 in the comp, had all the information needed to begin the final – there's no point in wasting time repainting it. So I retrieve that layer from the previous Photoshop file, increase its size, and continue working on it here. My first step is adding the darker notes to the scene, specifically the planes and cliffsides that are facing us, as well as the recesses of the windows.

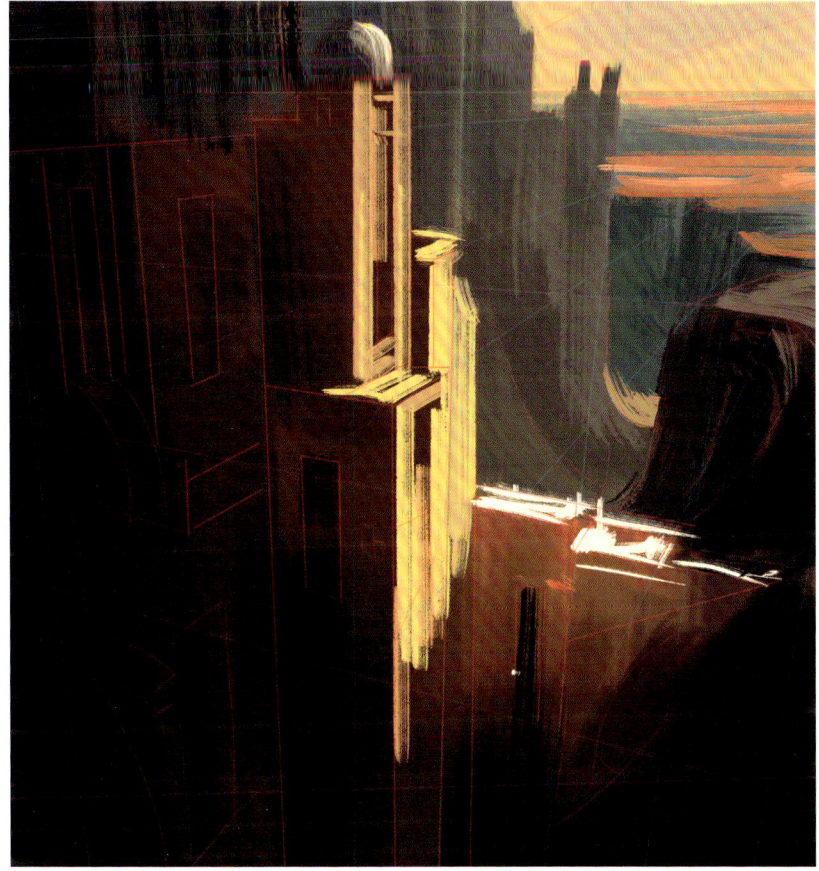

08. The lit areas begin to take clear shape

08. DIRECT LIGHT

And here's the fun part, when we get to officially dig into the direct light! I use a digital brush with a bit of streaky texture to emphasize the elongated verticals, and the color is a combination of the warm yellow of the sunlight and the red-brown of the stone. I know exactly where I want to place the light, since I was happy with the design of the comp. All I have to do is illuminate the front planes and let them cast shadows onto adjacent planes. I also indicate the warm light on the distant canyon tops, receding into the background.

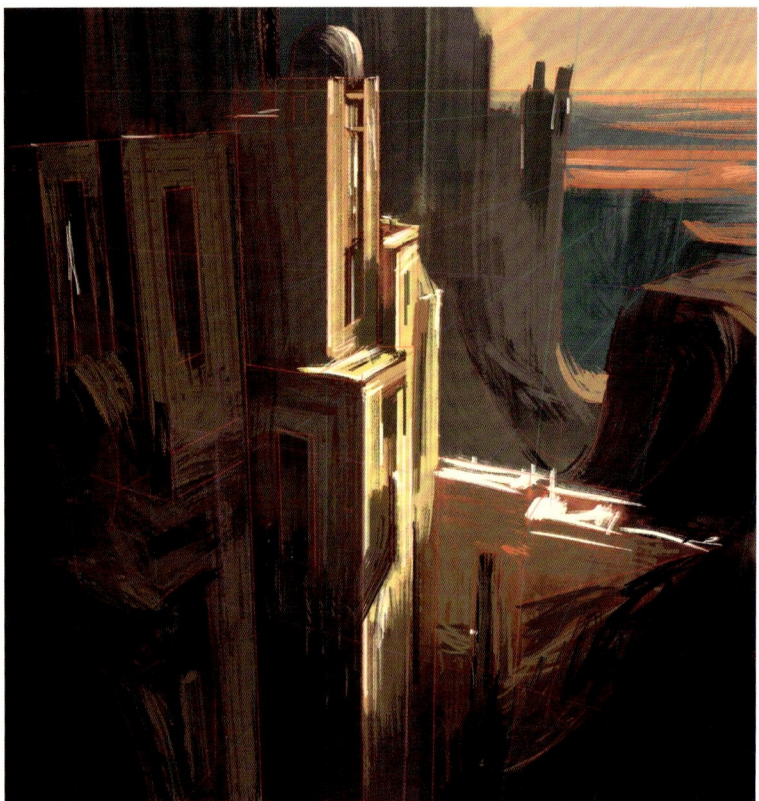

O9. Flesh out the shadowed sides with more detail

O9. SHADOW AREAS

Now we really need to dig into what's happening in the shadows, just as we achieved in the comp. I illuminate the shadow planes with cool skylight, as well as making sure I don't miss warm bounce lights. You'll notice that anywhere there's a bright light adjacent to a shadow, a warm bounce light appears in that area. These shadow hues are critical to the believability of the scene and its richness of color. I don't worry too much about technique at this stage – I just try to get something down that's headed in the right direction, knowing that it will be cleaned up later.

10. FINAL IMAGE

And speaking of cleanup, that's exactly what we do here to take us to the final image. Though there are still lots of brushstrokes and textures, I make sure those contrasts do not rise to the point of distracting from the overall purpose of the image. In the background I suggest a bit of warm light hitting the clouds and a very subtle, warm stream of light coming in to heroically illuminate the palace. I also add some reflected blues and cyans in the windows – these little bits of color contrast are very important accents within the overwhelming warmth of the buildings. And there's the addition of little white birds – everyone knows that when you're doing an epic environment it needs those little white birds for scale and visual interest. And we're finished!

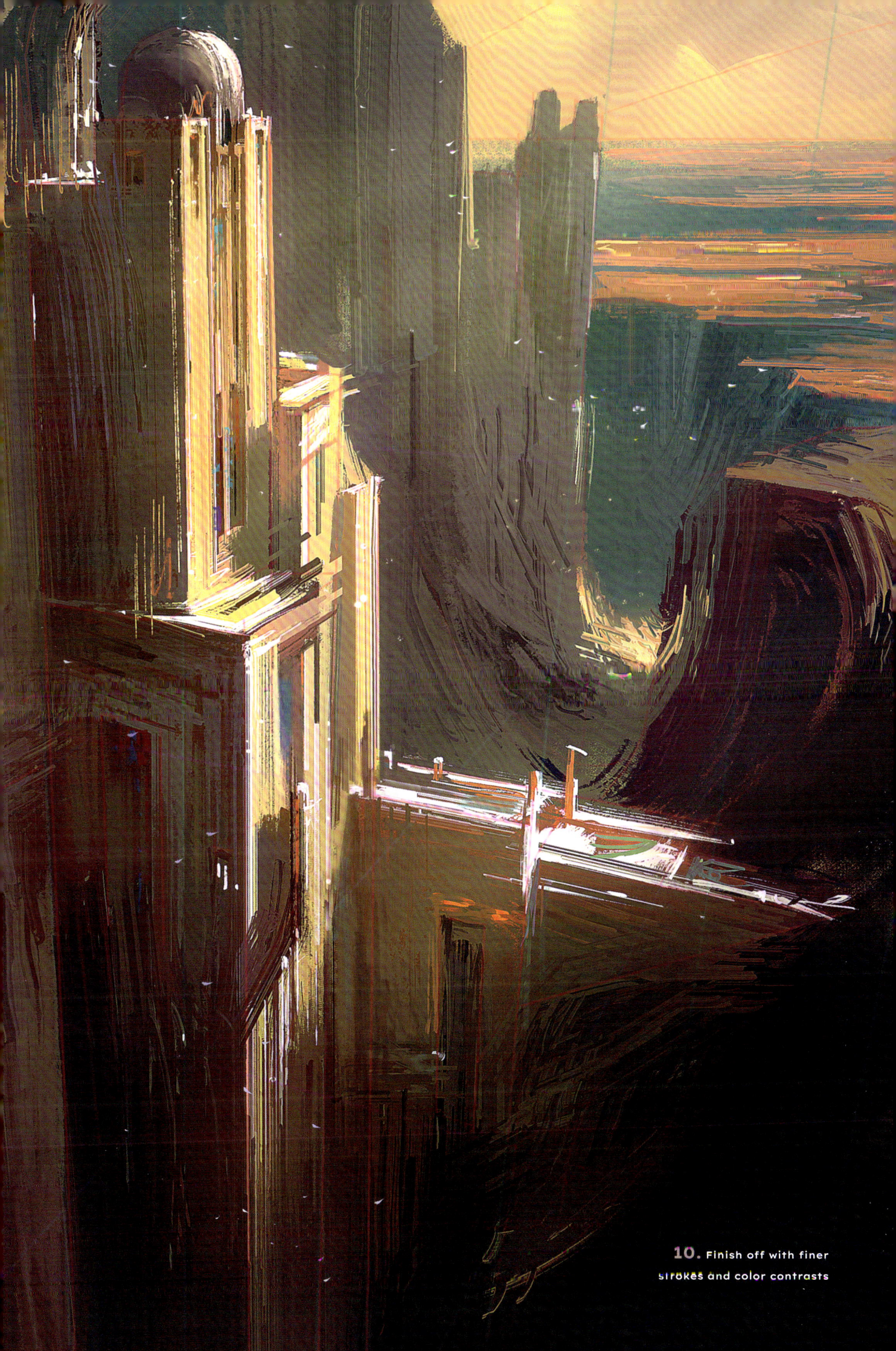

10. Finish off with finer strokes and color contrasts

RECOMMENDED EXERCISE:
SHAPE & LINE LANGUAGE STUDIES

We started this chapter asking, 'How do we give completely inanimate objects a sense of character and emotion?' and we've spent the entirety of it answering that question. It's critical for the quality of our work that we put these ideas into practice.

Assign yourself simple black-and-white sketches that try to create a range of mood and emotion just by using shape and line as primary considerations. Think of an emotion, then consider what shape and line language can help you render that emotion. I recommend that you think of five very different emotions and see how well you can target them using value, shape, and line. Here's a batch that I did, and I'm excited for the ideas that you'll come up with in your own studies.

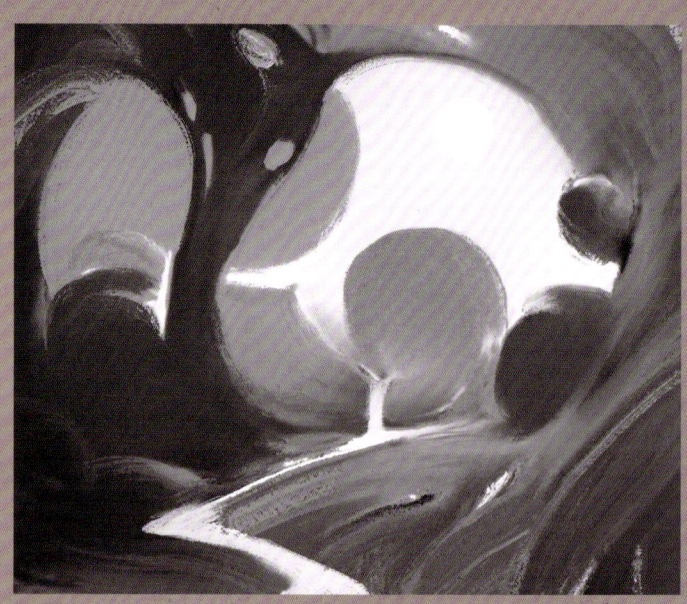

Inviting

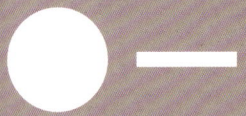

Calm

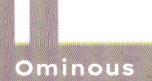

Ominous

Spooky

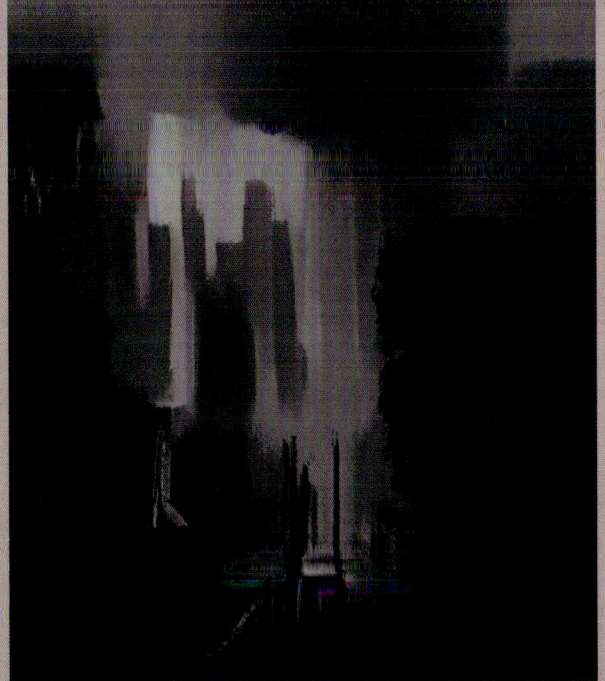

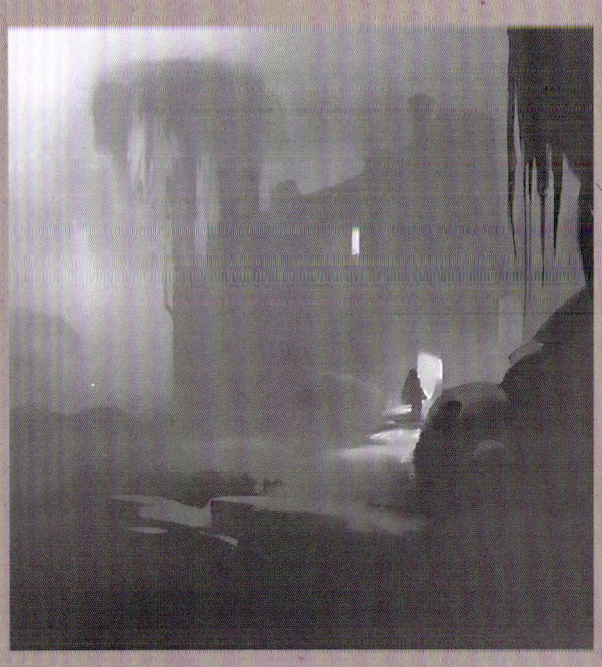

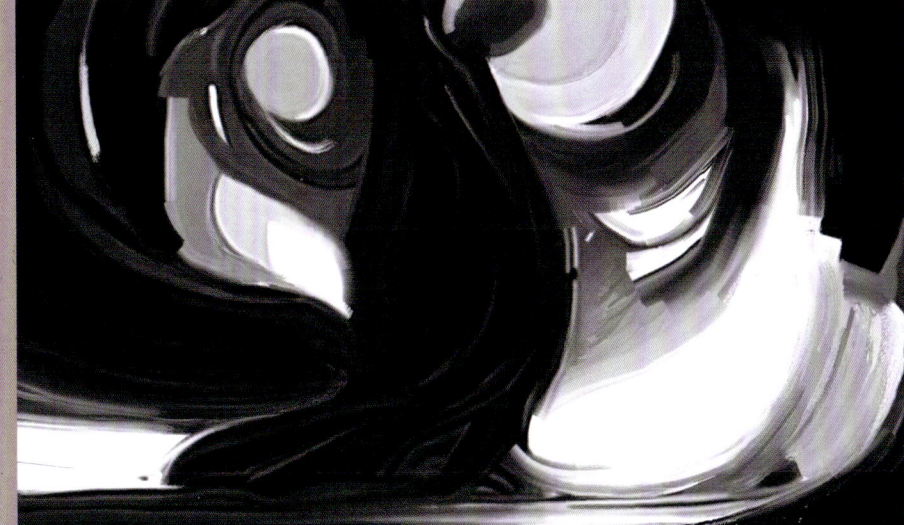

Whimsical

THE DESIGN OF SPACE

The spaces we create don't mean much to our audience if they're not filled with potent emotion.

THE STAR WARS TRENCH CONUNDRUM

The movie *Star Wars* came out in 1977 when I was eight years old, and for kids of my generation it was the defining movie experience. It was especially true for me – I grew up in a very small town where there was no movie theater, so we had to travel a long distance to see any movies. So *Star Wars* was one of the few movies that I saw during that period, and man, it made an impression! I came home and I drew *Star Wars* every day for years.

Many years later, VHS tapes came out, and you can guess the first movie we bought – *Star Wars*, of course, and it was still great. I was a teenager by this time. I remember watching the ending where Luke Skywalker and his band of heroes fly down into a trench to avoid surface guns and line up on their target. I remember saying to myself, 'Wait a minute, did they really have to come down into that trench, miles and miles and kilometers and kilometers in front of that target, all the while getting picked off one by one by the TIE fighters? I mean, couldn't they come down just enough to get in there, line up, take their shot, and get back out?'

It would be ridiculous if it were an actual military action, but this is not a military action. This is a movie. And it's not just any part of a movie – this is the grand finale. If you want a successful action thriller, you have to get the audience on the edge of their seats. They have to be deeply invested. This is the moment that decides if Luke Skywalker and his heroic resistance will succeed or fail, and everything is riding on that.

Let's put this in the context of the real world at the time. If this movie does not succeed, then there is no George Lucas. He doesn't found Industrial Light & Magic to create wondrous and innovative visual effects. There's no *Indiana Jones*. The entire movie landscape of the world is diminished if *Star Wars* is a flop. And it all comes down to that one moment in the trench. So it might not make military sense, but it makes movie sense. If Luke Skywalker is in a tight situation, then the visual designers of the movie put him in a *physically* tight space to help the audience feel the tension. You put the audience in the *Star Wars* trench, where evil feels inescapable, and only through great power and great skill can they maneuver their way to success. Through the design of space, you have a movie.

Because, as I've said many times in this book, what we do doesn't mean much to our audience if it's not filled with potent emotion.

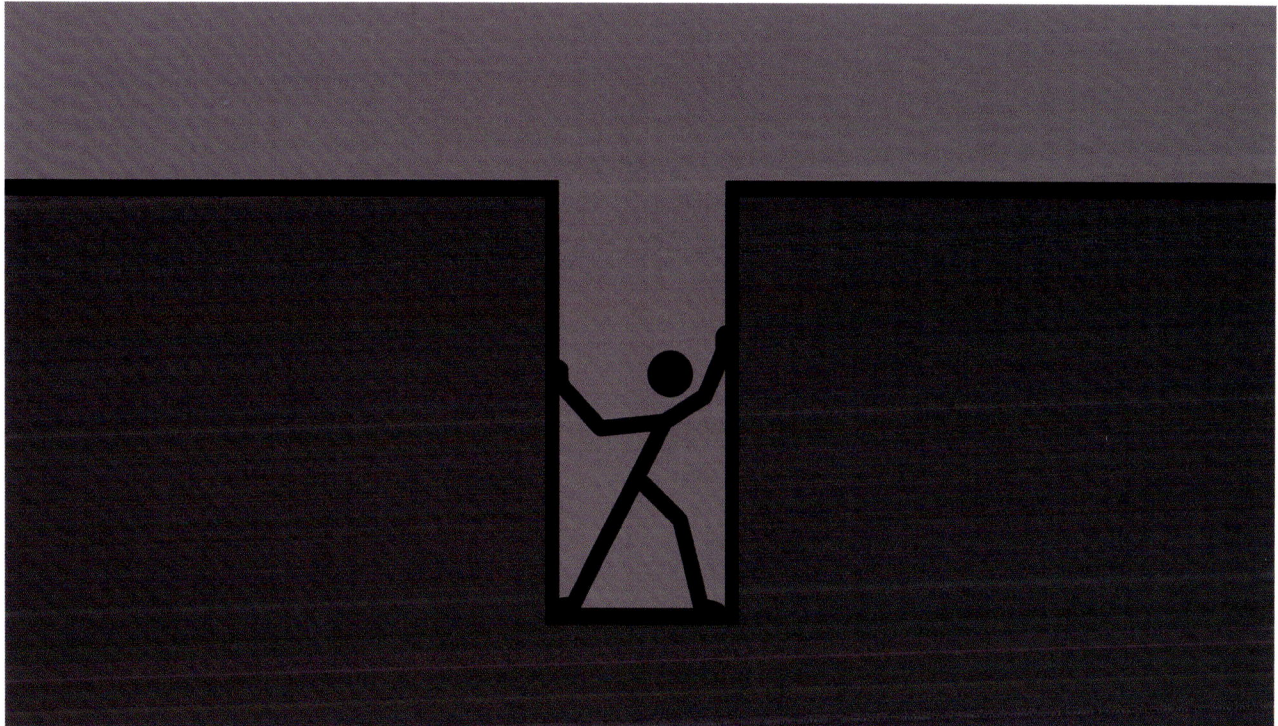

△ Trapping the hero in an enclosed space helps to heighten drama

THE SPIRIT 'TRENCH'

I really enjoyed working on the DreamWorks movie *Spirit: Stallion of the Cimarron*. I love landscape painting, and for a couple of years I got to paint scenes of the grand expanse of the American West. The movie begins with mustangs roaming wild and free in that setting. We did our best to paint it that way, with layers and layers of landscape moving into the distance, giving the impression that no matter how many rises you climb, there'll be more waiting for you in the distance. And we created our own '*Star Wars* trench' in this movie. Let me explain.

Spirit takes place during the settler expansion of the 1800s, when the freedom of the wild mustangs is threatened. Humans discover our main character, Spirit the mustang, and attempt to capture him. It's a moment of great emotional threat in the movie. So what do we do? We do the *Star Wars* trench scenario! Spirit is chased into a very tight canyon, which creates the same kind of emotional tension for the audience as in *Star Wars*. The verdant green hills turn to dust and brown cliffsides, the warm sunshine turns to cold gray light, and the space goes from expansive to claustrophobic. It's the emotional

change that this moment in the movie needs. It's another example of the emotional importance of space in environment design.

And since we're several chapters into this book, let me continue to push the importance of emotion into every subject we tackle. The goal of this book is to turn you into not just a highly capable artist, but a highly sought-after artist. Your potential clients see tons of work on social media, and they review hundreds of portfolios, many of them quite good. So what does that mean for you?

It means that when they come to your portfolio, they can't just *see* it. The moment they open it, there has to be a flash of light and a thunderclap that they will never forget. They'll want to immediately hire you. The only impediment is that they're fearful they might not be able to meet the rate of an artist such as you. That's the dream! So let's keep digging into every possible way to create clarity, artistry, and emotion in our work. In this chapter we'll keep our focus on the emotional qualities of space.

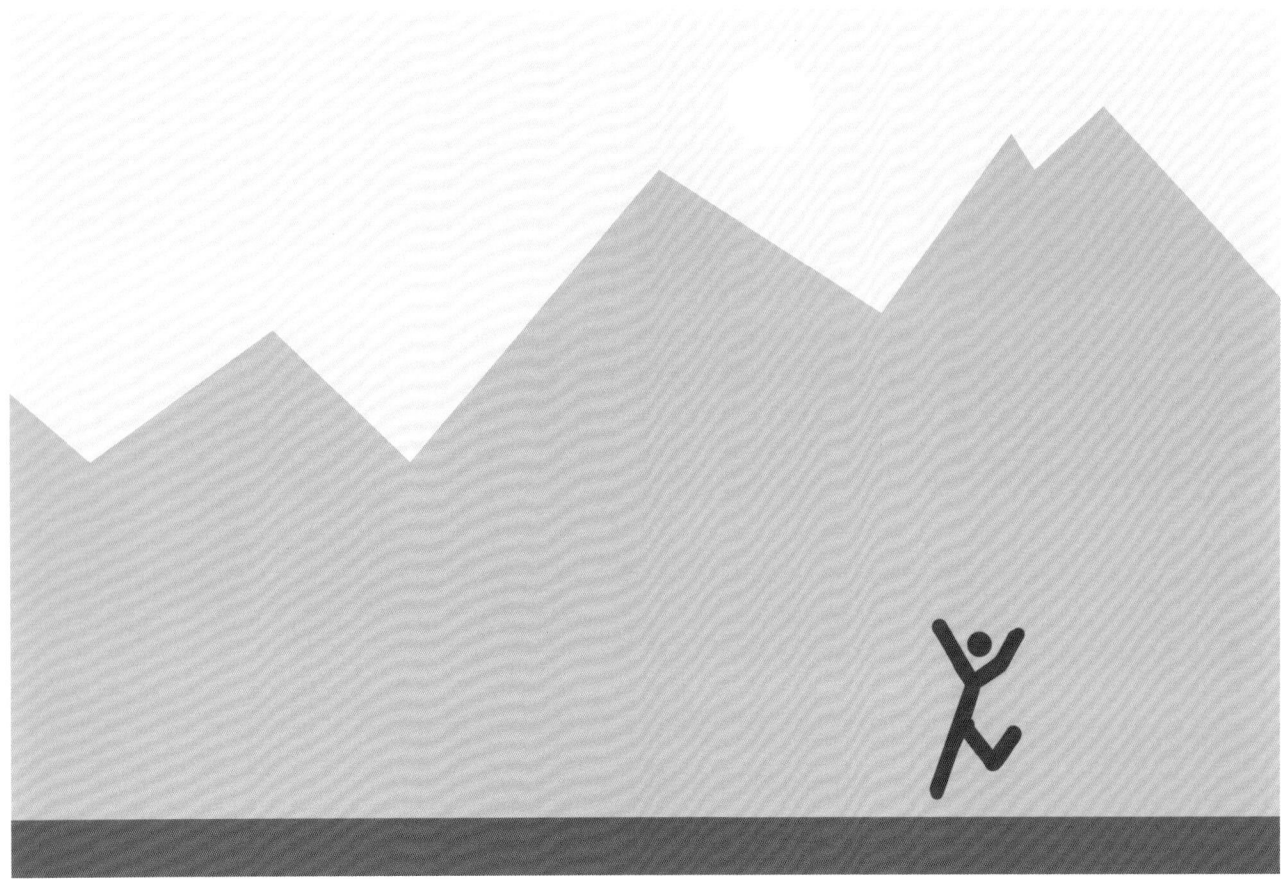

△ A wide-open space evokes a very different feeling!

CREATING THE ILLUSION OF SPACE

Let's begin with the most direct and useful ways to create space, and then we'll quickly get to the application of these ideas to storytelling and emotion. I created this rusty disk for you in Photoshop so I could carefully lay out our initial ideas. On the nearer, advancing side I placed hot temperature, high texture, and contrasting light and shadow. On the receding side I did exactly the opposite: cool temperatures and low contrast. In real life an object like this wouldn't naturally have these effects, but you and I are not in the business of telling the truth – we're in the business of telling a whole lot of little white lies that together create a greater truth. The purpose of this example is to show as much depth as possible, so I've emphasized and exaggerated those elements

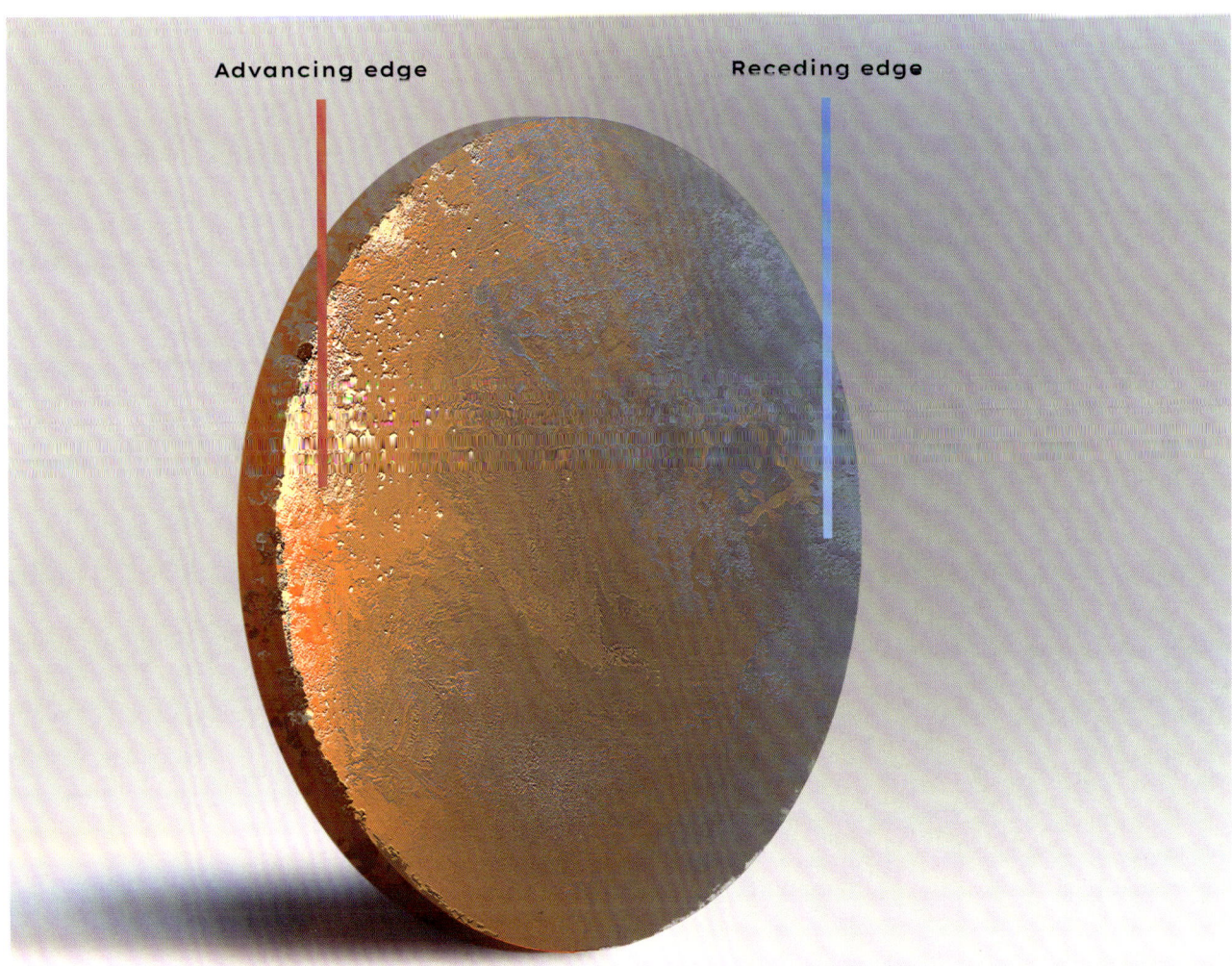

△ Temperature, contrast, and texture create depth and space

You and I are not in the business of telling the truth – we're in the business of telling a whole lot of little white lies that together create a greater truth.

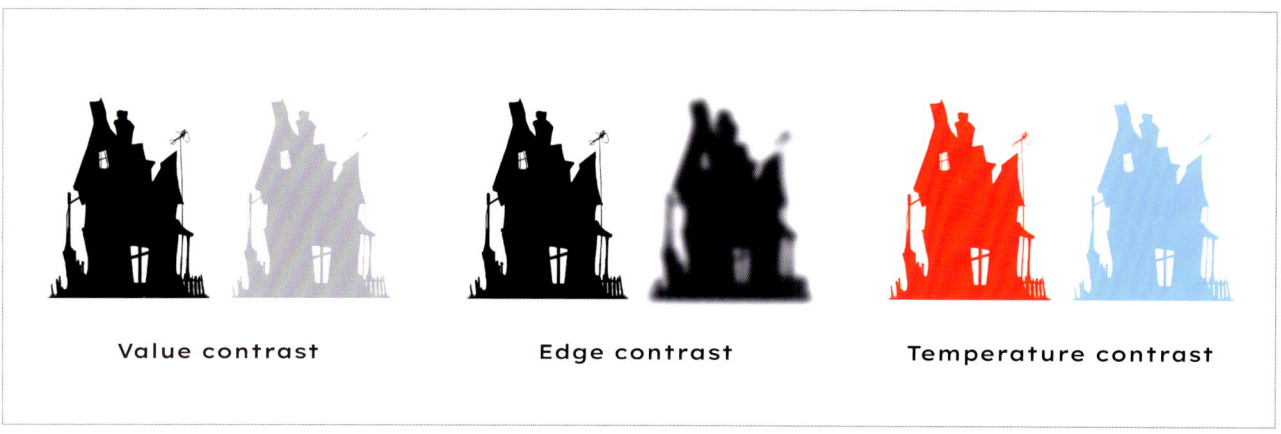

Value contrast   Edge contrast   Temperature contrast

01. Three different ways of creating space with contrast

01. CONTRAST

Let's make further use of the little haunted house you saw in the chapter on the design of value (see page 60). Here we're using three different kinds of contrast to do the job of creating space: value contrast, edge contrast, and temperature contrast. Notice how the houses with lower contrast are the ones that drop further away in space.

02. OVERLAP

Overlap is such a simple and fantastic way of creating space, as you'll see in upcoming examples. Every one of these gray squares is exactly identical in shape, size, and value, yet they feel like they're receding in space. Simply overlapping them was enough to do the trick.

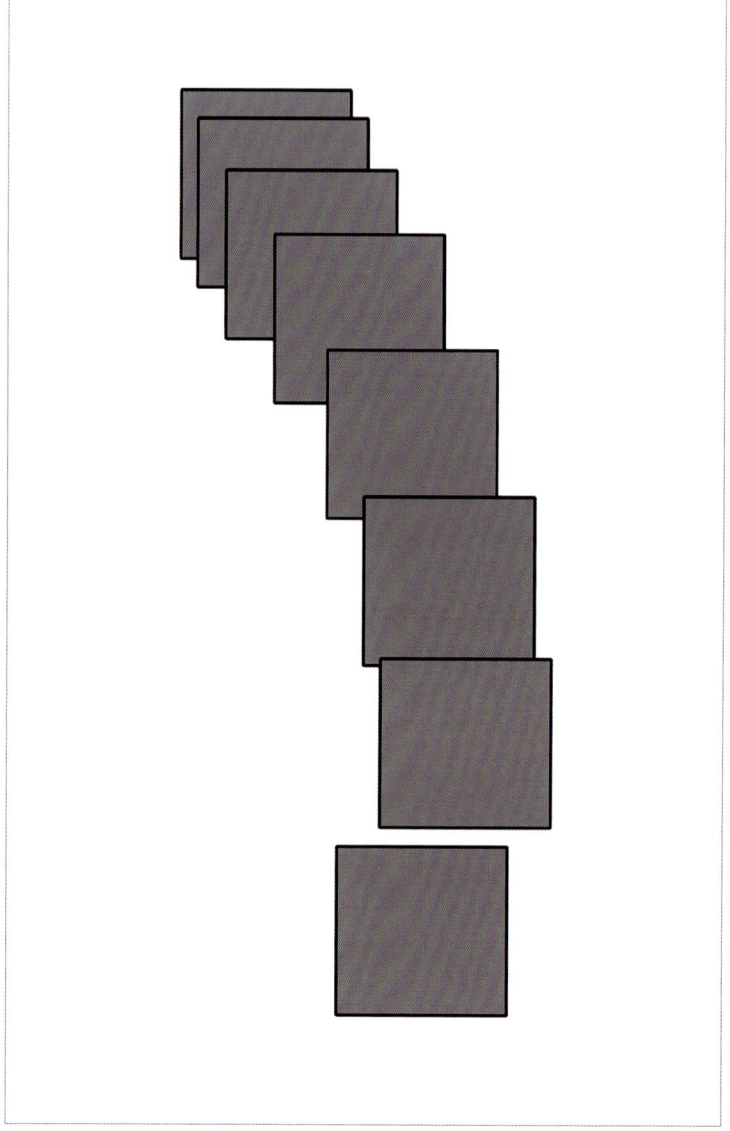

02. These squares are all exactly the same!

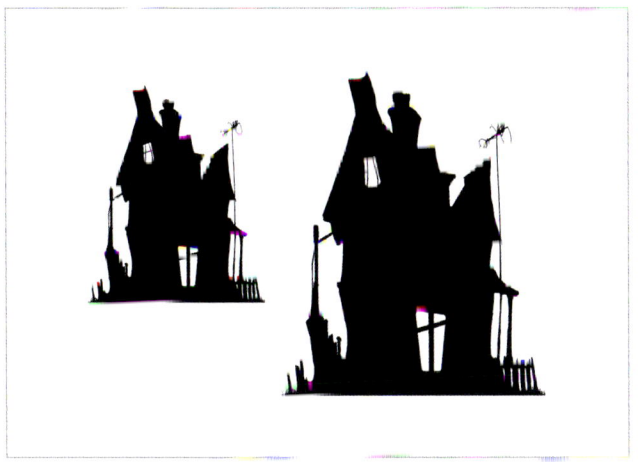 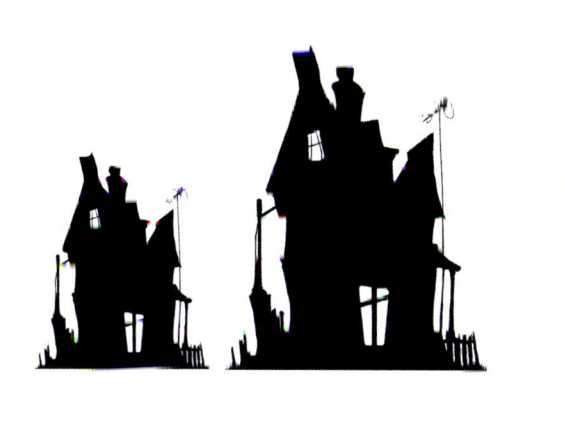

03. Create space using the position of objects relative to each other

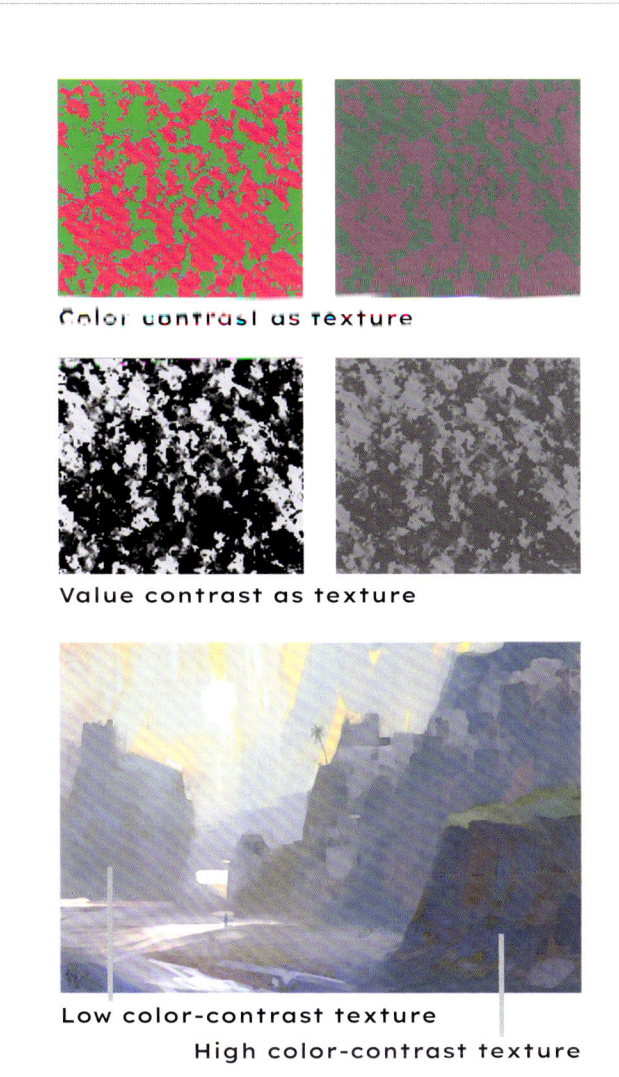

Color contrast as texture

Value contrast as texture

Low color-contrast texture

High color-contrast texture

04. Texture can vary widely in value and color contrast

03. RELATIVE POSITION

The idea of relative position is especially useful when working in a more graphic style. Simply raising an object creates the illusion that it's farther away. A lower relative position makes an object look smaller and closer. This happens because a higher object is usually closer to the eye-level line, which is a more natural position for a further object.

04. TEXTURE

We can apply these same ideas to texture because areas tend to advance in space if they have more texture contrast in their color and value. The misty landscape illustration shown here puts these ideas into practice – I'm able to create the illusion of great distance by using contrasting texture.

Simply putting higher contrast in the foreground and lower contrast in the background can create the illusion of great distance.

SPACE IS A STORYTELLING TOOL

Now let's see how we can use these ideas of space for storytelling purposes. The first interior sketch below floods the room with warm light, making it the focus of the scene. But what if the story demanded that the view to the exterior was the area of interest? A simple value and temperature shift tells us we need to be paying attention to the outside.

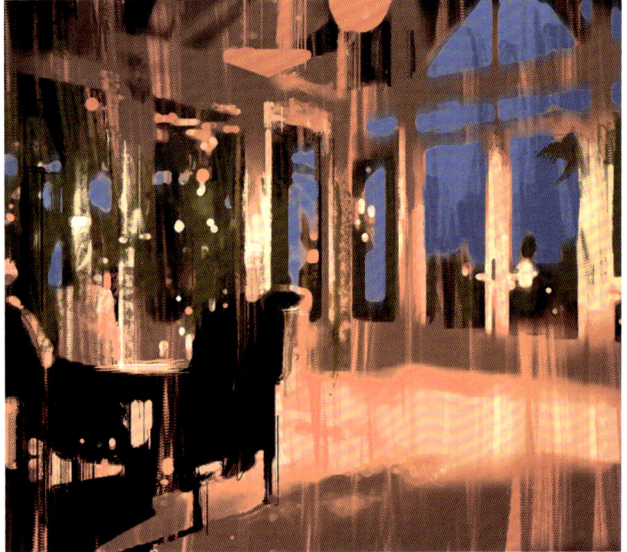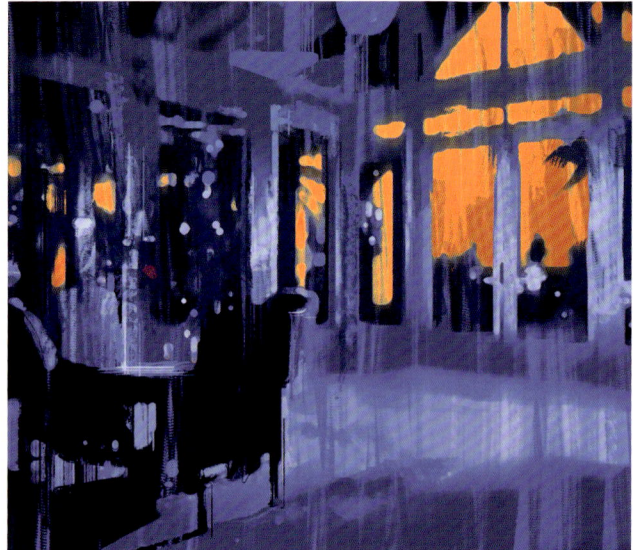

△ Same space, different emphasis

01. FOREST SCENE

Let's further illustrate these ideas with a simple forest scene. In my sketchbook I roughed out a little idea pulling the viewer toward a simple tree shape at the center. I suggested some receding layers in the foreground, as simply as possible, and kept the area behind the tree soft and low-contrast. I used this sketch to flesh out a completed study of the forest with an expansive sense of depth, which you can see on the opposite page.

The bottom-right image charts all the different elements I used to enhance the quality of space in this environment. Note that they include warm foreground accents, many layers of overlapping planes, and distant atmosphere with softer edges and cooler temperatures.

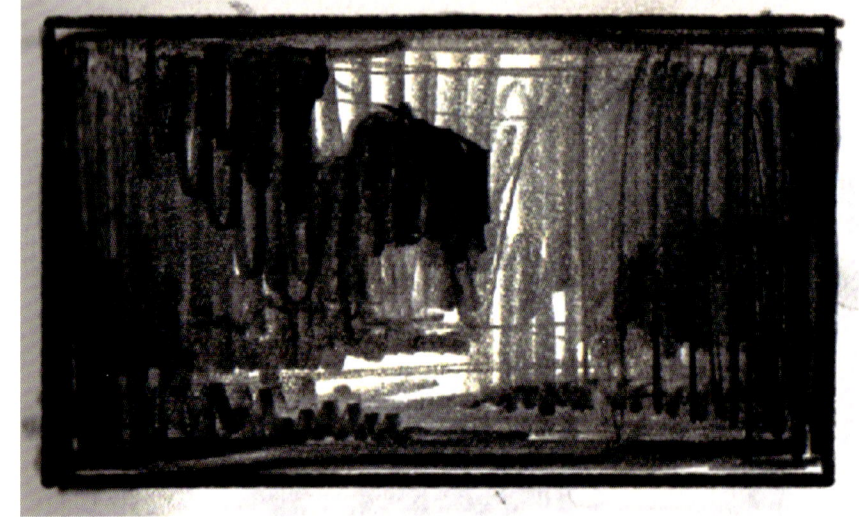

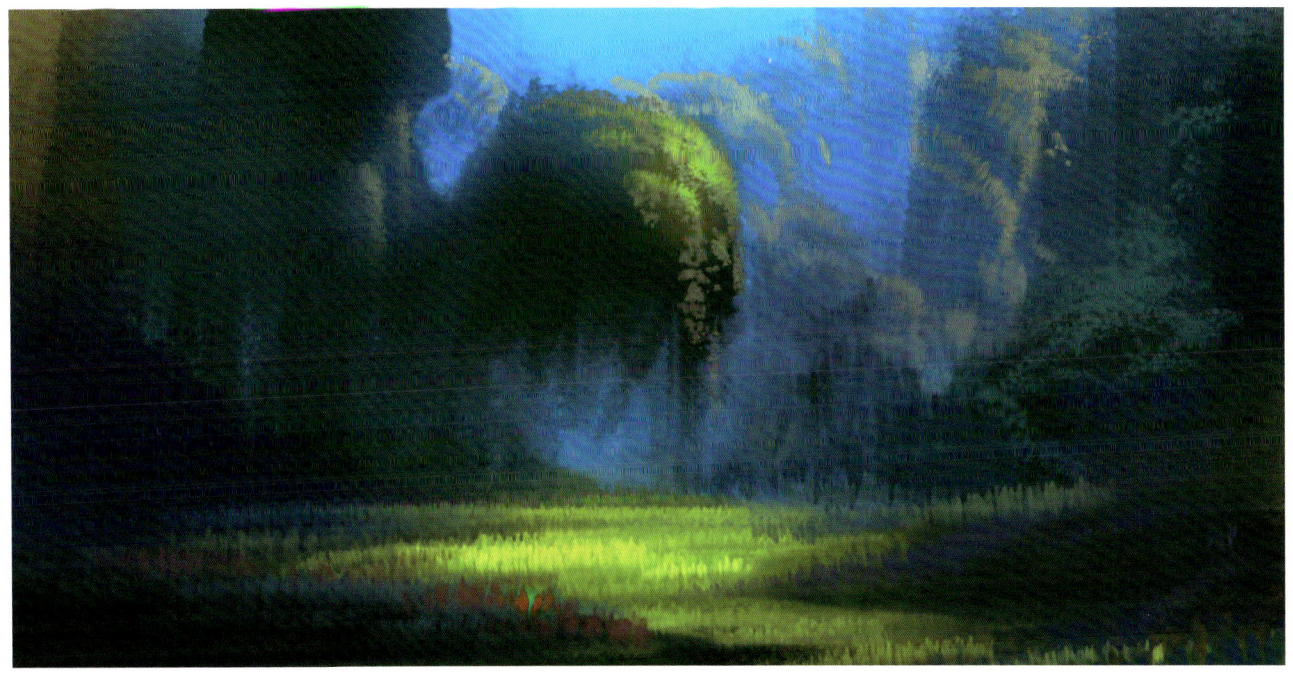

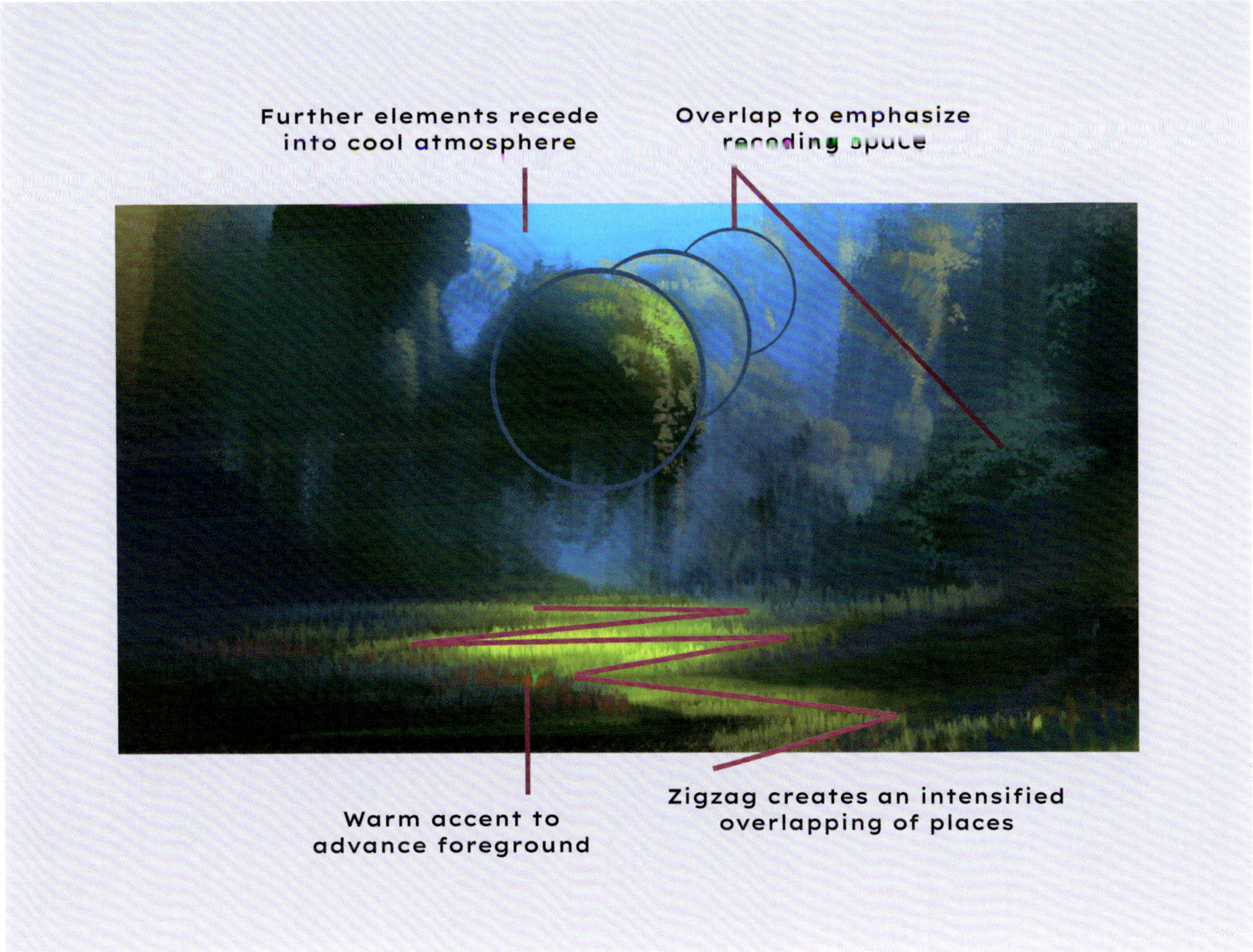

Further elements recede into cool atmosphere

Overlap to emphasize receding space

Warm accent to advance foreground

Zigzag creates an intensified overlapping of places

01. This forest scene uses several techniques and elements to create space

02. PATHWAYS

I had the wonderful opportunity to work in Japan and was mesmerized by the cherry-blossomed landscape surrounding temples and shrines. I had a hard time getting my paintings of these complicated scenes to have a clear sense of space until I realized I needed to add pathways. Pathways carry us through an environment – they wrap around from front to back, creating layers of space while giving a solid grounding to an otherwise confusing landscape. I've noted the pathways here in red and orange. Imagine what a jumble this landscape would be if not for the clarity and the sense of space they create.

Pathways carry us through an environment – they wrap around from front to back, creating layers of space while giving a solid grounding to an otherwise confusing landscape.

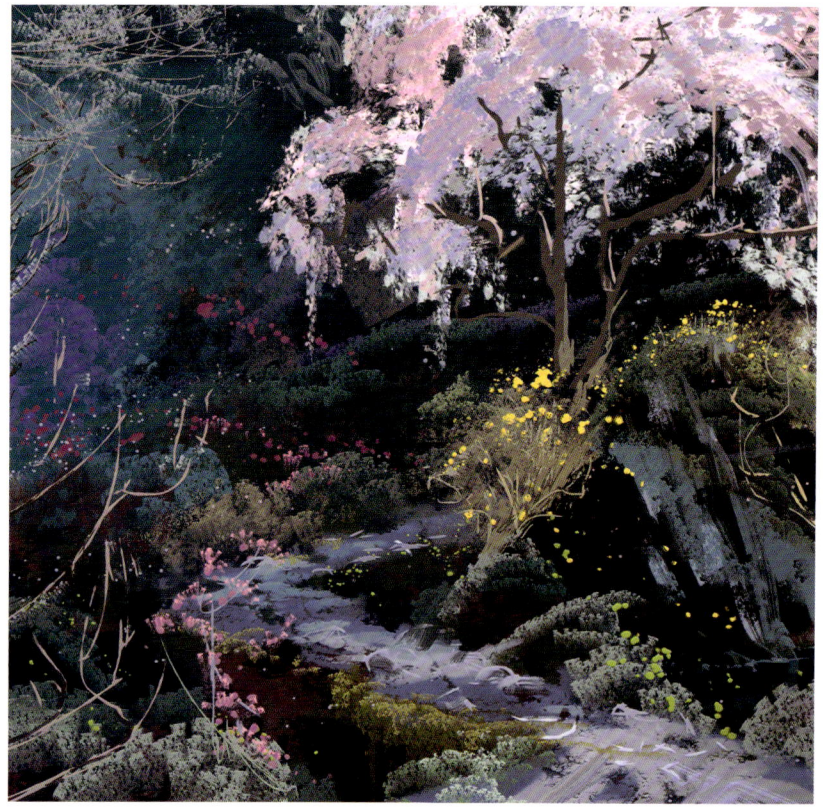

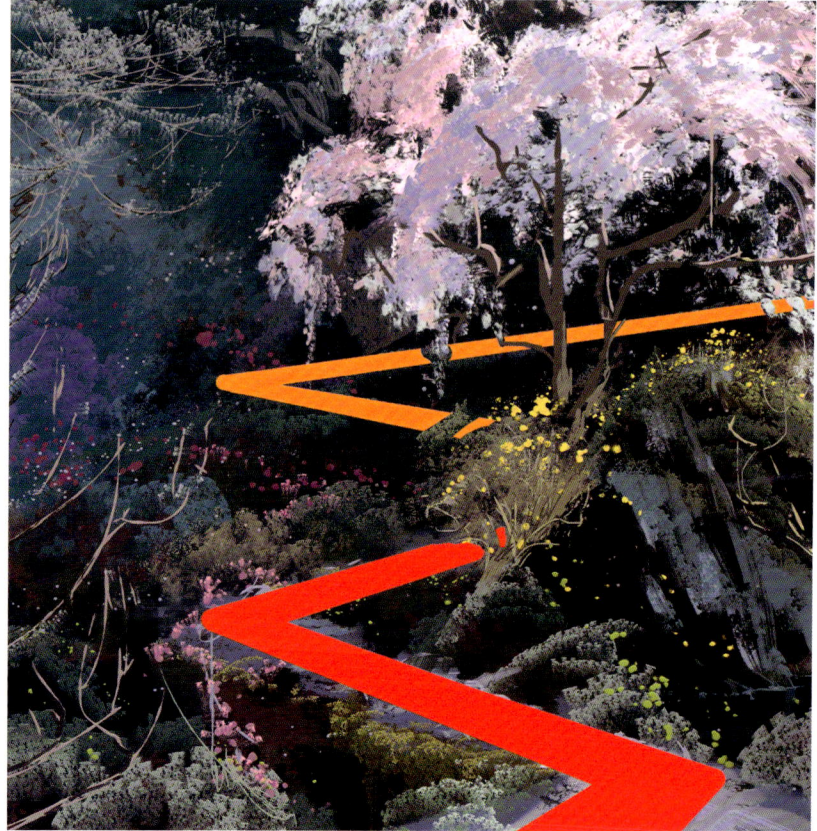

02. Devise a pathway to give clarity to your environment

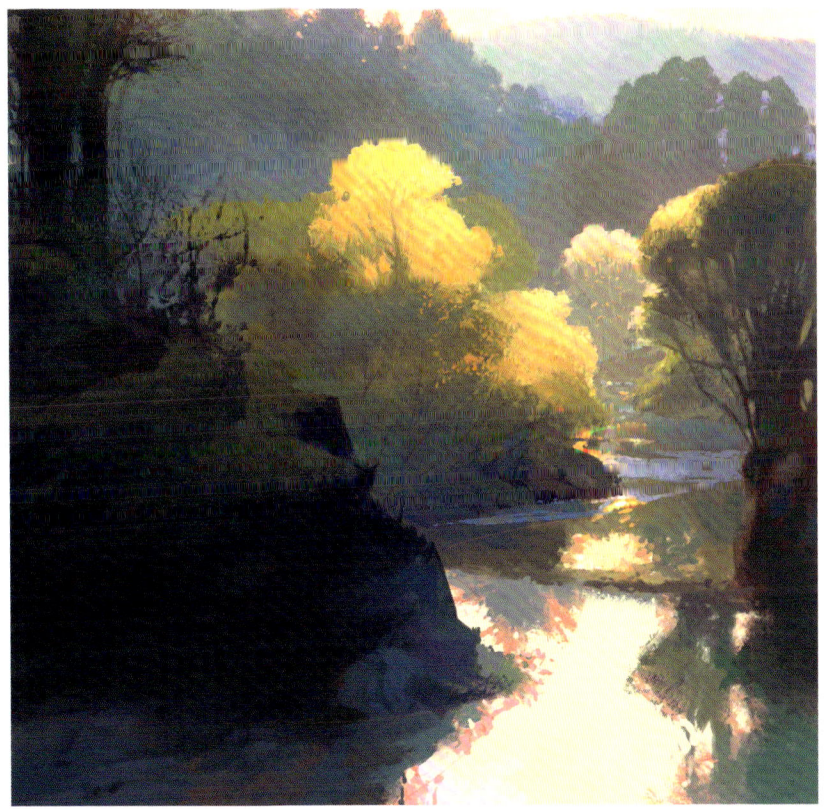

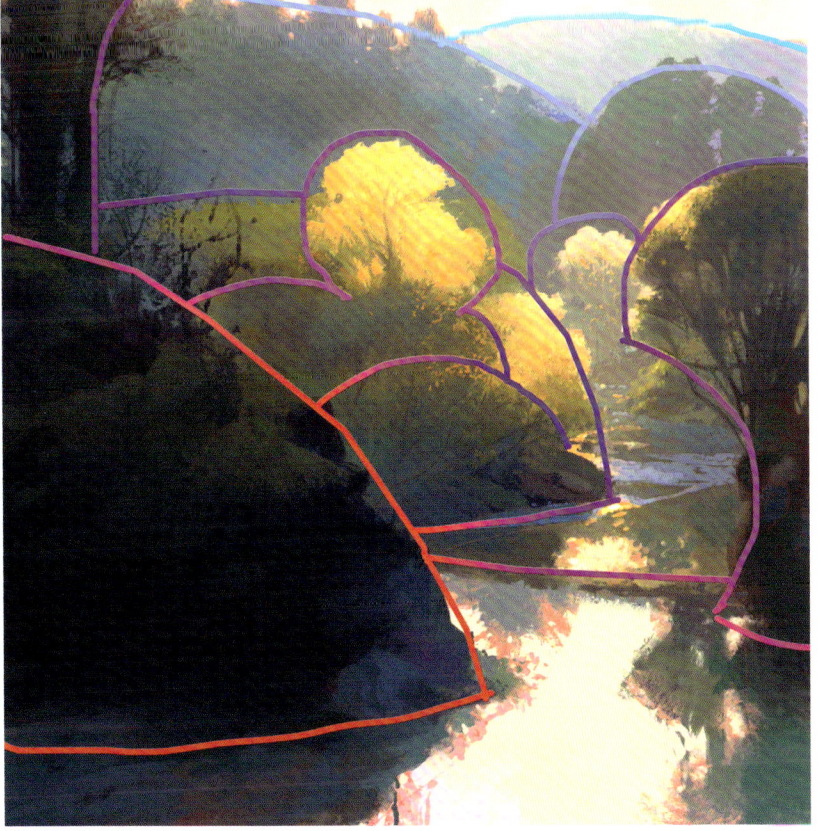

03. Layers of overlapping landscape create depth along this river

03. LANDSCAPE LAYERS

I love painting head-on views of streams and rivers as they weave from the foreground into the distance. They automatically create valuable effects of space, the same as the pathway in the previous painting. For this painting I was very careful to take advantage of this effect and emphasize as many overlapping layers of landscape as possible. I've outlined each of those major layers for you here. Whether the layers happen to be warm or cool, hard or soft, the overlap clarifies where they are in space. It's just like the simple overlapping of squares shown on page 98.

04. OVERLAPPING SHAPES

Let's review another example of overlap, but this time in a completely imagined and stylized environment. This one takes inspiration from the great Disney animation artist Eyvind Earle, an artist I can't recommend strongly enough for your studies. The more graphic quality of this image lends itself to an obvious overlap of shapes, and it does so in two ways. First, the more graphically defined local colors of objects create lots of opportunities for overlap. Second, the simplified layers of landscape create a clear overlapping of space.

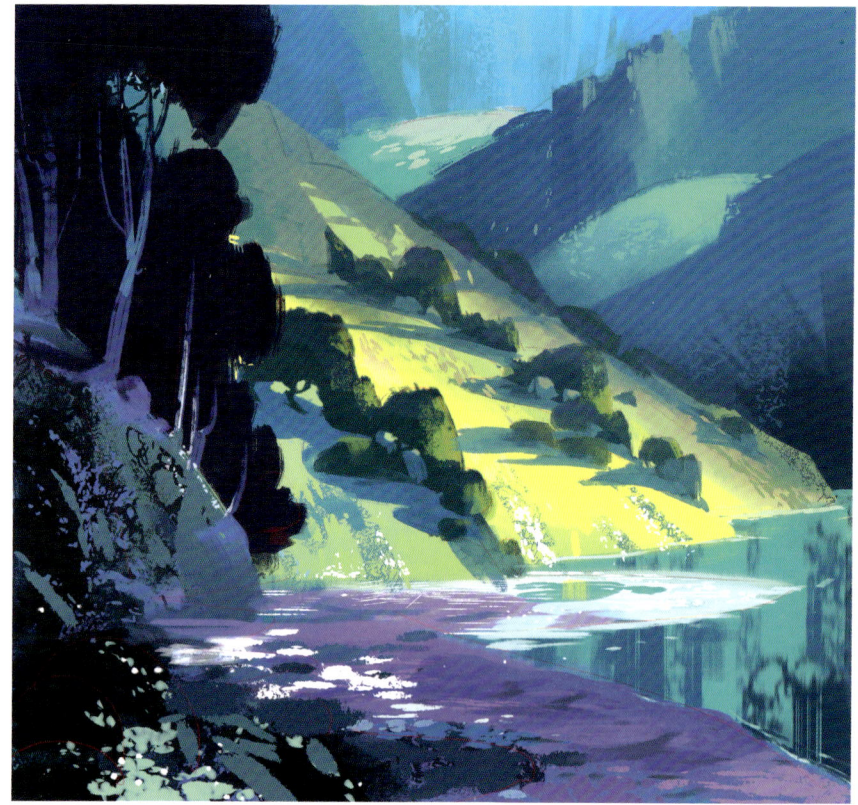

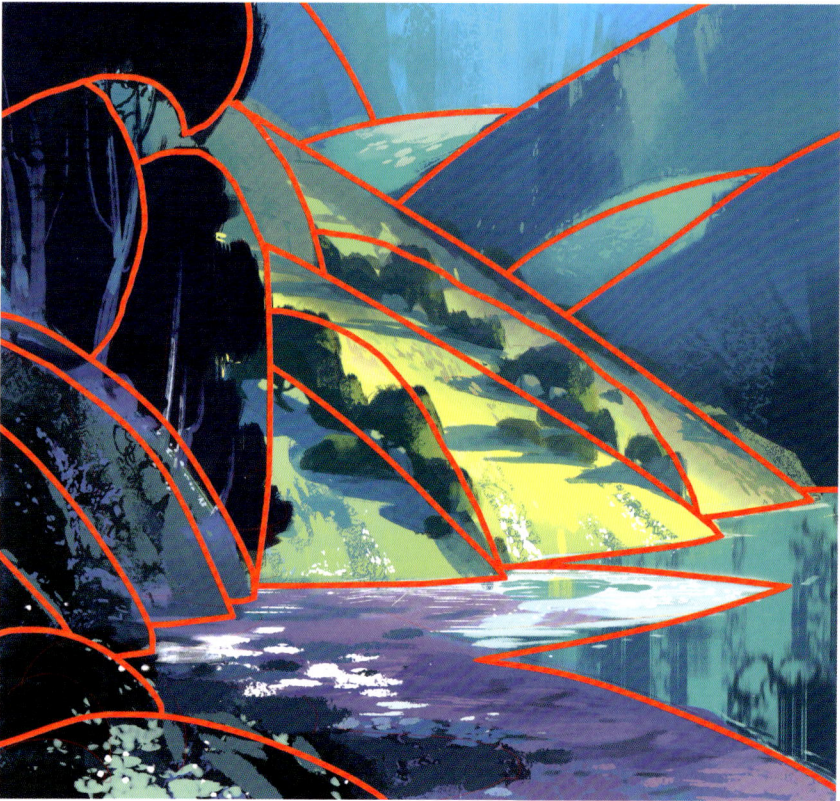

04. This landscape shows space through overlapping layers of clear, distinct shapes

THE DEPTH OF ATMOSPHERE

Let's look at a series of images to familiarize ourselves with the space-intensifying qualities of atmosphere. First, a straightforward tonal example. Since mist and atmosphere diffuse light, distant elements become more luminous and lighter in value. Here I've used the darker foreground as a frame that lets us look out into deeper

space, as if through a window. This approach, combined with the overlapping shapes and the value changes, gives us an immediate quality of space. It might be of interest to you that this was a typical approach we used in DreamWorks' *How to Train Your Dragon* movies, which were often monochromatic and value-driven.

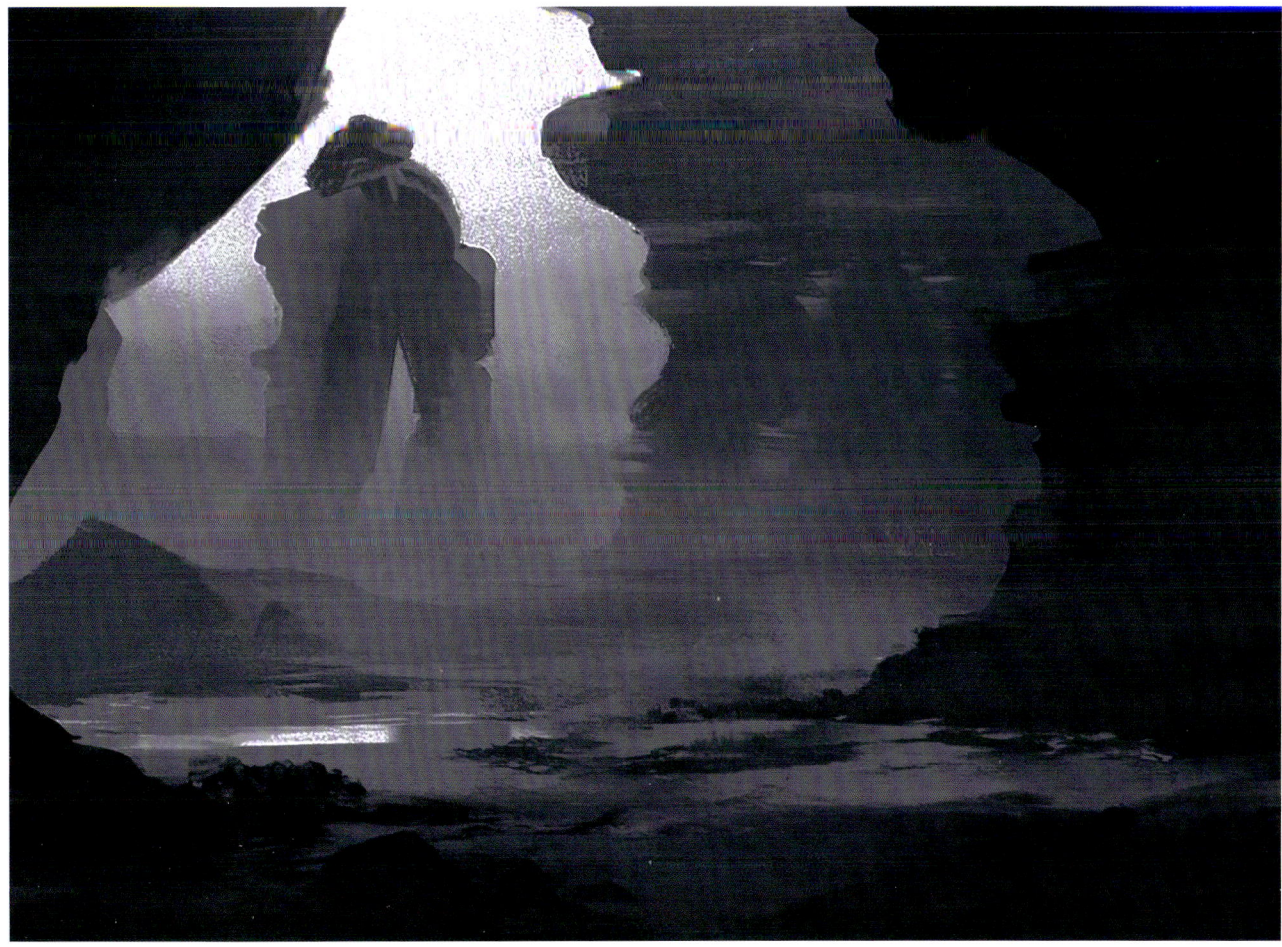

△ Atmosphere causes objects to get lighter with distance, creating depth with value

01. MISTY SUNRISE

I'm excited to show you this one because this is the environment I grew up in. In the fall season we would get misty mornings such as this. As the sun came up over the trees, the backlight would fill the environment with gorgeous luminosity. I've included this painting as a contrast to the previous monochromatic one – it has the same quality of objects getting lighter into the distance, but it's filled with color. This happens because the sunlight is warm, the skylight from above is cool, and the foreground has rich local colors of greens, ochers, and oranges.

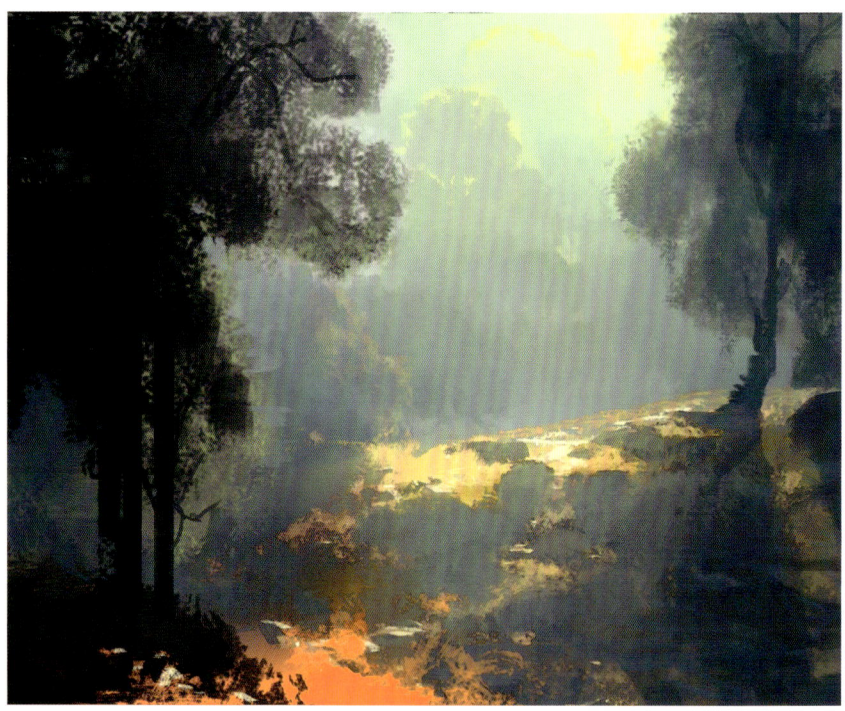

01. Combine atmosphere and color to create rich atmospheric space

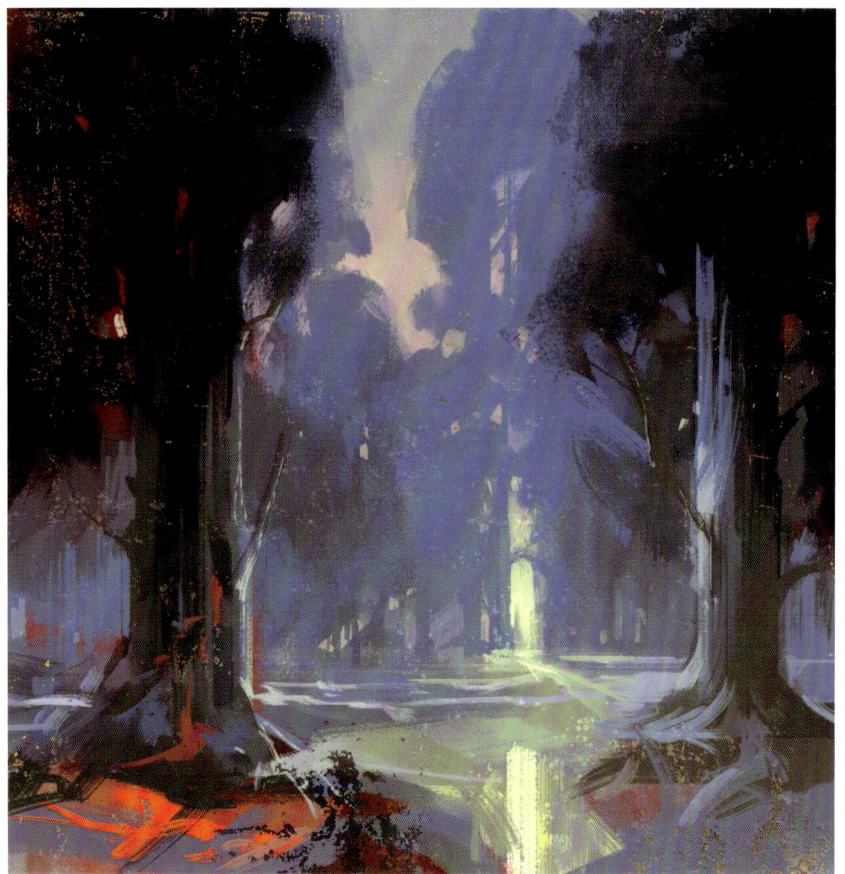

02. The same principles apply to otherworldly light sources and color palettes

02. MAGICAL LIGHT

And here's an imagined environment making strong usage of atmospheric space. This one has an invented shaft of green light in the distance, almost as if it's magic, and this green focus drives the color palette of this image. I've used a blue-purple for the distant atmospheric trees because it contrasts nicely with the green. Had I used cyans, like in the previous image, they would be too similar to the green and the green would lose its magic. Again, I've used some real heat in the foreground to emphasize the quality of space – this time a vivid red to create maximum contrast with the green.

ADDING 'BANDING' TO THE MIX

This rocky environment illustrates most of what we've talked about thus far with the addition of the idea that I call 'banding'. First, let me point out that the shoreline and the rocks zigzag through space, allowing each object to overlap with the next for an immediate quality of space. In terms of temperature, this image uses the same idea as the two previous ones: it has a highly exaggerated warm temperature in the foreground and very heightened atmospheric blues and cyans in the background. And note the texture: the image has texture throughout, but the foreground texture is much larger and more pronounced, as indicated here.

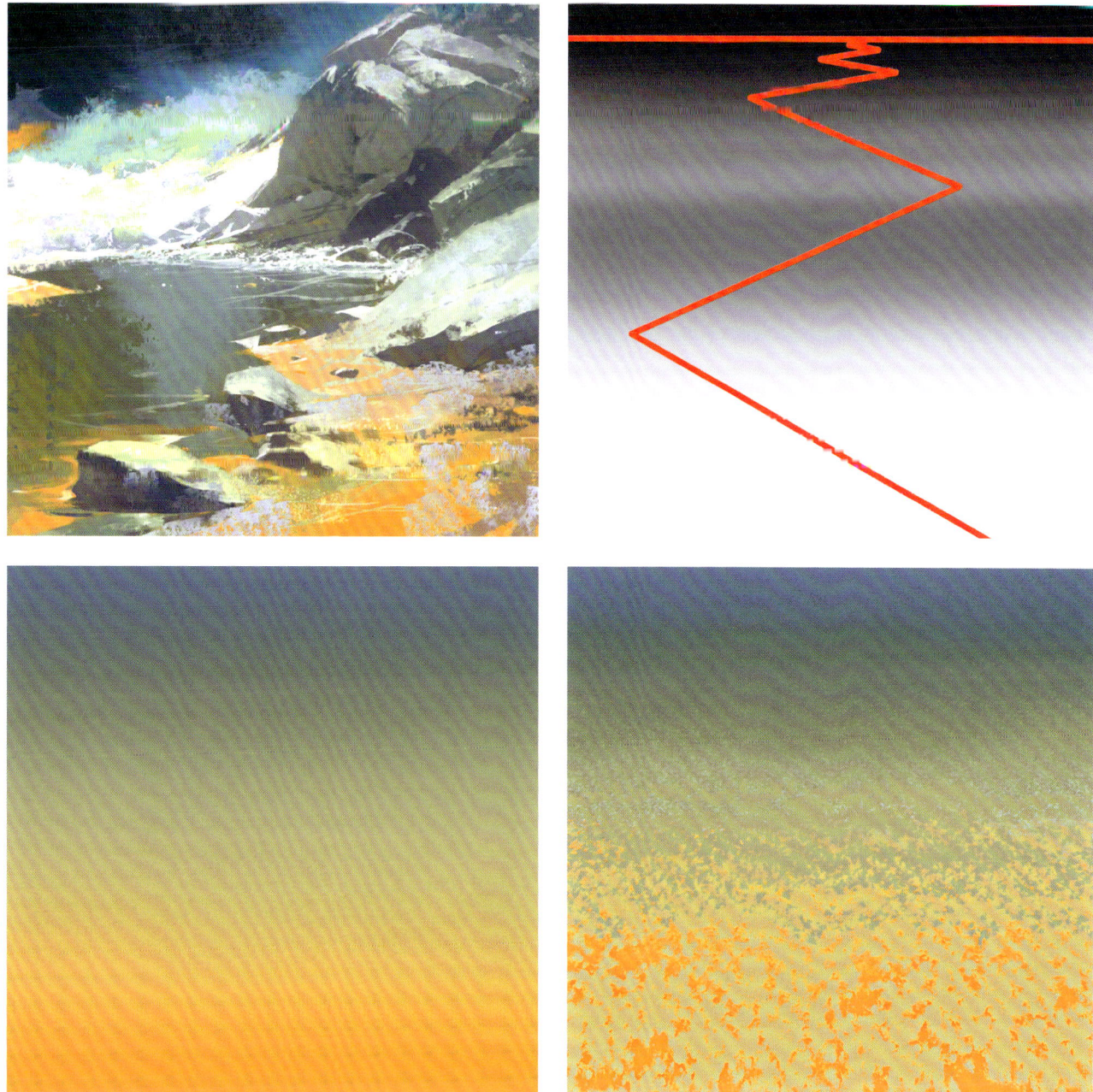

△ Zigzagging overlap, temperature, and texture create space in this scene

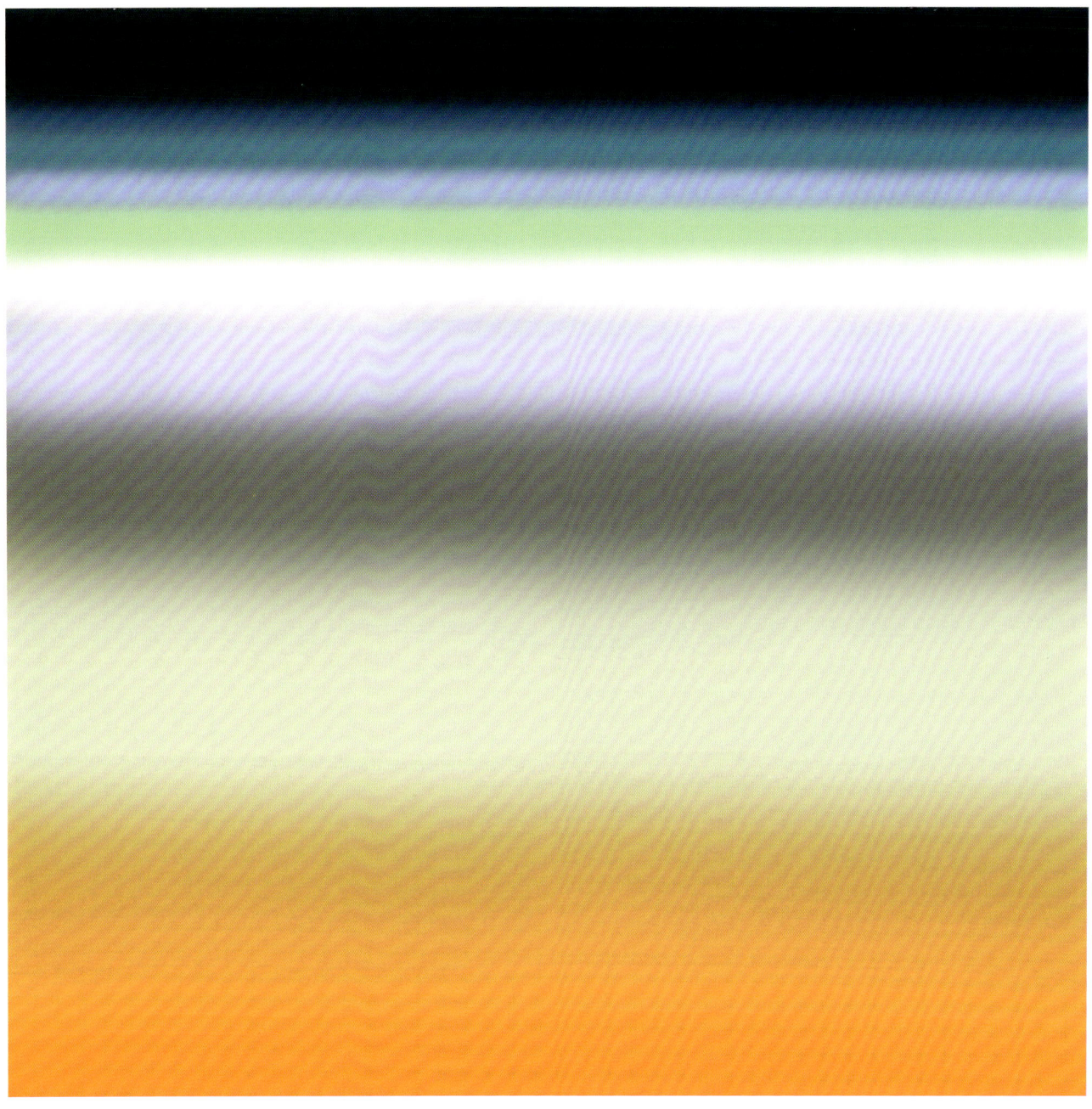

△ Using 'bands' of color and value adds depth and variety to an image

WHAT'S BANDING?

This simplification indicates the banding of color and value that I use moving into the distance. Banding is where you use light, shadow, and local color to create a variety of groupings that overlap each other, moving into the distance. If you feel your environments are overly simple and need a little spatial excitement thrown in, banding might just be the thing.

If you feel your environments are overly simple and need a little spatial excitement thrown in, banding might just be the thing.

A FULL JOURNEY
IN A SINGLE IMAGE

Remember, we're talking about the design of space, not just for its own sake but also as a storytelling tool. Here's an image to emphasize that idea. I think almost anyone would take a look at this image and understand that it has a starting point and a destination. Here we are in the foreground, but we've just got to get to the end of this journey to find out what that mysterious glow is all about.

This is an image filled with rocks, earth, clouds, and all kinds of stuff, but every one of those things is designed to serve a greater purpose. They're designed to put you on that path and take you on a journey to solve the mystery of what's going on at the top. I've created a simplified version of the image here to zero in on that quality of purpose.

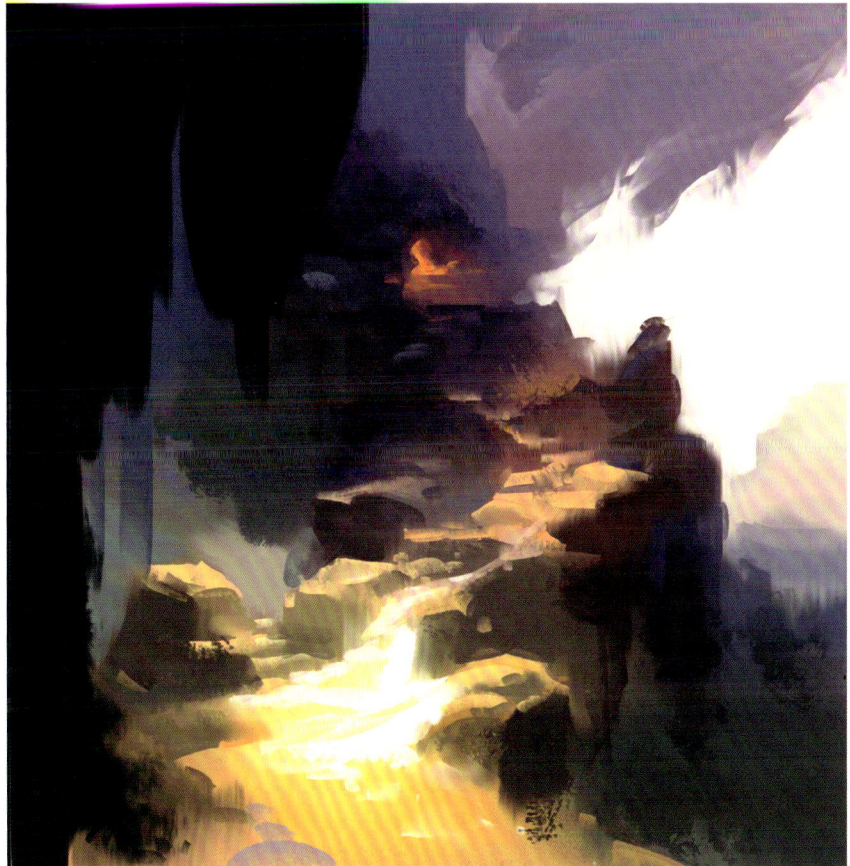

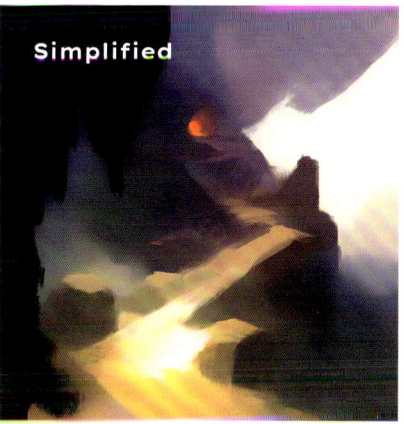

Simplified

△ A landscape with a destination will engage the viewer's curiosity

SPACE & STORYTELLING THROUGH POINT OF VIEW

Let's talk eye-level line. The eye-level, the horizon, and point-of-view line are always the same thing, but I'll go ahead and refer to it as the 'eye-level line'. It's important for us to decide early on the position of that line because it has a dramatic influence on our audience's perceived emotions about a scene. Let's take a look at three different scenes to illustrate this.

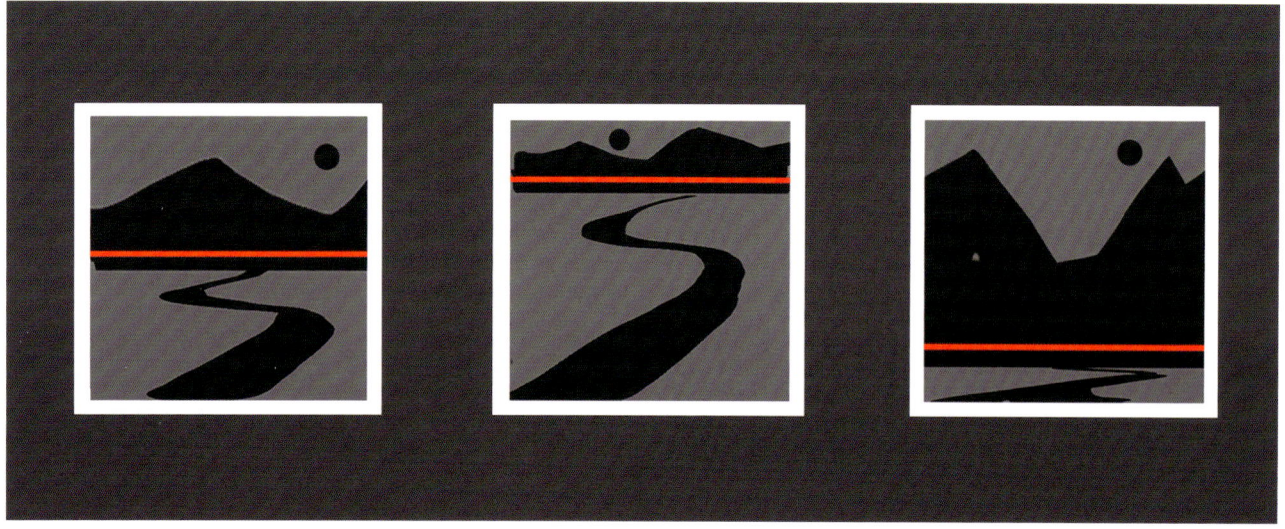

△ Examples of eye-level/point-of-view lines

The eye-level line has a dramatic influence on our audience's perceived emotions about a scene.

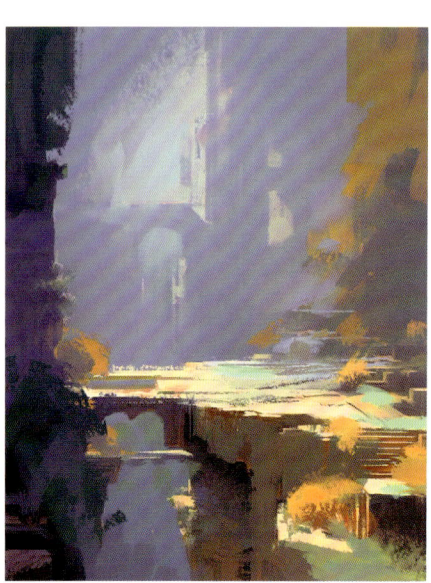
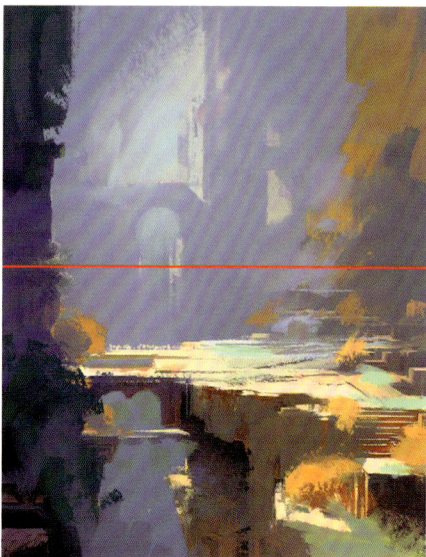

01. This eye-level line sets us in the environment at a central level

01. CENTRAL EYE-LEVEL LINE

For this scene I've chosen to place the eye-level line right about in the middle because it's a vertical scene. It's all about the amazing vertical expanse of the chasm, so it's important we're at an eye level where we can look deep down into space and equally look upward at the ascended cliffsides. A central eye-level line serves the needs of the environment.

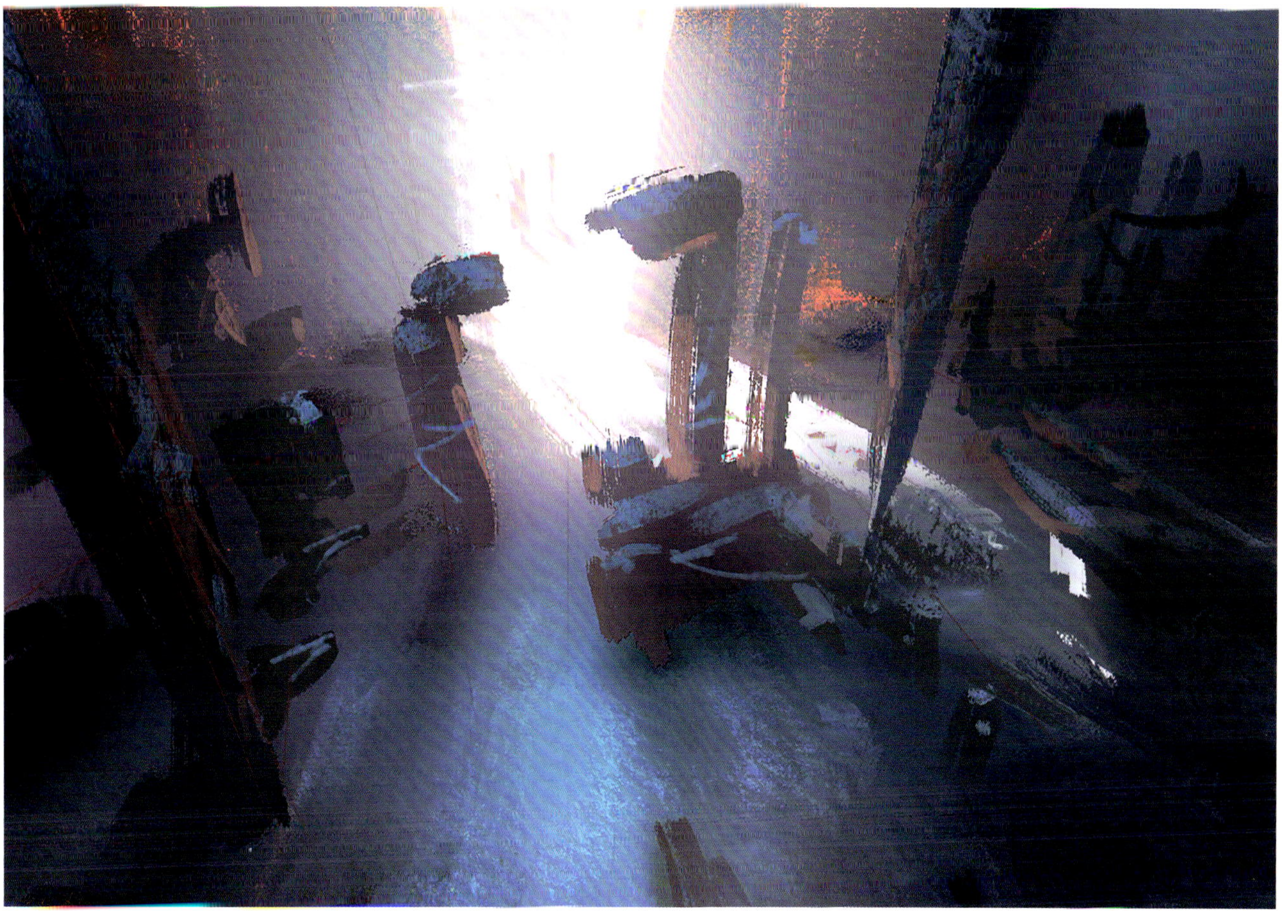

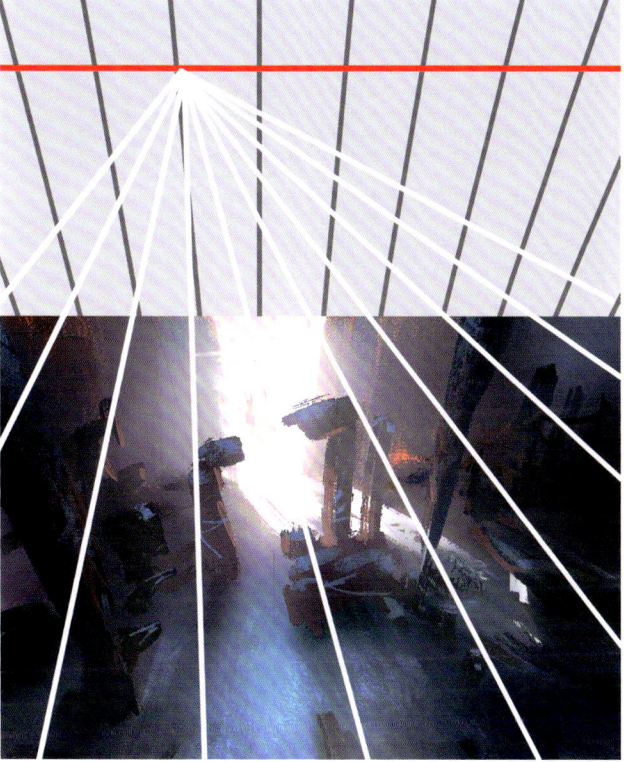

02. This eye-level line is
high off the canvas, placing
us above the scene

02. BIRD'S-EYE VIEW

This downward-looking scene has an eye-level line so high that
I've charted it out for you with perspective lines. The red line
shows where the horizon would be if we could see all the way out
to it. People call this a 'bird's-eye view' or an 'omniscient view'.
I think the term omniscient view is particularly appropriate
because it gives a sense of power to the viewer – we're able to
observe without being threatened by events down below.

111

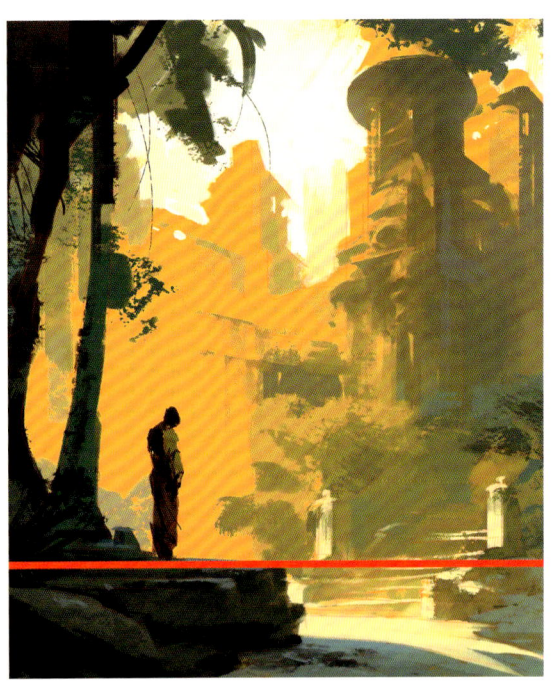

03. BUG'S-EYE VIEW

Instead of a bird's-eye view, people like to call this very low eye-level line a 'bug's-eye' view. It's very much the opposite of the omniscient view, looking so far upward at these buildings. It can convey a dominant and even ominous feeling – and *feeling* is the important word here because, as usual, it's all about emotion.

The spatial design of a scene is not just about creating depth – it's an emotional storytelling tool. Choosing the point of view for an environment is a major storytelling consideration.

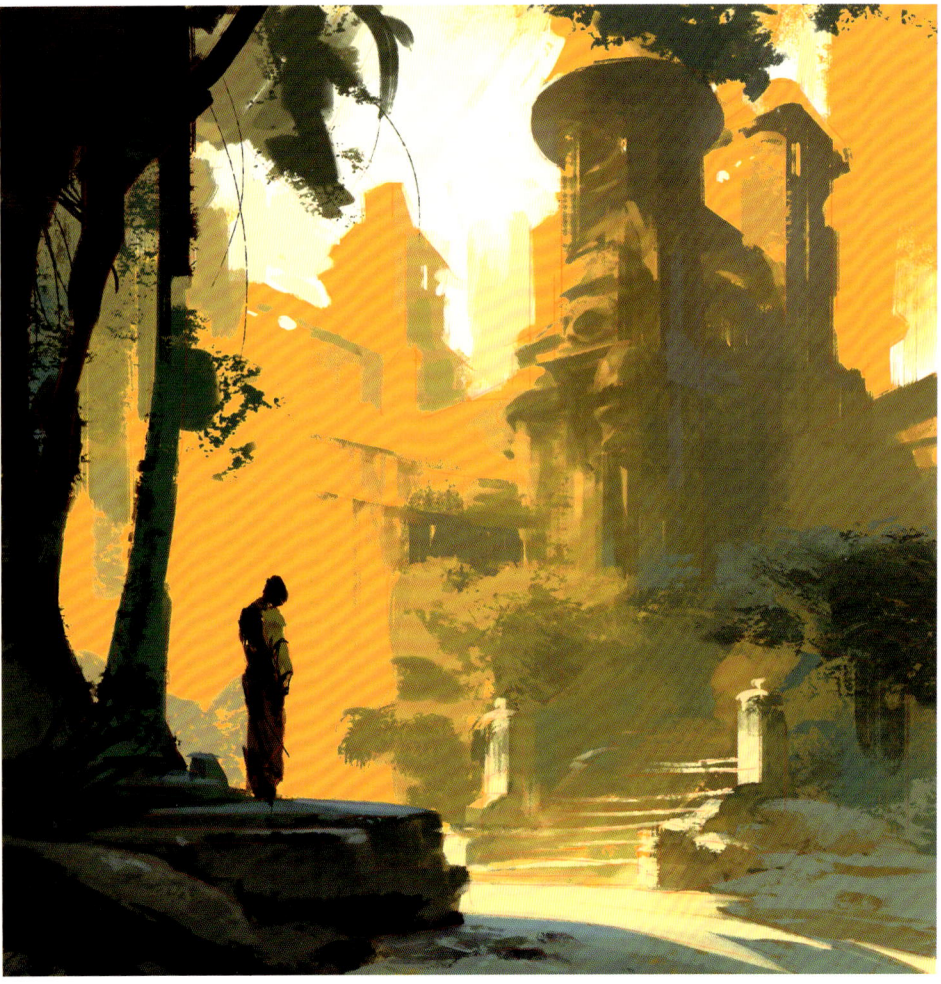

03. A lower eye-level line sets us near to the ground, looking upward

PERSPECTIVE CHOICES

For each of the three environments we've looked at, I've shown the eye-level line, but let's also look at the type of perspective that would serve each scene best. One-point, two-point, and three-point perspectives all have different effects and advantages.

01. ONE-POINT PERSPECTIVE

This first image is a destination scene we're being led to the archway in the center. So I chose straightforward one-point perspective for this scene, as shown below.

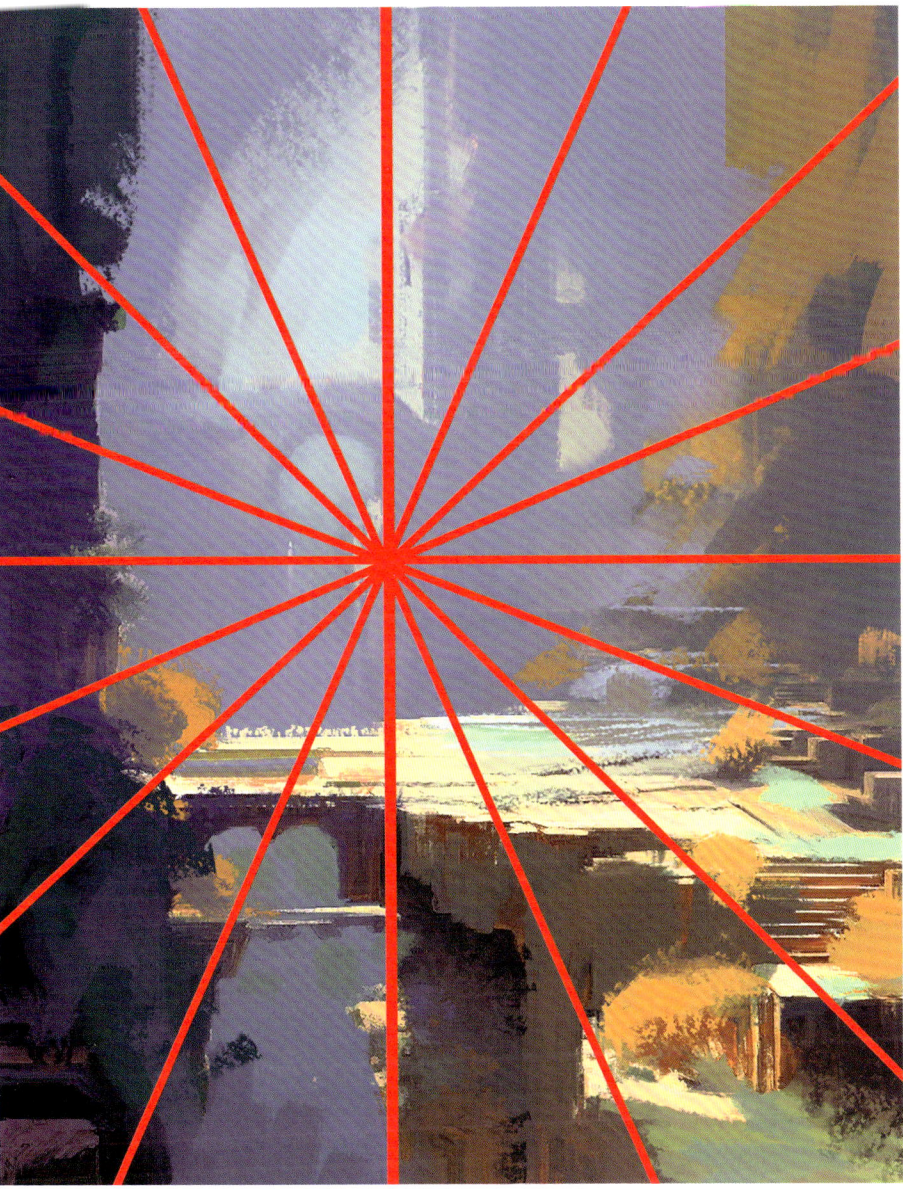

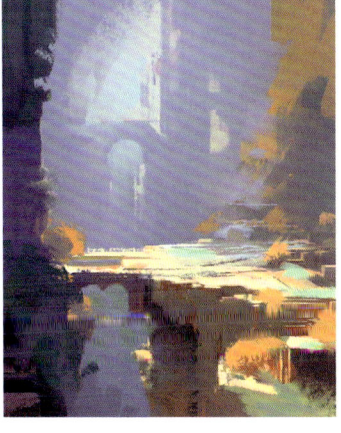

01. One-point perspective is the most simple and direct

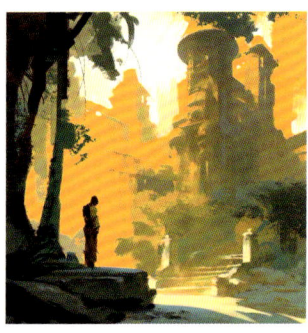

02. TWO-POINT PERSPECTIVE

For the bug's-eye view I chose two-point perspective. This is because I felt the steepness of the perspective lines, rising upward from side to side, would give the architecture a strong presence.

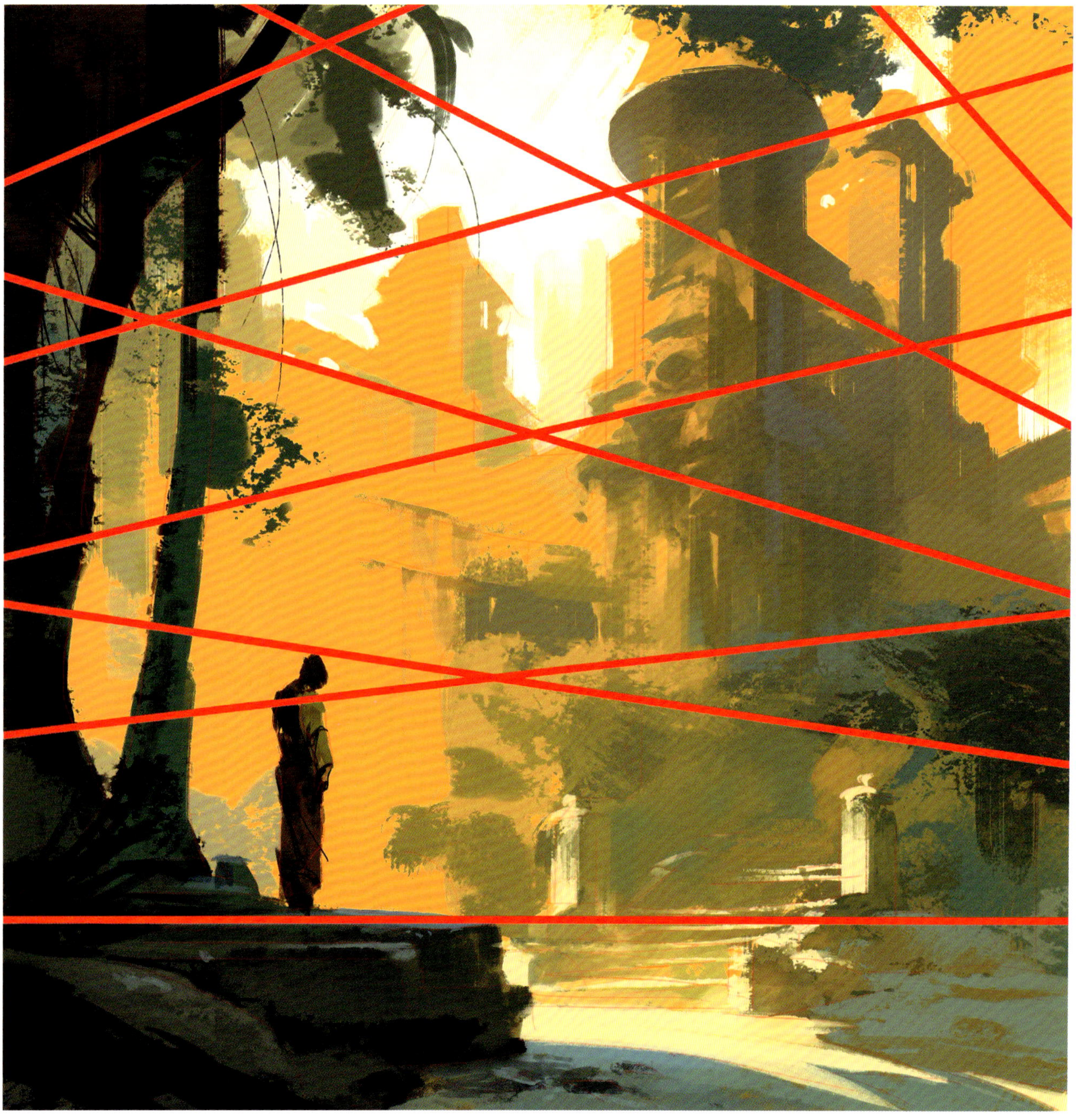

02. Two-point perspective can give the subject a strong physical presence

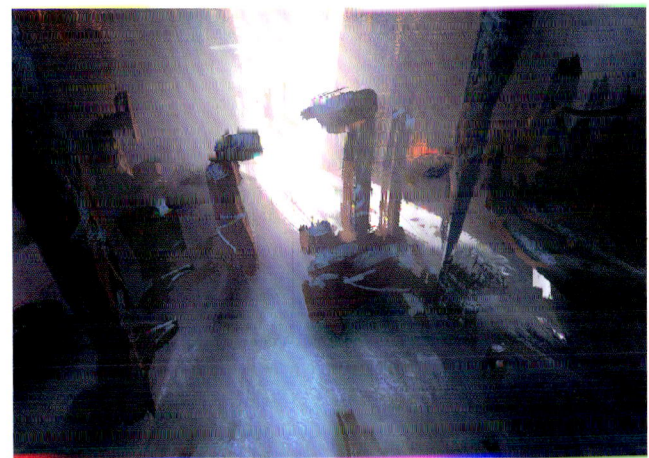

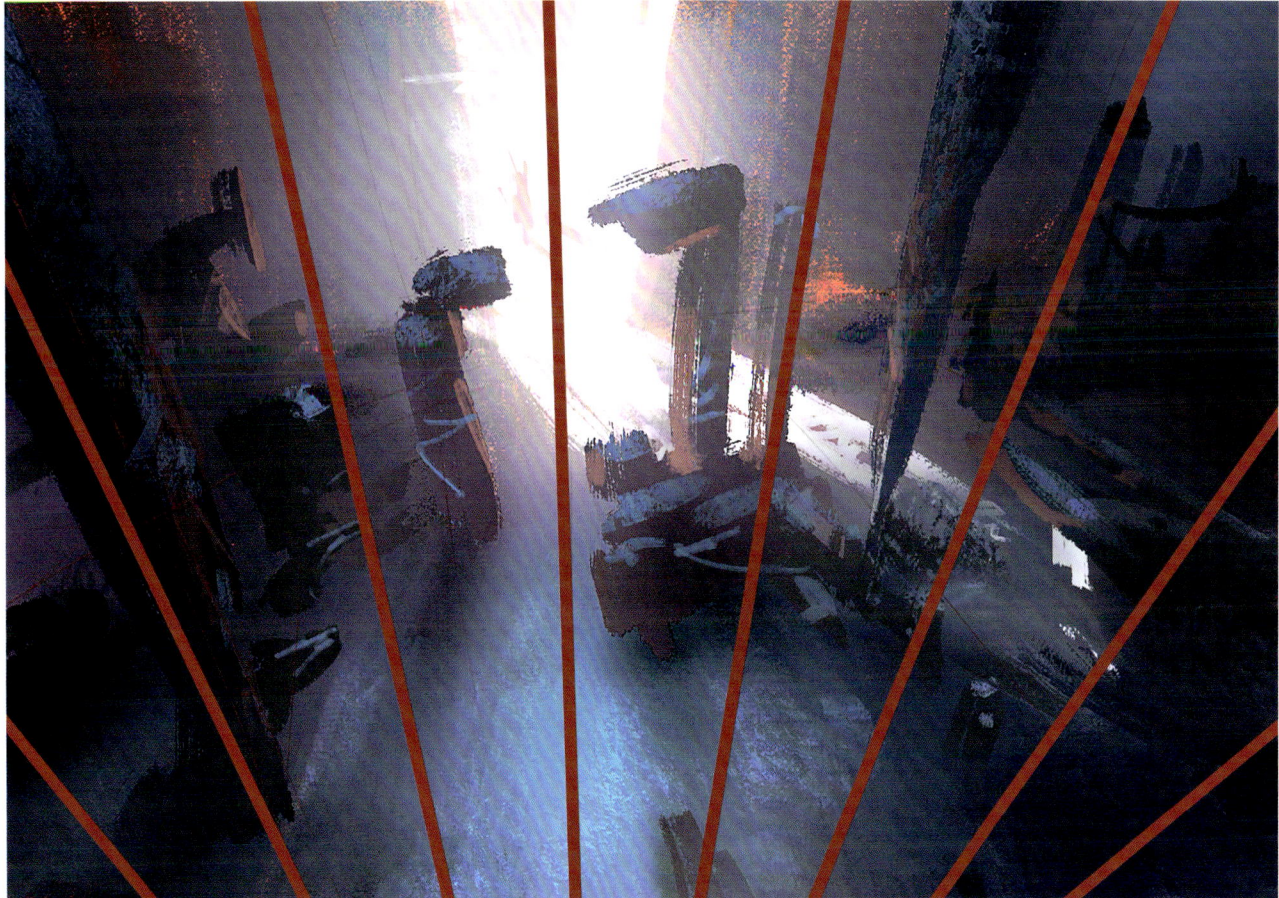

03. Three-point perspective can create the most dramatic space

03. THREE-POINT PERSPECTIVE

Back to our omniscient view. Creating the effect of 'looking down from on high' was so important for this scene, so I chose a three-point perspective with strong vanishing lines converging downward.

BREADCRUMBS

Is this a circle or is it a bunch of dots? Well, to humans it's a circle because our brains are primed to complete patterns. This quality helps us succeed in parsing the visual world and successfully making our way through it. We tend to connect the dots, or breadcrumbs, so to speak. You know the *Hansel and Gretel* fairy tale? If you aren't familiar with it, I'll explain shortly. To be more precise, psychologists call it a 'gestalt', an official term for this idea, and it's a valuable tool in visual storytelling.

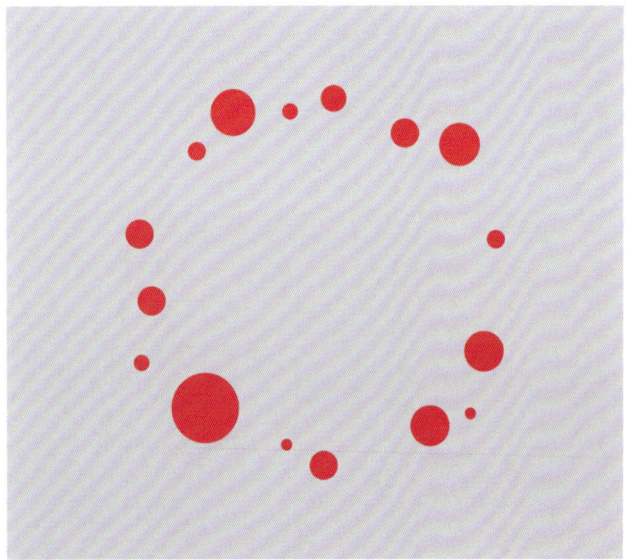

△ Gestalt: identifying a whole that's more than the sum of its parts

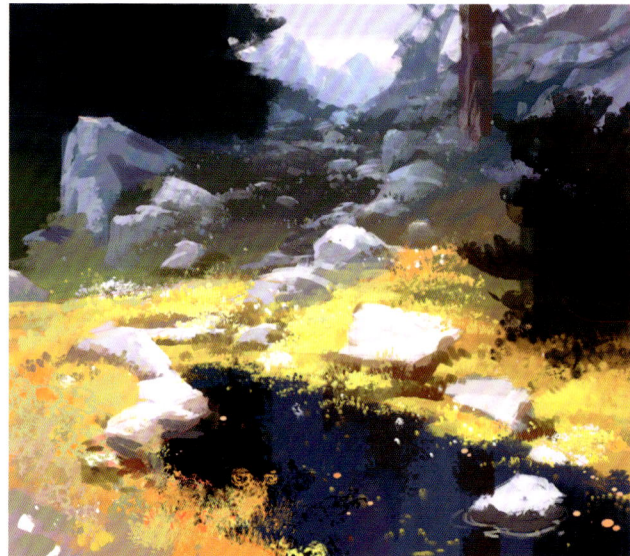

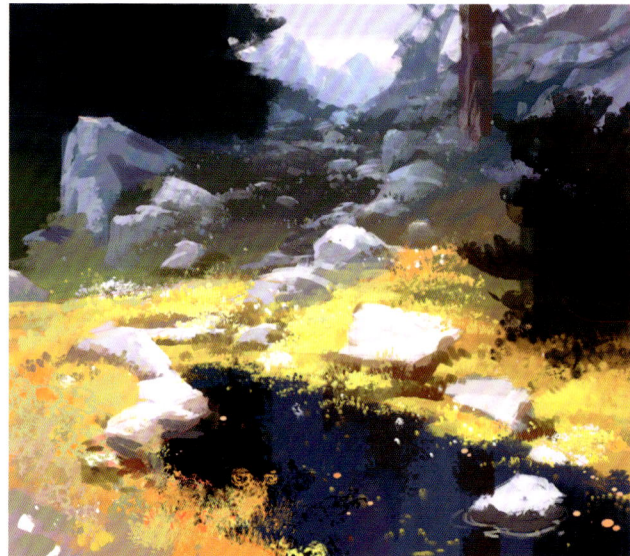

01. 'Breadcrumbs' lead the viewer through the environment

01. LEAVE A TRAIL

We must be our viewer's guide through our environments, carefully designing a hierarchy of importance – because if everything is equally important, by default everything is equally *unimportant*. Let's say you're designing a video game where the characters can travel in any direction but, to progress, they need to get to a specific location. You need to lay breadcrumbs to guide them, so to speak. The whole *Hansel and Gretel* thing was that Hansel dropped breadcrumbs as he traveled an unfamiliar path, so he could follow them to find his way back. This scene drops breadcrumbs: the rocks and boulders are somewhat random, but overall fall into a pattern that leads us up the hill to a specific destination. We're helping the audience, or our players, discover what's next. It's simple but powerful.

We must be the viewer's guide, carefully designing a hierarchy of importance – because if everything is equally important, by default everything is equally unimportant.

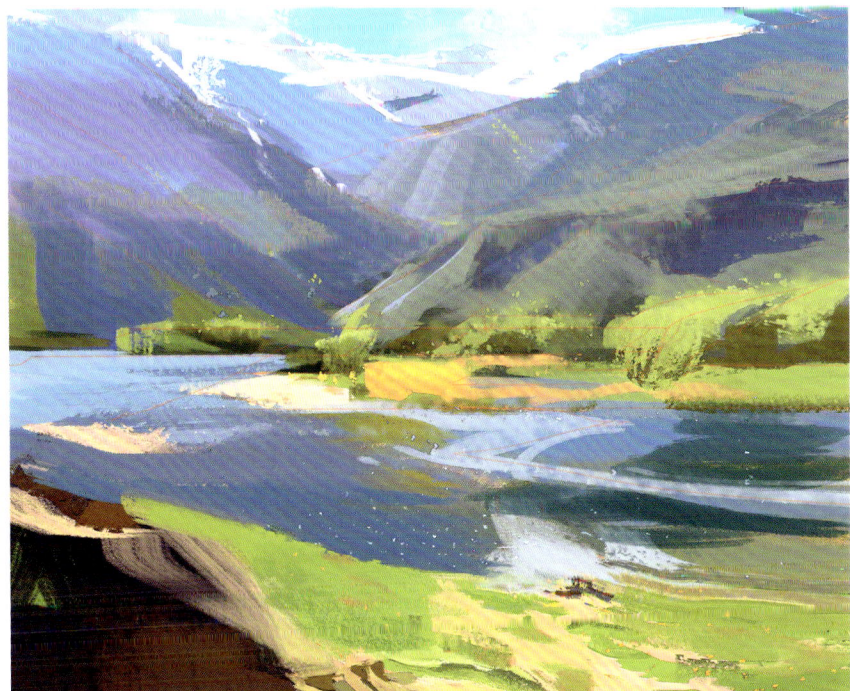

02. GUIDING PATH

In this landscape study, I really wanted the viewer to experience the full environment, so I suggested a path to carry them through it: from the foreground, into the mid-ground island, then weaving through the background mountains, all the way to their peaks and beyond. I carefully laid breadcrumbs in the form of trails, water reflections, a warm accent of grass, and a pass through the mountains to where they meet the clouds.

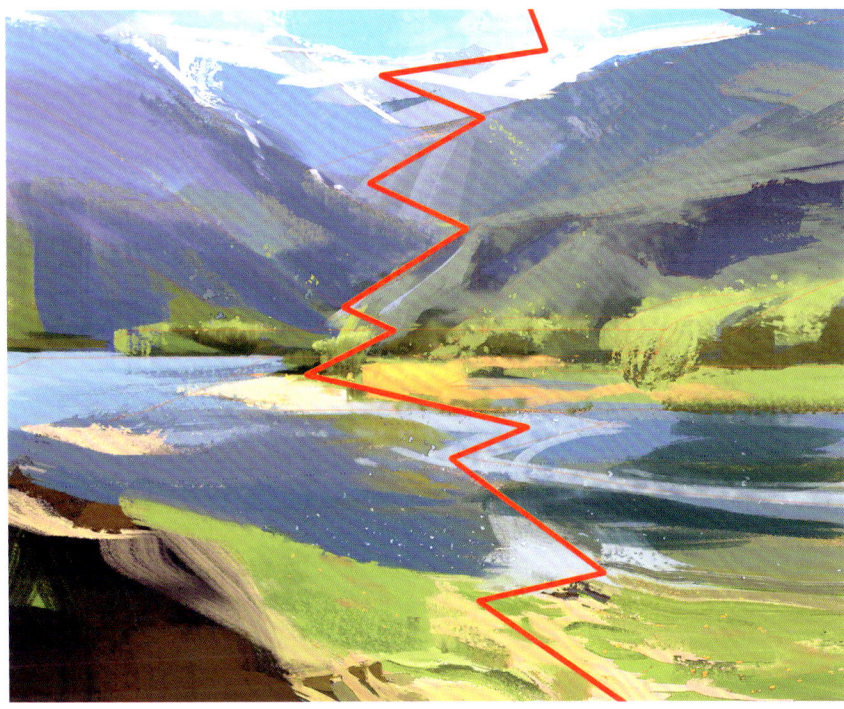

02. Breadcrumbs help guide the viewer along a pathway

BACKGROUND CONNECTIONS

The idea of connecting less-important areas of a subject to the background is something I really love. I picked this up while I studied charcoal figure-drawing. It would drive me nuts trying to get the three-dimensional forms to read in an interesting way on the two-dimensional surface of my paper. I found that if I laid a tone on the most distant parts of the figure, and let that same tone continue past the outline into the background, it made those parts seem farther away. I started trying that same idea in landscape painting to create the illusion of space on a flat canvas and it worked beautifully.

In this first example, I really wanted the entrance of the building to stand out as being profoundly important. I put just about every trick into it that we've discussed thus far, but it just wasn't enough – I wanted to go all the way with this thing! So I took the furthest and least important parts and gave them a color and value that continued right into the background. Since we perceive the sky as being very far away, it gave a great distance to the affected architecture.

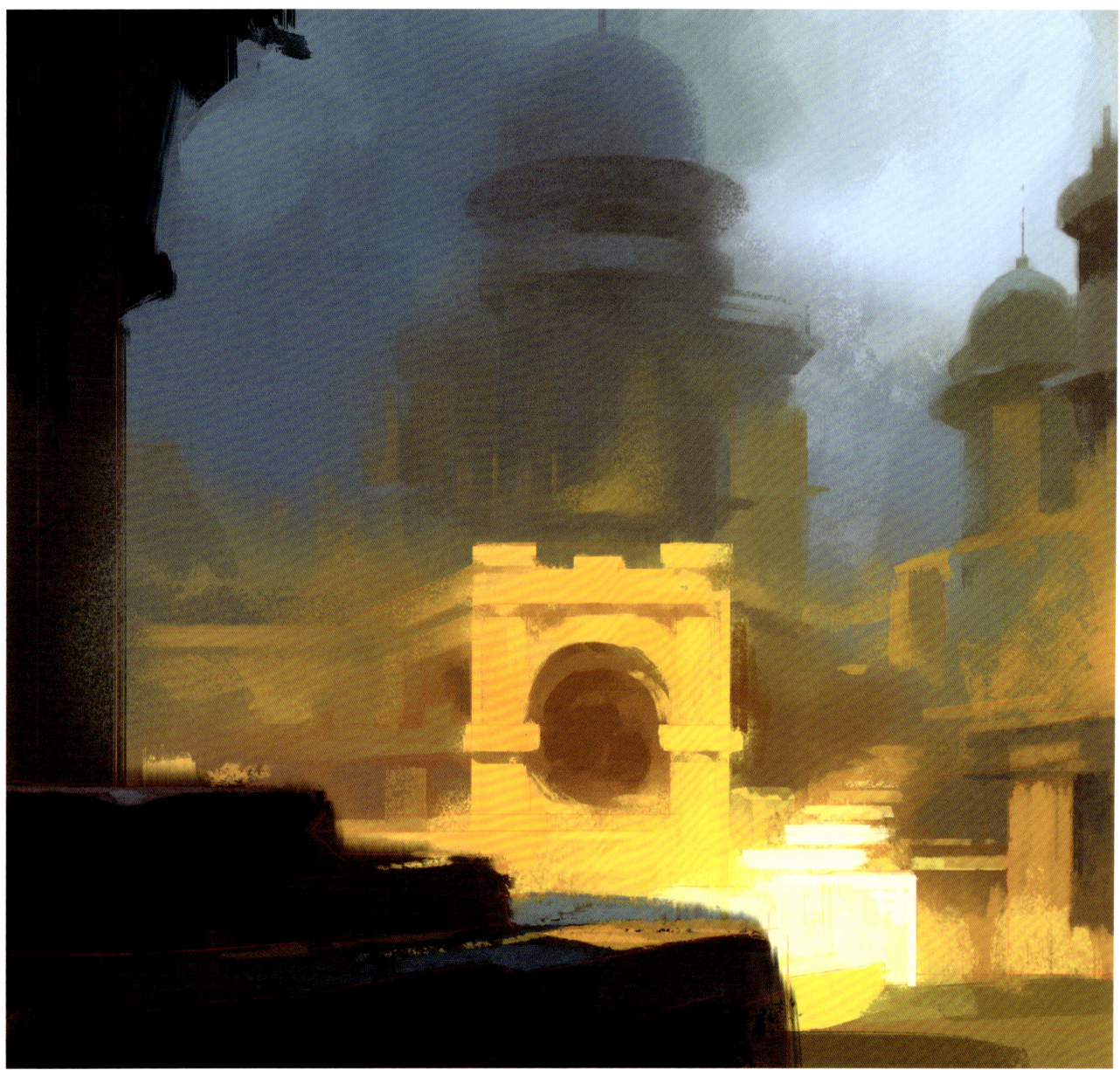

△ I try pushing distance by connecting architecture with the background through color and value matching. Success!

I had to tight to find ways to get my figure drawings to read as three-dimensional forms on the two-dimensional paper. I realized the same breakthroughs applied to creating space in environments, and it gave me a whole new set of ideas. The lesson here? It's not just about environment practice – do your life-drawing studies!

ATMOSPHERIC TRICKS

Here's another one where I'm using the same trick, but in the midground. With this water pavilion, I really wanted the front columns to project out toward us and have a strong presence. So as the columns receded further away, I made their color closer and closer to what's behind them. It's a short-distance atmospheric effect that usually doesn't happen in real life, but it's a very effective way of conveying importance and depth in a short-distance subject.

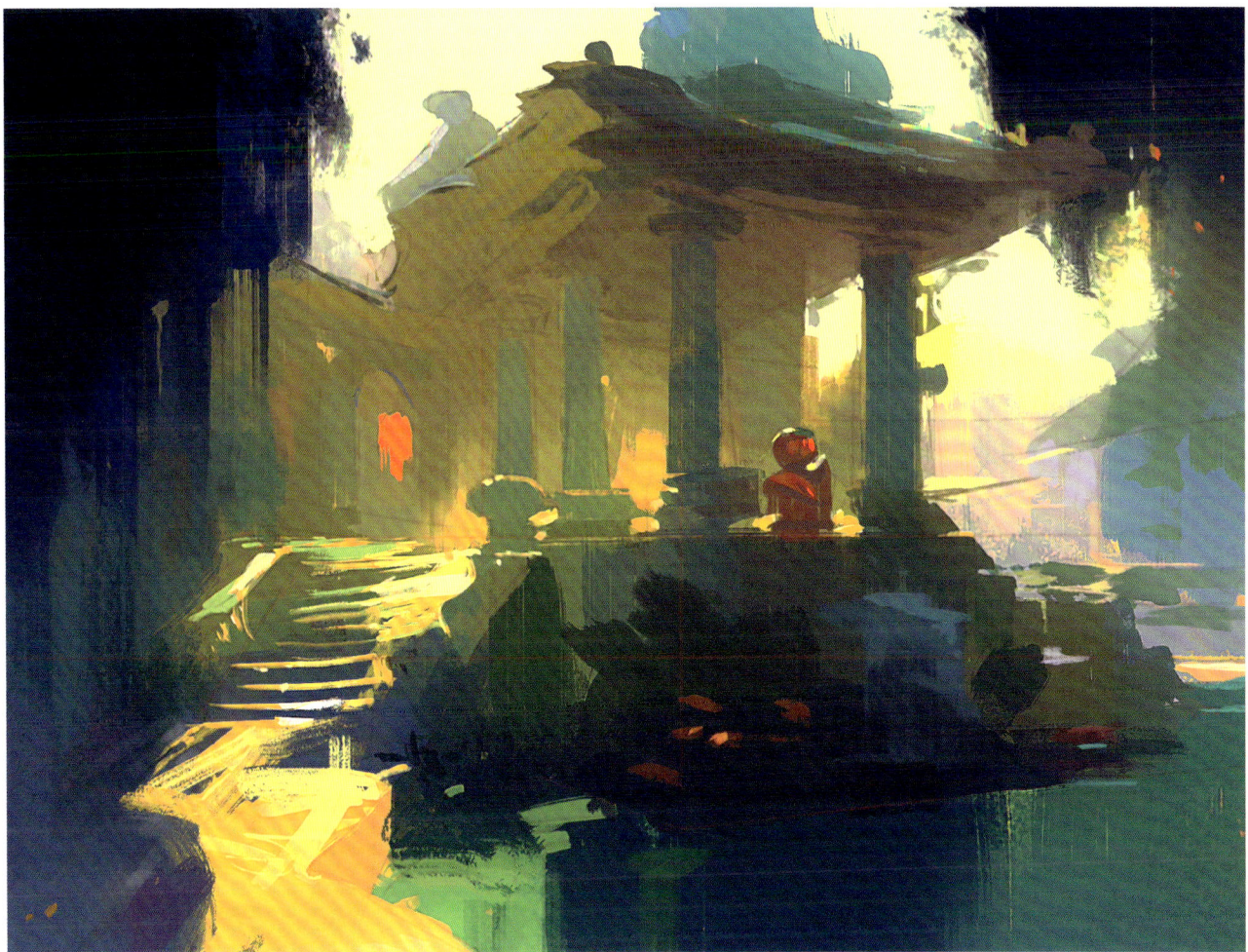

△ This effect takes some liberties with physics, but makes a powerful visual impact

IT ALL COMES BACK TO STORYTELLING

Many years ago, when I was a college student, I watched the movie *Citizen Kane* with rapt attention. The movie was so old and yet it was so visually well-crafted. Frankly, I was in awe. Those movie makers were so sophisticated to my as yet untrained mind.

For instance, I've suggested in the graphic below a female figure in the foreground and a male figure in the distant background, representative of a scene in the movie. The main character is a wealthy businessman, living in a large mansion with his wife, and they're having serious marital troubles. The filmmakers could have had one character say, 'Sweetheart, I feel like there's a great emotional gulf between us,' but that would've been heavy-handed and laughable. Instead, they placed a physical gulf of space between the characters, making the couple have this difficult conversation across a great distance in the ballroom of the mansion. The filmmakers didn't say it – they made us visually feel it. Genius!

Good filmmakers often avoid using voice-overs or characters telling us something. Rather, they find visual ways of getting us to feel the story emotionally. The latter is more subtle and more powerful.

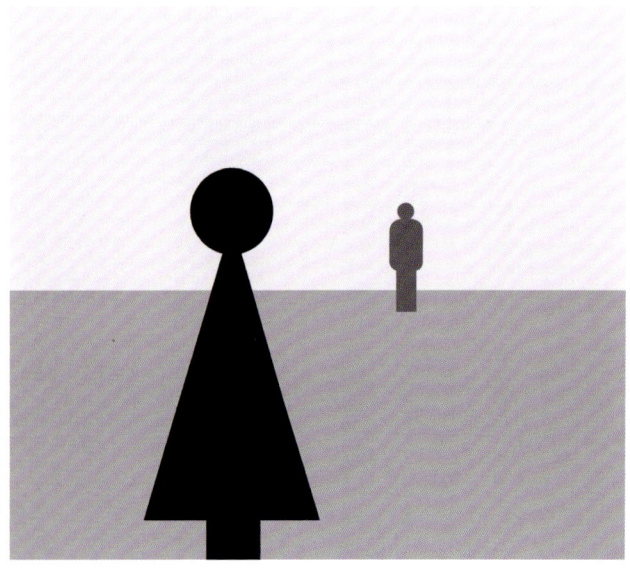

△ What does this tell us about the relationship between two characters?

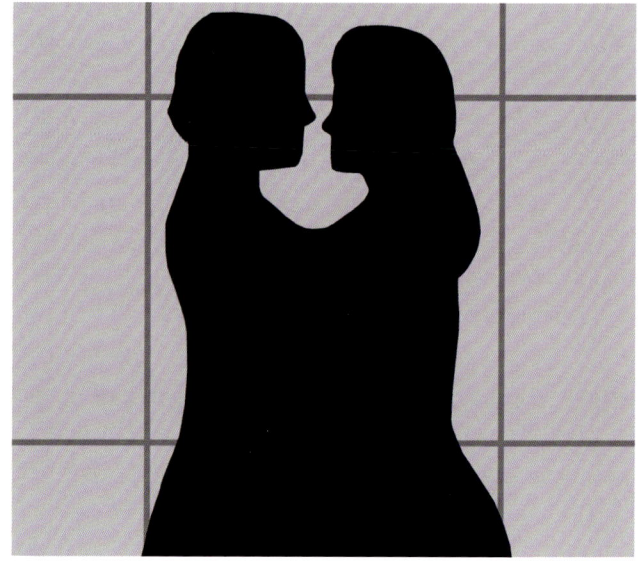

△ This conveys a very different relationship between two characters

VANITY FAIR

At another time, I was watching *Vanity Fair*. There was a scene in the movie of an embrace, a moment of great intimacy. I noticed that rather than being in a wide-open space, the moment was set facing a flat wall, squared off, like a large framed painting. The actors acted the part of intimacy, and the flattened design of space intensified it.

FLAT SPACE VS DEEP SPACE

Now let's talk about flat space versus deep space as emotional storytelling design elements. To do that, let's get back to our blue gorilla friend who we met in the previous chapter. The cool, squared-off environment is very passive. It's so shallow that not much action could happen here. That's what makes the idea of flat space so useful when we need to convey moments of passivity.

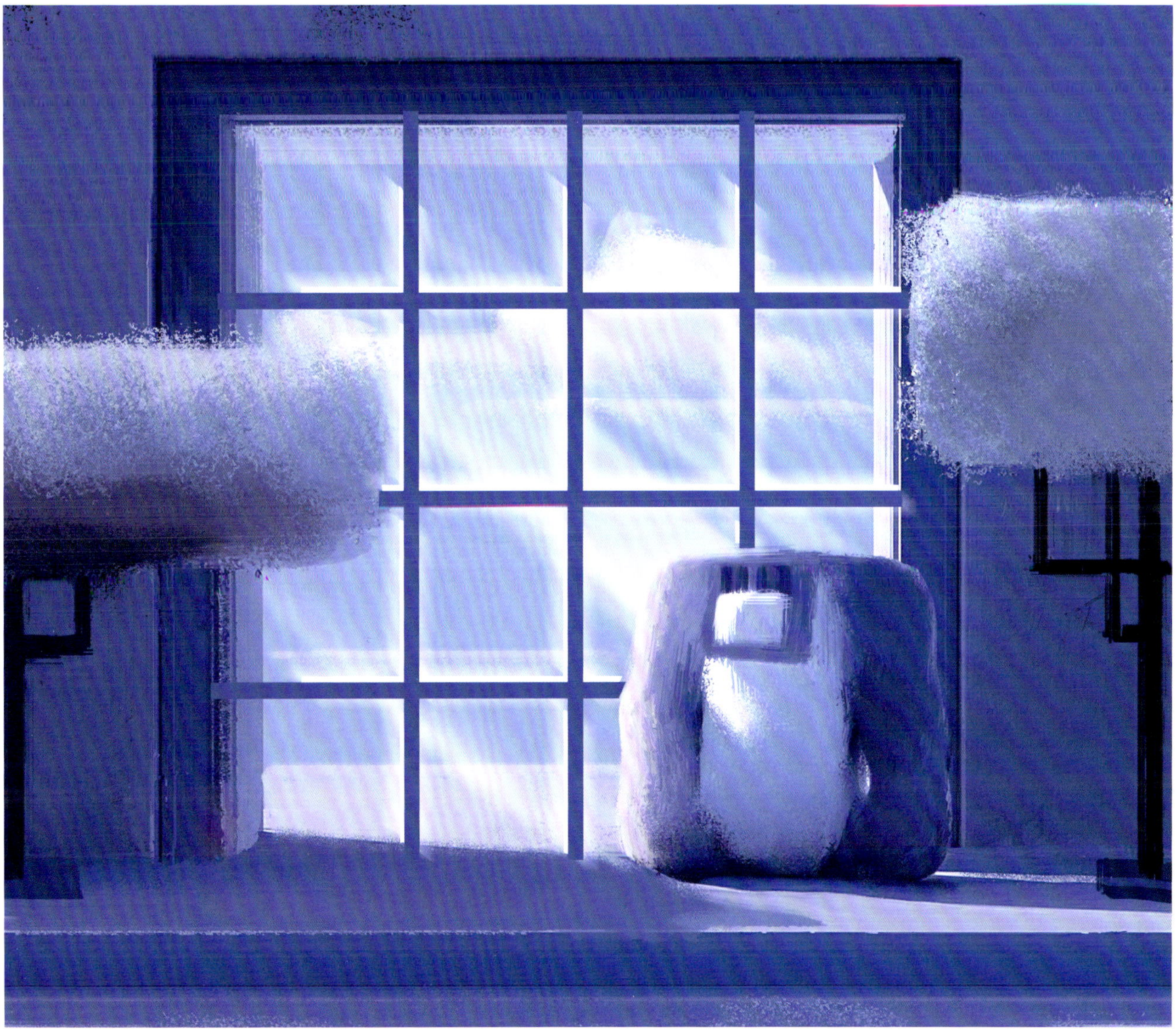

△ This flat space doesn't have room for dynamic action

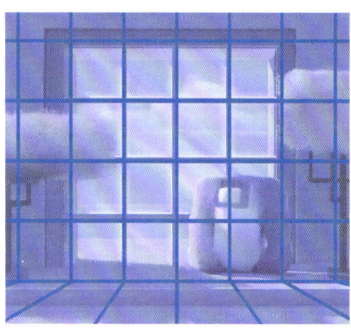

01. SPACE FOR ACTION

The jazz musicians say, 'If you wanna get up, you gotta get down,' and it's true! If you want to take your audience into explosive excitement, then you need hot, deep space where all the action you need can happen. We've taken the action and the heat about as far as it can go here, and yet there is a way to double its potency. Your scene can start off by taking your audience all the way down to cool, passive, flat space, then move away from it to action-packed deep space. It makes an amazing rollercoaster ride for the audience.

It's like jazz musicians say: 'If you wanna get up, you gotta get down.' Take your audience on a wild rollercoaster ride!

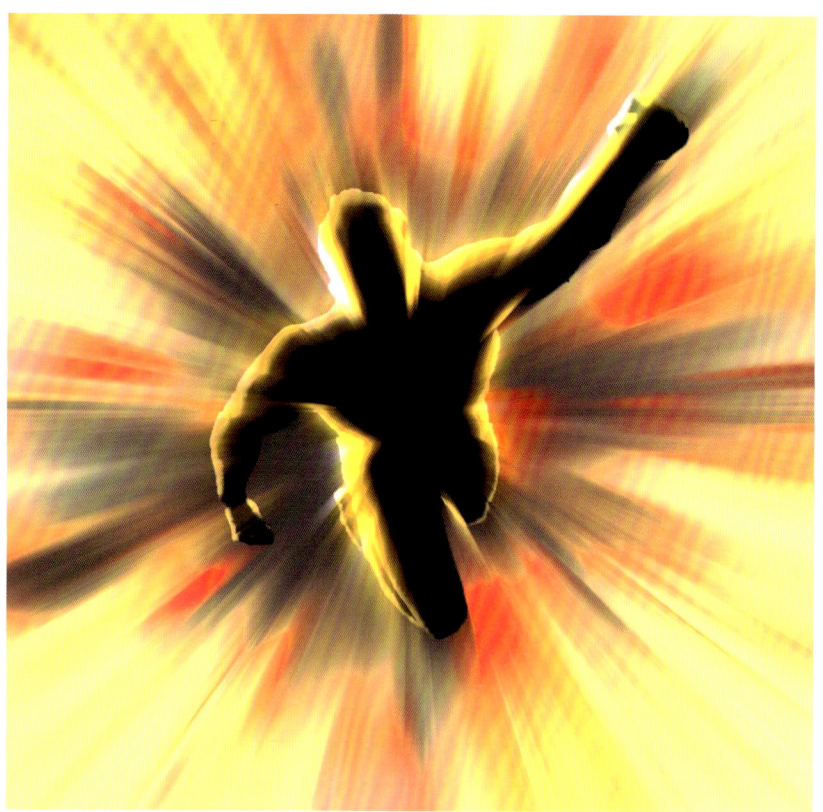

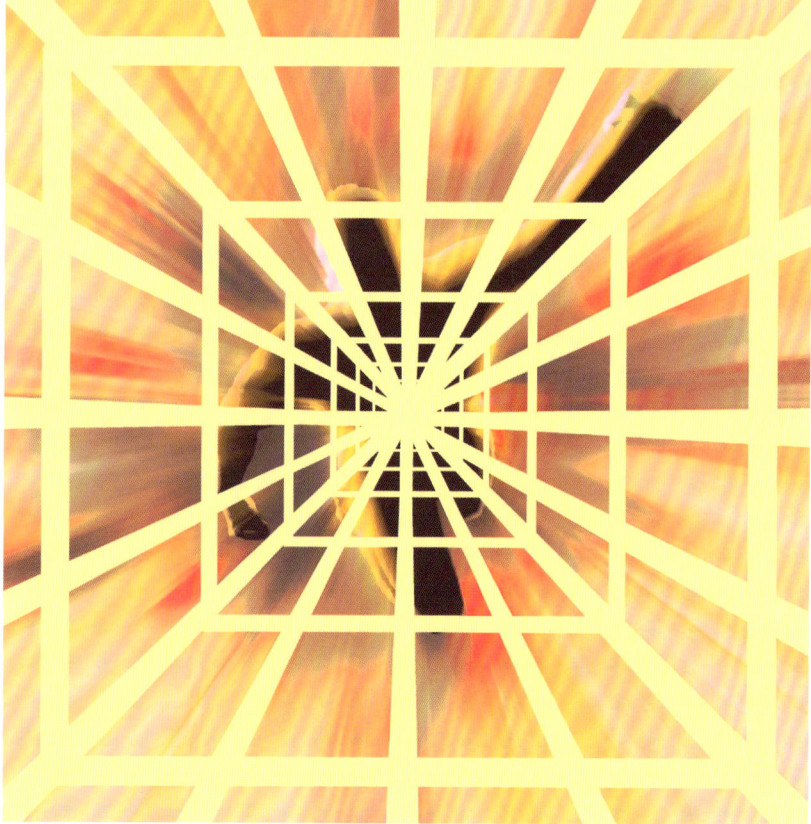

01. This deep space allows for big, explosive action to unfold

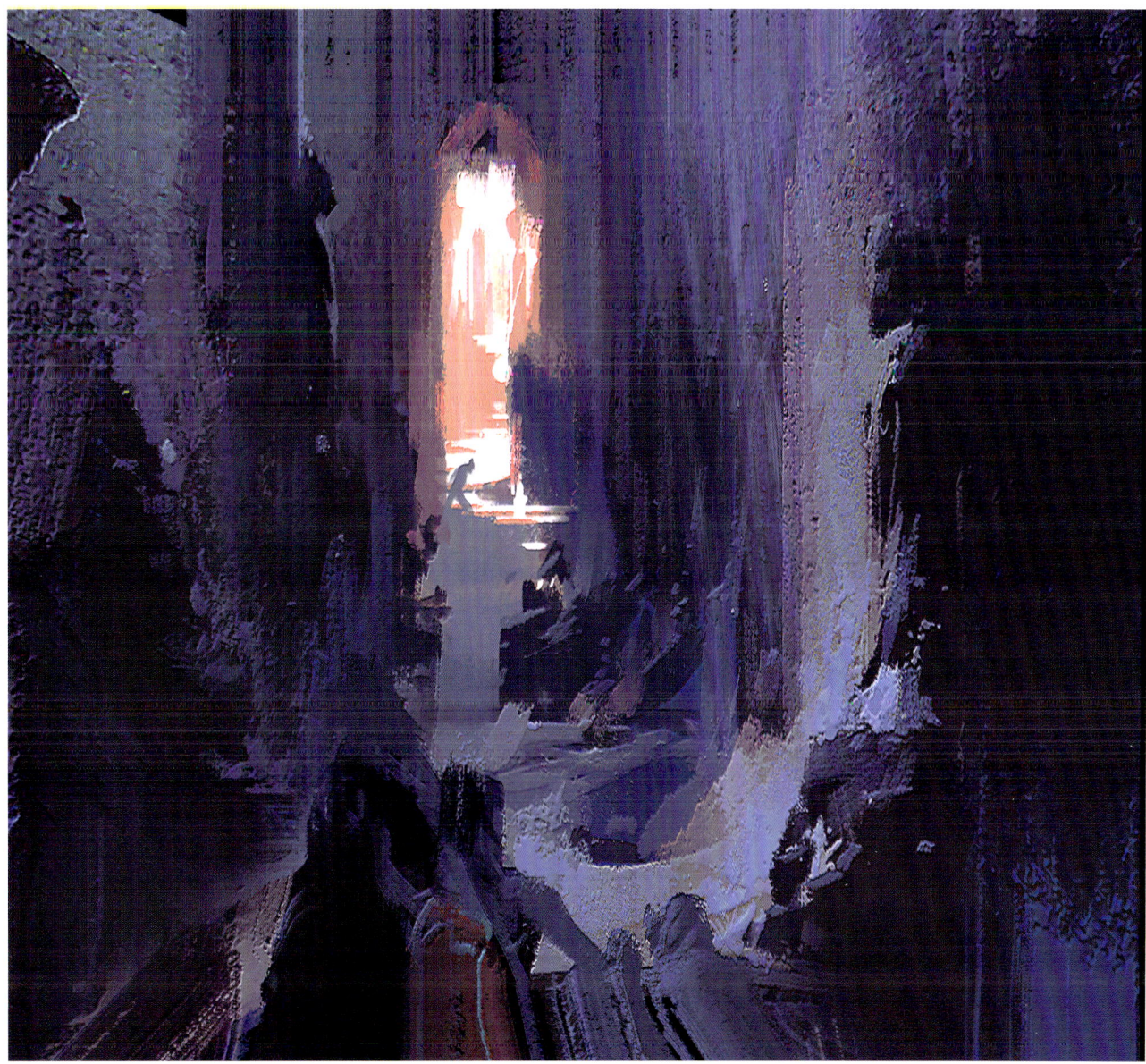

02. A long, narrow tunnel is a different kind of deep space

02. ENCLOSED SPACE

Be thoughtful and creative in your space design; there are many interesting ways to combine our ideas to get a wide range of emotional effects. Here we have deep space, but it's tight and claustrophobic. Horror movies often use something like this to convey inescapable evil.

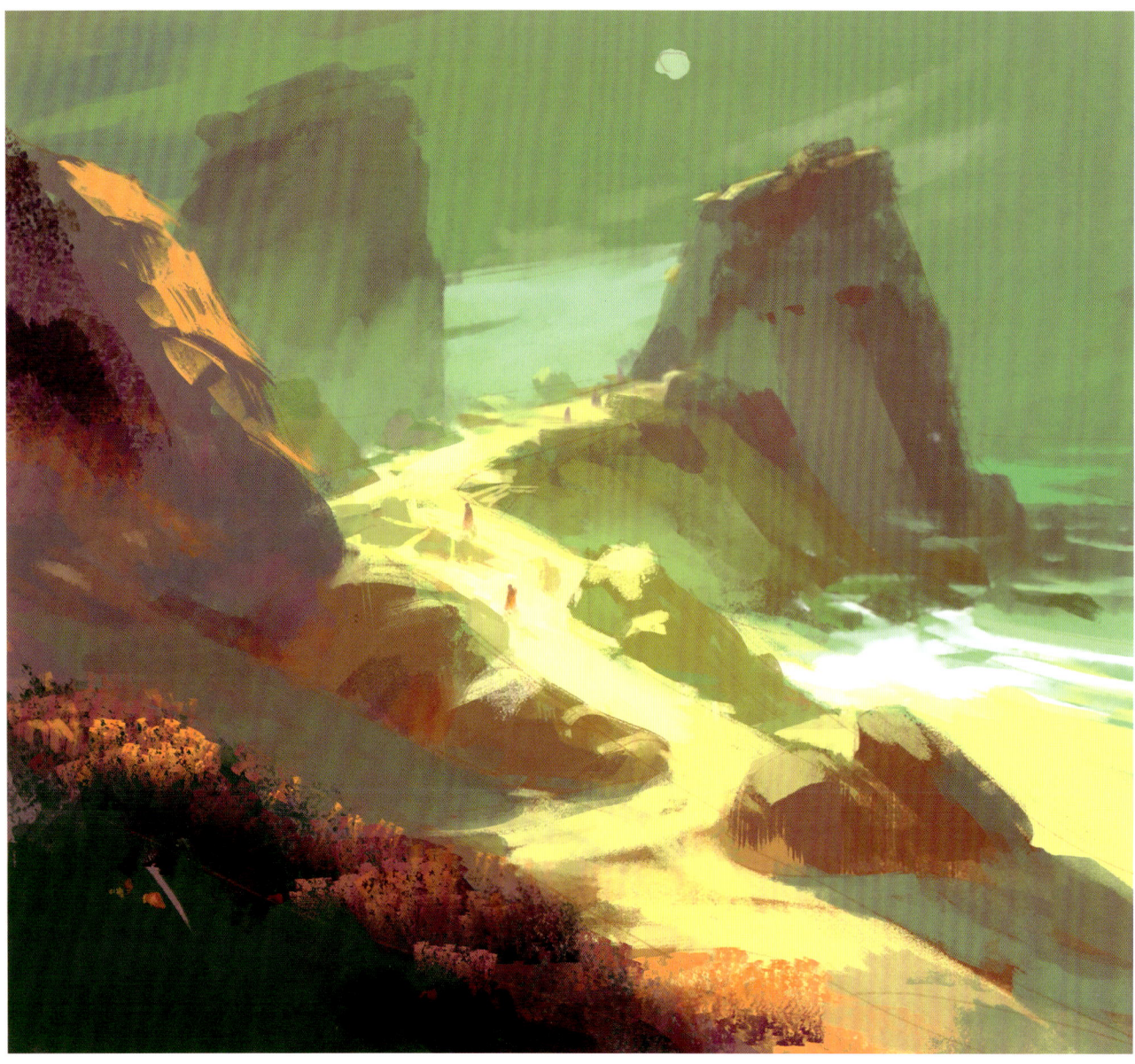

03. This space is deep but open, inviting us on an adventure

03. OPEN SPACE

And here we have a zigzagging pattern taking us out to an interesting destination. The foreground color directly contrasts with the background color, and the background shapes begin to take on the atmospheric color of the background, giving them a deeper sense of space.

DON'T FORGET INTERIORS!

We've discussed flat space, but we haven't spent much time specifically talking about interiors. It's easy to create flat space in an interior, but what about deep space?

For this interior painting, I'll take us back to the inspiration behind *Citizen Kane*. The story was reportedly based on William Randolph Hearst, a real life wealthy media magnate in the early 1900s. He built a real castle on the Central Coast of California, which has since become a museum, Hearst Castle, a place I've visited many times. I hope you can, too, someday – it's on the beautiful San Simeon coastline, all alone in the hills leading down to the beach. Hearst populated the surrounding landscape with various herd animals from all over the world. Zebras and the like still graze there today.

So, back to this painting. It's inspired by photos I took of the interior of Hearst's palatial mansion. Even though this is not a huge room, I've used the idea of banding to give it a breadth of space. We move from the Oriental rug shadowed in the foreground, to a passage of light which moves us to the staircase and its ornate balustrade, up to a wall lit by candles, and deeper into mysterious shadow. This is meant to be a journey as intricate as some of the long-distance environments we've looked at previously.

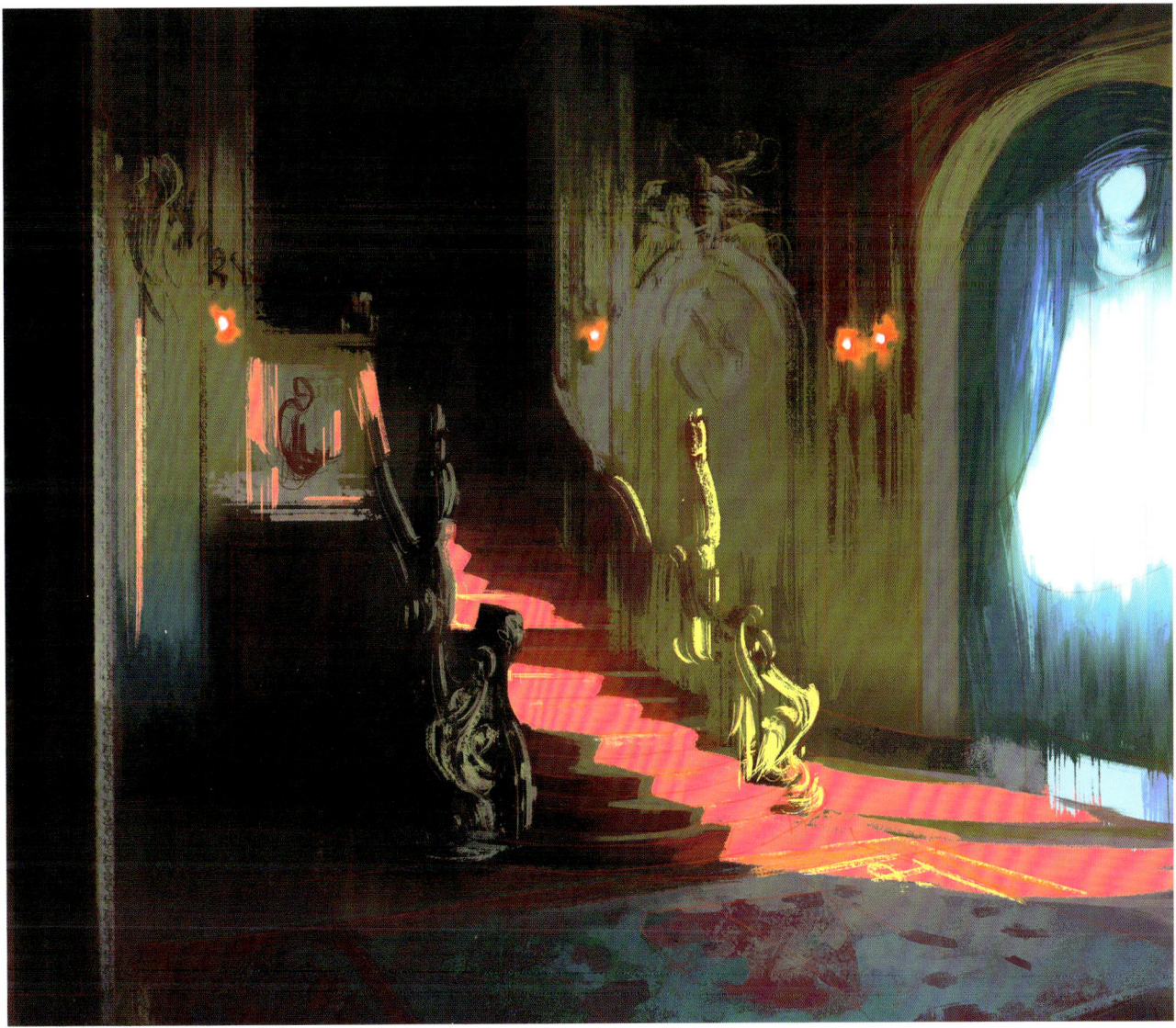

△ Even a relatively small interior location can have deep, atmospheric space

01. PROOF OF CONCEPT

This scene has a lot of depth, but wait a minute – I thought distant backgrounds were supposed to be cooler? What's going on here? You see, the environments we create and the story moments that unfold in them are a careful balance of competing contrasts. In this scene I wanted to bring a unique quality of attention to the subject, so I put the figures in a contrasting cold light, since they are the focus of our attention. To get that to work, I made the surrounding background a contrasting warm temperature. Sometimes the demand of our subject forces us to go against convention. I'll show you a specific example in the next scene.

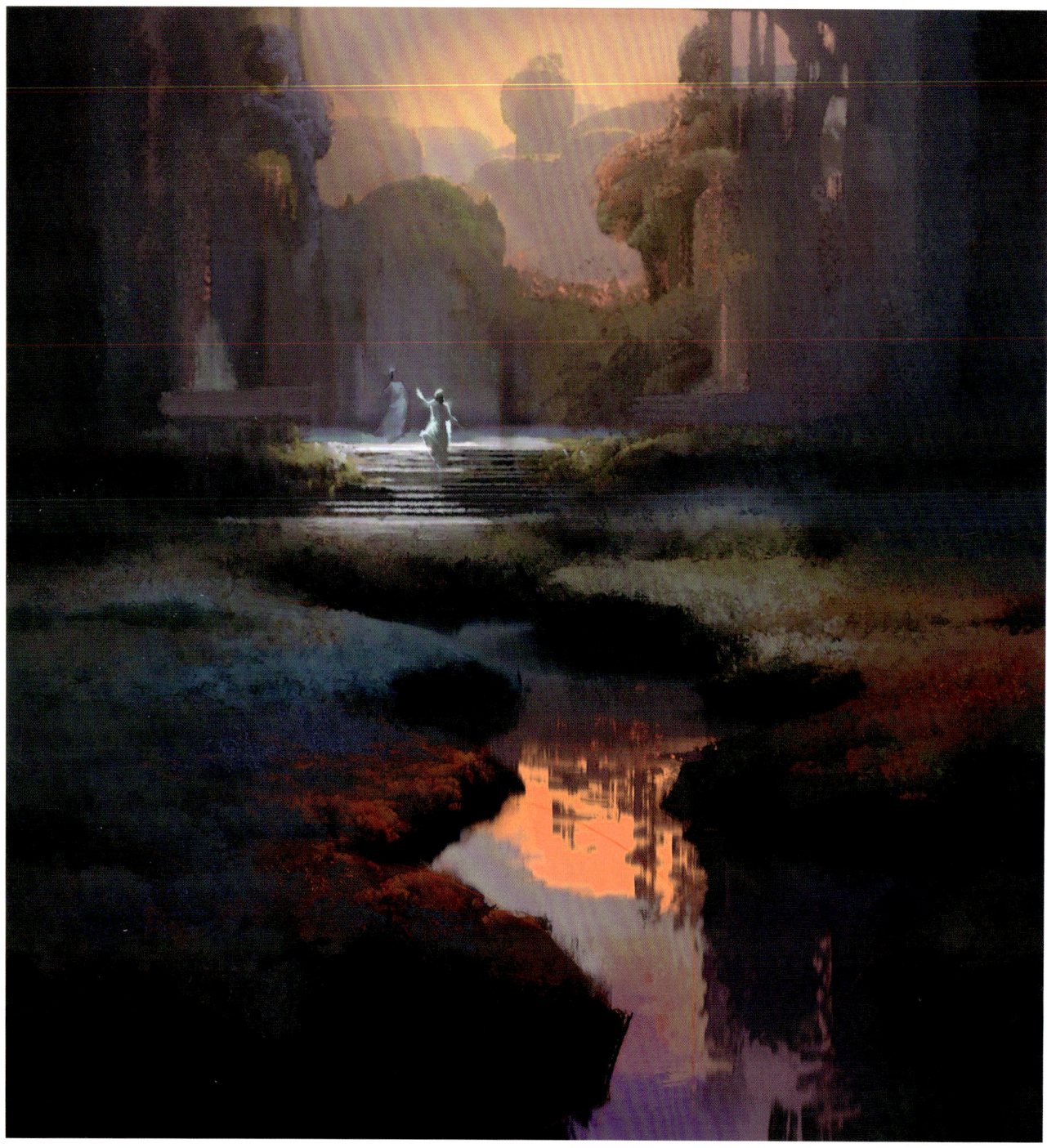

01. Sometimes we must break the rules to help tell the story

Sometimes the story we're telling forces us to go against conventional wisdom. You can go contrary to some of the space-creating elements discussed in this chapter, as long as you emphasize many others. The cumulative effect will still work.

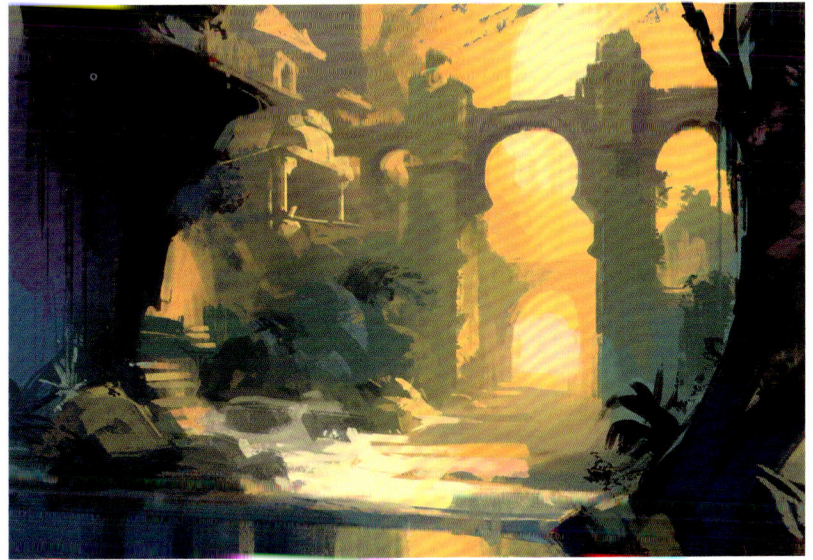

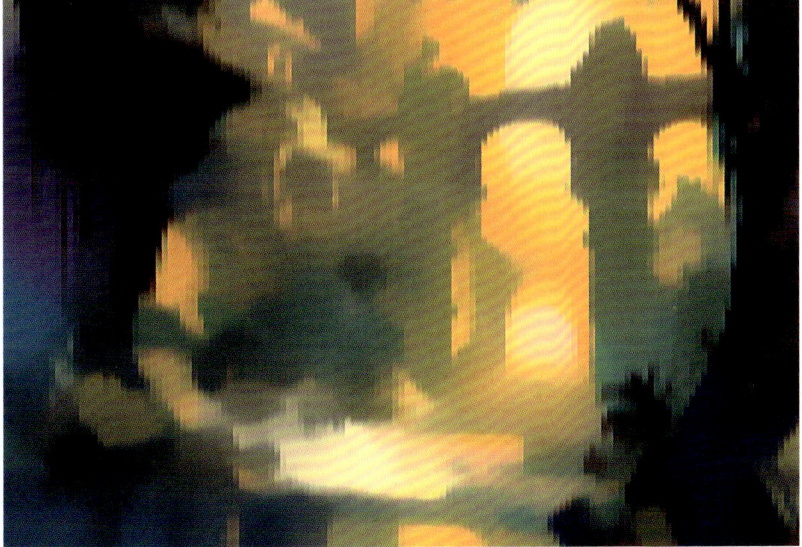

02. Stacking some familiar techniques allows you to throw in a wild card

02. STACKING SOLUTIONS

Let's do an experiment here. Let's take the concept of warm background temperatures from the previous scene and push it to an extreme. I've created a scene that does the opposite of the general wisdom. Instead of starting out with warm light and hot local colors, moving into layer upon layer that gets gradually cooler, I've done the exact opposite. I've created layers that start cold in the foreground and get warmer and warmer as they recede in the background. Can this work? Can we still get a deep sense of space in this scenario? We can!

We don't want to have a formula where we do the exact same thing in every single scene we create. We need variety. I refer to my solution as *stacking*. If you stack up three or four depth-creating devices, you can throw in another that goes completely against convention and it will still work. This is very important because our responsibility is to tackle any kind of environment and give it any kind of story and mood. We can't employ the same solutions over and over and still get the variety we need.

DEMONSTRATION: DESIGNING SPACE

Let's demonstrate our ideas step by step now. In this project I'll create a scene of intricate ruins in three-point perspective, as seen on the cover of this book.

01. PERSPECTIVE GRID

I start by creating a three-point perspective grid that has an eye-level line high up above for a strong downward omniscient view. I stack up the blocks of the ruins so that I have a strong foreground surrounding a courtyard with some elements receding to the left and right of the screen.

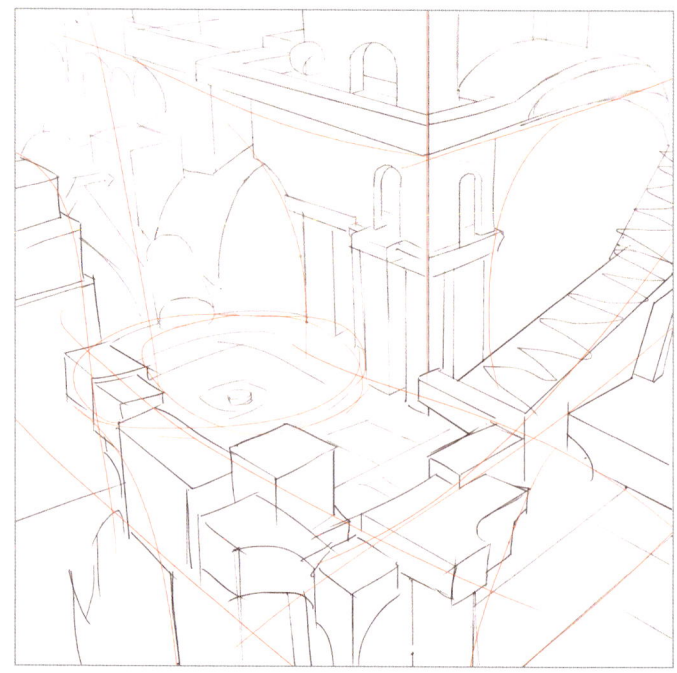

01. Start with a rough perspective drawing

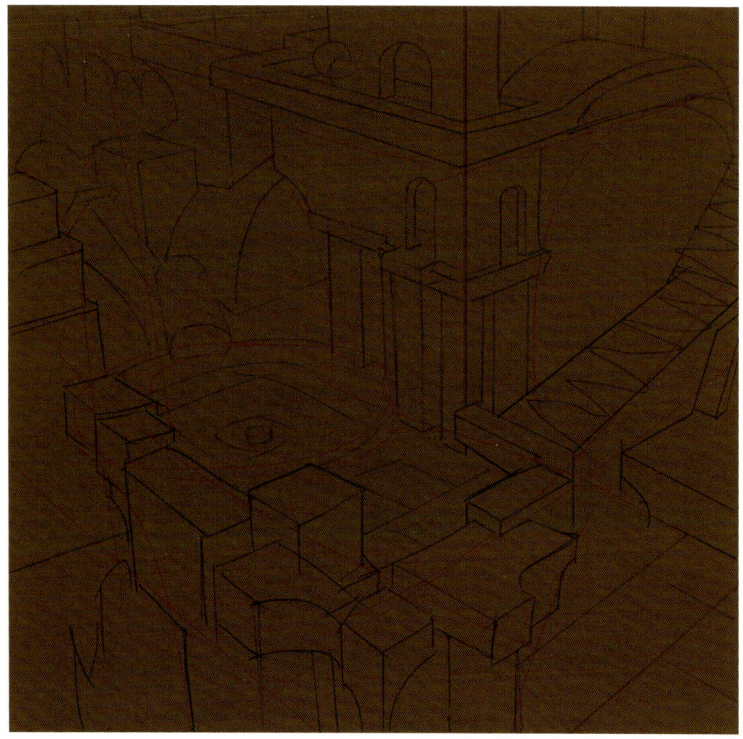

02. An earthy umber base sets the tone

02. BASE COLOR

A general color helps me get going. I want this to be an earthy scene, so a nice raw umber should do the trick. If you're not familiar with the colors referred to as umber, imagine a yellow that gets shifted darker and darker until it's a deep yellow-brown. These are the umber tones.

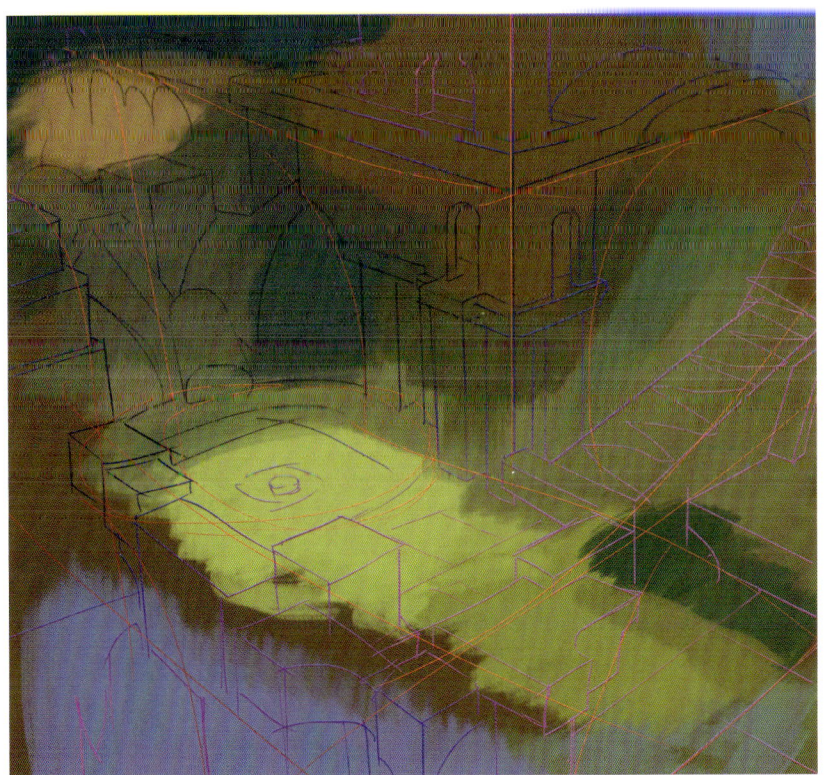

03. Add local colors, letting the base color shine through

03. LOCAL COLORS

I move forward by loosely adding local colors and a bit of atmosphere. I keep the browns of the buildings, add a green courtyard overrun with wild grass, and then add cool colors at the top and bottom where the perspective moves away into distant atmosphere.

04. GROUPING

Now I get more specific and make sure the various groupings here are defined. I keep the foreground in shadow as a nice depth contrast, and lighten the building so the deeper surrounding areas can plunge into shadow.

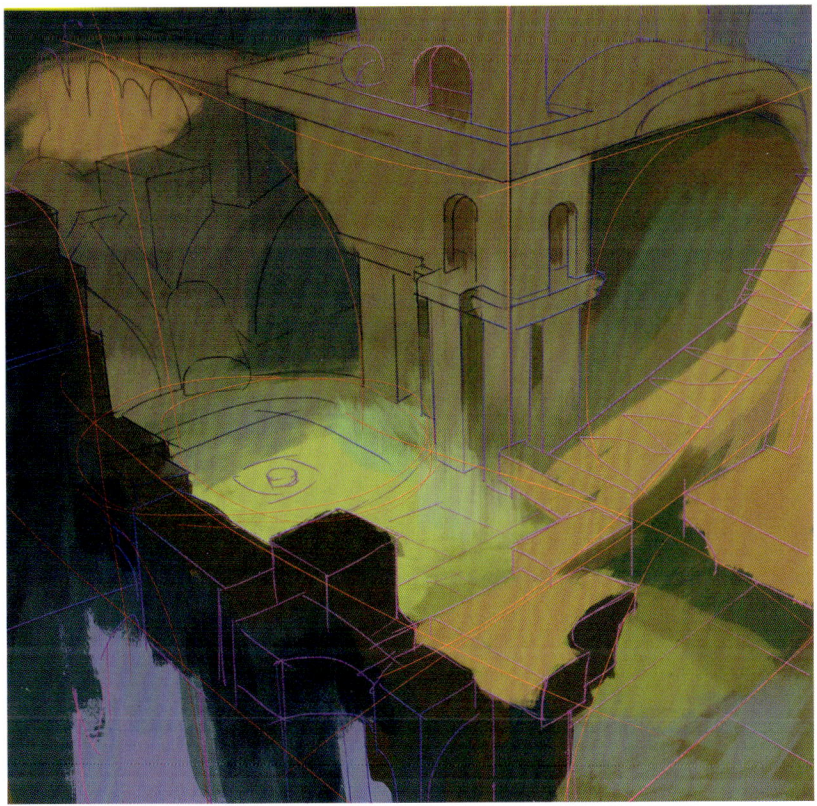

04. Group areas of the scene together with contrast

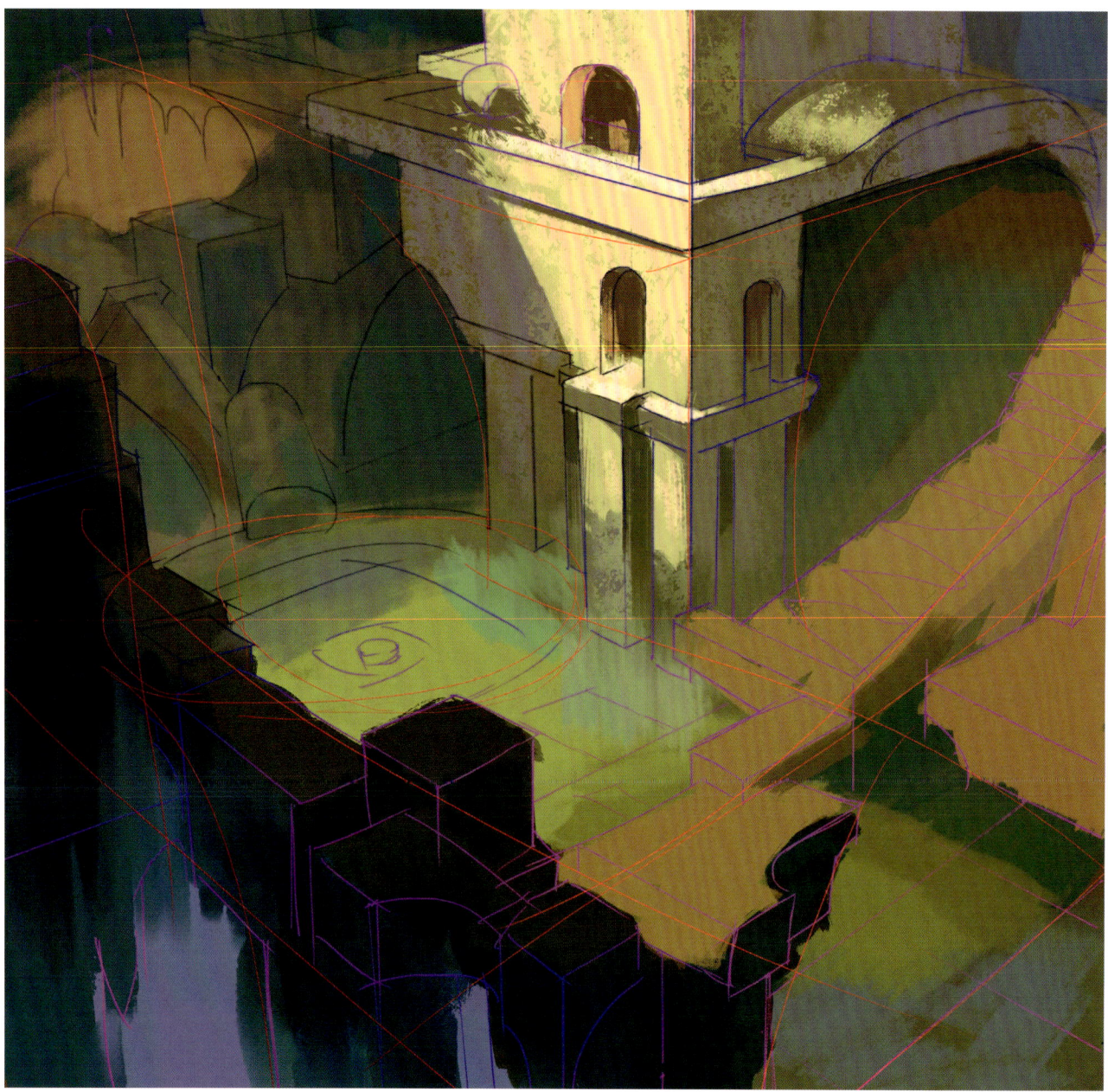

05. Illuminate the focal building with bright light

05. LIGHTING

It's time for light! I want to set up a lighting direction that will be most useful to me, as the center architecture will be the focus of this piece. So I design the light as if there are tall ruins or obstructions out of frame to screen left, casting a shadow onto the building. This gives me the lighting that I need and the diagonal shadow gives a bit of action to the image.

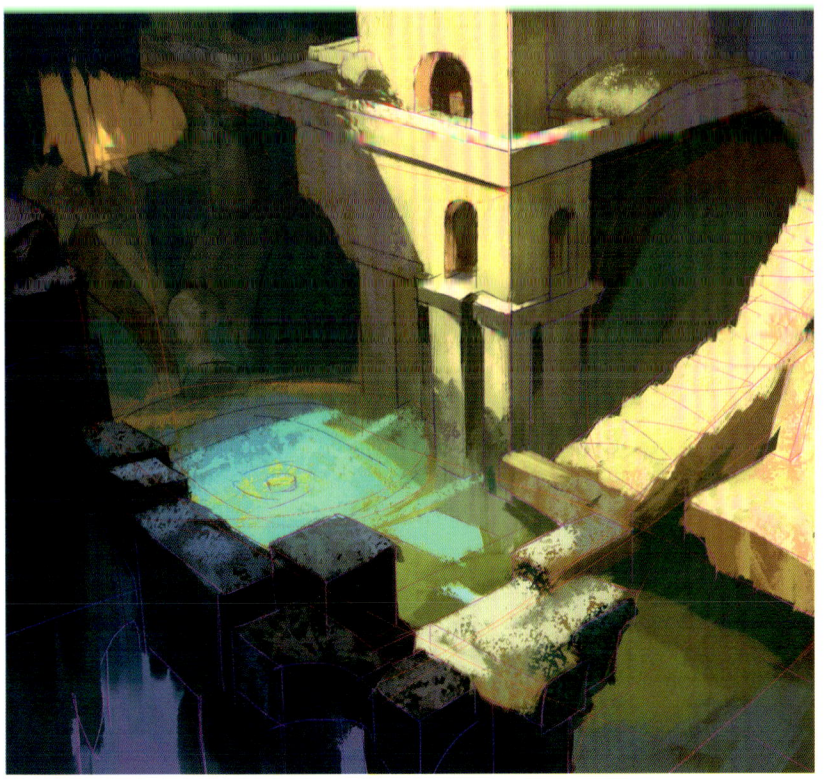

06. THE POOL

I start suggesting that there's still water in the courtyard pool – you know, a residue of rain or something, any excuse to get interesting contrast in the scene! Those blues and cyans really help bring the scene to life. Without them I'd just have brown, green, and gray, and the place would look kind of dead. I also expand the surrounding lighting to reach the adjacent stairs.

07. DETAILS

We're ready now for some detail work. I have two primary goals: I want to emphasize three-dimensional planes and I want to add rugged textures to give a quality of age to the place. As I go along adding these, I also add moss and brush to be sure the place has an abandoned, overgrown look.

06. The pool adds a pop of cyan that makes the scene come alive

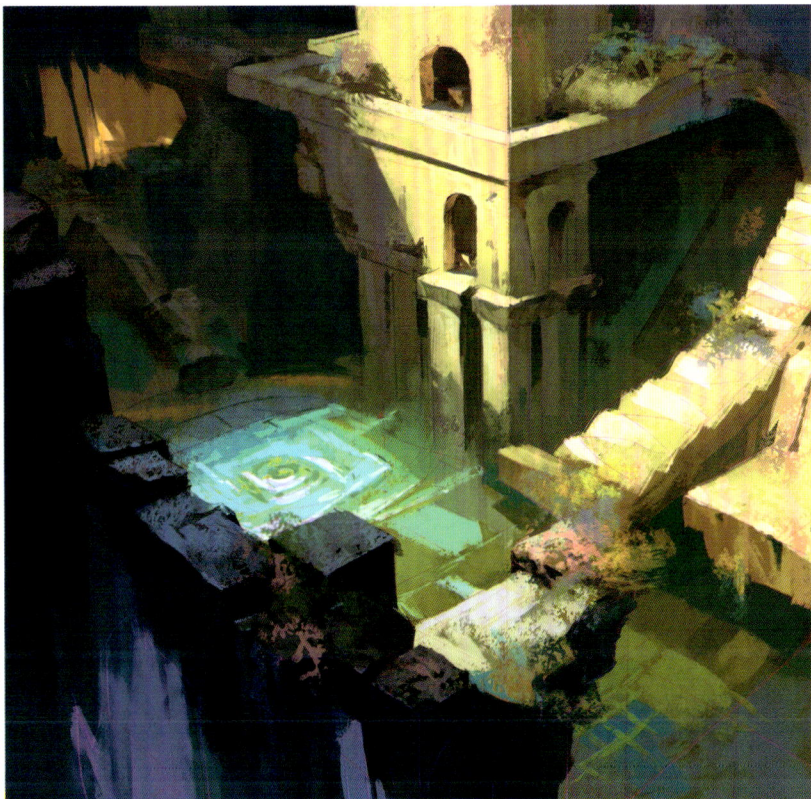

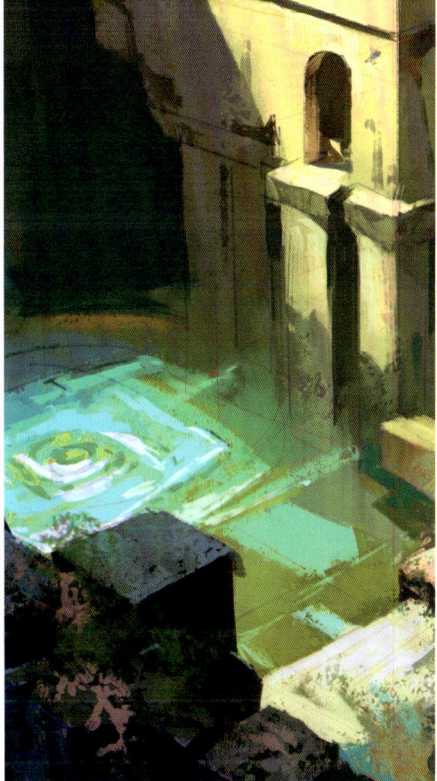

07. Add more three-dimensional form and some overgrown flora to the architecture

08. FINAL IMAGE

Let's bring this bad boy to a finish. To do that, I sharpen important edges, the ones that need to thrust out toward us, especially in the foreground and the central architecture. I crisp up the texture and add more overgrown foliage. You could probably sense my excitement about the colors in the pool in the previous step, and I guess my excitement couldn't be contained, because I felt the color needed to be pushed even further for variety. I suggest flowering plants and mosses that produce red, yellow, and magenta flowers. Then I throw in a white bird to give a little life and action to the scene, and voilà – we're finished!

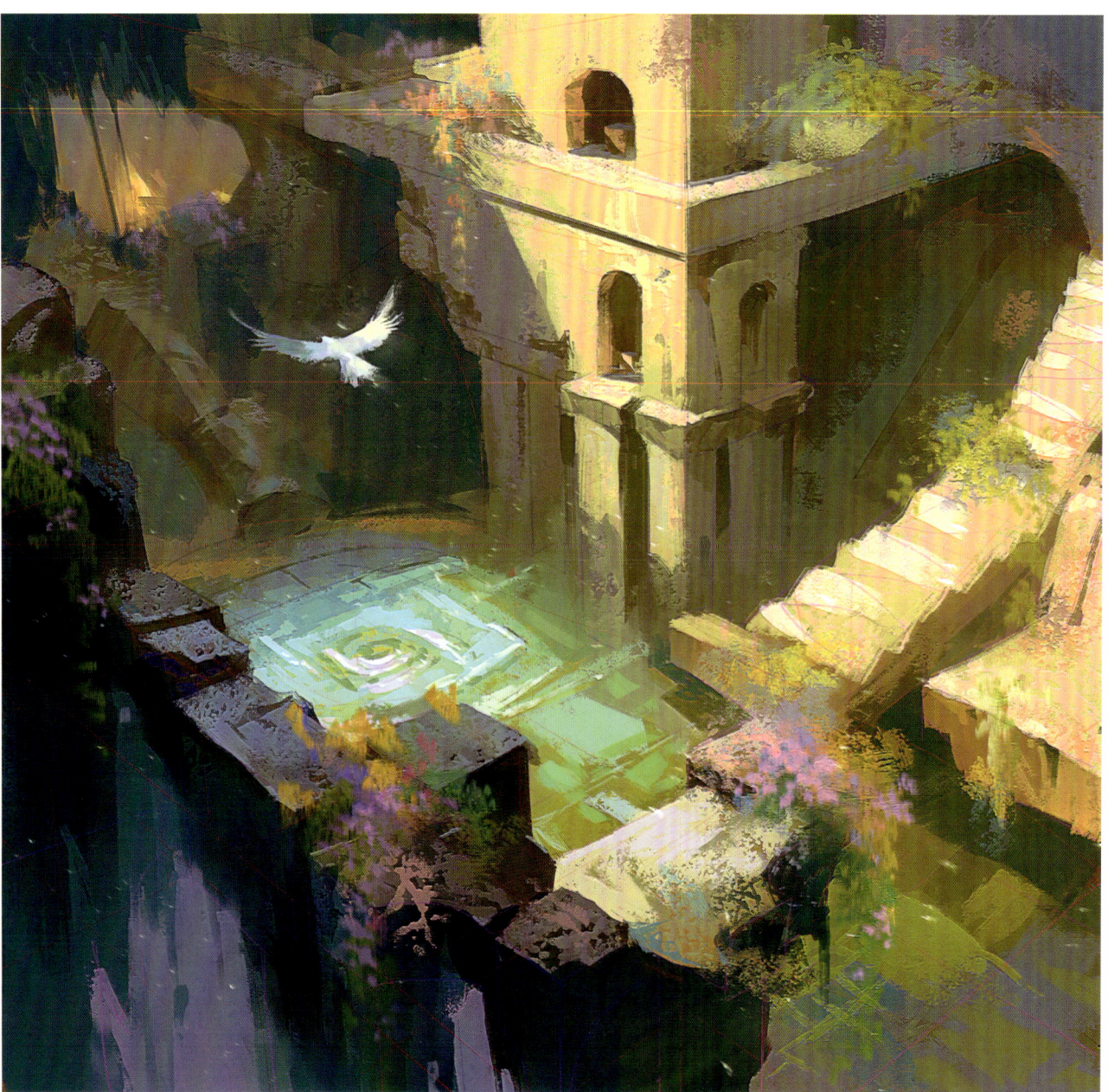

08. A bird and colorful flowers finish off the scene

RECOMMENDED EXERCISE: SPATIAL STUDIES

Almost every image you create will feature a setting of some kind, which means you'll always be dealing with the design of space, and you've got to be good at it!

So in your daily practice, set aside time to do quick little studies that put the principles we've covered here into practice. Rough out something that moves from warm in the foreground to cool in the distance. Rough out something that uses the 'breadcrumbs' idea. Try a space that feels close-up and intimate, another that suggests vast distances, and so on. Have fun with it!

Here's a checklist for you to cover:

- claustrophobic versus wide-open space
- warm advancing temperatures versus cool receding temperatures
- high-contrast advancing textures versus low-contrast receding textures
- overlap
- value contrast
- edge contrast
- relative position
- banding
- placement of the eye-level line
- one-point, two-point, and three-point perspective
- breadcrumbs
- attaching less-important distant objects to the background
- intimate space versus distant space
- flat space versus open space

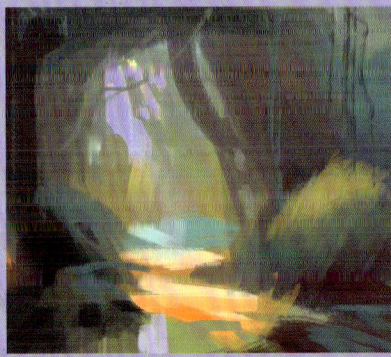
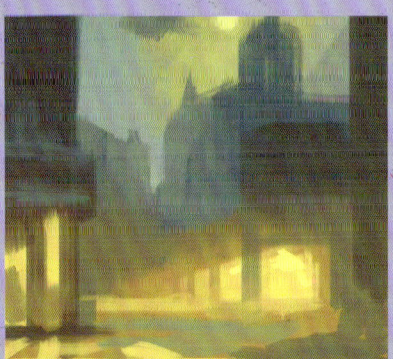
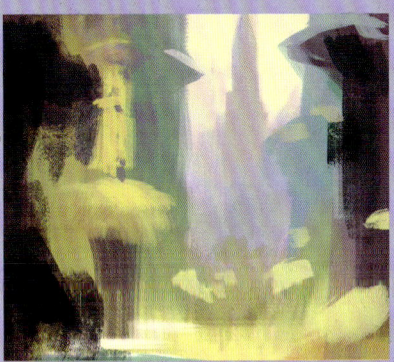

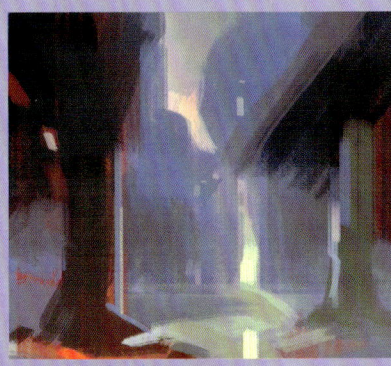
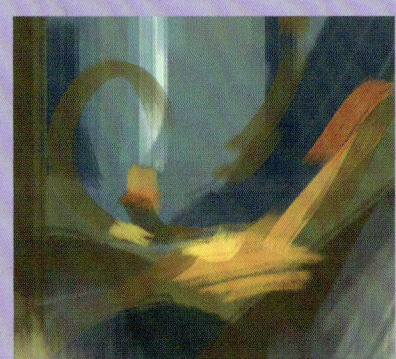
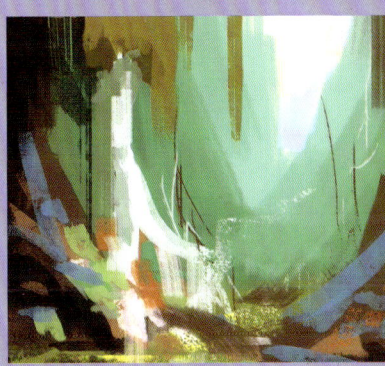
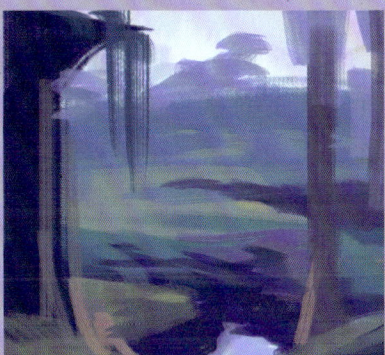

△ Practice as many different approaches to space as you can

THE DESIGN OF ARCHITECTURE

If you're designing an asteroid, should it have a more realistic potato-in-space look, or can you take creative liberties? If you're illustrating a science text, then go with the potato, but if you're making a movie, go crazy!

THE ARMAGEDDON ASTEROID

Here we go with a brand-new subject! I'll have to walk a tightrope on this one, because I'll be writing on the subject for you with great authority, when the truth is I have very little expertise on it. I didn't go to architecture school and odds are you didn't, either.

We simply don't have the knowledge that a trained architect would have, and yet the majority of environments we create will include architecture. Now you can reasonably say, 'Wait a minute, Nathan. I paid good money for this book, plus I'm devoting my precious time to it, so there has to be some real value here for me!' Well, what I can do is teach you how to pull the same con with your clients and audience that I do with mine – a con they will actually love you for! It all comes back to emotion. In our business, nothing is actually real, but if our audience feels it emotionally, then it seems real to them.

Let me tell you the story of an argument I moderated between my dad and the production designer of the DreamWorks movie *The Prince of Egypt*. In 1998, I was working on that movie and went back to my parents' home for Thanksgiving. That night, after we had gotten ourselves fat and happy feasting on Thanksgiving dinner, we watched a movie on TV called *Armageddon*. In it, Bruce Willis and his band of unlikely heroes take control of a space shuttle, fly into space, and place a nuclear charge on a looming asteroid to blow it into harmless pieces.

Well, my dad is a professor of both geology and astronomy, and as we watched this movie, he got angrier and angrier. We watched Bruce Willis traverse dangerous and awe-inspiring environments on that asteroid. It had incredible protrusions of rock with crazy and dangerous-looking giant crystalline structures. It was piled with amazing visual design. So a commercial break comes up – this was the nineties, remember – and my dad puts the TV on mute and says, 'This movie is ridiculous. All that stuff on the asteroid wouldn't have lasted the first ten million years in the solar system due to constant impacts, and here we are four and a half billion years later. This is ridiculous! I can't take another minute of this. I'm going to bed.' But then he peeked back through the doorway and said, 'And another thing. Those steaming vents that are popping up everywhere, so powerful they're blowing people off into space – that's not an asteroid, that's a comet! That's what happens when a comet comes into solar orbit closer to the sun and starts to vent. A nickel–iron asteroid does nothing like that. Good night!'

Well, the designer of the asteroid was an artist named Darek Gogol, and it just so happened that same artist was the production designer on my current movie at the time, *The Prince of Egypt*. Funny coincidence! (A production designer is the director of the

visual aspects of a movie.) The next morning, I told my dad I knew the very guy who had designed the asteroid, and he said, 'You tell him that his asteroid doesn't even remotely resemble reality!' and so that's exactly what I did on Monday morning when I got back to work. Darek is a guy with a big personality and a big voice, who originally came from Poland. He has a strong accent and speaks with a strong authority, so he nearly shouted, 'Well, what does your dad want me to do? Design a giant potato in space? Because that's exactly what real asteroids look like!'

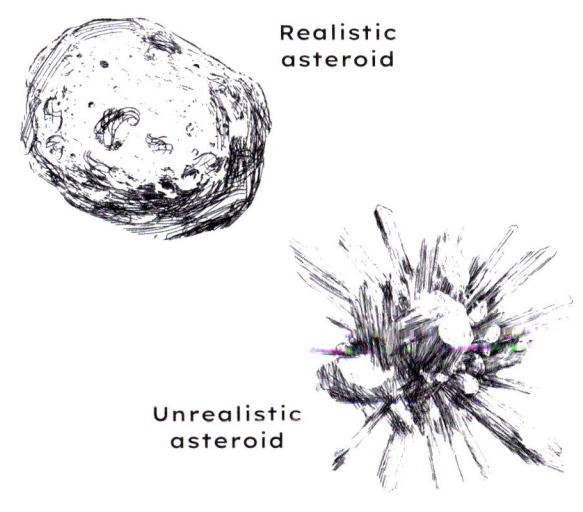

△ Which of these asteroid designs will excite the viewer more?

And there we have it: the scientist's point of view and the artist's point of view. Who is right? If we're in a science classroom, my dad is right, but if we're watching a movie, Darek is right. This brings us back to the scam. With our lack of technical knowledge about the intricacies of true architecture, how do we fool our audiences to suspend their disbelief for what we're showing them? You already know the answer because we've been driving at it every chapter of this book thus far: we give the architecture a profound quality of emotion! Really, the answer is that simple – just like Darek Gogol did for his asteroid. I invite you to look back to the chapter on the emotional language of shape and line (page 74) and everything else we covered there, because it all can and should apply to architecture.

In this chapter, I'll begin by showing you how to give your architecture a basic geometric believability, then how to bring that profound emotional believability into it, and you'll be all set.

STACKING BOXES

Here's a quick jumble of architectural shapes that's starting to have a little intrigue and visual interest, but it's nothing more than a few stacked blocks and a little perspective. We won't need a whole lot more than this to get basic structural believability and visual interest into our architecture. But how can we take this kind of raw simplicity and turn it into a pleasing finished product?

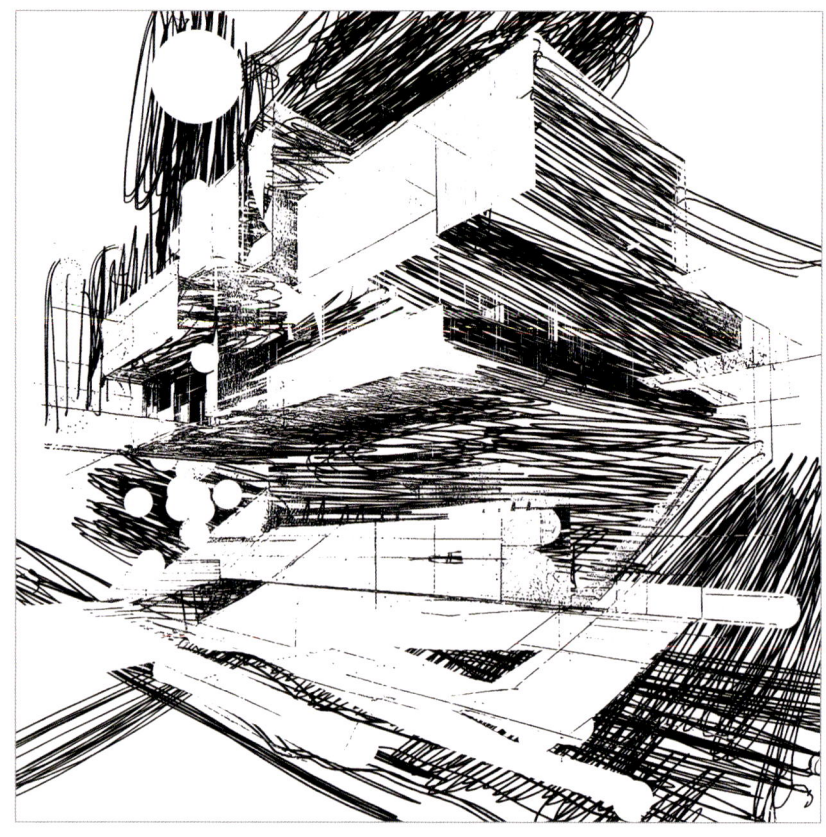

△ There's a rough idea here, but how could you take it further?

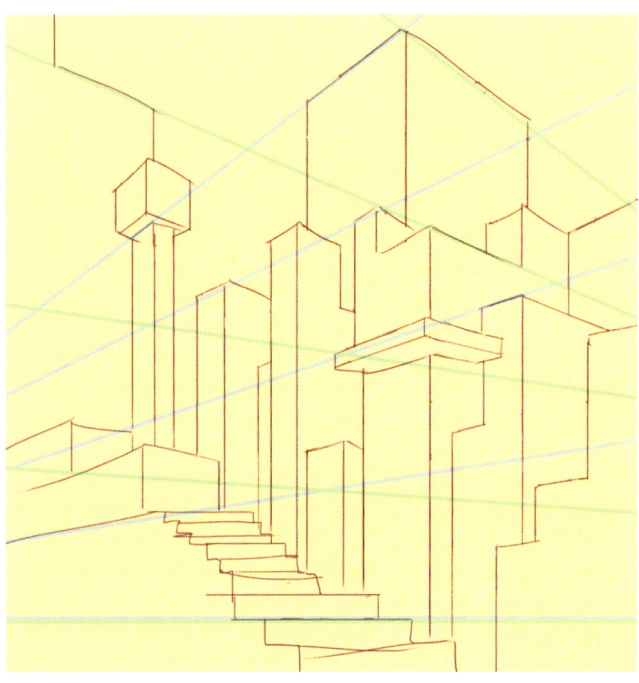

01. Stack very basic geometry in a suitable perspective

01. BLOCKS IN PERSPECTIVE

All we have to do is stack blocks. Isn't that essentially what architecture is? I try to stack them in an interesting way: I have a monolith to the right of the center with some active shapes around it to give it a bit more attention. The steps help lead us in and give us a bit of a journey, and the tall column over to the left provides visual balance against the mass on the other side. All of this is conforming to a steep two-point perspective – it's that bug's-eye view again, which gives an extra sense of importance to the buildings.

There's no reason a person would need to use my specific technique, but it's fun for me and keeps me engaged in the process. I stand by the principles taught in this book but, as for techniques, find the ones you enjoy and that keep you coming back for more.

02. LIGHT & SHADOW

Now let's throw a little fun artistry at it and play with light and shadow. I choose a lighting direction that gives a firm illumination to the central area, then mask out the planes that would catch the light. I scribble linework into the shadows and background to try and find a simple but interesting vignetted composition. I like where this is going! There's no reason a person would need to use this specific technique, but it's fun for me and keeps me engaged in the process.

03. COLOR FINAL

Here's the fully finished illustration. I've kept the light and shadow shapes and vignetted composition, and used simple warms and cools to get some visual interest into the scene using color. The warms and cools are doing double duty here, because they also add believability to the 3D nature of the structures. The warm local colors of stone receive warm direct sunlight, which bounces brilliantly into the adjacent shadows. Other shadow planes that face outward or upward receive cool skylight for a nice contrast to the warms. Just add some more warm and cool in the background, and we've got it! And it's nothing more than stacked blocks.

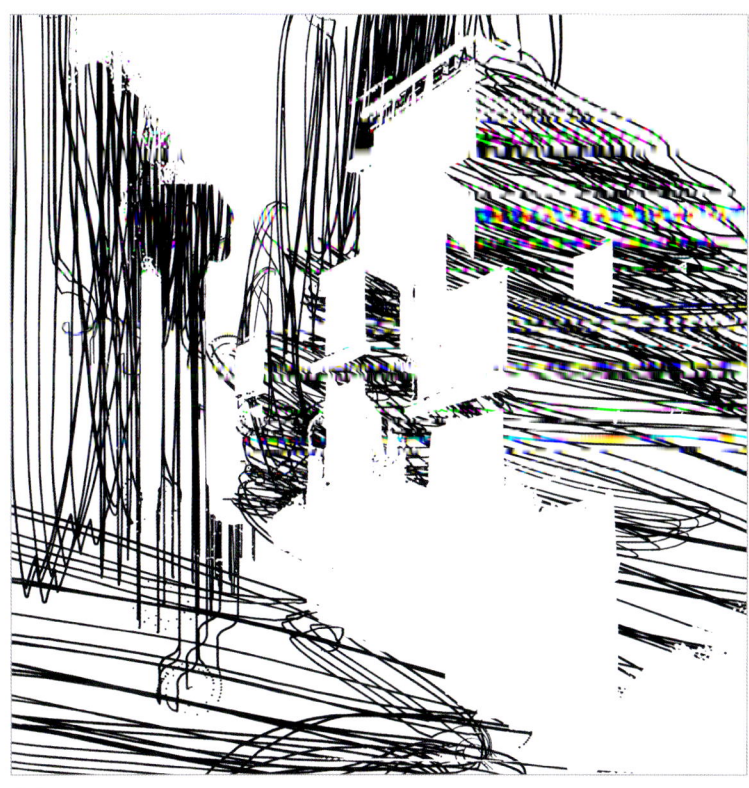

02. This approach is a fun way to create light and shadow shapes

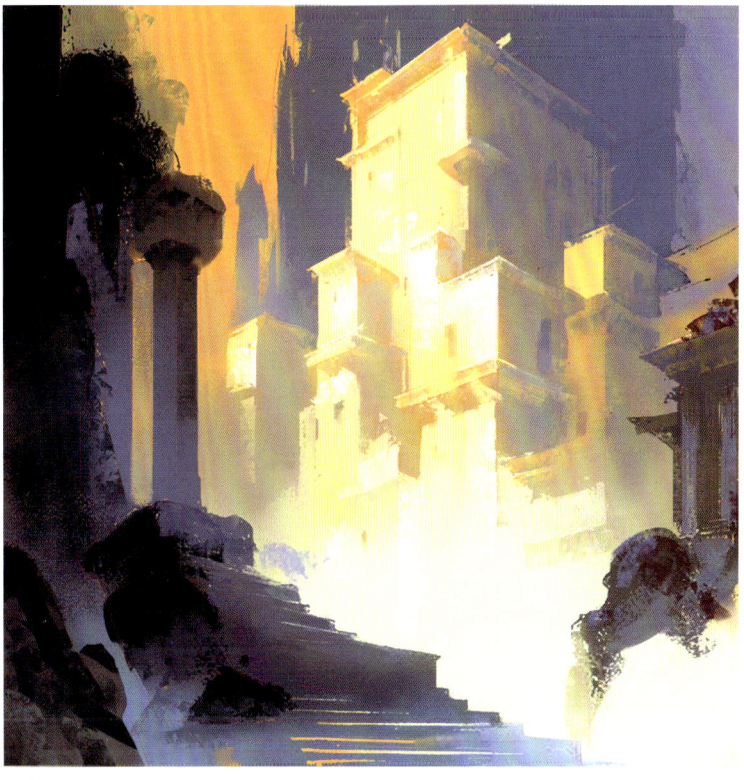

03. The color image builds on the strong foundation of stacked forms

04. Let's try a scene on an even more epic scale!

04. ANOTHER EXAMPLE

I mentioned *The Prince of Egypt* in this chapter's introduction. I worked on that project way back in the nineties, but I've never lost my love for the big architectural epic quality of that movie. So let's stack more blocks but throw in an old-world Egyptian vibe and see what we can get. I go through the same process of trying to stack up shapes in an interesting way, then adding some quick linework to try out light and shadow.

05. THE RESULT

And our simple stacking of blocks brings us to this! I hope you like this painting and, if you do, you'll be glad to know that I'll take you through the step-by-step process of creating it on page 162.

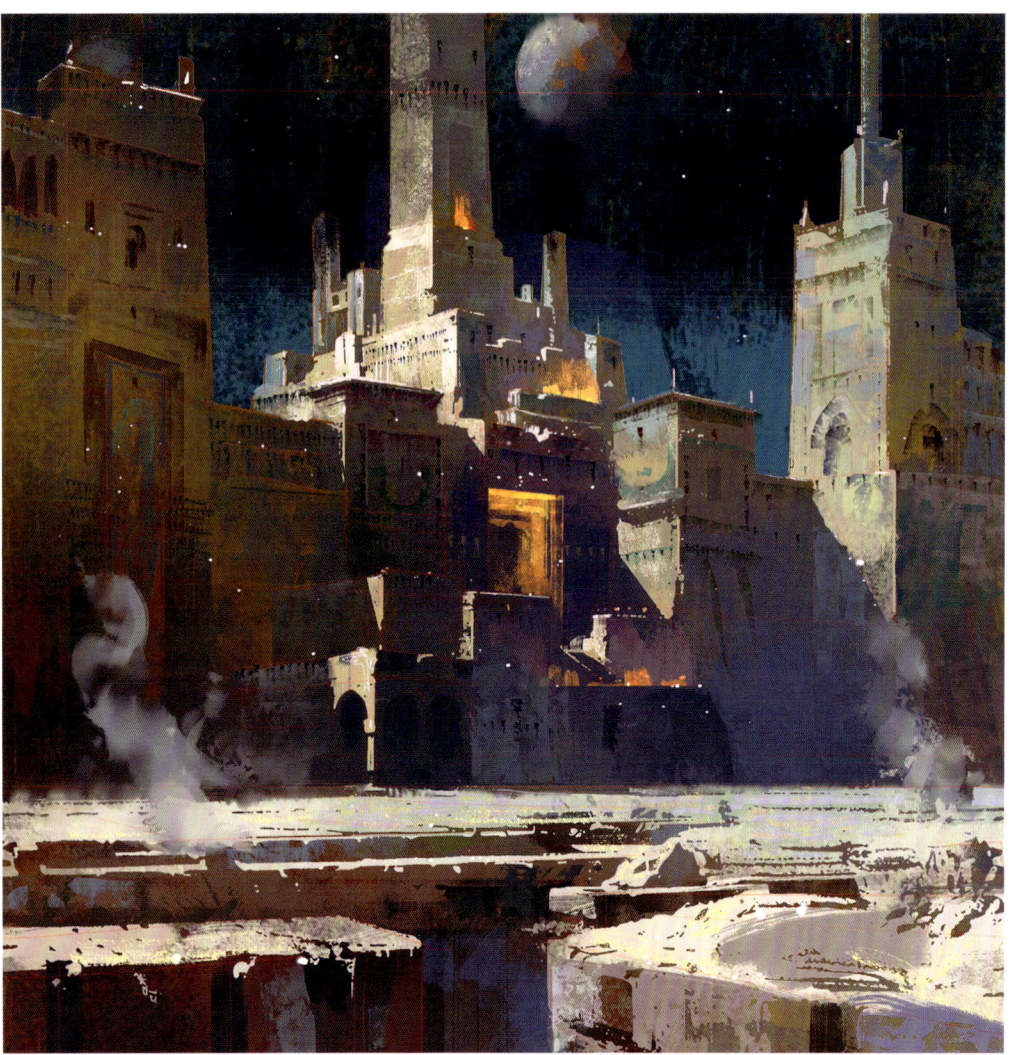

05. You'll see how this painting was made later in this chapter

IS IT ALIVE?

Now we need to get back to one of the central themes of this book, which is *purpose*. For every environment we've created, we've had a reason for doing it. We've had a *purpose*. So it makes sense to be sure that all aspects of the environment serve that particular purpose, whatever it may be. And that's why I broke out Photoshop and painted up these weird shapes for you. They're kind of nonsensical and yet we look at them and know there's some sort of *purpose* being conveyed. They were either made by someone or they're alive, like a fungus or something. The meaningful repetition here conveys purpose, which is a simple but powerful idea. Let me illustrate this in the next couple of environment studies.

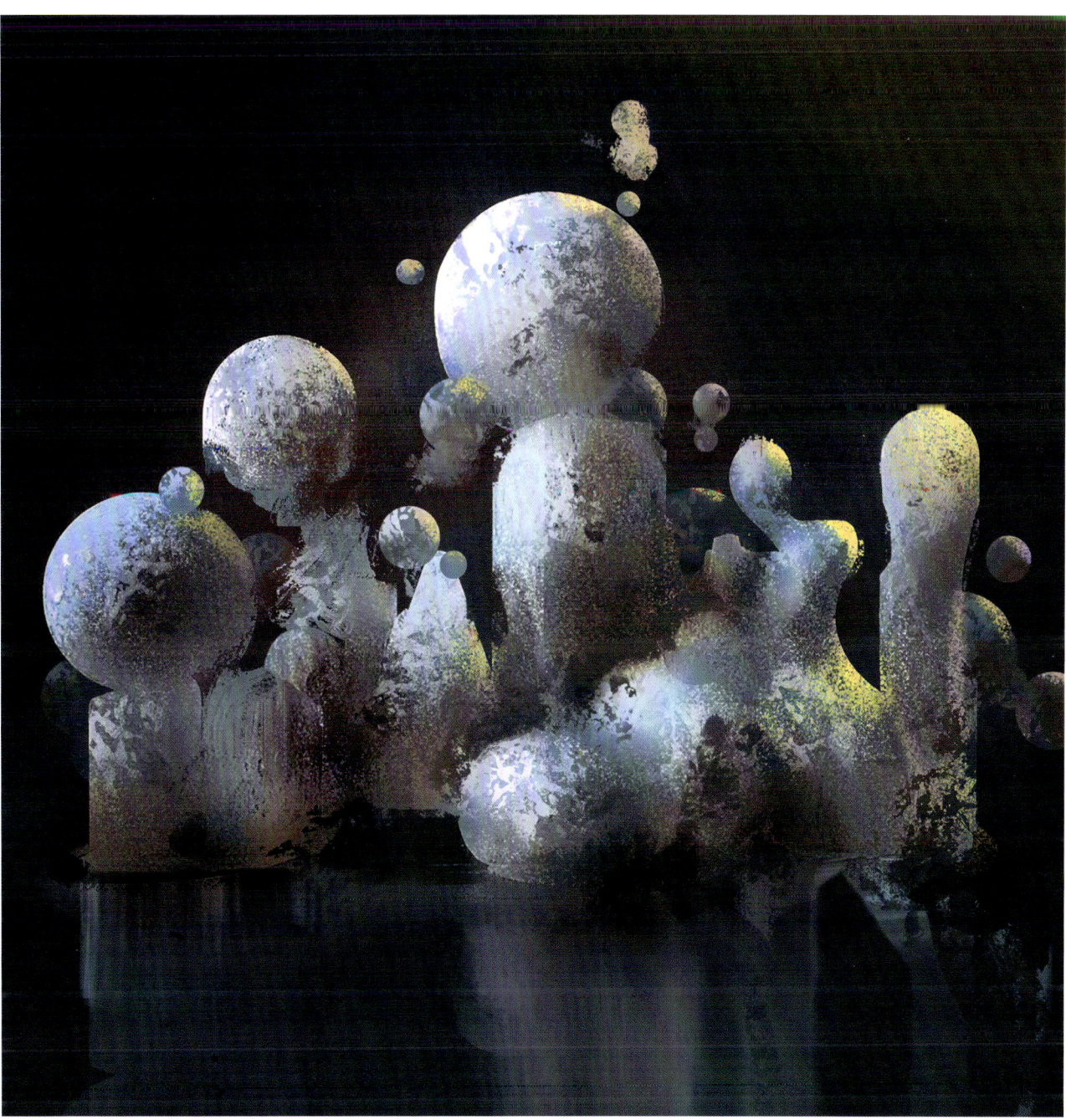

△ This image is mysterious, but it feels intentional – it has purpose

01. ALIEN PATTERNS

My favorite kind of science-fiction novel is one where a trained biologist writes a well-crafted story about aliens of some kind, because aliens are the ultimate 'mystery wrapped in an enigma'. Aliens are intelligent but how can you ever know their true intent? They say that they're here to help, but are they lying? There's no way to know – the thing about aliens is *they're alien*. So you see an image like this and you know there's purpose there, but you don't know what that purpose is. There's a drive to find out because people love a mystery. Getting your audience to want to know more about what you're doing is a powerful thing.

Over the years, it's been fun for me to rough out weird little alien environments in my sketchbook or in Photoshop. All I need to do is get a little of that meaningful repetition, that quality of purpose, and the audience knows that they're seeing something strange and alive – or that something strange and alive made what they're seeing! This environment is made of fun colors and textures, with a similar repetition of spheres as in the previous image.

02. MORE REPETITION

Here's another one I did some years back. We'd come back from a trip to the beach and I had gotten a bit bored with my ordinary sketches. I started stacking up spheres to create alien shapes caught within an eerie green mist. Don't worry if you don't like science fiction or aliens – this simple idea of conveying purpose through repetition can strengthen the intentional quality of any architecture. All you have to do is set up a visually interesting theme and then play on it through meaningful repetition.

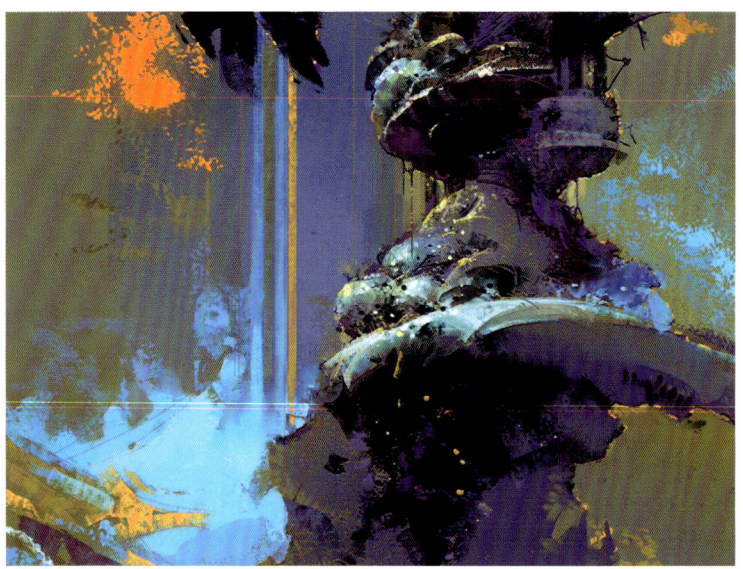

01. This structure could be made by aliens – or be an alien itself

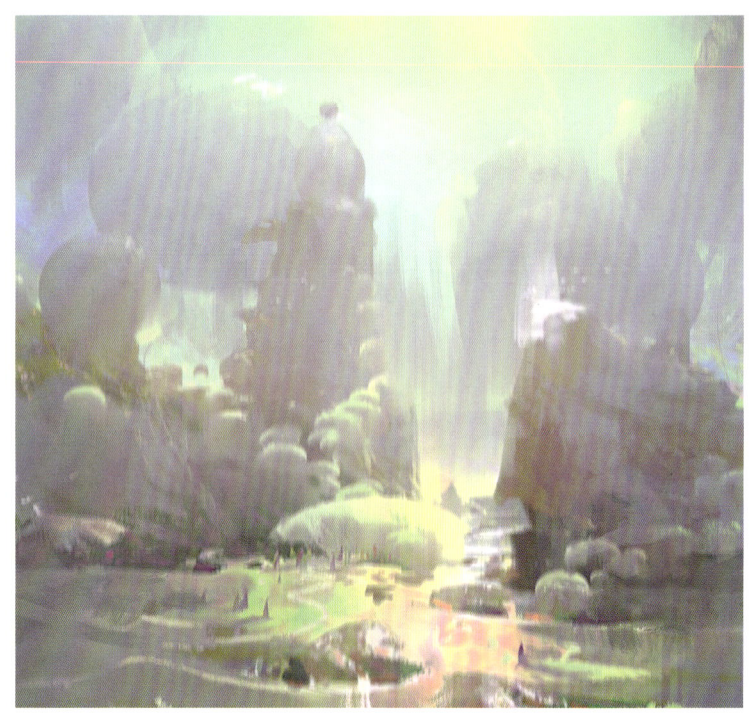

02. Repeated shapes make this landscape uncanny and intriguing

You can give a purposeful quality to your architecture, even if it's a nonsensical alien subject. All you have to do is set up a visually interesting theme and then play on it through meaningful repetition.

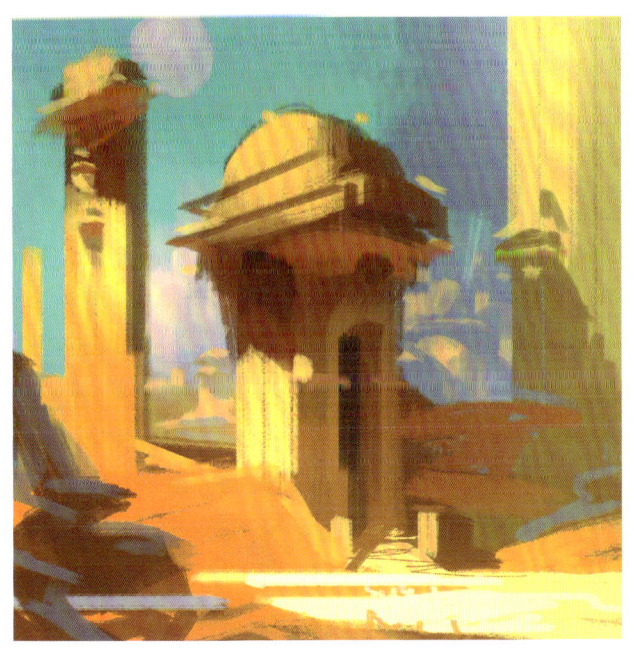

03. It works for non-alien environments, too!

03. FAMILIAR FANTASY

Now I'm bringing my ideas a little more down to earth. This sketch is more familiar in its shapes but just different enough to suggest fantasy. It uses the same kind of simple repetition as before, with rounds and verticals.

04. CONVEYING STORY

Here's a similar place where the purpose is to suggest a story is unfolding. The characters are walking toward a destination through a courtyard, purposefully framed by elements of architecture and foliage. Look at how simple the architecture is – it's just a variety of domes with light and shadow, but it's organized to suggest that this is an important destination. There's something going on there worth traveling to.

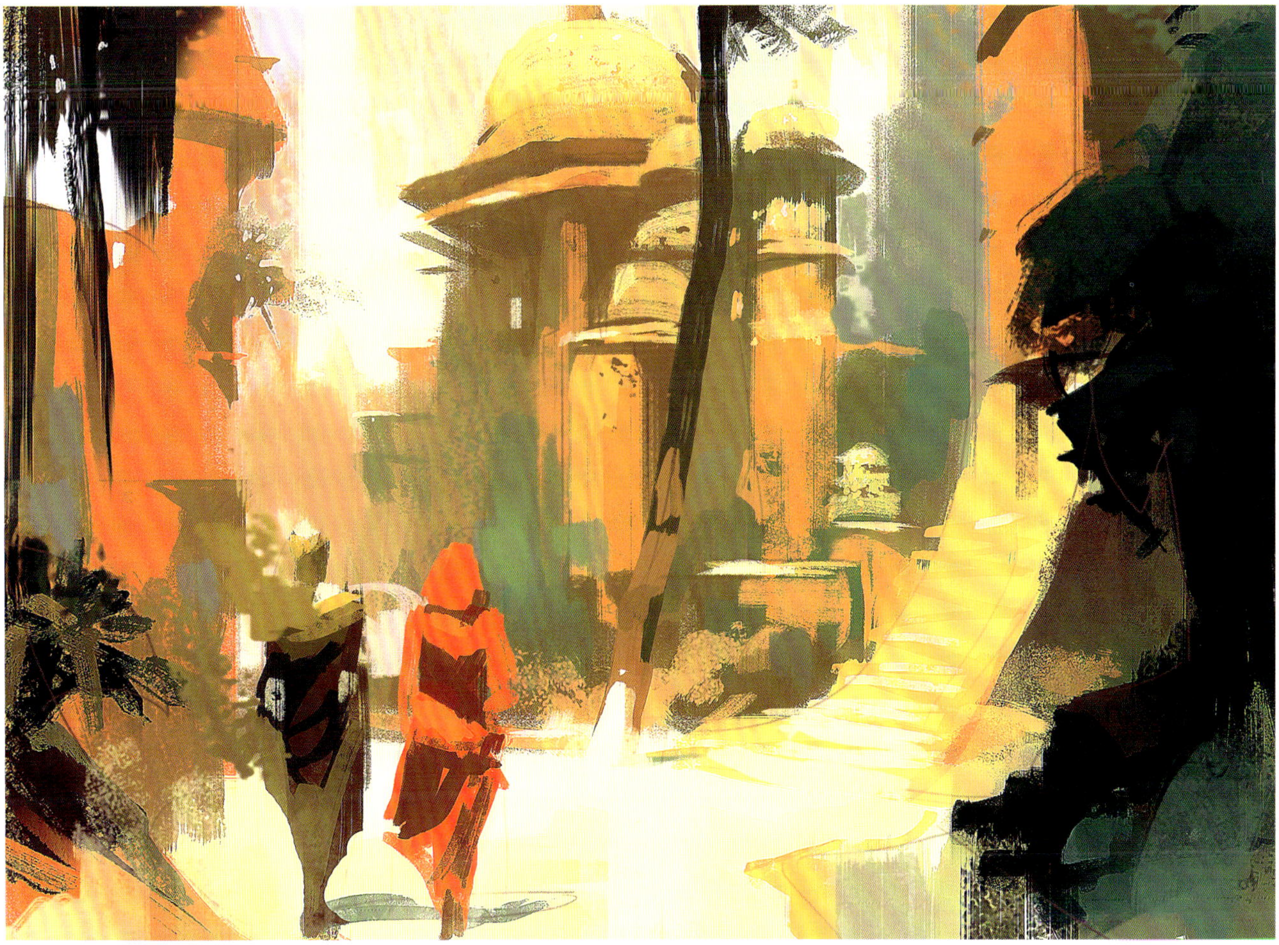

04. Repetition makes the building feel important

WORLD ARCHITECTURE

I did say that you and I are not trained architects, but that doesn't mean we don't need to do any architectural study. Giving your architecture a particular geographic style can give your audience an immediate sense of where they are or what kind of history or culture you're presenting to them. So architectural styles of the world, throughout history, are something we must have a firm grasp on. Making those styles immediately clear and iconic is a critical skill as well. If your experience is lacking in this regard, I invite you to immediately start doing a survey of world architecture and its history.

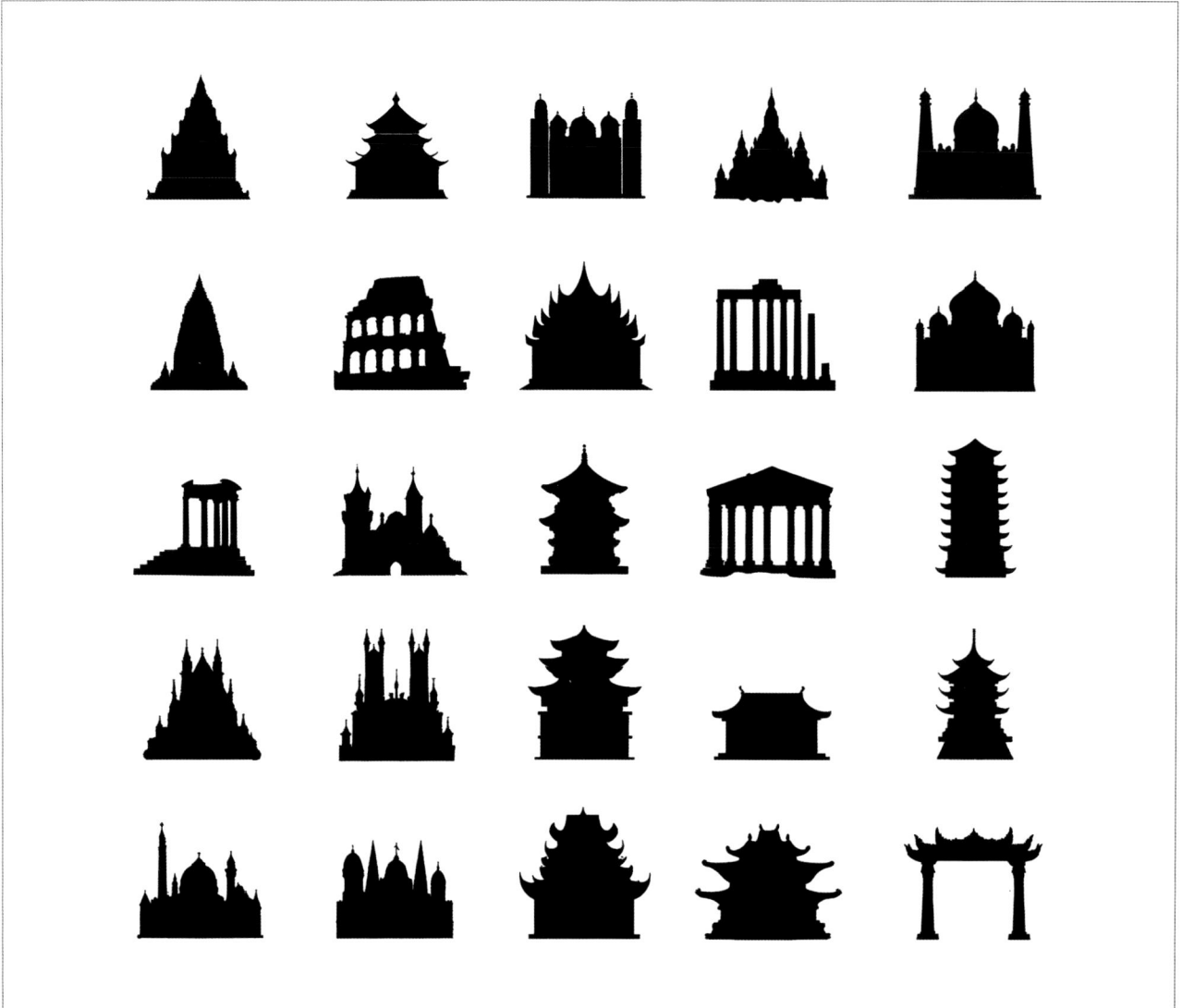

△ It's still important to have a strong grasp of real-world architectural styles

The styles of world architecture are something we must have a firm grasp on. They give our audience an immediate sense of where they are, and what kind of culture or history we're presenting to them.

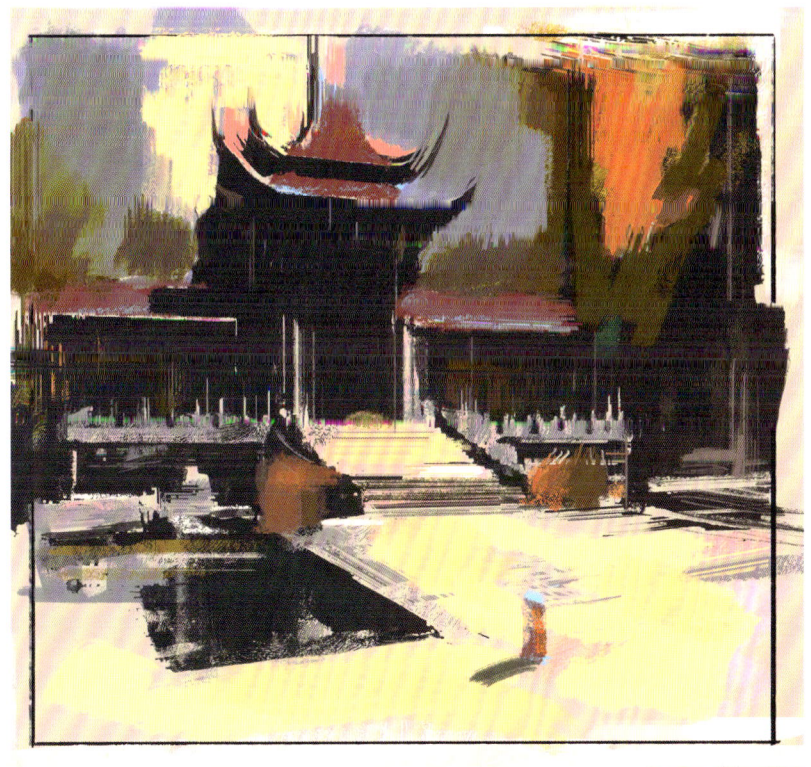

01. Architecture can quickly clue the viewer into geography or country

01. SENSE OF PLACE

Here's a quick study. Everyone immediately knows we're somewhere in East Asia. If we were to add characters in old-timey costumes, we would have a sense of the time period as well. Our environments represent somewhere in time and space, imaginary or real, and we can give that to our audience at a glance.

02. MYSTERY

Now I'd like to show you a few images that have a mere *suggestion* of architectural style, yet still enough to let the audience know what kind of environment they're in. This first one is a story sketch of two characters passing through a mysterious location. What kind of location? The broken Moorish architectural shapes tell us that this is an exotic and rare location, like a ruin – a clear tell that adventures are bound to happen in a place such as this.

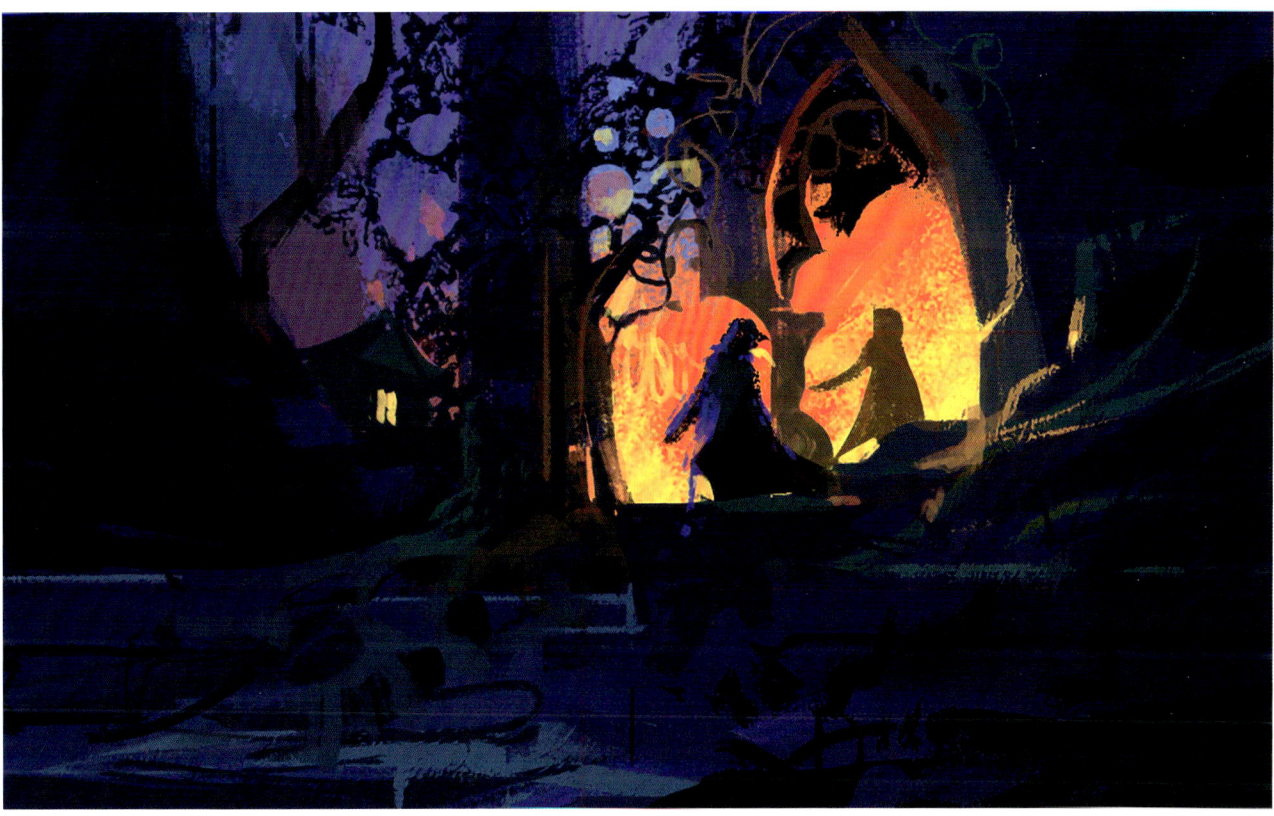

02. Sometimes a hint of architectural style is all you need!

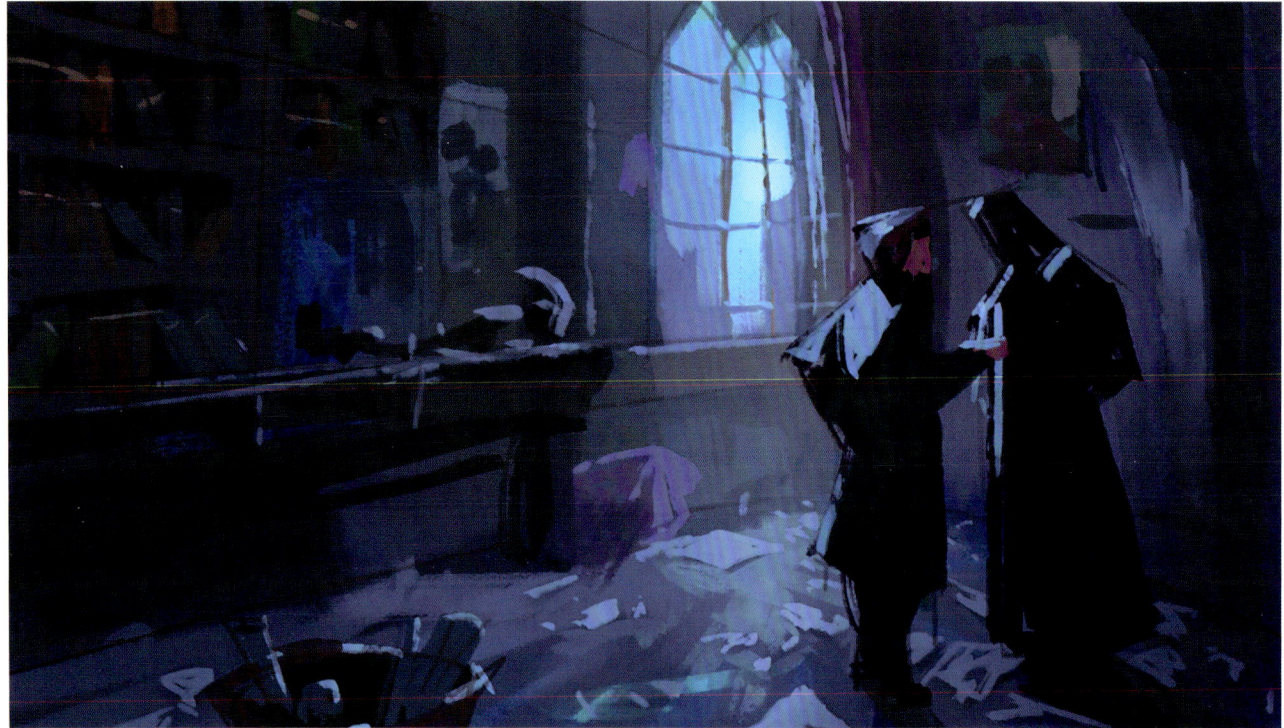

03. The shape of a window can tell us what kind of a building we're in

03. NARRATIVE

The environment of this story sketch is nothing more than a messy room with lots of books, but the window all by itself tells us this is no everyday room. It must be in a castle or mansion – a place that goes beyond the kind of environment where we spend our everyday lives. A place where stories and events unfold that are worth our interest and attention.

04. PAST & PRESENT

A wonderful way to think about architecture is that it often indicates to us what kind of people live there. Architecture conveys the character of the people who built the place, and the current state of the architecture tells us what kind of people live there now. This image is just some invented architectural shapes to have fun with, but I included Gothic-styled ornamentation for that bit of intrigue I've been talking about. Including a mysterious monk in the mix fits the 'gothic monastery on a mountain' vibe.

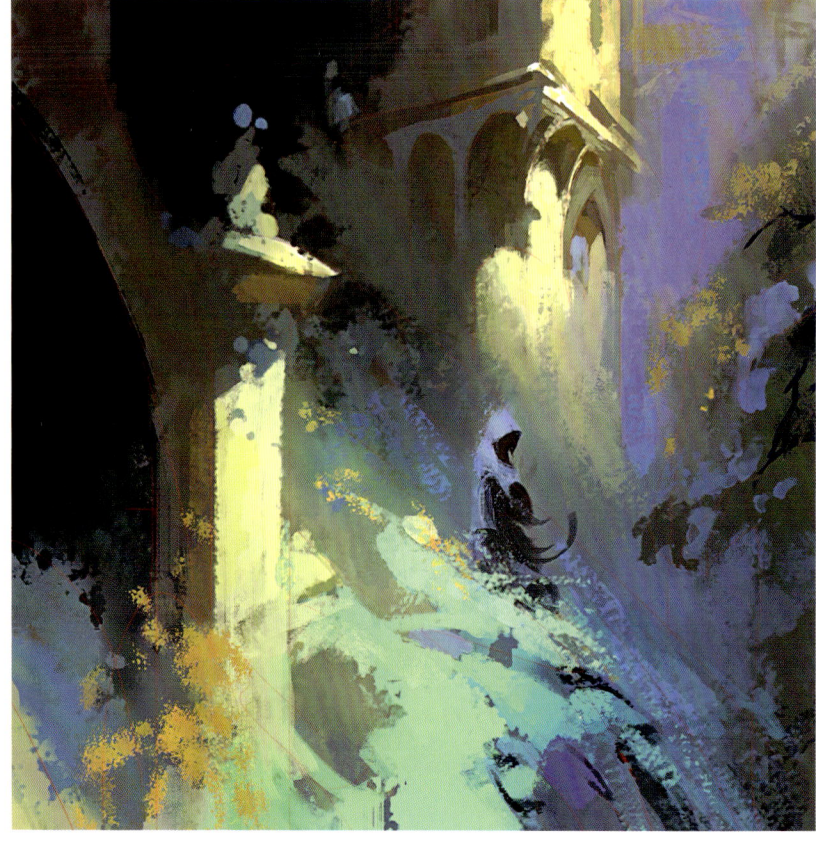

04. Architectural styling gives a sense of history to a location

A wonderful way to think about architecture is that it indicates to us what kind of people live there. It tells us about the people who built it, and the current state of the architecture tells us what kind of people live there now.

WONDERFUL WINDOWS & DOORS

Imagine you're illustrating a lone spaceship out in the deep reaches of the cosmos. With no point of comparison in empty space, there's no way for your audience to understand how big the ship really is, is there? Is it a small ship for a single pilot?

Or is it a giant superliner? The simple solution to this problem is windows! We intuitively know how big a window tends to be, and that immediately gives us a point of reference for scale. Be sure to carefully size your windows when designing any human space.

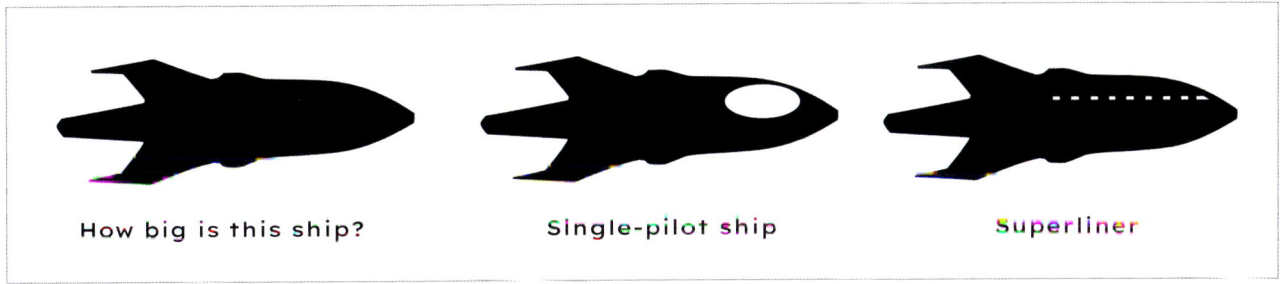

How big is this ship?   Single-pilot ship   Superliner

△ Changing the windows completely changes the scale of this spaceship

We intuitively know how big a window tends to be, and that immediately gives us a point of reference for scale. Be sure to carefully size your windows when designing any human space.

01. WINDOWS & DOORS

Let's bring the idea of spaceship windows back to our topic of architecture. The idea is exactly the same – we can convey the scale of an unfamiliar building simply with the size of its doors and windows. That brings us to another important point about designing architecture, which is that many students struggle with painting buildings. They can be so complex and take forever! What do you do when you need to paint quick and loose? What information do you leave in and what information do you edit out? If you place your emphasis on the simple geometry of the structure, and indicate doors and windows, you have most of the information you need.

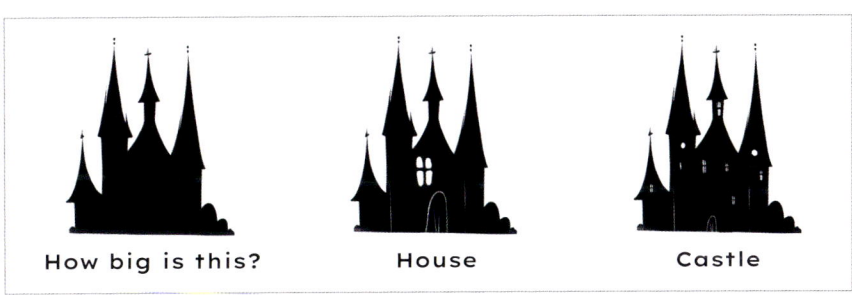

How big is this?   House   Castle

01. See how windows and doors alter our impression of this building?

02. PURPOSEFUL COMPOSITION

Illustrators often need to work quickly to meet deadlines, especially in the production of an animated movie or video game, so I've put together this example of working out a quick architectural environment. The architecture here is not much more than the stacked blocks and doorways we've been discussing since the beginning of this chapter. For visual interest and structure, I threw in some trees, an ornamental pool, and simple light and shadow. Note that there's a specific composition here: I'm leading the viewer to the centerpiece of the architecture as shown. That brings us back to the idea of purpose; I made sure this environment is more than buildings, water, and trees. I made sure it has a central quality of *purpose*.

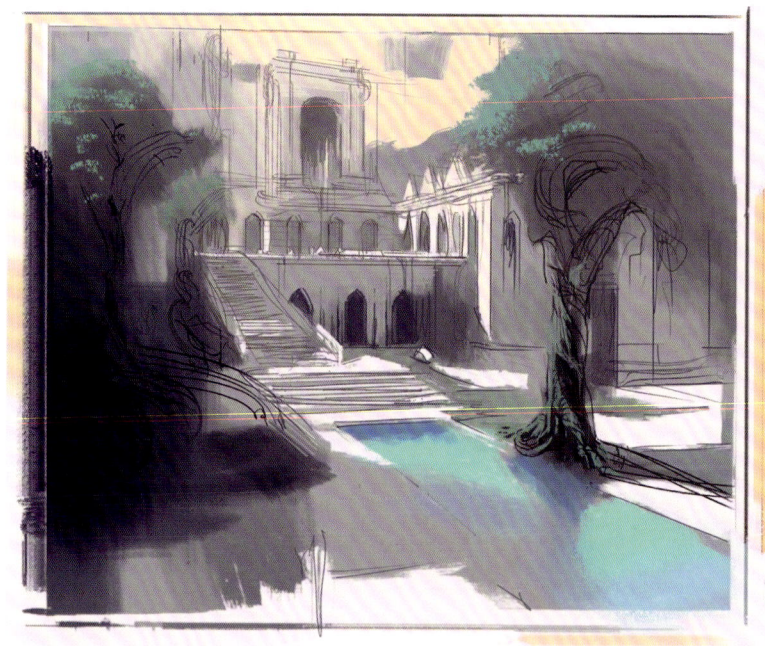

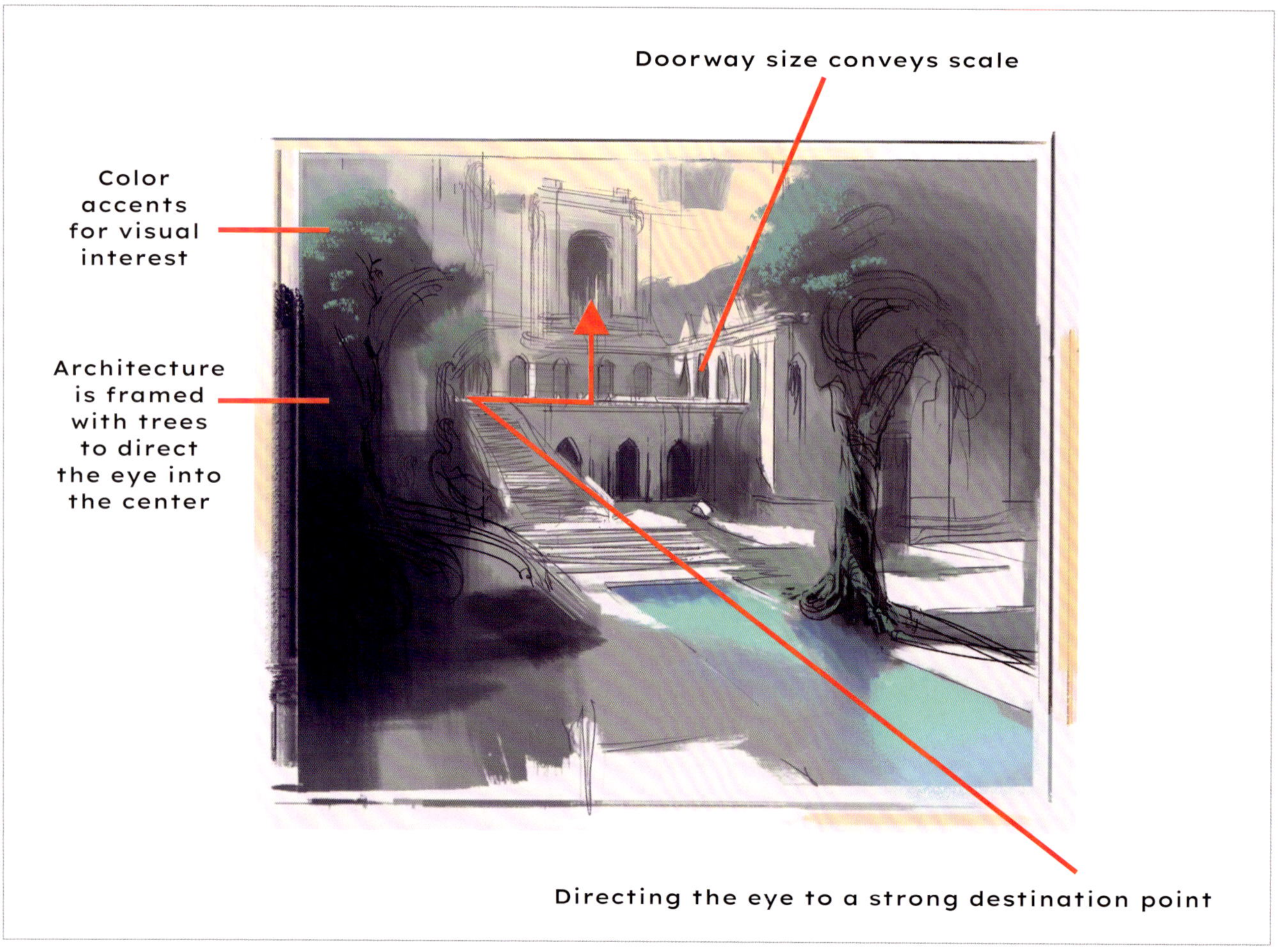

Doorway size conveys scale

Color accents for visual interest

Architecture is framed with trees to direct the eye into the center

Directing the eye to a strong destination point

02. Strong visual choices give this image purpose and direction

03. ANOTHER EXAMPLE

Here I've fleshed out an environment idea that has the same thinking described in the previous image. This time it goes into full color, value, and atmosphere. Its purpose is to convey a boat journey down the canals of a mysterious ancient ruin, with the destination opening up in the distance, and it's a combination of each of the ideas we've been talking about thus far. It has the stylings of the ancient stone architecture found in southern Asia, doorways that give us a sense of the scale, and lighting that emphasizes the purpose of the image.

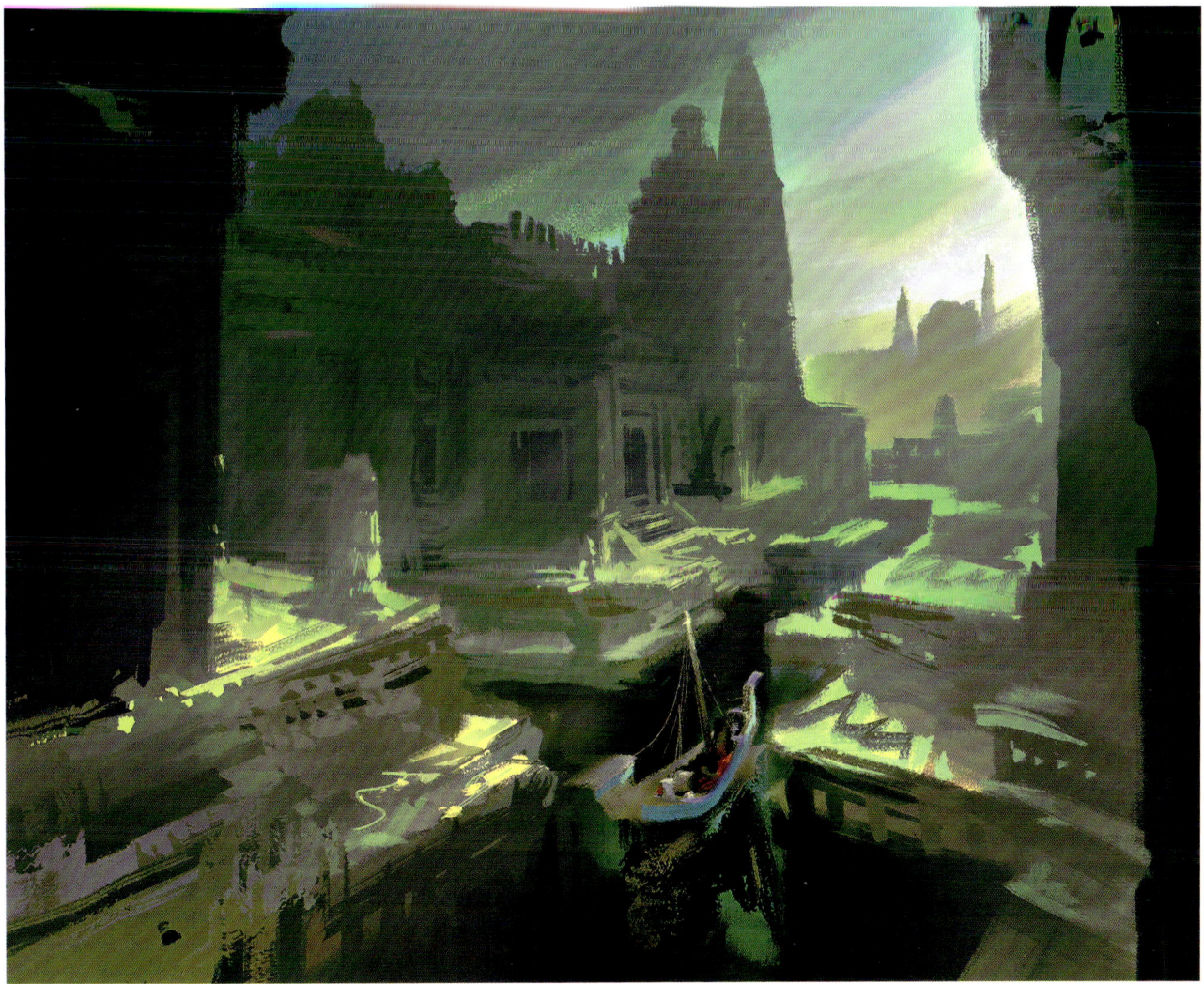

03. This image is more rendered than the previous, but still follows the same principles

IT ALL COMES BACK TO EMOTION

Let's keep our central themes of purpose and emotion going. Here's another batch of buildings, this time designed to indicate emotion. I'm relying on familiar tropes here – our simple elements of shape and line design. Diagonals have more action, sharp triangles are more threatening, rounded shapes are friendlier, and so on. This group is in black and white for the sake of simplicity, but that creates a challenge for us, as plain black silhouettes tend to carry an immediate negative impression. So let's move to color for the next batch of images.

01. COLOR THUMBNAILS

Look at how much more emotion these images carry by virtue of their color choices. Warm colors tend to feel inviting and lively, cool colors may be a bit more mysterious, and high-contrast black-and-whites can seem a bit more dangerous or spooky. Experiment with this and have fun with it. See what qualities of emotion you can create out of a simple architectural silhouette.

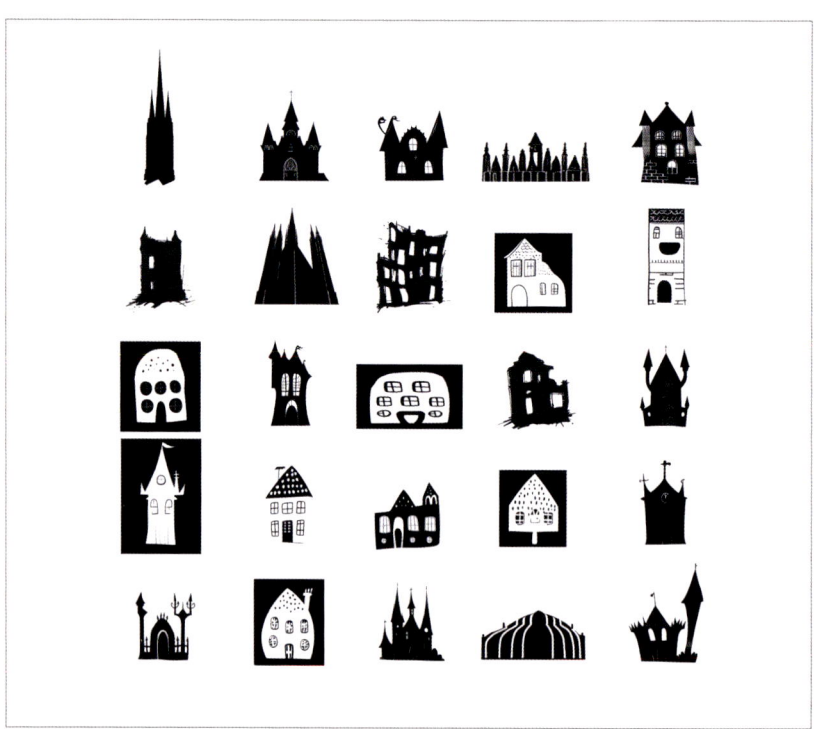

△ Even as thumbnails, these buildings convey distinct qualities of emotion

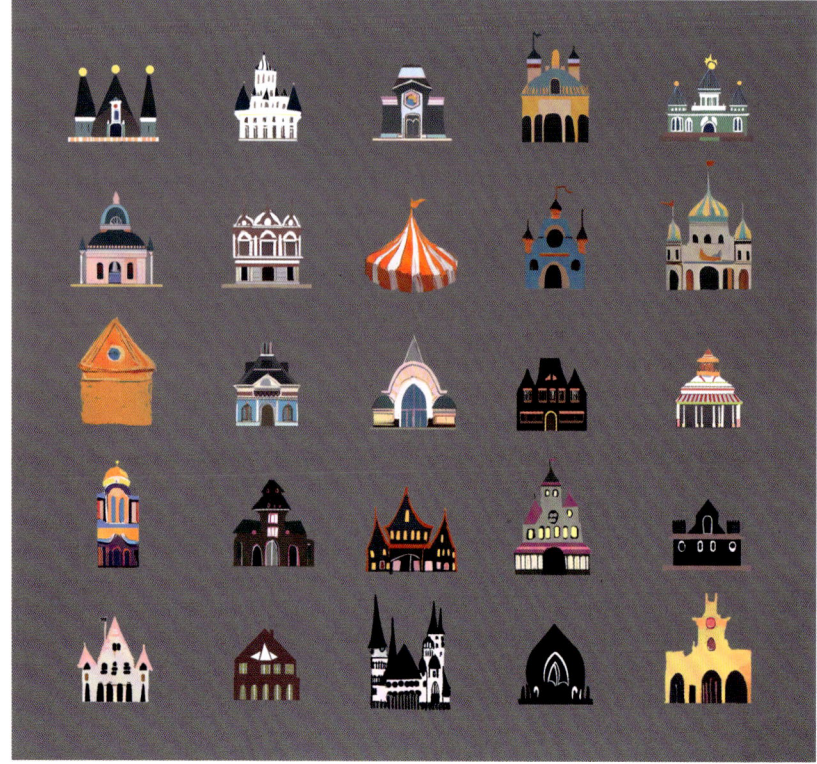

01. Colors imbue these buildings with a stronger emotional presence

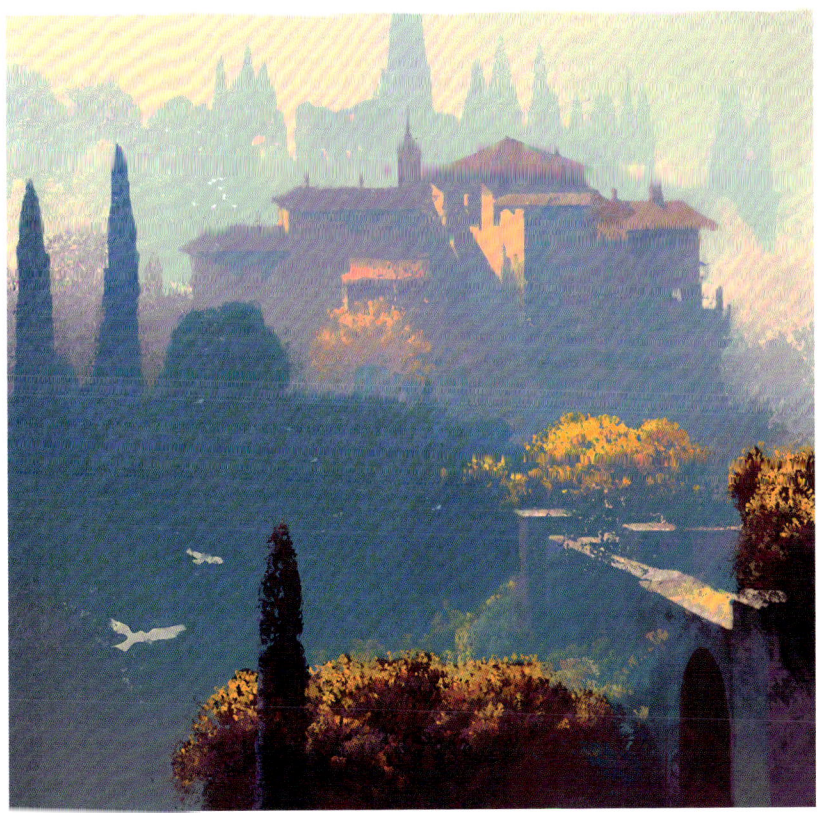

02. Strong silhouette and local color contribute to the Tuscan environment

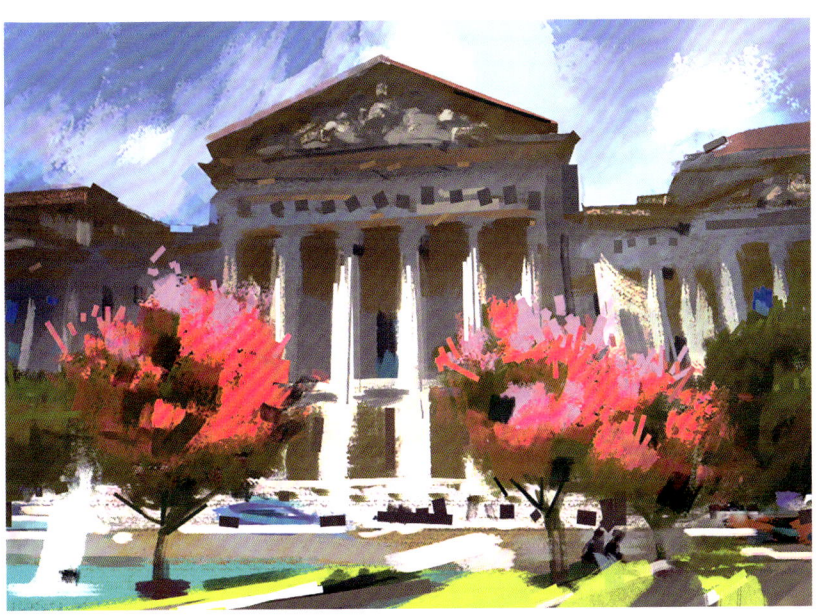

03. The focus here is conveying the bright grandeur of the museum's architecture

02. FLORENCE STUDY

We have a whole chapter on environmental color coming up soon, so I won't jump the gun here, but let me show you this example of applying architectural silhouettes and colors to a full environment. Here's a painting inspired by a trip to Florence. It has full light and shadow but is centered around two color ideas: the local colors and the warms and cools of the light and atmosphere. Our environments are usually a combination of believability and imagination, which is definitely the case for this scene. I chose warm local colors and lighting to grab your attention and pull you to the palazzo in the distance, and I exaggerated the cool atmosphere to accentuate the warmer colors. We design color toward the purpose of our environment. Purpose, purpose, purpose.

03. SMITHSONIAN STUDY

Let's pull it back around to emotion again. Here's a sketch I did of the Smithsonian National Museum of Natural History in Washington, D.C. The architecture comes from the neoclassical period, associated with nation-building, and is expensively designed. It makes the statement that this place is of great importance, of great stability and permanence – all-around just letting you know that 'Hey, we aren't kidding around here.' It was built at the time when the United States was a new nation and was building itself up and communicating its ideals.

So always keep in mind that architecture is meant to communicate. It communicates the ideals of the original builders, and its upkeep (or lack thereof) communicates about its current residents or purpose. And the Smithsonian is well kept-up!

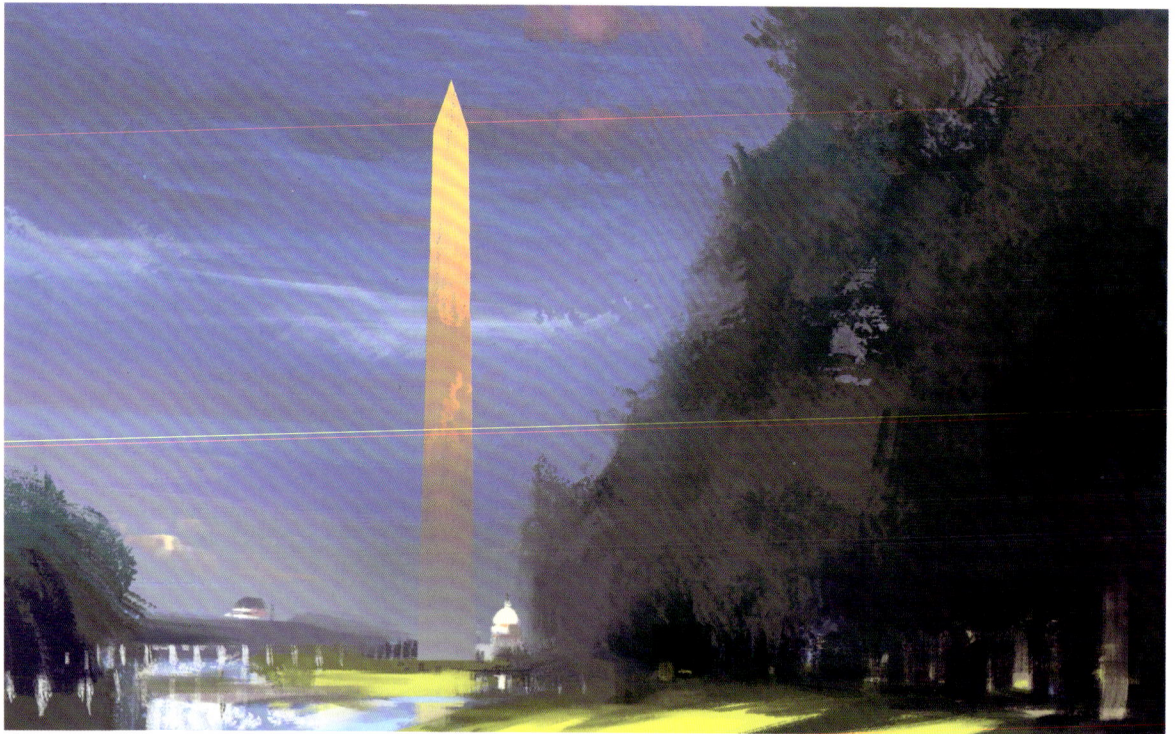

04. Exaggerating real-life qualities accentuates the purpose and presence of the monument

04. MONUMENT STUDY

I promise I'm not turning this chapter into a travelogue, nor is it intended to be a tutorial on sketching from life – I'm hoping that a few real-life examples will set the stage, and then we'll move back into imaginative environments! This is another monument I painted on my trip to Washington, D.C. I don't think it needs much discussion – the purpose of this obelisk is clear. Just note that the lighting and sky weren't like this in real life. I emphasized and exaggerated them to accentuate the purpose and emotion of the environment.

05. STYLIZED CITYSCAPE

Now we'll bring the same thinking to this invented and wildly exaggerated cityscape. I did the same thing here as in the previous image, emphasizing the height and breadth of the skyscrapers as they proudly rise up into the sky out of the darkness of the city below. Even though it's a blue-sky environment, I pushed it into quite a dark blue to make the warm highlights of the buildings shine. I planned the purpose and the emotion of this study before I began and then threw everything I knew at making those two things happen.

06. DARK & THREATENING

Let's stick with tall and engaging architecture, but with a completely changed emotion now. By adding sharpened shapes to the key building in the background, and spooky atmosphere and lighting throughout, we have a completely different mood and emotion than in the previous environments.

> If an architectural element needs to stand out, don't shy away from contrast. If the architecture is light and warm, make its surroundings dark and blue. Don't shy away from contrast design because it's not 'real'. In our line of work, it's how the audience feels that is the reality we target.

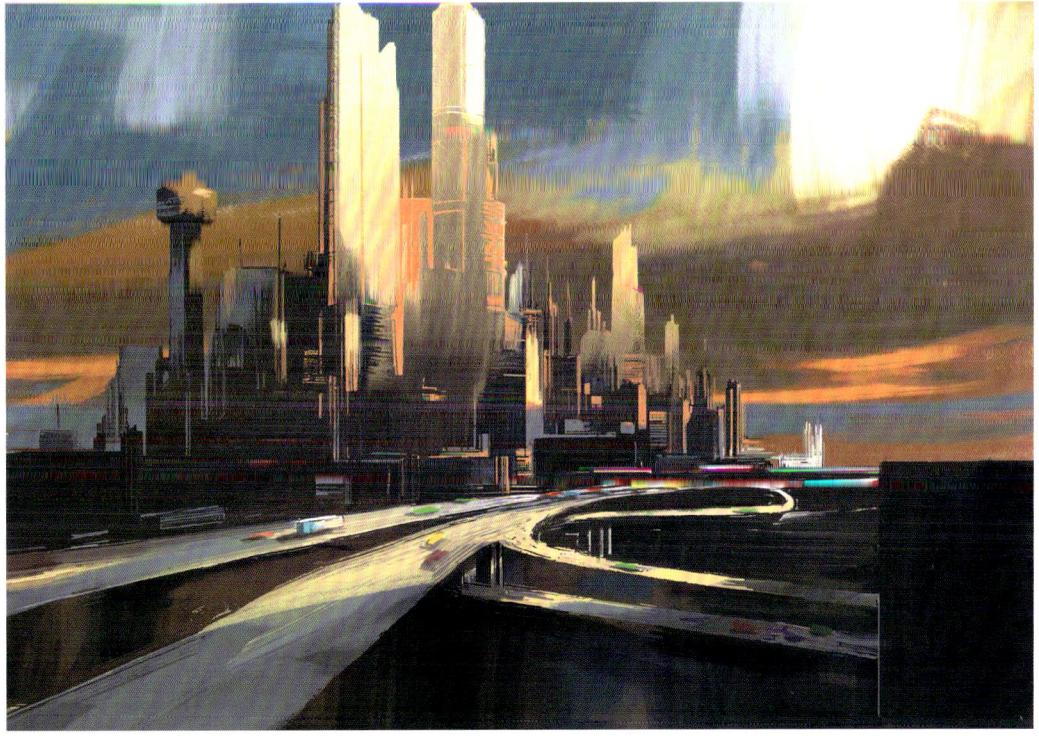

05. Heightened color and contrast make this city scene feel vast and dramatic

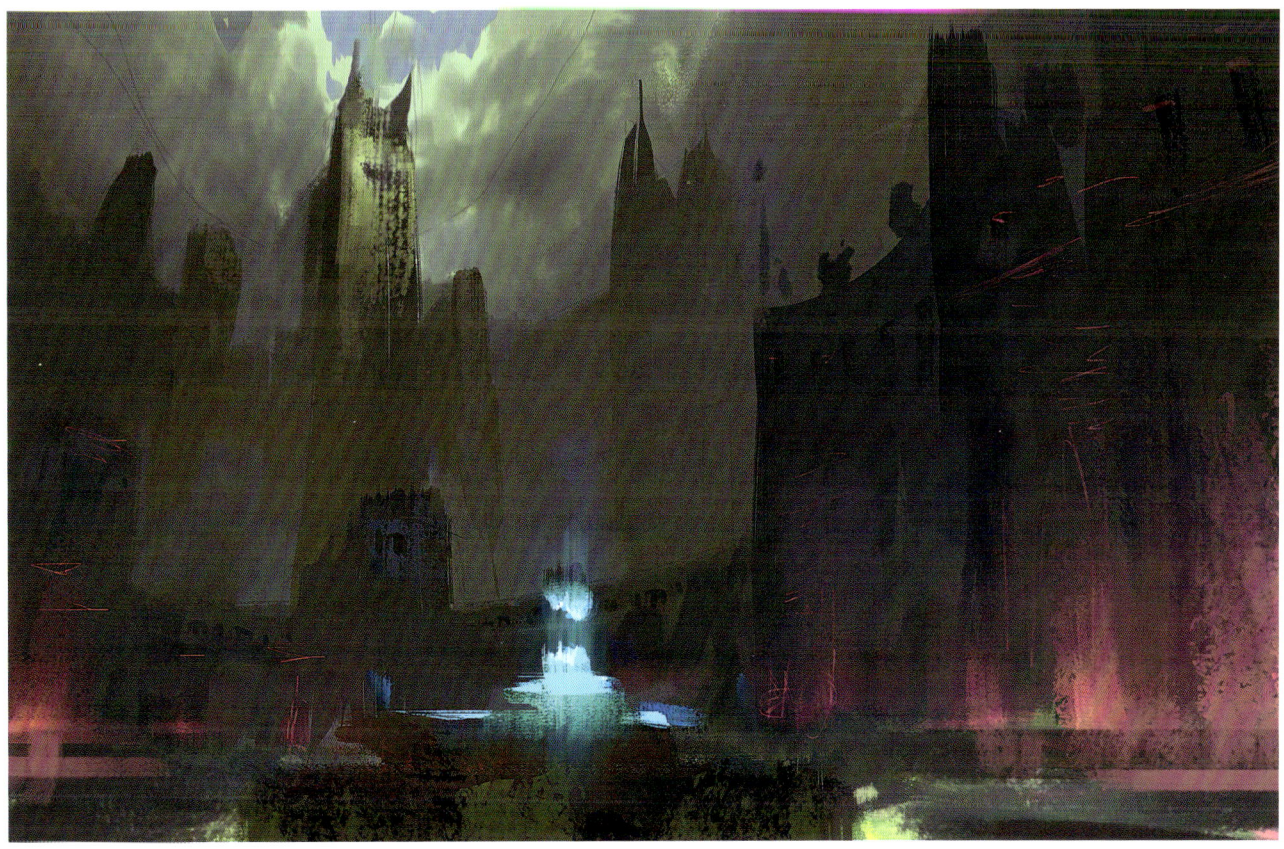

06. Sharp silhouettes and red up-lighting give this location a hellish menace

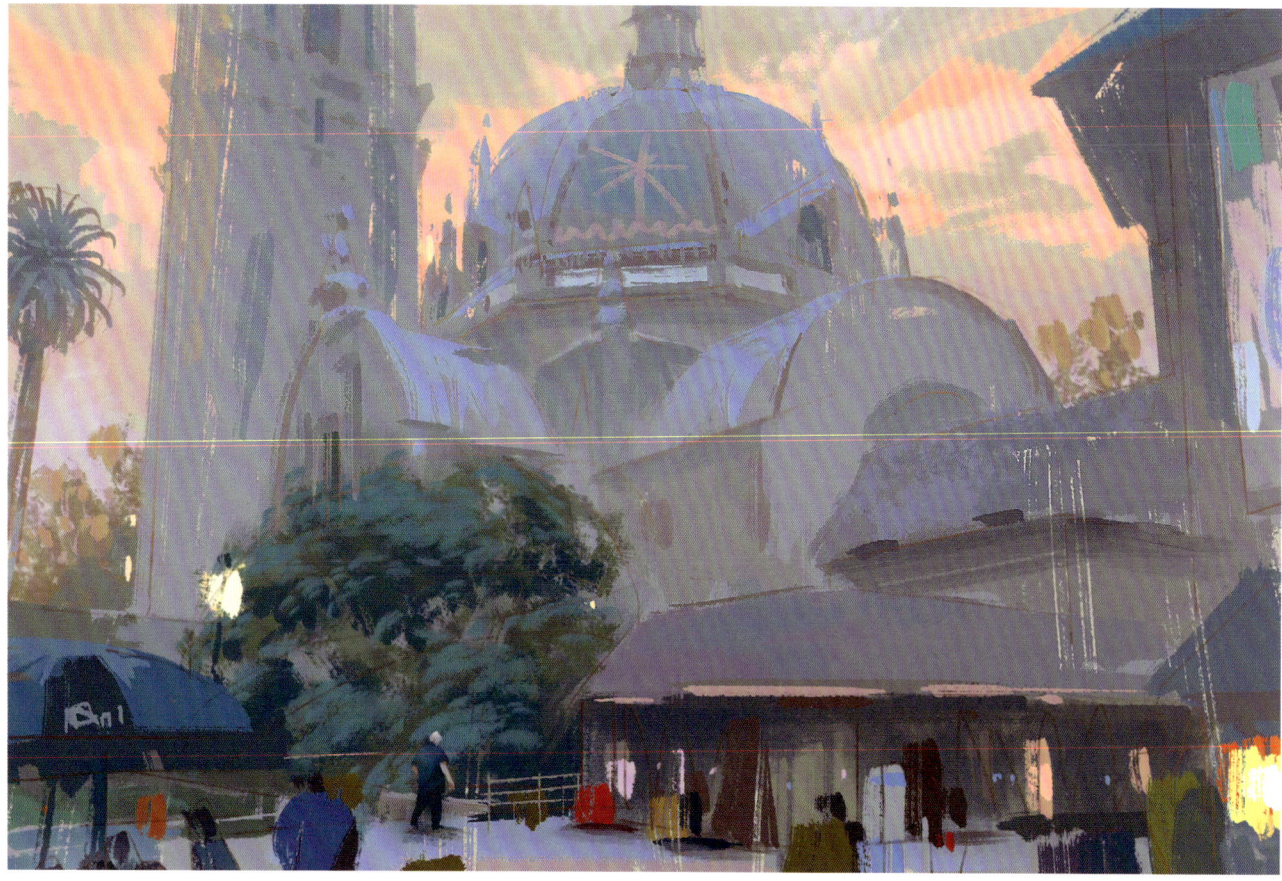

07. Round shapes and a soft, warm glow make this location feel appealing and welcoming

07. WARM & INVITING

There's a bit of enhanced atmosphere and lighting again in this architectural study, but I designed it in such a way as to be inviting rather than frightening. This was done by emphasizing more naturalistic warms and cools combined with more rounded, inviting shapes.

08. EERIE & DECAYING

We can't have too much happiness, though, so let's get back to spooky to prove we can do it whenever we need to. Here's a decayed environment with crumbling architecture and a few triangular rooftops thrown in as well. The way I tweaked the color palette is especially important – I pushed the shadows into less natural greens, with plenty of sour yellow-ocher throughout. The green water is very exaggerated, as is the atmospheric purple in the distance. It's only the orange accents of the trees that keep this scene from being too 'icky'.

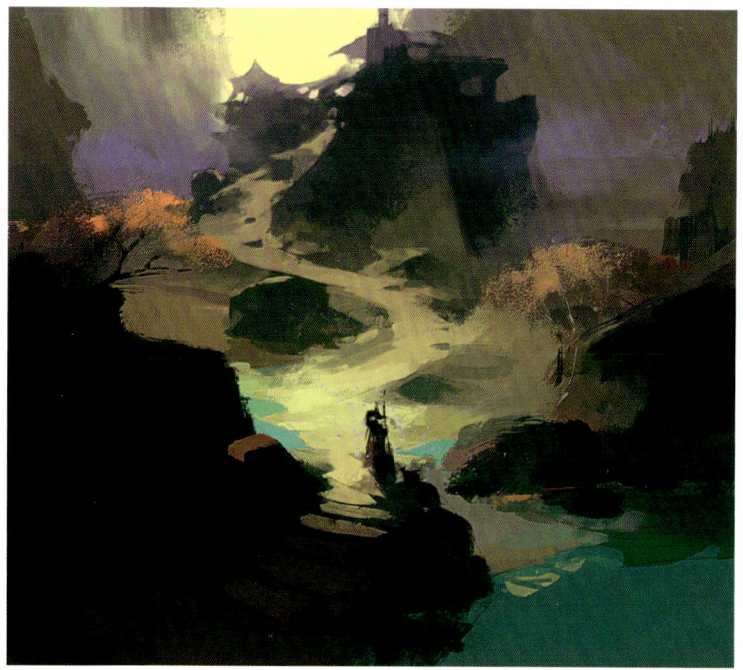

08. Vivid greens and dark yellows make this place feel creepy and poisonous

MAKE US FEEL IT!

'A big heavy stone block? Why is this in a chapter about architecture?' Well, that's exactly the right question, because this is indeed a heavy stone block. Remember, everything we design should visually communicate what the subject is. So if you need to render a very heavy stone block, it should sink into the ground to immediately convey its extraordinary weight. Our architecture should do the same – not necessarily sink into the ground, but it should immediately communicate information about itself.

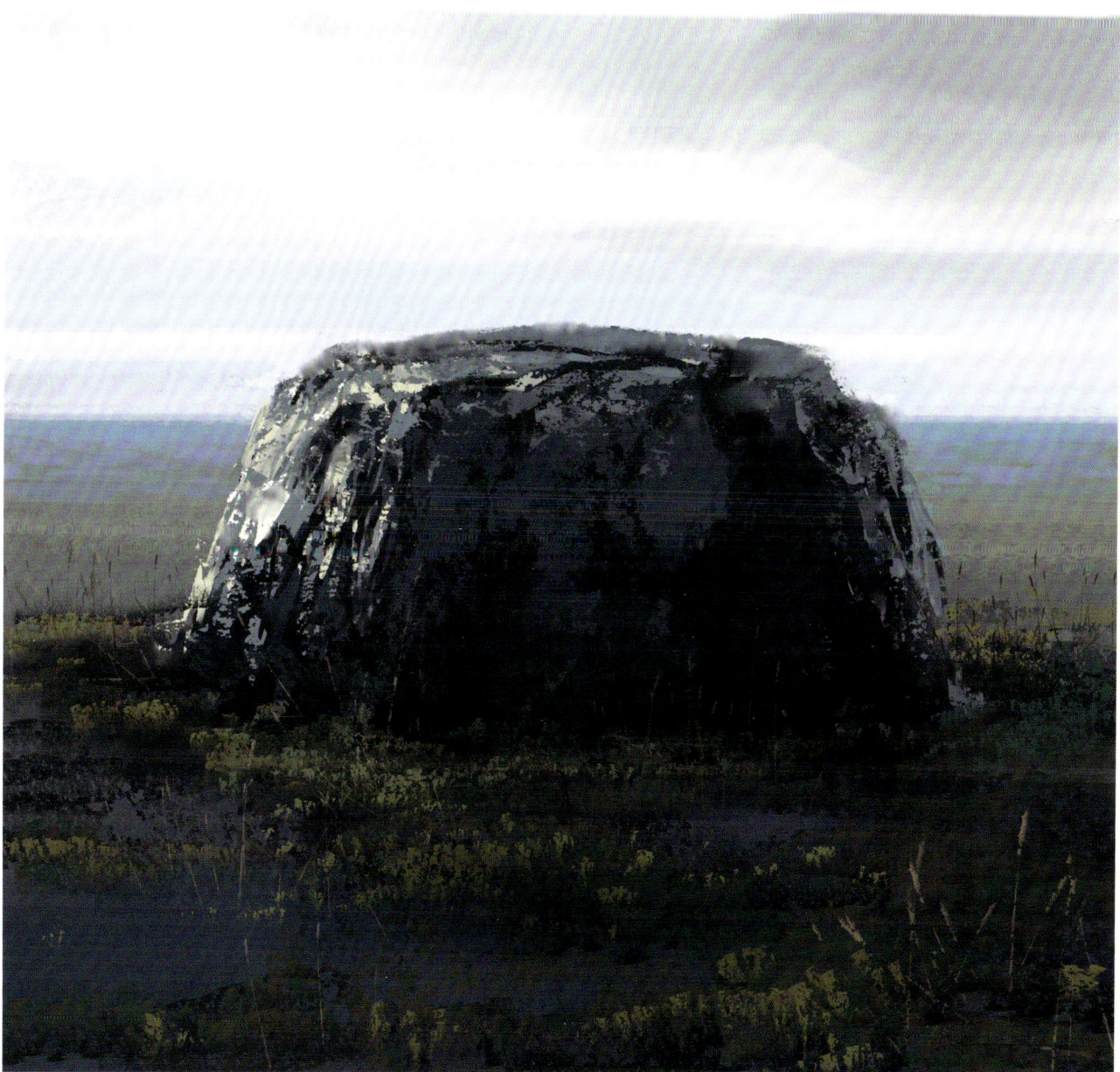

△ We instantly understand the weight of this huge stone

01. STURDY LONGHOUSE

Let's keep pushing our architecture to powerfully communicate. This Viking-like structure insists that it is the sturdiest building you could ever make out of natural materials. Just like the previous stone block was heavy, this building is *sturdy*. You could build this thing right on the fjords of Norway and throw wind and rain, sea and tsunami at it, and it will stand firm. This is very much like our approach to architecture back when I was working on DreamWorks' *How to Train Your Dragon*. We had Viking characters that could withstand everything nature could throw at them and, on top of that, they had to survive the attack of dragons! If you have a chance to watch that series, you'll see that the character of the people is displayed by the architecture they build.

02. STONE KEEP

Here's another display of permanence, since I'm having a great time with this. This structure is a simple cylinder but is designed to communicate purpose and emotion. It's a winter keep built with stones quarried at the root of mighty mountains – it can withstand all the weight of snow and tempest that Mother Nature can throw at it.

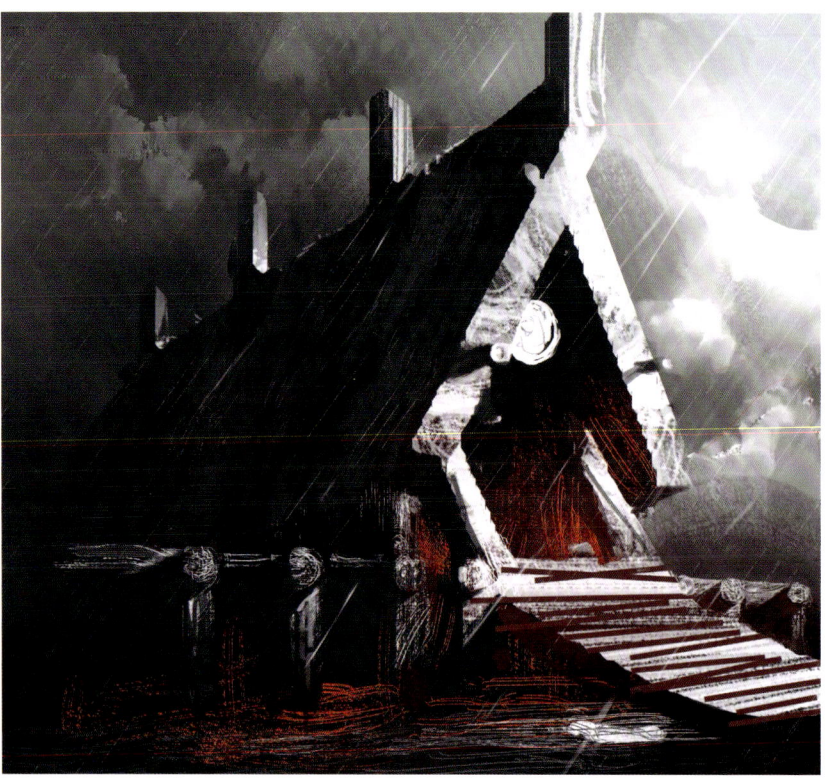

01. This building feels strong, rugged, and immovable in structure

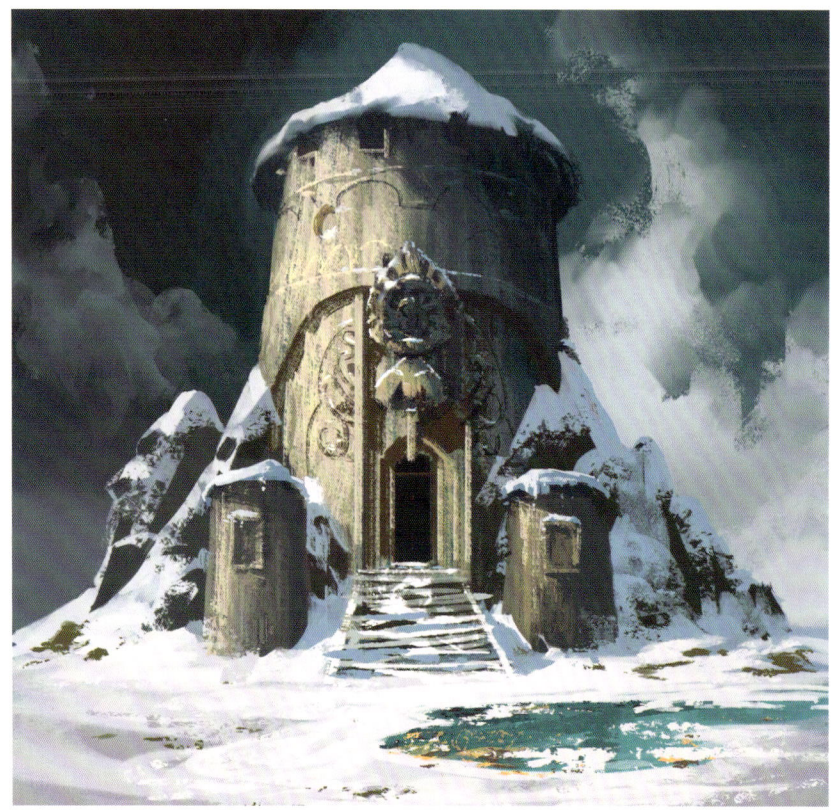

02. This example looks powerfully sturdy, too, but uses very different shapes

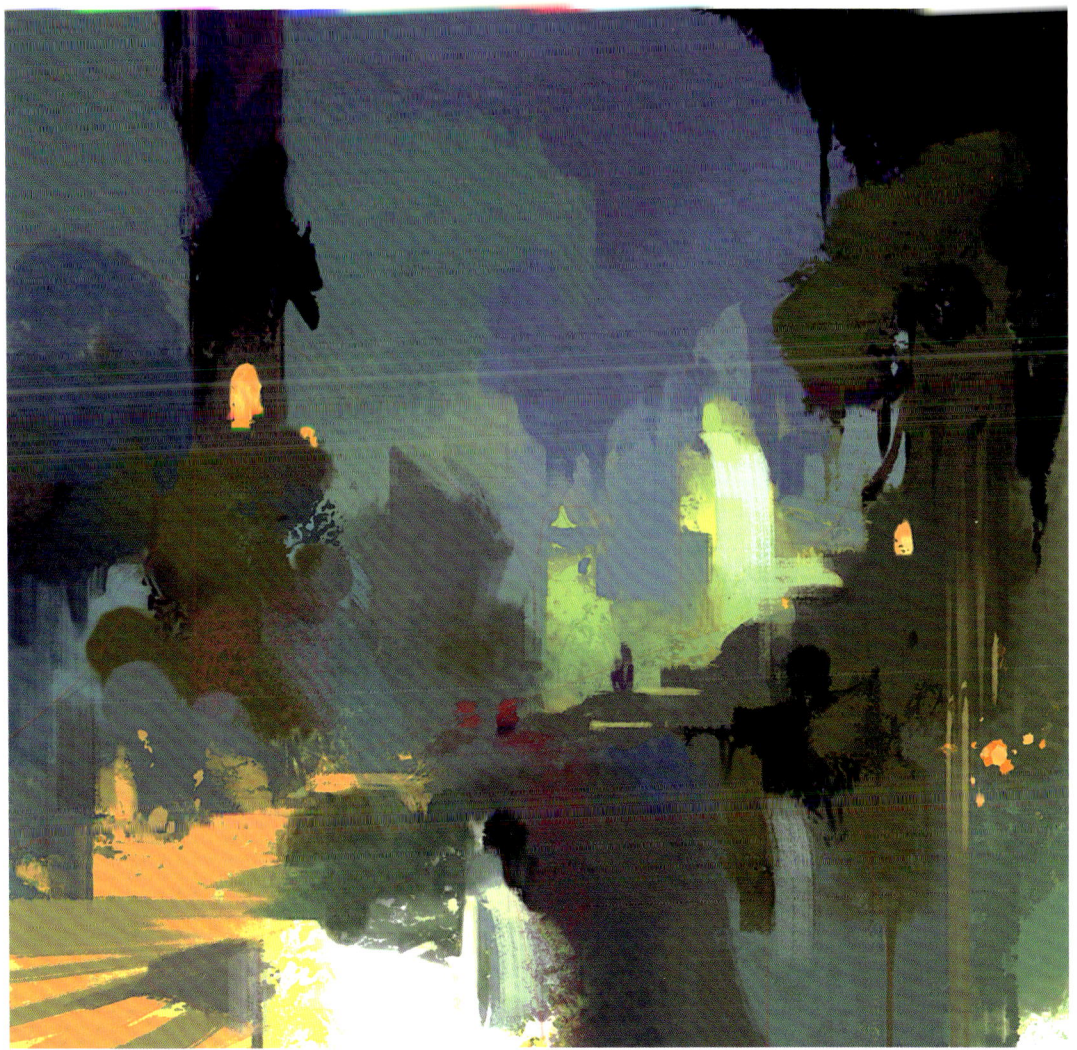

03. This environment feels both built and organic – the two qualities are completely blended

03. BUILDINGS & NATURE

Many years ago, I got a phone call that I've thought about a lot, because it was about a great opportunity and I wasn't able to take advantage of it. The phone call was from an art director I had worked with at DreamWorks, and he was now calling me from the other side of the world in New Zealand. He was starting as an art director on the *Lord of the Rings* movies, and he was inviting me to come join him and work on the project! What an amazing opportunity, and what a shame that I wasn't able to accept it. I was on a three-year contract with another studio and I wasn't able to get out of it.

When I finally saw the first movie, I thought it was beautifully designed, which was upsetting because obviously they did just fine without me! Of particular beauty was the Elvish city of Rivendell. Not only did it look great, but it communicated just the right thing. You see, the majority of people who watched the movies had never

read the books, and didn't have the extensive backstory of who the Elvish people were. They didn't know that they were an ancient race of people who were wise and at one with their natural environment. The genius of the architectural design wasn't just its ornate organic quality, but also how you couldn't tell where the natural environment ended and the built architecture began. That transition was seamless, and that quality instantly told us who the Elvish people were: we immediately felt that they were a people at one with nature.

Let me now get to the sketch shown above. It was quick and simple, but I was thinking about this quality of a made environment where you can't tell where nature ends and the buildings begin. I was just having a little fun with the idea of a meaningful repetition of organic-looking structures and weaving them into a composition.

04. Another take on combining nature with built elements

04. CAVERN DWELLERS

Here's another environment intending the same blend of nature and architecture, this time with stone rather than foliage. My intention here was to create the feeling that we're inside some kind of giant cave where the people have built up the stalagmites into dwellings, and now there's a thriving community illuminated by fires and torches.

THE ROLE OF FOLIAGE

Let's use this environment as a reminder of the importance of foliage. Architecture is almost always groomed with foliage, so it's an important consideration along with any architectural design. Always ask yourself, 'Is this foliage highly ornamental and groomed, or natural and grown in?' For this scene, I wanted to create the contrast of a clean, vertical building rising up out of a surrounding chaos of foliage. The next image will go much further with this idea.

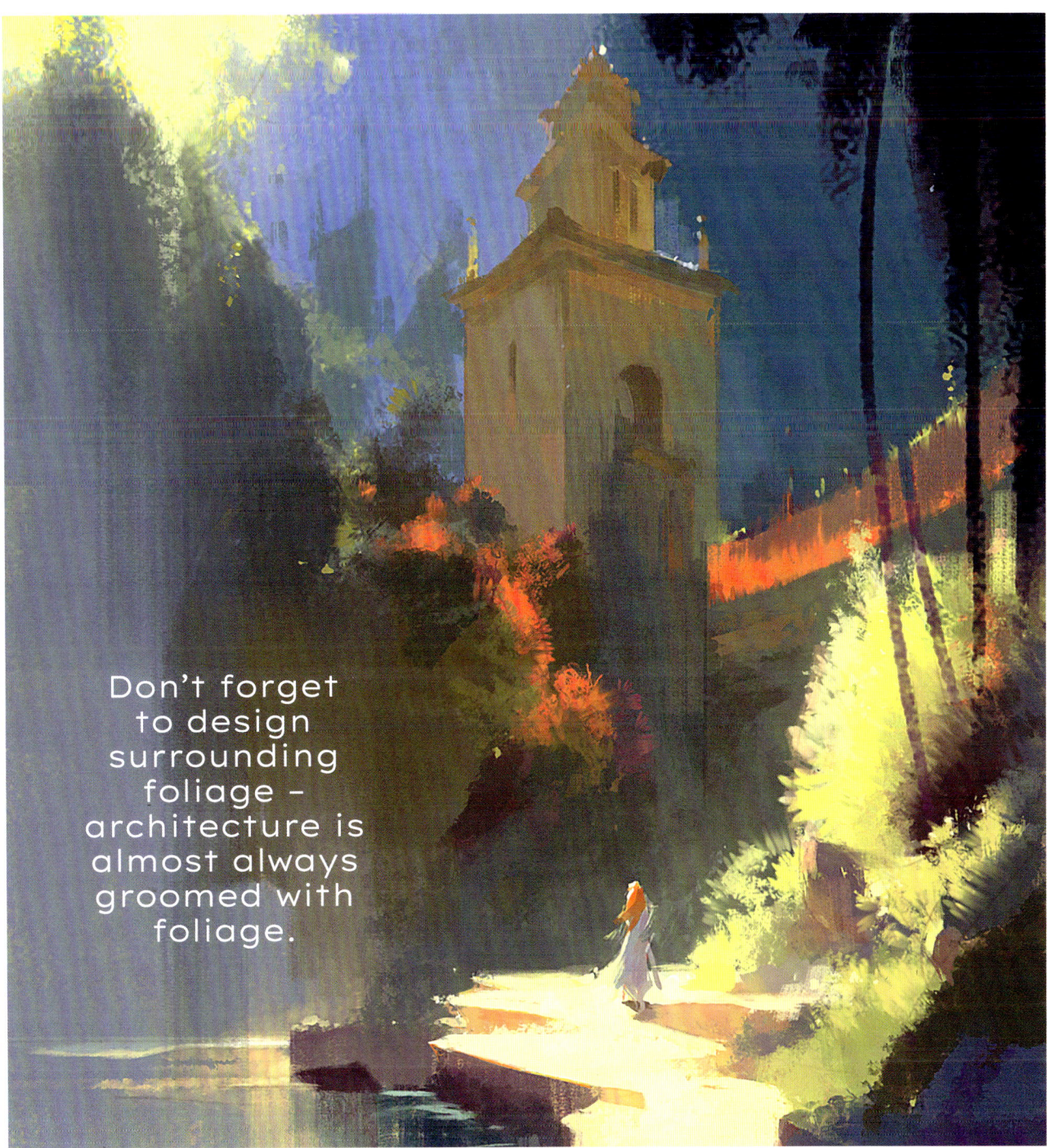

Don't forget to design surrounding foliage – architecture is almost always groomed with foliage.

△ The architecture contrasts with the shapes and textures of lush foliage below

01. EVERGLADES

This ruined wooden structure was inspired by a trip to the Florida Everglades, where you would occasionally see an abandoned structure out in the swamps. I wanted the scene to be attractive, with a sparkle of sunshine, but leave no doubt that the building had been derelict for many years. That's made obvious by the building's state of decay, and even more so by the way that foliage is overgrowing it, slowly taking it over year by year.

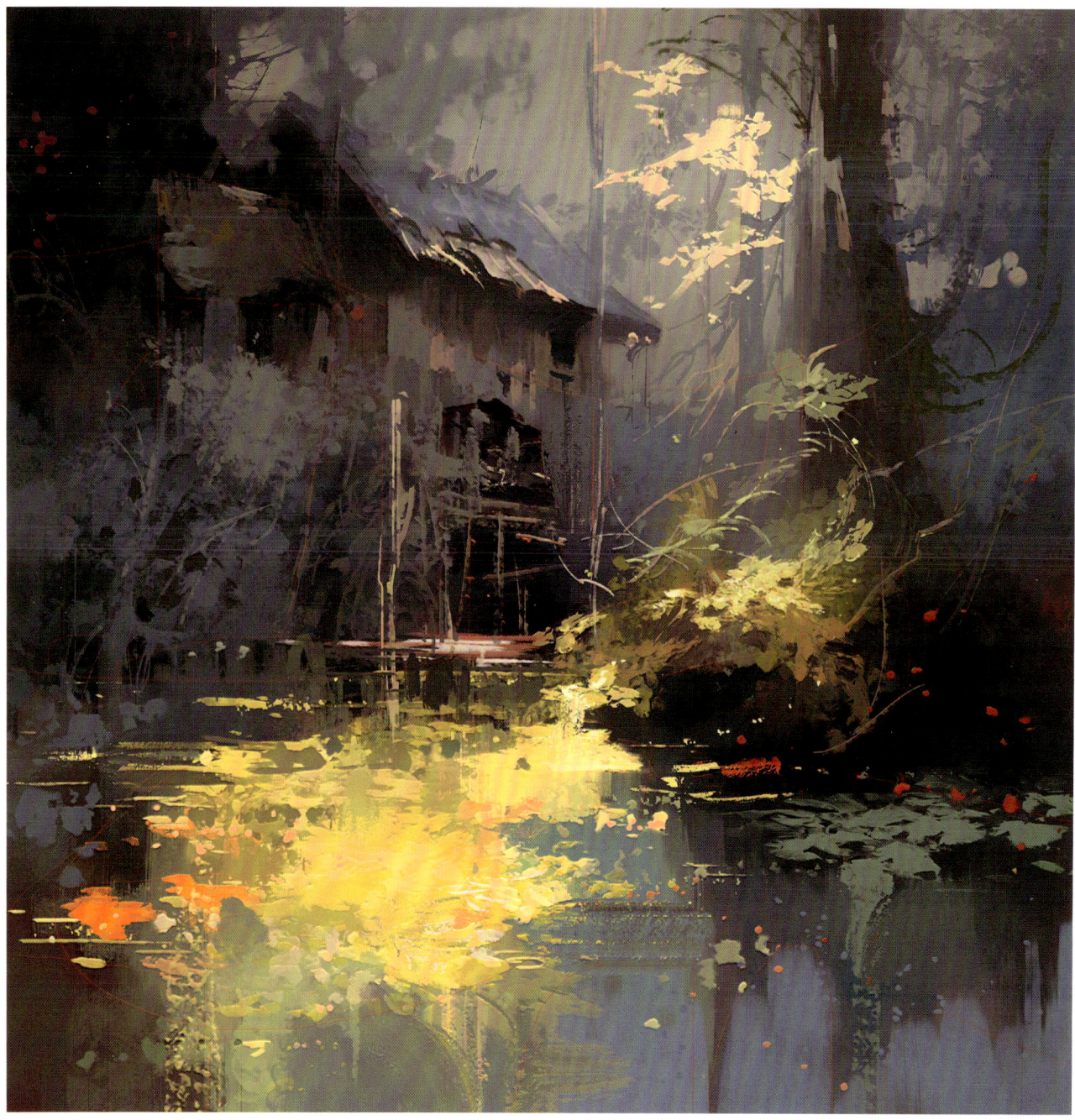

01. This location feels sunlit and appealing, yet still derelict and overgrown

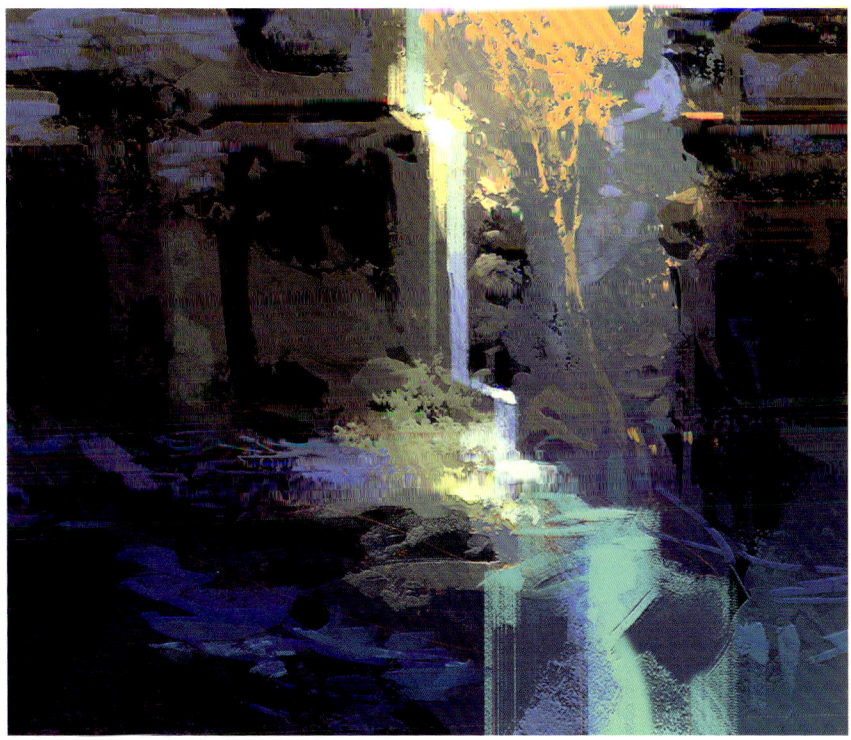

02. Enhance reference with your imagination
to add intriguing twists and details

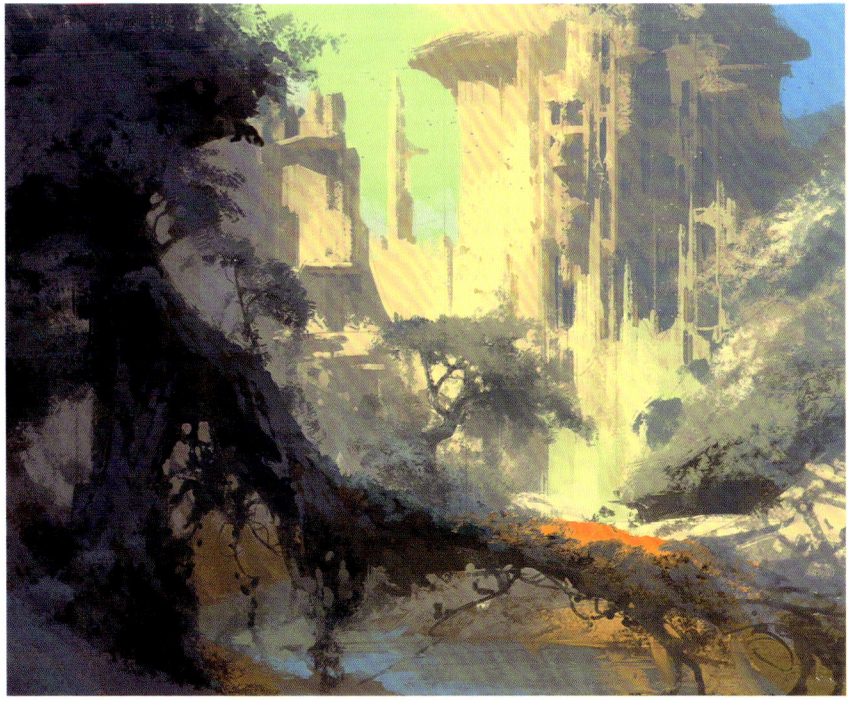

03. Foliage still applies on this alien world!

02. TEMPLE RUINS

Have you ever seen photos of the ancient ruins in Cambodia? They're the ones where banyan trees grow right up out of crumbling stone buildings, with roots intertwining throughout. If you're not familiar, look up the ancient temples of Ta Prohm. This is a place I got to travel to way back in the nineties, when Cambodia had opened up to tourism after a very difficult history. I was utterly amazed. It may well be the most intriguing trip I've ever made.

Here's a sketch I did digitally many years later, looking at some of my photos. Was there really a waterfall coming down the side of one of the buildings? Nope. But I needed a cyan-green accent to make this picture work, and I needed an exotic quality of visual interest along with all the texture and foliage, so I took the artistic liberty and put it in. My point is that architecture can do, and be, anything that serves our particular needs. Let your imagination run wild!

03. ANOTHER PLANET

OK, green sky, weird architecture, unfamiliar environment... Nathan must be trying to take us to an alien planet again. Yeah, I probably am.

ARCHITECTURE AS CHARACTER

Here's a fun and useful idea: architecture can be treated the same as character design! Character designers are great not just because they draw well, but most of all because they imbue their characters with telling information. A well-designed character is often one whose personality we understand at a glance without any written or acted explanation. This whole chapter I've been begging you to do the same thing with architecture – to imbue it with visual information. I believe that every piece of architecture we design should be given at least a little of this kind of consideration. It won't always be appropriate, but when it is, it will be a home run for you. So ask yourself, 'What's the gesture and the attitude of the architecture? How is my audience meant to feel emotionally about it?'

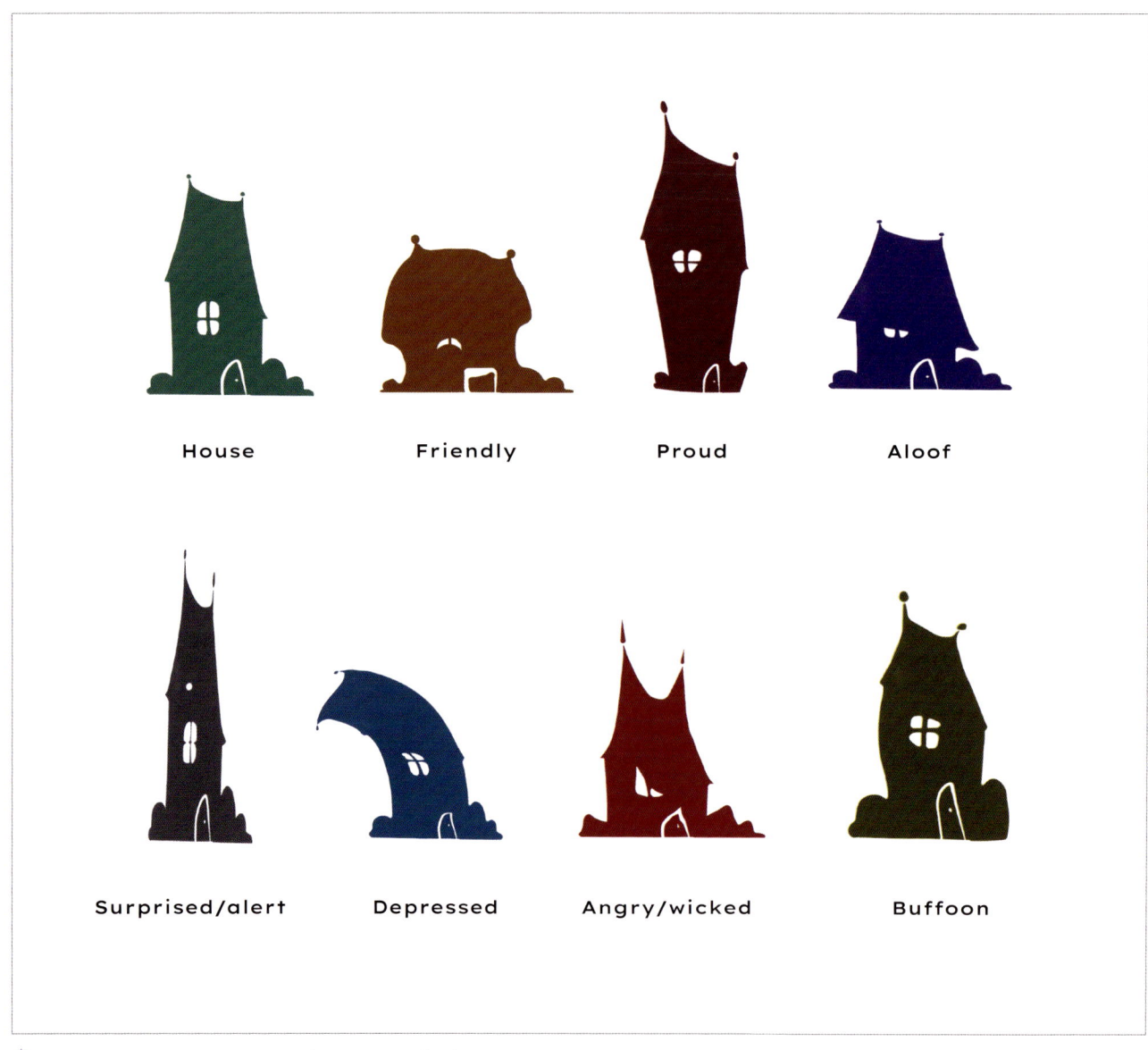

House   Friendly   Proud   Aloof

Surprised/alert   Depressed   Angry/wicked   Buffoon

△ Architecture can be imbued with personality in the same way as characters

Architecture can be treated the same as character design!

PROOF OF CONCEPT

Let's take a couple of interior scenes that feature a staircase, and give them two completely separate emotional qualities of character.

The first is designed with local colors, lighting, and golden ornamentation that suggest a place of great wealth, comfort, and abundance. The second staircase is something very different; its creepy styling and color palette feel more like a road to ruin. Like nothing good will come from a climb to the top of this staircase.

The differences between the two are obvious, but let me point out the rounded quality of the first image and the sharp, pointed quality of the second. The creepy staircase image has the quality of decay in its rendering and uses an exaggerated three-point perspective to give the spatial impression that the walls are oppressively leaning in on you. Emotion, emotion, emotion.

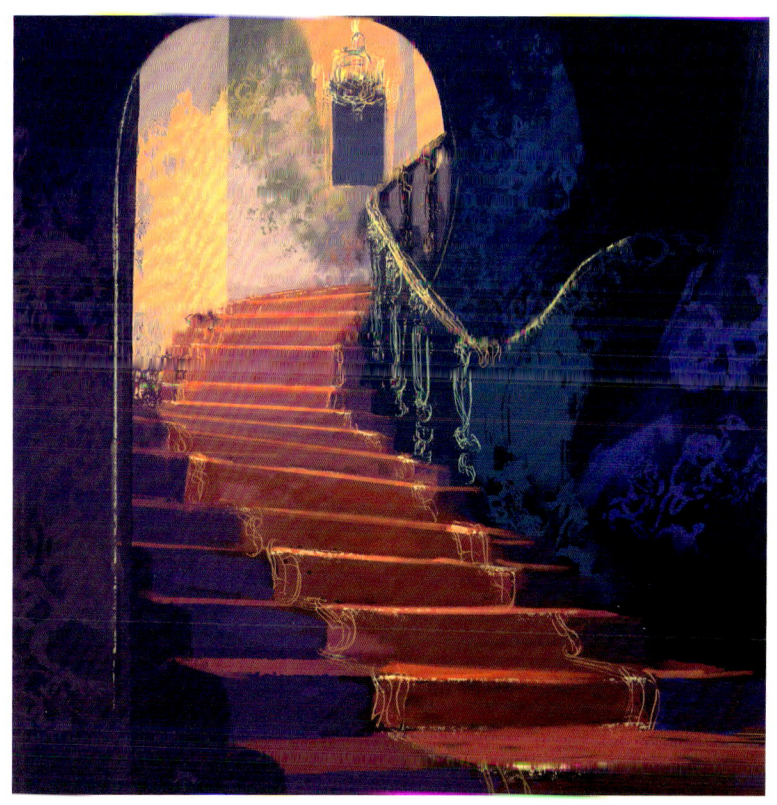

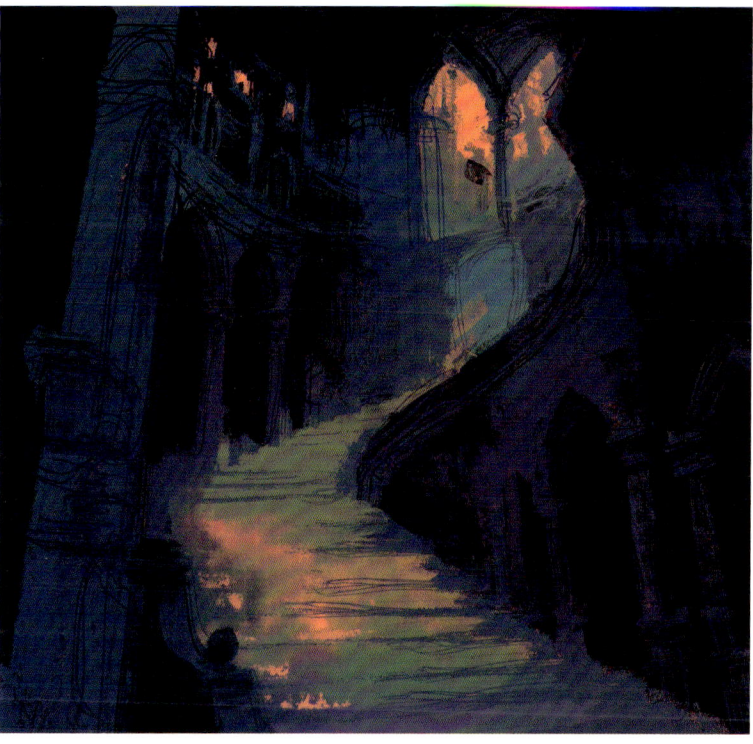

△ Two scenes with very similar architecture but very different emotion qualities

DEMONSTRATION: EPIC DESERT PALACE

Here's the desert palace we studied at the beginning of the chapter (see page 138). As promised, I've broken it down step by step for you.

01. PERSPECTIVE GRID

The first step is to set up a perspective that will best serve the image. I used the word 'epic' in the title, so I'd better deliver on that quality. I can do so by carefully placing the eye-level line as discussed in the previous chapter on space (page 110). The eye-level line is low in the picture plane to give the effect of looking up at these vast vertical structures.

02. STACKING BLOCKS

The process of constructing the architecture is exactly what I described earlier in the chapter – it's not much more than stacking blocks. There is a quality of purpose taking place here, though; the central area will be most important, so I place a more intricate variety of shapes there to draw our interest. Note that I also create a big gap in the ground plane below the city, also located in the center. This is to grab our attention and pull us in, to reinforce the central area's interest.

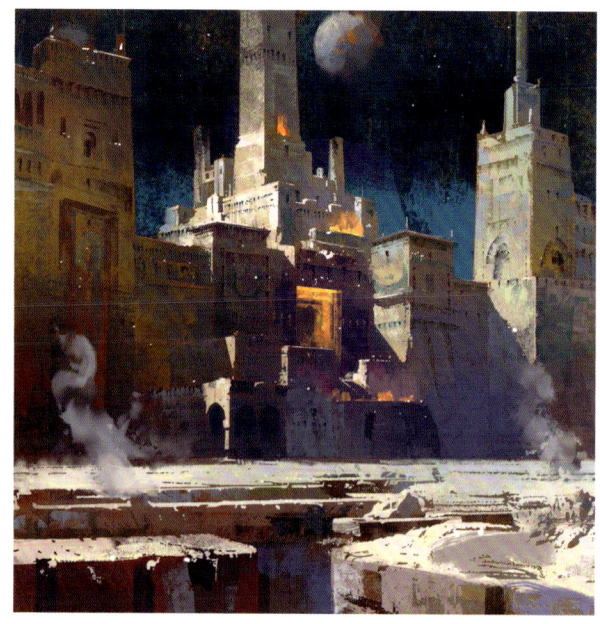

△ Let's get into the process behind this image we saw earlier

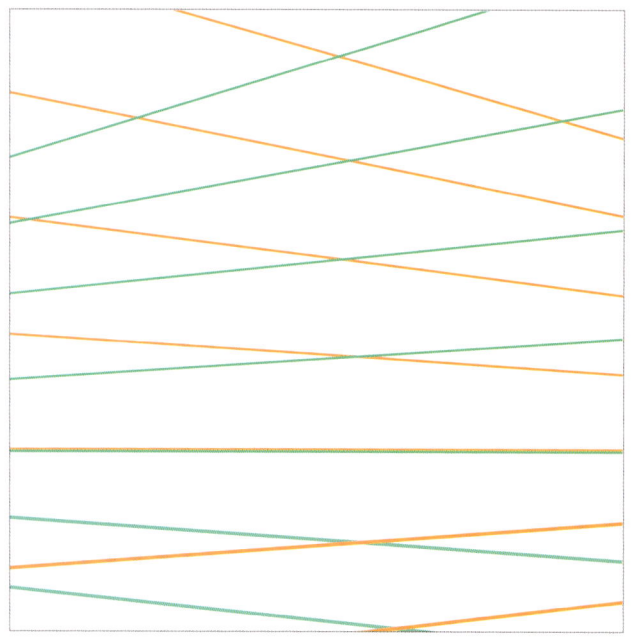

01. A low eye-level line will make the buildings feel vast and impressive

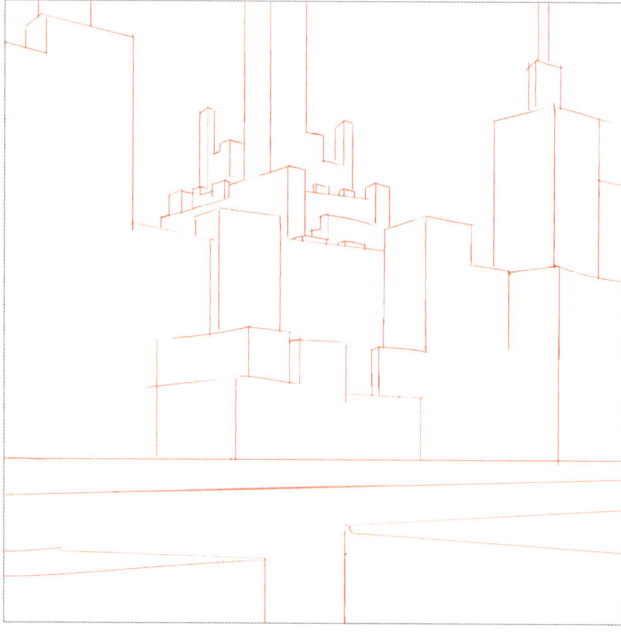

02. The blocks are simple, but the focal area still has more detail

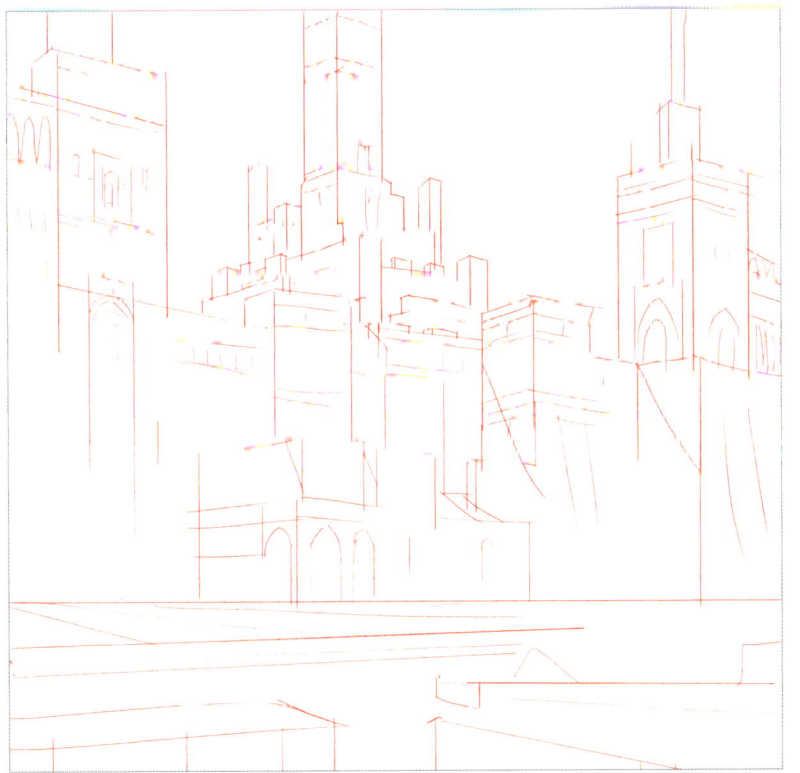

03. The vast scale of this palatial building is now becoming clear

03. WINDOWS & DOORS

We're now ready for a little detail work, primarily windows and doorways, plus a little ornamentation. Remember that windows and doorways are, in most cases, the most important elements for depicting purpose and scale in architecture.

04. BACKGROUND COLOR

A very simple step here, but highly useful: I carefully choose a grounding color for the background. The background color choice depends on the needs of each particular environment you create. In this case, the architecture will be primarily in shadow, so I choose a shadowy version of the local color of the stone building blocks and ground.

04. A deep red-brown color will serve the rest of the painting well

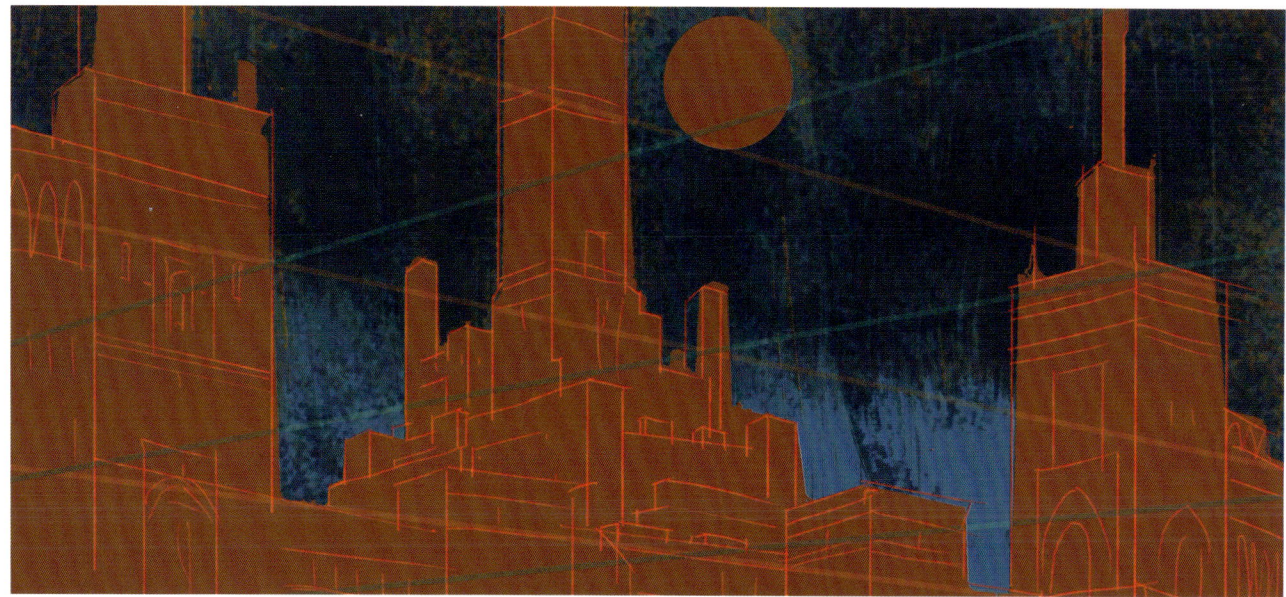

05. The value of the buildings will be a little tricky, so placing the sky first is helpful

05. ADDING THE SKY

Another simple but valuable step: laying in the general color and value of the sky. There is no rule that one should do the sky first, or work back to front – once again, that would be determined by the needs of the environment. In this case, my architecture will be forming a silhouette that's lighter than the sky, even though the building is a shadow value. Establishing the sky first will help the architecture in both light and shadow to group together as one structural subject. It will give the environment clarity.

06. HUE & VALUE

Next up is the addition of hue and value variations in the stone. The upper areas of the buildings are warmed with bounce light from the direct light that will be painted into the ground shortly. Why is the bounce light way up there and not closer to the ground? We can't see the cast shadows on the ground from this vantage point, but we can see that the light only hits the ground starting a way out from the buildings – so there would be no bounce light at the palace's base. And why are the darker values so blue when the local color of this stone is warm? It's because atmospheric cools would accumulate in areas not influenced by the warm bounce light. Once again, we want an epic quality of scale here. The buildings are very distant and yet still huge in the picture frame.

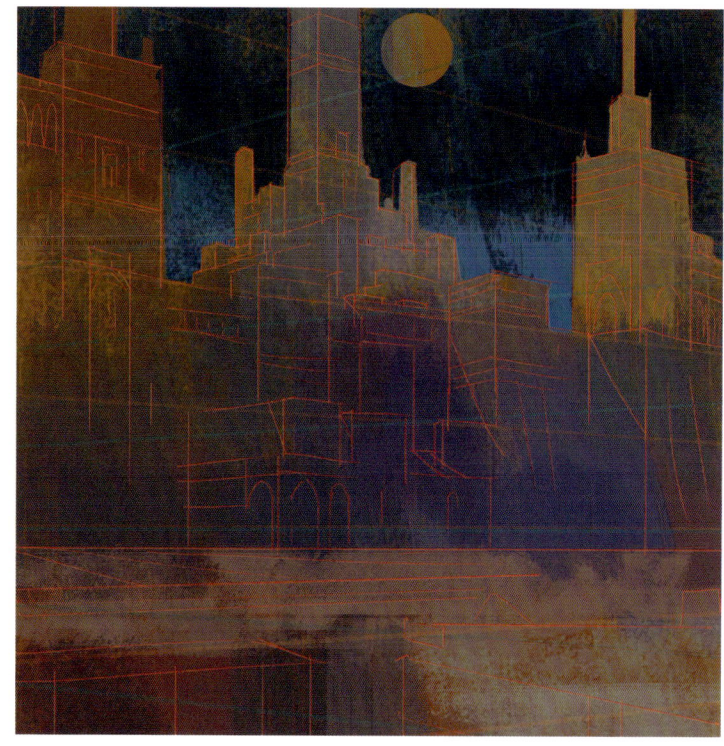

06. Cool shadows will make the palace feel distant, emphasizing its vast scale

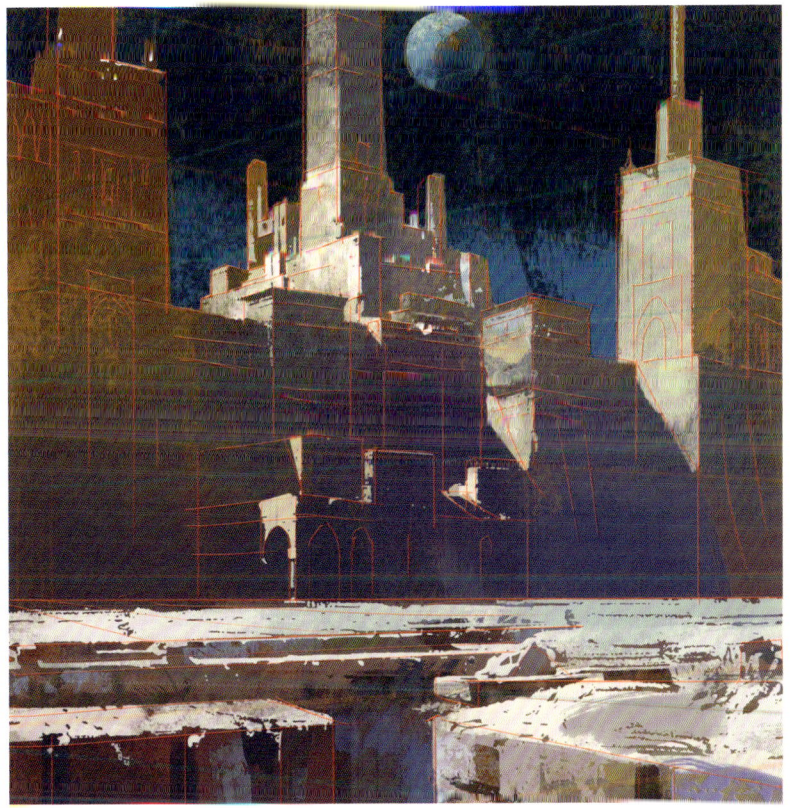

07. LIGHTING

And now for one of my favorite parts: adding the masses of light. This building is natural stone, so I want subtle variations of value and temperature in the light, but the values still need to be similar enough to have a strong quality of grouping. It's as simple as lighting up rectangles, indicating where the side planes are in light while the front planes remain in shadow. I've chosen a roughly 45-degree angle for the light, so I guesstimate how shadows will fall across adjacent blocks at that angle.

08. DETAILING

Time for detail work, and by now you know the drill: concentrate on doors, windows, and important ornamentation. At the same time, be careful not to get so aggressive with the rendering that it breaks up the simple grouping of the shadow mass. I've been working toward a clearly grouped quality for the massive architecture, and I don't want to ruin that now!

07. Only the side planes are lit, casting shadows at an angle

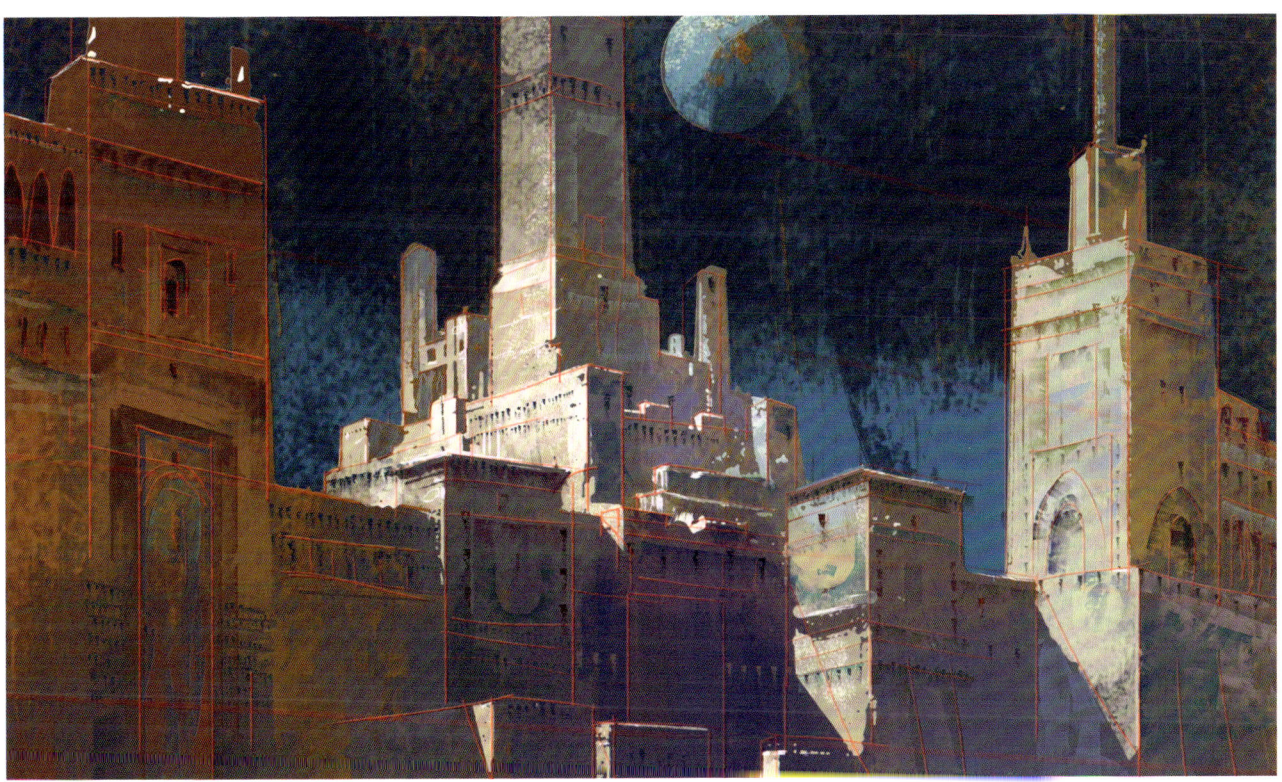

08. Add detail without disrupting the strong value structure of the image

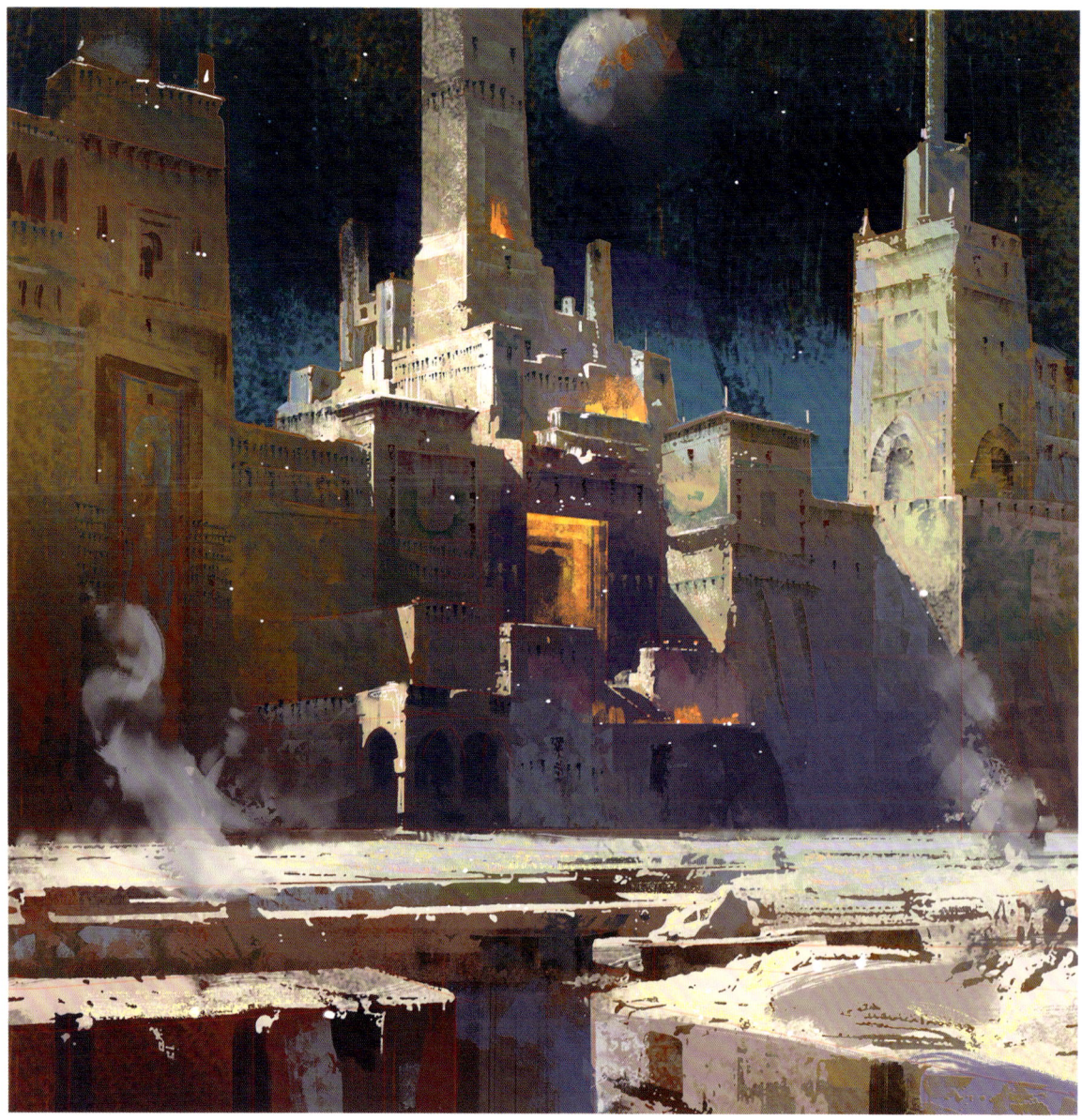

09. Firelight, lit windows, and swirls of dust finish off the scene

09. FINAL IMAGE

And now for the final touches. This is not an abandoned ruin but an active palace where people live and thrive, so let's light up windows and indicate activity. I include firelights on the terraces to show that people are out and about. Oh, and I haven't mentioned the moon yet – that's in place to give a little extra visual interest and mystery. I initially had it quite cyan-blue, but it began to feel out of character with the rest of the scene, so I push a little more gray-purple into it. I also give a lost edge to its shadow side to convey its great distance.

And last I add a couple of dust plumes into the foreground. These help in two ways: they create a little extra layering, so that the mid-ground directly overlaps the background for an extra feeling of space, and their position frames the central, most important area of the environment.

This painting may initially have looked overwhelming and complicated, but do you feel more confident seeing this very simple step-by-step process? I've spent my entire career trying to figure out how to make complicated subjects highly manageable for ordinary people like you and me – I hope you found this organized process to be helpful.

RECOMMENDED EXERCISE:
UNIQUE & EMOTIONAL ARCHITECTURAL DESIGN

This beautiful piece of architectural design is not my work! I wanted to show it to you because it utterly succeeds and was done by one of my very talented students, Anastasia Shiyankova, who is now a successful working professional. Her work can be seen at artstation.com/anshi

Here's the assignment: create an imaginative element of architecture that has a purposeful and unique quality. State the quality of purpose and emotional tone first, then create your design. Your work must have a unique quality – for instance, it can't feel the same as something that can be Googled or that your audience could see in real life. This is how you maintain your relevance as an artist: you create for them something they cannot get in their everyday lives. The only way they can get it is by coming to you!

A useful way to begin is by designing simple silhouettes to work out your idea. Any additional props, elevations, or iconography are a useful addition to the assignment. Even though it is commonplace for us to include shadowy mystery and atmosphere in our illustrated environments, that must not be the case for this exercise. This architectural element must be illustrated with great clarity so that it is model ready. By 'model ready', I mean that the drawing could be handed to a 3D modeler in the pipeline of an entertainment project, and they could create an entire 3D model intuited from only your drawing's single point of view.

This is all about purpose, emotion, clarity, and uniqueness. If your architectural work shows these skills, then you'll be a valued artist and illustrator.

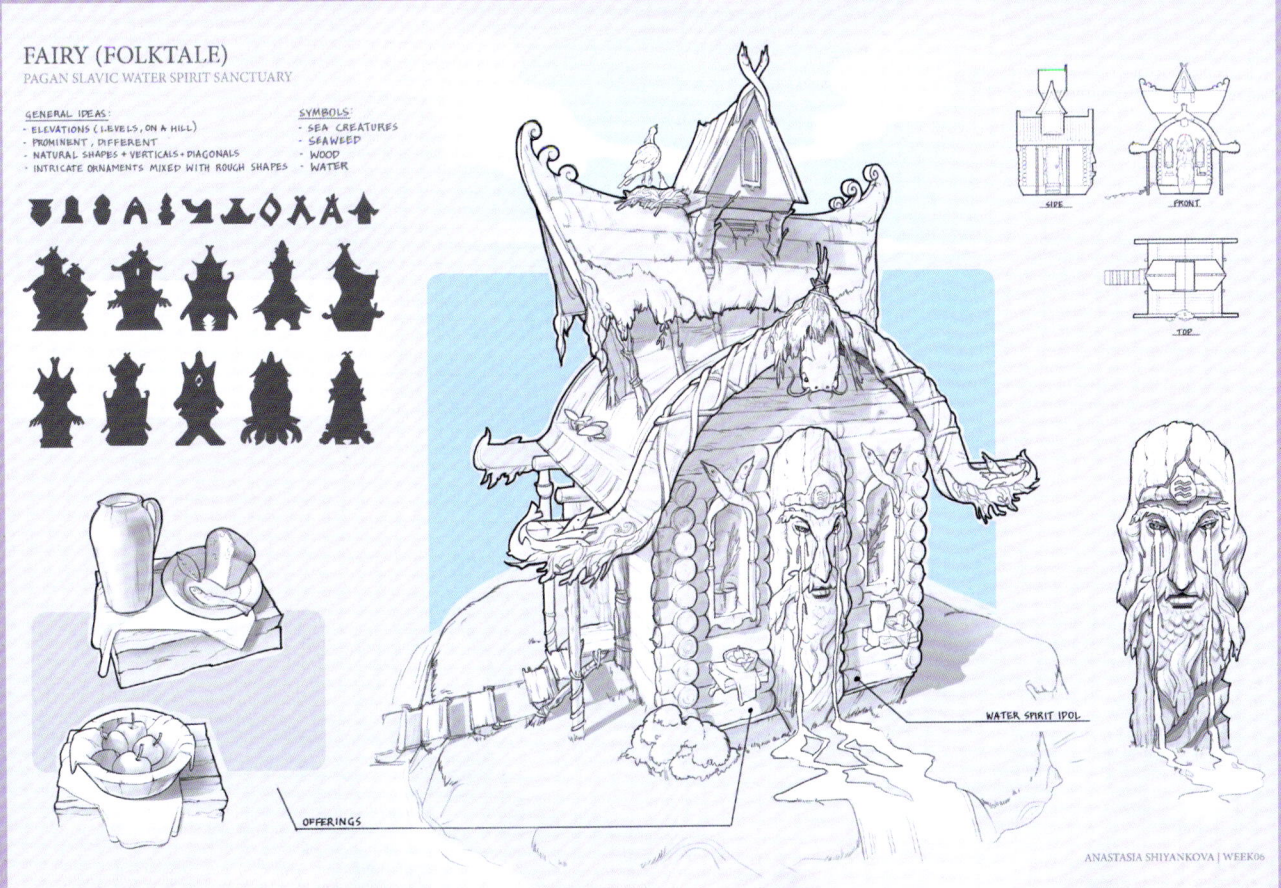

△ See more of Anastasia's designs at artstation.com/anshi

Image: *Pagan Slavic Water Spirit Sanctuary* © Anastasia Shiyankova

BIOME

We live in a fascinating world, a place where masses of land and entire continents have their own distinctive look as a result of millions of years of meteorology, geology, and the influence of life in all its grandeur. It's unbelievably complex, beautiful, and wonderfully dangerous. This is the environment.

CALLE DE LA MUERTE

Many years ago I was on a trip to Costa Rica, and getting to where I wanted to go required travel through the mountains on a road called Calle de la Muerte, which translates to 'road of death'. This was obviously a genius move on my part: the name was a clue to the likely outcome of this venture, and I spoke just enough Spanish to know better (this was before there was such a thing as Google). I was aware that the road was known for extreme cliffs, switchbacks, and washouts, but I figured if I drove slowly and during daylight I should be fine.

There were indeed washouts at many of the hairpin turns, but there was always a narrow lane available. I was doing fine but the drive was taking much longer than expected. Still, there was plenty of daylight left! That's when the heavy, tropical mountain fog came rolling in and visibility went down to a few meters. I was in real trouble. I was moving at barely a crawl. If I had to stop for the night, someone else could come up behind me and not see my vehicle until it was too late. It was a white-knuckle drive as I started down the mountain. Just as I was about to lose hope, the fog suddenly disappeared – it was essentially a low cloud hovering against the mountain, and I had dropped below it. I was able to make it to my destination that night.

We discussed earlier in this book the cataclysmic quality of the environment. I was glad to not be the cataclysm that day but, between the dangerous mountain travel and visiting an active volcano, crashing rocky shores, and tropical rainforests, Costa Rica has a biome different than any place I had visited and has informed my work ever since.

We live in a fascinating world, a place where masses of land and entire continents have their own distinctive look as a result of millions of years of meteorology, geology, and the influence of life in all its grandeur. It's unbelievably complex, beautiful, and wonderfully dangerous. This is the environment. Let's explore the visual uniqueness of individual biomes in this chapter.

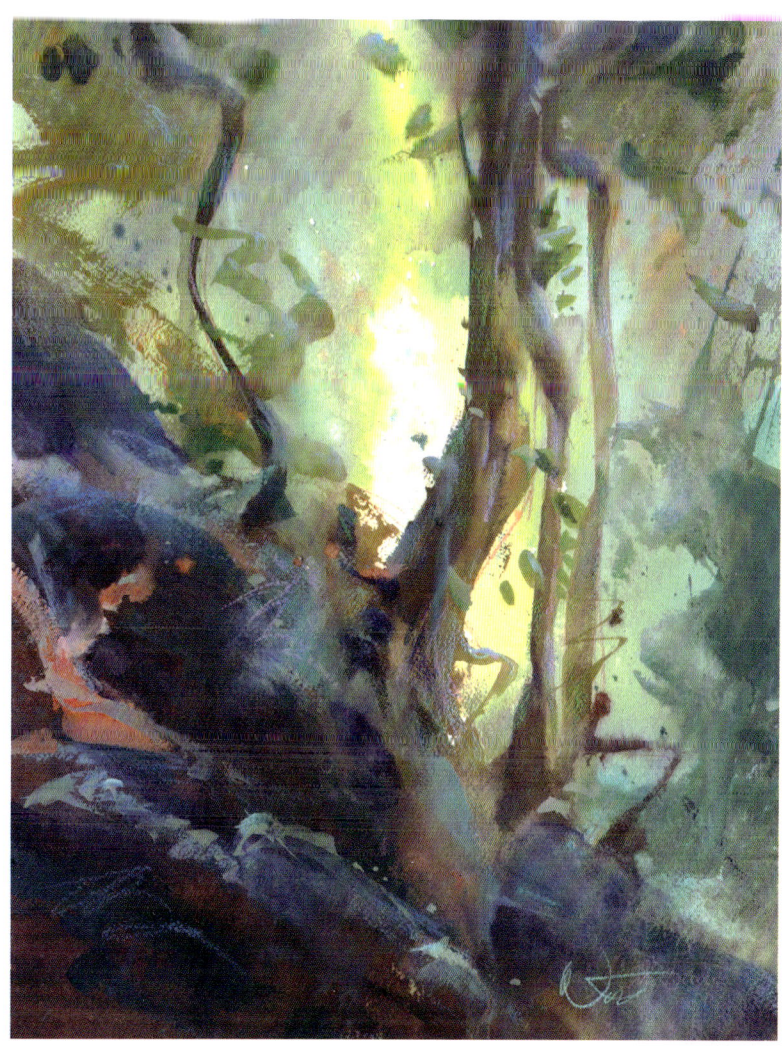

△ The choice of biome will dictate many exciting features and qualities of your image

Choosing the right environmental biome for your story is critical to giving your audience the best experience possible.

UNIQUELY IDENTIFIABLE BIOMES

To warm us up to this subject, I've created a series of images representing very different and uniquely identifiable biomes, from deserts to rainforests and more. Notice how each has its distinctive characteristics and all the various emotions that come with them. Spending time in a desert? Bring plenty of water.

Spending time in a swamp? Bring plenty of bug spray. As an artist, choosing the right environmental biome for your story is critical to giving your audience the best experience possible. Often you'll need to rely on clearly identifiable elements and clues, which this chapter will cover in detail.

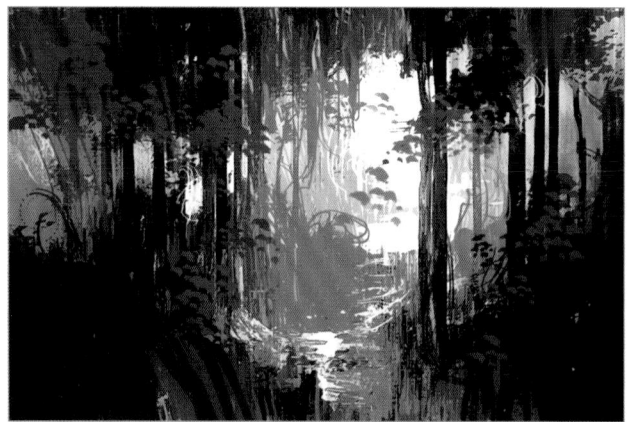

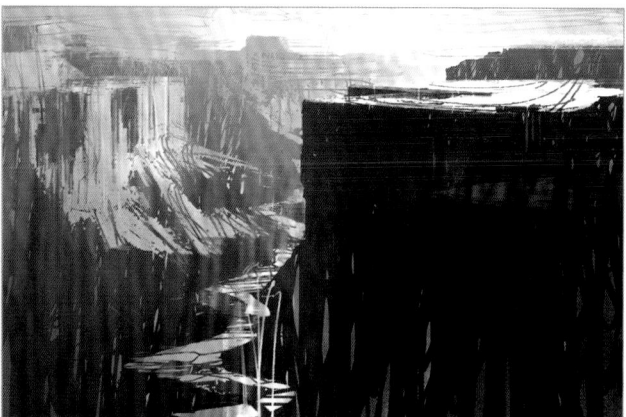

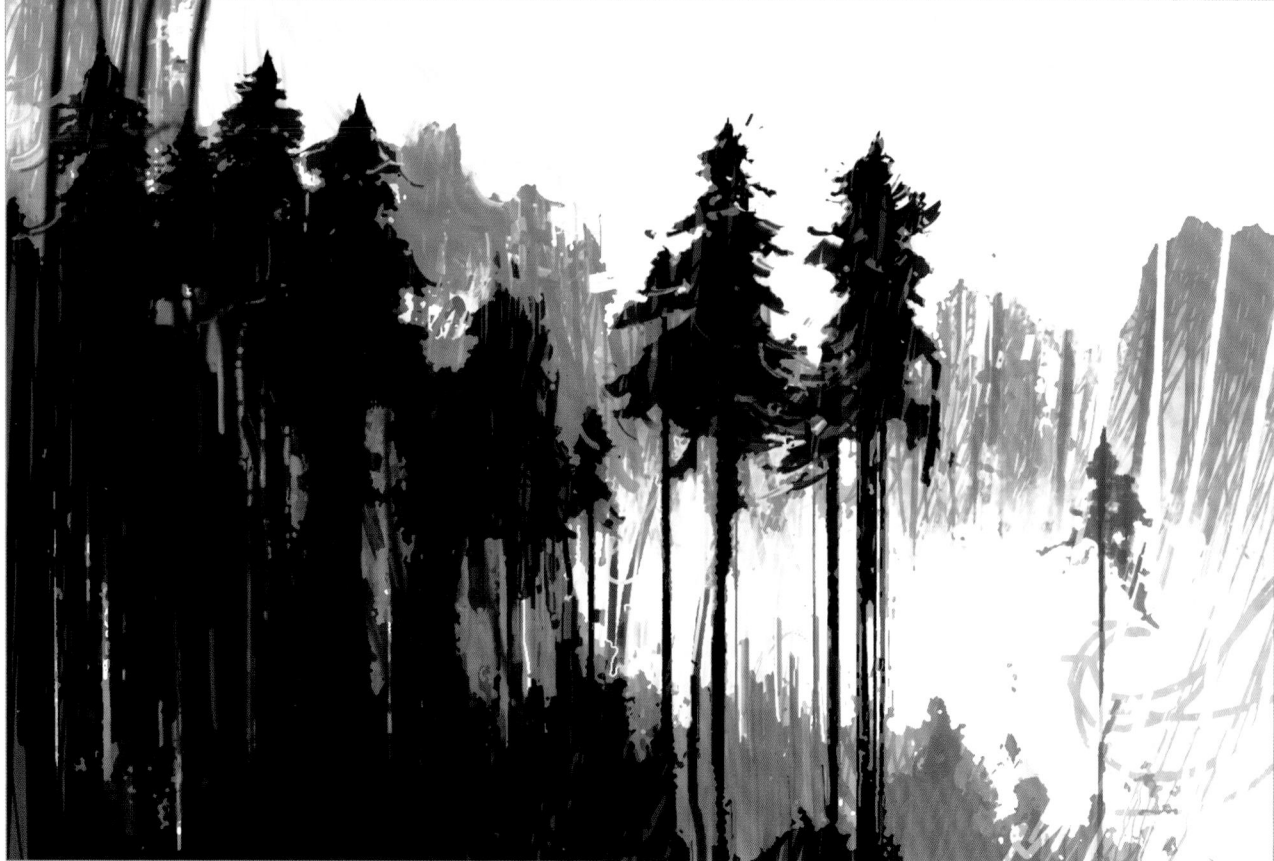

△ What feelings or associations come to mind when you see these biomes?

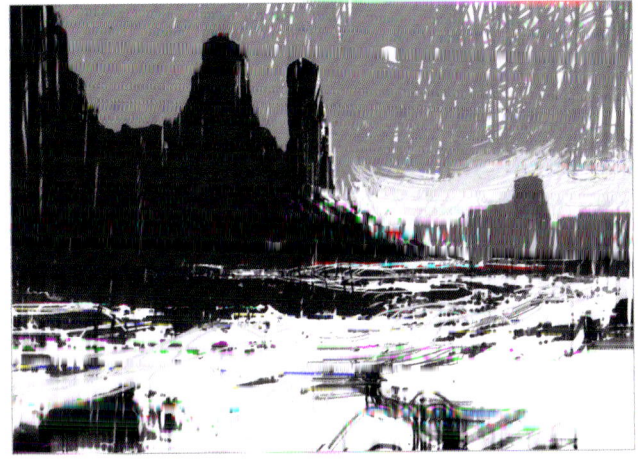
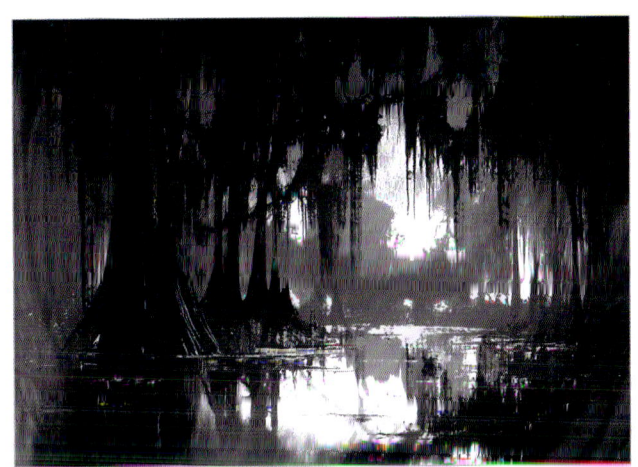
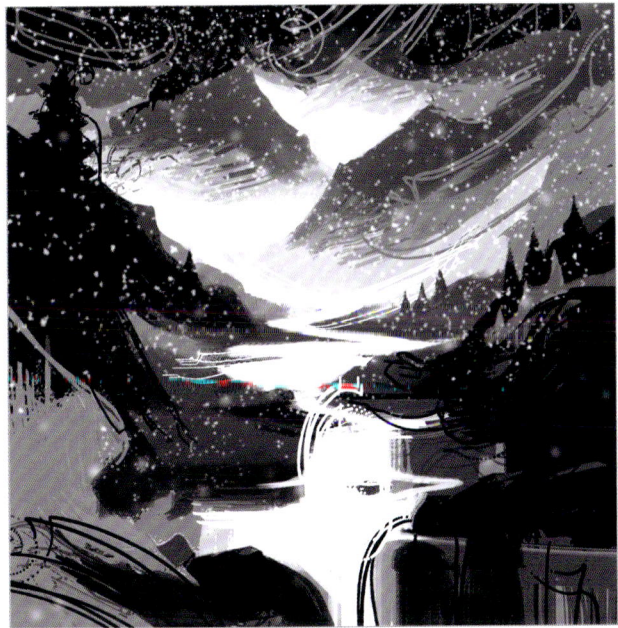
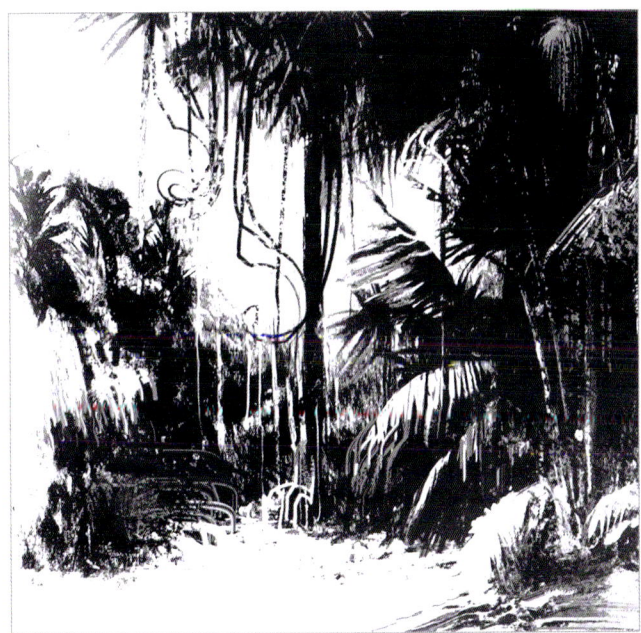
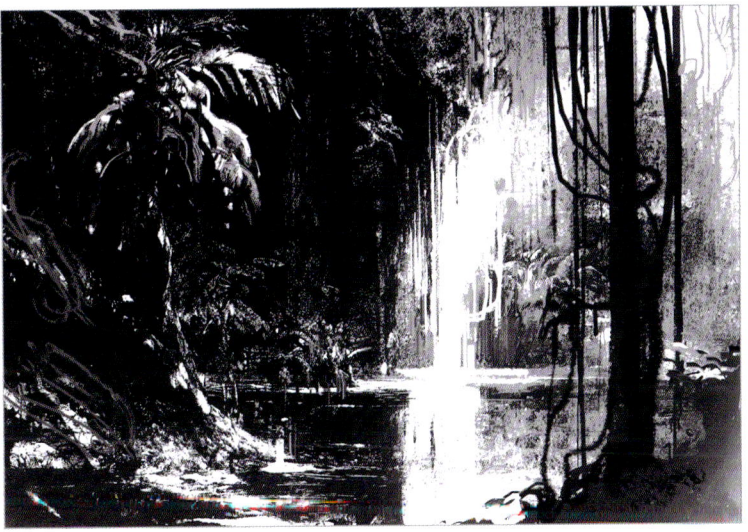
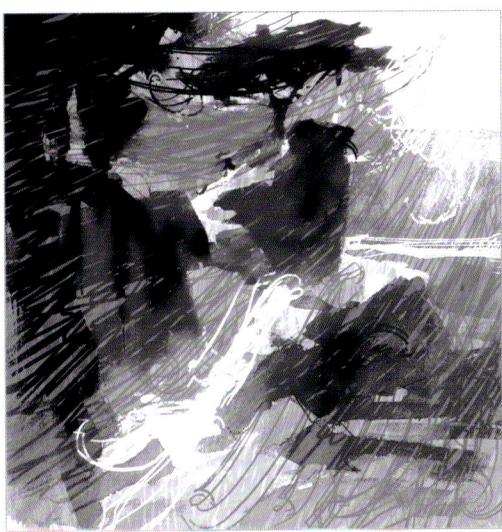

TREES!

Since we're studying life that is instantly recognizable as belonging to unique biomes, let's start with trees. We might not be able to name all these trees, but we instantly recognize the continent, biome, or even specific country that they come from, from Asia to the swamps of Louisiana. Even the strange fat tree, third from the right below – many non-Africans still recognize it as being unique to that continent. (It's the baobab tree, if you care to look it up!)

Remember in the previous chapter, when we said that architecture can be designed to inform us what kind of people live in a place? It's the same with biomes. Unique biomes often hold unique cultures, which is a powerful storytelling tool. And trees are often the core element to recognizing a biome.

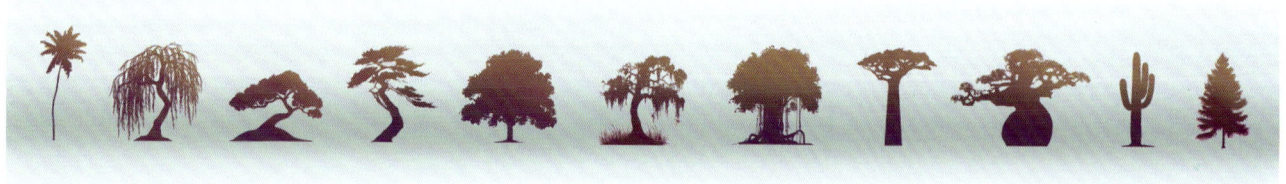

△ Trees can be a unique indicator of biome, continent, or even country

Unique biomes often hold unique cultures, so clearly identifying a biome can inform us of the people who live there.

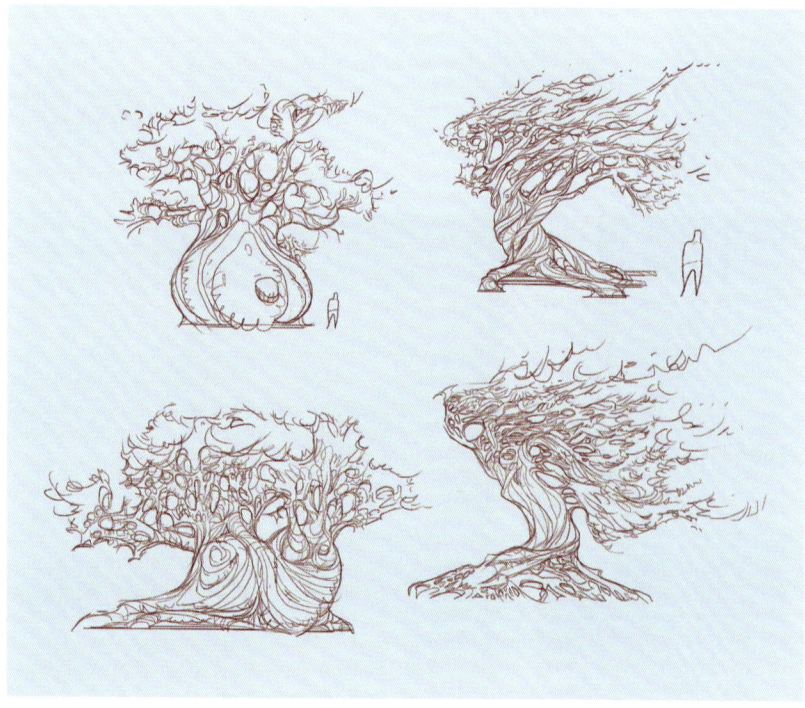

△ The thick, bottom-heavy baobab versus the dramatically windswept cypress

Let me present two further examples on the left: the African baobab tree and the North American Monterey cypress. See the distinctive thicks and thins, and the twists and turns? Trees and foliage can be treated very much like portrait caricatures. You know those really fast portrait caricaturists at the fair? That's something I did many years ago, so I can speak to it. The trick is to immediately identify any unique characteristics of the sitter and emphasize those. The sitter has a long nose, sharp eyebrows, and a double chin? Exaggerate those features wildly on a generic head, and everyone will say it looks just like the sitter. Foliage, especially trees, can be treated in this same way. We can and should emphasize its distinctive qualities.

One tree is fat and simple on the bottom and thin and spindly on the top, so just emphasize those qualities and you've nailed it. The other looks like it's in heavy wind even on a calm day, with twists and turns showing that it grew against that constant force. Exaggerate that windblown quality with twisting and turning trunks and, again, you've nailed it!

TWISTS & TURNS

Humans have always used braided materials to make ropes and tethers of great strength. Even super strong modern materials, including steel, are braided to create impressive holding power. It makes sense that nature uses the same trick – living structures in nature are always working against the forces of gravity and weather, so they have to grow strong!

Braiding is such a successful strategy that you see it in very different biomes all over the world. If we're going to be great environment designers, we've got to create living structures of fantastic living authority. It's just our luck that these twisting and turning shapes are delightful to look at and design with.

Here is a rope that's simple and somewhat random, and a tree that uses the same type of braiding. I dare you to draw a tree like this with complicated braids from imagination, without looking at the reference. If it's a complete disaster then you're in good company, with me and most of the others out there who just can't do it without practice. If you get it on the first try, you're a visual genius!

Once you've tried this out on your own, I invite you to copy these sketches. Let yourself get a feel for how this works. Then invent your own tree – you can look at the one below as reference to help. You and I have to be really good at this if we're going to be true environment designers.

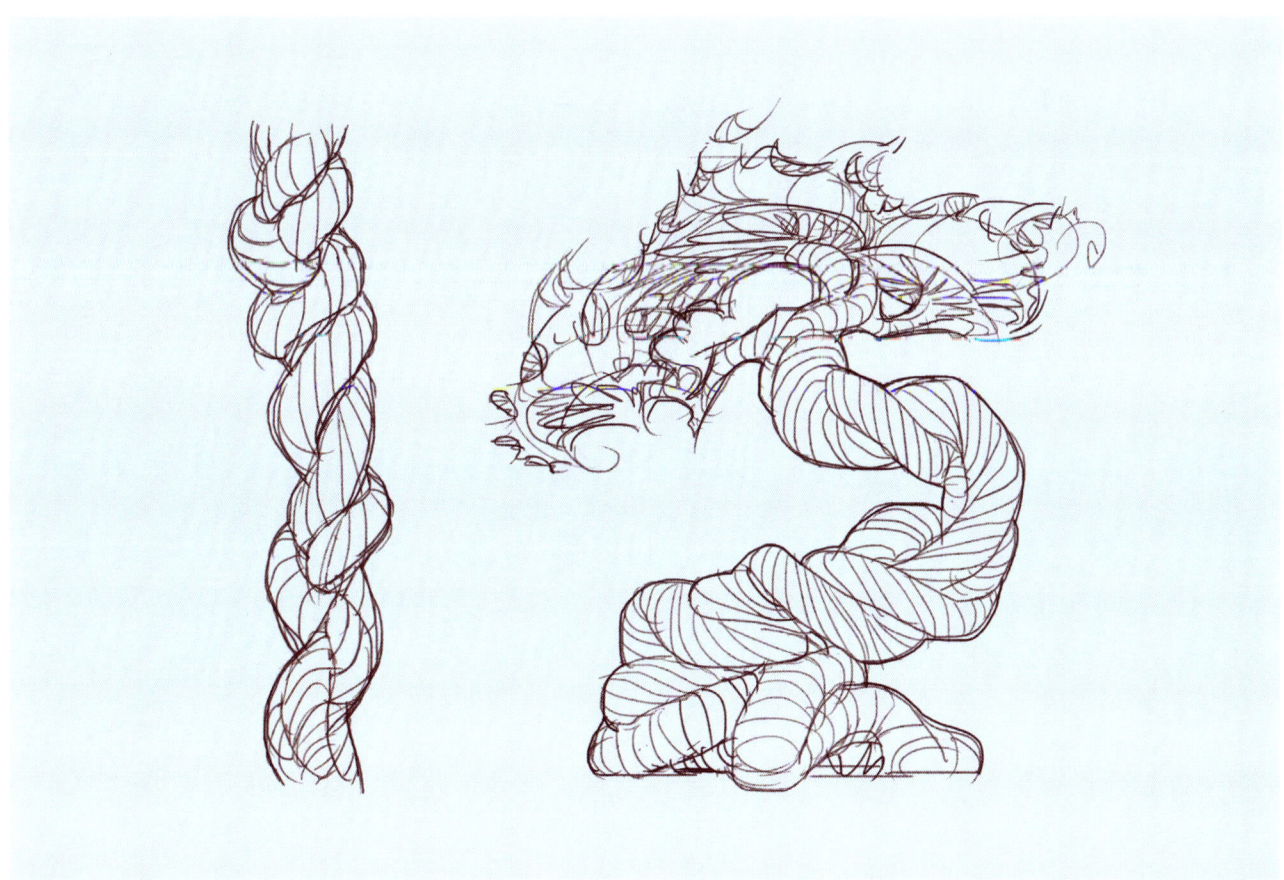

△ We can use nature's twisting patterns in our art

Braided materials have great strength, and nature uses this trick to fight against weather and gravity. Luckily for us, these twisting and turning shapes are delightful to look at and design with.

BIG IDEAS IN LITTLE TREES

Here's a batch of more naturalistic trees, the kind you most commonly find in East Asia. Another area of study I invite you to take part in is the study of bonsai trees. Not only do they twist and turn like ropes, but they also angle back and forth, balance and counterbalance. This is another common solution nature has for the forces of gravity and weather. Straight up-and-down trees can be very powerful and very successful, but they must often grow very

big and use a lot of resources for structural strength. The kind of balance and counterbalance seen below is an alternate strategy that uses fewer resources and results in smaller trees. Bonsai trees are tiny, but there are many trees that are several meters tall that follow the same pattern. I had an opportunity to visit Japan recently and was in awe of these brilliantly grown and groomed trees.

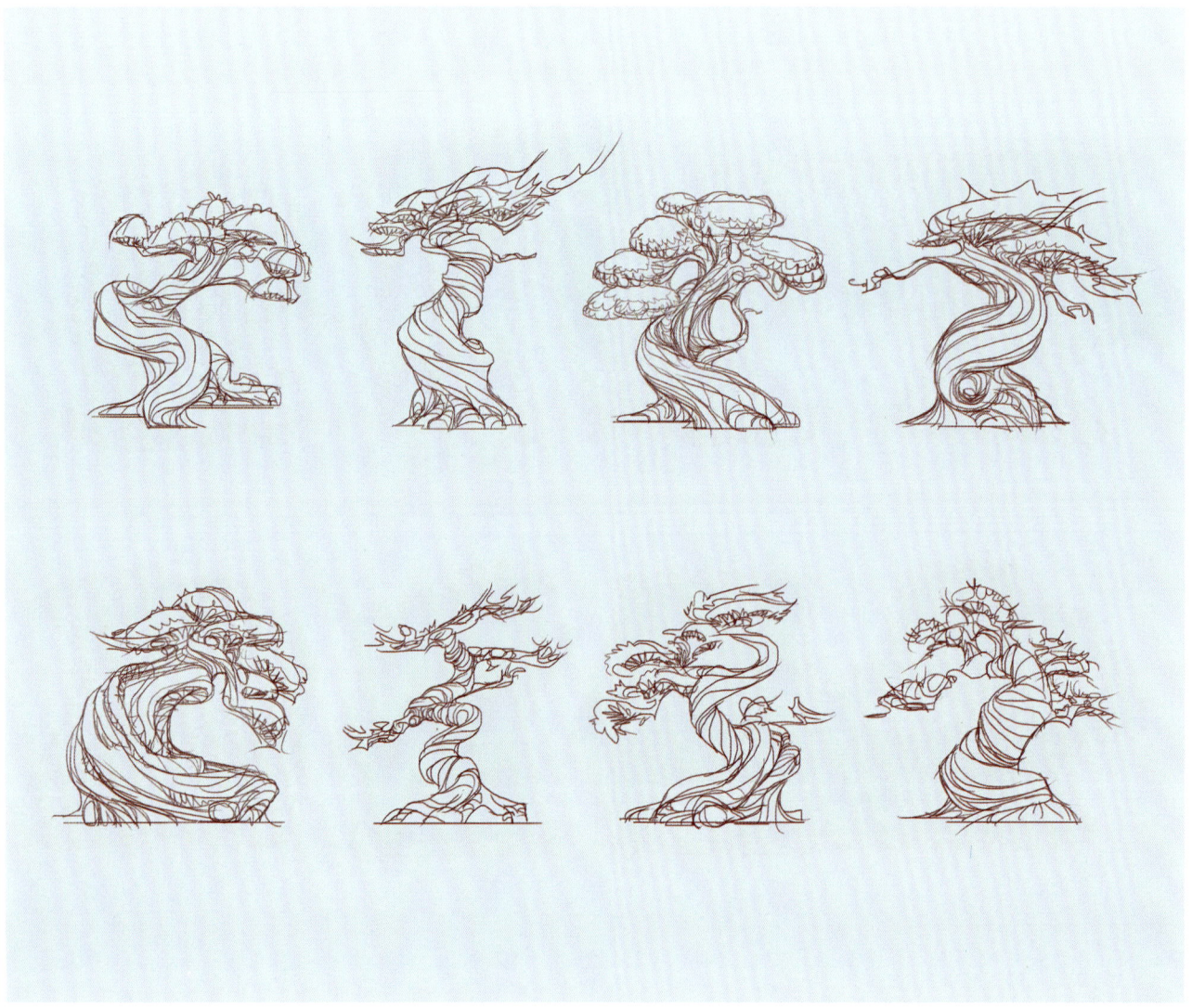

△ Many trees, both wild and cultivated, grow in dramatic shapes

The back-and-forth angles of balance and counterbalance are another common solution nature has for the forces of gravity and weather.

BIOME AS CHARACTER

You might have noticed that some of these trees almost seem like a figure in a contrapposto pose. Some have arm-like branches reaching out, and a crown of leaves at the top. Remember when I encouraged the idea of caricature on page 173? We're taking that to an extreme in the example on the right – our audience will pay far more attention to a figurative tree, like this, than a random one. As designers, any visual that commands our audience's attention and evokes emotion is a winner. That's probably the twentieth time I've said that in this book, but I won't stop saying it, because I want you to be one of the best designers in the world.

01. CARMEL-BY-THE-SEA

Now let's put all of this to the test and paint up a real tree that has strong visual interest. I've done so much with trees found in Asian biomes that I'm now switching back to the North American Monterey cypress. I love these trees! I only have to drive a few hours to find them along the coast but the most prominent place is a community named Carmel-by-the-Sea. I hope you have a chance to visit there someday but, until then, here is a seaside example that has been dramatized for your enjoyment.

02. CALIFORNIA LIVE OAK

Let's keep moving to different kinds of trees so that I'm not too repetitive. Here's a gnarled and delightful California live oak. Again, it's based on a real tree that I came across, though I've exaggerated it. But look at the fight here – look at how this tree has scratched, clawed, dug, and used every resource it could to live! It's emotional and evocative.

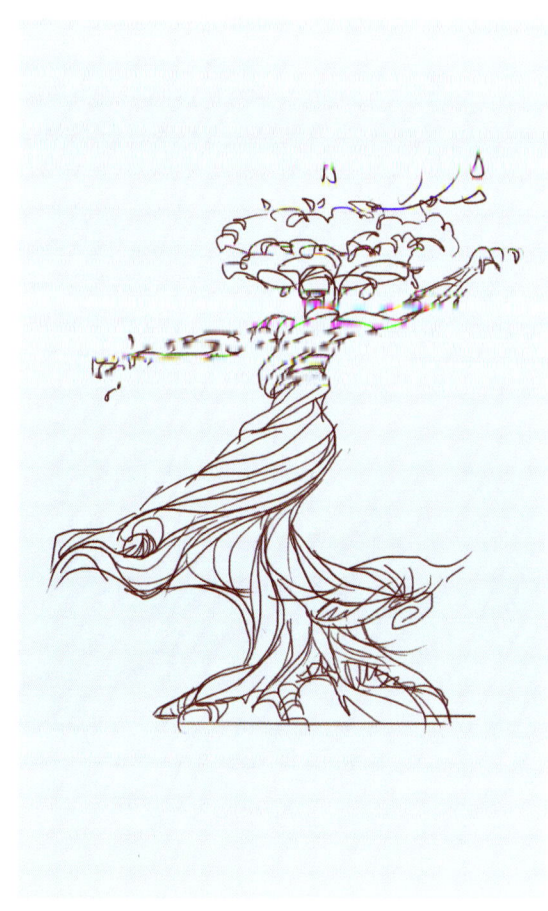

△ Can you see the humanoid figure in this tree?

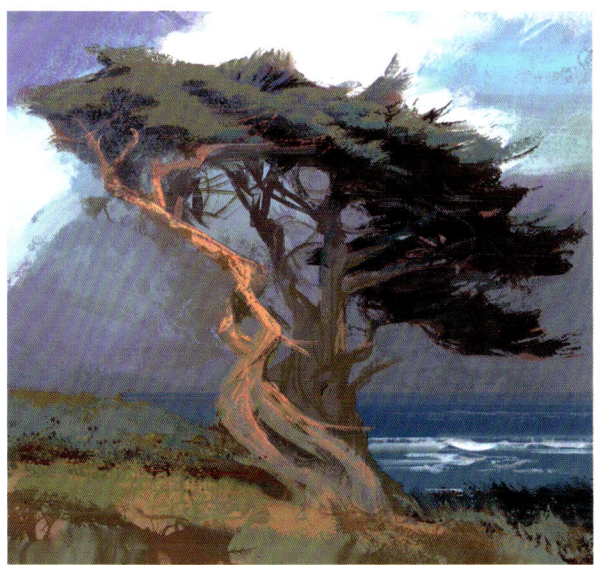

01. Cypress trees such as this one can be found on California's West Coast

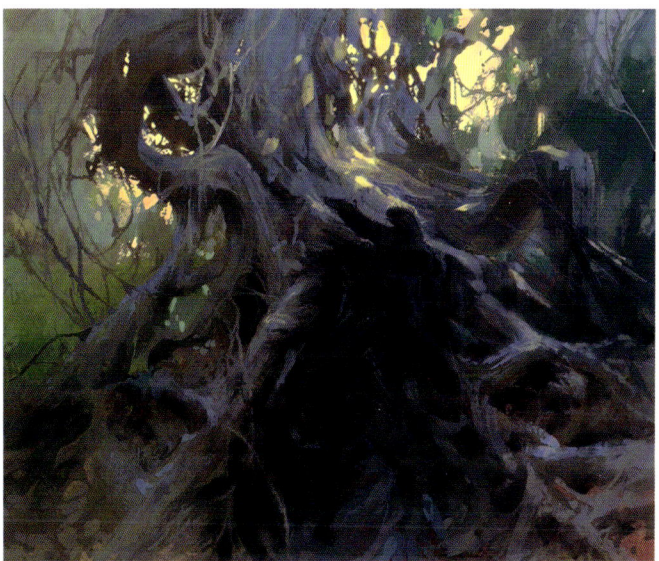

02. The toughness and resilience of this old oak come through in its shapes

SKETCHBOOK OBSERVATIONS

Let's move forward into simple design ideas that we can learn from nature. As we proceed through this chapter, look out for these qualities and how I've applied them to natural subjects. Using these techniques and visual tools – balance, rhythm, and two kinds of contrast – will become second nature with study and practice.

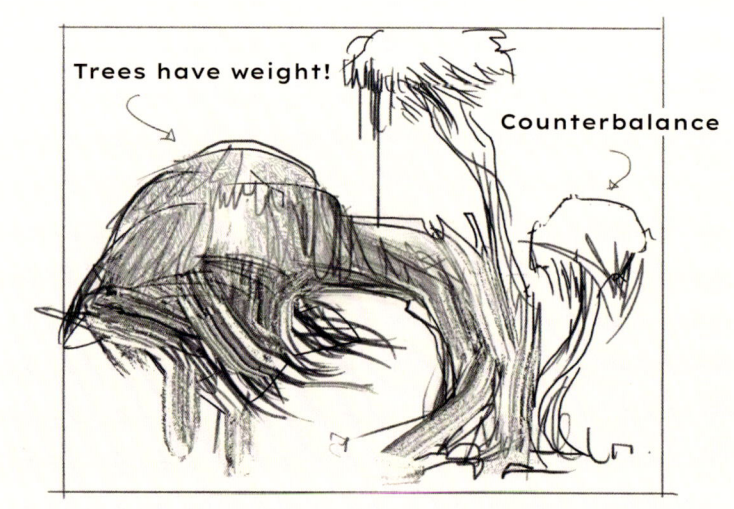

01. As with gravity in real life, we naturally seek balance in compositions

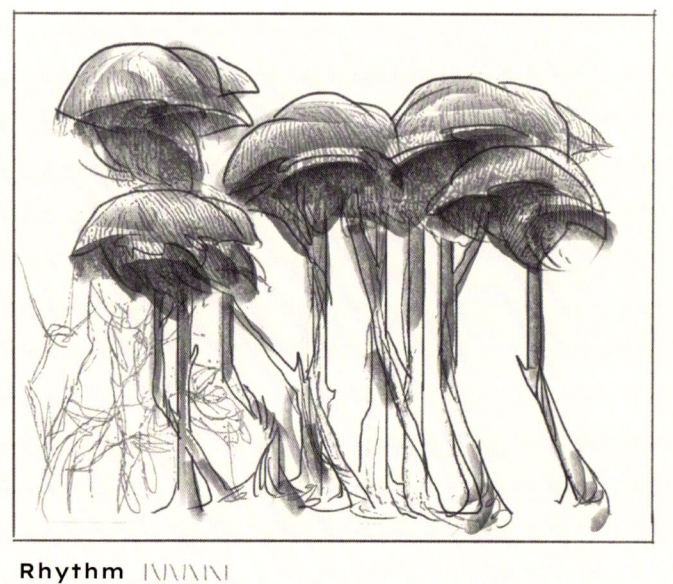

02. Intentional repetition creates a pleasing sense of rhythm

01. BALANCE

This first one is simple: nature deals with great weight. It's an important consideration as you design. One useful way to design with it is to have a counterbalancing visual weight. We've been dealing with structural balance and counterbalance, but human beings also crave this quality in picture composition. I taught this principle in *Artists' Master Series: Composition & Narrative*, an excellent book on composition, but I'll also mention it here in simple terms. If perceived visual weight is unbalanced in a picture, it often makes the audience feel discomfort. Why? Because, every moment of our lives, our bodies unconsciously work against the force of gravity. It's an unconscious need we have, and we impose it onto pictures. There are always exceptions, but visual balance is an important principle of which to be aware.

02. RHYTHM

Next is rhythm. I define visual rhythm as the meaningful repetition of elements in a picture. Don't these simplified trees just *feel* like they belong together, as if there's a purpose here? 'Purpose' is another term I use over and over to emphasize meaning in a picture. These trees have repetitive canopies and the trunks only have two angles: vertical and a repeating diagonal. We'll put this into action shortly in another rendering of oak trees.

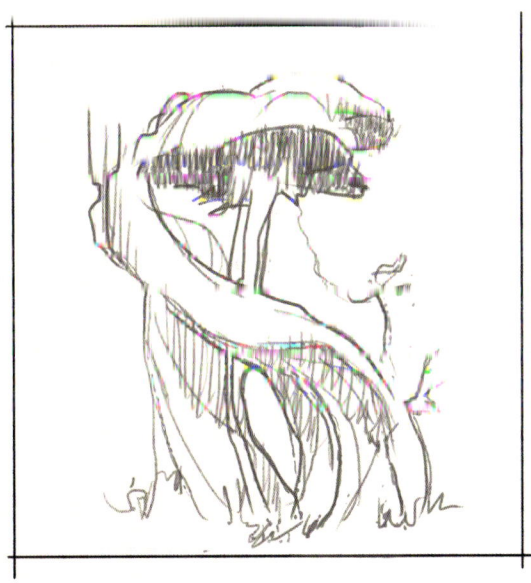

03. DIRECTIONAL CONTRAST

Twists, turns, and straights are delightful together. They are three different qualities where each one gives the others a little uniqueness, as you can see when three contrasting trunks are placed together.

04. SCALE CONTRAST

How do you make something look big and husky? You could just make it big, but there's a way you can double this impact without changing it in any way. Simply add something tiny for contrast, and you will instantly have an exaggerated sense of scale.

03. A juxtaposition of contrasting shapes is immediately engaging

Big tree

Small tree

04. These trees exaggerate each other's sizes when placed together

A MEANINGFUL REPETITION

Now we get to the heavy stuff. It's fun to make nature crazy and gnarled, and maybe that's enough, but we can make that craziness feel really good by applying rhythm: a meaningful repetition. You can see in the red-lined version that all of this craziness conforms to only two angles and then a ground plane. This idea relates to the reason why people often enjoy a graphic, cartoony style. Those styles replace all the chaotic possibilities of shape and angle with just a few carefully crafted ones, giving the subject a simple clarity and a more direct quality of purpose. If you ever paint an overly active biome and it's just a mess, try to apply this simple idea. It might just turn you into a design hero.

People enjoy graphic cartoony styles because they replace all the chaotic possibilities of shape and angle with just a few carefully chosen ones. This gives the subject a simple clarity and a more direct quality of purpose.

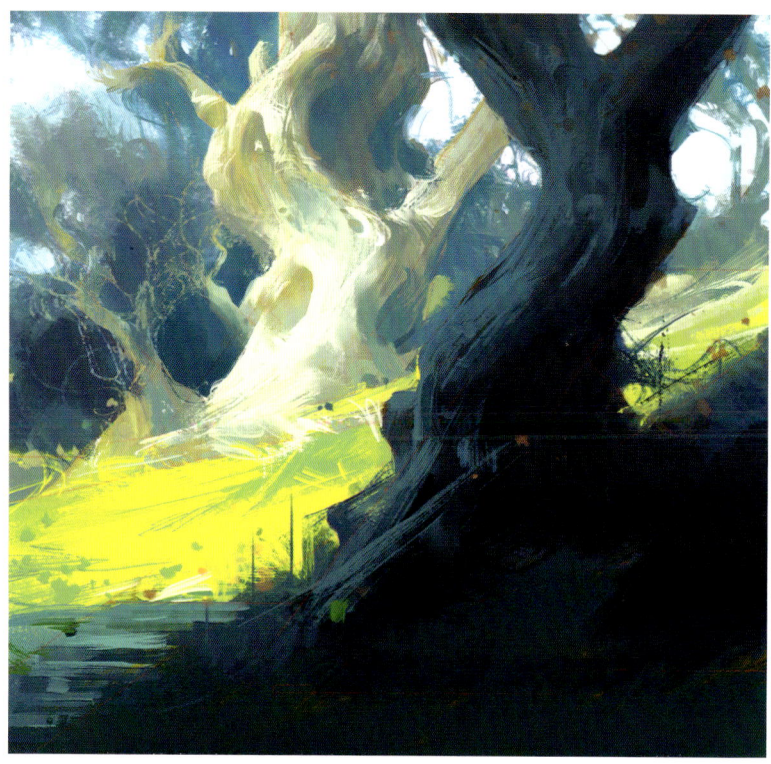

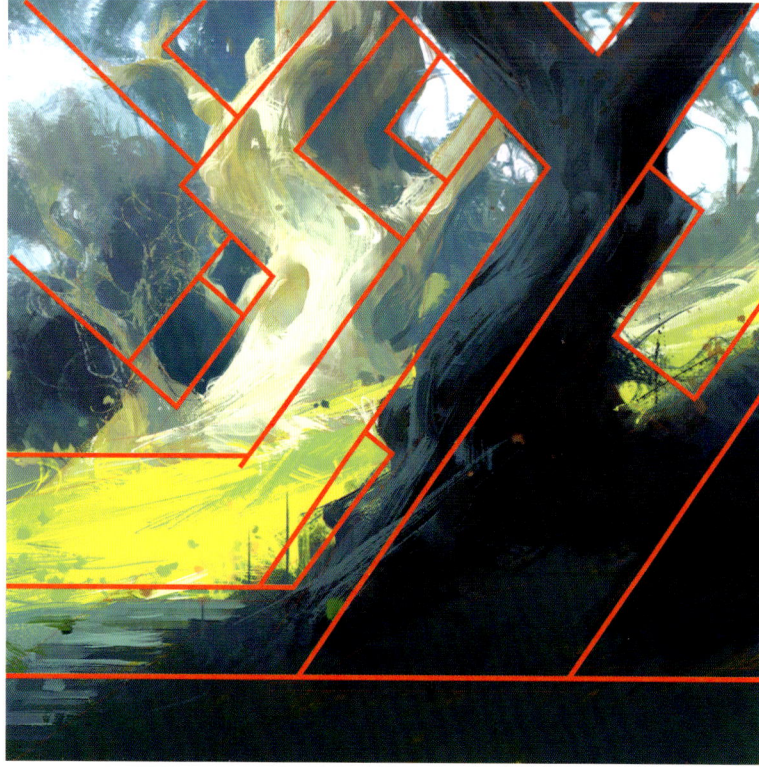

△ Adding rhythm and repetition can make your environments more appealing

EARTH'S CARPET

In a forest, the ground is a huge part of the ecological biomass; the material that falls to earth there is rich in nutrients. Small creatures, plants, lichens, and fungi fatten themselves on it. As they break it down, nutrients are returned to the soil, which feeds the next wave of plants. The resulting layers of colors and textures on the ground can be awe-striking.

01. GALÁPAGOS HIGHLANDS

Let's travel to another unique biome. I recently made a trip to the Galápagos Islands – the misty highland area where all of those amazing hundred-year-old tortoises live. This is a sketch of the quality of biome in that place: misty and magical. The point I wanted to make here is the importance and the intricacy of the ground, which is lush and varied, as mentioned above.

02. FOREST FLOOR

Here's a rendering of a forest floor, this time of a pine forest. I did it to illustrate in detail that idea of the splendor that exists right under our feet. As you design an environment and create the quality of a biome, I encourage you to include careful design of the ground itself.

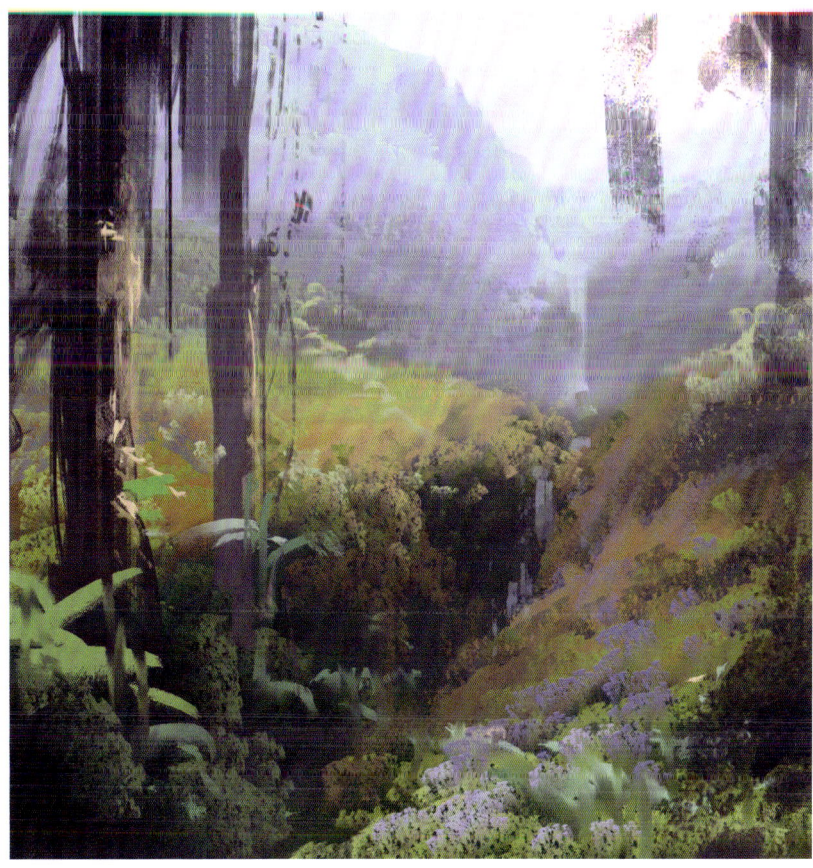

01. No, there are no tortoises to find in this sketch!

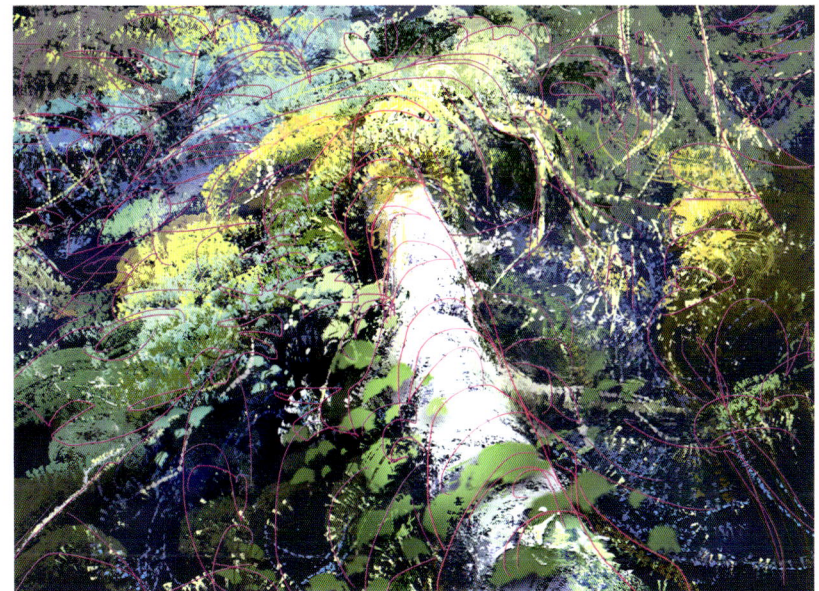

02. Don't neglect the ground as an element of your environments

GREATEST HITS

Now I'd like to share with you a gallery of a great variety of biomes, with the hope that you'll see the uniqueness of each and how much they differ from each other. Some are sketches of real places as they really are; some are sketches of real places but exaggerated and caricatured; and some are completely imagined, as we often do in the art industry. I invite you to carefully study what makes them distinctive from one another.

01. STILL WATER

This image takes us back to the Galápagos highlands. For me, the takeaway from a biome like this is the active textures contrasted with the overall stillness of the place. The quality of *stillness* can be visualized by the placid surface of the water.

02. EVERGLADES

Now let's travel to the swamps of the Everglades in Florida. The location is characterized by fluffy Spanish moss growing all over the trees, so I emphasized that aspect. The overall color palette of the biome is yellow-red ocher, which is the reason for the wildly exaggerated greens in the background – it emphasizes the unique palette of warm earth tones. As per usual, I was identifying what's unique and accentuating those qualities.

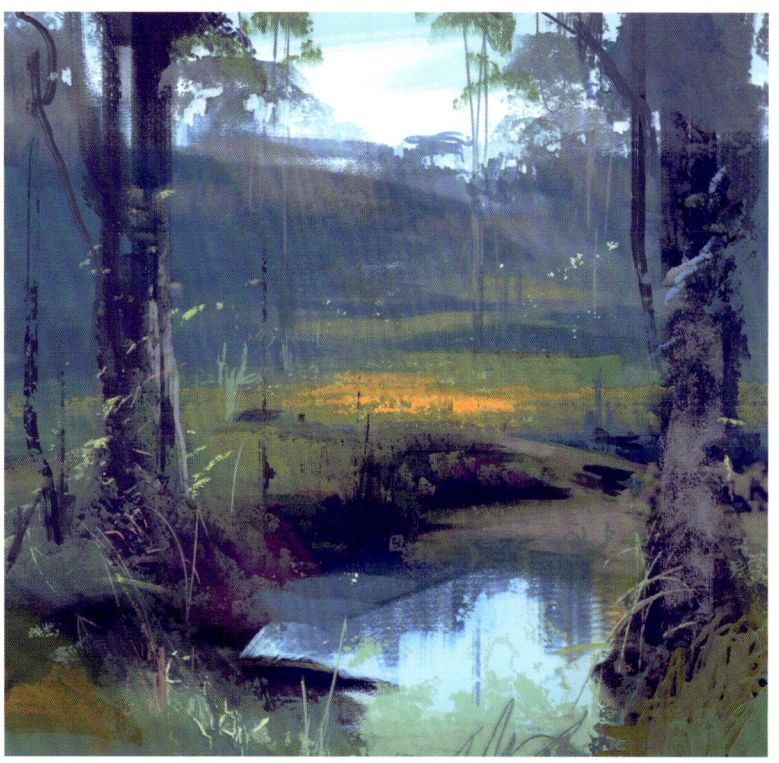

01. Tranquil water contrasts with busy foliage

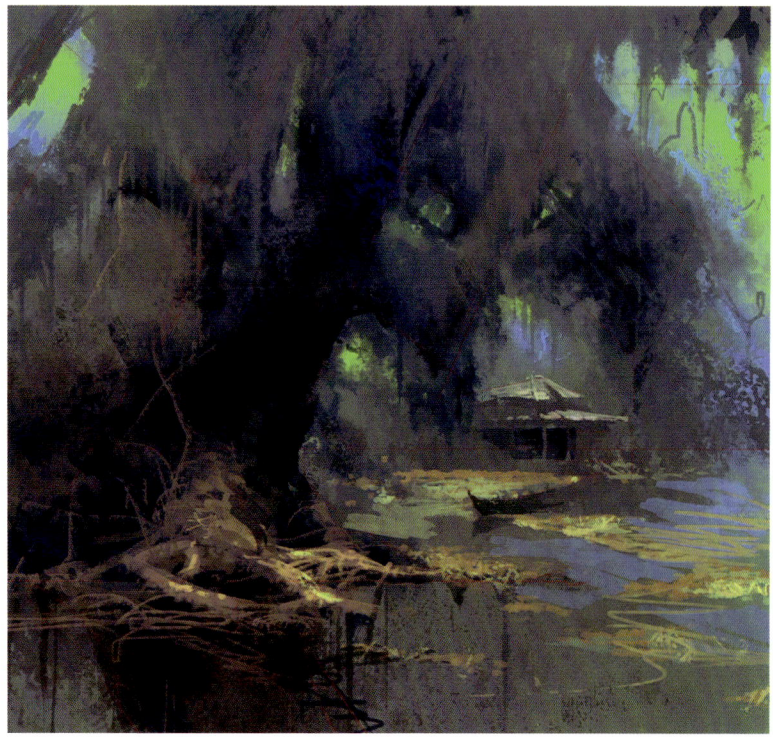

02. Soft textures capture the location's mossiness

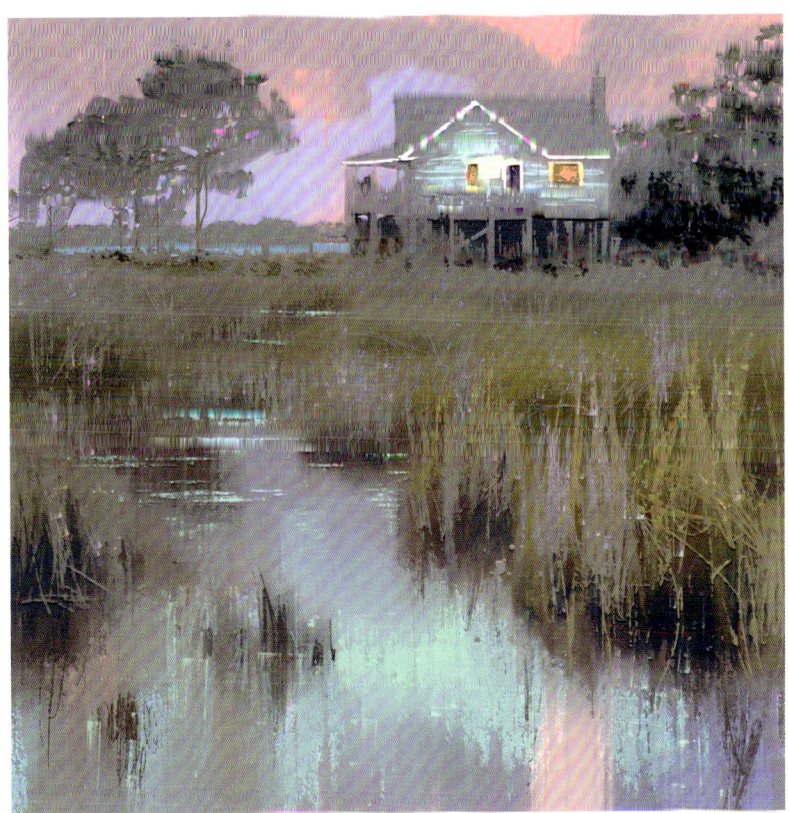

03. The architecture tells a story of life in this biome

03. NORTH CAROLINA

And now the swamps of North Carolina. The marshy quality here is very distinctive, but I think the biggest tell is that the house has to be built up on stilts. That one element gives us visions of storms and floods, and of nature just overall doing its thing.

04. UTAH

Here's the winter wonderland of Utah. This is a real spot, though I've made it more graphic for design purposes. In a place like this, the weighty drifts of snow settle in triangular patterns atop the pine-tree fronds. It's an opportunity for unique design work in our environments.

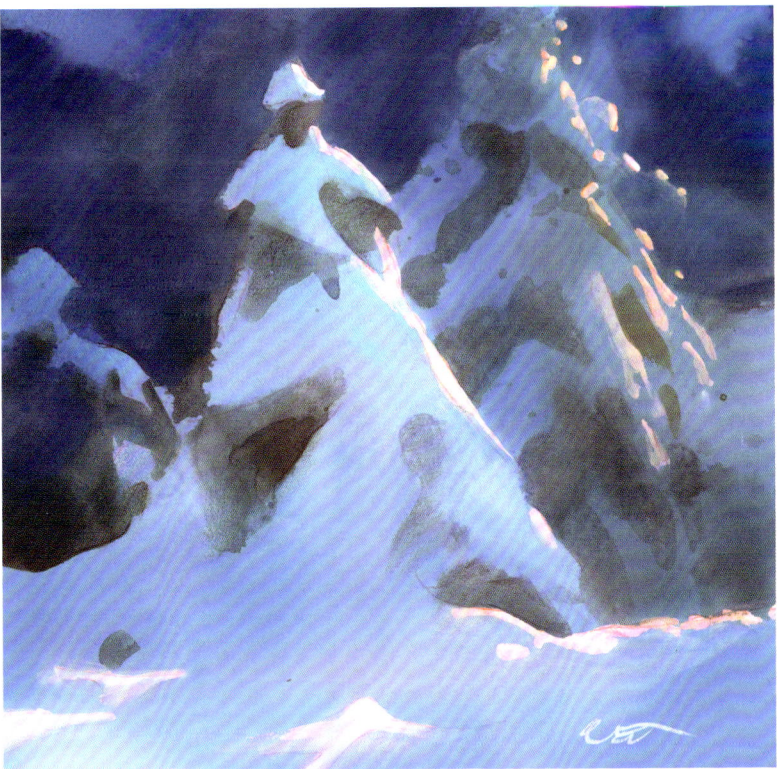

04. Drifts of snow pile up gently on these angular trees

05. ANGELES CREST

The rocky granite pools of Angeles Crest, California, are a place where one thing forcibly carves its way through another. You can think of the design opportunities like this: rounded, light, cool-gray stones surrounded by dark, warm, gritty earth and scrub trees. It's a potentially metaphorical and emotional subject.

06. YOSEMITE

Though this is inspired by a real place that I visited – Yosemite National Park, California – I did a lot of moving mountains! I carefully worked out the placement of the granite mountains in dappled sunset lighting, and of the pool beneath reflecting those colors.

You can think of the Yosemite Valley as a giant version of the stream bed above. In this case, a giant glacier tore through the valley and left huge white granite boulders in its wake. And thank goodness for us it did – Yosemite is one of the wonders of the world. I took advantage of the repeating triangle shapes in the geology and the conifers, and I also carefully placed the white boulders and river reflections.

I went a little crazy with purple accents everywhere. I still like them but it's possibly overdone. (Maybe I was thinking about working at Blizzard Entertainment at the time – an inside joke that some of you out there will get.)

07. THE ANDES

The vertical mountainous biome of Peru as viewed from Machu Picchu. You'll recall that in the chapter on the design of space (page 94), we discussed framing our environments in a way that best suited their distinctive qualities. This demanded to be a vertical composition. Note that the mountains are so high that we don't even see the sky! If a biome or environment is steeply vertical, be sure to emphasize that special quality.

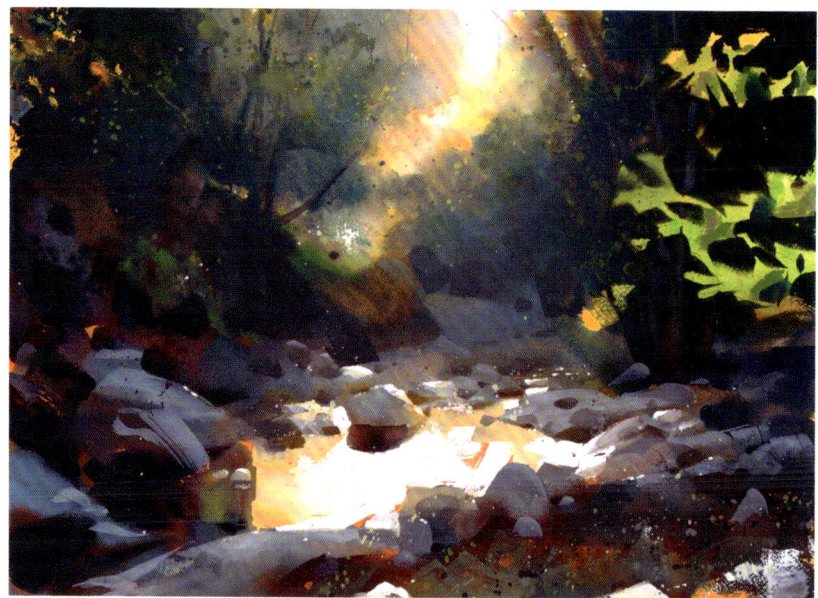

05. This location is full of vibrant and intriguing contrasts

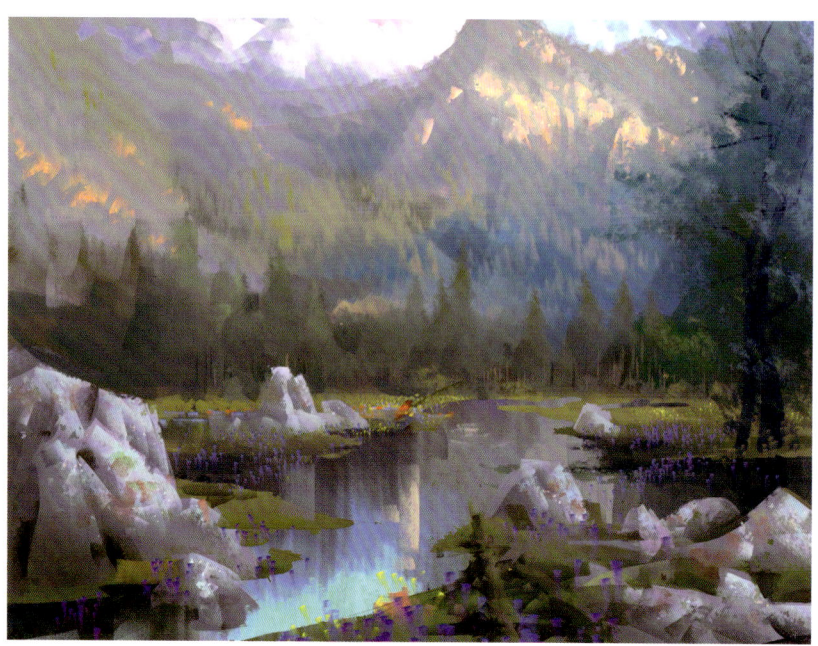

06. Repetition and careful placement play key roles in this scene

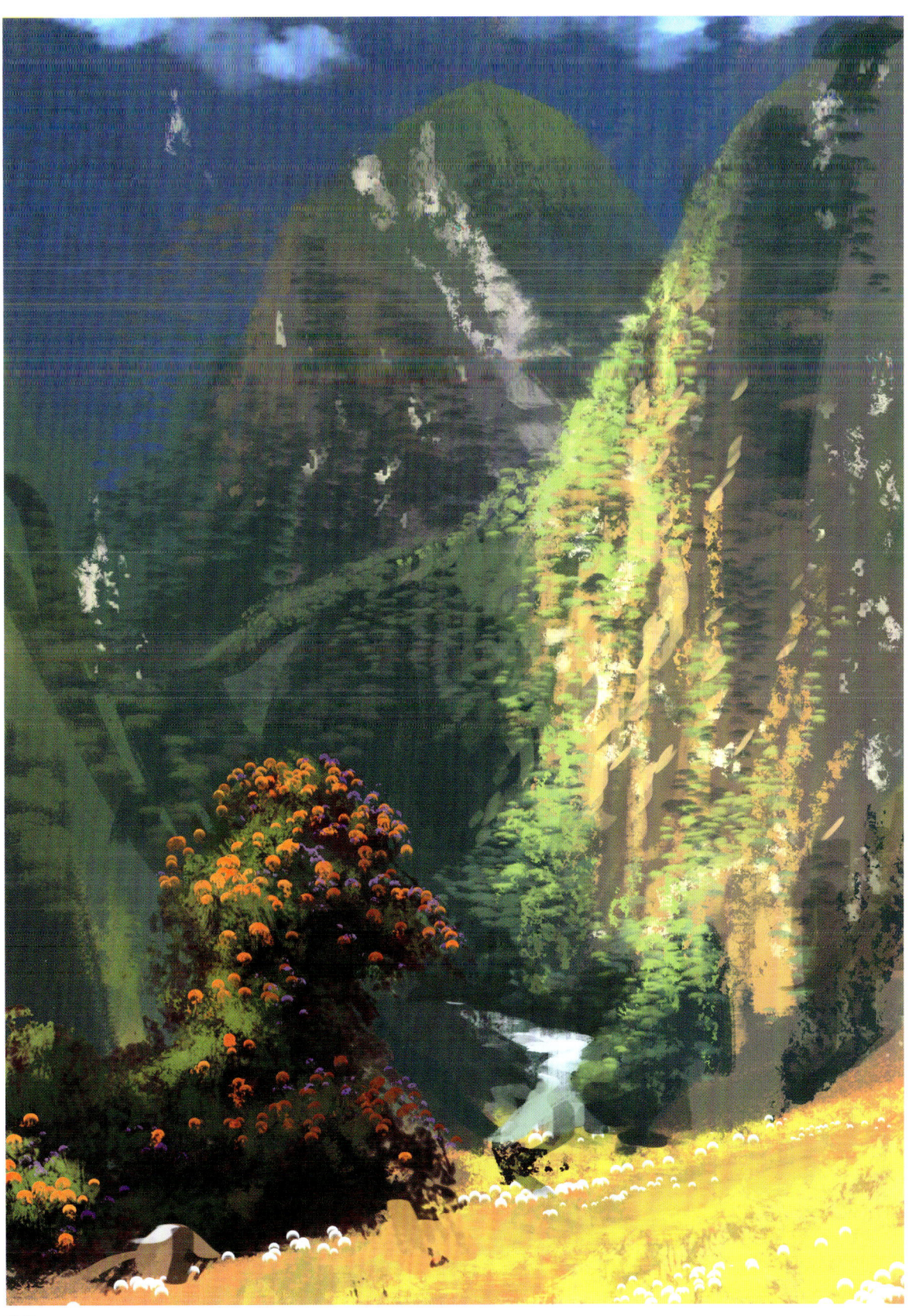

07. Taller image dimensions help convey the towering scale of these mountains

08. SIERRA NEVADA

This one is from a hike through the Sierra Nevada mountains. I moved the river into a good position where it would lead the viewer toward the mountains with glittering reflections. An important part of the beauty of this place is the backlighting that fills the atmosphere with luminosity – but that's a product of lighting, not of the biome specifically, so it will be addressed in a future chapter on atmosphere (page 327). But the distant atmospheric blues hold half of the ingredients of the richness of this biome; the warm ocher of the grasses that grow across the valley floor creates a wonderful warm/cool contrast.

09. ANOTHER SWAMP!

Swamps again. One reason I like swamps so much is the readily available reflections. Water is everywhere and so its placement can be carefully designed to catch reflections that serve the picture best. Don't forget about water in your biomes! Also, take note of all the mats of fallen leaves and debris, and the new life growing on it. This can be a unique part of your design.

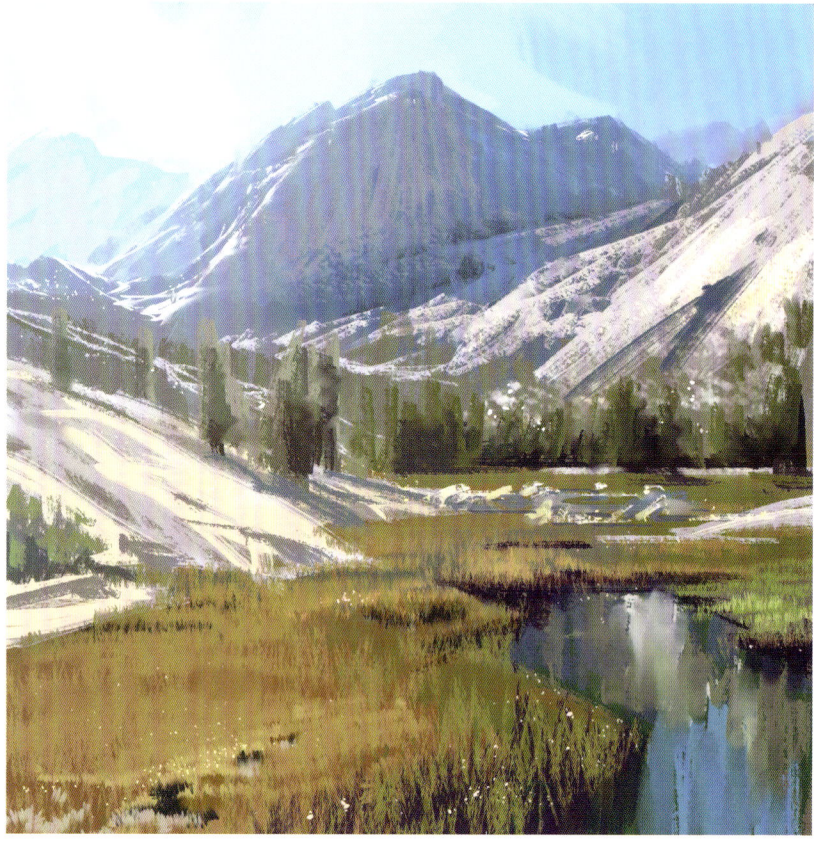

08. Warm grasses contrast with the soft, cool-blue atmosphere

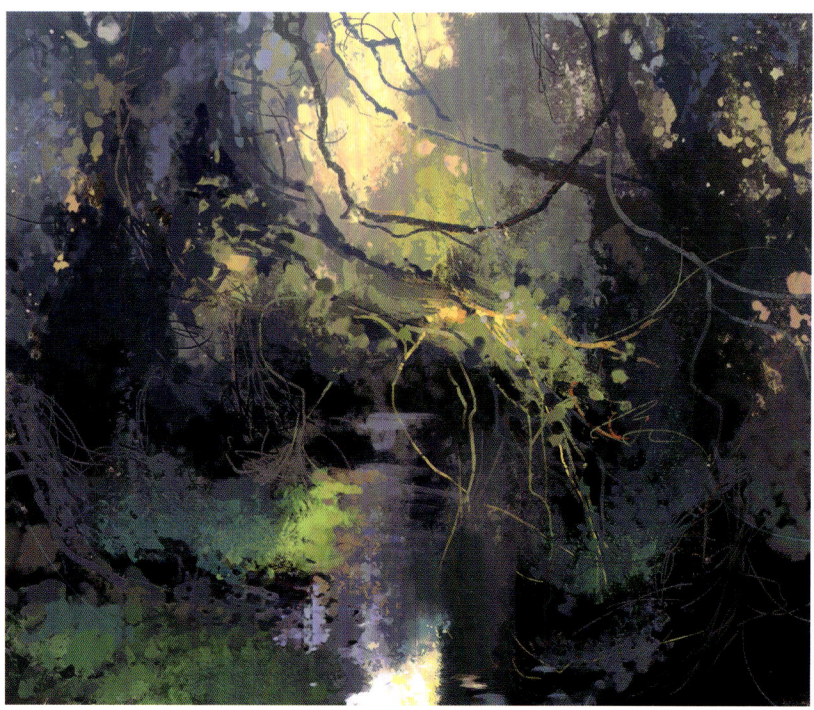

09. Water and rich, dense plant life make swamps a particularly exciting biome

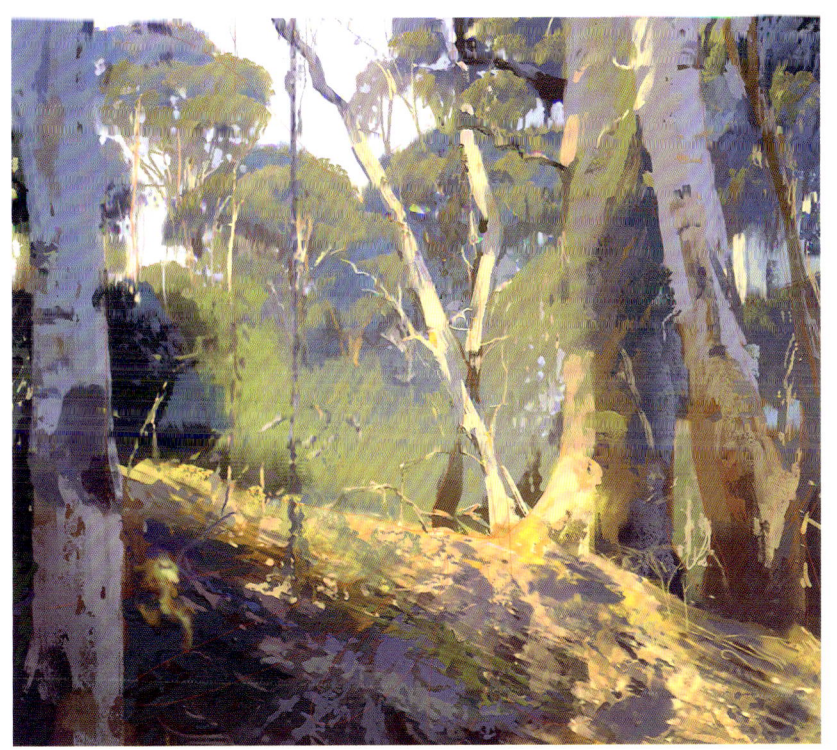

10. These eucalyptus trees have distinctively smooth, pale trunks

10. EUCALYPTUS TREES

Since I'm in love with white tree trunks, the eucalyptus forests of coastal California are a constant source of inspiration. Your audience is used to seeing mostly dark trees, so treat them to this for a change.

11. LAKE SCENE

This lake image emphasizes the idea of grouping. When elements are scattered, they have less importance. When they group and clump together, they have a greater feeling of purpose, as these groves of trees do.

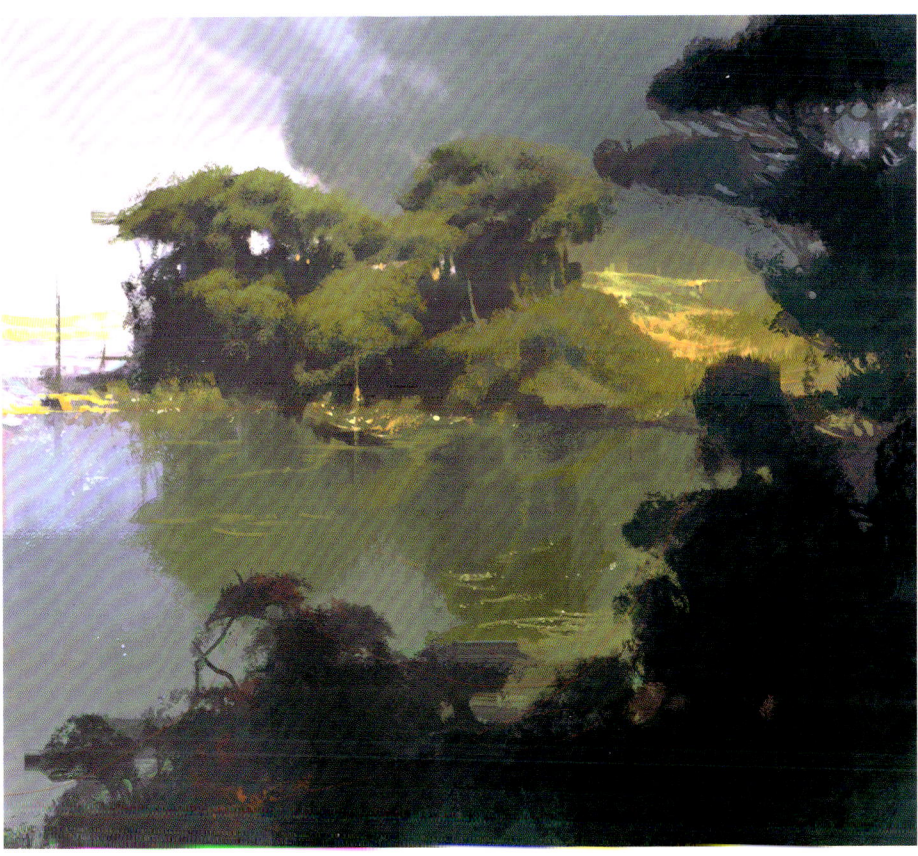

11. Use grouping to your advantage when placing environmental features

Rainforest trees are fighting for their lives.
They're pushing their way upward in desperation to
get as much sunlight as possible at their crowns.
Show your audience that primal upward reach!

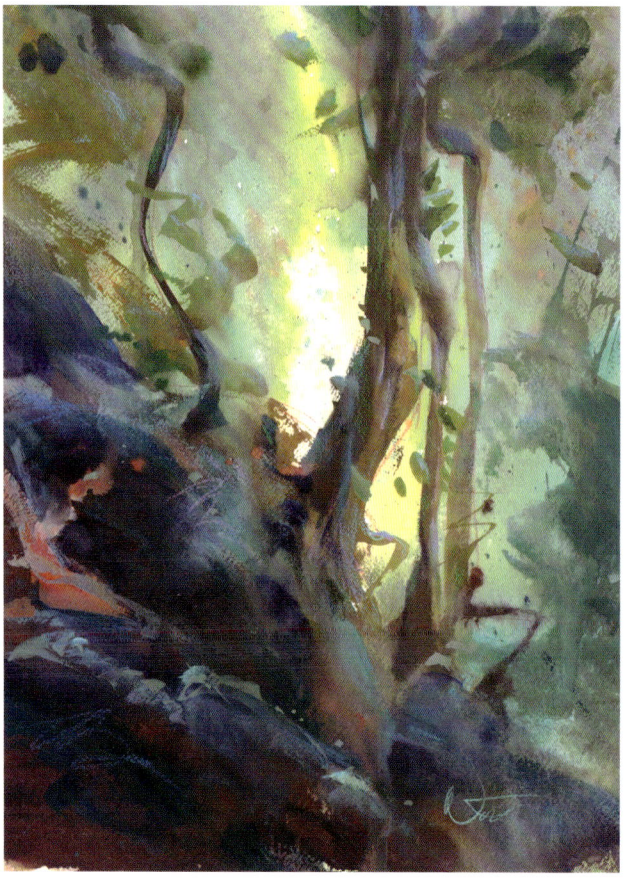

12. The need for sunlight is a
powerful factor in a tree's growth

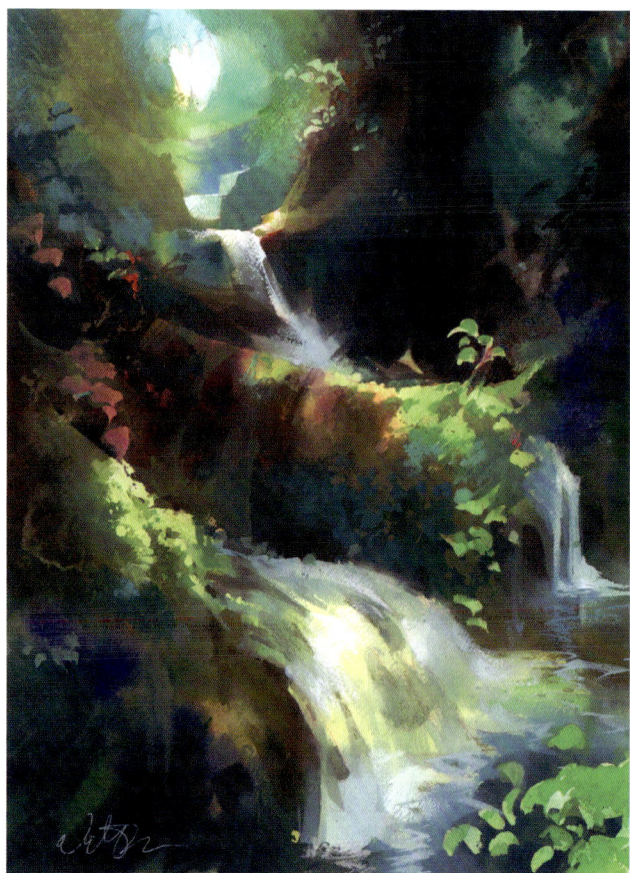

13. You can make strong design choices
even when illustrating from reality

12. COSTA RICA

I mentioned a trip to Costa Rica at the
top of this chapter, and this watercolor
is one of the results. I risked my life for
this, so I hope you like it. Remember, these
trees are fighting for their lives. They're
pushing their way upward in desperation
to get as much sunlight as possible at their
crowns. Show your audience that primal
upward reach!

13. O'AHU

Let's stick with rainforests. This is a fun
exaggeration of scenery at the windward
side of O'ahu. In what way is it exaggerated?
The direction and counter-direction are
carefully composed for an appealing
composition, and the bands of red and
green, though truthful to the original,
are carefully placed to keep the interest
toward the middle.

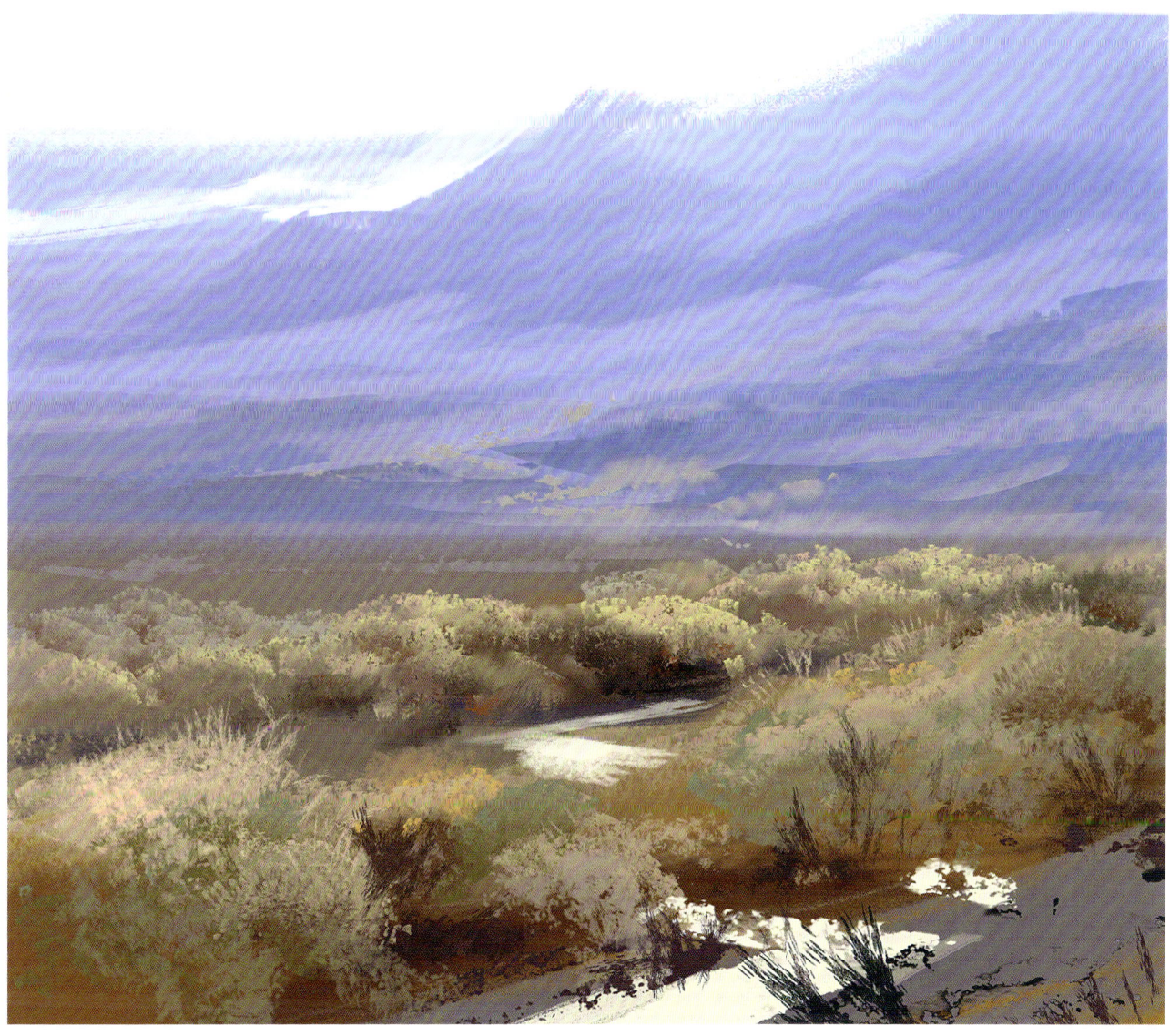

14. This composition's tranquil beauty belies one of the hottest places on Earth!

14. DEATH VALLEY

I guess I just have this penchant for flirting with the forces of nature, because this is Death Valley, California, a place that I have visited and painted many times. I tried to time my visits in the more temperate spring and fall seasons, but I was once there in the dead of summer and the temperature measured 122°F (50°C) in full shade after the sun had set. It's a unique and beautiful desert biome rich in color and texture, but don't hike there alone in the summer – it's called Death Valley for a reason.

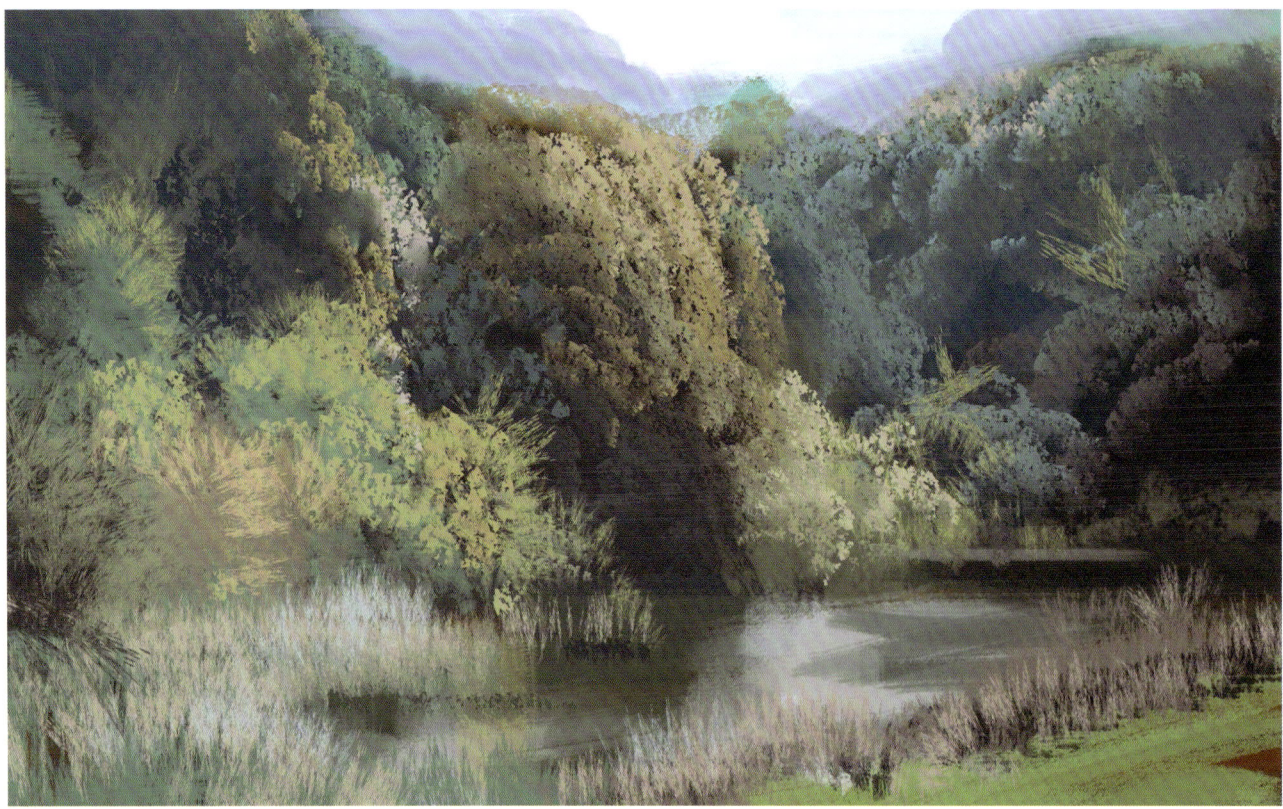

15. These swamps are rich with foliage colors and textures

15. NORTH CAROLINA

And now back to the swamps of North Carolina. This is a quick pass to explore the rich textures of the location. The area is nearly entirely green, but look at how very many different *shades* of green there are.

16. HISPANIOLA

Here's the tropical fiesta of the Dominican Republic, from the Caribbean island of Hispaniola. This is another place with an extraordinary range in shades of green. The thing to pay attention to here is translucency: leaves and fronds in nature often have a translucent quality where direct sunlight passes right through into the shadow side. That's what's happening in the upper center – that brilliant yellow patch is a backlit palm frond. That's the takeaway I'd like you to get from this image: look for the translucent qualities in nature. There is a real glow of life in such materials.

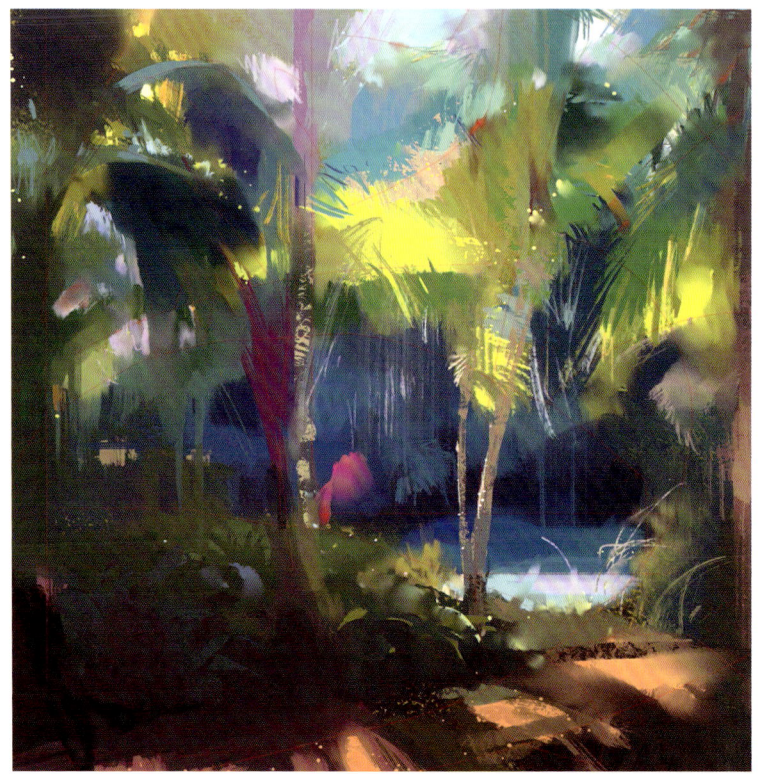

16. Always observe how light interacts with translucent materials

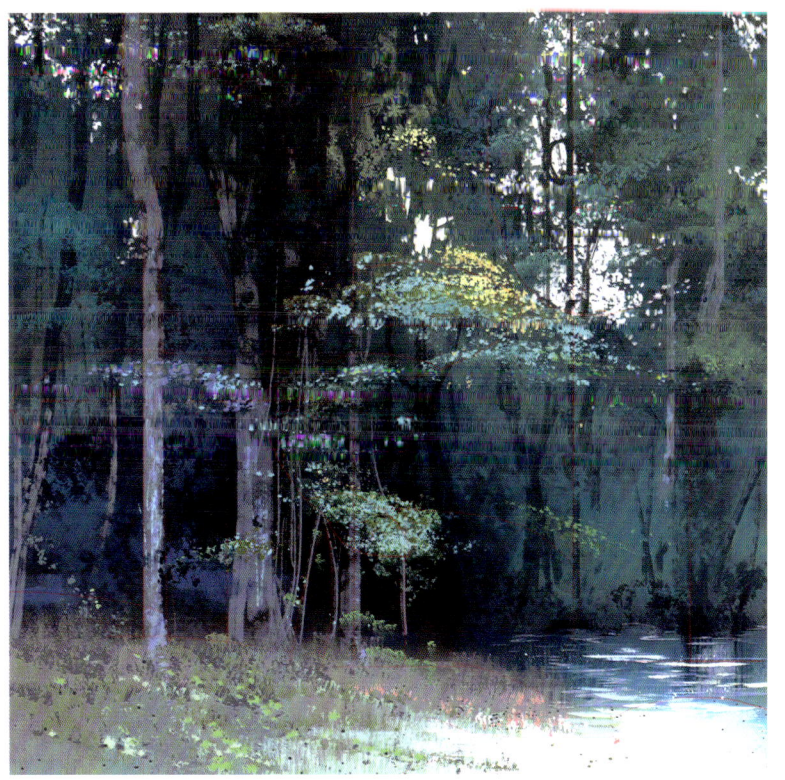

17. Rhythm, grouping, and active versus passive are qualities of this environment

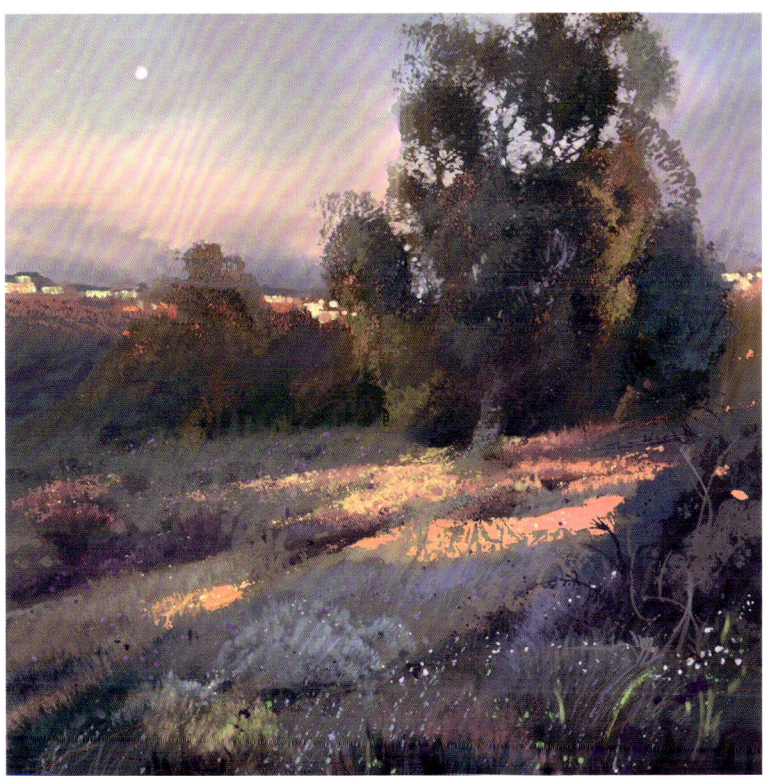

18. These hills are rich with variety, texture, and color

17. SWAMP FOLIAGE

Back to North Carolina, again! Notice the rhythm of the leaves, weaving their way down from top to bottom, and the grouping of the trees. The background is kept simple, dark, and massed to support the glittery sprinkle of leaves and light.

18. SOUTHERN CALIFORNIA

These are the beautiful rich hills of home in southern California. In fact, this whole biome is at the core of what caused me to become an artist. I wandered these hills as a kid and could not believe the iridescent colors at sunset. I wanted to become an artist and to figure out how the color of otherwise bland foliage could be so intensely ornamental. Dusk accentuates the color but, in any lighting, it's a rich tapestry of contrasting local colors.

189

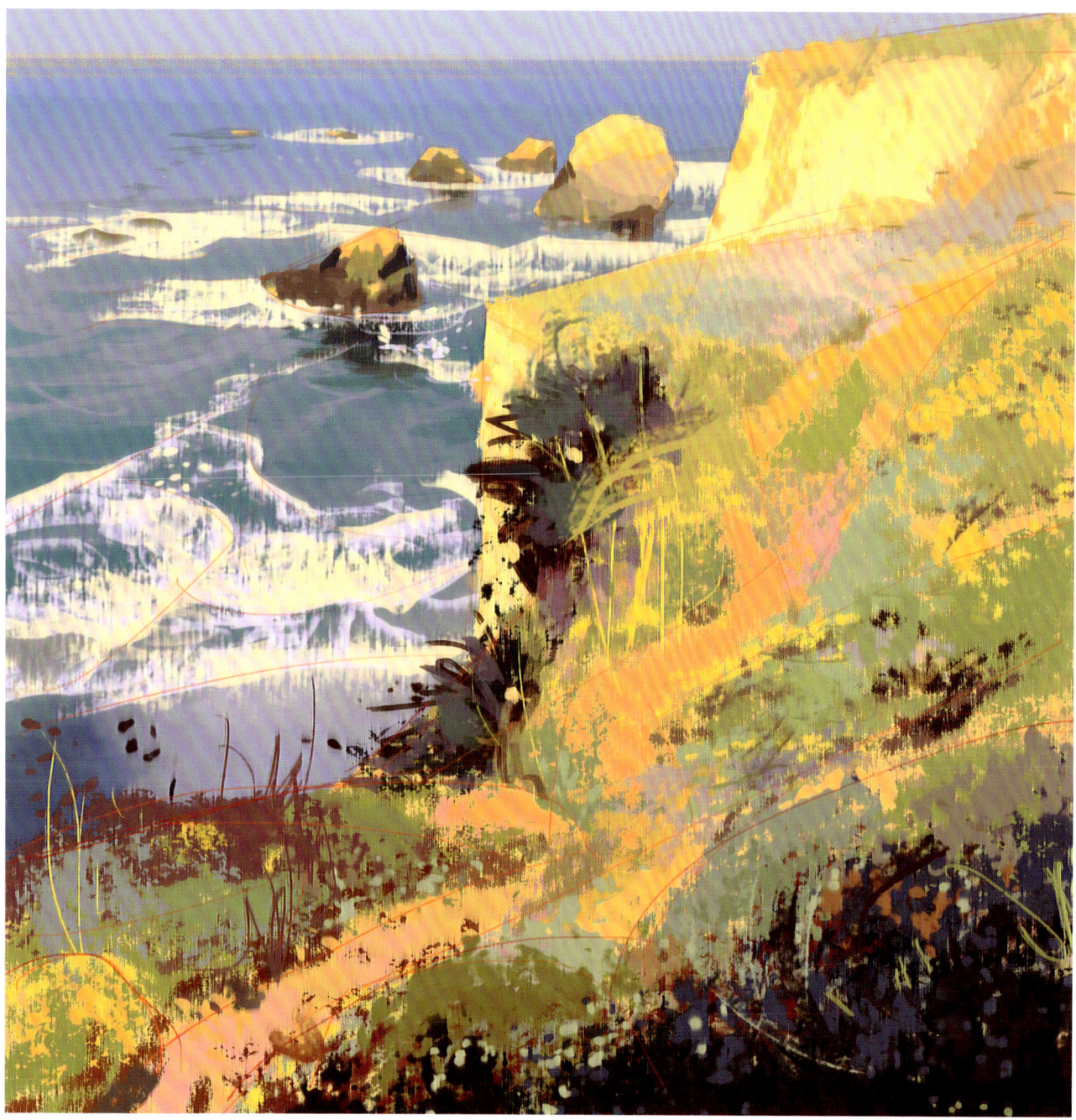

19. This image is vivid with contrast in local color, texture, and shape

19. CALIFORNIA COAST

Another favorite biome: the California coast. The takeaway of this one is the contrast of the yellowed ornamental ground colors with the blues of the ocean and sky.

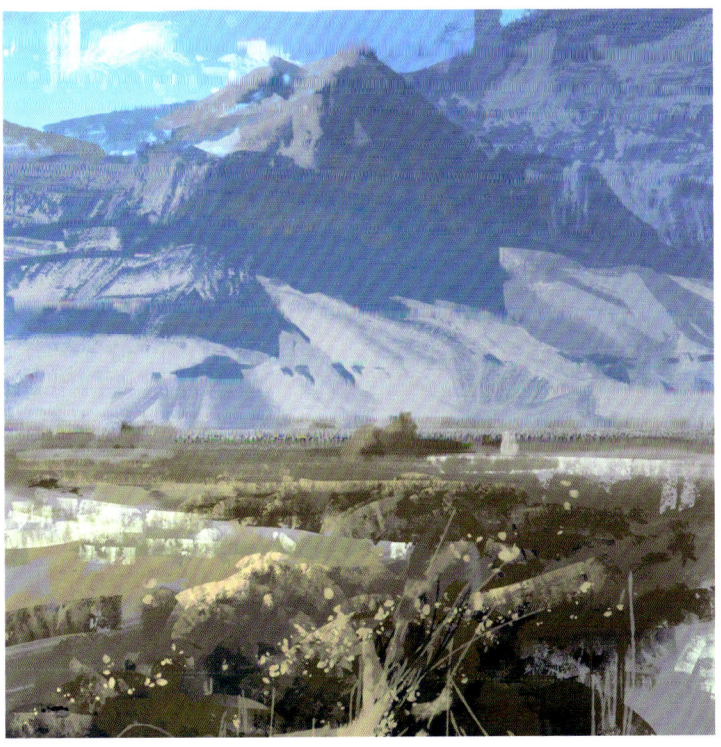

20. The mountains offer remarkable patterns of light and shadow

20. NEVADA

The remarkable shapes and patterns of the desert mountains of Nevada. A mountain range like this, half in light and half in shadow, can be molded to create patterns to powerfully serve the needs of the story unfolding in your desert environment.

21. THE LONE CYPRESS

Earlier I was telling you about the beautiful biome of Carmel-by-the-Sea. This is a famous spot there called Lone Cypress. Hopefully the emotion of the place speaks for itself.

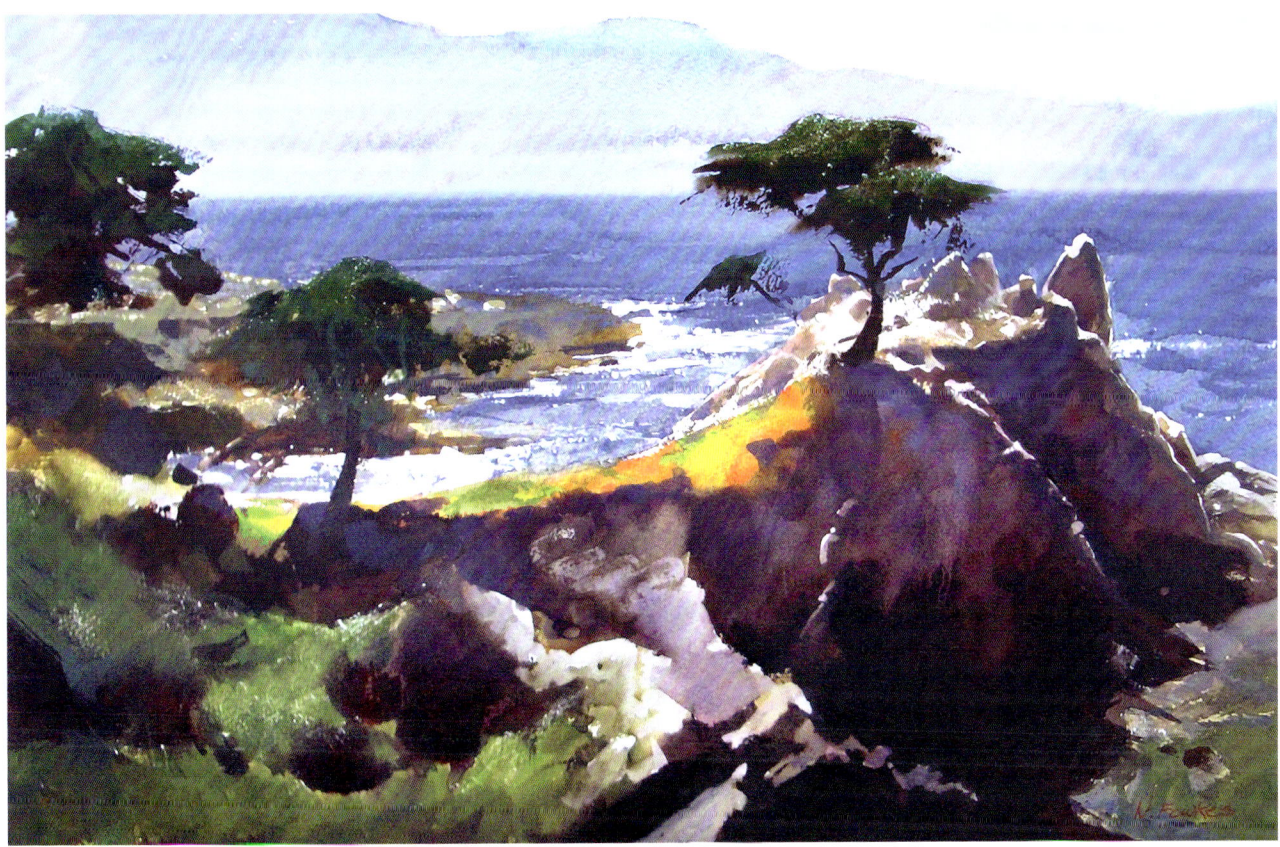

21. This distinctive cypress tree has become an iconic landmark

INTO IMAGINARY LANDS

For this one I visited the birch forests in Utah and fell in love with white tree trunks (again). Here they are in all their glory, and I did sneak a stream of water into the ground plane. This particular study has been pushed into a fantasy realm – the stylized shapes and colors are a departure from reality for illustrative purposes. We must study the realities of nature but, at the same time, our audience demands that we take them to places they can't get to in real life. Places they can only get to through us. This is how we hold our value as artists.

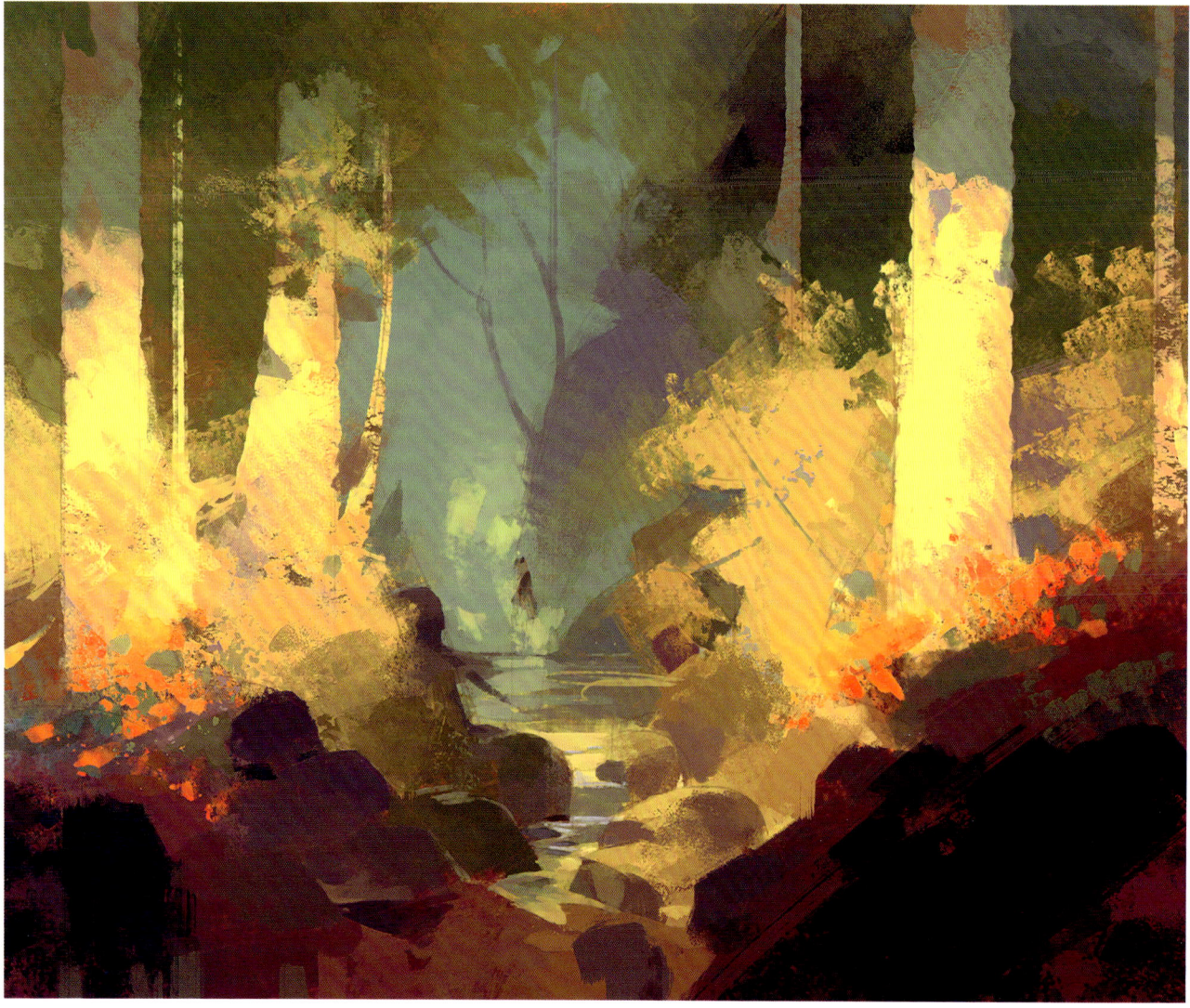

△ Though this scene has its roots in a real location, it's stylized to dramatize the emotional experience

01. A SETTING FOR ADVENTURE

The paintings I've shown up to this point have been illustrations of specific biomes, but they haven't necessarily been imagined story illustrations. So what's the difference? A landscape painting is an illustration of a place; an entertainment-art environment is an illustration of a place *for a story to unfold*. That's the feel we're getting into with these last few images. This one is meant to create an upbeat mood and take us on a journey. We are firmly placed in the foreground, but are invited to travel into the distance, following the winding brook to explore the copse of trees.

02. A FANTASY SCENE

This image is obviously fictionalized. The goal was to create a beautiful but unsettling environment where the next thing that happens in the story might be really good ... or it might also be really bad. If you look carefully, you'll see which one of those outcomes it's headed toward.

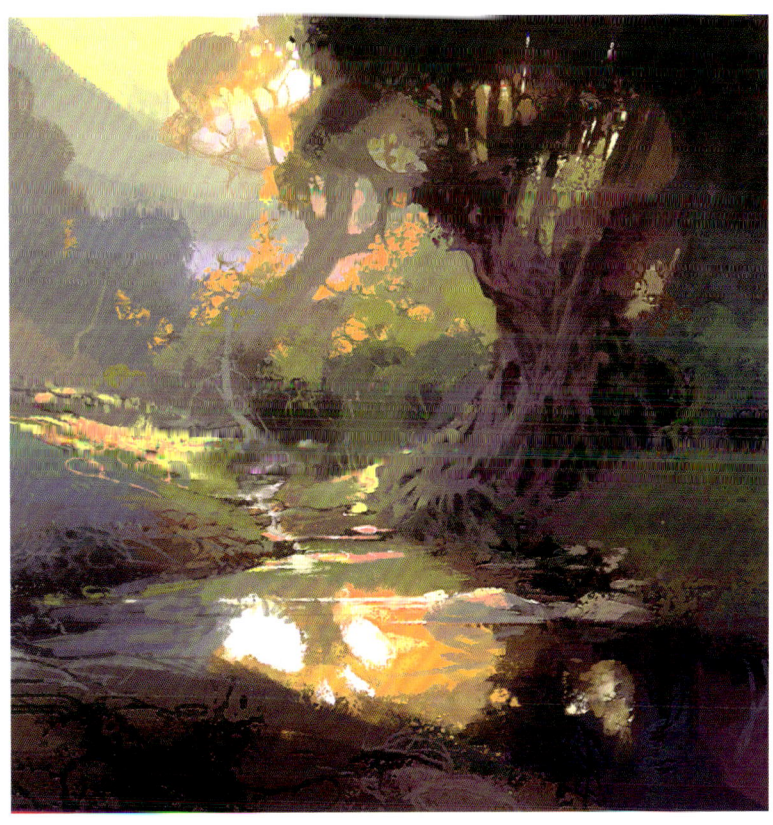

01. This is a location with room for the viewer to be drawn into a story

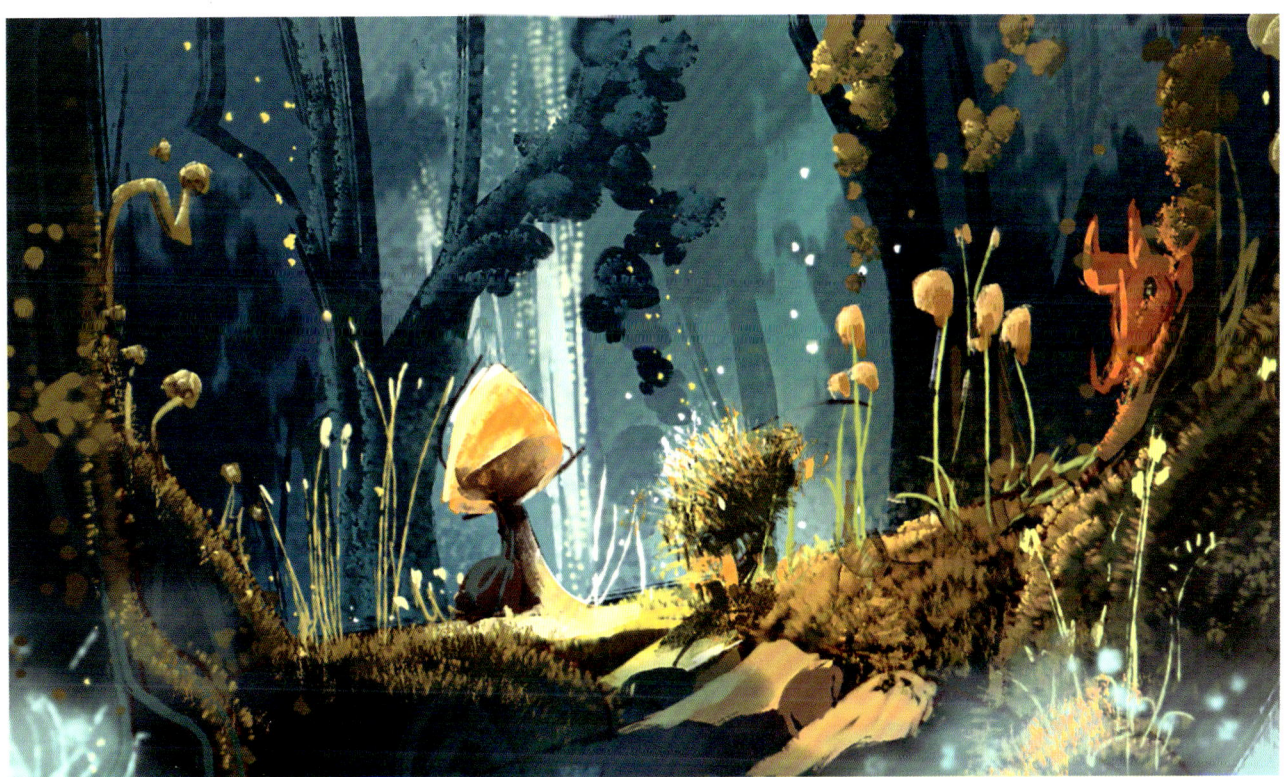

02. This setting combines a warm, magical ambience with an air of menace

DEMONSTRATION: STRANGE FOREST

This image will be the demo for this chapter. It uses the qualities of biome that we've covered so far to create a sense of place, mood, and emotion. Let's dive in and do this bad boy!

01. ORANGE BASE

We'll start with orange because it will be a critical aspect of our color palette. I want the picture to have a distinctive ground plane, so I work the perspective out enough to make that area clear. Then I plan to surround the forest floor with a frame of trees that will lead us into the distant background. I don't need to get too specific as long as I have the big shapes and the big idea established here.

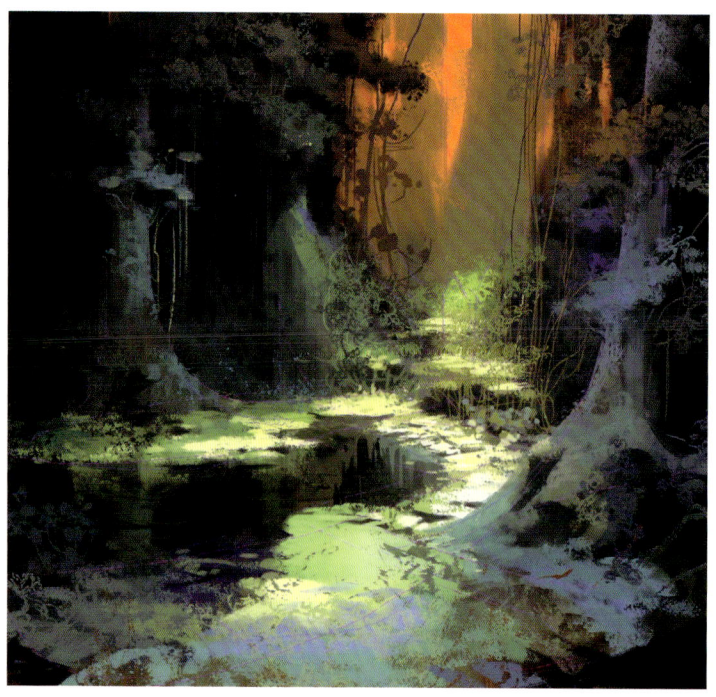

△ Look closely and you'll recognize many of the biome elements we've discussed

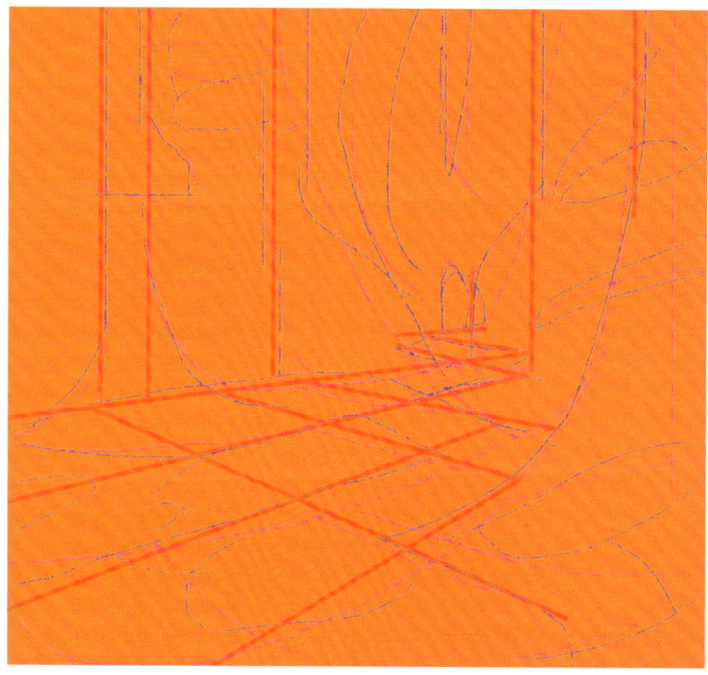

01. Start off with an orange base color and rough perspective drawing

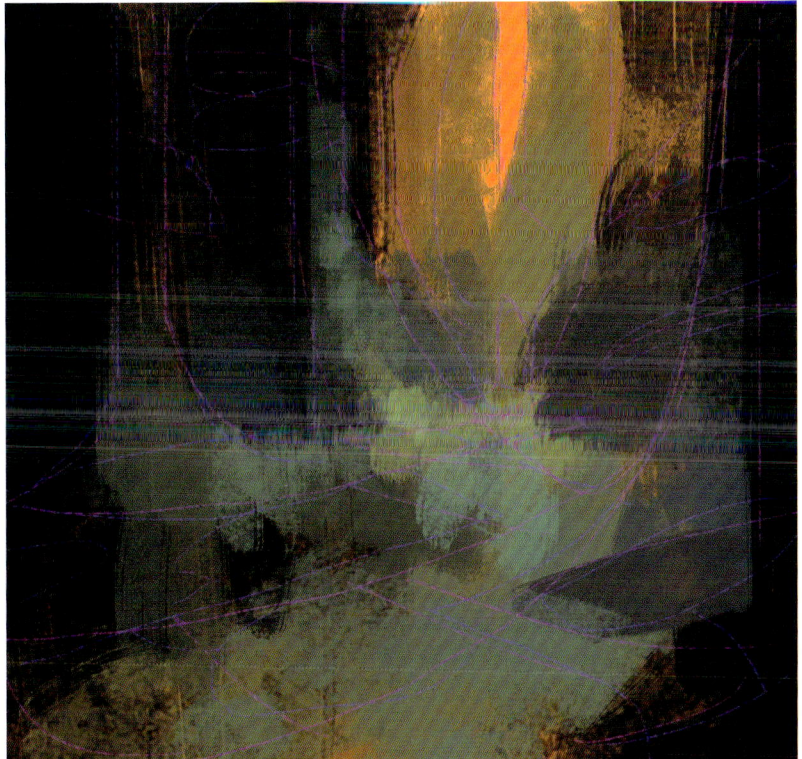

02. Block in shades of green undergrowth and framing shapes of the trees

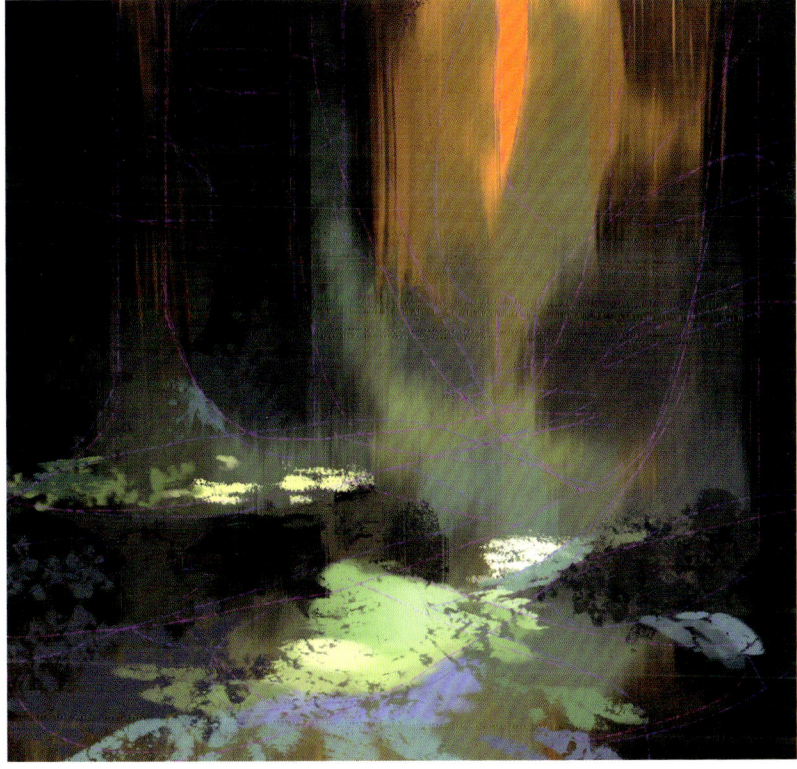

03. Sunlight breaks through the canopy to light the ground and pool

02. ROUGH COLORS

We're ready to dive right into the massing of color. I want the ground plane to have that rich neutral green of plant life, and the surrounding trees need to be dark as a framing element. I make sure those darks have some reds in them to keep them alive. The ground plane is illuminated with cool skylight filtering down from above – we'll add direct sunlight shortly. I also have some of the lighting creeping up the trees to establish them more specifically. One thing I'm doing here at the beginning is working toward an imaginative, unexpected quality in the scene and color palette. We'll talk color details in the next chapter, but the thing I'm upending here is the expectation that warmer colors will be in front and cooler colors will be in the back. I'm doing just the opposite.

03. DAPPLED LIGHT

Now let's add focus with direct lights. I want the new light passages to have texture and presence, so my first step is to create softness by putting a vertical blur on what I've already done. I start adding lights as if I'm beginning a pathway through the forest floor. The light is passing through a canopy of foliage above, so it will have a broken and dappled quality. It's hitting green foliage and warm earth, so those will be my color choices in the central area. The surrounding cool lights act as a nice complement to the warms. Finally, I begin to add the suggestion of a pool in the lower middle and left. Notice the reflections indicated there.

04. FOLIAGE

Next I mass in more light for greater impact in the picture. The lighting continues up the tree trunks, but as more of a blue skylight since those areas are less important. As I get up into the trees I sprinkle the suggestion of foliage. I'm using some specific brushes for textures, but the truth is you can use just about anything that has some texture. I'll get more specific on these techniques for you in the chapter on my process for achieving the 'wow factor' (page 360).

05. DETAILING

And this is our final step! It's primarily a matter of refining the lighting and weaving some fun brush and shrubbery into the scene. Hanging vines and strands are an important addition to the foliage – they help get the creepy factor. And I want you to notice how carefully the temperature and the value of the lighting are controlled. I mentioned the direct light on the ground softening into cool ambient light as the foliage and trees move upward, and I've stuck to that very carefully. The reason is our constantly discussed topic of *purpose*: the lighting pulls us down into the ground plane, then leads us off into the distance so we can have a grand fantasy adventure in this mysterious, decayed forest. Mission accomplished!

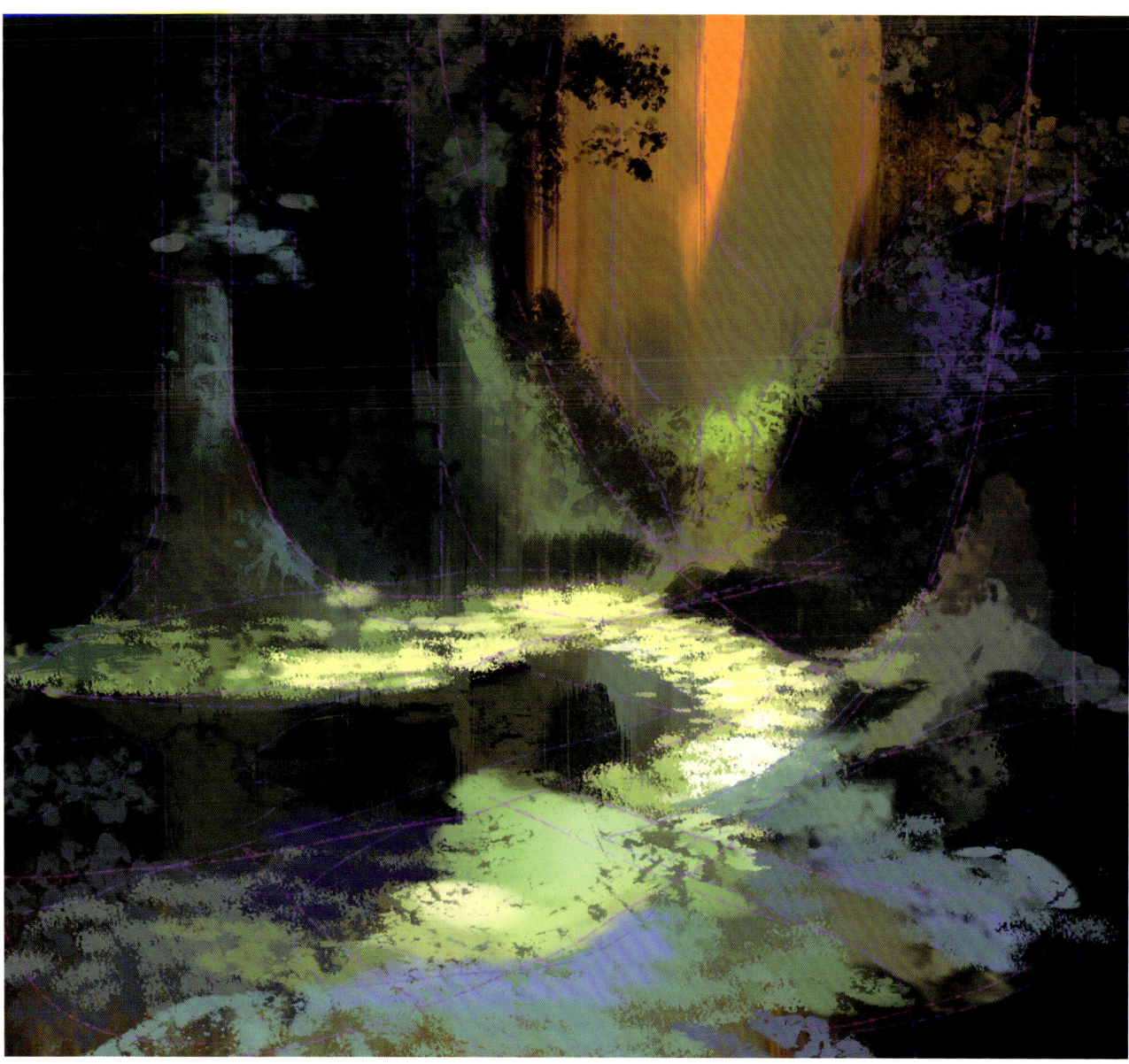

04. The higher trunks and foliage shift to a cooler, dimmer light

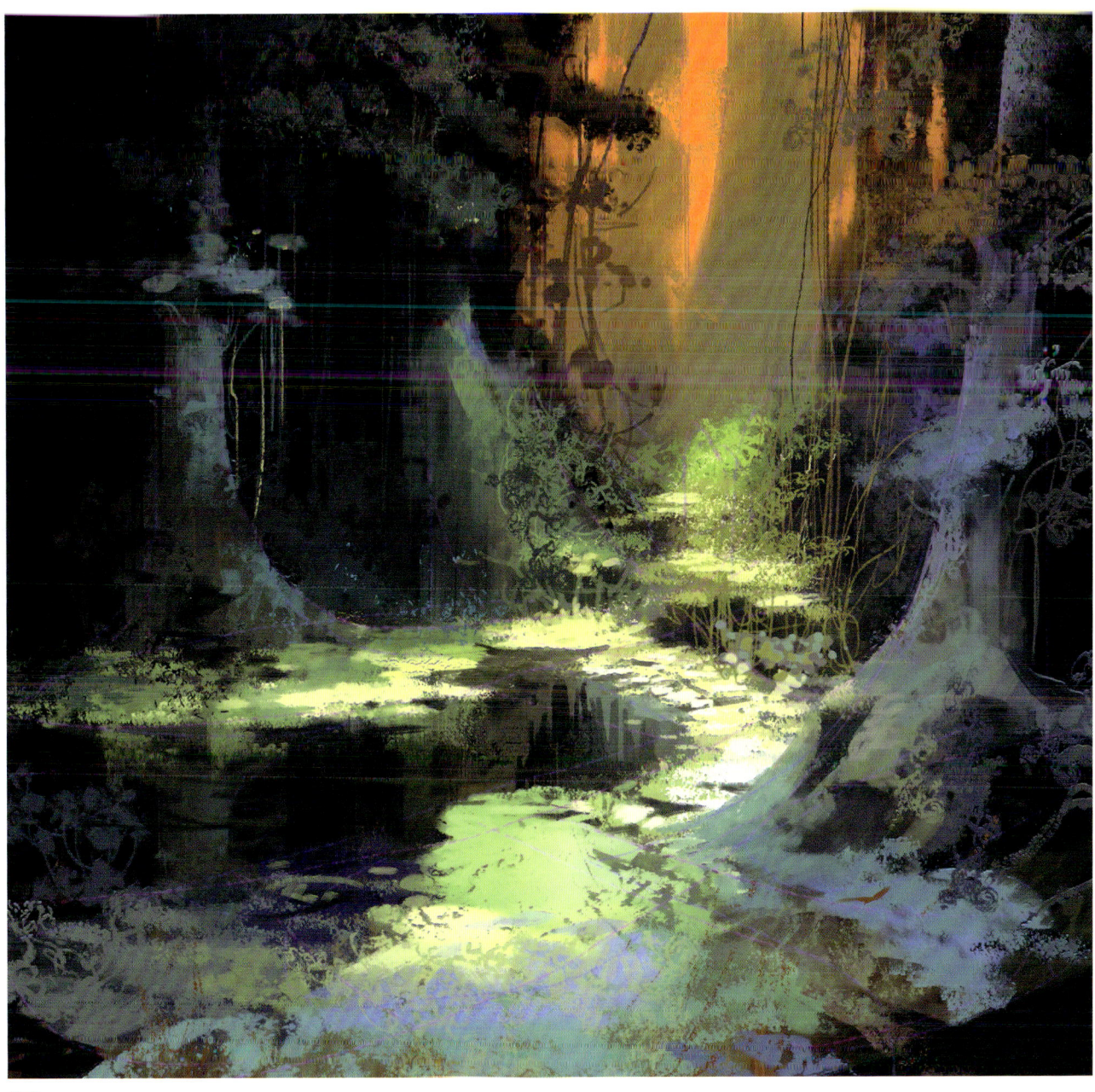

05. Tangled vines and scribbled shrubbery make the scene feel eerie and alive

The environment is carefully crafted so that
we can have a grand fantasy adventure
in this mysterious, decayed forest. This is
the goal of biome development.

RECOMMENDED EXERCISE:
NATURE SKETCHBOOK

At this point in the book, it will come as no surprise to you that I love sketchbooks! But you may not have guessed the level of my obsession. I have hundreds of them – many are full and many are just waiting to be filled. You can see a stack of them here. I've experimented over the years and found the types that I like, but that doesn't mean you will have the same preferences. You likely already have sketchbooks but, if you're not completely happy with the papers you're currently working on, try some new ones. I tend to prefer heavy paper stock, especially papers thick enough to take pencil, pen, and watercolor. I love both white paper and toned paper but, in the end, the key to successful sketchbooking is that you must enjoy the process! If you don't, you won't come back to it often enough for it to be an effective form of exploration. Better to enjoy what you're doing than engage in some kind of 'proper' study.

I've learned over the years that the sketching I enjoy most is using a brush and water, so most of the pages you see here are using the ink/brush process that I showed you in chapter 71. When you sketch, don't worry too much about what I prefer. Many of you will prefer linework rather than tonal work, and that's a fine choice. Once again, any medium and process that you enjoy, which keeps you coming back for more, is the right approach.

One last reminder: since there's neither the time nor the means to render every aspect of the biome you're sketching, the caricaturing we discussed on page 172 might just be the solution for you. Happy biome-sketching!

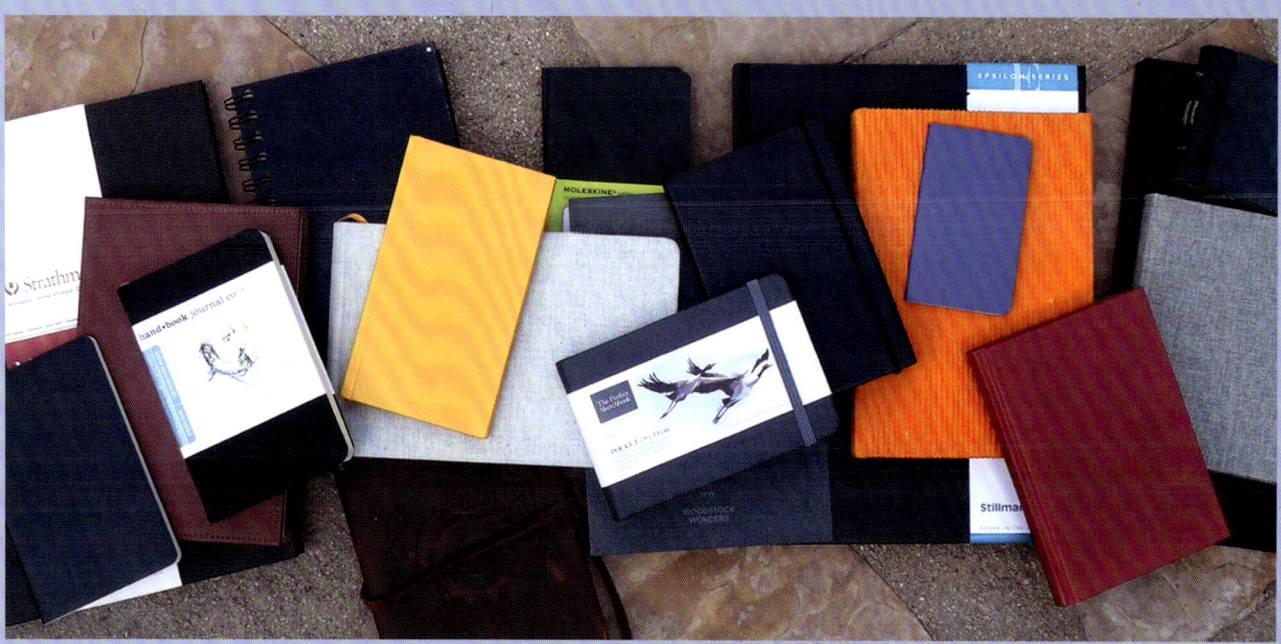

△ Just a few of my many sketchbooks

The key to successful sketchbooking is that you must enjoy the process! If you don't, you won't come back to it often enough for it to be an effective form of study.

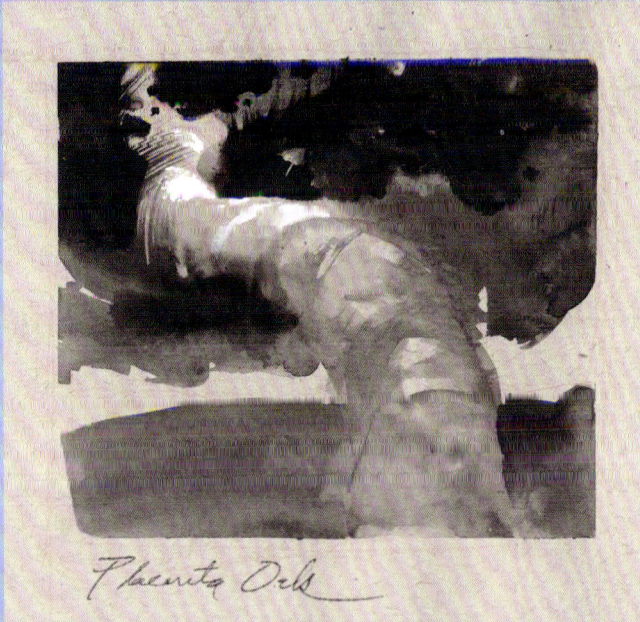

Placerita Oaks

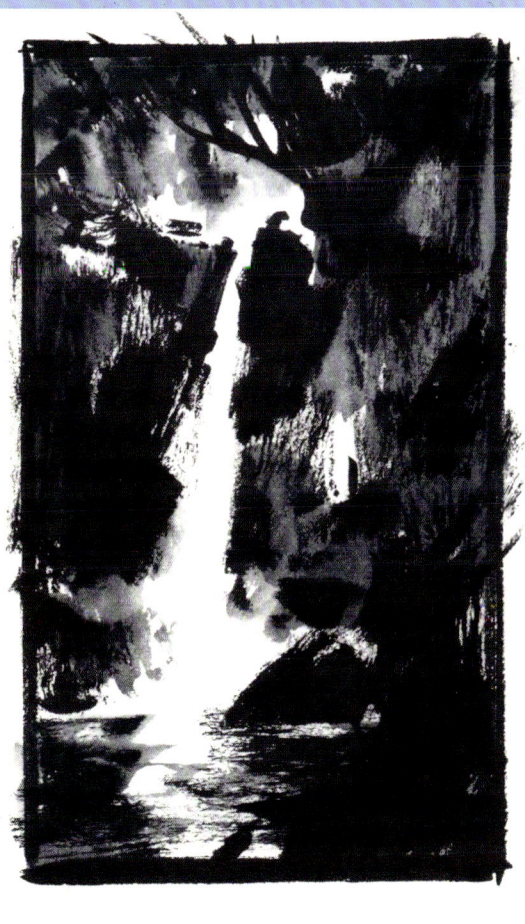

The Waterfall

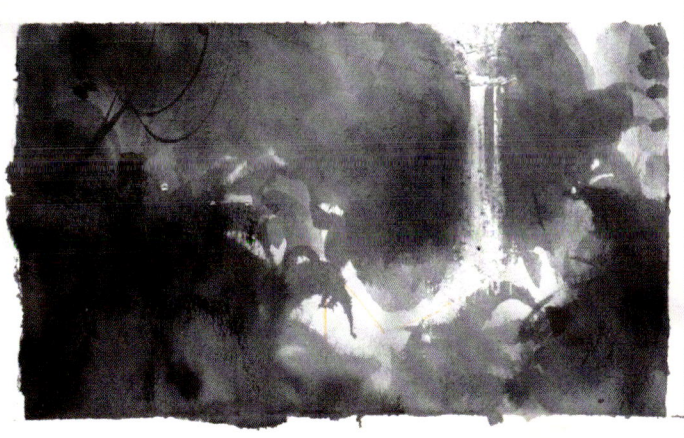

Falls

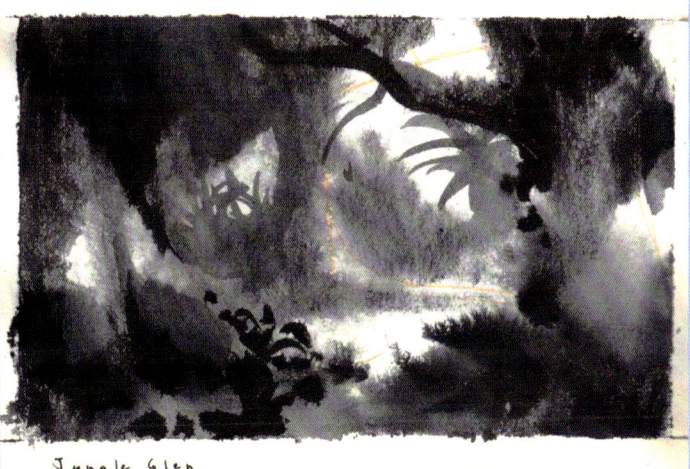

Jungle Glen

△ Some of my nature sketches using a prefilled inkbrush and water

PROP DESIGN

Everything that appears in an entertainment-
art project, such as an animation or a video
game, has to be designed by somebody.

NEW KNOWLEDGE

In the first chapter of this book, I relayed the experience I had in art school where I changed my direction to imaginative art with a traditional foundation. But even after changing, there was a required course that I dreaded. The subject was nuts, the instructor was nuts – it was a fine-arts theory course that threw everything I was interested in out the window for something that was, to me, murky and indefinable. I was sure it was going to be a distraction from what I needed to do ... but, boy, was I wrong!

Throughout the course we looked at all kinds of crazy artists, subjects, and art films – some were not my thing, but many more eye-opening. We took regular field trips to destinations of interest around Los Angeles. One of those places was a back-alley furniture restoration warehouse. It was a place where a remarkable crew would acquire old pieces of furniture that had really good bones and use them as bases to create and upholster something completely new. Some pieces were straightforward beauties of craftsmanship and others looked like they came out of *The Nightmare Before Christmas*. Each was one of a kind.

I had never thought much about how far furniture could go, so this experience and the entire course ended up being of great value to me. For this reason I've chosen furniture for some of our primary examples in this chapter. There's little more ordinary and mundane in our environments than a sofa, but a good prop designer can turn that sofa toward any mood and emotion that they need. And this is true for all props. We've already asked the question, 'How can we take inanimate objects and imbue them with great emotion?' and this chapter will be a further exploration of that subject.

EVEN A TINY PEBBLE

I was once on an animated movie project where I was handling the design of a particular sequence. One of the 3D modelers approached me about a moment where the main character absently kicks a pebble while he's thinking. The modeler was asking what the pebble should look like, as it had to be created as a 3D asset. It was a legit question. Should it be round and innocuous? Should it be really sharp, as if the character might inadvertently snag his toe? Everything that appears in an entertainment-art project, such as an animation or a video game, has to be designed by somebody. All such objects are considered 'props', and prop design is a formal part of the design and development process. This means that we need to be good at designing props in such a way that they can be passed to 3D-modeling and texturing artists to create the final production assets. Concept environments can sometimes be rendered in a loose and suggestive way, but prop art is the opposite – it usually needs a tight finish so that 3D artists completely understand what qualities to give to the prop. Let's begin.

How can we take inanimate objects and imbue them with great emotion? A good prop designer must be able to achieve this.

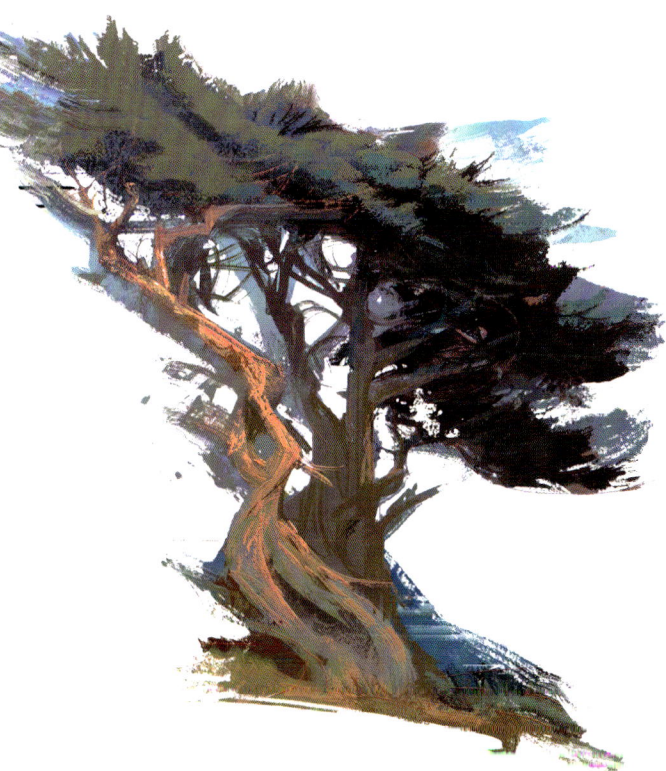

BASIC REQUIREMENTS

As a generic example, I've put together this ornamental perfume bottle in the same way it might be done in the production process. Everything here is painted two-dimensionally in Adobe Photoshop. First is the simple design including shapes and local color. It's useful to show this baseline version, so we can see the design without it being obstructed by highlights or varying qualities of the material.

Speaking of which, what material is the object? What are its surface qualities? We need to render those qualities, as shown in the second graphic, and then show the full 3D form of the prop. This is enough information for any good 3D modeler to create the model as a final production asset.

Our prop renderings need to contain enough information that any good 3D modeler can recreate the object as a final production asset.

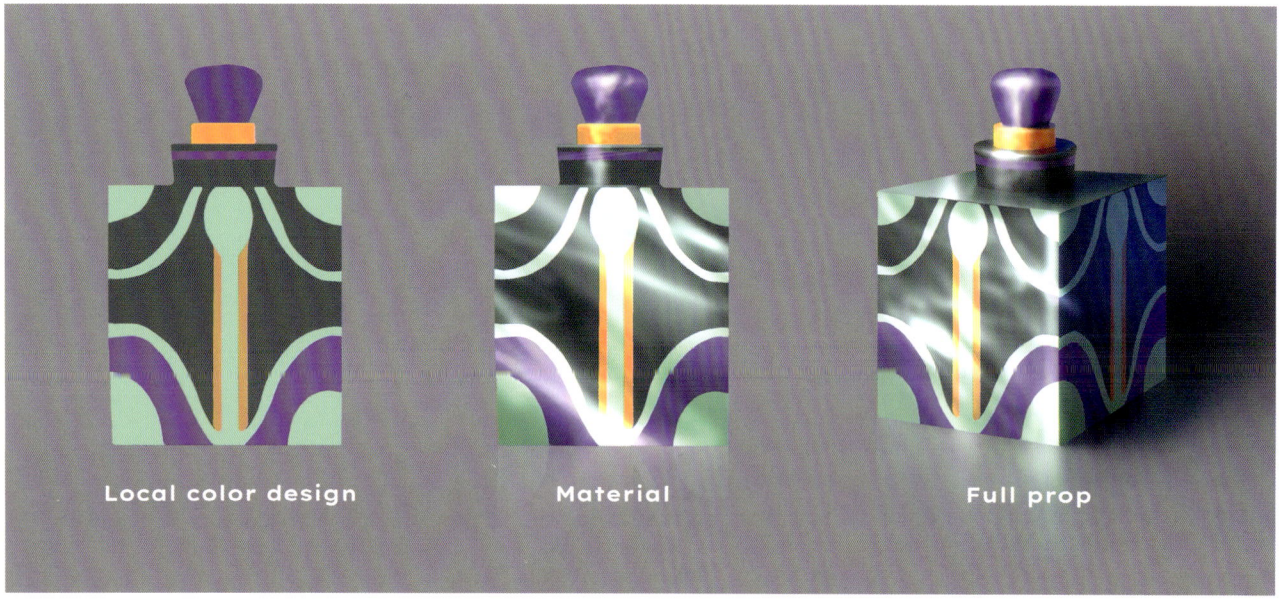

Local color design   Material   Full prop

△ Visualizing a three-dimensional object to pass on to a 3D artist

01. MATERIALS

Now here's the challenge: if we need to be able to render any possible prop, we must be able to render any possible material. How are transparent or translucent materials made to look real? What about magic, like a material that has its own inner glow? How do you render that? Here are a few examples. You can find references of just about any material online. I recommend that you practice, practice, practice, to be proficient at this. That'll be the recommended exercise for this chapter, so we'll revisit the subject shortly.

02. CREATING PROPS

As we become proficient in rendering materials, we need to put that experience into practice with props. For instance, let's say our main character is an alchemist who has an assortment of cork-stopped glass bottles filled with potions. Or perhaps we're working on an animated story of Thomas Edison, and we need a weird attention-grabbing light bulb. The list goes on and so does our batch of props. Leather, paper, steel, and so on – we need to work them all out to help tell our story.

If we need to be able to render any possible prop,
we must be able to render any possible material.

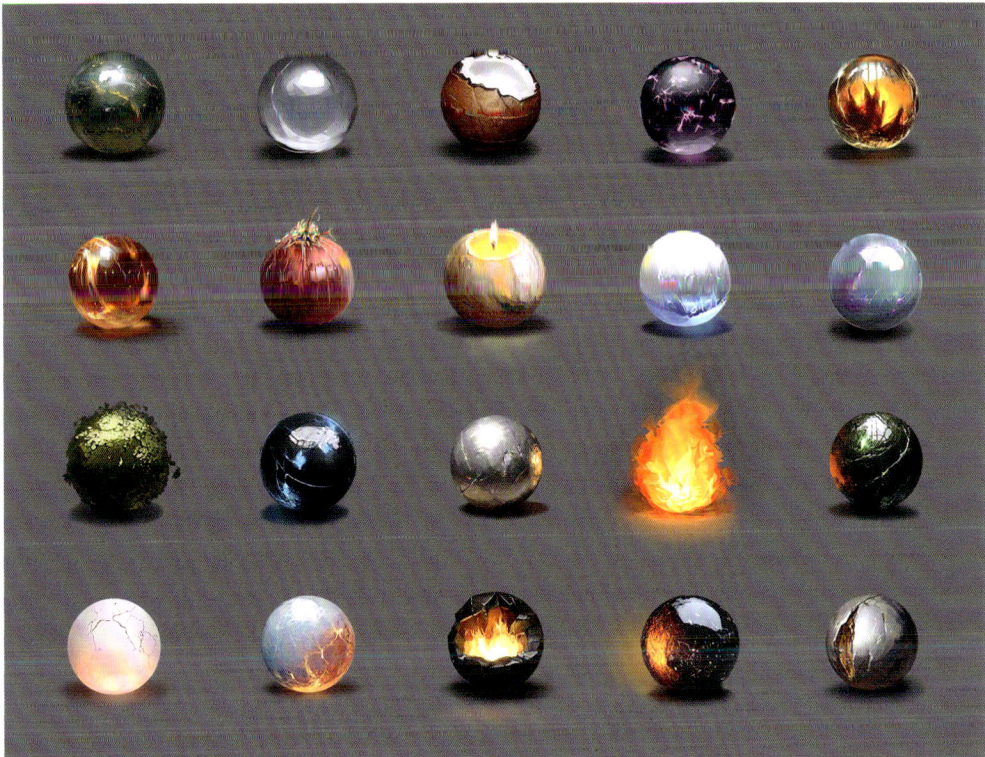

01. Just a few examples of the many, many materials out there!

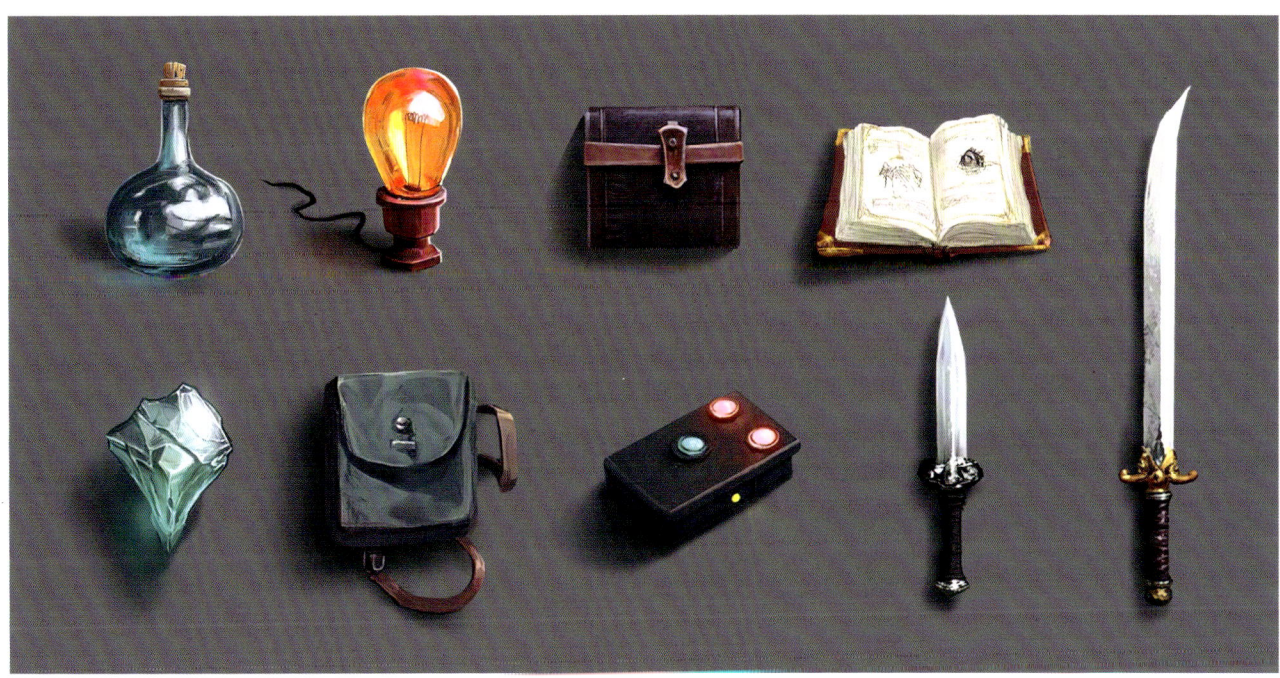

02. Props often require multiple material considerations

MODULES

Let's expand our props to a modular building. Buildings are props, too! For this first example, we need to pull out all of our powers of design and rendering, because this is the home of that crazy alchemist that we were just discussing.

The building needs a design and rendering that fits that character, so we have stone, wood, metal, painted fabric, and magic. Individual buildings and structures need to be carefully worked out – it's useful to render them from this elevated point of view to offer the most information about form and materials. A straight-on point of view would limit us to the front and side planes, but an elevated view shows us three planes – top, front, and side – that will give 3D modelers the best information about structure.

01. ANCIENT RUINS

Now let's continue with the same idea but we'll get more complex. Don't worry about the complexity too much – just think back to the previous chapter on architecture, where we built complicated structures with nothing more than stacked blocks. This module is the same. Here we're going for very heavy stone ruins that have stood for a thousand years or more, and where mystery and magic still abound. Rugged textures, cracks, and invasive foliage all lend themselves to this great sense of history. This whole thing is made of beige stone, so to keep visual interest I'm using green magic, warm lighting, and blue-purple skylights in the shadows for a variety of color.

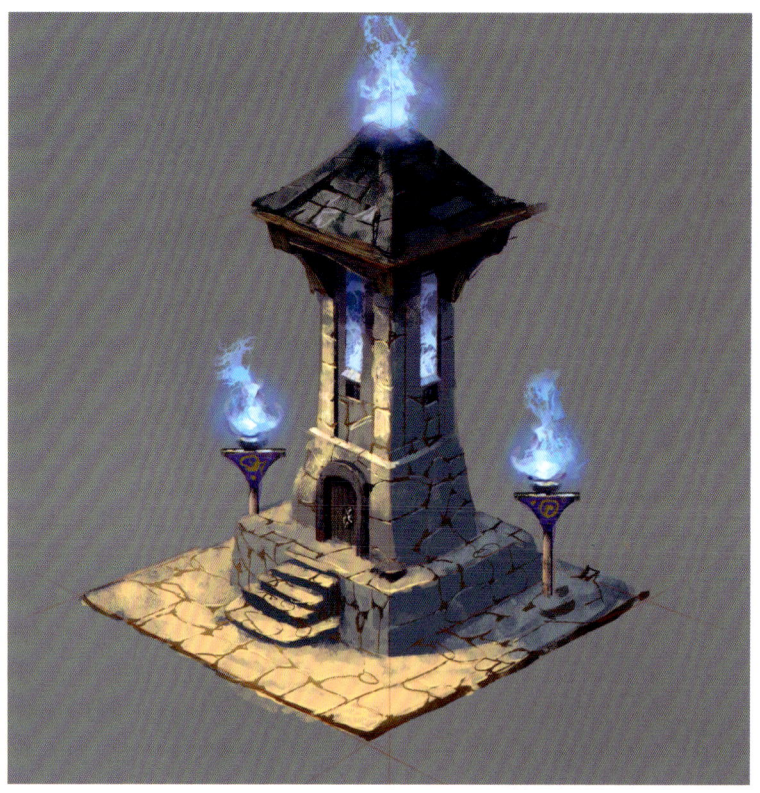

△ An angled top-down view conveys more information about the design

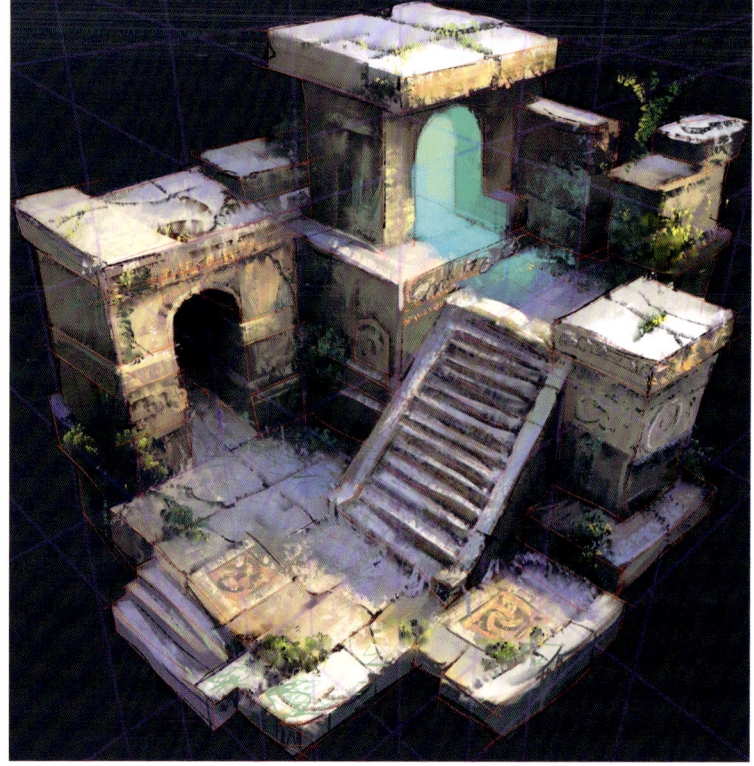

01. This place looks solid, heavy, ancient, and overgrown

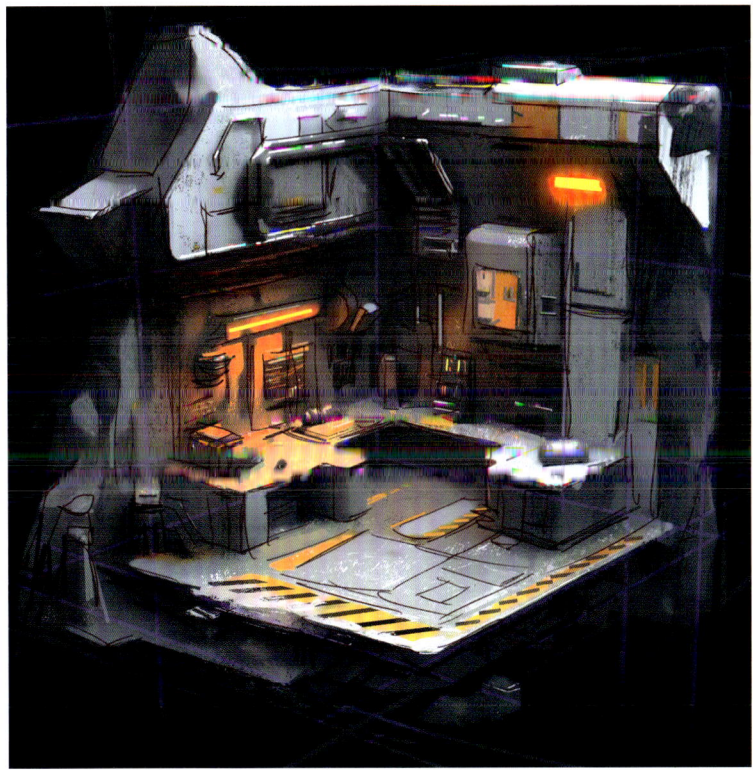

02. This image presents a cross-section of one side of a room

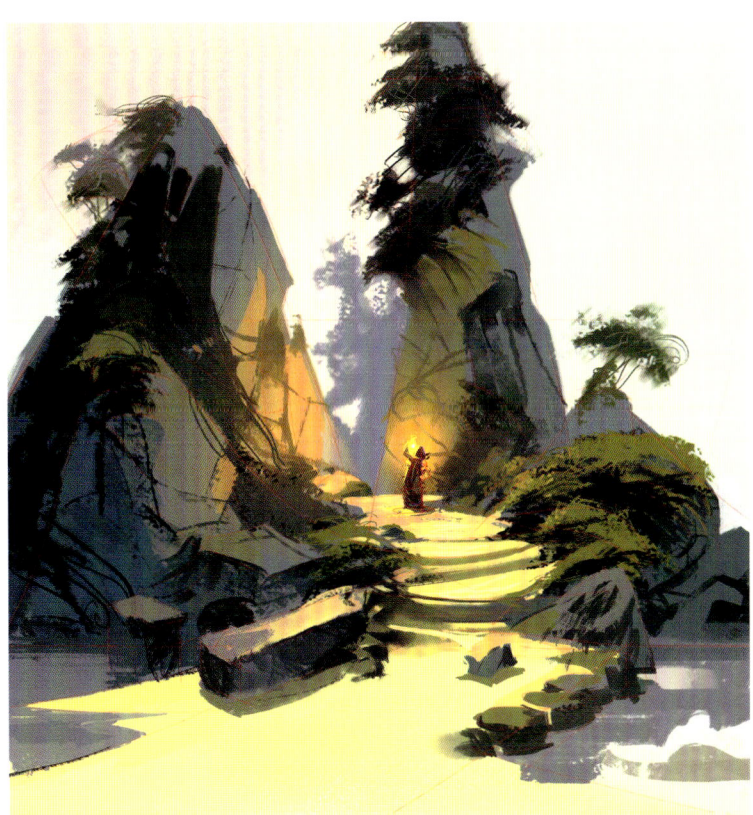

03. The module approach can be used for landscape locations, too

02. FUTURISTIC ROOM

We haven't dealt with an interior yet in this chapter, so let's tackle that now: a techie interior space, very functional, maybe for a lunar colony or some such. For design purposes, interiors are often presented as modules in a cross-section view such as this. Imagine that I had also painted up the opposite view of the room; at that point we would have a full understanding of the interior space, the director would (hopefully) give it a big thumbs-up, and then the designs would go down the pipeline to be modeled and textured. This is the process we usually use for interiors in the formal design and development portion of a project.

03. LANDSCAPE

In the previous chapter we studied the intricacies of biome and how those can be adapted to the needs of a story. We're now putting those ideas into action. For instance, this torch-bearing traveler is making his way through a mysterious landscape that reminds us of rock formations in China. The production pipeline will need a location prop illustration such as this to lay out the design and flavor of the location.

AN EMOTIONAL COUCH?

Now back to the topic that we apply to every subject we tackle: the idea of emotion. At the top of the chapter, I promised to apply this concept to furniture, and this is our big moment! Furniture is a huge part of the design of interior environments and, as we always say, the designed interior tells us about the people who live there and the quality of the place. So here are a series of highly exaggerated and emotional offerings.

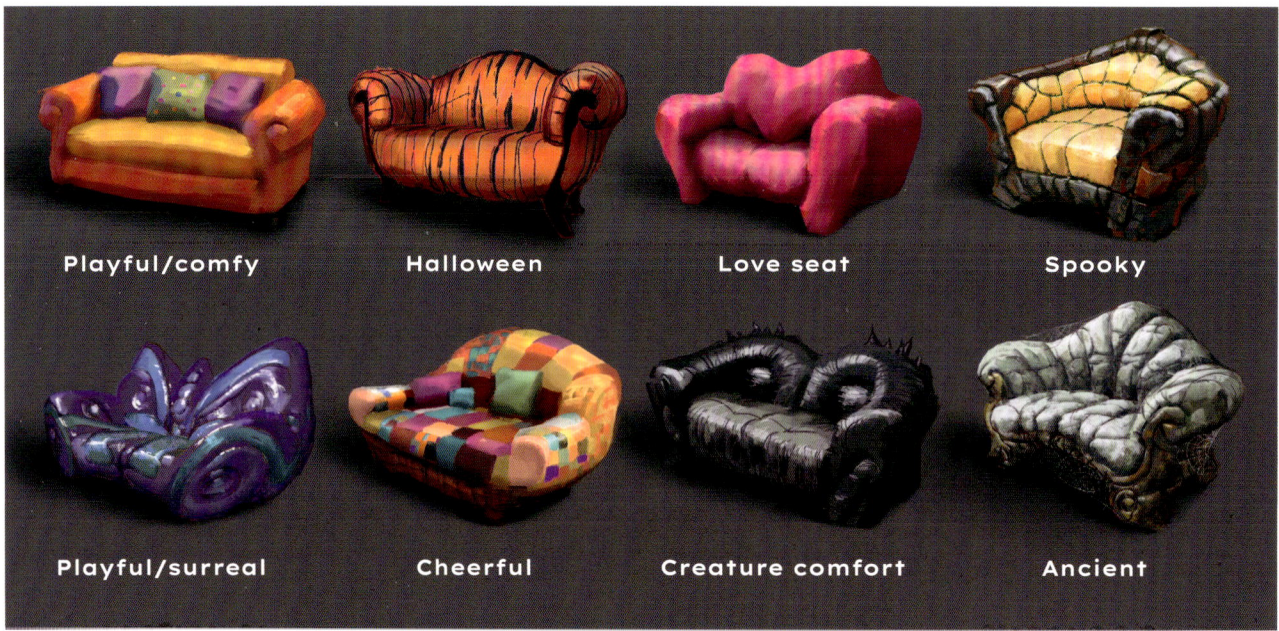

Playful/comfy   Halloween   Love seat   Spooky

Playful/surreal   Cheerful   Creature comfort   Ancient

△ Even a couch can be uniquely expressive, like a character in its own right

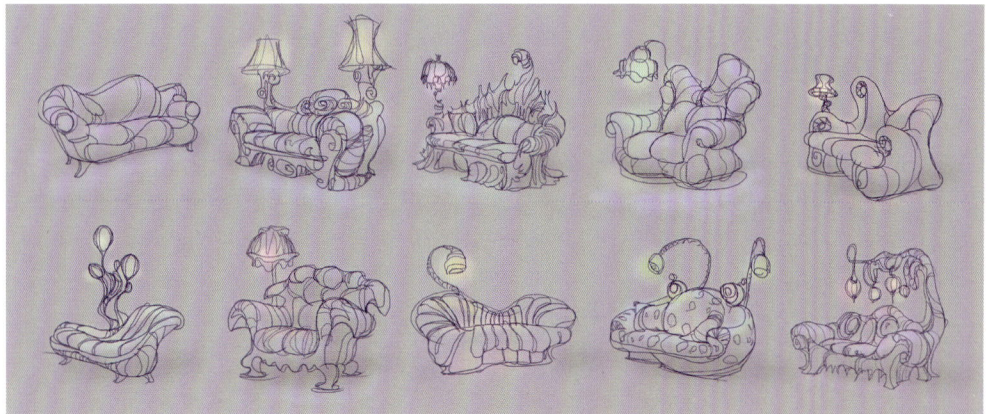

△ Exaggerating a simple couch into several variants

Possibilities are endless, even for something as seemingly ordinary and banal as a sofa.

PUSH, PUSH, PUSH!

As concept artists, we have to tackle so many different kinds of emotions and stories. We need the ability to push our props toward any and every emotion and design possible. So let's keep going because the possibilities are endless, even for something as seemingly ordinary and banal as a sofa.

THE PROP PAGE

Since props are meant to inform the entire production pipeline, a formal 'prop page' is the expected form of presentation. Here's a tree design prop page for an invented movie that I'm titling *The Deed*. It would be something like a gritty 1800s Western set around a Spanish-style mission, featuring a California cypress like the ones we analyzed in the previous chapter (page 175). This page is meant to contain enough information that the tree can be developed in 3D space. It contains a loose color rendering to give the overall feel of the tree, a silhouette with a figure to give scale, photo references for the modelers and texture artists, and an environmental illustration to give the context in which the tree is placed. In a production, every major prop is given a prop page such as this.

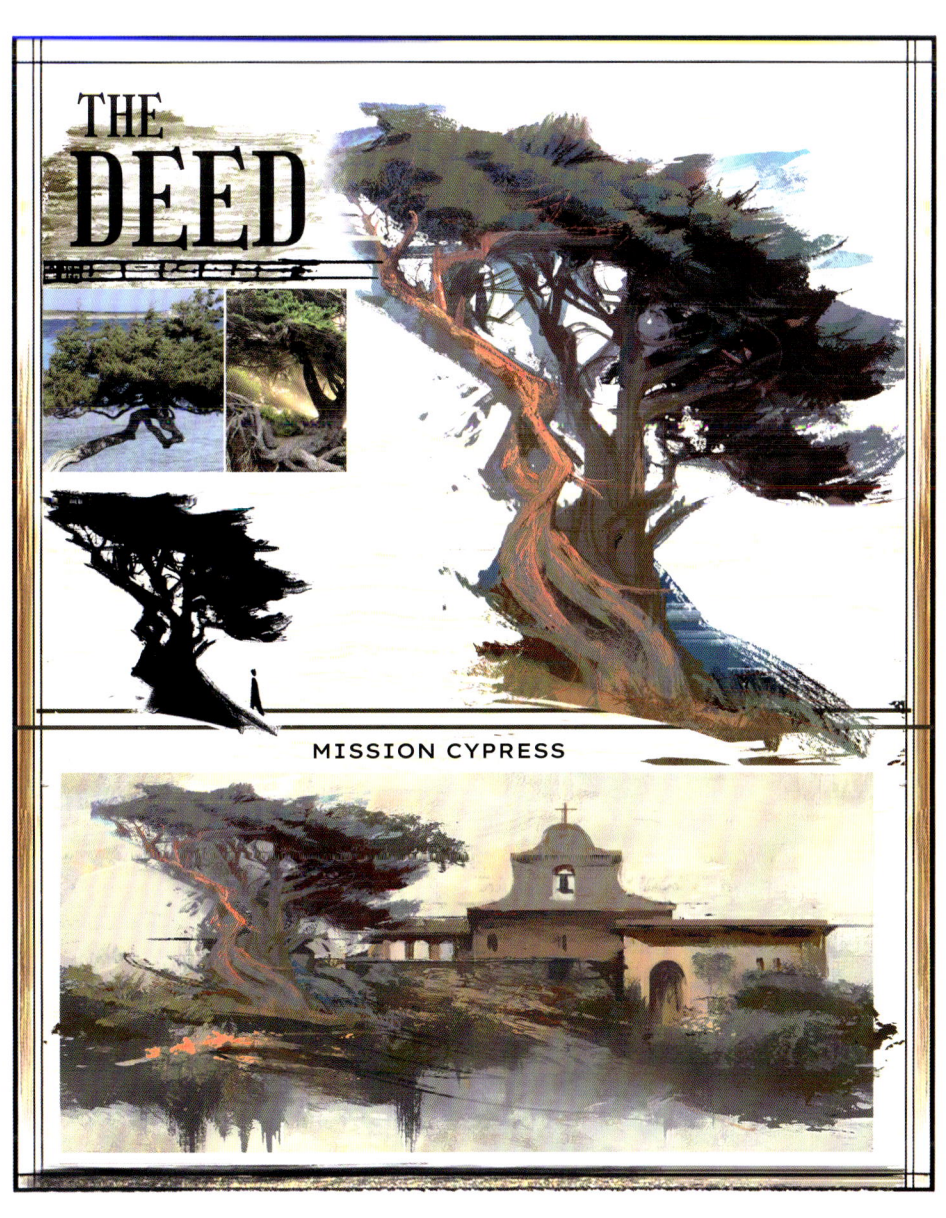

△ A 'prop page' helps to contextualize a prop design for 3D artists

DEMONSTRATION: ARCHITECTURAL MODULE

For our demo, let's design an architectural module. On the right is the image we'll be creating. Here's the purpose and sense of emotion we're targeting: an old hermit has built this structure to live away from it all. The stairs and high entrance discourage visitors and protect from inclement weather and lurking animals. The building is chunky and a bit clumsily put together, but made out of sturdy materials capable of holding it steady over the years. It's also slightly cartoony to keep us from taking it too seriously. Let's begin.

01. BASE COLOR

The architecture will be primarily warm, so I want to start with this cool, neutral green as a simple backdrop. I've noted previously that props and prop modules are best shown from a point of view where we see three planes, rather than just the two we would get from a human's height. In this case, I set the eye-level at the very top of the picture, so we'll be looking down toward the building, allowing us to see top planes, front planes, and side planes.

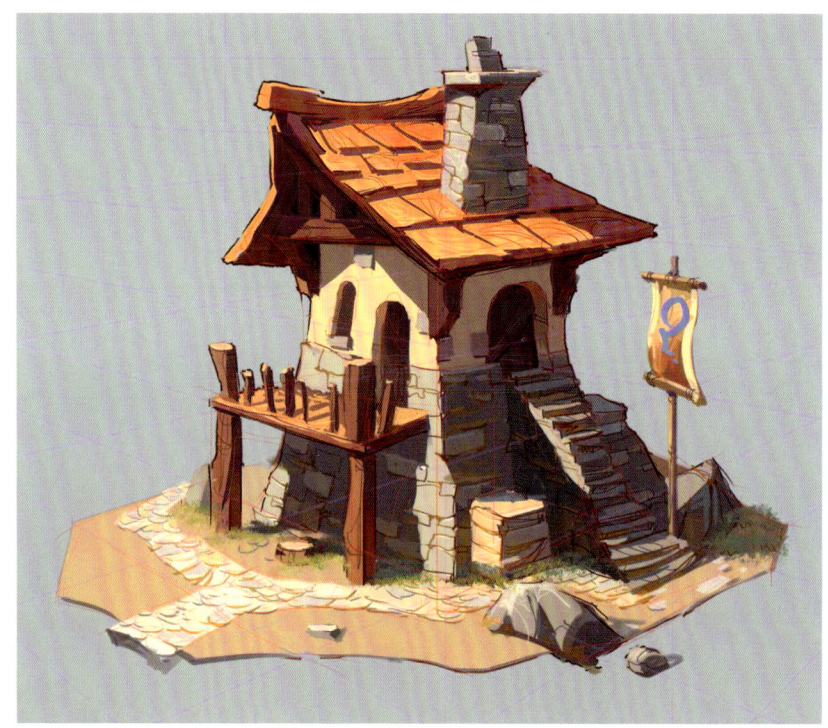

△ Who might live in this crooked but sturdy little house?

01. The background color and perspective grid

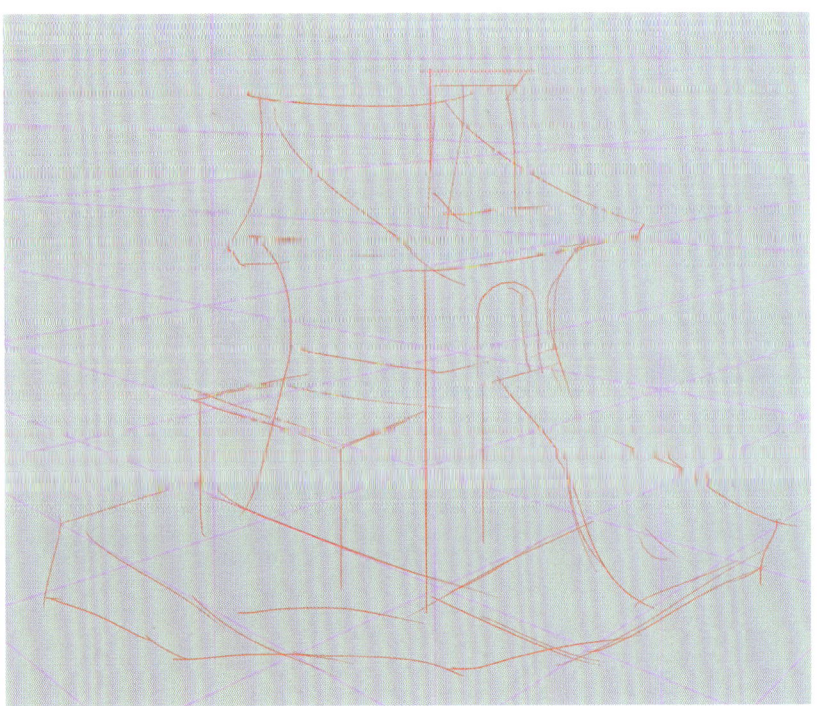

02. Rough out the architecture according to the three planes

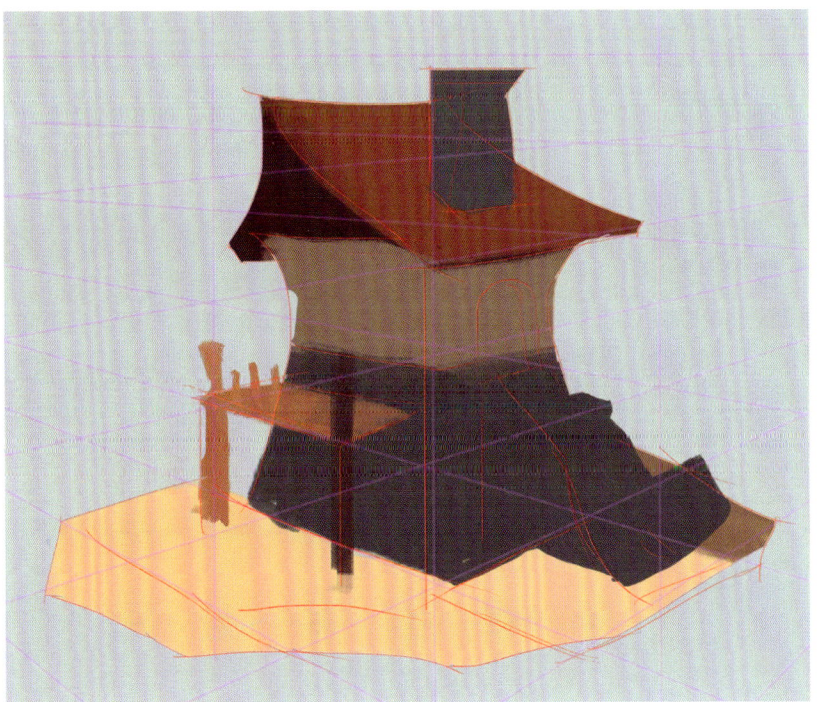

03. Block in local colors for the whole prop

02. SIMPLE DRAWING

I start with a very simple drawing to establish the basic three-plane structure and work out the overall placement and silhouette of the building. I indicate the high staircase and entrance on the right, as well as a rough wooden deck to the left. I show just enough of the ground plane to give the building a solid footing and have some room for a pathway surrounding it. Chimneys are very important for structures like this – they let us know this is not just some kind of shed or storehouse, but that someone lives here and needs to warm themselves through the winter.

03. LOCAL COLORS

In this step I block in the basic local colors. The house will have a redwood shingle roof, a stucco or painted top layer, a stone lower layer, and a dusty ground plane. The redwood is most important for visual interest, as it gives the prop a nice pop, and the stone base is most important for structure.

04. STRUCTURAL DETAILS

I don't need to make a huge leap here – I just need to be sure that the module is prepared for the illusion of light that'll follow in the next step. So I add windows and a door, as well as a few important stones, beams, and knick-knacks around the building. The roof supports are important here as well, as it's a heavy roof and the structure is meant to be sturdy; the wooden buttresses holding up each corner are a critical addition.

05. LIGHTING

I want to keep the lighting straightforward and simple. There's nothing wrong with complicated and challenging lighting, but that's not what a prop is about. Props are about clarity. Side-light coming from the left at about a 45-degree angle will give a nice clarity to the three-plane structure. So I simply add a warm and brightened version of the local color with sharp cast shadows. It's a simple addition and yet it gives tremendous clarity and visual interest to the building.

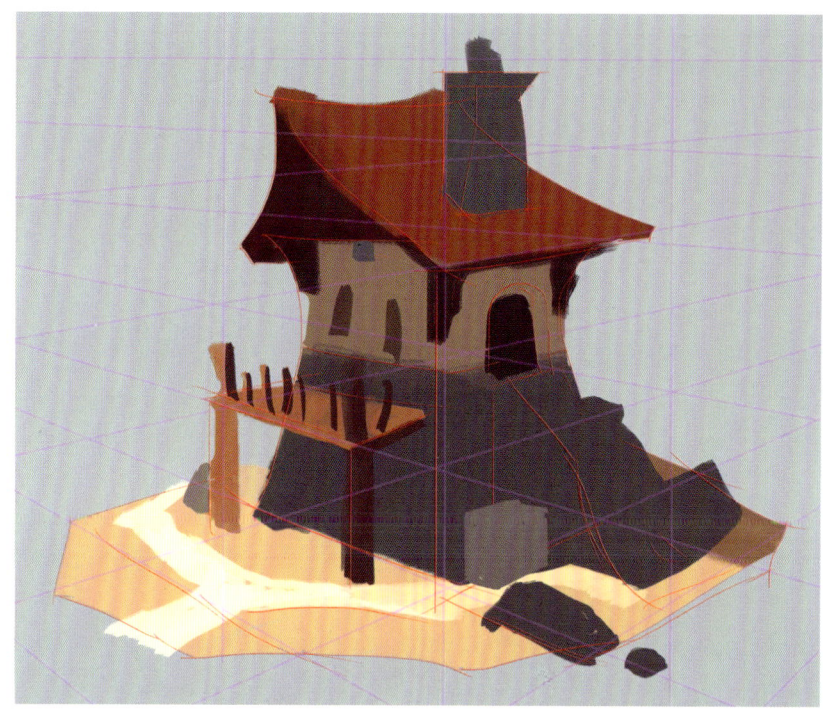

04. Bring in some extra features and important architectural details

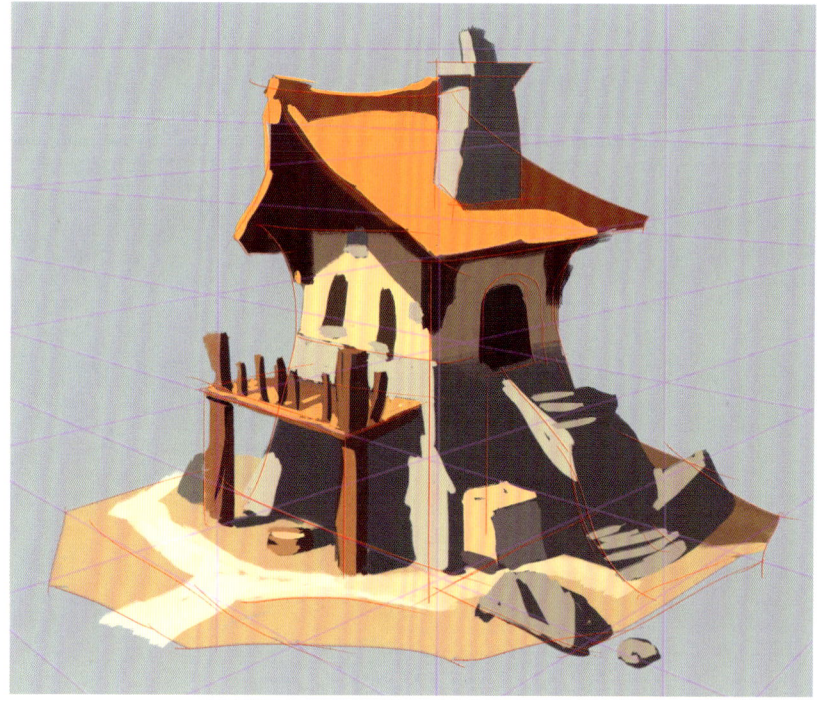

05. Simple lighting really makes the prop feel three-dimensional

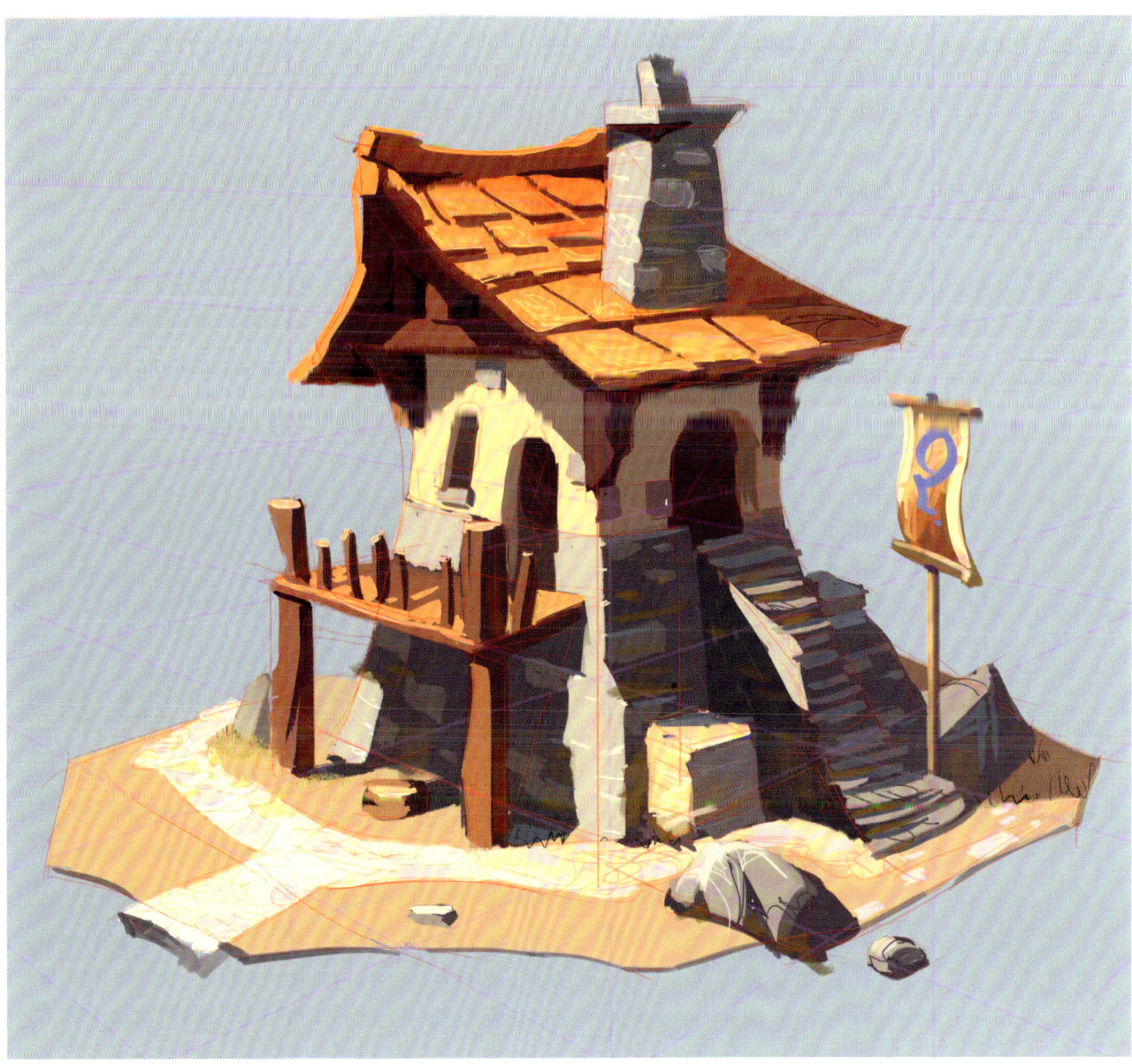

06. Small details and nuances give the building a more lived-in character

06. VARIATION

Now I'm ready to suggest some of the subtle variations that I've been avoiding thus far. The quarried stones that form the base need an individual quality, so I indicate that some are slightly different colors and values from one another. I do the same for the stones that make up the path around the building. The lighting needs a little natural believability, which means that direct lights will bounce into adjacent shadows and cooler skylights will illuminate top planes in the shadows. I indicate those as is appropriate. I also indicate the roof shingles. They're huge, which is something I often avoid because it can cause scale confusion in a building, but in this case they lend to the whimsical and cartoony quality needed for the emotion of the building. Also, there's that banner thrown up at the stairway entrance. This could say anything from 'Old man Chiggins lives here' to 'Get off of my lawn!' Truth be told, though, it's really done to create visual interest.

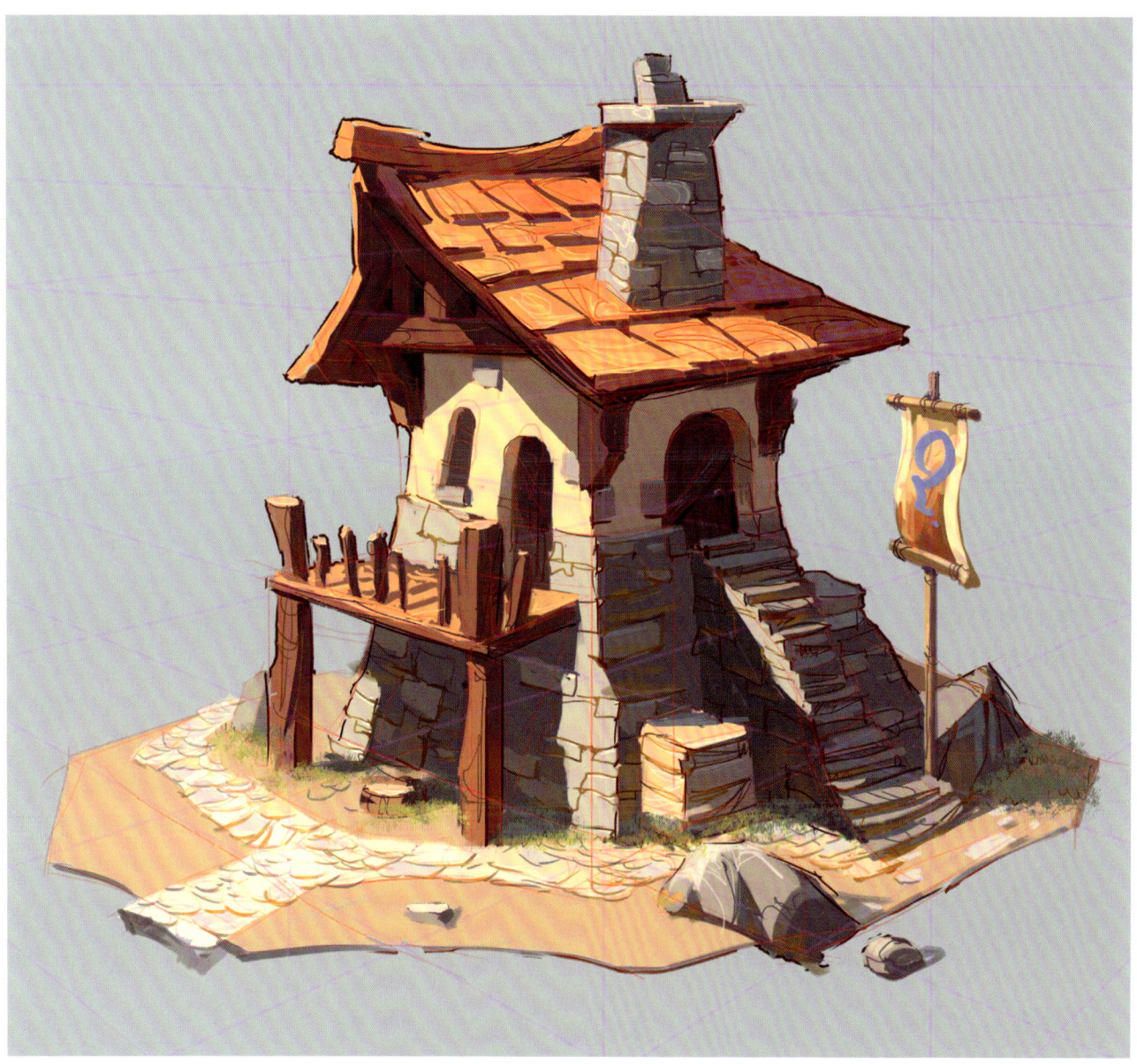

07. Linework clarifies the design and ties everything together

07. LINEWORK

And now our final step! This step is simply a matter of linework –
it's a quick way to convey structure without having to spend forever
rendering. I work my way around significant individual objects,
like stones, wood beams, doorways, shingles, and so on. My final step
is to work a rugged outline around the entire image. This helps it
feel like one singular object rather than a bunch of cobbled-together
materials. And we're finished!

RECOMMENDED EXERCISE: SPHEROID RENDERING

We looked at materials earlier and know we've got to practice, practice, practice! I recommend that you paint a copy of each and every one of these elements and even add more to the list. You could render a sphere made of leather or a head of lettuce – anything you can think of that will heighten your rendering prowess. Remember, a big part of what we're doing is making ourselves as valuable to our clients and our audience as possible. There may be technology that can do quick rendering for you, but if you know how to quickly do your own renderings, corrections, and paint-overs, you'll have made yourself valuable above and beyond what can be done by tech alone.

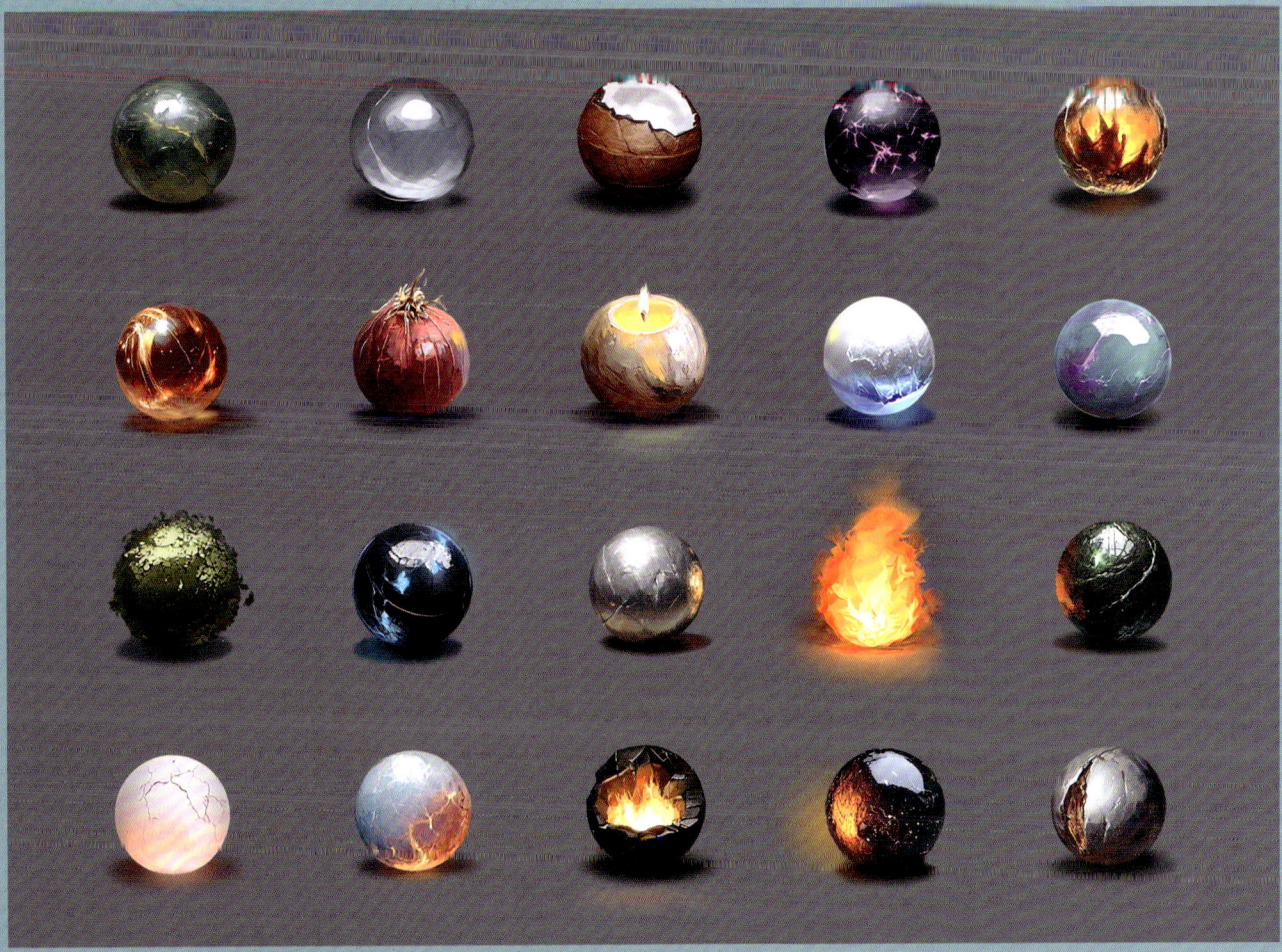

△ Practice rendering as many materials as you possibly can

A big part of what we're doing is making ourselves as valuable to our clients and our audience as possible. Even with all the tech that can do quick rendering for us, we must know how to do our own renderings, corrections, and paint-overs to quickly meet the demands of the director and the production.

ENVIRONMENTAL COLOR

We live in challenging times for artists, which means we have to know how to really push the limits – so let's push color as far as we dare.

EMBARRASSING CONVERSATION

As you know by now, my work is the design of animated movies. I also teach a class or two each week, and one of my favorites is a color-design course for entertainment-art students. I have really great students but, because they're coming through a learning curve, there's a common mistake they make in thinking about color. For example, maybe they've heard about the idea of a color triad from other artists and teachers and want to try it out. Our conversation goes something like this:

Student: *For this image I'm planning on using a color triad.*

Me: *Great, I'm in favor of you doing that, but can you tell me why a triad is a good thing to do?*

Student (with a bit of a deer in the headlights look): *Well... my favorite artist is so-and-so, and they said that they like to use a triad for their color palette design, and I really like their paintings, so I plan to try it as well.*

Me (as the conversation starts to go in a circle): *Great, I like that artist's work too, but why does a triad look good?*

Student: *Well... maybe it's because a triad limits the color palette... you know, like a limited-palette painting.*

Me: *OK, maybe that's a good idea – but, again, why? I mean, the amazing world that we live in is filled with a chaos of colors, so why is placing limitations on all of that beauty a good thing to do?*

This is where the conversation usually ends because the student doesn't know why a triad, or any other particular color palette design, really works. They've simply heard a favorite artist or teacher refer to it. **If you've heard of a great-sounding idea but don't know why it works, do not use it!** First, study exactly *why* it may work, so that you can use it appropriately and effectively. The good news is you're about to get the answers on why any particular color palette works (or doesn't).

> Color design needs a unifying quality so that it can be designed to a purpose, and it needs enough variety to hold our visual interest.

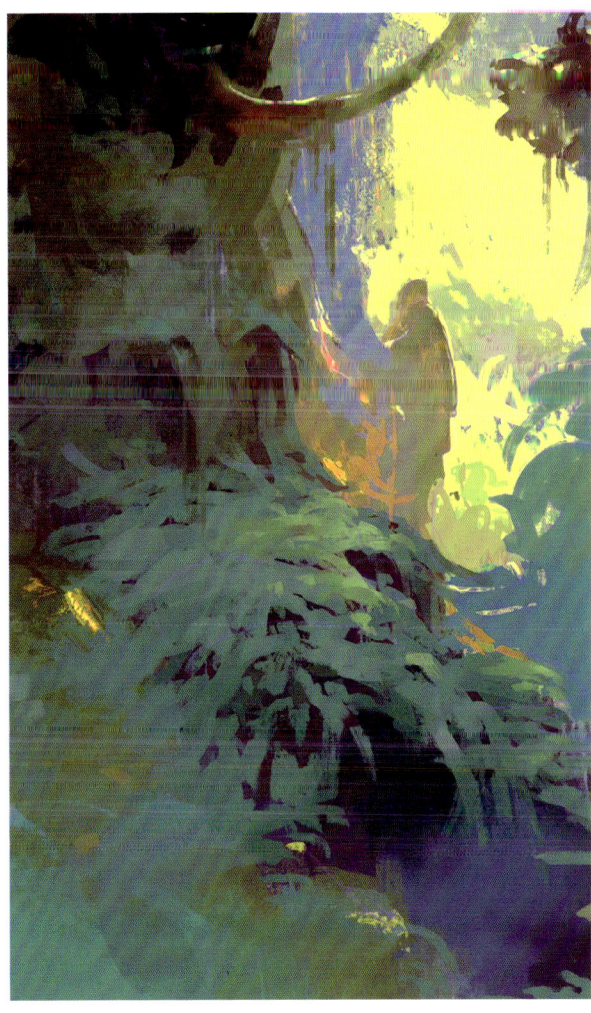

△ The purposeful use of color helps us to tell stories

UNITY WITH VARIETY

Here's the answer and it's so simple. We all love visual contrast, but if everything is in constant high contrast to everything else, then there's no purpose, no organization, no meaning. Only chaos. We're visual storytellers – everything we do needs meaning. Color design also needs a unifying quality so that it can be designed to a purpose. This is why some organizations of color are useful – they have unity with variety at the same time. That's the key: unity with variety. So a color triad (which I'll discuss shortly), or any other designed color palette, is simply one idea of many on how to organize color to have unity with variety.

That's color theory in a nutshell. That's it, that's the whole thing. All your pain and suffering over disastrous color is over and there's nothing but blue sky ahead!

THE OBJECTS THAT MAKE UP AN ENVIRONMENT

We'll start with a quick refresher to be sure we're all on the same page with terminology and why we see colors the way we do. Here we have two different objects: one made of green foliage, the other of warm stone. These are lit directly by sunlight, with the brightest highlights closer to the color of the light source. The half-tone lights tend to be more the local color of the object. In the shadow we have light bouncing in from adjacent illuminated areas; this 'bounce light' tends to have a quality of warmth. In the areas of shadow facing outward and upward, we'll often see the influence of cool skylight. Don't forget that the sky is an actual light source, though far weaker than direct sunlight. These are the color basics for the objects that make up an environment.

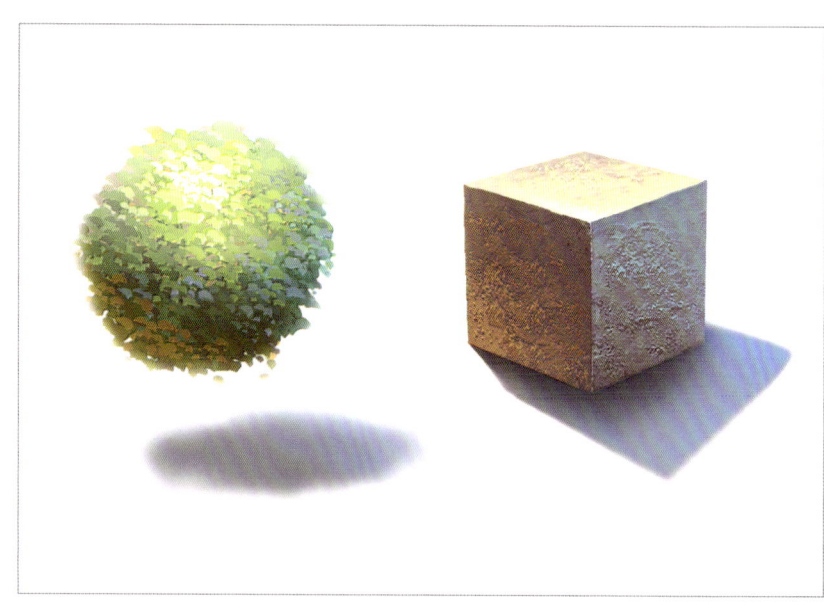

△ Any environmental objects you design will have some basic lighting qualities to take into account

LOCAL COLOR VS LIGHT-SOURCE COLOR

Next we need to distinguish between local color and light-source color. Here's a simple show and tell on the difference. The middle block is exactly the same material as the left one, but it's lit by a purely red light source instead of natural sunlight. The image on the right is also very red, but not because of light – it has red local color. In this chapter we'll be dealing with local colors in combination with the color and quality of light to create the colors that make up our environments.

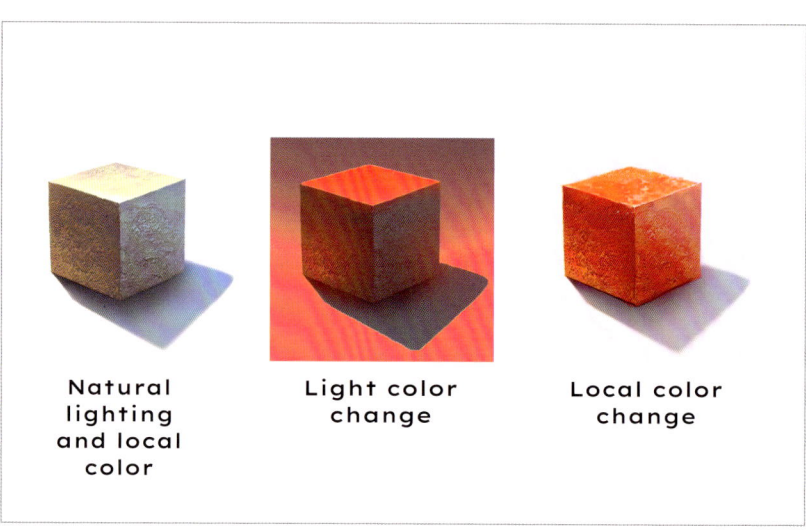

Natural lighting and local color

Light color change

Local color change

△ There's a big difference between a cube lit with red light and a cube with a red local color

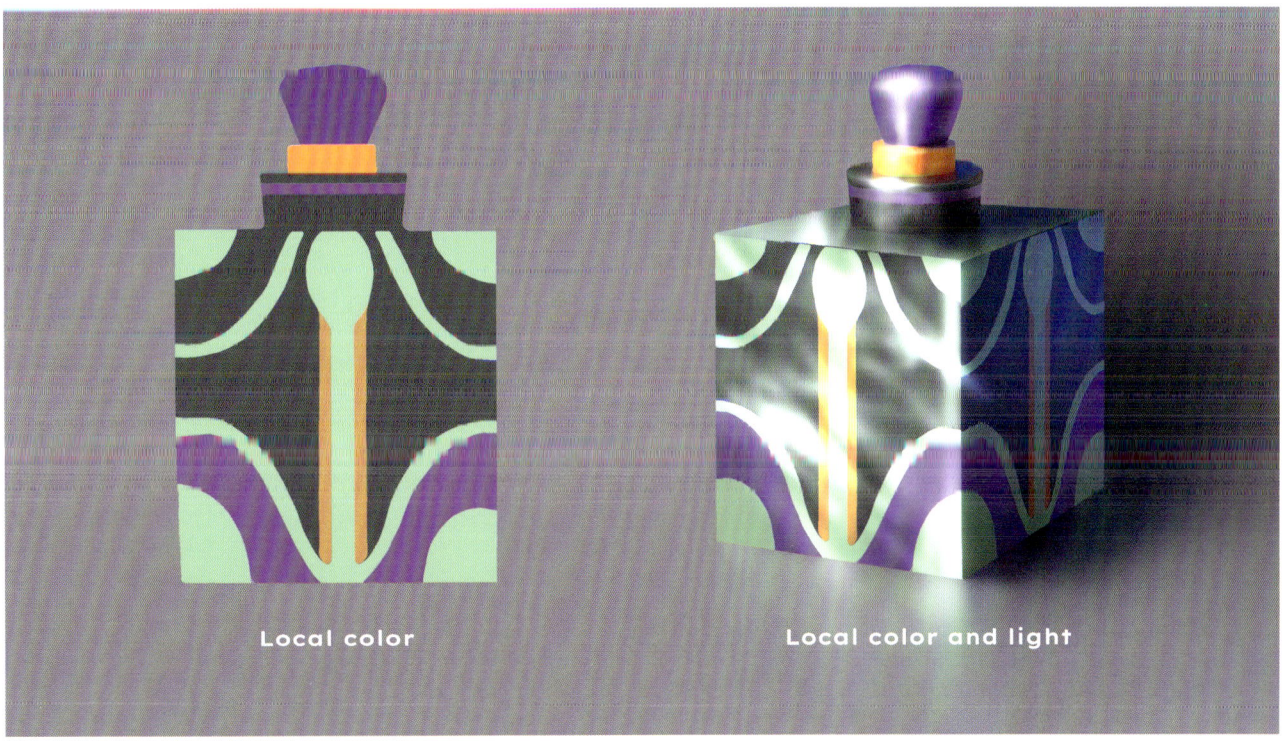

Local color

Local color and light

01. Local color is the color of an object regardless of lighting

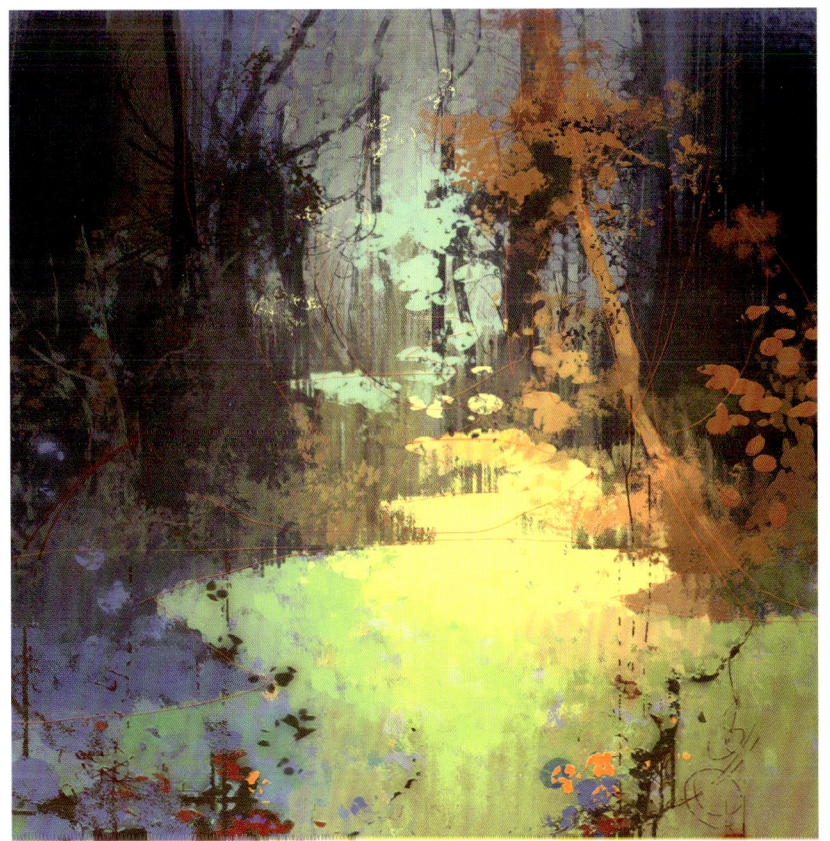

02. This image is driven more by local color than lighting

01. OBJECT EXAMPLE

Remember this image from the last chapter? I've added it to help put all of this in context, because this is what we're talking about here: local-color design combined with lighting for the final effect.

02. LOCAL COLOR

This image and the next two help show the difference between local-color design and lighting design in an environment. This one is inspired by a visit to the swamps of Florida. I was fascinated by the local colors in the swamp and wanted to do an environment designed around the visual interest of local colors. There's certainly lighting here, but this painting is not at all about lighting design – it's all about *local color* design.

To create believable color, our basic considerations are the local color of the subject and the color of the light source.

03. LIGHT COLOR

During that same trip to Florida, our family visited Walt Disney World. My very first job in the mid-nineties was designing for theme-park shows – I'm always fascinated to see how the lighting is handled on the indoor rides, since that was once my job. The Disney Imagineers do a brilliant job of designing vivid palettes of colored light to create a wondrous experience for the visitors. I did a series of abstract sketches inspired by these lighting palettes to get a better feel for their vivid quality and wanted to share it with you here. Unlike the previous image, this is not *local color* design. This is the design of colored *light sources*.

04. LOS ANGELES COUNTY FAIR

Let's continue our exploration of design based on light-source color. The Los Angeles County Fair is quite a vivid experience at night, so I took some photos for reference and did this painting to encapsulate the experience. There is a little bit of local color present here, but far and away the color palette of this environment is created by colored lights. I think we've covered the difference between local color and light source color in environment design pretty well now and can move forward into full color-palette design.

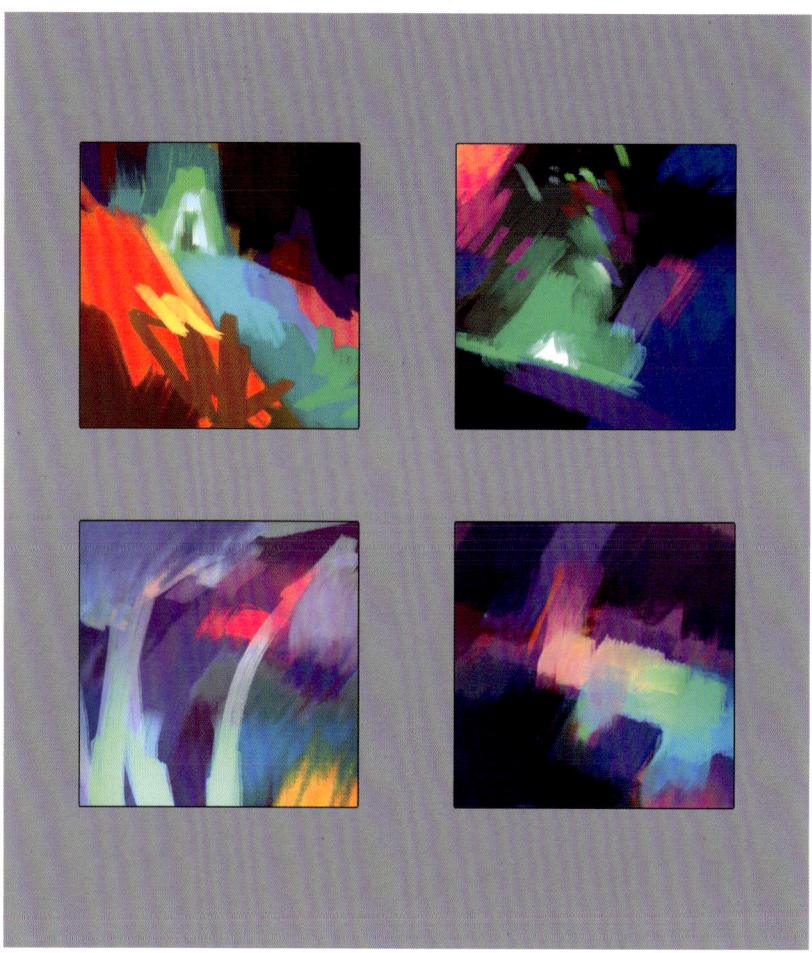

03. These studies focus on capturing vibrant lighting colors

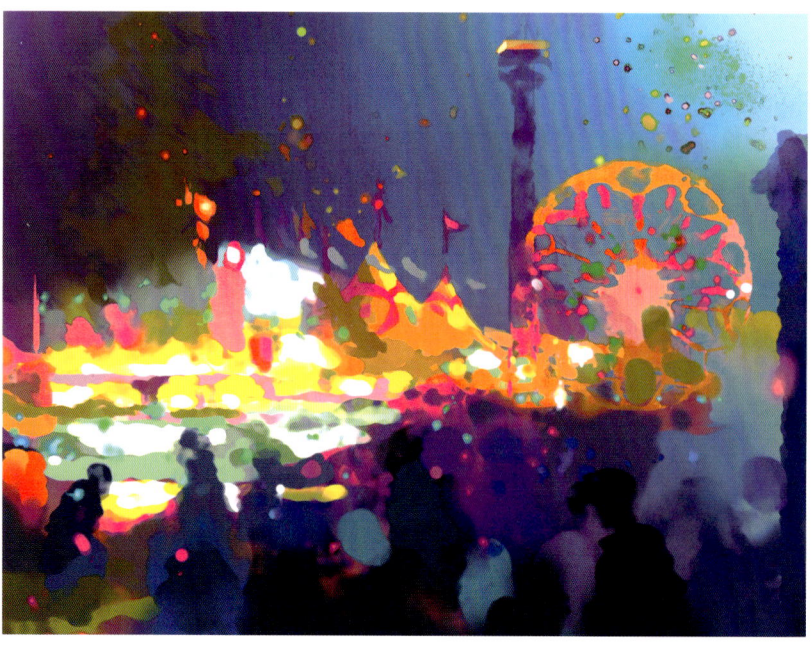

04. Another vivid example of a lighting-driven environment

BACK TO UNITY WITH VARIETY

I've mentioned 'unity with variety' as a foundational principle several times now, but let's officially put it into practice. We'll do it by sticking with the Los Angeles County Fair for our subject. Here's another painting from the fair and it was incredibly challenging. It was challenging because there was chaos everywhere: textures, details, every local color you can think of, not to mention people screaming at you to come spend money at their booth.

How could I possibly manage such a situation? The answer was with careful design of unity and variety in the scene. There happened to be a crew of workers wearing cyan T-shirts and that contrasted beautifully with all the reds and oranges of the tents. I decided I would center my painting around the contrasting relationship between those warm and cool colors.

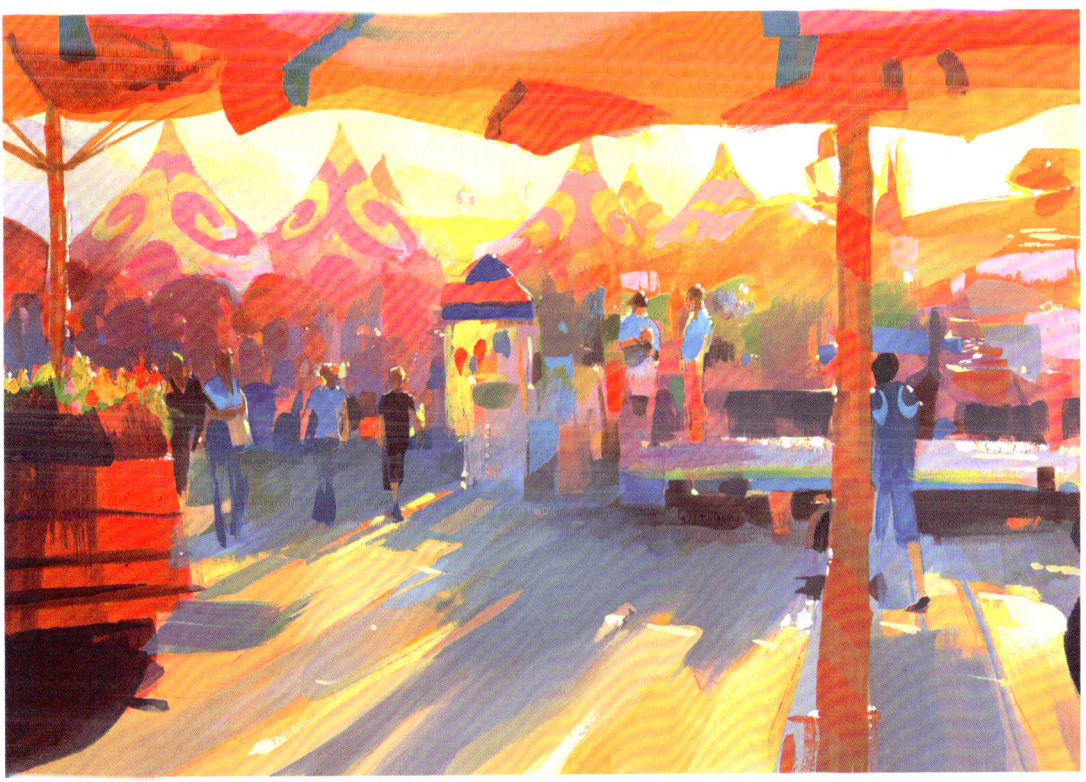

△ This image shows the use of unity (warm yellows, oranges, and reds) and variety (cool cyan)

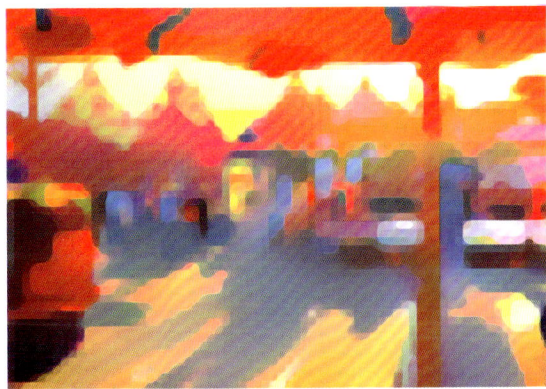

01. Here you can easily see the clear grouping of warms and cools

01. SIMPLIFIED VERSION

This simplified version blends away the noise so that you can see the color relationships directly. Despite the chaos going on inside the tents, I carefully grouped their color and value as I painted; then I made sure the blue and cyan shirts contrasted nicely against that backdrop. There were some beautiful cool temperatures in the shadows coming down from the sky, which helped me get rich contrast as well. The majority of the image unifies around warm colors, but they would quickly get boring with no contrasting elements. The shirts and shadows give me just what I need for unity with variety.

02. COLOR WHEEL

Let's prepare to chart out our county fair scene on a color wheel. A color wheel is useful because it arranges colors in terms of their contrast, which is the way that we perceive them – differences in hue help us distinguish one object from another, which helps us survive and thrive in the world. A color wheel arranges colors with the greatest contrast opposite each other: the yellows opposite the blues, the reds opposite the greens, and so on.

The color wheel also helps us chart out the saturation of each color. When opposite colors are blended together, they neutralize each other, creating gray. So at the center of the color wheel is a pure neutral gray, and I've shown how the hues transition toward this neutral center.

In a nutshell, a color wheel helps us design how our colors contrast from one another. It can help us design the unity and variety of our color choices.

03. COLOR CHART

Now let's chart out the color relationships I'm using for my painting of the county fair. I have a range of harmonious warms and neutrals – they *unify*. As we move across the color wheel, we have the strong and direct *contrast* of cyan. This arrangement shows that the palette of colors for my painting has *unity and variety*.

A color wheel helps us design how our colors contrast from one another. It can help us design the unity and variety of our color choices.

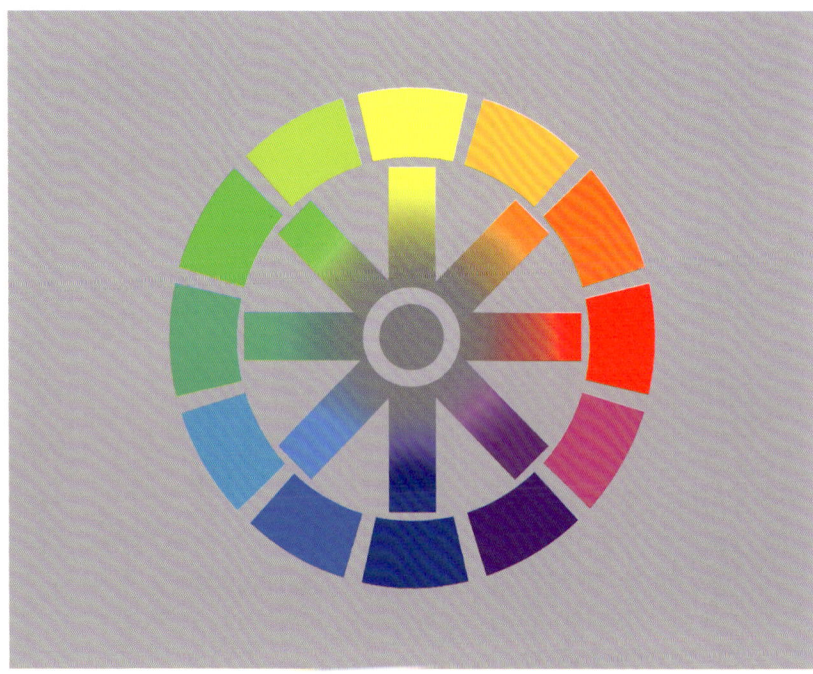

02. An example of a color wheel

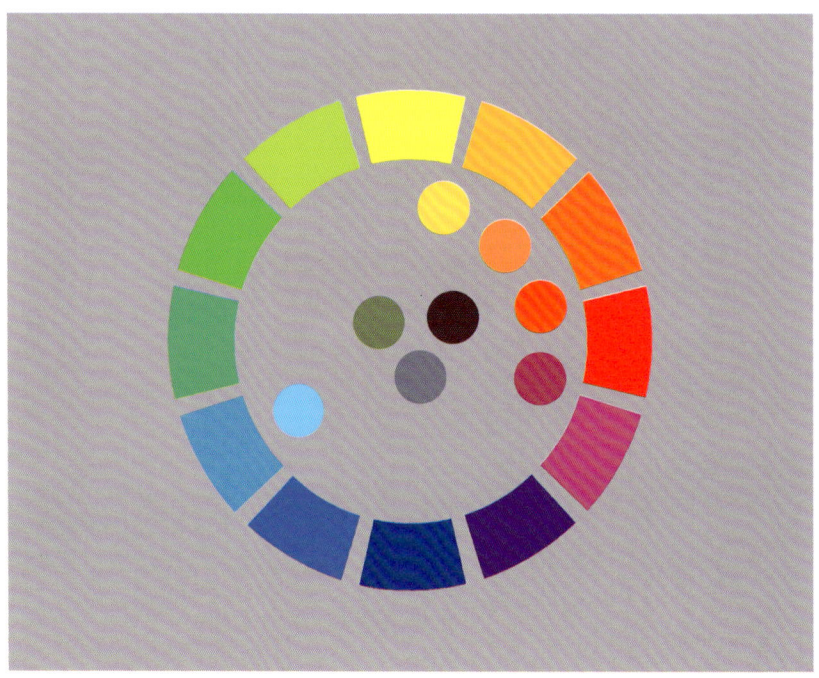

03. The color palette used for the county fair painting

04. A SIMPLER EXAMPLE

If you're still a bit confused by 'unity with variety', let me show you in a way that I think will clinch it. Looking at this chart from left to right, the first grouping has very low contrast – it has unity and very little variety. There's a time and a place for low-contrast color palettes like this, but they get boring real fast. The middle image has no unity at all – it's nothing *but* variety. There's no purpose, there are no meaningful relationships, and everything contrasts from everything else. The final image is an example of unity *and* variety working together. It's an attractive grouping of colors that's easy on the eyes because it doesn't bore us and doesn't induce seizures! It strikes a 'best of both worlds' balance. You'll see this abstract color palette come to life in the next image.

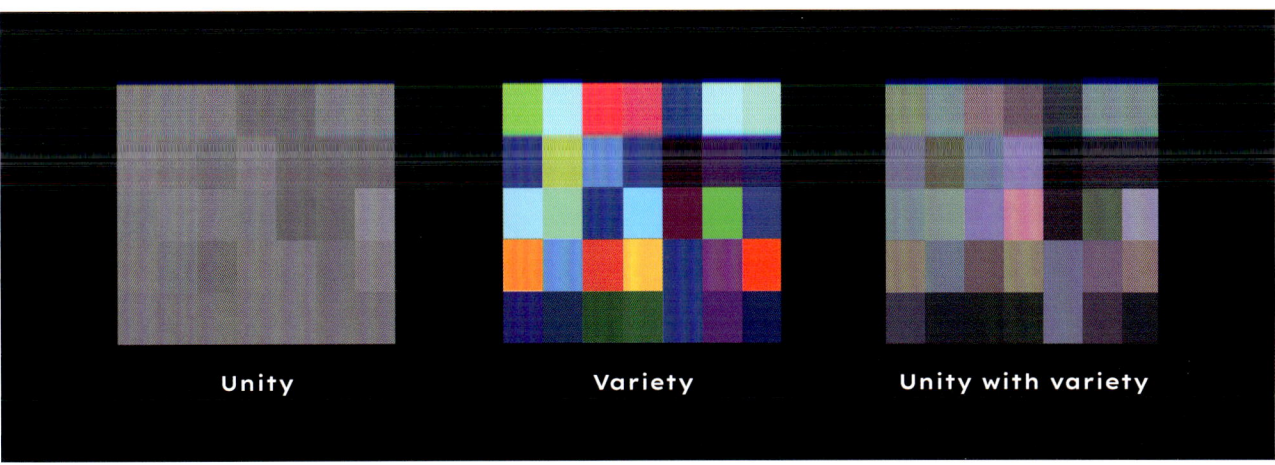

04. Without a balance of unity and variety, an image will be either boring or chaotic

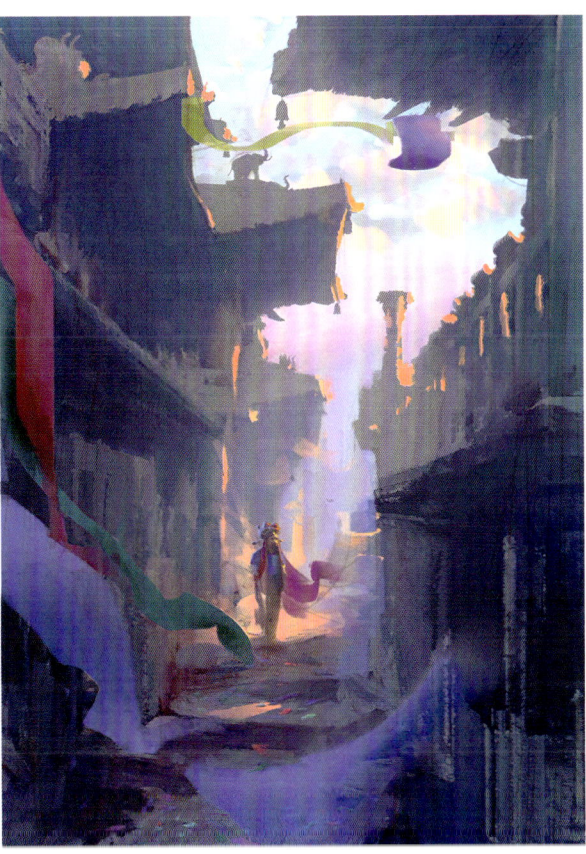

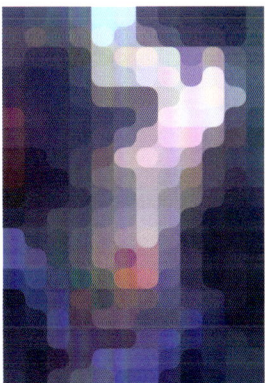

05. See how clearly the color design comes across in the tiled version

05. ATMOSPHERIC STREET

This painting is designed to draw you into the environment and lead you to the character in the middle. Color is a big part of that design. To help us set aside the subject matter and just see the palette of colors used, I have created a tiled version of the image as well. Notice all the harmonious neutrals with just a few accents of more saturated color. Let's start with the orange-red accent at the lower center; now notice the adjacent green just to the left of it. These two colors have a strong contrast with each other, helping direct our attention. Next, notice the blues a little further out – these help frame those essential warms by giving them even more contrast.

06. STYLIZED FOREST

Is this topic still seeming complicated? No worries – let me go over another very simple version of the idea. This cartoony scene has cool temperatures in the background that graduate to neutral purples in the foreground, with the singular accent of orange to the lower right. This palette gives us a harmonious environment full of unifying colors with a spot of red-orange contrast for a hit of visual interest. And like the previous example, I've tiled the image so you can see past the subject to the simple color relationships. What you're seeing here is textbook unity with variety.

07. CHARTING THE SCENE

Let's return to the color wheel to chart the colors of that forest scene. The grouping of cyans and neutral purples has a unifying cool quality and the spot of red gives us the contrasting heat. 'But wait, Nathan, aren't you supposed to go straight across the color wheel to create contrast? Why did you use a red instead of the opposite golden orange?' Remember, we're not following mindless rules – we're creating harmony and contrast in whatever way suits the needs of the picture. I didn't want a hyper-contrasting yellow-gold. I felt like a pale red would give us all the contrast we needed in the context of this very cool environment.

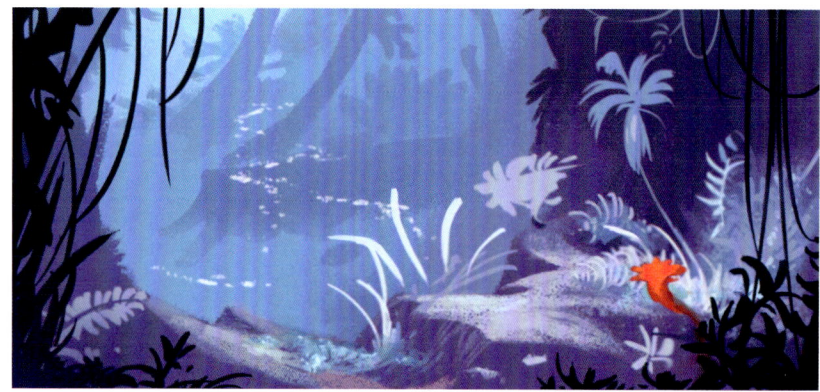

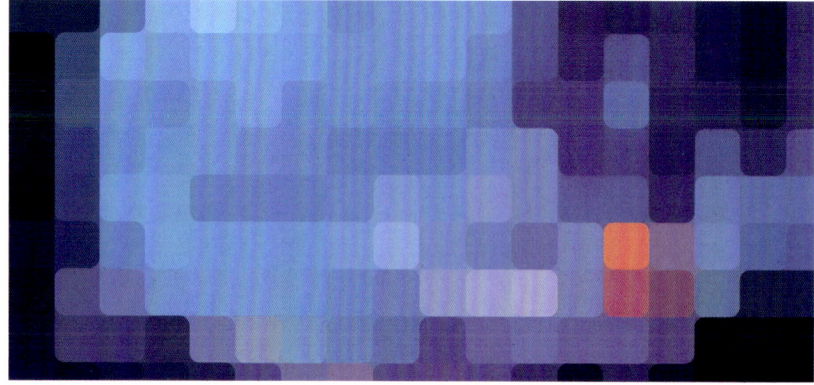

06. The tiled version shows the underlying theory

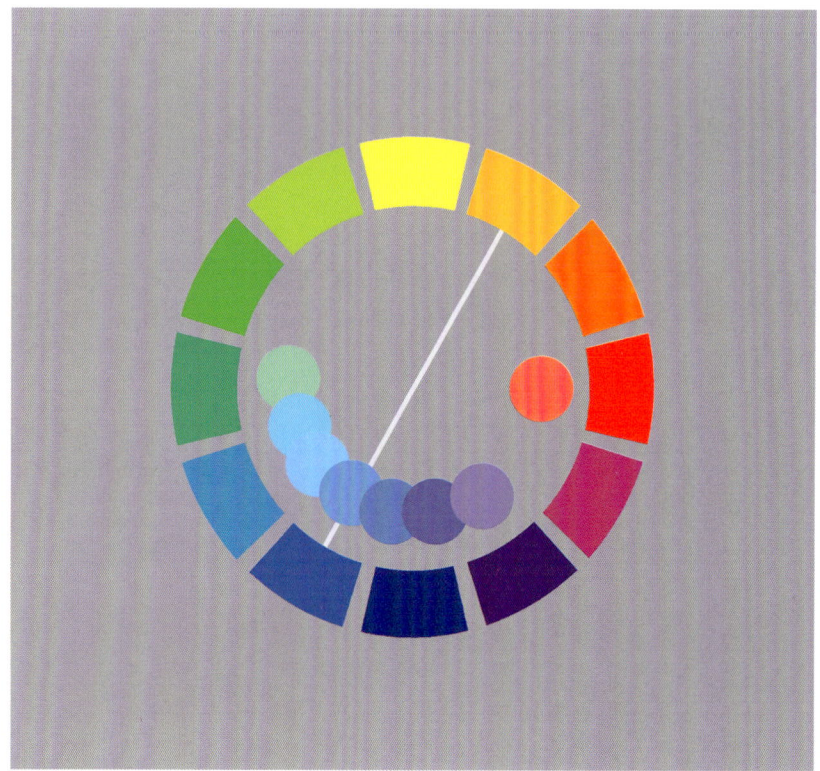

07. Plotting the previous image's palette on a color wheel

TWO-COLOR PALETTE (SORT OF)

'Sort of? Why are you only *sort of* committing to this color palette?! Color is already hard enough without this kind of ambiguity – give me specifics so I can learn this!' This is very reasonable and common thinking, but it's not useful. Why? Because the human eye has been shown to perceive about 2.3 million color variations. Do you really want a specific library of 2.3 million possibilities for you to juggle? It's not possible. In fact, counting every potential combination of those 2.3 million colors runs you into the trillions of possible color combinations. Yikes!

This is why the *unity with variety* approach is so useful. You, as the artist, get to decide how much harmony you want to bring into your color palette, or how much contrasting variety. It's a simple way to manage the overwhelming complexity of color.

This painting is centered around two colors: green and magenta. That gives it tons of potential for variety, but that would be so painfully predictable. To keep things interesting and playful, the greens slip toward yellow in some areas and toward cyan in others; the magenta toward burnt orange and toward purple in other areas. These changes have a logic that goes beyond just a desire for variety. The cooler colors are created by skylight in the shadows, and the warmer colors are created by bounce light in the shadows. And so the whole thing centers around two colors, *sort of*.

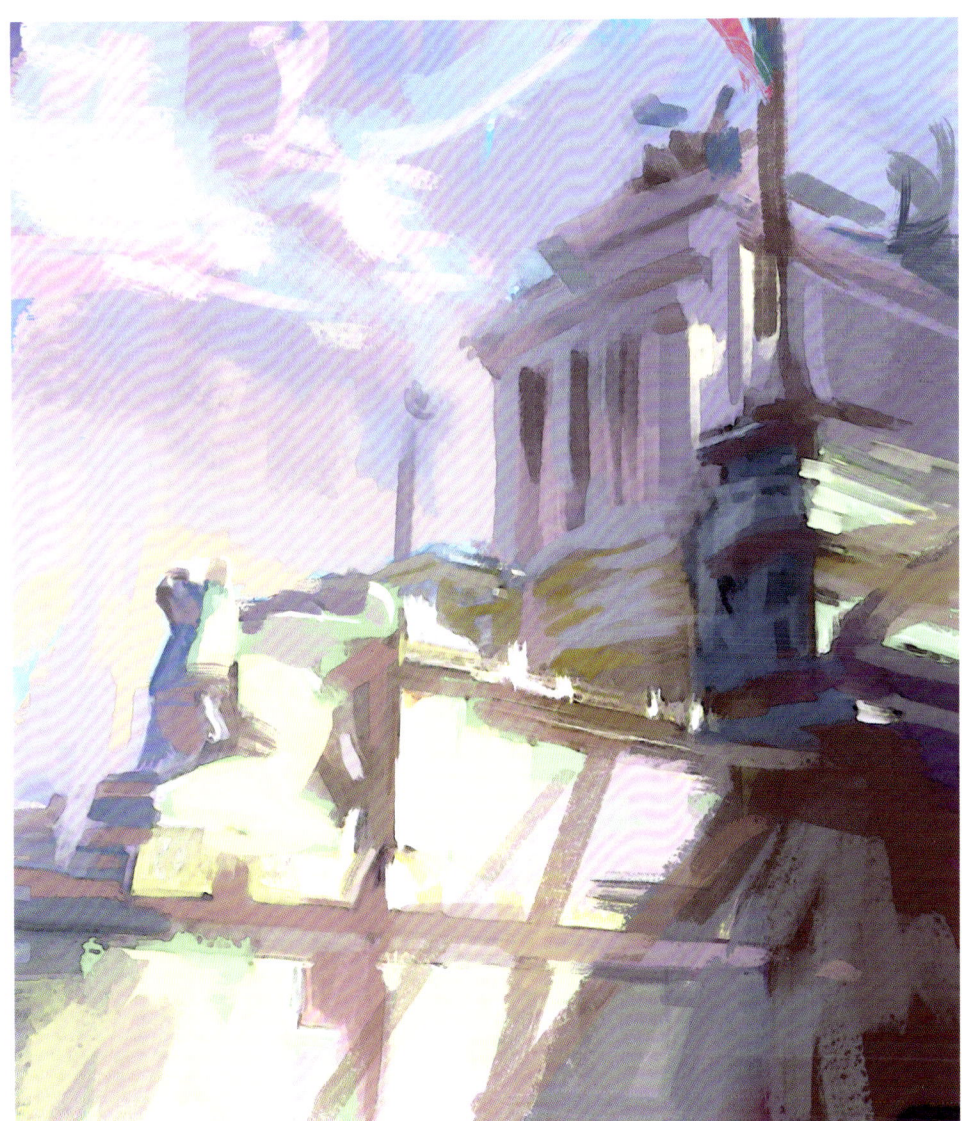

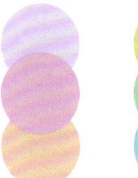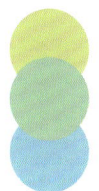

△ This image is focused around 'just' two colors but is still full of variety and subtlety

THREE-COLOR PALETTE

Let's advance into a three-color palette – again, *sort of*. There are lots of subtle things going on here, but there are three distinctive colors that have tons of contrast from one to another: **greens, purples, and golds.** The majority is made up of very neutral variations of these three colors. More saturated accents are reserved for the more important areas: the pathway, the tree, and the adjacent purplish background. And it's the purple background that's the clincher. By itself it's just purple, and the adjacent tree is potentially boring, with only pale greens and dull ochers. But put those two contrasting color groups side by side and they become magic. This is the beauty of designing color relationships.

Adjacent colors can be individually boring, but give them a little contrast from each other and they become magic. This is the beauty of designing color relationships.

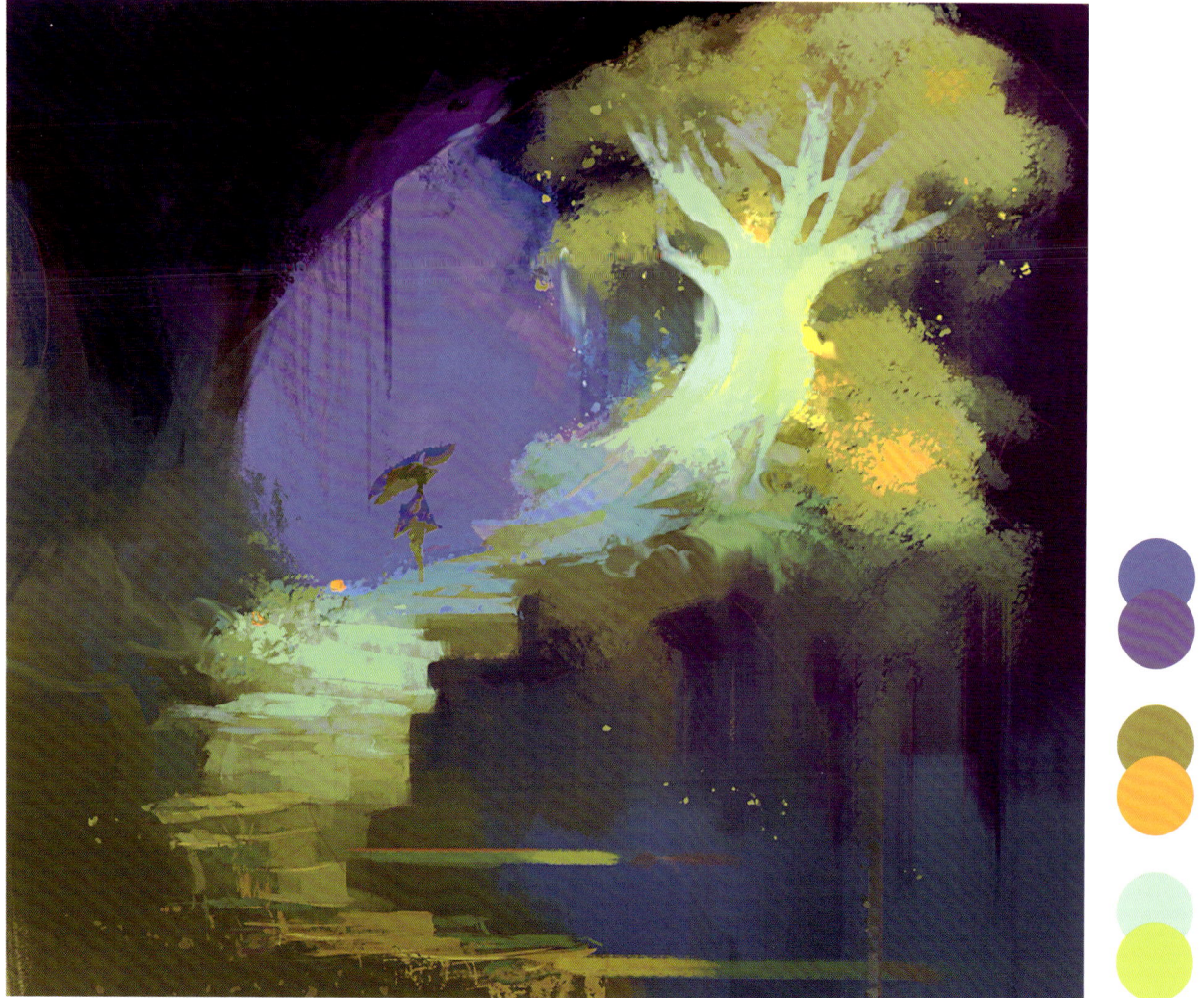

△ This image is driven by three neutral/saturated color pairs

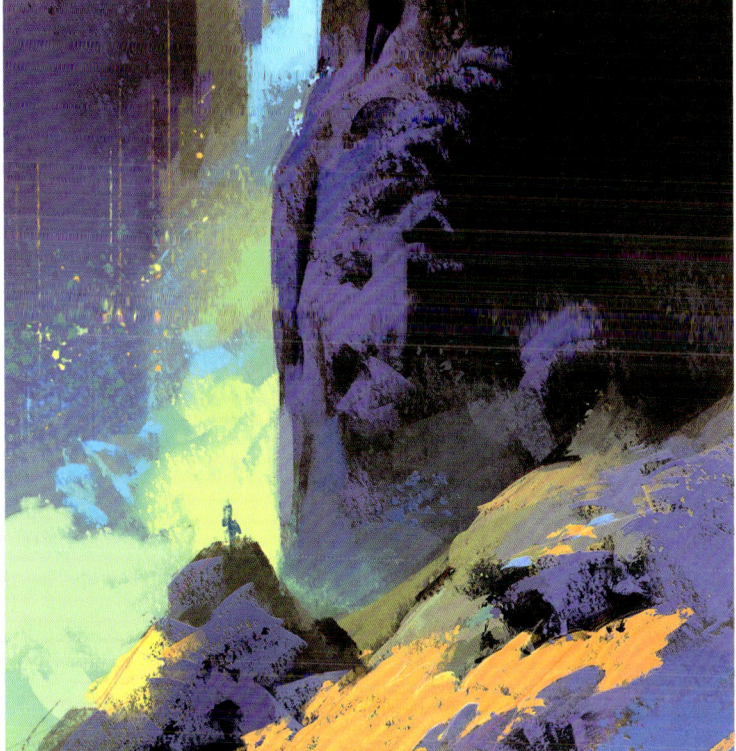

01. These colors may seem outlandish but they're really just heightened versions of reality

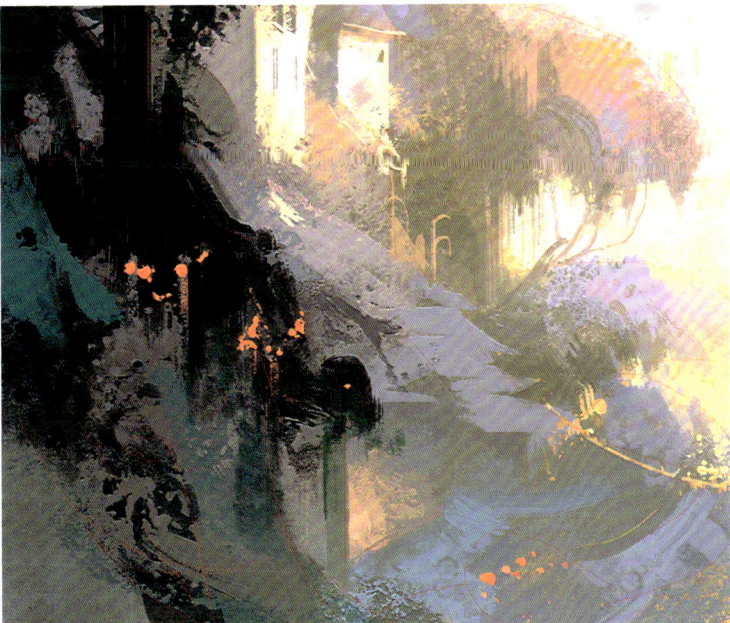

02. This take on the 'green, purple, orange' palette feels completely different

Highly exaggerated color is most believable when it's an exaggeration of what really happens.

01. EXAGGERATING REALITY

Many students ask the question, 'How do I exaggerate color without losing control of it?' The answer is wrapped up in this image. Highly exaggerated color is most believable when it's an exaggeration of what really happens. For instance, sunshine is slightly warm, so I've made it orange-gold here. Skylight is somewhat cool, so I've made it vivid purple. Blue skylight and yellow sunlight passing through mist can take on a hint of green, so I've exaggerated that as well. And I've kept these choices organized – this is primarily a three-color combination.

02. LUMINOUS COLOR

Let's keep going with this idea of designing exaggerated color into our environments in a way that really engages our audience. This environment is intended to be vivid and luminous and yet it's primarily made of very neutral gray. Once again, it's the sunshine and the skylight that saves it. The sunshine is an exaggerated orange and the skylight an exaggerated gray-purple and cyan. For contrast, there's a bit of green local color in the foreground. This image is centered around straight-up green, purple, and orange.

FINALLY, THE TRIAD PALETTE

For a straightforward color exploration, let's put together another image founded on the contrasting nature of green, purple, and orange. For this image I'm not going to worry about local color – I'm just going for a lively expression of unity with variety.

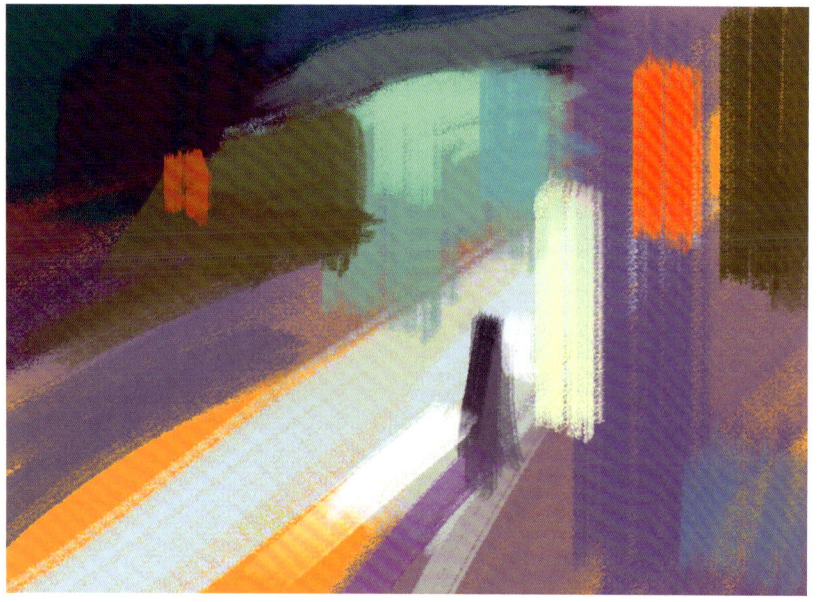

01. A rough color sketch using a triad palette

01. ROUGH SKETCH

I rough out my idea of a pathway headed from indoors to outdoors – I'm just making an abstract composition using three colors.

02. THE COMP

Now let's look at the finished idea. We would still call this a 'comp' – it's certainly not a polished, finished image – but it has all the information it needs to move forward from the idea phase. And it's all based on three contrasting colors. You'll have noticed that the images so far are most often made of more neutral colors with smaller accents of saturated colors, and that's certainly the case with this one.

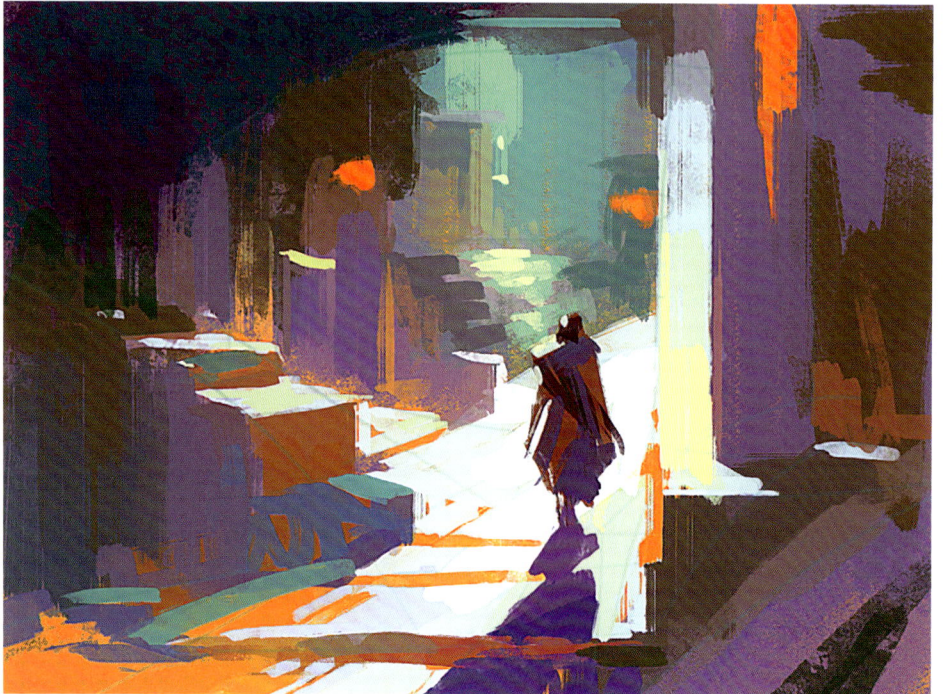

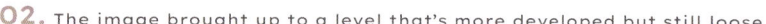

02. The image brought up to a level that's more developed but still loose

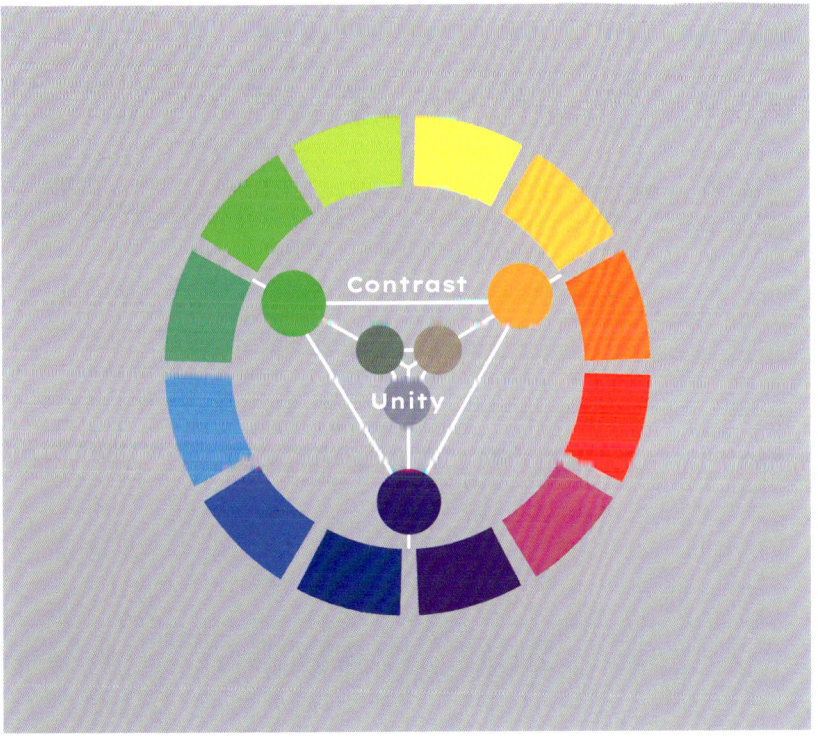

03. Charting the unified and contrasting color trios on the color wheel

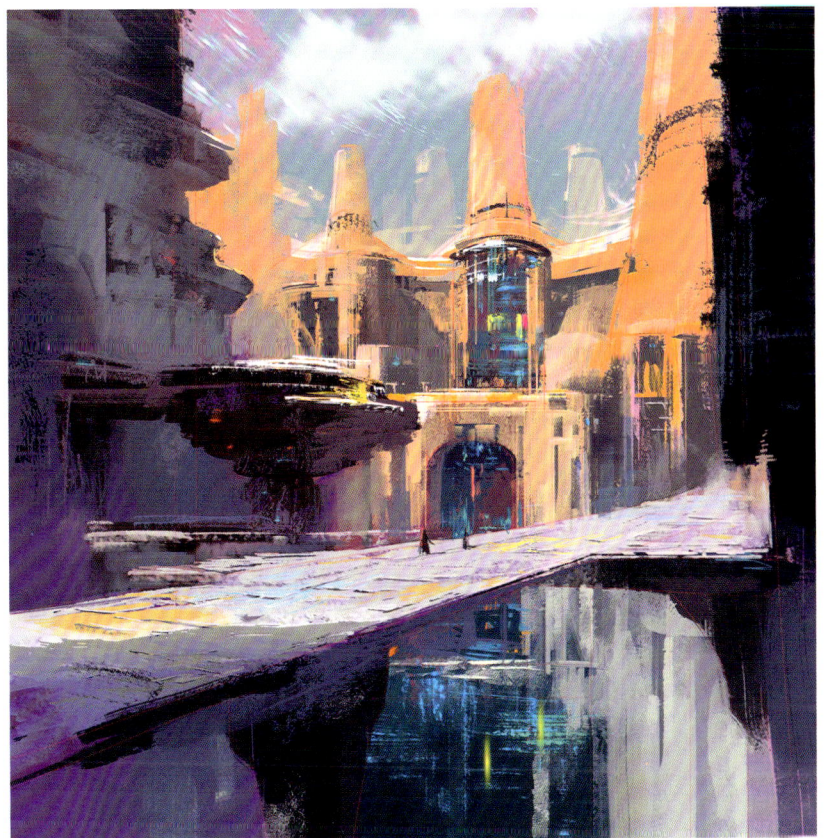

04. A more developed example using the green-purple-orange triad

03. COLOR CHART

So let's chart out this idea on the color wheel. At the top of the chapter we asked the question, 'Why is a color triad a good thing?' Let's answer that in more detail now. A 'triad' of color is three colors equally distant on the color wheel; they have as much contrast from each other as any three colors can have. This is great because it gives us tons of variety – one of our two components in the 'unity with variety' equation. And if we use desaturated versions of those same three colors, as shown on the color wheel, we get lots and lots of rich neutral colors that unify. Then we have what the human eye craves: groupings of color that meaningfully unify, but have enough contrast to be engaging.

By the way, since I've shown you many images with lots of neutrals and limited saturation, I plan to completely break that idea in 'Emphasis through saturation' (page 234). Keep your eyes open for it – we must never fall prey to using one formula!

04. CLEANER CONCEPT

The previous painting used a triad to create a loose concept idea, but I wanted to use the same kind of palette for a more finished environment. This painting is at the level that's typically expected when we present an environment concept to whatever studio or client we might be working for. I'll leave this one up to you – look through it and see how the triad of colors has been used.

And one additional note to help us avoid being formulaic: I leaned on green, purple, and orange in the last several images because I really love that combination, but I don't want to give the impression that a triad means green, purple, and orange. It absolutely doesn't! A triad is any three hues that are equally distant from each other on the color wheel. Red, yellow, and blue would be another example of a triad.

TURNING MUD INTO MAGIC

In this simple chart, look at the warm rectangle on the center left. There's nothing special about it – in fact, it's just kind of muddy. But a good artist can turn mud into magic in an instant. For the square on the right, I've taken the exact same brown and surrounded it with a dull, boring, poke-your-eyes-out, *dead* blue color – except this is where the magic happens. Because there's just a little temperature contrast, the muddy brown suddenly becomes a richly warm golden color that's alive with possibilities!

This is one of the reasons many people get lost in color as they paint landscapes and environments. They want their painting to be full of vivid colors, so they put down vivid colors everywhere. The result is so loaded with sugary saturation that you have to turn away from it for fear it might trigger diabetes. The secret to painting natural environments is in the grays. Keep them desaturated but give them a little bit of temperature or hue contrast, and then they'll have the magical vibrancy you're looking for.

01. COLOR PERCEPTION

Let's prove that neutral colors affect each other in a rich and useful way in an actual environment. Here I've circled three colors, each of which feels as if it has a cool temperature: a cyan, a cool green, and a cool purple. But look at the color charts below: I've surrounded those sampled colors with a version of what we 'see' them to be. I've surrounded the perceived cyan with an actual cyan, the perceived cool green with an actual cool green, and the perceived cool purple with an actual cool purple. The colors aren't at all the cool temperatures they seem – they all have tremendous warmth.

In a painting, no colors exist in isolation. Colors have an extraordinary influence on each other. I wanted this to be a harmonious painting unified by its warmth, but I didn't want it to be hot, sweaty, and boring. It needed a little contrast. So as I added color accents, I knew not to use saturated, cool colors – subtle temperature variations would do the trick. Careful control of color temperature is a hugely useful way to design our color palettes.

The secret to painting natural environments is in the grays. Keep them desaturated but give them a little bit of temperature or hue contrast, and then they'll have the magical vibrancy you're looking for.

 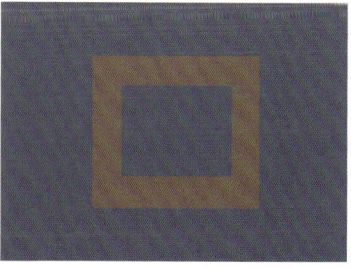

△ Changing the surrounding color completely alters how we perceive the central brown

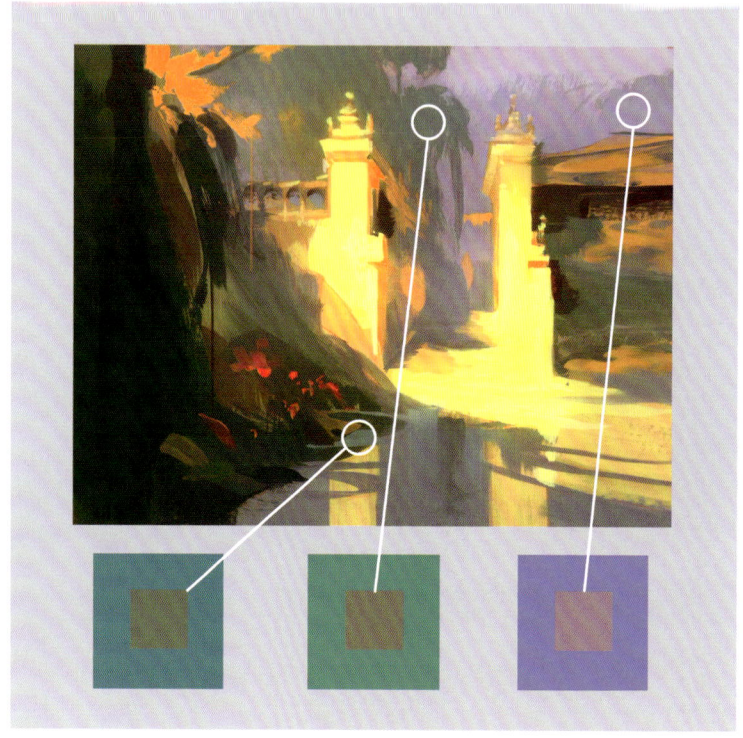

01. The image's overall warmth makes the 'cool' colors appear much cooler than they actually are

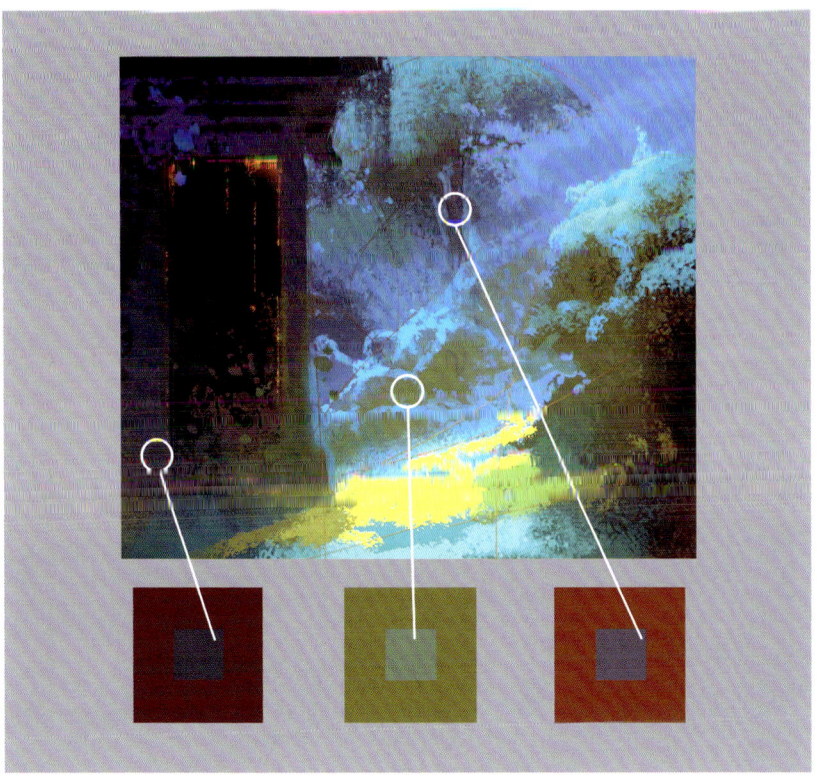

02. Colors that appear deep and warm are actually cool and desaturated

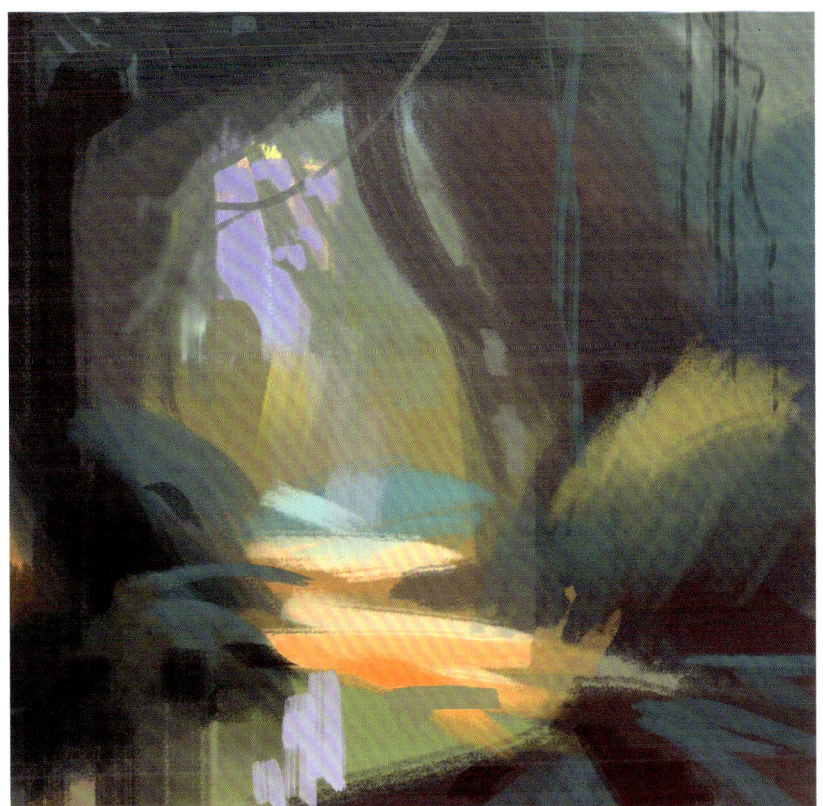

03. Color temperature adds to the illusion of depth and distance

02. WARM ACCENTS

Now let's look at the color relationships in a predominantly *cool* painting as a proof of concept about color temperature relationships. I've circled three spots that have a clear feeling of warmth within the context of this painting. There's a warm red-purple on the wall of the building, a warm yellow-ocher in the shadow of the bushes, and a warm brown in the bark of the middle tree. Again, I've surrounded them with actual versions of the colors they *seem* to be, and something very different emerges. In this new context, those sampled colors are not warm at all – they're very cold.

So once again, our environments are often made up of subtle relationships of color hues and temperatures. This is a quality of color that we must firmly understand and be good at.

03. CREATING DEPTH

I wanted to show you this comp because it has a solution in it that I use frequently. Color temperature plays a big part in creating a sense of space and depth in our environments; we tackled this subject in the earlier chapter on space (page 97) and I wanted to review it again here. The background in this study takes on a rich, cool, purple quality in contrast to the rest of the environment. In particular, I pushed a hot local color into the foreground, not just to emphasize the space of the scene, but also to create a rich visual interest of warm and cool color temperatures.

04. REVERSING THE NORM

Next let's play with color temperature in unexpected ways. You'll recall that in the chapter on space (page 126) we looked at how you can 'break the rules' of color temperature by strongly emphasizing other elements of depth. That's definitely the case in this environment study – it flip-flops the usual idea of heat in the foreground and cold in the background. I believe the depth still works because of the extraordinary number of overlapping elements taking us back to the distant opening. But it's still the warm and cool accents that give this environment its visual interest. Foreground stones with hints of warm local color are dappled with vibrant blue atmospheric light. Strong accents of gold and yellow-ocher give an exciting contrast to the blues, and *kaboom* – we have unity with variety creating a dynamic and engaging color palette!

05. TEMPERATURE ADDS EXCITEMENT

I love the challenge of taking a subject that has bland local colors and finding a way to bring in some visual excitement, as I did with this fantasy architectural environment. Here we are in a desert kingdom where everything is made of beige sandstone – how very boring. So I simply have the furthest masses of architecture made of a material that's a bit more of an orange-beige, and then I fill the shadows of adjacent planes with the contrasting cyan skylight. And voilà, we have an exciting temperature contrast even though our local color is limited.

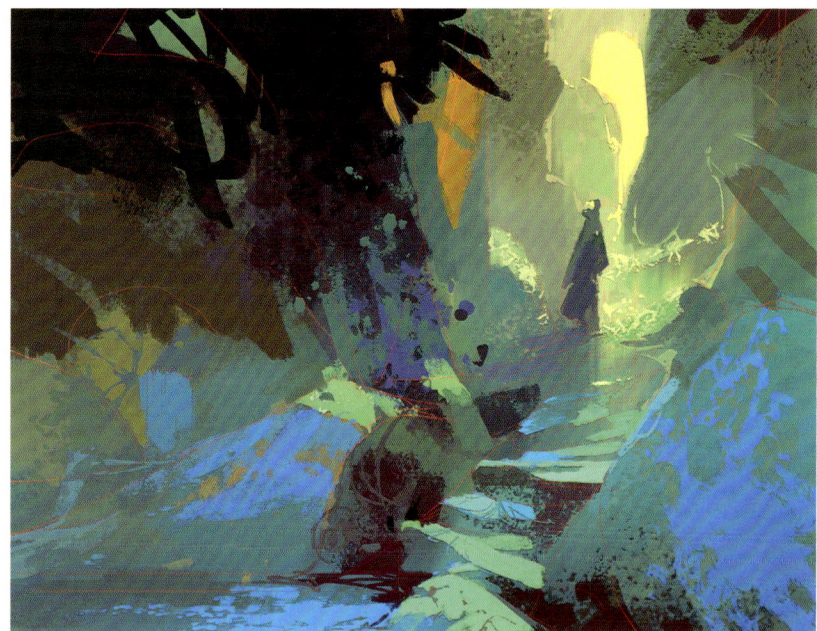

04. Using warmer colors for the distant background is uncommon but still possible

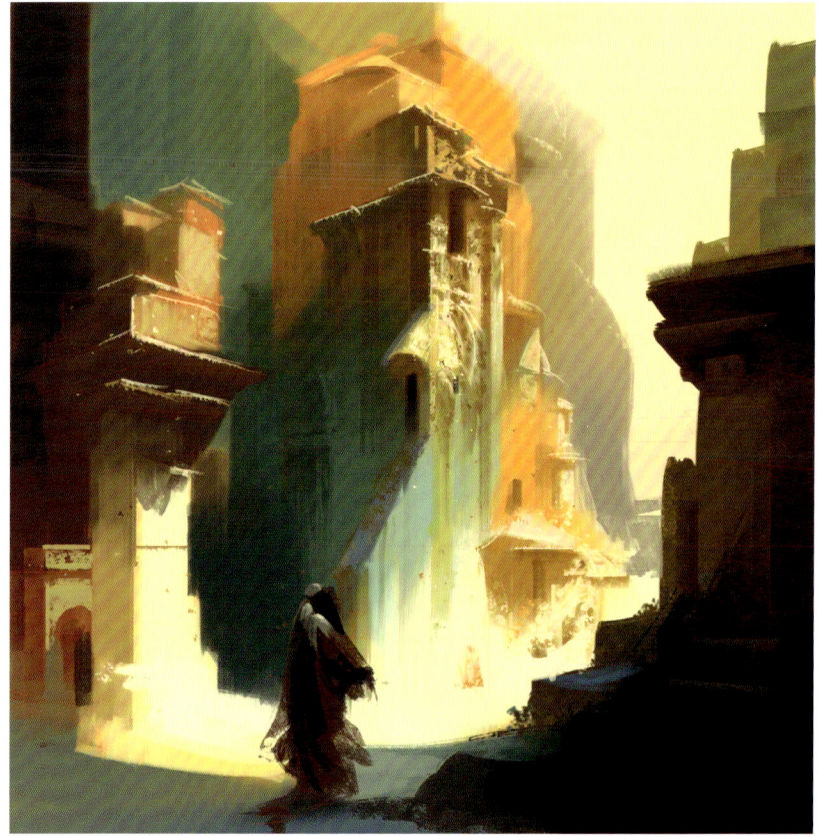

05. Find opportunities to enrich a dull-colored scene with vibrant temperature

THE COLOR SURPRISE!

I've been excited to get to this section because this is one of my favorite things in color. So let me ask, have you ever seen a painting where many of the colors didn't make logical sense but still worked? And not just worked but looked really *great*? While I was coming up I remember seeing some fantasy paintings that had such an effect. Back then I didn't understand what it was all about, but on further exploration it was quite a simple cheat.

The abstract painting below holds the answer: if something is important, you simply surround it with contrast. I've noticed in my many years of teaching that when students want more contrast they automatically go to value contrast, turning their environments into dark silhouettes against blown-out backgrounds. There's nothing wrong with this, though it's overly common and predictable; light against dark is nothing more than that. I've found that hue contrast carries more richness and more subtle possibilities than value contrast, as there's such a wide range of hues we can play against each other.

For clarity, I've charted out the color relationships for this abstract painting here on the color wheel. You can see that it's a very straightforward hue contrast.

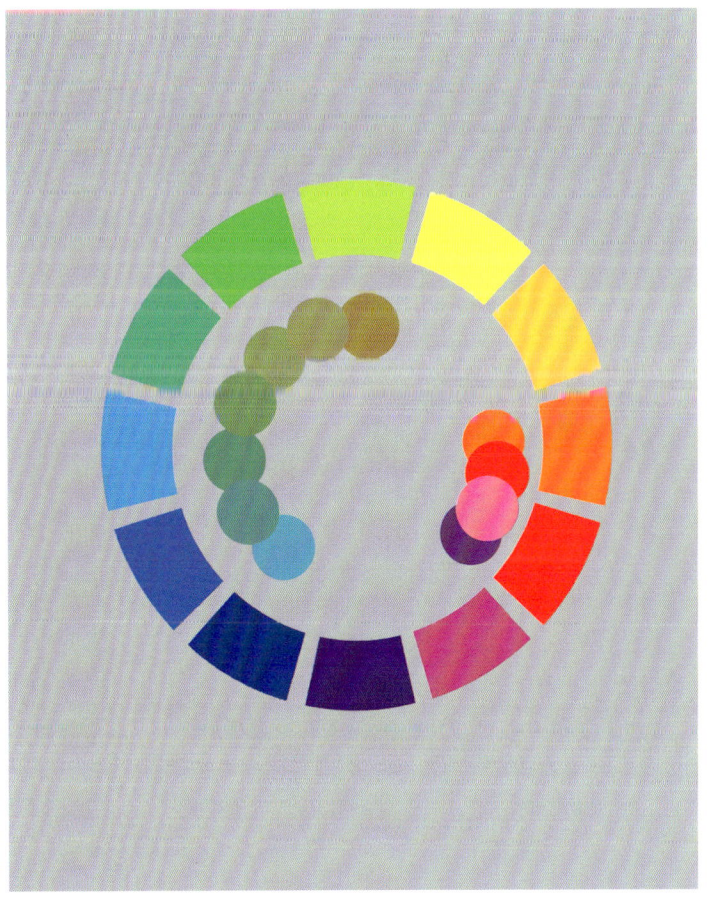

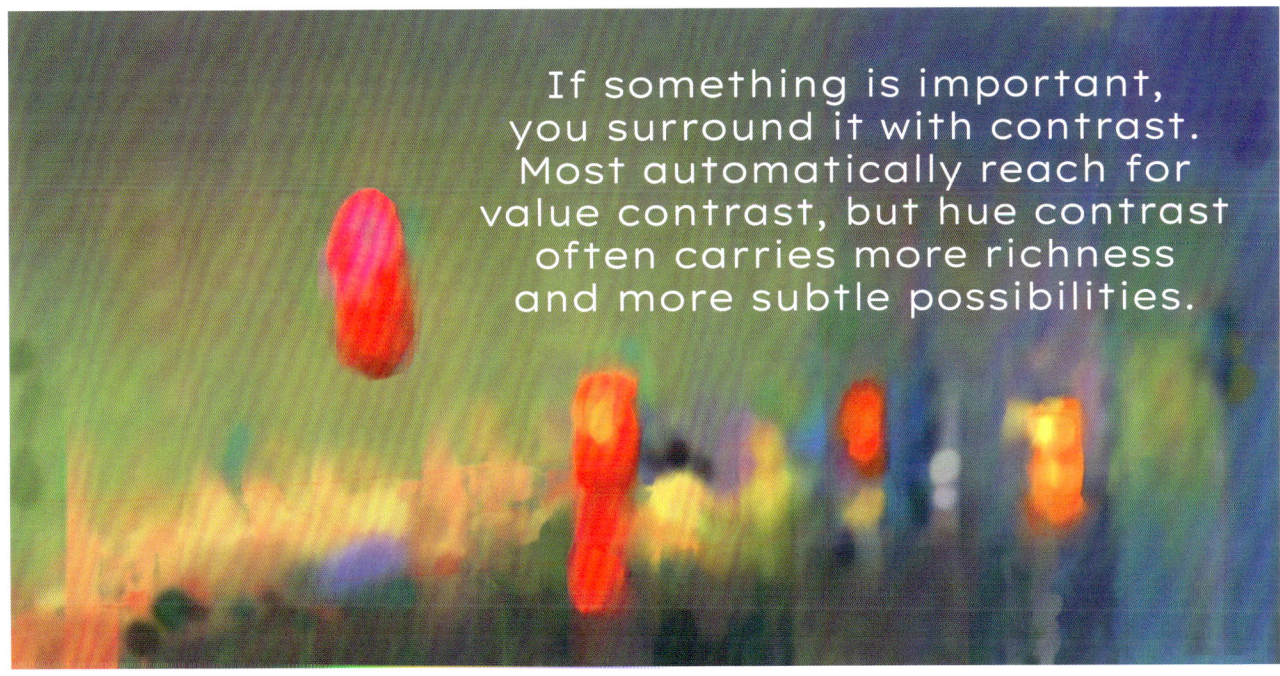

If something is important, you surround it with contrast. Most automatically reach for value contrast, but hue contrast often carries more richness and more subtle possibilities.

△ Instead of defaulting to value, we can use hue to create exciting, unexpected contrasts

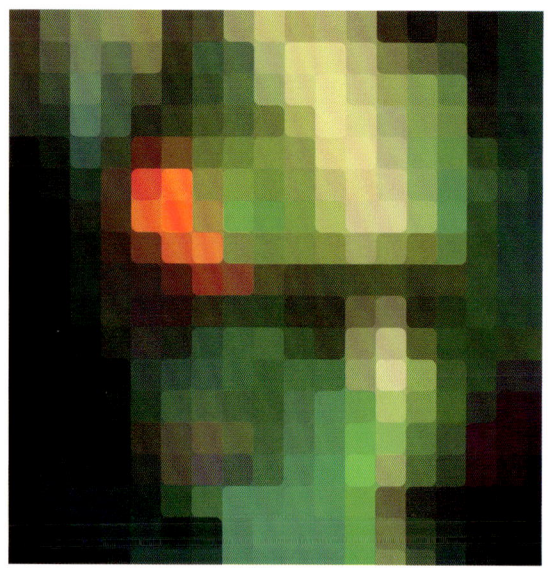

01. JUNGLE RUINS

Now let's bring this abstract idea to the case of these swampy jungle ruins. They're green, and not just *sort of* green – they're crazy green! There is a real-world justification for these colors: the ruins could be overgrown and mossy, plus the water could be casting a caustic greenish light up into it. Either way, this is a wild exaggeration, but it's all by intentional design. I want that flowering shrubbery to inescapably rock your world, and the way to do that is to make it really, *really* red. But that's not nearly enough. I'm looking for an extreme of color here, and I can only get it by leaning heavily on a contrasting color – in this case, green.

To make the exaggerated simplicity of this color palette readily apparent, I've made a tiled version of it on the left. This way we stop looking at leaves, windows, and individual details and just see the overall color relationships.

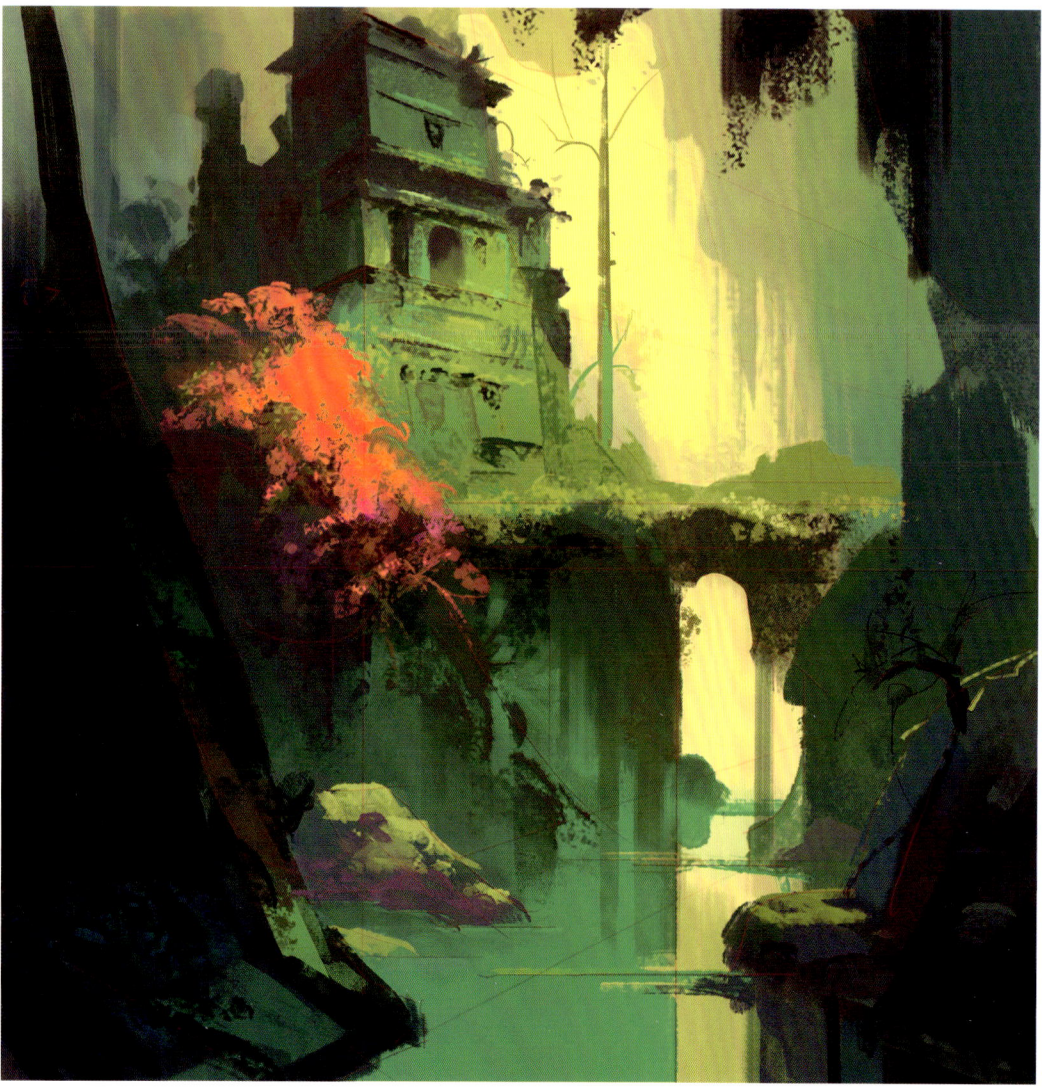

01. The red foliage is all the more vivid for being surrounded by strong greens

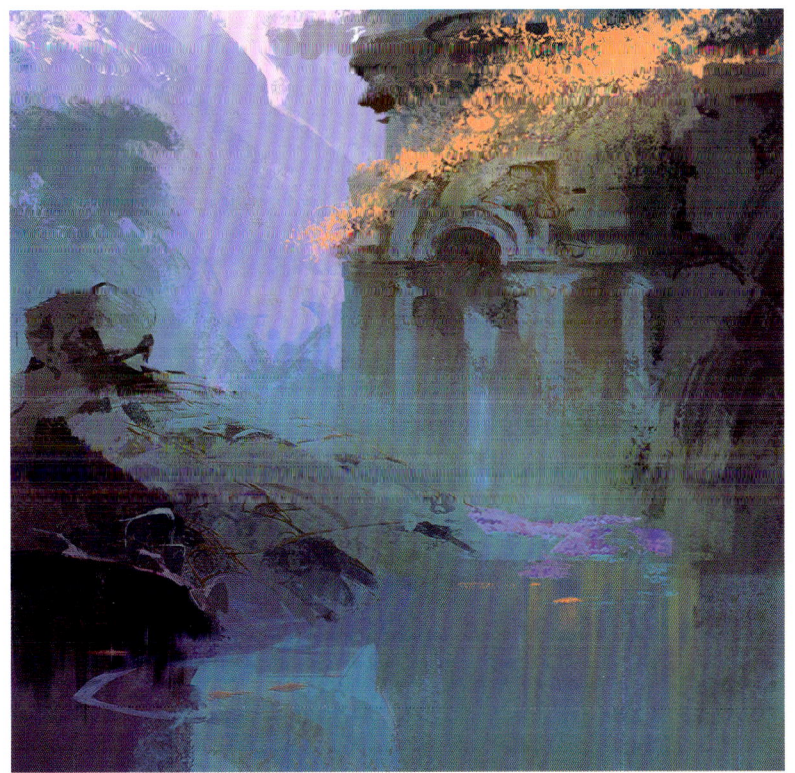

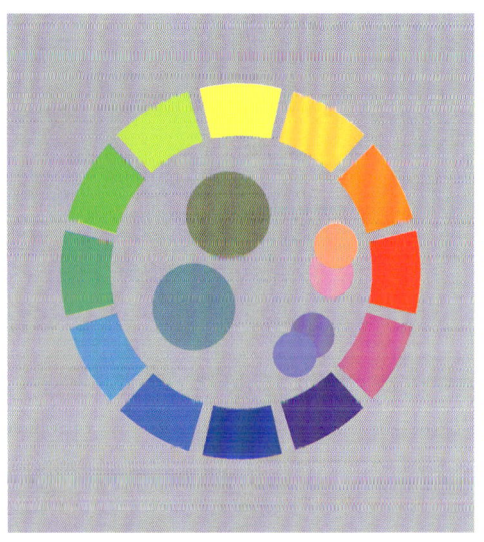

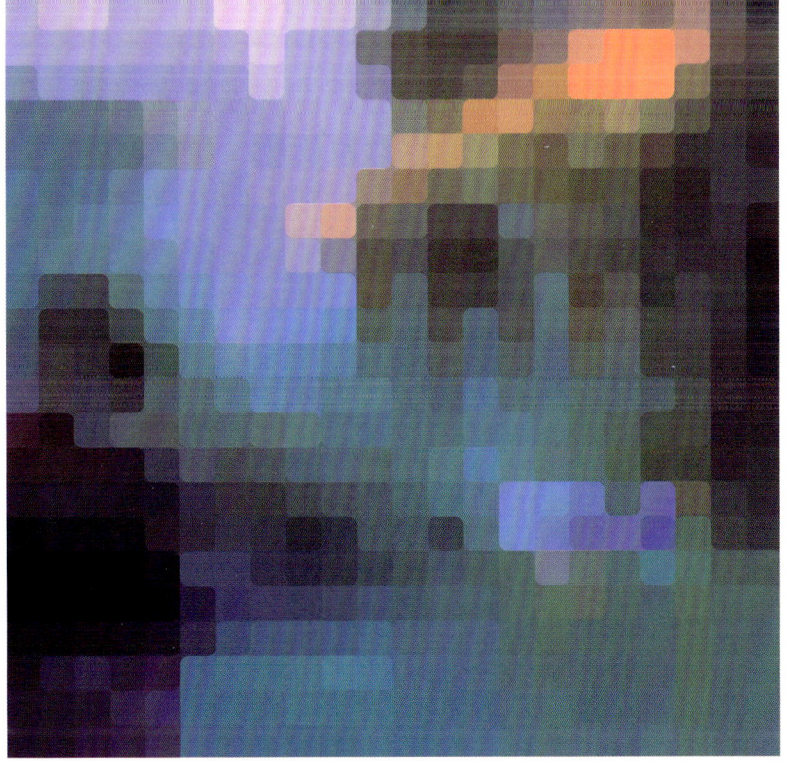

02. An image can contain more than one surprising color choice

02. EMPHASIZING HUE CONTRAST

The 'color surprise' can be designed any way we want. It doesn't have to be just one surprise – the environment can have multiple intriguing color accents. But the more we do this, the more complicated the color design becomes.

Let's stick with ruins, since they're such a mysteriously fun subject. This scene has similar warm foliage to the previous example, but with less hue contrast to the adjacent color – it's orange foliage alongside a warm neutral green. This still has a pleasant contrast but what I'm *really* setting up is for those greens to gradate cooler and cooler down to the water to contrast with a magenta accent.

You can see the color relationships clearly in the tiled version and I've further laid it out for you in another color wheel. We have an overall harmony of cool temperatures with the contrast of magenta and cyan, and a contrast of orange and warm green. Some might refer to these color relationships as split-complementary or some such – it's not a bad thing to do, but there are so many subtle possibilities that these labels make me nervous. They can cause us to revert to an exact formula rather than subtly adjusting to the needs of the picture.

EMPHASIS THROUGH SATURATION

Let's continue our endless quest to find even more ways to create visual interest in our environments through color. Here's another abstraction I've made for you, titled *Family Dynamics*. We will all have the tendency to rest our focus on the vivid red accent to the right of the scene. This image is very unlike the contrasting hues of the previous images – this entire scene is made almost exclusively of reds, yet it still works. This is why I make such a big fuss about not getting caught up in a trick bag of formulas, but rather finding

intriguing ways to create color contrast with both hue and saturation. Everything here is based on red, but neutral versions of the color except for our one hero accent. It pops because it's more saturated than any of the other reds.

You can see this worked out on the color wheel: we move all the way from the neutral center to the saturated accent with no other hues needed.

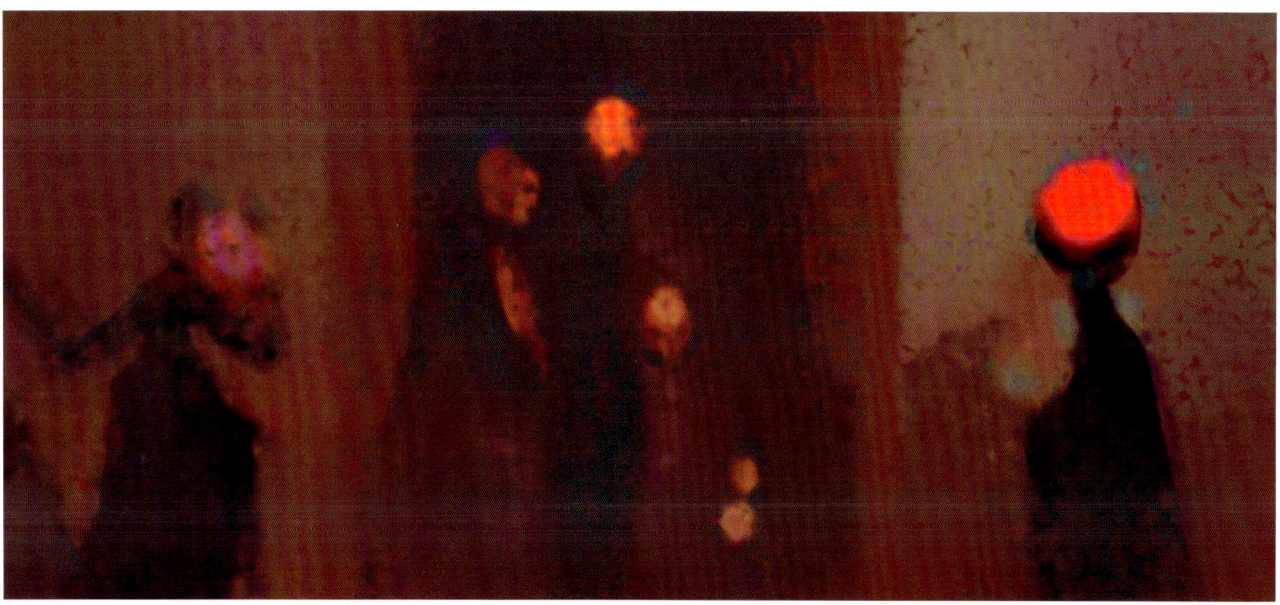

△ You can use saturation to create emphasis within a single hue

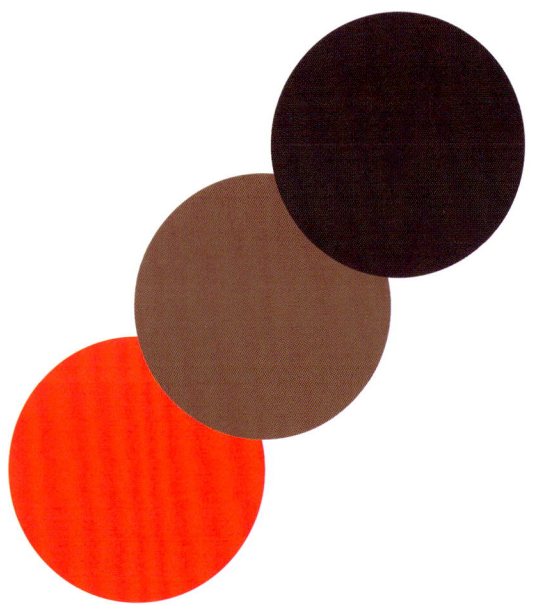

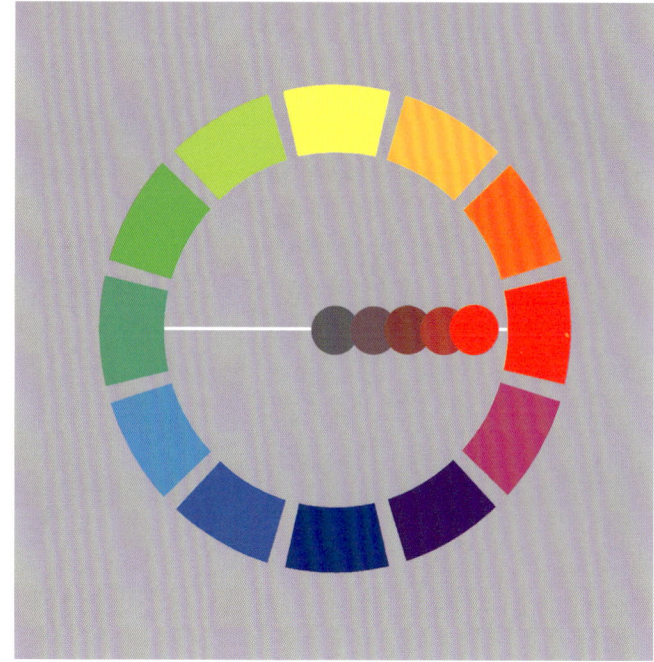

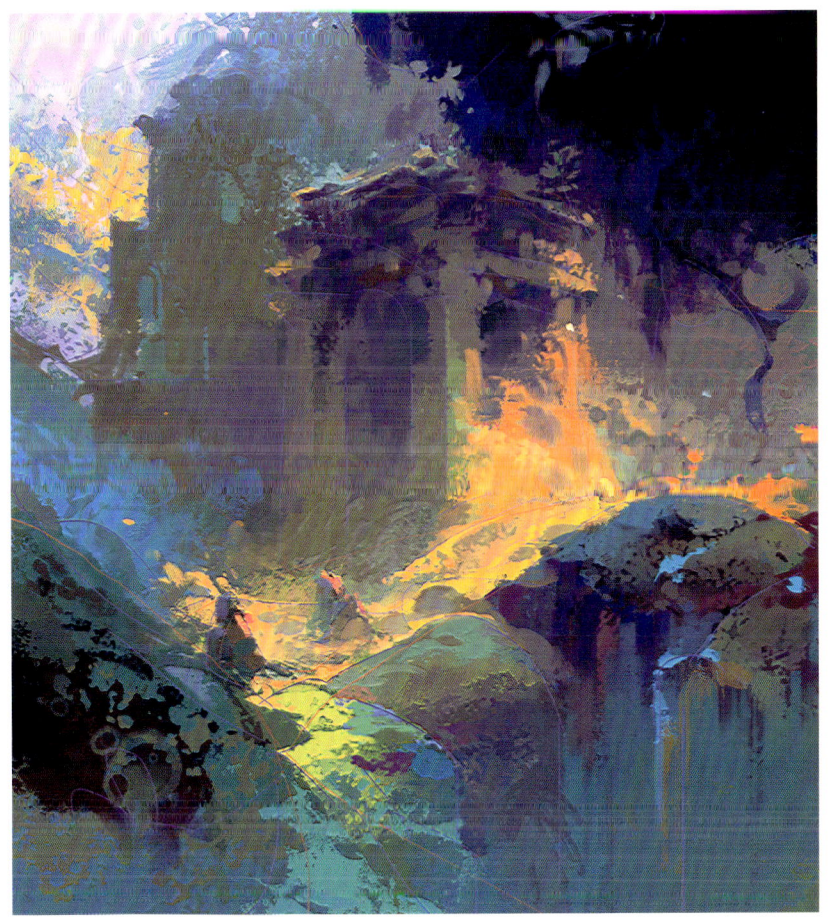

01. The local color of the buildings and foliage is less important here than the light-source colors

01. COLORFUL LIGHT

We're back in the ruins again because they're so much fun to paint! In this environment we have a combination of the ideas that create visual interest through color, including saturation contrast. The thing that's different about this image, compared with the previous handful, is that the color contrast is specifically created by light-source color rather than local color. We have lots of tools in our toolkit!

02. SCI-FI SCENE

Here's some sort of alien-planet situation where we have an obvious saturation contrast. And those saturated red circle things – are they local color? Are they a light source? It doesn't matter, they're sci-fi! It just matters that they have an intriguing contrast. They have a *color surprise*.

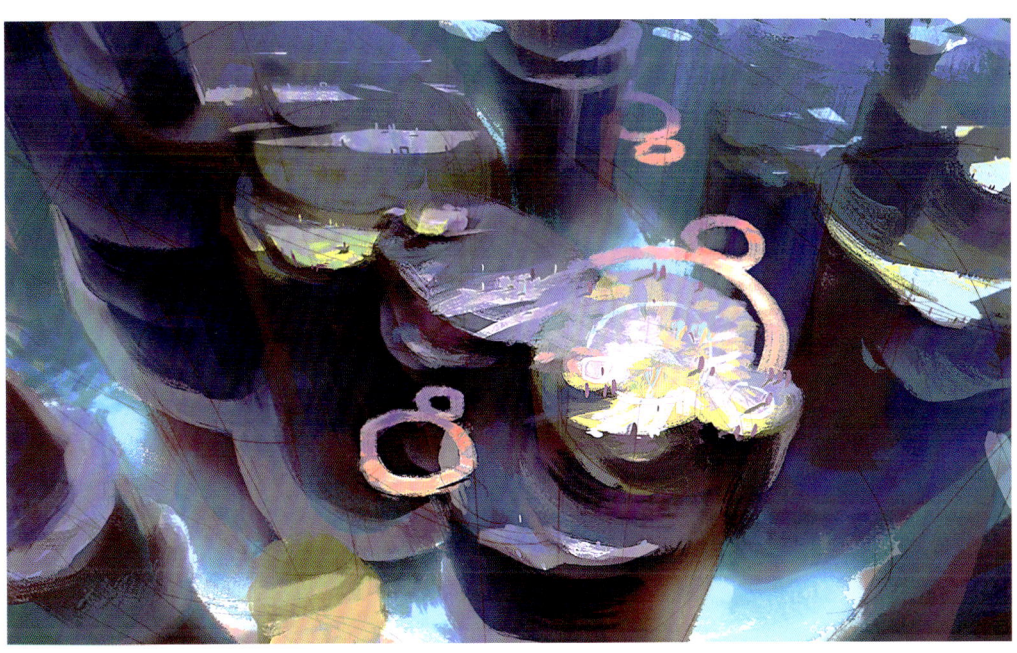

02. The saturation contrast here comes from areas of punchy red and cyan

ENVIRONMENT DESIGN THROUGH COLOR ACCENTS

Our big, simple idea so far in this chapter is unifying some aspects of our environment so that we can make other parts more important through contrast and variety. This gives our environments a great sense of purpose – it's how we tell stories and inform our audience about the environment. Is anything in the environment worth greater attention? Of all the elements in an environment, which one might be most important? We need ways to answer these questions to tell our stories and make our environments engaging to our audience. You've seen that we can do it beautifully through accents of color contrast.

Below are a color rough and a more worked-out version of an environment concept, including a silhouetted character lurking back in the jungle. Even though the figure has no detail and is nothing more than a silhouette, our attention still needs to be pulled toward it. The silhouette is backlit against a glowing yellow light, which is my first pass at creating contrast. I also have tons of jungle foliage in shadow, which gives me an overall cool green, so if I add orange accents to the figure I create a vivid color contrast.

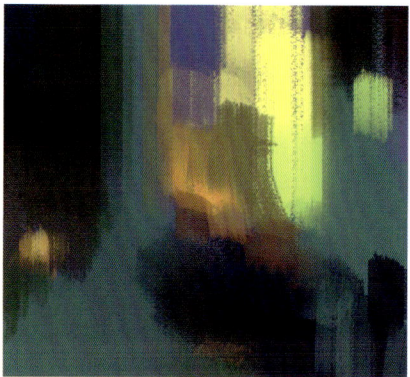

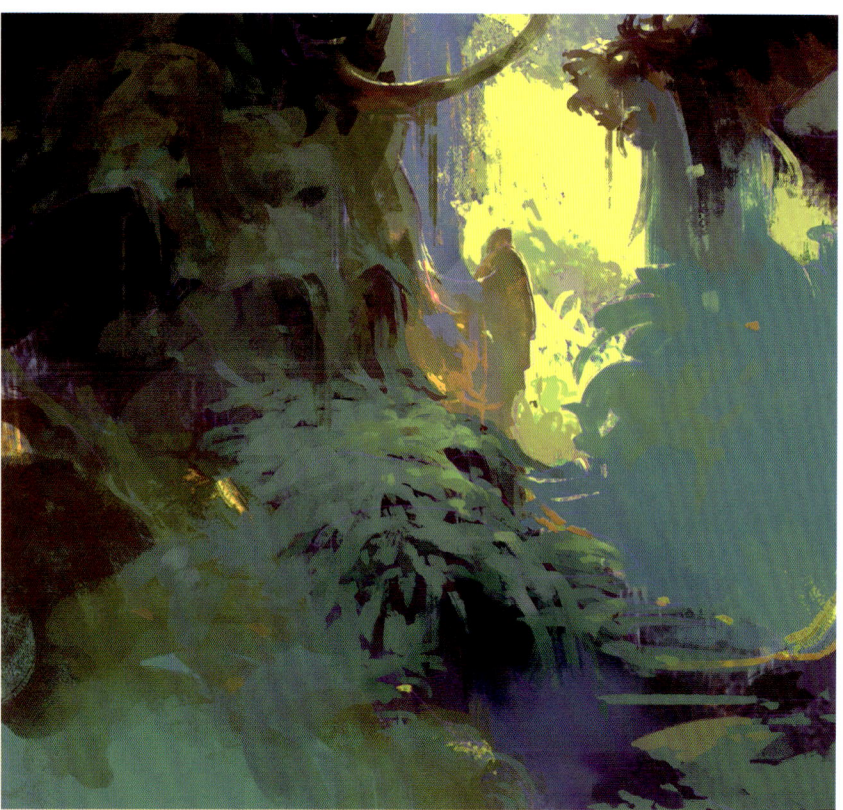

△ The color accents highlight what's most important for suggesting a story

Of all the elements in an environment, which ones are most important? When we've identified those, we need a whole toolbox of ways to give them special visual importance so that we can tell our stories and make our environments engaging.

GALLERY OF COLOR CONTRASTS

I'd like to take you through a series of images to give you a wide range of examples of useful color accents in environments. Let's start with this somewhat surreal-seeming landscape. It feels surreal because the color palette is an uncommon one compared to real life, but you'll find that the basic concept of it is familiar by now – it's a straightforward 'green, purple, and orange' triad for the most part. It's also a destination painting, meaning it's designed to feel like it's leading you somewhere. I need to make that 'somewhere' interesting, even if it's distant and abstract, so I do it with a simple color accent. I make the backdrop a vivid fantasy orange and then make the silhouetted outcrop a contrasting cool temperature.

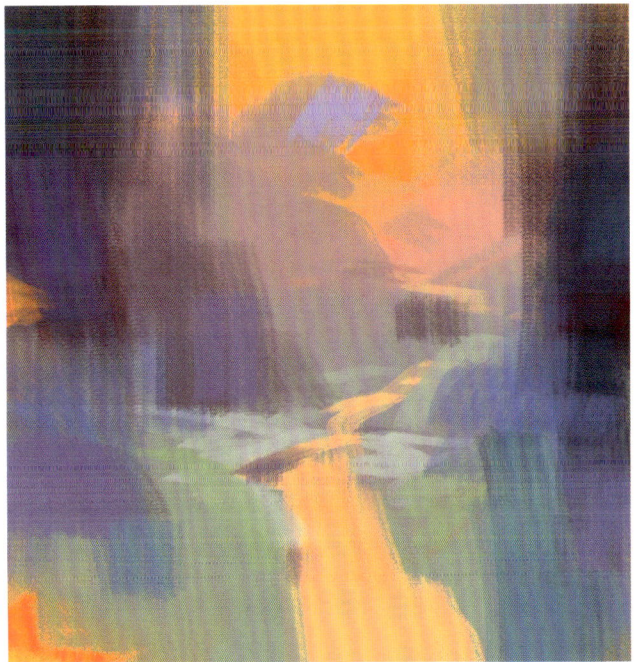 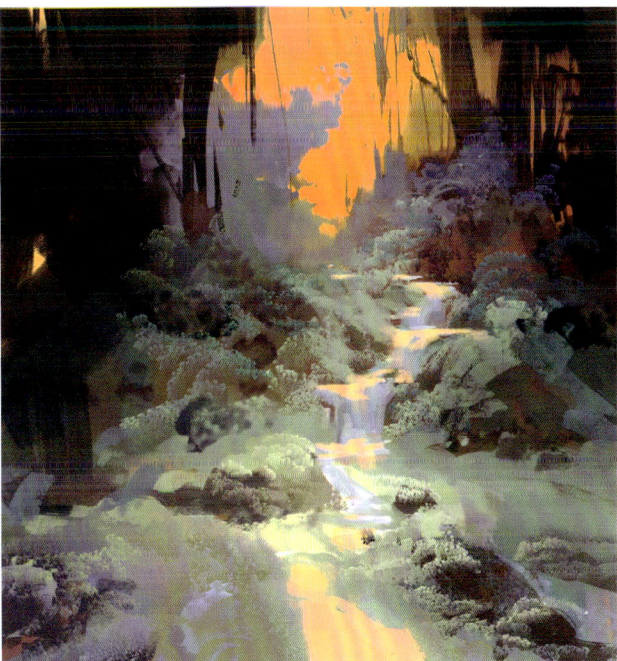

△ This scene draws the viewer into the vibrant orange distance

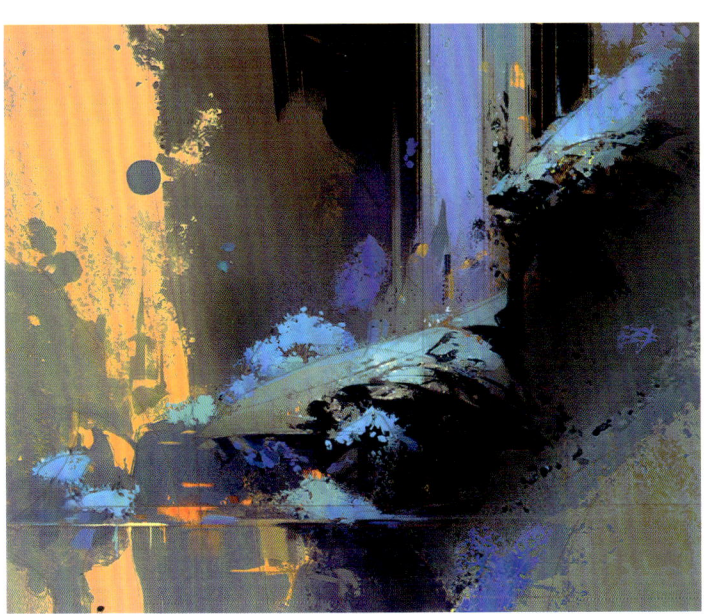

01. BLUE PLANET

Another sci-fi image. Everyone knows alien planets are bound to have blue foliage, so let's use that as a major color accent in this very brown world. Remember, if your painting turns to brownish mud, it's an easy fix – just find places where you can add cool accents and the mud will turn to magic!

01. Blue accents look extra vivid and alien against the surrounding browns

Learn everything you can about environmental color design, then use every bit of color trickery possible to create the most engaging environments.

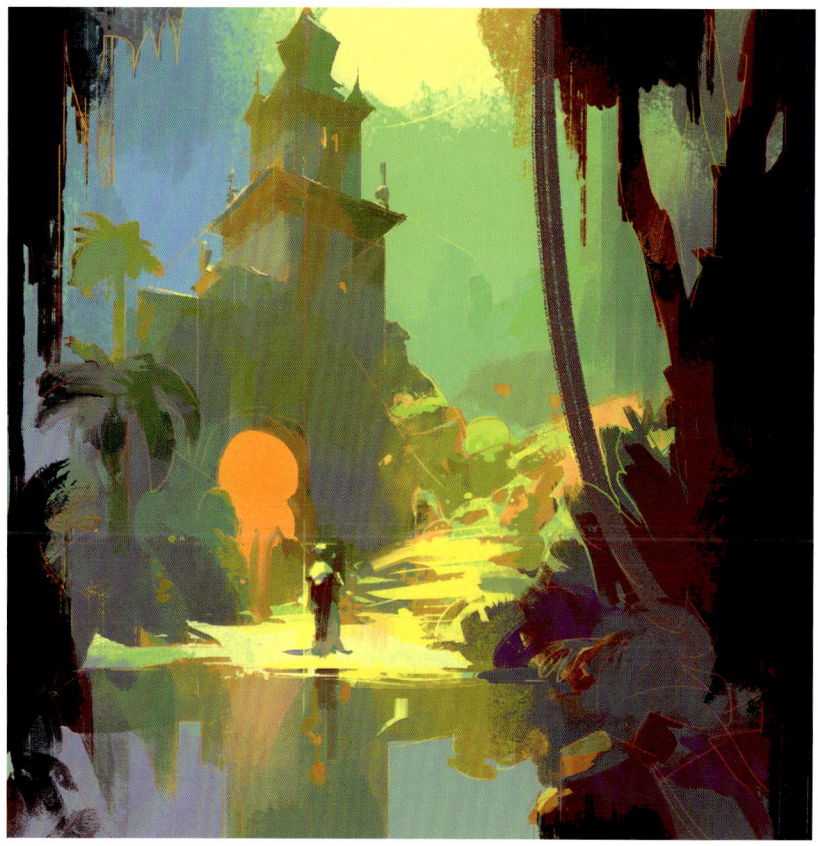

02. GREEN ATMOSPHERE

I started this chapter discussing the possibilities of local color versus lighting color. The previous image was about local color contrast, but this example has very little local color in it. The bold colors are nearly exclusively created by lighting and atmosphere. The vivid green in the upper center background might be unexpected to many viewers. It's definitely exaggerated to serve as a relief from all of the brown, but there's also a justification for it – as yellow sunlight and blue skylight intermingle in the thickness of distant atmosphere, they blend together to create a hue that has a hint of green in it. I've simply taken this idea and wildly exaggerated it for theatrical effect. Whatever it takes to create an engaging picture!

03. JUNGLE FOLIAGE

Here I was playing around with big fronds of leafy green jungle foliage. I wanted to make them seem extra special, so take a wild guess at what I did next. Yep, I surrounded the green outgrowths with magenta! This once again goes back to the idea of turning mud into magic – we have mostly gray-greens and neutral magentas here, which are boring by themselves, but real magic when you put them together.

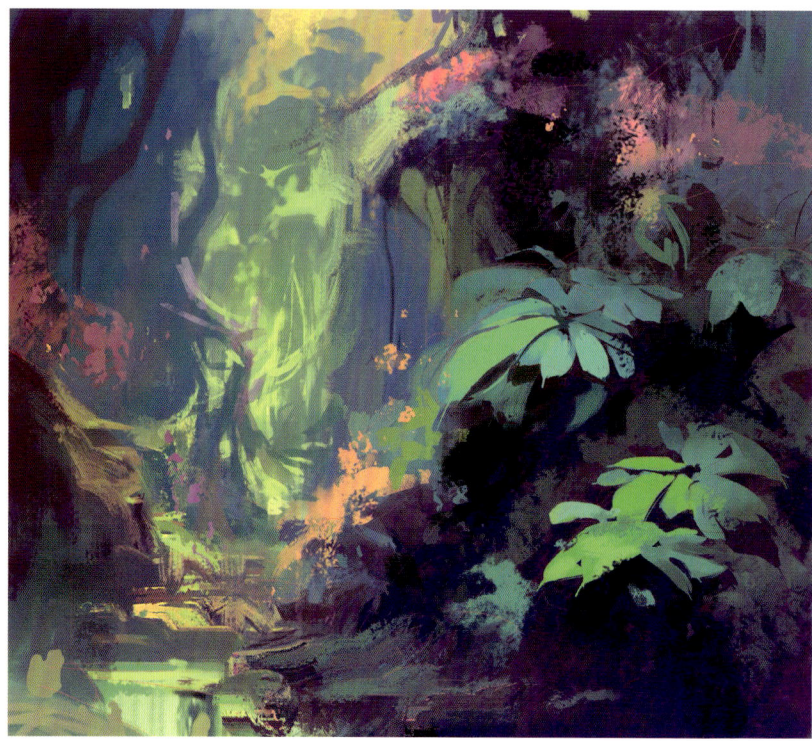

03. A magenta backdrop makes the green undergrowth extra vivid

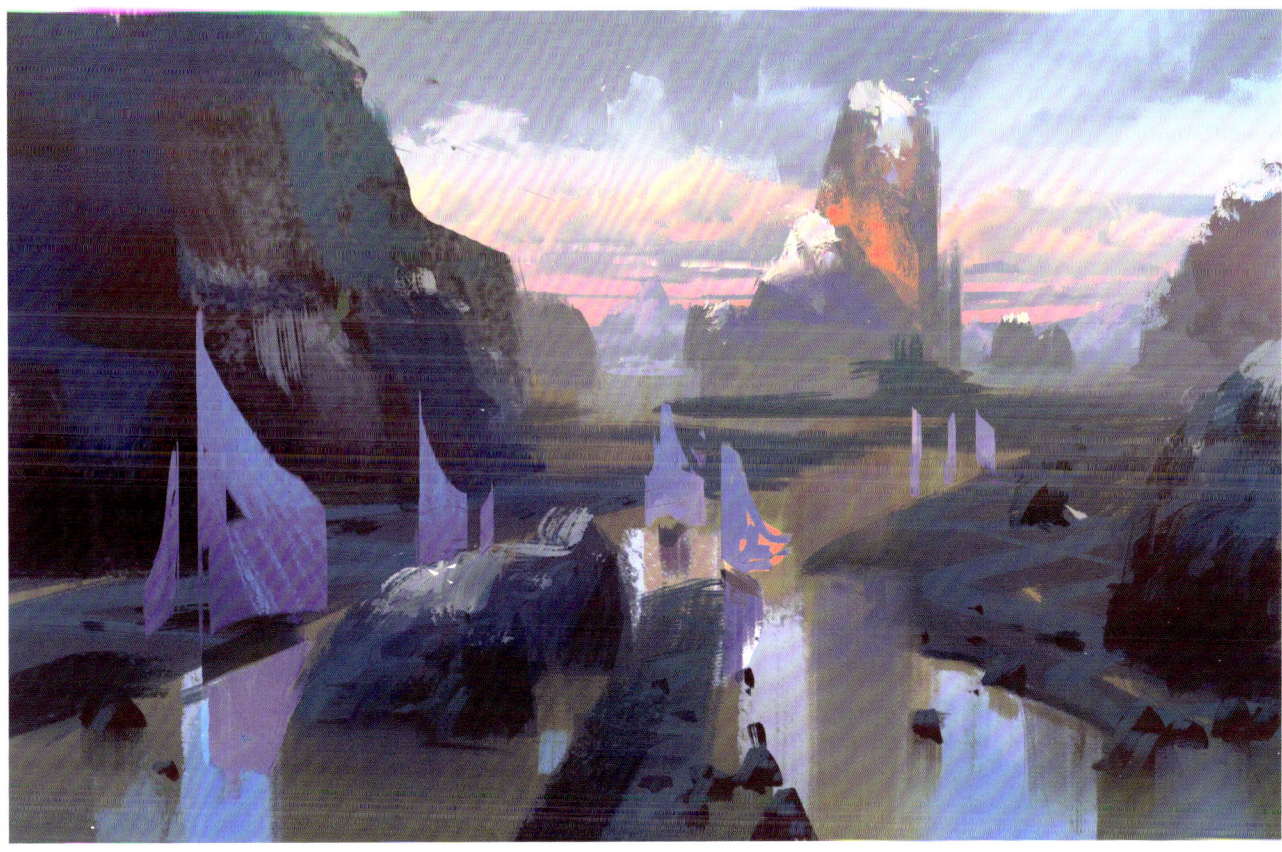

04. The boats' sails lead the viewer through an environment of greens and browns

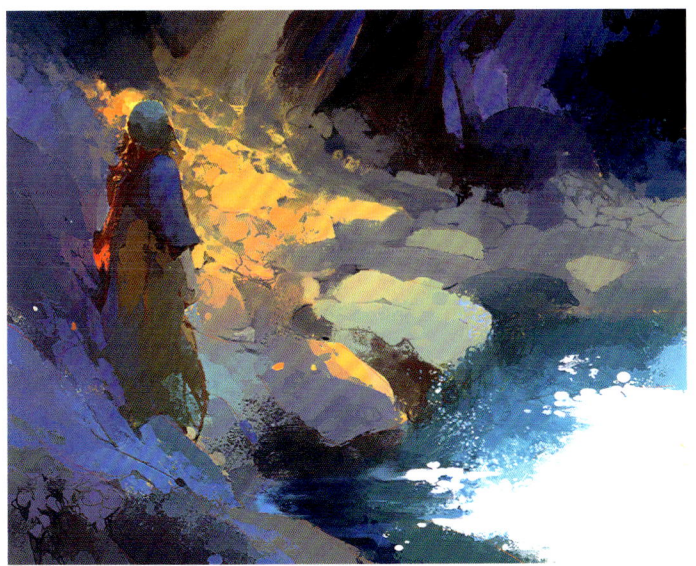

05. This image employs multiple contrasts grouped close together

04. SAILING BOATS

Let's take our audiences on another journey by sprinkling breadcrumbs of color hue to guide them toward a distant destination. In this image those 'breadcrumbs' are the sailboats. Their local color is magenta with cool skylight, which is primarily saturation contrast, but I've also made it an issue of hue contrast by adding neutral greens nearby to emphasize the boats' importance.

05. ADJACENT CONTRASTS

Let's wrap up our gallery of color explorations with a couple of images that have singular focal areas. They use multiple color contrasts to guarantee the viewer's attention. This one is inspired by the line from a Robert Frost poem: '*The woods are lovely, dark and deep ...*'. To bring our attention to the figure, I use both local color and light-source color to amp things up. The woman has red hair and a shirt with a blue local color. Cool skylight gives her cap a cyan accent and warm direct sunlight adds a golden pool of light adjacent to the figure. This grouping of multiple contrasts locks us into the purpose of the image.

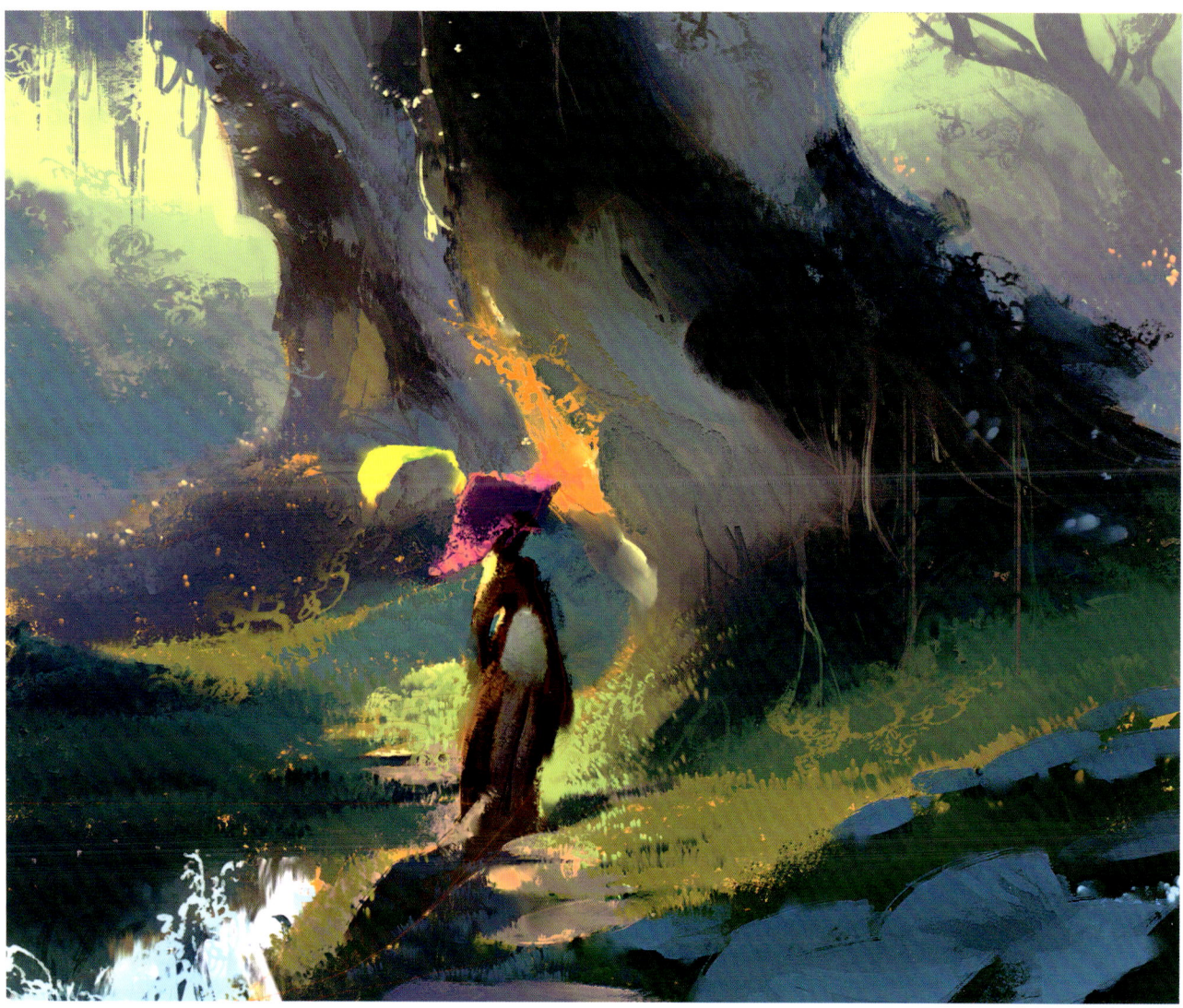

06. This image uses contrast in both its local and light-source colors

06. ONE LAST EXAMPLE

And let's do it one more time. What are the accents of local color and light-source color in this example? I know you're great at identifying color accents by now – I'd like you to observe the figure and identify what local color and light-source colors are accentuating this primary focus of the image.

OPTICAL COLOR-MIXING

Let's add some more magic to our bag of tricks in the form of optical color-mixing, because it can be very special. The idea is simple and one you're no doubt familiar with: some colors mix to create other colors, and this can be done with very small dots of different colors without any kind of blending. You can see that illustrated in our first example: we take a pure yellow and a pure cyan and place dots side by side. If we're standing far enough away, or if the dots are small enough, they optically mix in our vision to create a very convincing green.

The same can be done to create optically mixed neutrals. In the chart below, I've used a triad of orange, green, and violet. These three colors optically negate each other and give the impression of a gray. For comparison, I've added a grayscale version so you can see that they're not so terribly different from each other.

OK, so why bother? Why not just paint a green and a gray instead of taking so much time to do this optical-mixing circus stunt? I believe the next page will give us the answer.

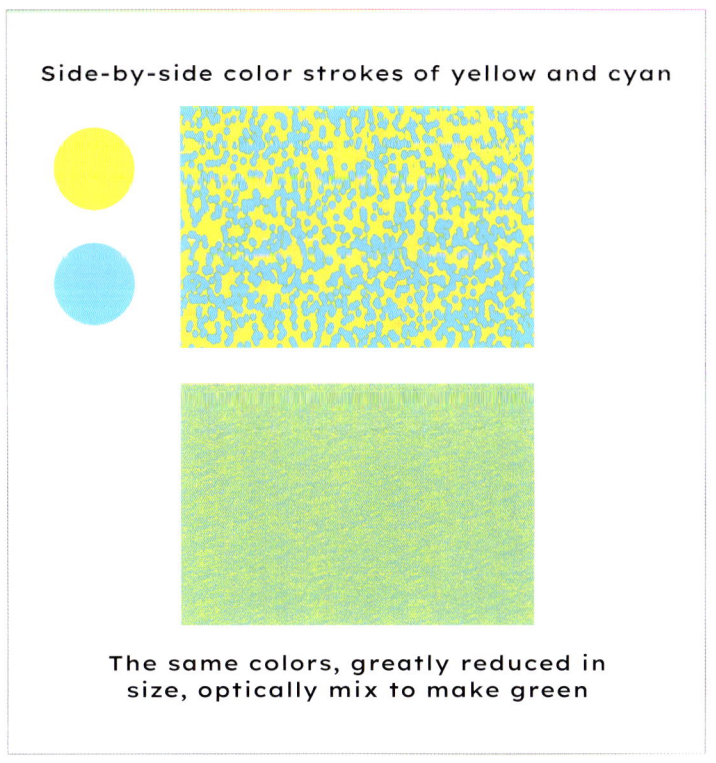

Side-by-side color strokes of yellow and cyan

The same colors, greatly reduced in size, optically mix to make green

△ In optical mixing, our eyes mix a new color for us

Side-by-side color strokes to create an 'optical' gray

Three contrasting hues are used, each with an identical value

The same image as above but shown in grayscale

The same colors but shown only in grayscale

△ An 'optical' gray and pure gray are pretty similar – but not exactly the same!

01. POOR MAN'S IMPRESSIONISM

Here's a birch grove at dusk. It's filled with varieties of warm and cool light filtering through the sky and atmosphere onto the local colors. To capture this, I've applied something I call 'poor man's Impressionism'. It's a technique where I simply use textures to do the equivalent of the dot patterns on the previous page. It's fast and effective and has a more natural quality. Despite the fast pace of getting this painting done, my goal is for it to have a rich and luminous glow that mimics real light and atmosphere.

This scene shows how you can achieve that in a painting, simply use contrasting color hues that are nearly identical in value. The technique gives color a vibrating luminosity that mimics the experience of a real-life glow of light. This effect is referred to by artists as 'simultaneous contrast'. The discovery of this idea was the foundation of the Impressionist movement in the nineteenth century.

On the right, I've pulled out a few examples to show you the color relationships I'm working with. For instance, I wanted a luminous cyan in the sky, so I layered it on top of a magenta that's identical in value and let bits of the magenta show through. I used this effect throughout the painting – this way cyan is never just cyan, it always has something extra.

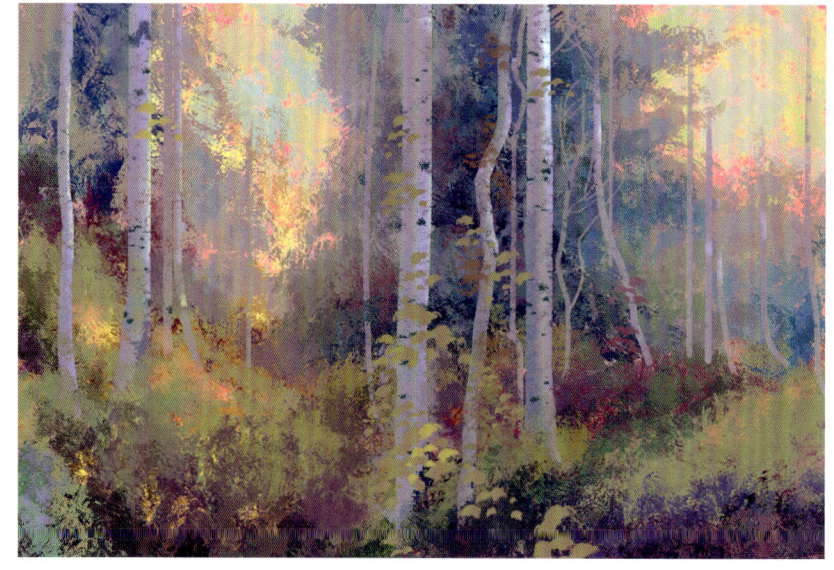

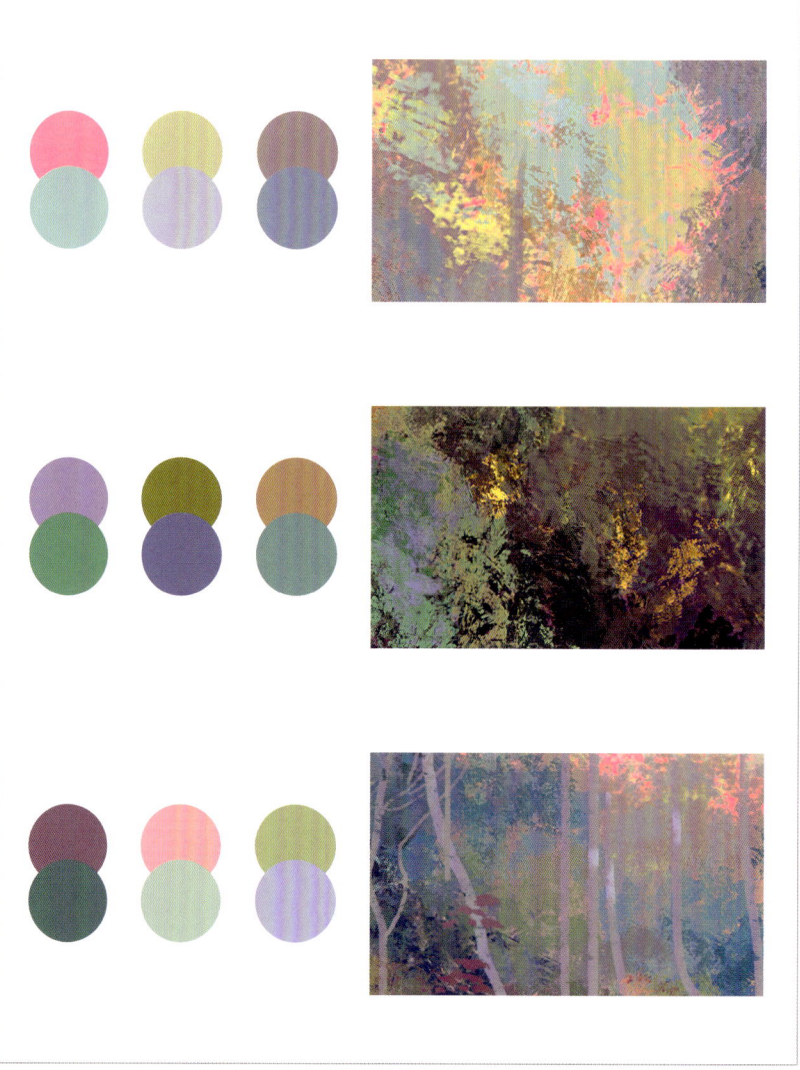

01. Using an Impressionistic painting style to create optical color-mixing

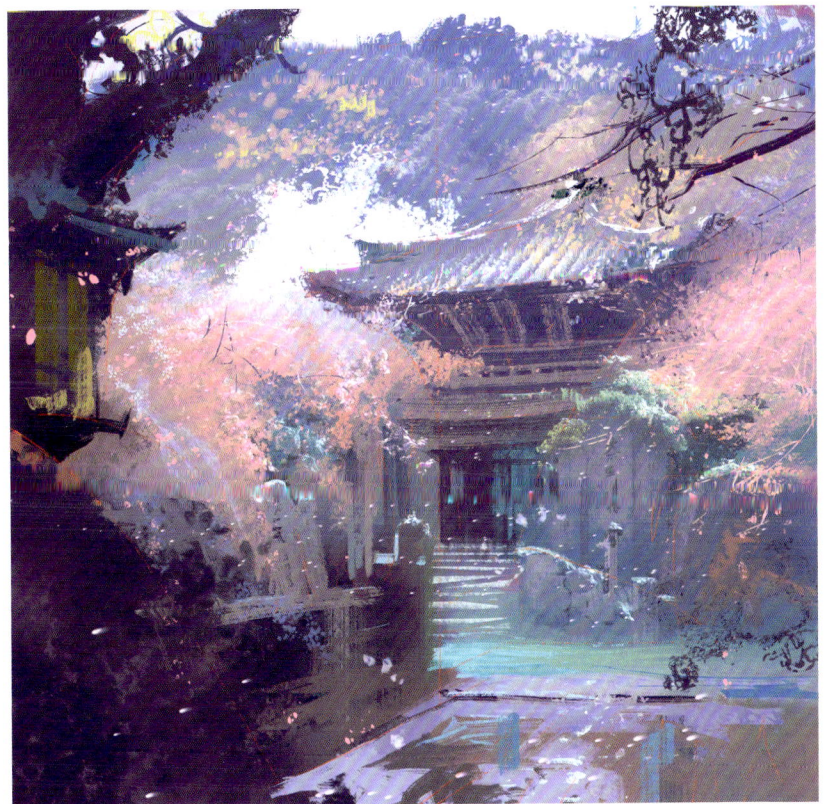

02. JAPANESE GARDEN

Here's another example featuring a Japanese garden environment where the many warm local colors, including blossoming trees, are brought to life by cool ambient lighting. It's a perfect opportunity for my 'poor man's Impressionism' technique. I've pulled some sections out for a close-up look at the layered colors, and I hope you enjoy the image.

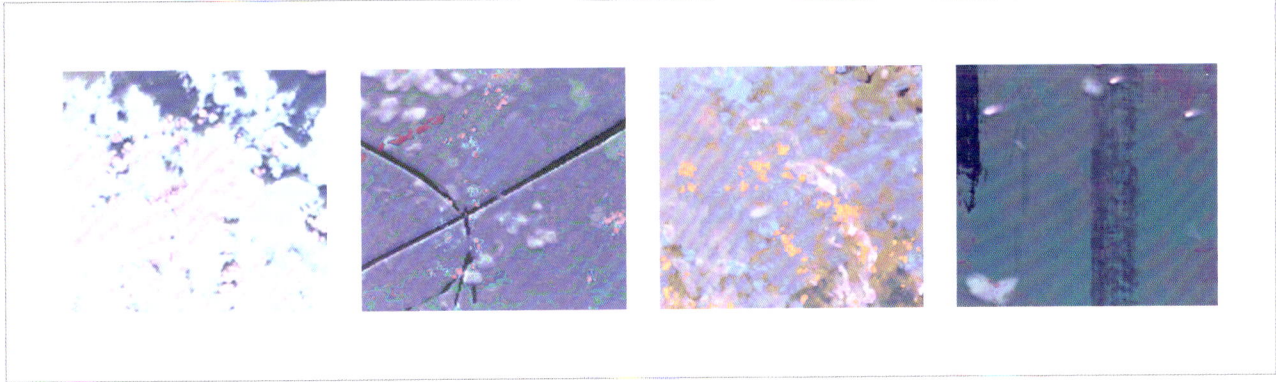

02. Optical mixing gives this image a dreamy glow and vibrancy

Why not just paint one color? Why bother taking so much time to do this optical-mixing circus stunt? Because the individually contrasting colors have a vibrating luminosity that mimics the real-life glow of light, even though you're only looking at a printed page.

EMOTION, ALWAYS EMOTION

Do these two images look familiar? If they don't, you skipped one of the most important chapters of the book – these were two of our images we used to explore the emotion of shape language (page 79).

I was being a bit tricky back in that chapter, as I used emotional color as well. I used red for the sharp and dangerous mountains and a quiet blue for the more stable and passive square environment, which I'm sure are obvious choices. Color is another of our primary tools to convey emotion, so let's dig into that idea.

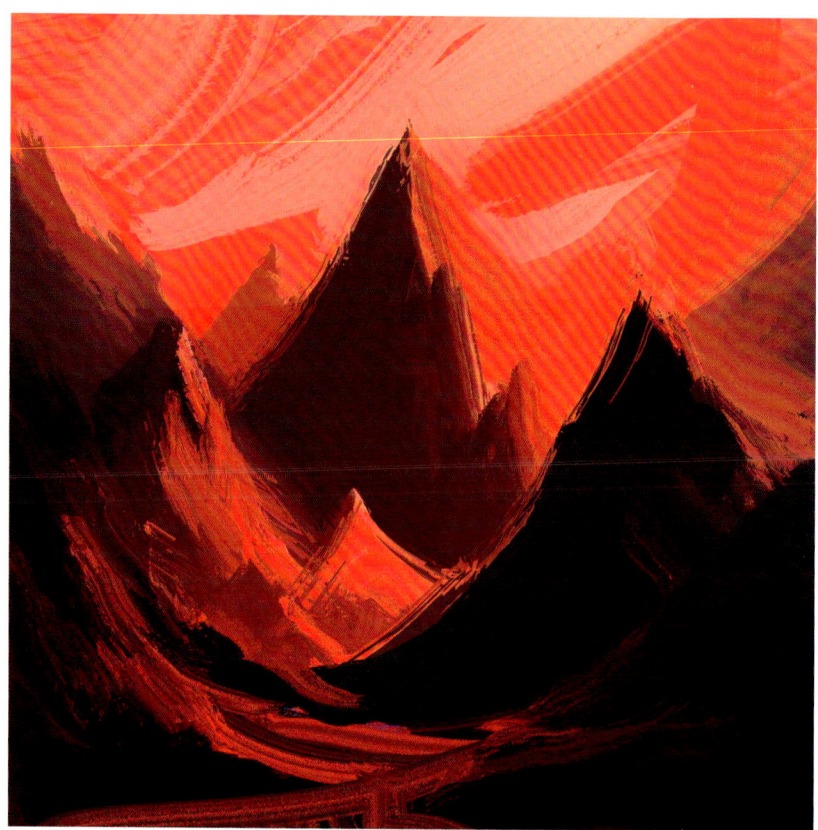

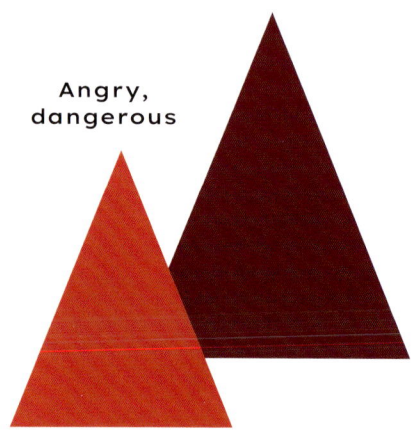

Angry,
dangerous

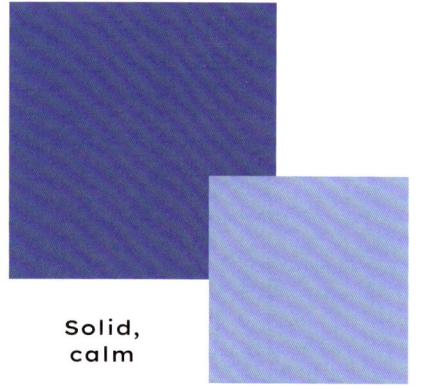

Solid,
calm

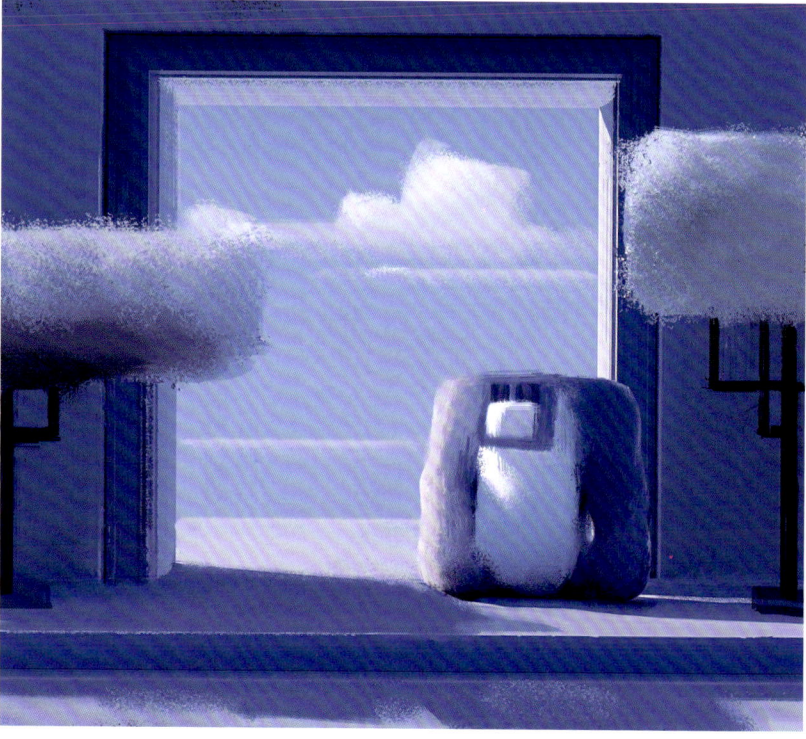

△ Color is one of our most powerful tools for conveying mood and emotion

01. THE EMOTION OF HUE

Simply arranging a color palette around a particular hue can be a strong emotional cue. Have a look at each one of these color groupings and notice how they feel different from each other in terms of emotion. There's a nice warmth to the golden one on the top left, but the red one feels angry. The green one on the top right feels almost supernatural – and the list goes on.

But don't forget that the *lack* of color can carry strong emotion. The white and gray example has a feeling of sterility, like a clean lab room. It also feels ashen, like the smoky aftermath of a disaster. And I think the black one speaks for itself.

There are single-hue environments that are very effective emotionally. We refer to this kind of color palette as 'monochromatic'. We'll get to some more examples shortly, but first we need to more thoroughly introduce the idea of color emotion.

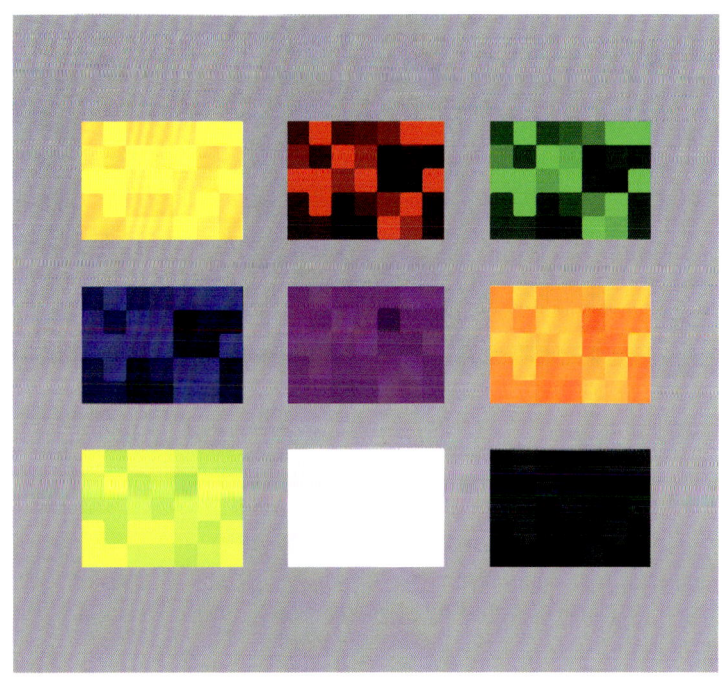

01. Each of these monochromatic palettes evokes a different emotion

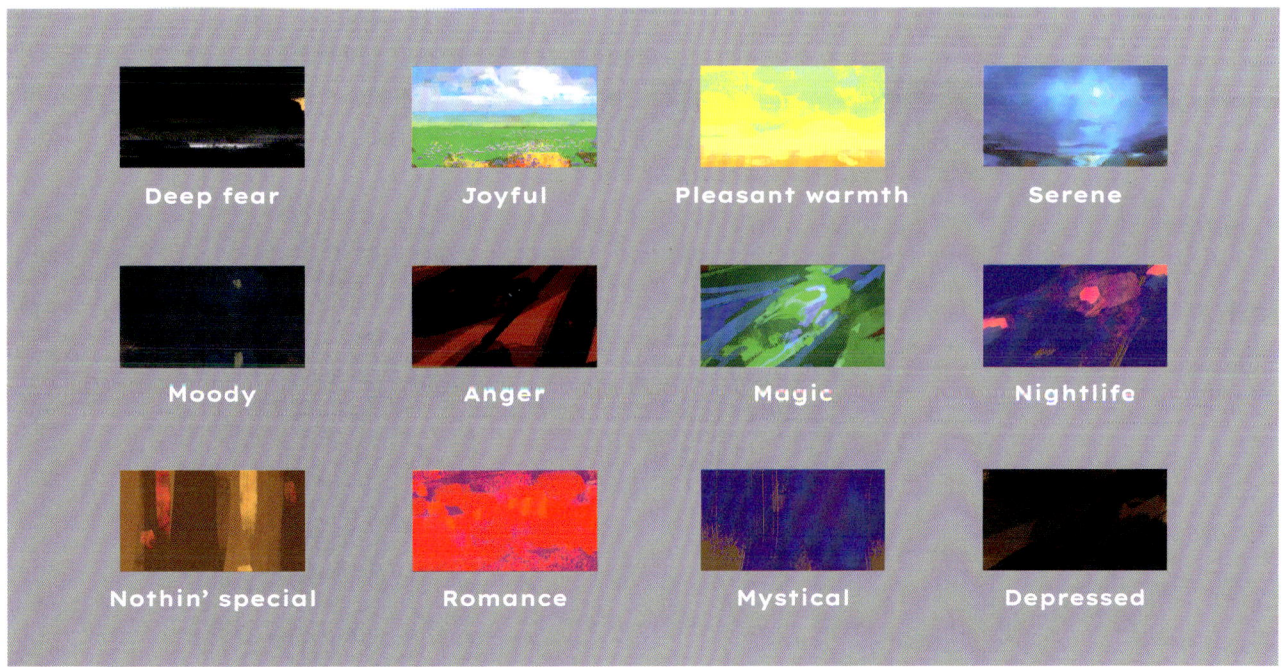

02. Expanding a palette with more color broadens the range of emotions we can capture

02. ENVIRONMENTAL COLOR EMOTION

Here I've expanded the color palettes significantly beyond just monochromatic combinations. Look at how much emotional range we can get! I invite you to take a careful look at each one of these, and at the labeled emotion, and think of how engaging your artwork will become as you apply intense color emotion.

MONOCHROMATIC COLOR

Monochromatic color palettes can be intensely emotional because they're just one thing. When we feel an intense emotion, it tends to edge everything else out. We don't feel happy and angry at the same time – in fact, we hardly think about anything *but* the emotion if it's intense enough. That's why a monochromatic color palette is so powerful and so simple.

Let's start with an image of great emotional intensity centered around only reds. For clarity, I've charted this color grouping on the color wheel for you. What mood does this palette evoke?

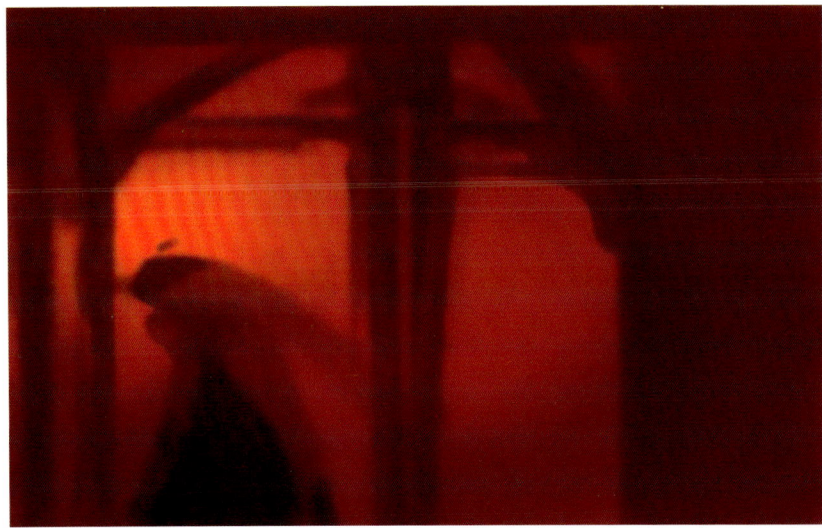
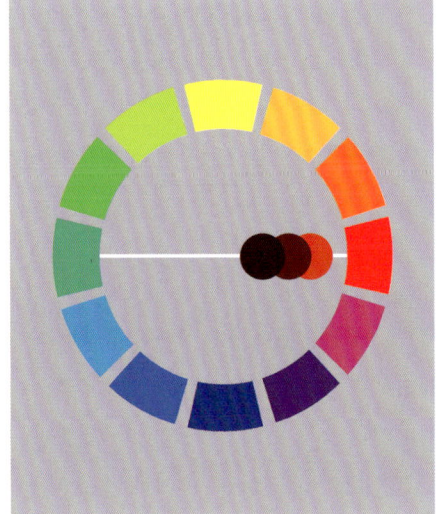

△ This monochromatic red scene has an angry, oppressive mood

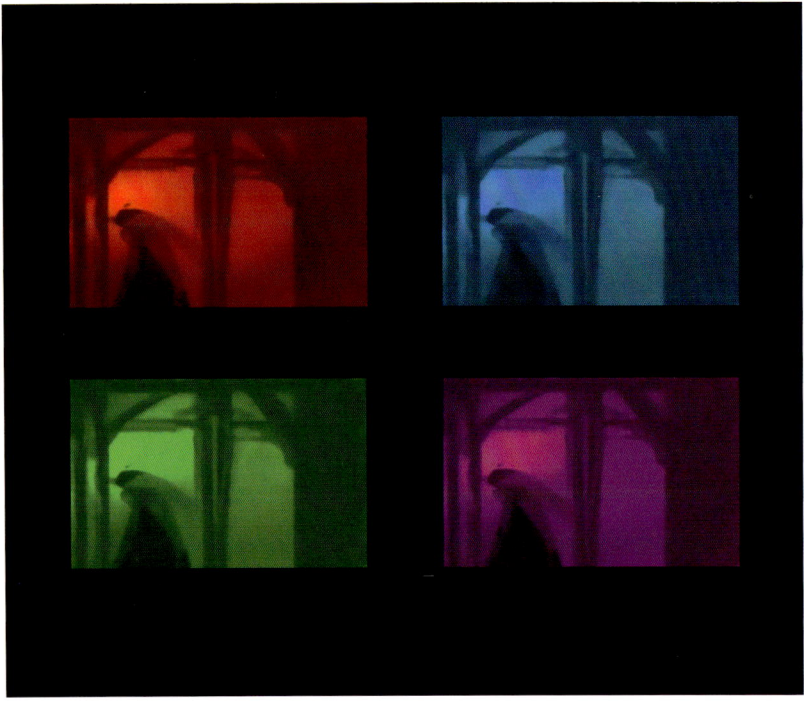

01. Changing the hue changes the mood

01. SAME SCENE, NEW HUE

Let's look at the same image but in different color hues and see what that does to the emotion. Notice how the images go from anger, to sorrow, to envy. These palettes are also monochromatic.

02. LIGHTEN THE MOOD

It's true that monochromatic palettes often fit best with negative emotions because of their overwhelming nature, but they don't have to be that limited. Here's an image that has a hint of hopefulness. It's a value-based image but the little bit of warmth heightens its visual interest and gives it a sense of hope. I've also charted this color grouping on the color wheel.

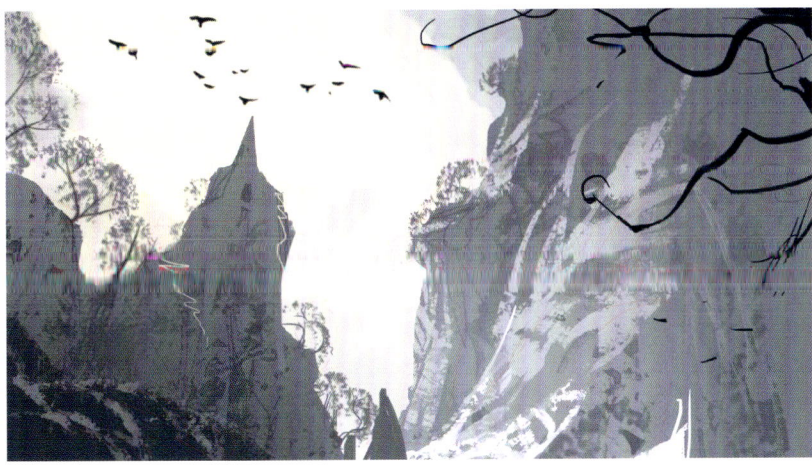
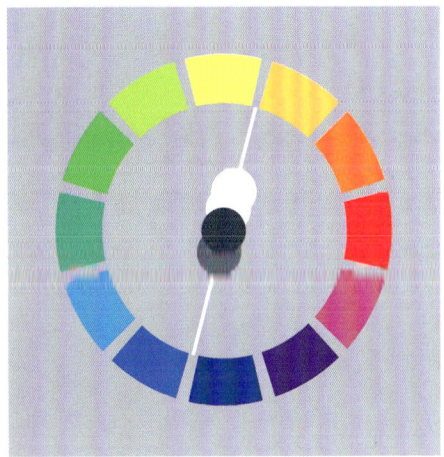

02. A monochromatic image doesn't have to be dark and heavy

LET'S ADD A BIT MORE COLOR

This would be a brooding monochromatic blue palette except for the hint of warmth added. Like the previous image, the warmth adds a bit of goodness in an otherwise questionable environment. Let's chart this out on the color wheel. Once again, we're not going straight across the color wheel to the vivid golds for contrast. This environment is meant to be much more subtle – it's meant to have more harmony. And how do we get that? It simply comes from colors that are closer together on the color wheel. Remember, that's how the color wheel is set up: the further the color, the more contrast, and the closer the color, the more unity. So I've used 'cooler warms', so to speak – they drift toward the reds and purples but are somewhat neutral. Harmony with contrast, unity with variety – however you want to refer to it, that's the key here.

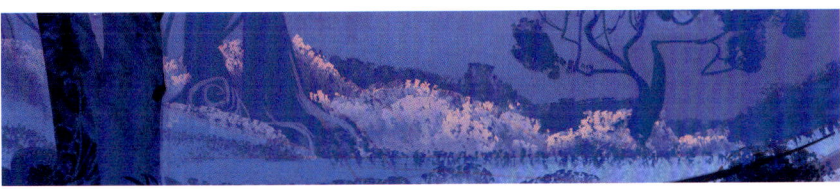
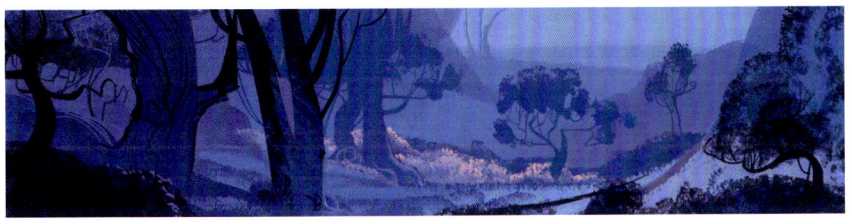
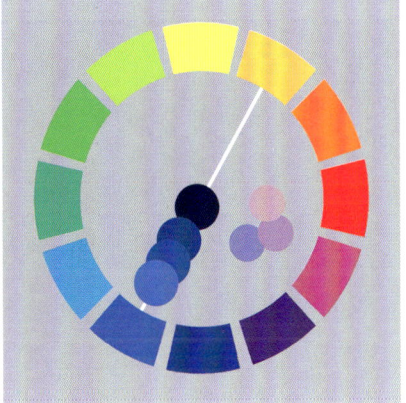

△ The pinkish color isn't the opposite of blue but it works to add warmth

01. COMPARISON

I've put two different versions together so you can see the difference in mood. We have an all-blue brooding image, which has a simpler, moodier emotion, and the version with a warm accent. Notice how the warm accent adds a more complex, positive quality.

02. EERIE ATMOSPHERE

Let's continue with images that carry an emotional tone, like this creepy example. Hanging gnarled roots in a hallway really tell you that things are not right, but we can go so much further by designing the color. Let's give the hallway an overgrown mossy green and add an eerie blue light in the distance – whatever's making that light is just not natural. We're continuing with the two-color combination to create our mood, though you'll notice a few red accents peeking through to add an earthy richness. I started out with a red grounding color and painted over that, so a few bits are showing through.

03. DREAMY ATMOSPHERE

We have a moody and poetic image here, also using a two-color palette. It confirms the point that more narrowly focused color leads to more narrowly focused emotion – in this case, an ethereal but somewhat melancholy mood.

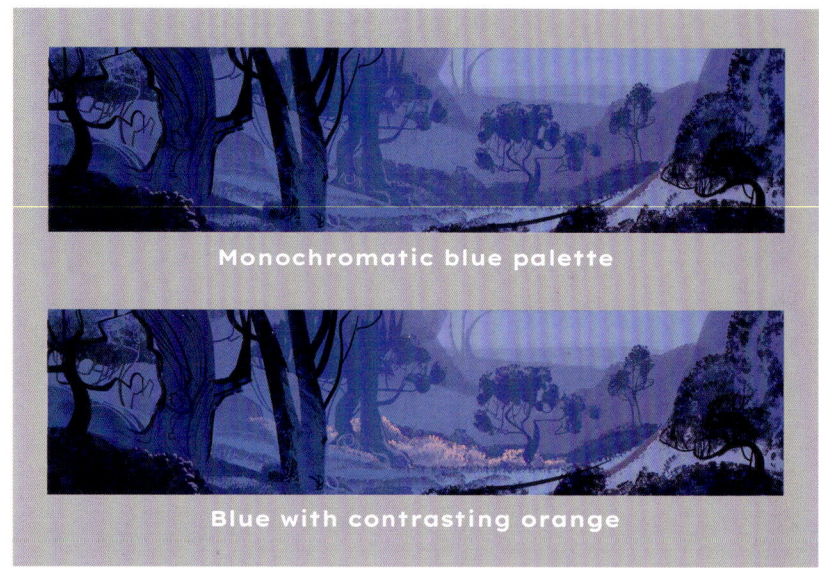

Monochromatic blue palette

Blue with contrasting orange

01. One simple well-chosen accent can change the whole mood!

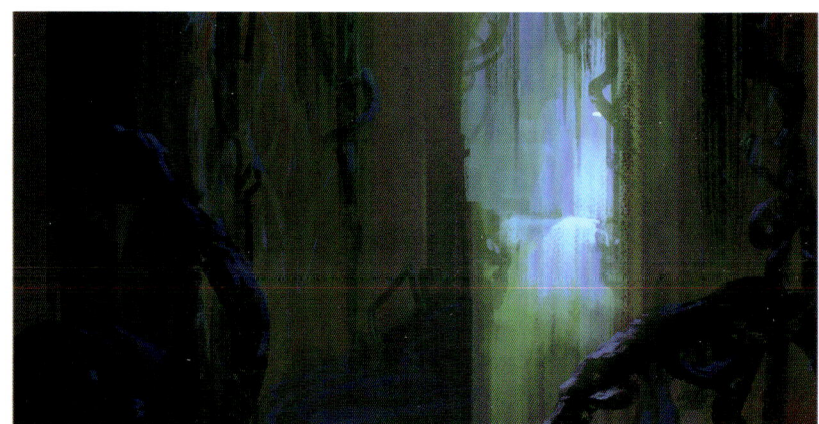

02. This scene is based around murky green with a supernatural blue accent

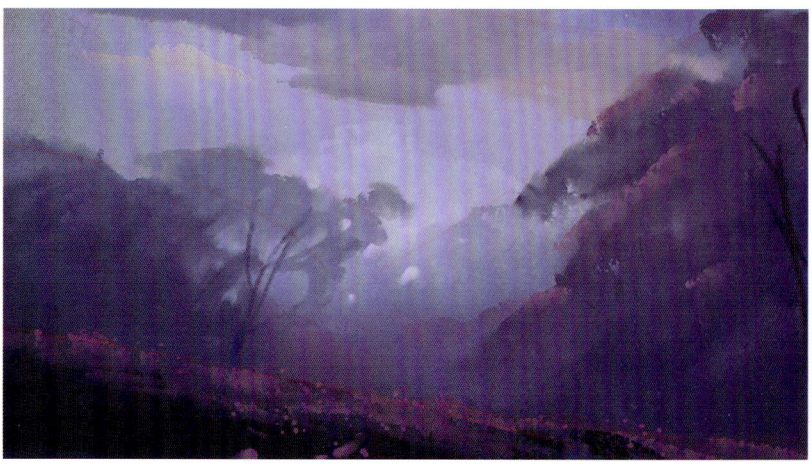

03. A very different example of a limited two-color palette

ANALOGOUS COLOR (AND BEYOND)

This next painting adds more hues while keeping a harmonious color palette. How is that done? You surely know the answer by now – harmony is achieved simply by using colors that have some commonality, as shown in this grouping on the color wheel.

Some refer to this as an 'analogous' color palette. We have plenty of variety in this color palette with greens, yellows, and golds, but they all have a grouped quality of *warmth*. This painting has unity with variety of color through an analogous color relationship.

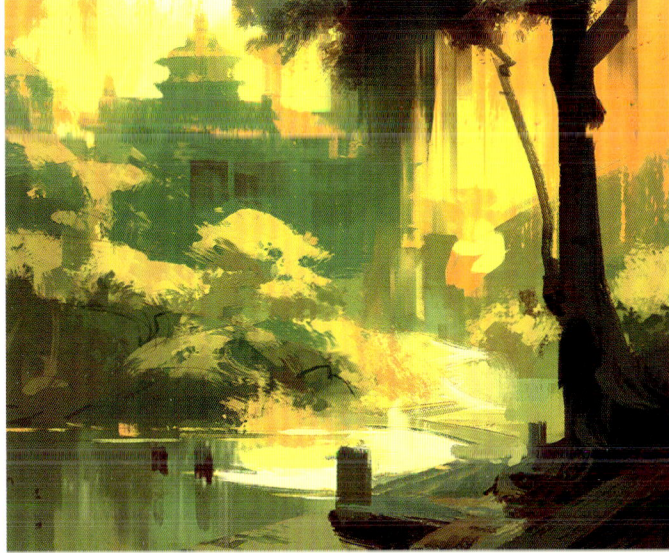 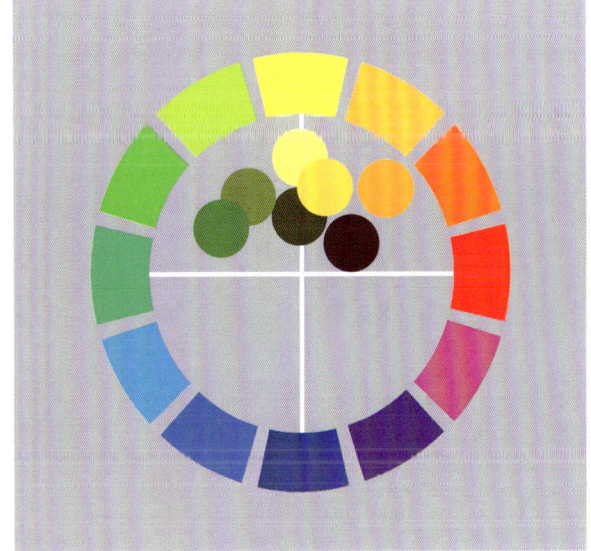

△ An analogous palette uses closely grouped colors for a harmonious effect

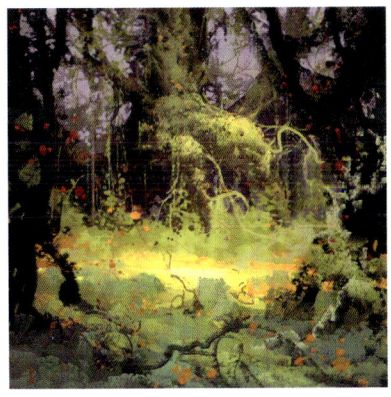 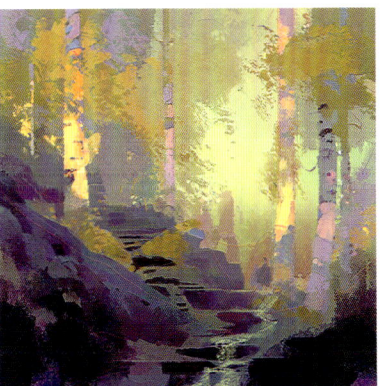

01. Go further than a simple analogous palette by bringing in rich color accents

01. ENHANCE WITH ACCENTS

Let's bring some local color back into the work by messing around with foliage. Here are two forest environments that have very different emotional tones. Much of this comes from the way the subject is handled. The first is filled with gnarled trees and roots with parasitic moss growing over everything; the second is an attractive birch-tree forest with a babbling brook running through the middle. As always, we accentuate the subject through the emotional use of color. The creepy image uses sour, desaturated colors with only small accents of saturation. The birch forest is much more saturated, with warm colors that are made even richer by accents of cool blue and purple. So now when the director tells you to make your scene creepier, or more rich and natural, you'll know exactly what to do!

So now when the director tells you to make your scene creepier, or more rich and natural, you'll know exactly what to do!

We live in
challenging
times for artists,
which means we
have to know
how to really
push the limits
– so let's push
color as far
as we dare.

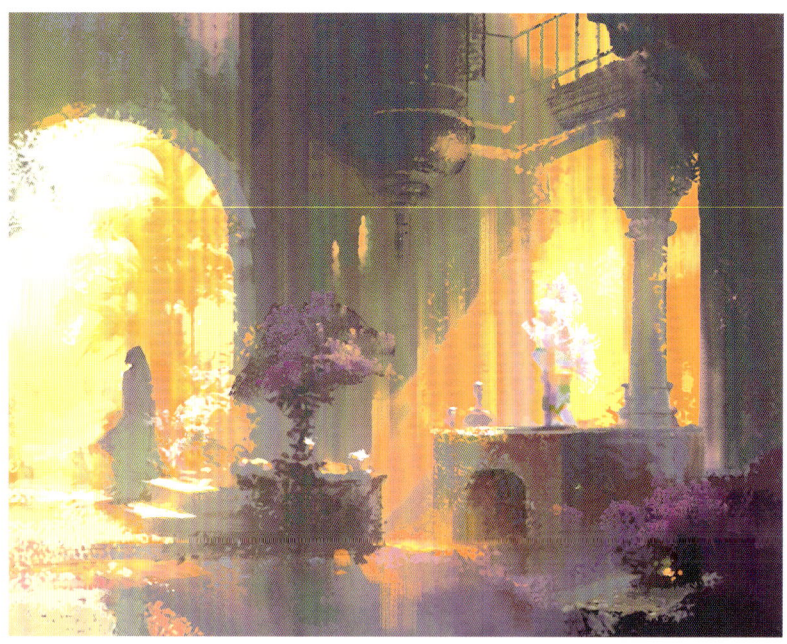

02. Hints of green shadow add coolness without being predictable

02. BE DARING

We live in challenging times for artists, which means we have to know how to really push the limits when appropriate. If we're creating images that are easily obtained or experienced elsewhere then we're irrelevant to our audience. But if we create experiences for them that they can't get anywhere else, things that they can only experience through us, then we are relevant and valuable. So let's push the luminous color in this image as far as we dare.

There's lots of color here, but notice that much of it is desaturated. Once again, it's the color relationships that keep those neutrals exciting and alive. In areas where shadows would be open to windows or the sky, I filled them with a cool color but not a blue, because blue wouldn't fit with the vivid warmth that I'm going for. Green is the key here – it feels cool relative to the magenta and orange but is warm enough to not distract from the luminous heat that I'm looking for. With practice, you can really 'trick out' color to get it to do anything that you need.

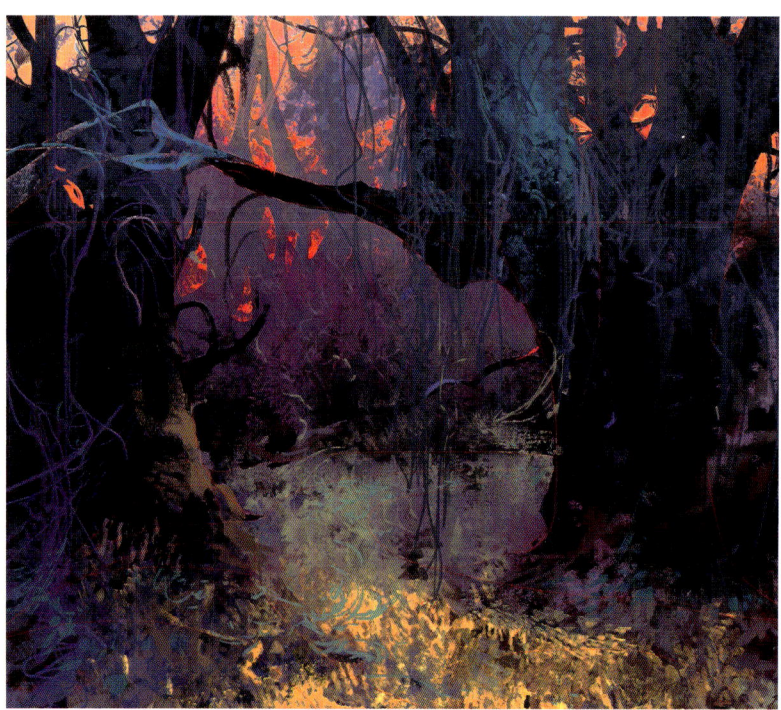

03. What are the dominant and accent colors in this eerie forest scene?

03. LEARN TO ANALYZE

I know the last two images were a little bit too joyful for some of you art ghouls out there, so I'll go back to another creepy image. I'll let you identify the color relationships in this one for yourself.

DEMONSTRATION: SPOOKY INTERIOR

Here's the concept we'll be making for this chapter's demonstration image. It's a classic Gothic interior where we'll be throwing in some spooky extremes of color to give the image a wild level of engagement. And here's the color wheel so that we can break down the overall palette of color choices. Some might want to call it a triad, and I guess that's technically true, but it's more about finding that dramatic quality of color that we're looking for. A two-color palette just won't do it, and four or more colors would take the painting to an out-of-control level, so centering things around three highly contrasting colors will give us lots of kick but enough harmony to keep a sense of eerie quiet in the scene.

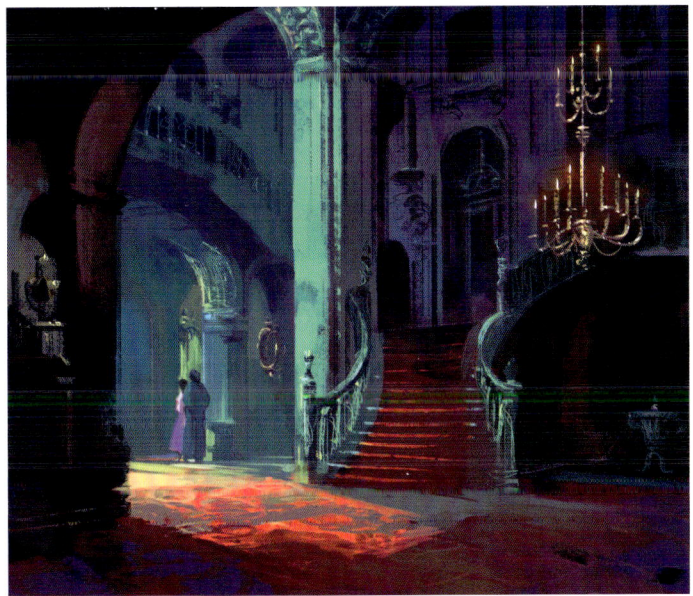
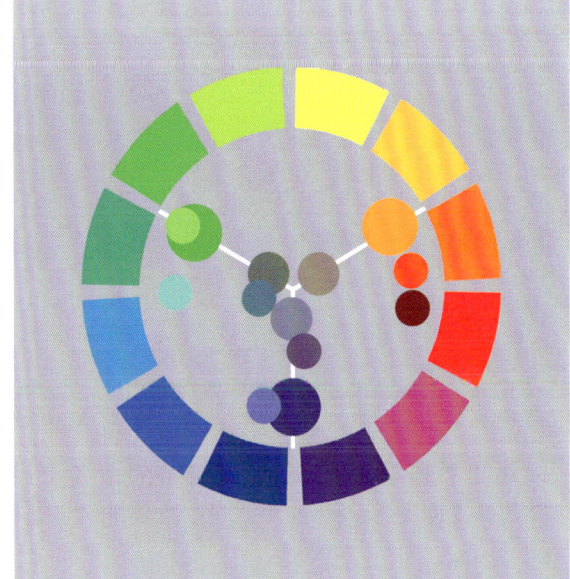

△ This darkly vivid interior is based around three contrasting colors

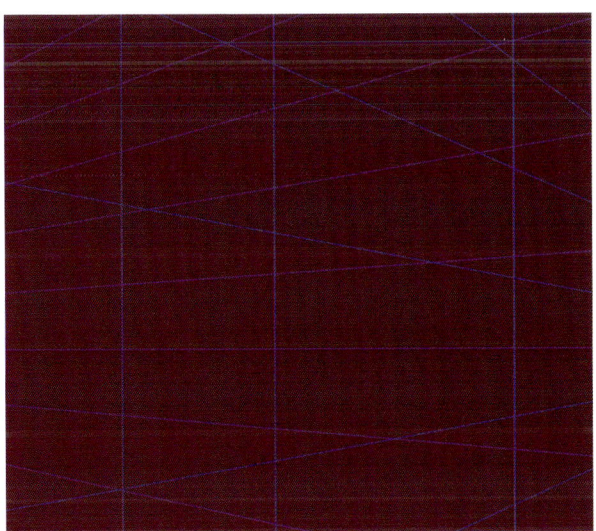

01. Start off with a deep, warm base color and perspective grid

01. BURGUNDY BASE

First I put down a deep red-burgundy color as a base for the blues and greens to contrast against. My local colors will be mostly warm, so having this underlying warmth already in place will help reinforce that. I also get my perspective established – I'm keeping the eye-level line well below the center of the image so that we're looking up into the room, giving it a feeling of scale and creating a looming quality.

02. LINEWORK

Since there's a good amount of architectural detail in the scene, I work out a careful drawing to be sure I keep everything in place. The image will center around the middle column and the adjacent staircase. There are a couple of figures in the distance to the left, which give the interior even more scale and depth – and a hint of gothic romance.

03. COLOR MASSES

Next up is some very simple massing of color. The middle-left needs to feel distant, so I put an atmospheric cool temperature back there. I also have the idea of cool light filtering down from above, so I rough out that transition on the top right. These give me the harmonious aspects of the color palette, so next I'm going to really wreak some havoc!

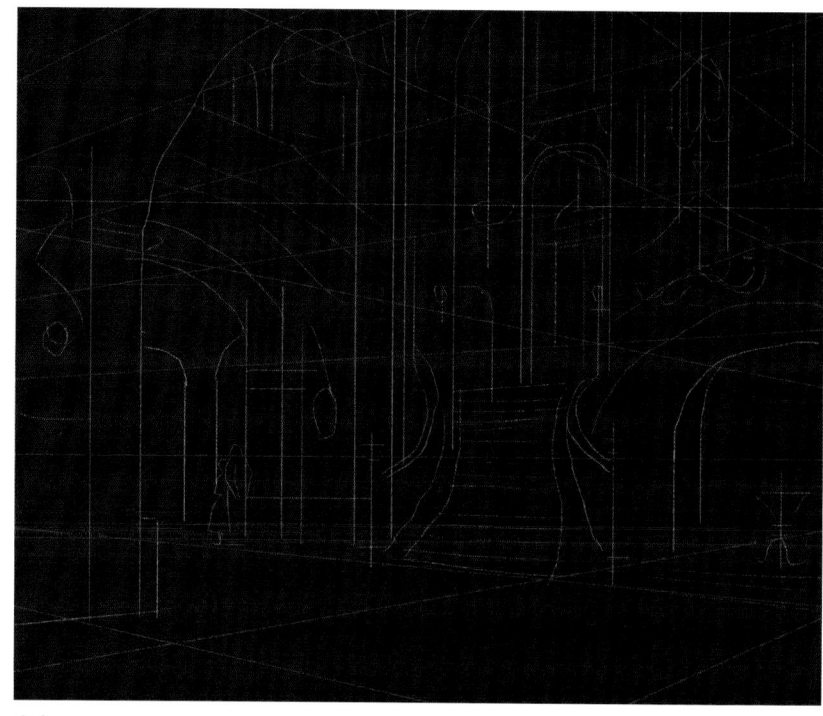

02. Plan out the architecture with a well-structured sketch

03. Begin blocking in the main areas of color

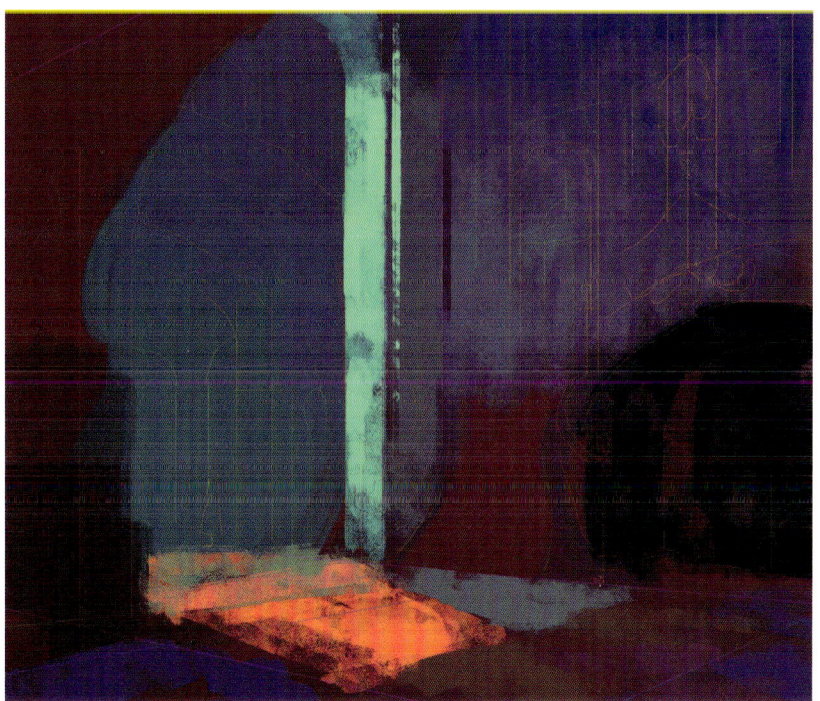

04. Introduce the most dramatic contrasts

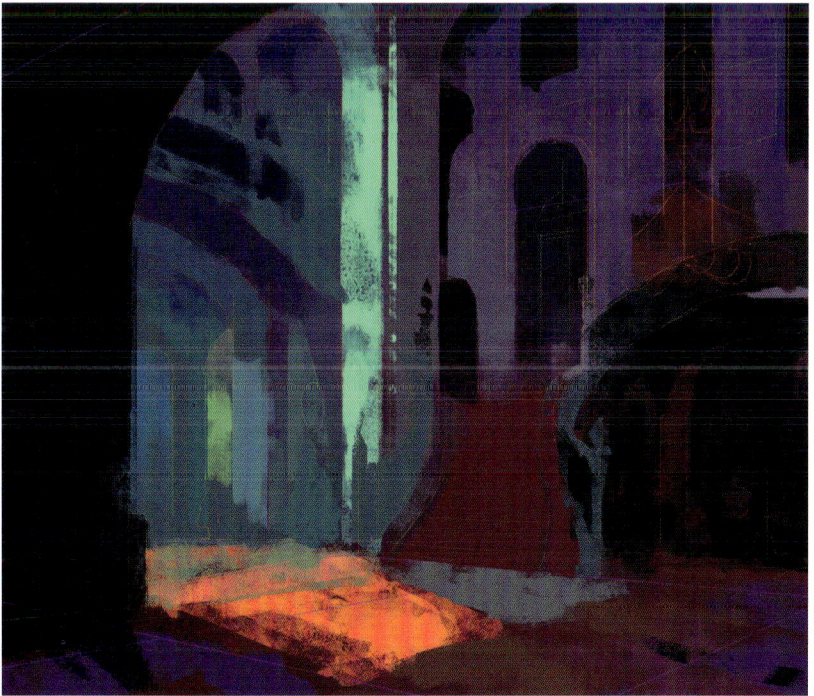

05. The scene takes clearer shape with the addition of dark areas

04. MAJOR CONTRASTS

Let's hit some of our major color contrasts. There's lots of color-cheating here, meaning I ignore what color and light would *really* do in favor of dramatic effect: the light hitting the center column takes on a vivid green quality, but I maintain the local color of the red-orange carpet down below as the light falls across it. The remaining reds are underpainting that will be mostly covered as we progress.

05. ADDING DARKNESS

This is the step where I get my major darks in. I've heard all sorts of rules about putting down darks first, or last, or when Mars and Jupiter align in the sky. It really depends on circumstance! Every painting has its own unique considerations and so rules go out the window. Since this is an architectural piece, it makes sense to work out the planes and the lighting first, then get in the major architectural elements (doors, windows, and staircases), so that's my approach here.

06. ARCHITECTURAL DETAIL

All the blocking-in has been about preparing the big masses so that quick rendering over the top is more likely to fall into place. That's exactly where we are now. I suggest detail with a brush that has some texture to help with the feel of old architecture. For now I intentionally focus on the center and center-right areas because the staircase and its surroundings are the focus of this environment. I keep the back area shadowy so that the staircase can emerge out of it. It then makes sense that there's lots of light falling across the staircase and banister to create those depth cues.

07. FINISHING UP

And now we're ready for our grand finale! As I wrap up the image, I keep my focus on what needs to be added to bring the image to a finish. What's the target? This is a color study to demonstrate how we can dramatize color for emotional effect, so I can't allow myself to lose sight of that. I make the green and orange lights group brightly against all the atmospheric shadow. I also add two important elements: the hanging chandelier and the two characters in the distance. These add to the emotional vibe of 'Gothic-horror romance'. With all the cool green in the distance, a magenta accent on the woman's dress is helpful for the overall vibrancy and impact of the picture. Finally, I need some visual interest on the far left to balance against the high contrast of the chandelier. Some sort of Victorian-looking shiny decoration there does the trick, and with that touch the image is complete!

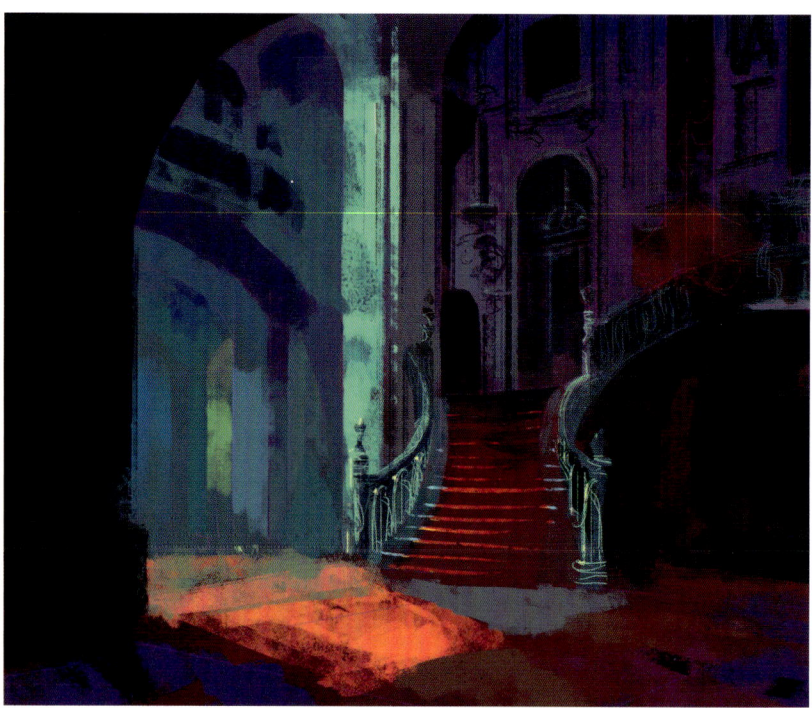

06. The detailing phase begins in the focal area around the staircase

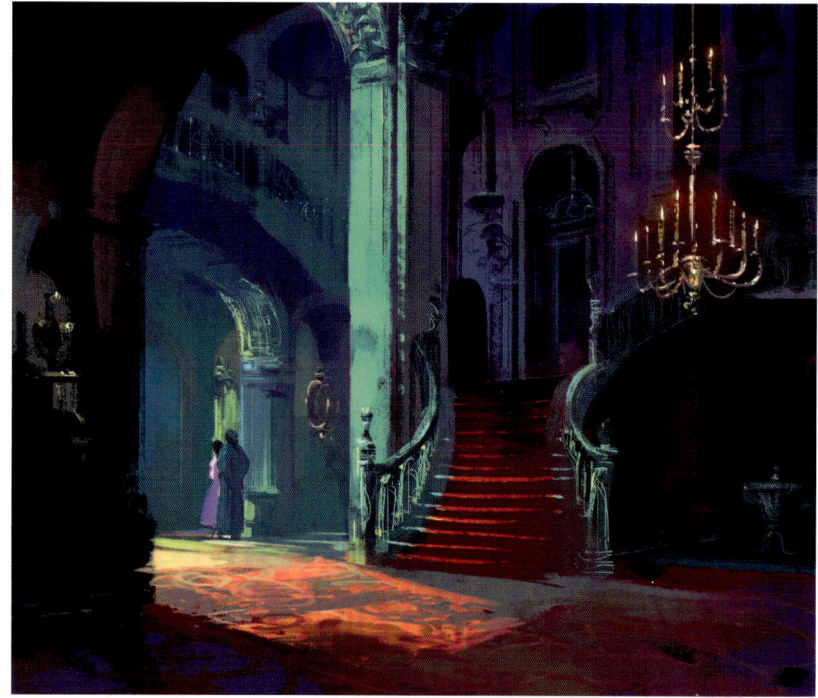

07. Finish up by detailing and balancing out the remaining areas

RECOMMENDED EXERCISE:
'UNITY WITH VARIETY' STUDIES

We've all had the experience where we want to get more color practice in, and we know we should, but it's cripplingly difficult to find the extra time or the energy. So we go with the idea of doing little half-hour practice studies, but there are times when even that half-hour goes beyond what we are willing and able to do. For me, doing personal practice daily is an absolute must, regardless of time constraints and exhaustion. That might make me sound heroic but it's just the opposite – sometimes I'll only take a moment to do a tiny abstract study like one of these. But every little bit helps!

These kinds of color abstractions free us from getting caught up in rendering subject material. Instead, we just work out color relationships. Doing a handful or even just one of these daily keeps up our chops and keeps a good habit alive. I invite you to do the same – maybe have the color wheel from this book handy and try to create unity with variety in interesting ways.

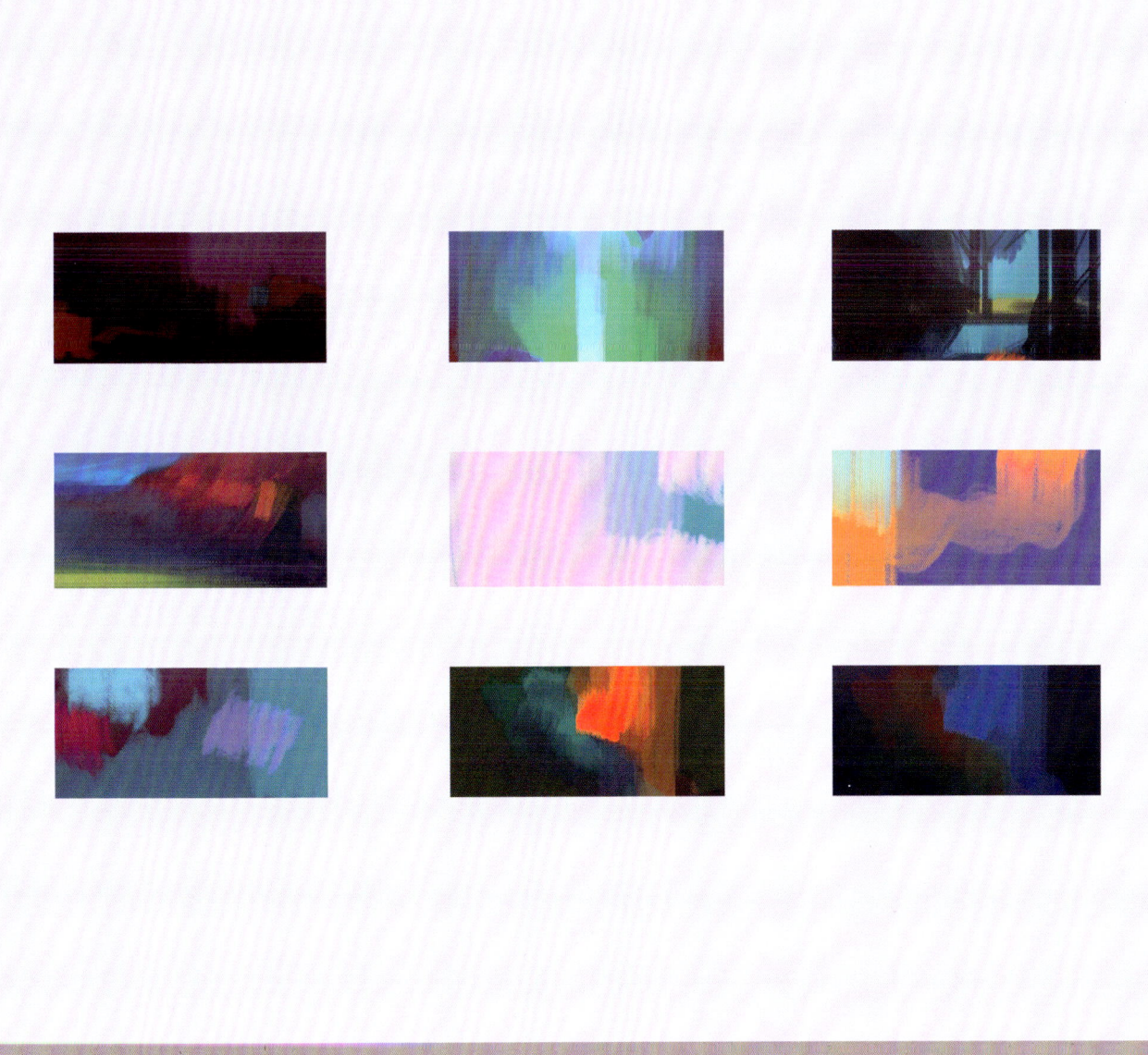

△ Even a tiny abstract study every day is a good habit to keep

ENVIRONMENTAL LIGHTING

Environments are not merely the rendering of a place. They are meant to be so much more: they are an emotional experience for our audience.

HOW I DISAPPOINTED THE DIRECTOR

Some years ago, I was working on a movie where I was in charge of identifying important story beats in the script, then doing quick paintings to create an overall 'visual story-beat board', as we called it. I was up most of the night trying to get these paintings wrapped up for a review with the director the next day.

The review was going pretty well, but then the director pointed out one important story painting and said, 'You know, I think we need to revisit this one. I'm just not feeling it here.' It was a moment where the main character was being chased through a jungle environment by foes armed with spears, intent on bringing him in dead or alive. It was meant to be a moment of great fear. And what had I done with all the amazing potential of the jungle environment? I had painted pretty dappled light softly filtering through the jungle leaves. *Ugh*. In the last hours of the night I had been working hard but definitely not smart.

The rule of thumb is that every aspect of an environment should be designed to serve the purpose of the painting. In this case the purpose was to convey fear and action, and I had lost focus. There wasn't much time to fix it, and I can't show you the image because it's proprietary to the studio, but let me describe the quick fix that saved me. I changed the light from soft, rounded, and dappled to long, sharp shards falling across the environment and characters at a diagonal angle. You remember my big song and dance about how action-packed diagonals are, right? Well, this was an action-packed story moment. I also changed the color of the light from pastel-yellow to red, and darkened the sky with angry, stormy lighting. The results were shocking in their 'fear factor' and all I had to do was adjust the lighting. Lesson learned!

The purpose of this book is to offer you solutions to make sure that you don't make the same mistakes that I did. Remember, environmental lighting design is one of your superpowers.

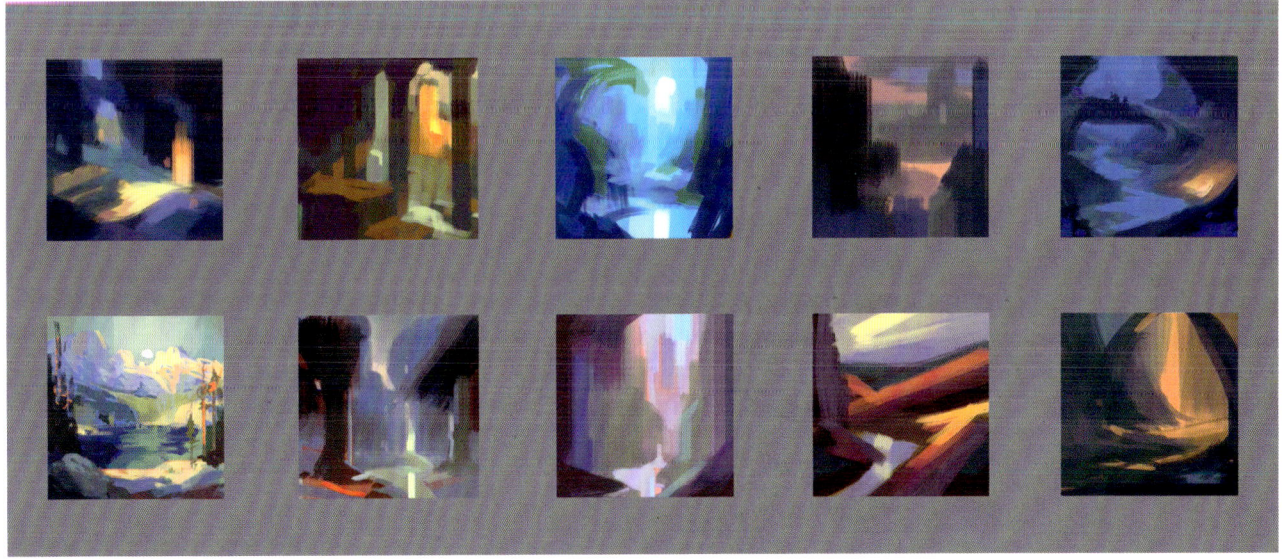

01. A sample of the small environmental lighting studies I make regularly

Environmental lighting design is one of your superpowers.

01. LIGHTING STUDIES

All of you know by now that I do constant studies to develop my ideas and abilities. Here's a page of such studies. This page is meant to introduce the idea that environmental lighting can have an incredible range of different moods and emotions. Let's now get directly to the how and why of environmental lighting to make sure you get good at this.

02. MOLDING ENVIRONMENTAL LIGHT TO YOUR PURPOSE

Let's do what I believe will be a useful reset. Remember these two images from pages 21–22, back when we looked at the design and development process? We established the usefulness of brainstorming the purpose and the emotion of our images and then executing. Take a look now at how very important the lighting design was for creating that quality of purpose and emotion. Both designs are castles, yet we ended up with two completely different vibes. In this chapter we will look at how and why lighting is one of our most powerful tools to create a range of purpose and emotion in our environments.

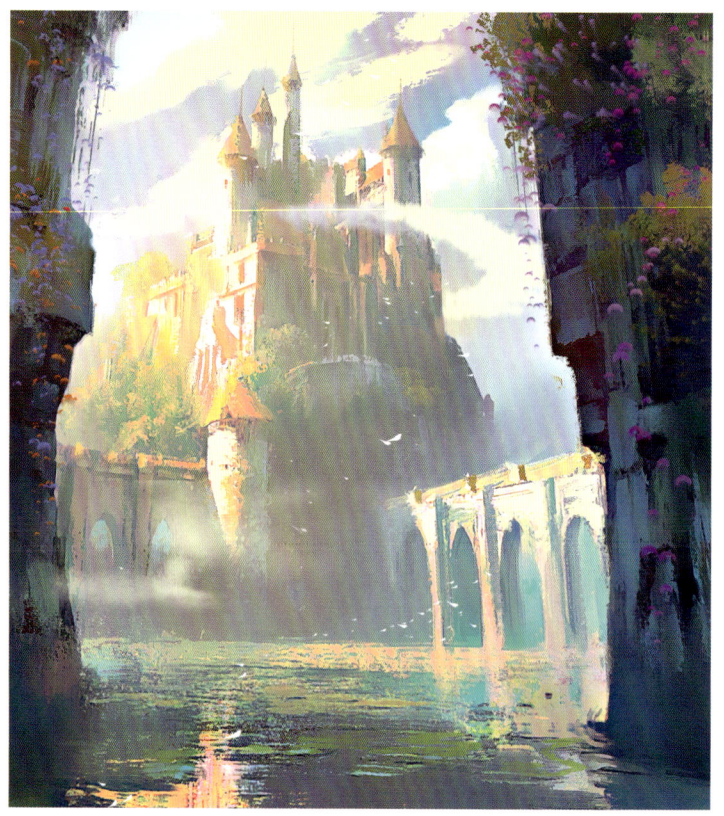

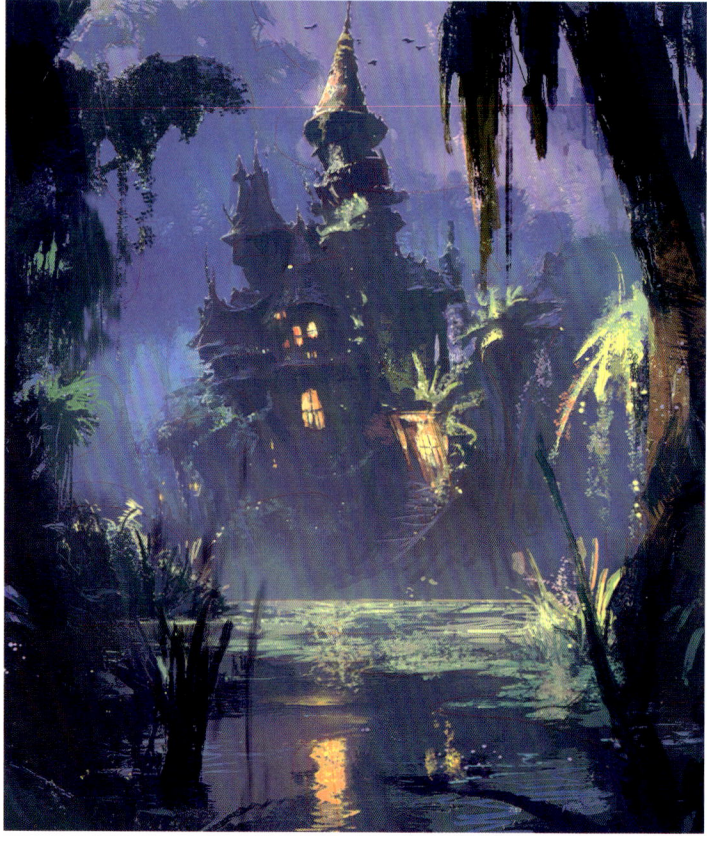

02. Same subject + different lighting design = very different vibe!

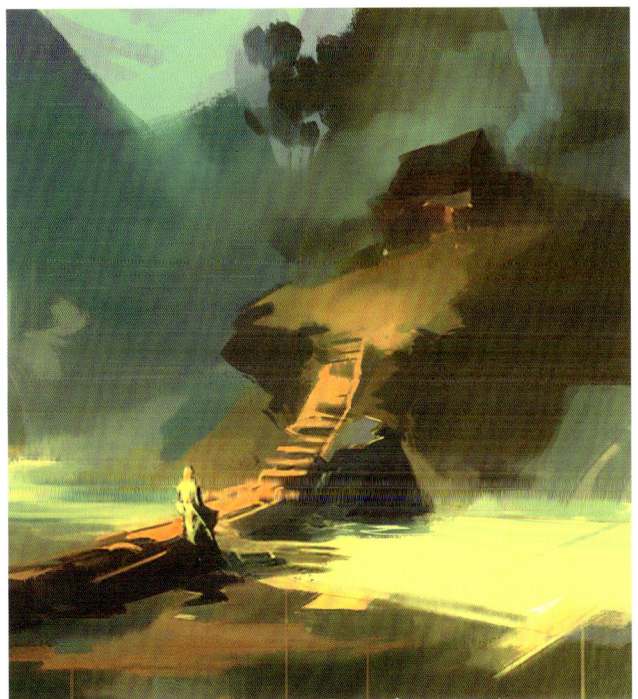 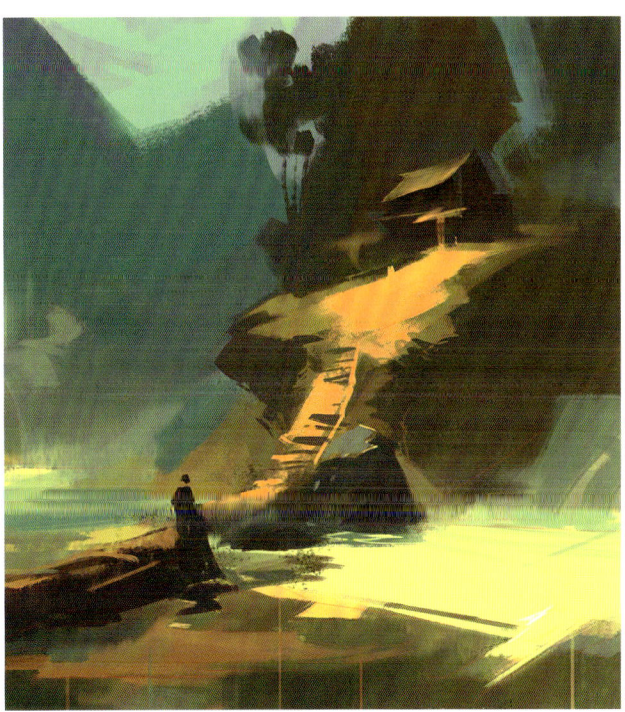

03. Changing the emphasis of the lighting changes the focus and story of this scene

If all parts of an environment are made to be equally important, then by default all parts are equally *unimportant*. Environmental storytelling requires a hierarchy of importance so that each place we create has a sense of purpose.

03. A TALE OF TWO HUTS

Let's look at two versions of the same environment with the lighting repurposed to create two very different qualities. Note how in the first image the lighting features the character – it's a scene about a character journeying to a distant hut cast in mysterious shadow. In the second image the lighting is molded to give the opposite effect. The lighting is taken off the character and focused on the hut and the pathway that leads to it. The character is still important – there's no escaping our impulse to look at a character first – but now we've placed the importance on the distant hut through lighting design.

I've made the point in this book that environments are not merely the rendering of a place. They are meant to be so much more: they are an emotional experience for our audience. The fastest way to kill this effect is to allow all parts of the environment to become equally important, because environmental storytelling requires a hierarchy of importance. These examples show how lighting is a key component to achieving this goal.

LIGHTING VARIATIONS

Let's now define our toolset of different kinds of lighting. We can do this by revisiting the mysterious obelisk we first saw on page 41. Keep in mind that lighting possibilities are endless, so this is not a complete list but rather a baseline to help us get started.

01. SIMPLE SUNSHINE

We'll begin with good old basic sunshine. Sunshine can be manipulated in many ways to suit our needs, especially in animation where we often cheat lighting for desired effects. For example, we might change the sunlight angle between shots to ensure consistent mood, even if it's not realistic. The audience won't notice, as long as the lighting quality feels similar across scenes. We do whatever it takes to get the shot!

02. AMBIENT LIGHTING

Ambient lighting is the kind you would get on an overcast day. Overcast light is useful for creating environments that are gray and moody – and that doesn't mean they have to be bland. In this example the rich variety of local colors complements the cool quality of the lighting.

Another important note about this lighting: it's not nearly as bright as direct sunshine, yet notice how this image is nearly as bright as the sunshine we just looked at. This is not a cheat – it's a legitimate presentation of overcast lighting. In real life our pupils simply open wider to let in more light, giving us all the brightness we need to survive and thrive in an overcast environment.

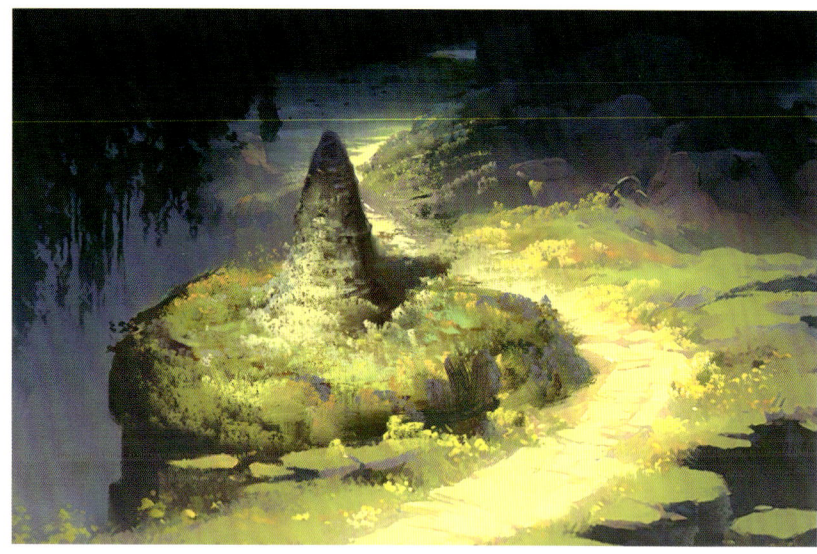

01. Sunlight is a naturalistic but versatile choice for lighting a scene

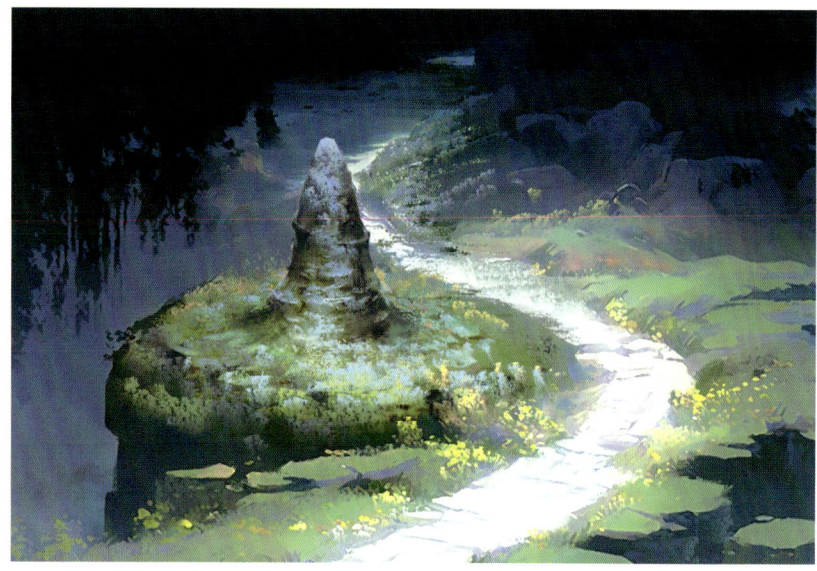

02. Overcast sunlight is softer, moodier, and doesn't cast strong shadows

03. MOONLIGHT

We'll explore varieties of nighttime lighting later in the chapter, but here's a little info about basic moonlight. I just referenced how our eyes adapt to any kind of lighting, and this is also true with moonlight – we can see surprisingly well in full moonlight. When lighting with moonlight, it's not the lit areas that are the key, but rather the shadows. In moonlit conditions the lighting is so dim that there is very little detail to be seen in shadows. So if you give your moonlight a neutral or cool temperature and limit detail in the shadows, you can have a fairly bright scene and viewers will completely believe that they're experiencing moonlight.

04. EXPOSURE

We're back to sunlight again but for a specific reason. You see two similar versions below but the difference between them is very important. When carefully designing light to serve the purpose of the image, whatever that might be, one critical consideration is this: Do I want the audience to see more information in the light, or do I want them to see more information in the shadow?

In the bottom-left image the light is toned down so that we can see whatever detail is needed in the light, and the shadows are dropped down in value and detail to reduce their importance. The bottom-right image is the opposite: the lights are intentionally blown out so they have no information whatsoever, and the environment becomes all about what's in the shadow.

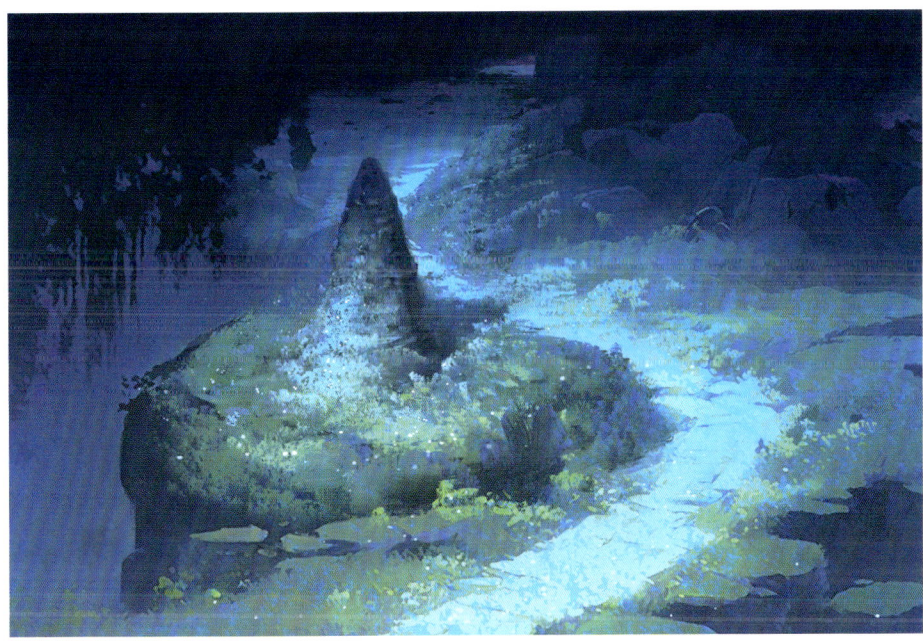

03. The key to a moonlit scene is limiting detail in the shadows

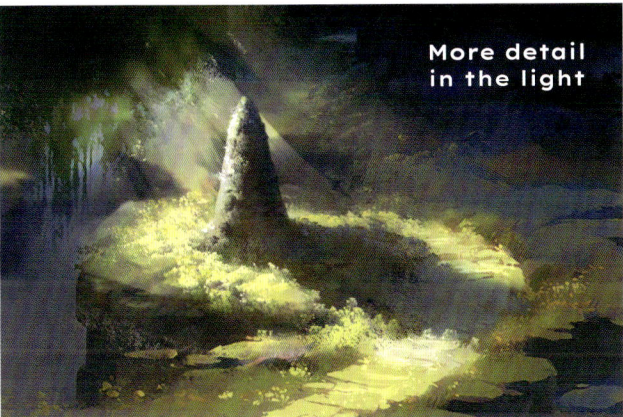

More detail in the light

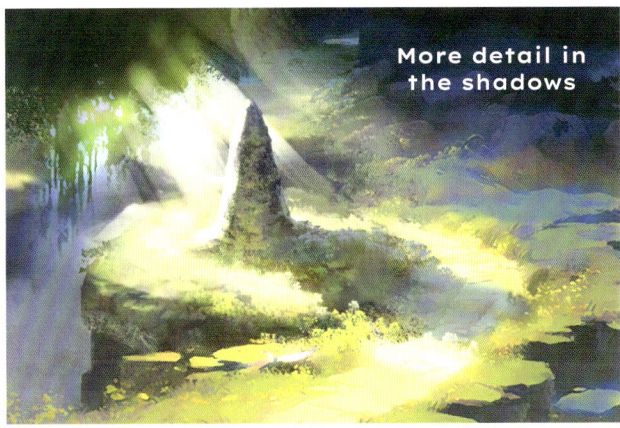

More detail in the shadows

04. You can create different effects by manipulating the detail levels in light and shadow

05. BACKLIGHT

Backlight, or rim light, is a powerful and immediate way to create contrast. You see the almost magical importance it gives to this weird spire of stone? And that's of course because of contrast. By now you know that I go on about the design of contrast, because it's so important!

06. OBJECT MATERIAL

The qualities of the materials that make up our environments are an important discussion in this book, so let's review another version of the stone spire made out of a completely different material. It has a quality of translucency – some of the light goes straight through the substance and emerges in the shadow. It's a natural gem-like effect that gives an almost supernatural quality to the environment.

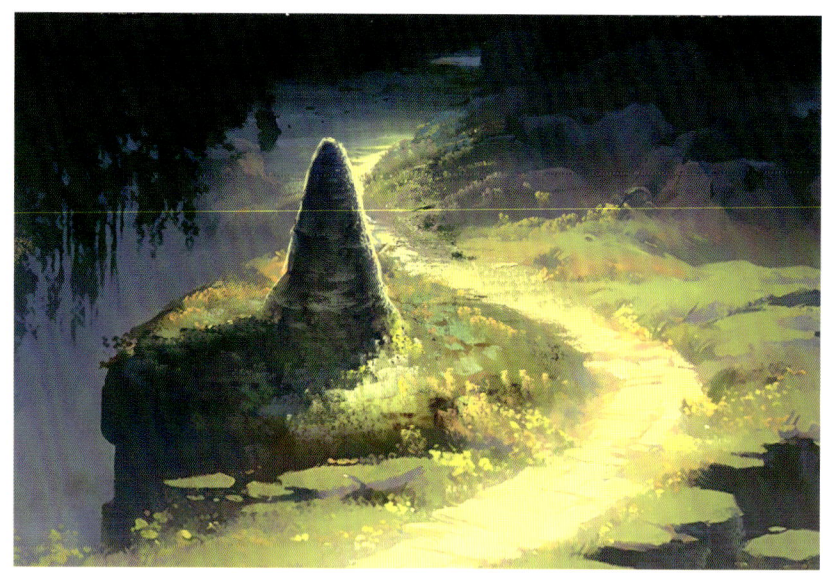

05. Backlighting creates an alluring rim around the subject

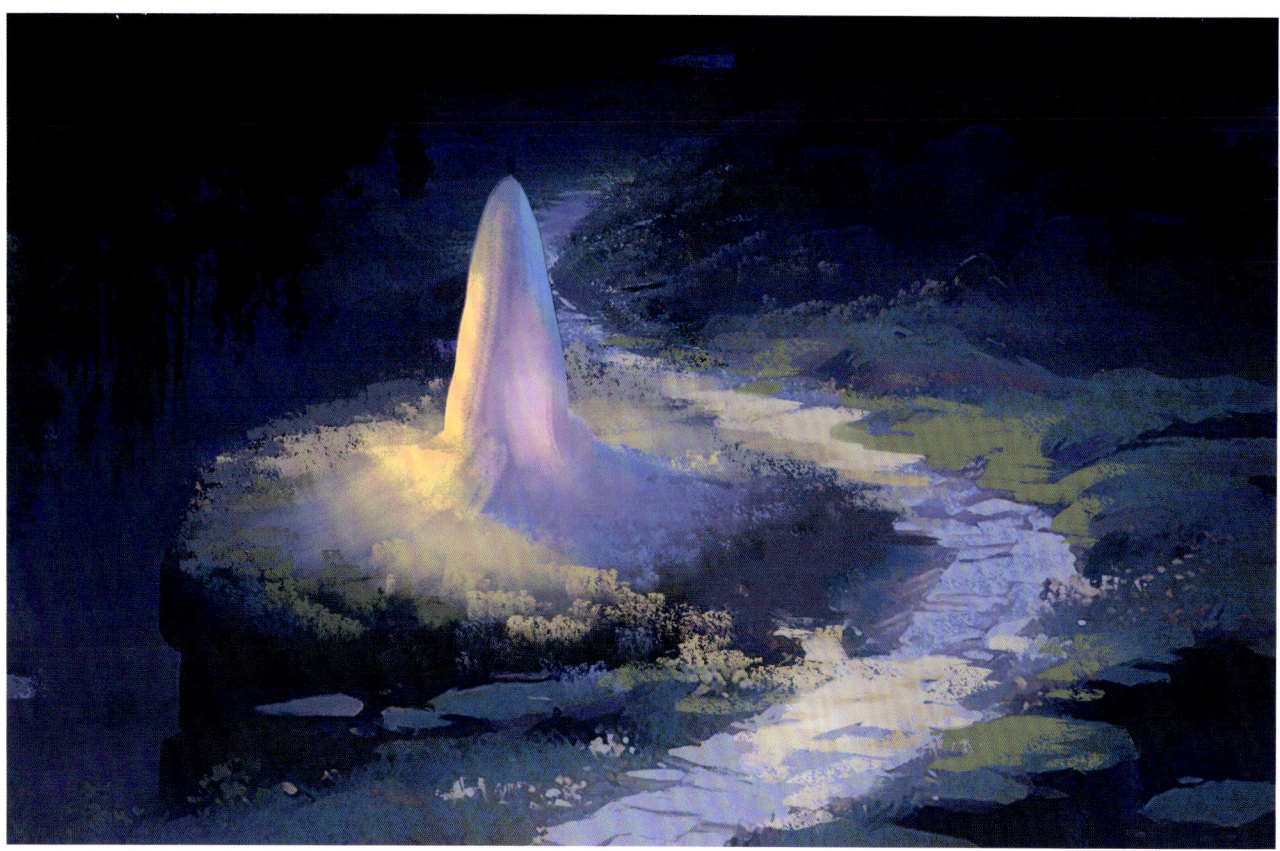

06. Our environmental lighting must also take surface and object materials into account

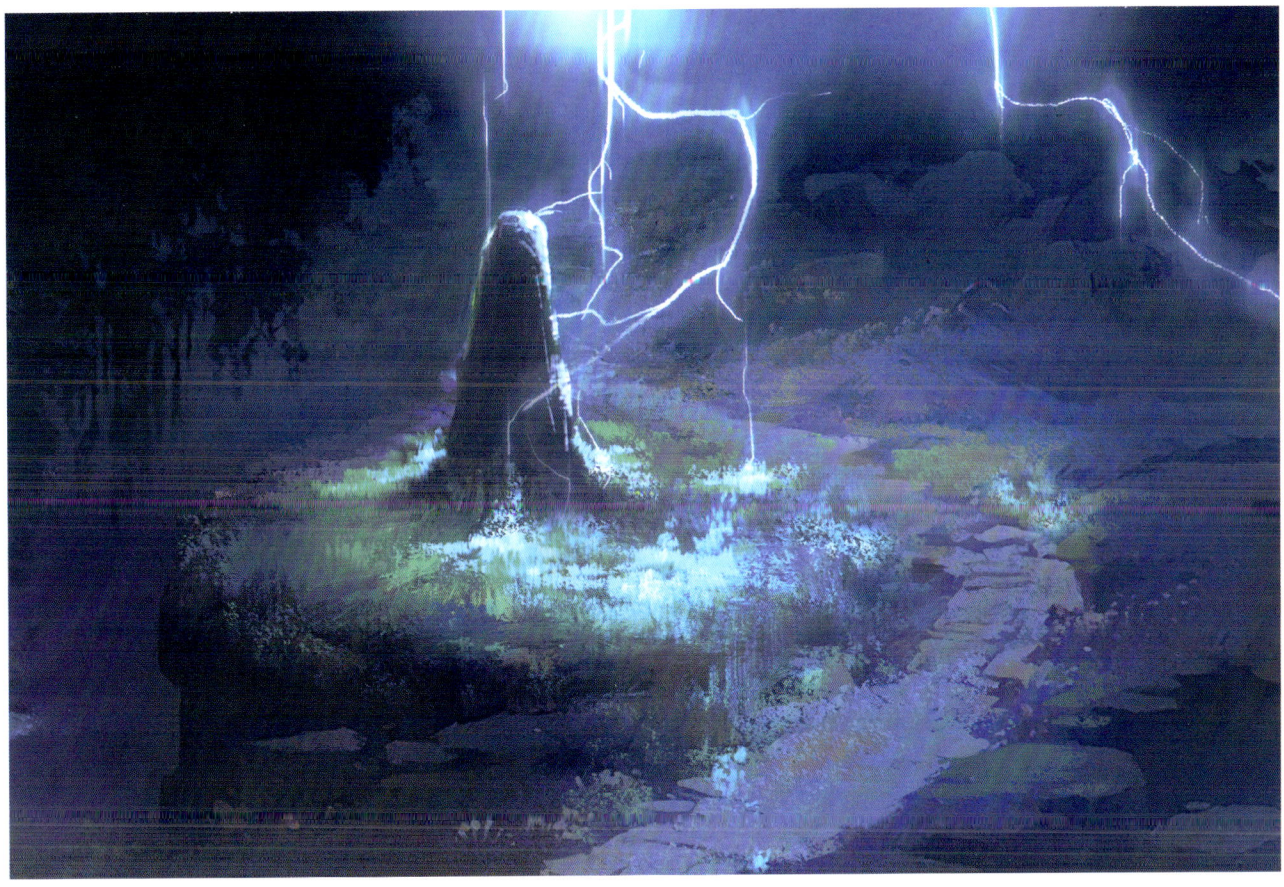

07. Weather effects can add a dramatic thrill to a scene's lighting

07. WEATHER

I don't want to jump the gun here, as the next chapter will be on weather and atmosphere, but extremes of weather can create crazy and exciting lighting effects. And of course all of us want to make crazy and exciting environments, so let's keep an eye out for where this type of lighting will work for us!

Extremes of weather can create crazy and exciting lighting effects. And of course all of us want to make crazy and exciting environments!

263

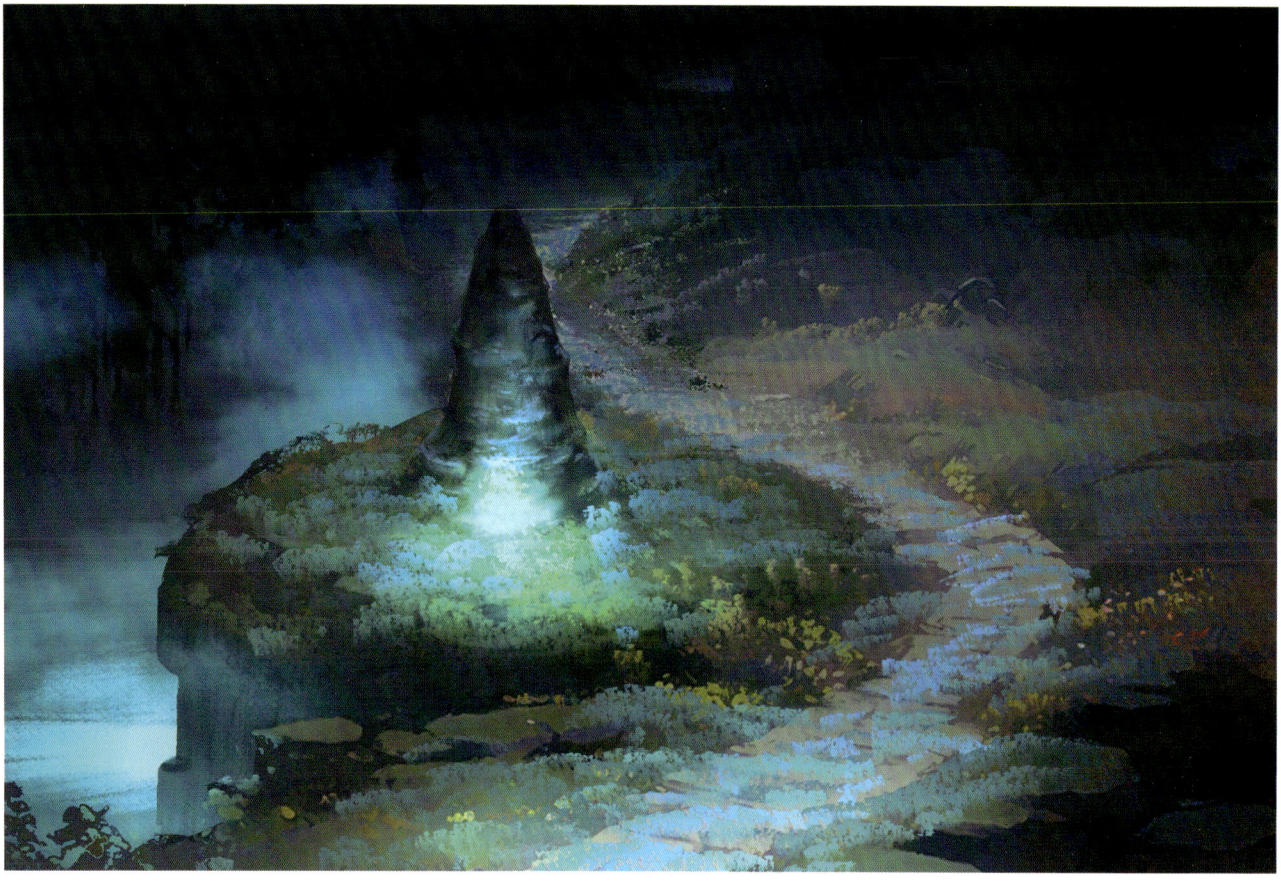

08. Underlighting lends itself well to an otherworldly or eerie effect

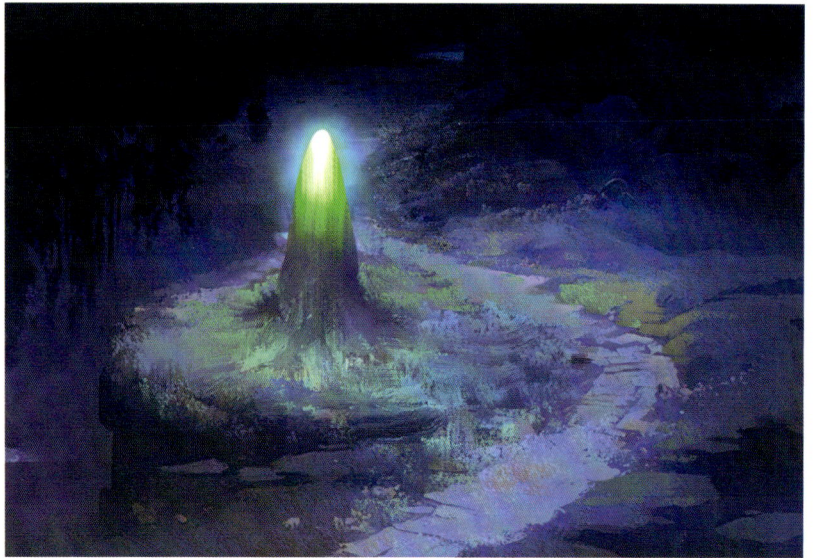

09. Fantasy and sci-fi allow us enormous potential for exciting light

08. UNDERLIGHTING

Underlighting is usually a result of intentionally placed artificial light, but in the worlds we create it can be a result of magic, hot lava, glowing mystical pools, and so on. Anything goes! I do understand there's not really a justification for the underlighting on the rocky prominence here, but it sure looks cool. To push the effect further I've treated the environment as if there's water below, with magical luminescence shining up into the surrounding mist.

09. SUPERNATURAL LIGHT

And since I keep talking about the magical effects of light, here's some straight-up magic light, or alien technology, or whatever we want it to be. This lighting isn't *natural* – it's *supernatural*.

BOUNCE LIGHT & SKYLIGHT

One of the powerful qualities of sunlight is the way it bounces into adjacent shadows. Its cool cousin, skylight, can also be used to enrich the lighting and colors of our environments.

01. BOUNCE LIGHT

Here we have warm light hitting warm surfaces and bouncing into other warm surfaces, then bouncing back toward us. What do we get? Warmth. A whole lot of it! And so this canyon is a study of carefully designed temperatures. Notice how I've also exaggerated cooler areas to let the heat of the distant shadows really pop. These temperature relationships created by sunlight and blue sky are a powerful weapon in our environment-design arsenal. There's no rule that bounce light is always warm, but it often appears warm relative to adjacent shadow temperatures. We can capitalize on the richness of this temperature contrast.

02. SKYLIGHT

Since the previous image features bounce light, let's look at the opposite now: cold skylight. Here is a study that also features warm stone. It's some sort of abandoned ruin with the pathway open to the sky. In the distance we see the contrasting heat of sunshine, but the foreground and mid-ground are completely filled with ambient skylight. This gives us wonderful potential for emotional contrast – cool light on warm surfaces is a delight for the eyes.

In fact, when I put on my portrait-painting hat, I like to have my subject illuminated by ambient skylight, because this cooler lighting on warm flesh is an absolutely wonderful temperature relationship. In a sense, environment design is the portraiture of landscapes.

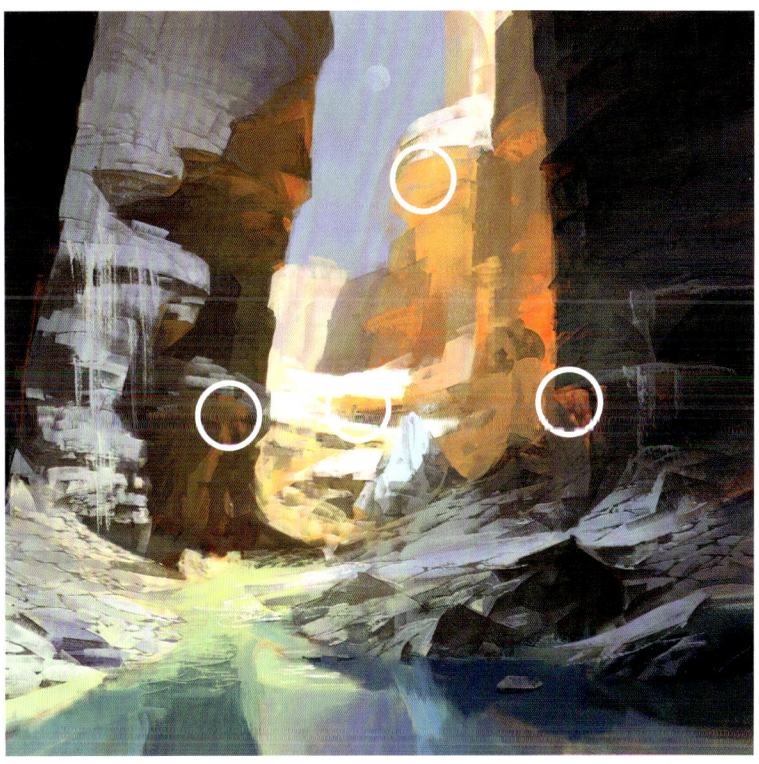

01. Warm bounce light (sunlight bouncing into adjacent shadows)

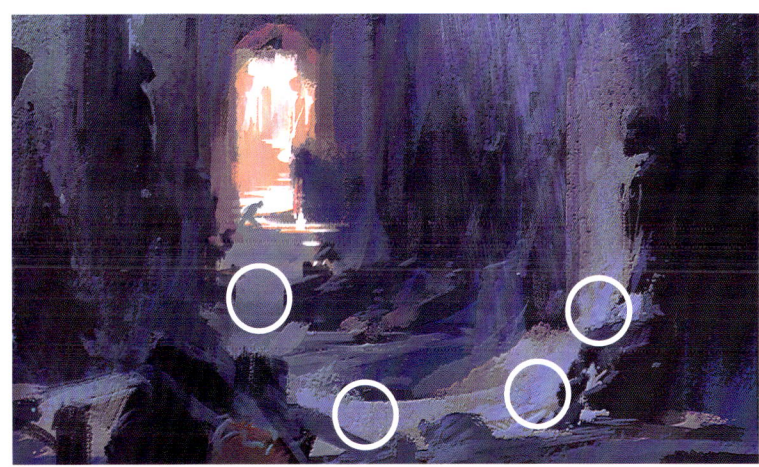

02. Cool skylight (atmospheric light)

Warm and cool temperature relationships created by bounce light and blue sky are a powerful weapon in our environment-design arsenal.

TRANSLUCENCY

Remember these spheres from the chapter on props? Here are two that have a useful quality of translucency. The one on the left transmits a great deal of light through its glassy substance, which creates a lensing effect where a pool of light shines right into the cast shadow. This is a rare effect in nature, but who knows – you might be tasked with creating an environment filled with giant crystals or some such, and this quality of light will come in handy.

Much more likely is the translucent quality of the wax candle on the right. You can see that bright direct light is shining on it from the right, cool ambient light is influencing the shadowy area on the left, and light is emitting from the interior as well. This is because wax is a slightly translucent material where a portion of the light passes right through it and emits out the other side.

It's possible you'll have candles in your environment – I can think of a handful of projects I've worked on that had candlelit moments – but it's much more likely you'll be dealing with the translucency of objects in nature, especially leaves and foliage. We'll take a look at those in the next images.

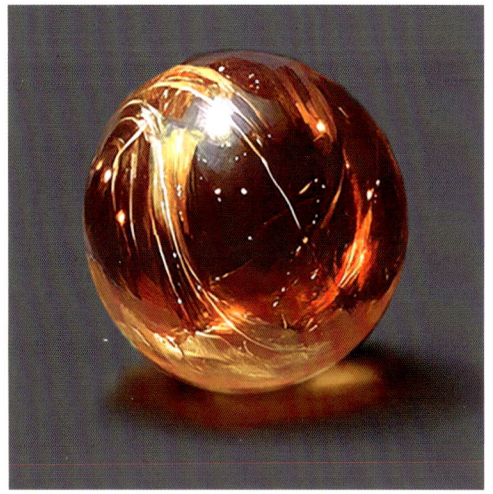
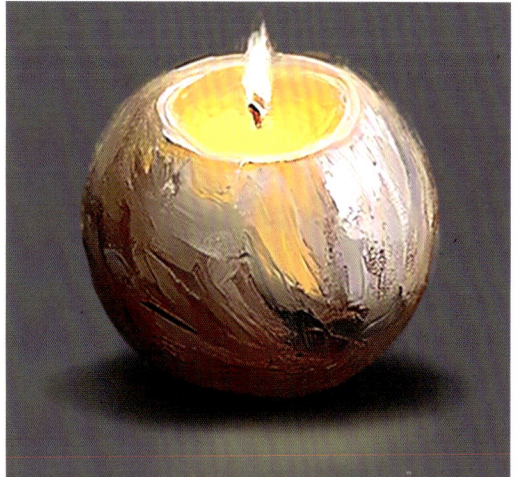

△ A transparent (left) versus translucent (right) sphere

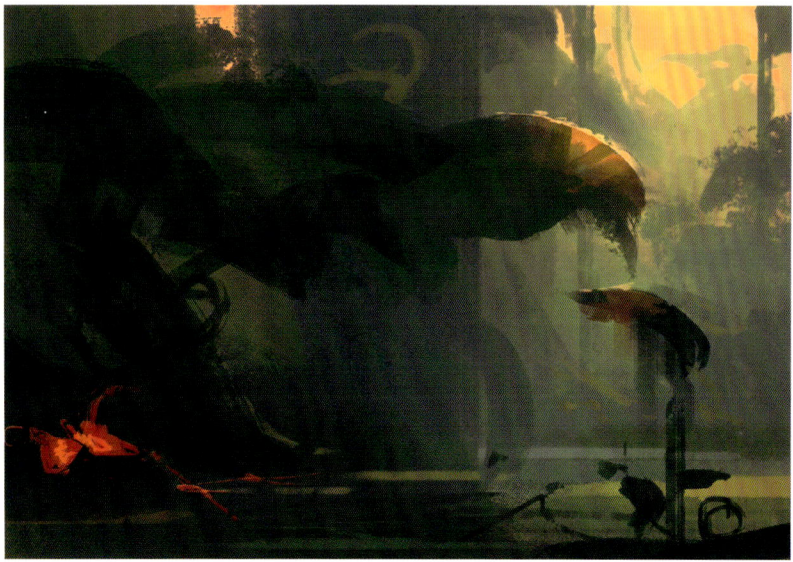

01. Backlighting transmits through the green leaf, creating a luminous glow

01. TRANSLUCENT FOLIAGE

Here's an idea I roughed out that features translucency as a key ingredient to the visual interest of the scene. I strategically placed a giant leaf as the focal area. It's backlit with sunlight and the thin material of the leaf transmits warm light. These warm accents are set against adjacent cool-green local colors and atmospheric blues, creating just the level of contrast I need to make this idea work.

02. RED MOSS

Let's look at another environment that takes this idea full send. Yes, this painting is about my funny little dodo character, but it's also about the lavish sense of visual interest created by the lighting. The dodo is backlit and silhouetted by light hitting the surroundings, but that's not enough – I really wanted this image to just light up like fireworks, except in full daylight! So I set up red backlit moss hanging from the tree, and what we're seeing is in fact its shadow side. It's transmitting so much light that it almost feels like a light source itself. You know by now that when we want something to feel intense, we surround it by its contrasting opposite, so I surrounded the glowing red with a darker atmospheric blue off in the distance. I also dramatized the atmospheric light on the greens in the foreground for the same reason.

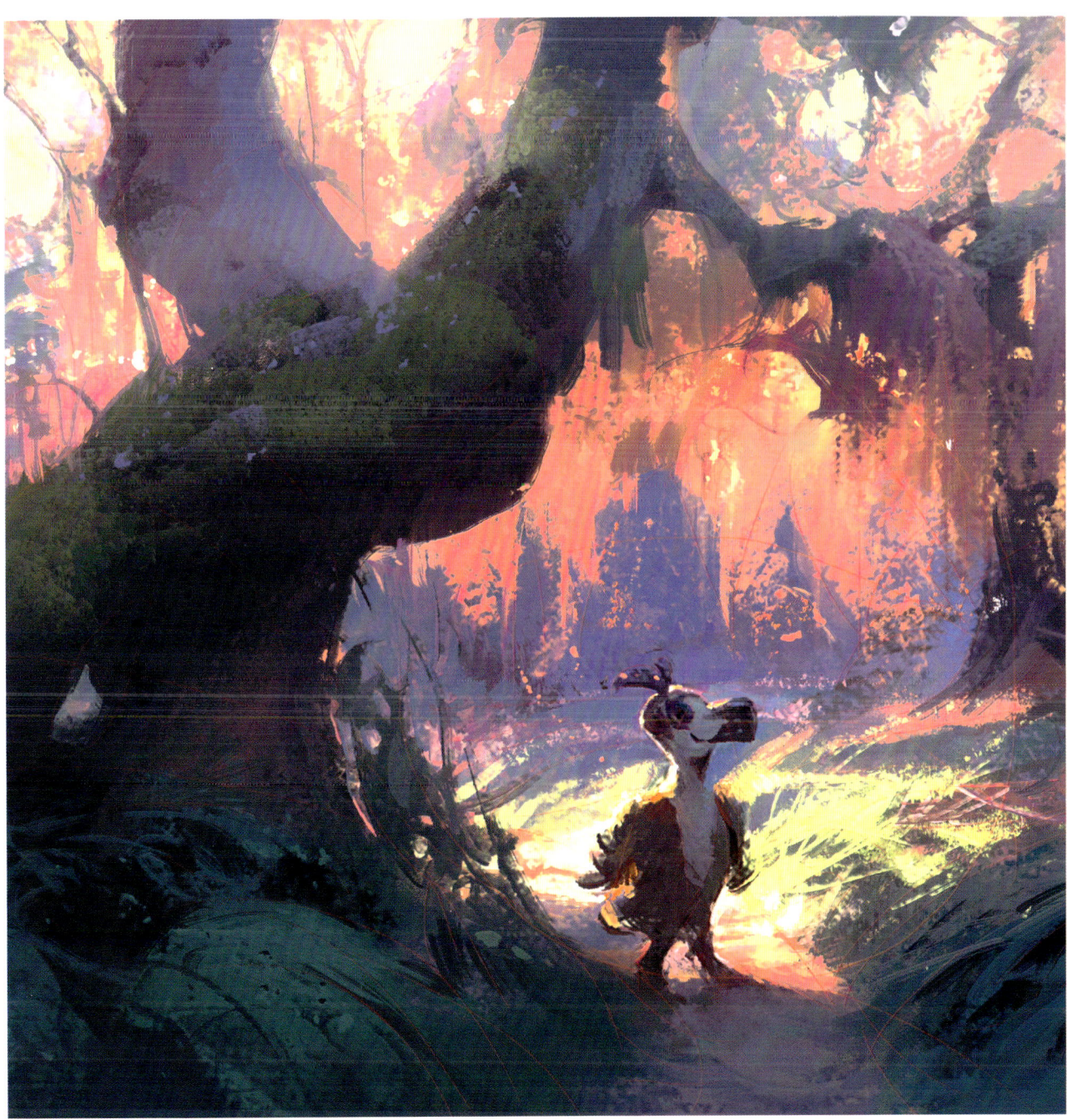

02. A cool background color makes the backlit moss especially vibrant

REFLECTIONS

A true environment designer knows the rules and how they're applied, so let's take a technical look at what reflections are and what they do, so that we can best put them to use. But let me tell you up front that I consider reflections to be a *design tool* and I ignore the technical rules all the time if it gives me a better picture. With that in mind, let's proceed.

01. HOW REFLECTIONS WORK

Imagine yourself standing in a shallow pond where the entire body of water is just a hand's length deep. If you look straight down, you can easily see your feet and the bottom of the pond, but the more you look outward, the more you see reflections instead of the bottom. This happens even though this pond is no deeper ten meters away than it is where you're standing. When light hits placid water at a shallow angle it tends to reflect, and at a steeper angle it tends to transmit through the water. The further you look outward, the more reflections you see, until they completely block your view of the shallow bottom.

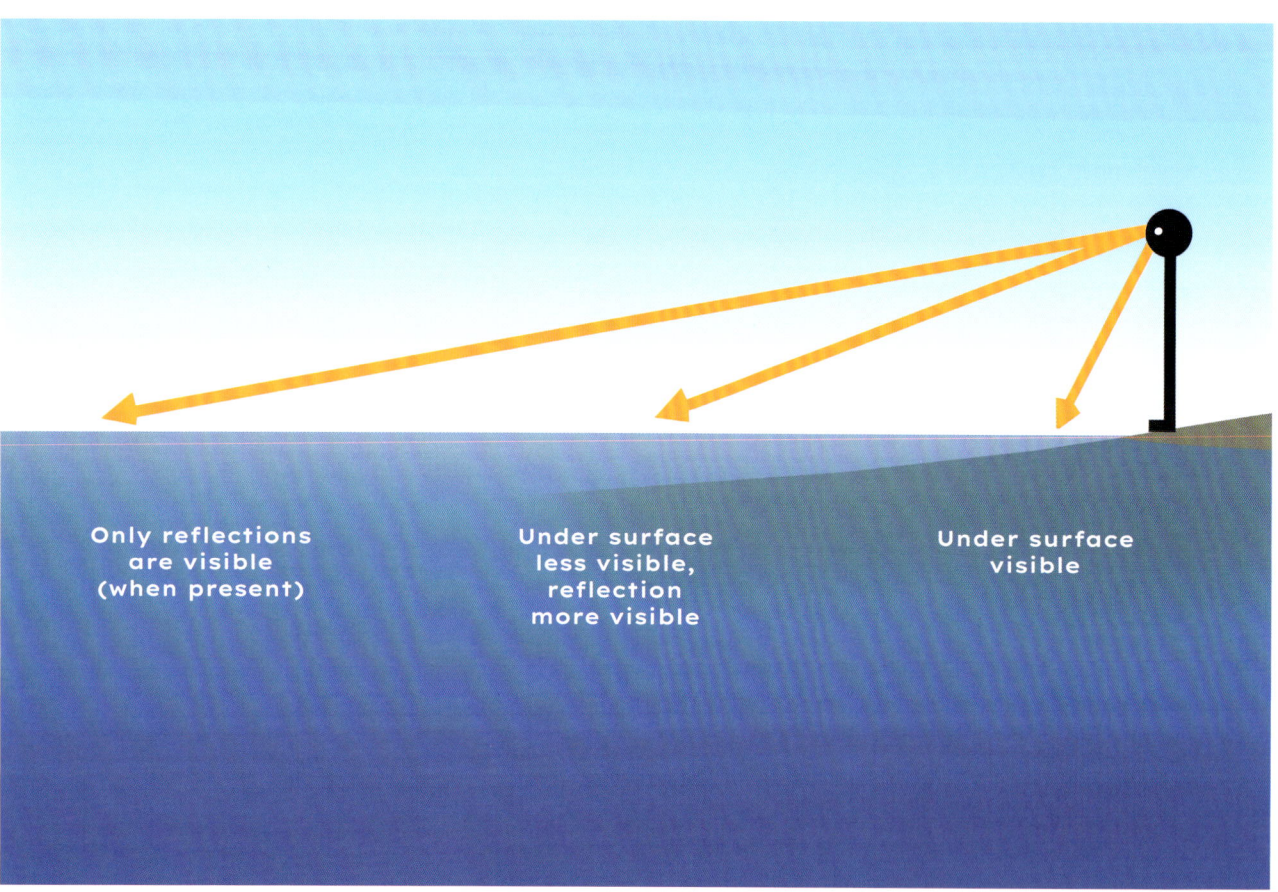

01. Distance and viewing angle affect the visibility of reflections

02. A CLOSER VIEW

Here's a point-of-view illustration showing my shallow pond with a distant mountain added. Most of us will look at this and have the impression we're seeing the reflection of the mountain, but that's not quite right. What we're actually seeing are the light reflections of the sky, the absence of which leaves the darker silhouetted shape of the mountain. Any light aspects on the mountain can certainly be reflected, but remember, *reflections are only made of light*. The darks we see are simply a reveal of the water itself.

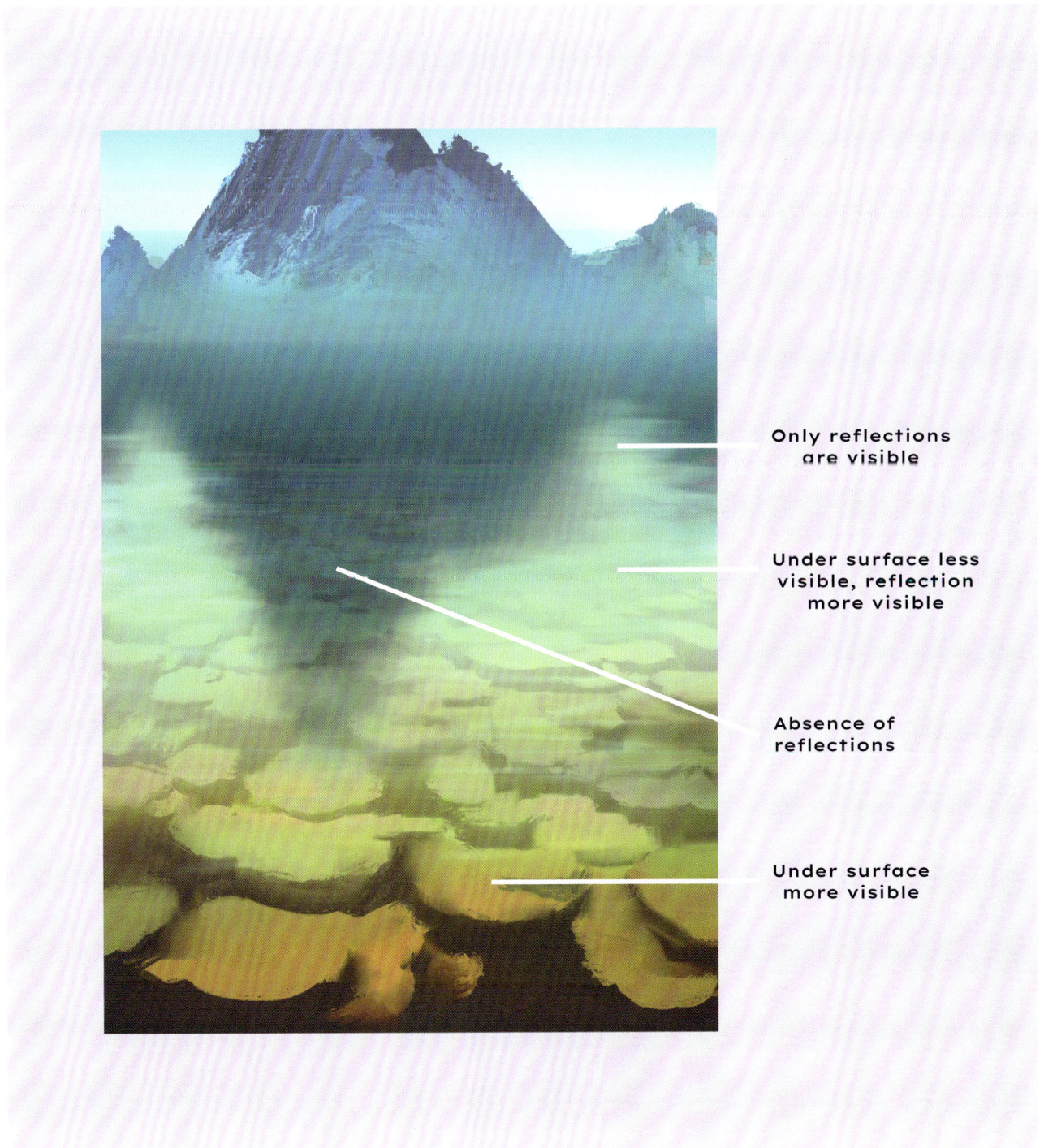

Only reflections
are visible

Under surface less
visible, reflection
more visible

Absence of
reflections

Under surface
more visible

02. The same phenomenon from the viewpoint of standing in the shallows

03. REFLECTIONS IN PERSPECTIVE

Accurate reflections require accurate perspective! An object reflects itself from the point at which it meets the plane of water, and that reflection follows the same perspective present in the environment. Any point on an object will reflect an equal distance below the water line as it is above. For reflected objects that don't actually touch the waterline, we would simply imagine where it would meet if the plane of water had continued.

04. TEMPLE POOL

Wouldn't you say that reflections are a great opportunity to paint more temple ruins? I'll take any opportunity I can, so let's fill the center of these ruins with rainwater that's collected in that neglected space and reflect the spires right into it. This puts into practice the perspective demonstrated in the previous image; this is where technical knowledge becomes picture magic. When an environment needs an additional shimmer of visual interest, I'll find an excuse to place water and reflections into it.

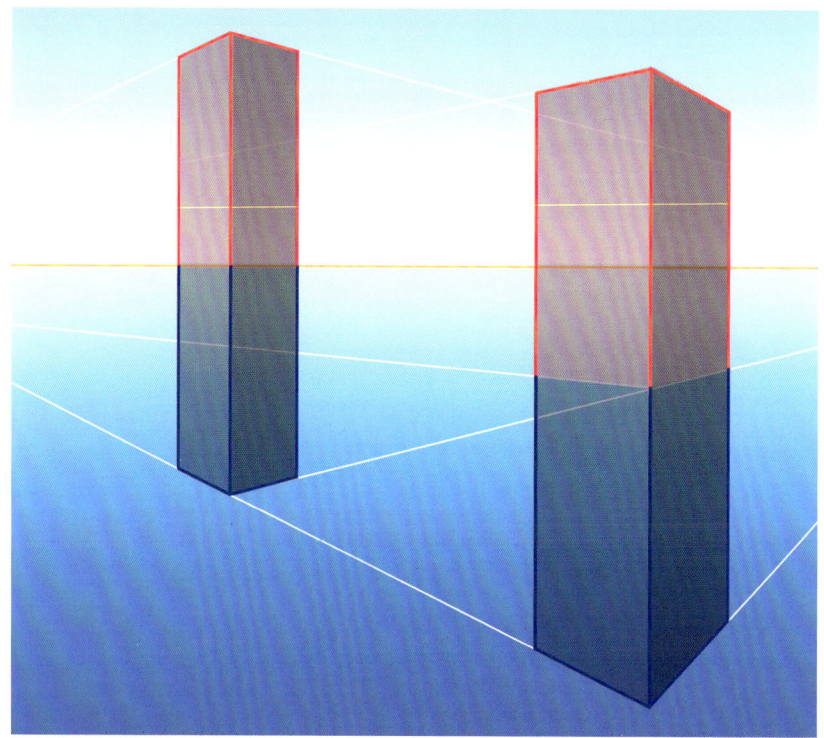

03. Reflected objects above the water (left) and touching the water (right)

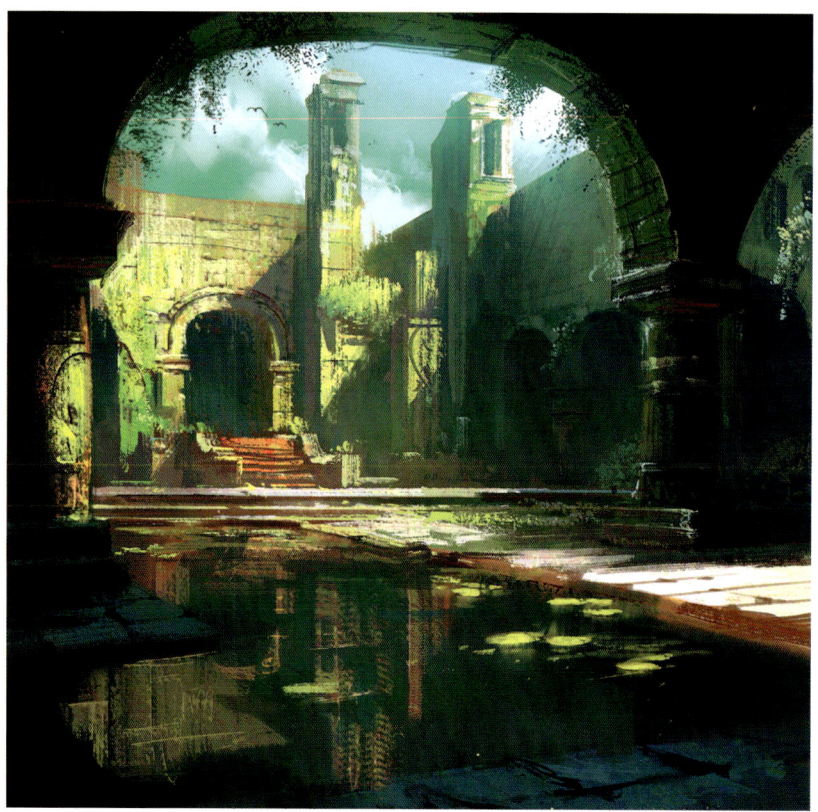

04. A reflecting pool makes these ruins feel even grander and more enticing to the adventurer

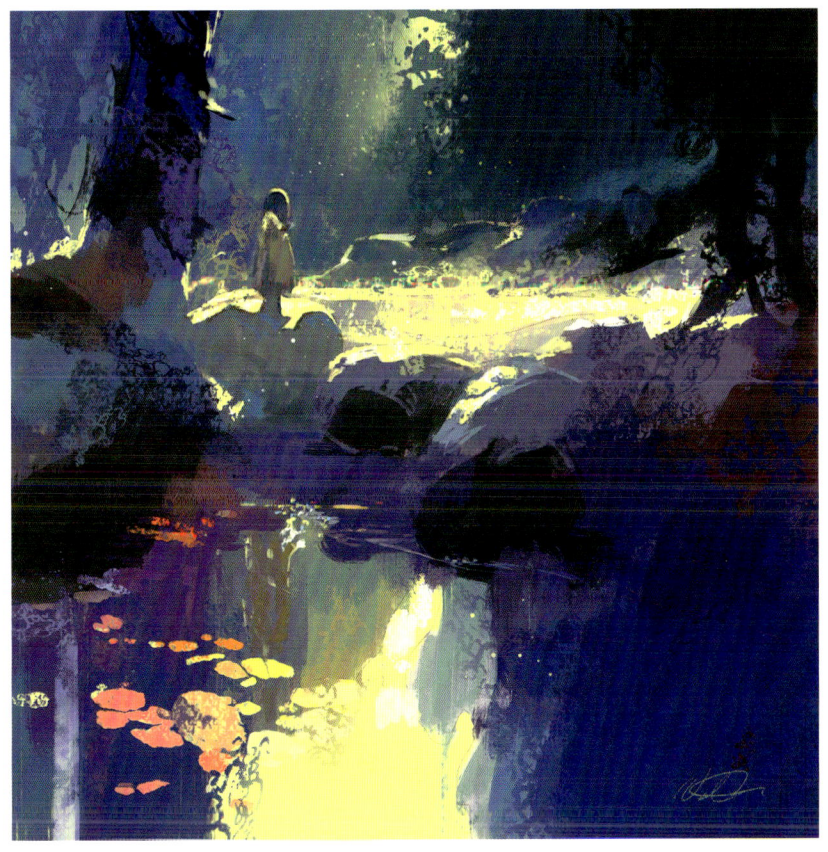

05. OUTSIDE THE FRAME

This image is about a little girl in a big environment. I intended to give it an overwhelmingly engaging quality through the lighting, a big part of which is the reflections. The place has a magical and mysterious mood as the sunlight streams through the foliage onto the land. The water shows us something that is otherwise completely out of frame – we see a reflection of the sky itself, which gives us all the luminous visual interest that we need. I've included a close-up so you can see in detail the abstract handling of the reflections here.

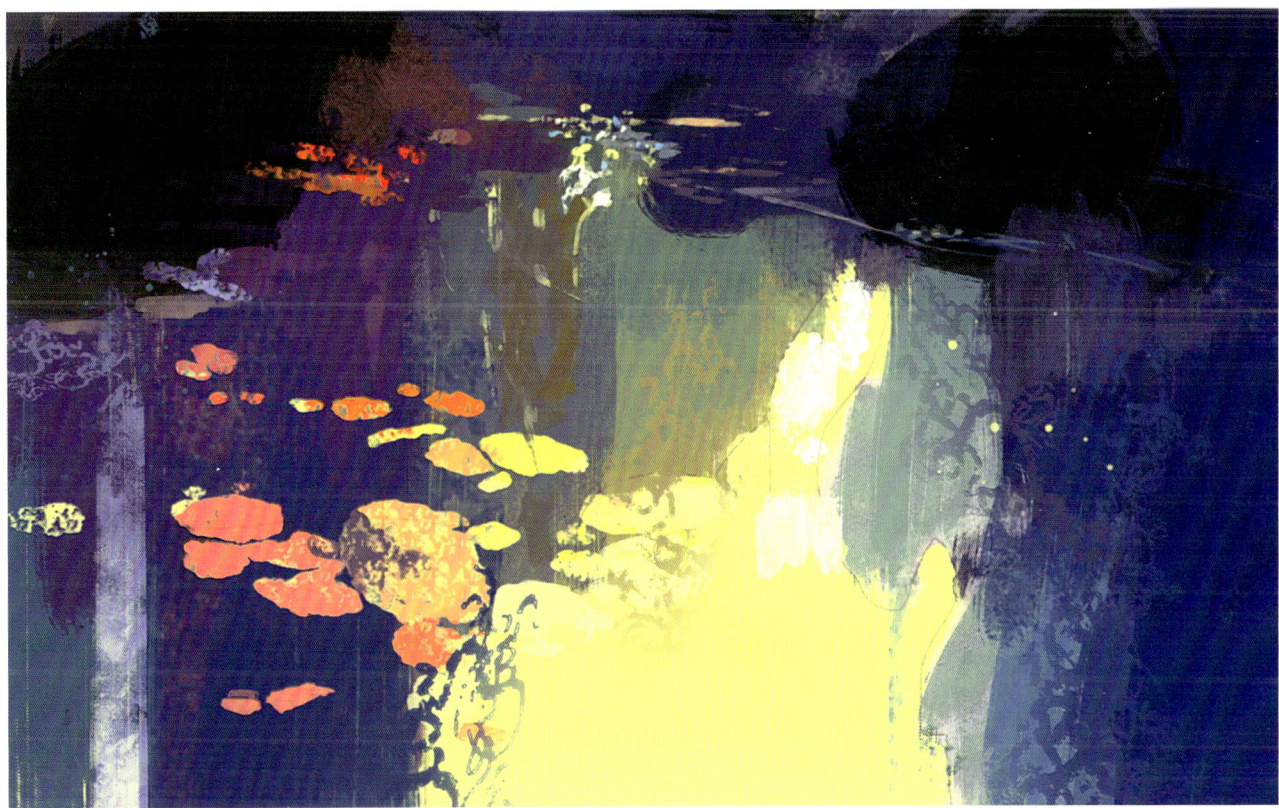

05. Here the water reflects parts of the location and lighting we can't otherwise see

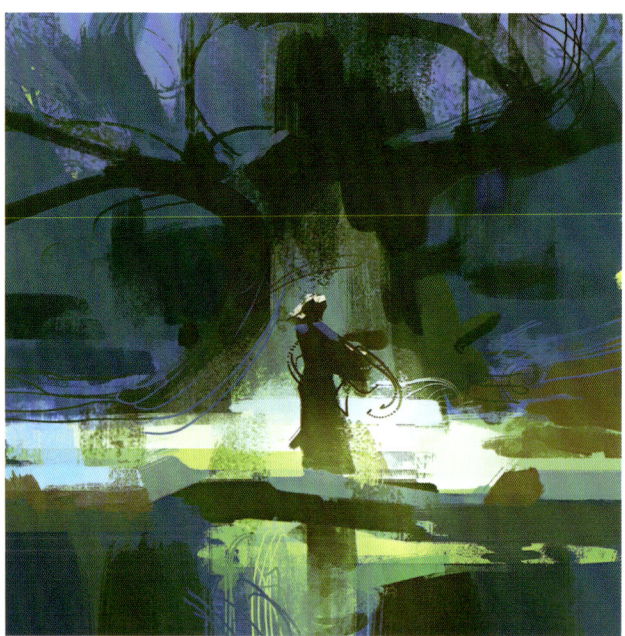
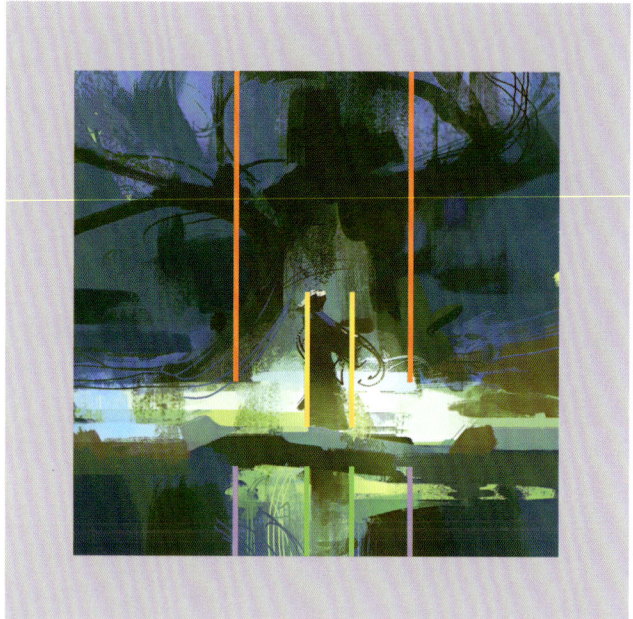

06. The reflections intensify the symmetry and central composition of the tree and character

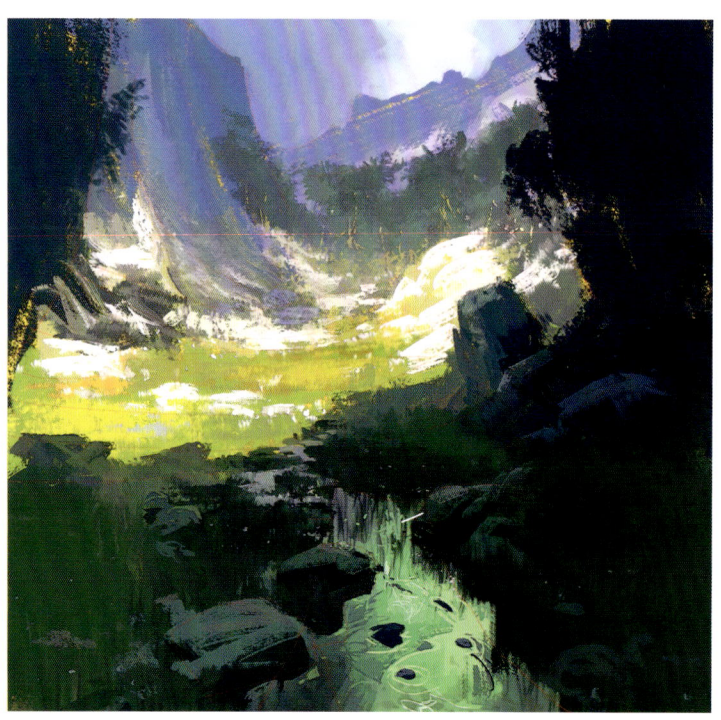

07. A reflective stream guides us through the shadowy foreground and into the landscape

Reflections, by their nature, double the impact of your subject.

06. DOUBLE IMPACT

In the sketch above, the centralized positioning of the character and tree gives the scene the purposeful quality I'm looking for. And guess what? If I add water, those centralized design elements are projected down into the foreground, which doubles their sense of authority.

07. DIRECTING WITH REFLECTIONS

Here's another handy trick I like to use with reflections. Sometimes areas filled with dark shadow need some life or visual interest, and reflections can give us exactly what we need. This is a painting inspired by a trek I went on through Sierra Nevada, though much is exaggerated and invented. I didn't want to just reproduce the environment – I wanted to recreate the emotional experience of the journey.

It was of critical importance to set up the passages of light and the layers of mountain and foliage to create a quality of *journey*. The vivid reflections in the foreground stream fill that space with contrast and visual interest – the effect is almost like an arrow, sending us forward into adventure!

LIGHTING TEMPERATURE

Let's look further into the idea of warm and cool temperatures of light that I introduced earlier. Here's a sketch that uses both temperatures to create depth and visual interest. We have the feeling of purposeful travel across a stone bridge to reach a mysterious location shrouded in cold light. This is often the key for environment design: to pique our audience's curiosity about a place and visually give them the means to travel there. I've included a simplified version so you can clearly see how the distant cool platform is framed by contrasting warm light and the bridge that connects them.

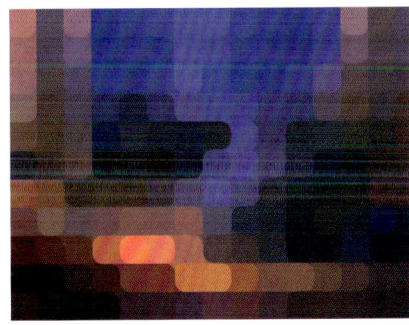

Sometimes the key to a successful environment design is to pique our audience's curiosity about a place and give them a visual means to travel there.

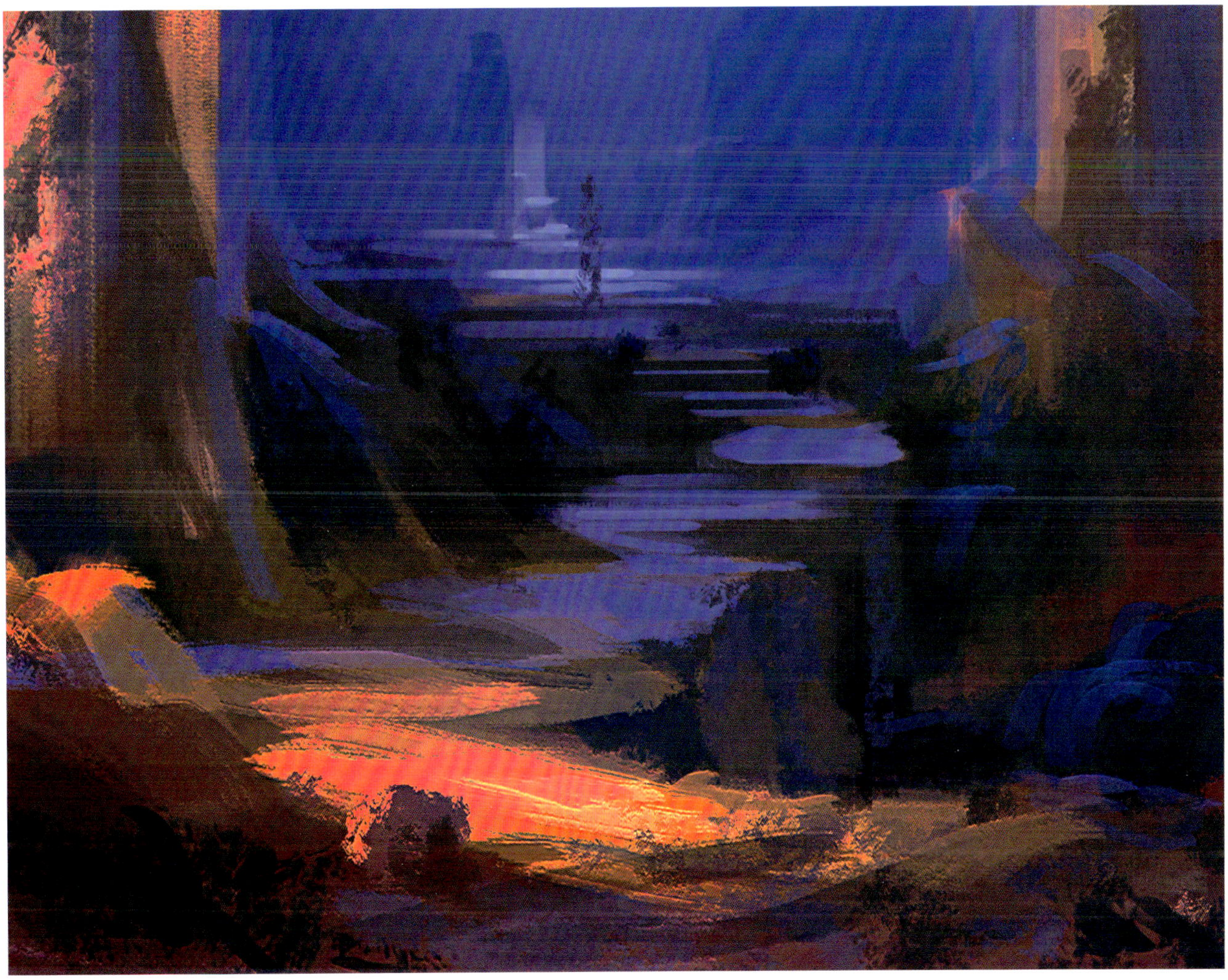

△ Warm and cool light create depth and atmosphere that intrigue the viewer

01. TEMPERATURE CONTRAST

Now let's look at temperature contrasts to create a sense of purpose in our environments. Here we have a small band of travelers in a pool of warm light, nearing their destination of the tall towers. My goal here is to lift the viewer's eye up to the crest of the towers through the use of contrast. There are many ways I could have achieved this, but I wanted a mysterious shimmering quality of atmosphere in the scene. My solution was to put a strong blue atmospheric light on the towers and surround them with a contrasting warm light, as if the sun is shining through a volume of mist. And there's that single orange window glowing at the top of the tower, too. This image is about two things – a group of travelers below and the tower crest above – and I've used temperature contrast to bring attention to both.

02. WARM/COOL LIGHTING

Here's an image that's simply about the beauty that can be created through warm and cool lighting. This environment has very little local color – it's almost exclusively about rich warm and cool light strategically placed in the foreground and background. I hope you enjoy it.

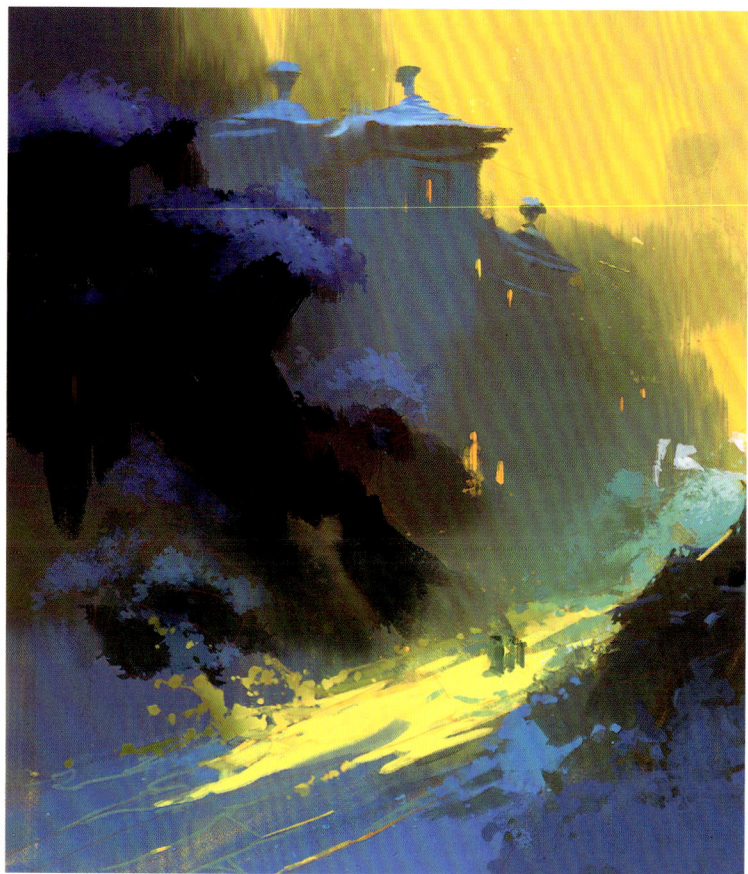

01. The temperature contrasts and reversals of color highlight the important elements

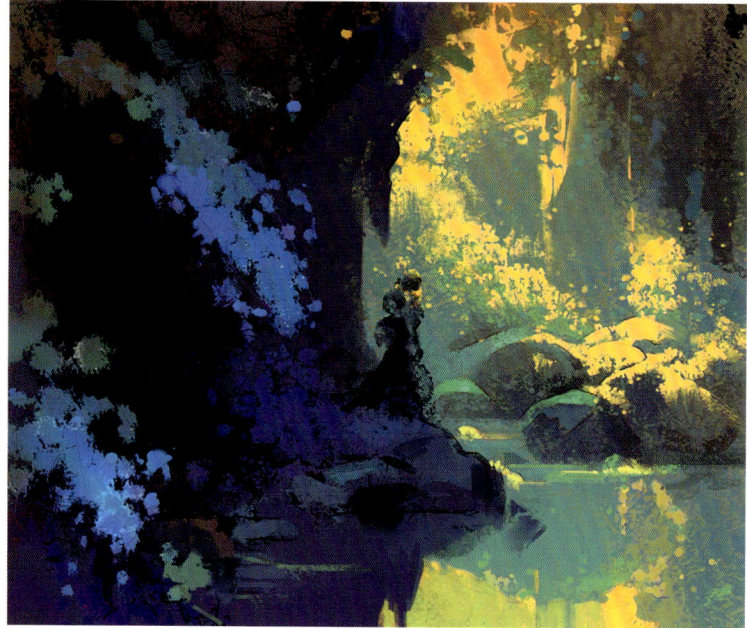

02. This image is built on the rich, beautiful contrast of warm and cool

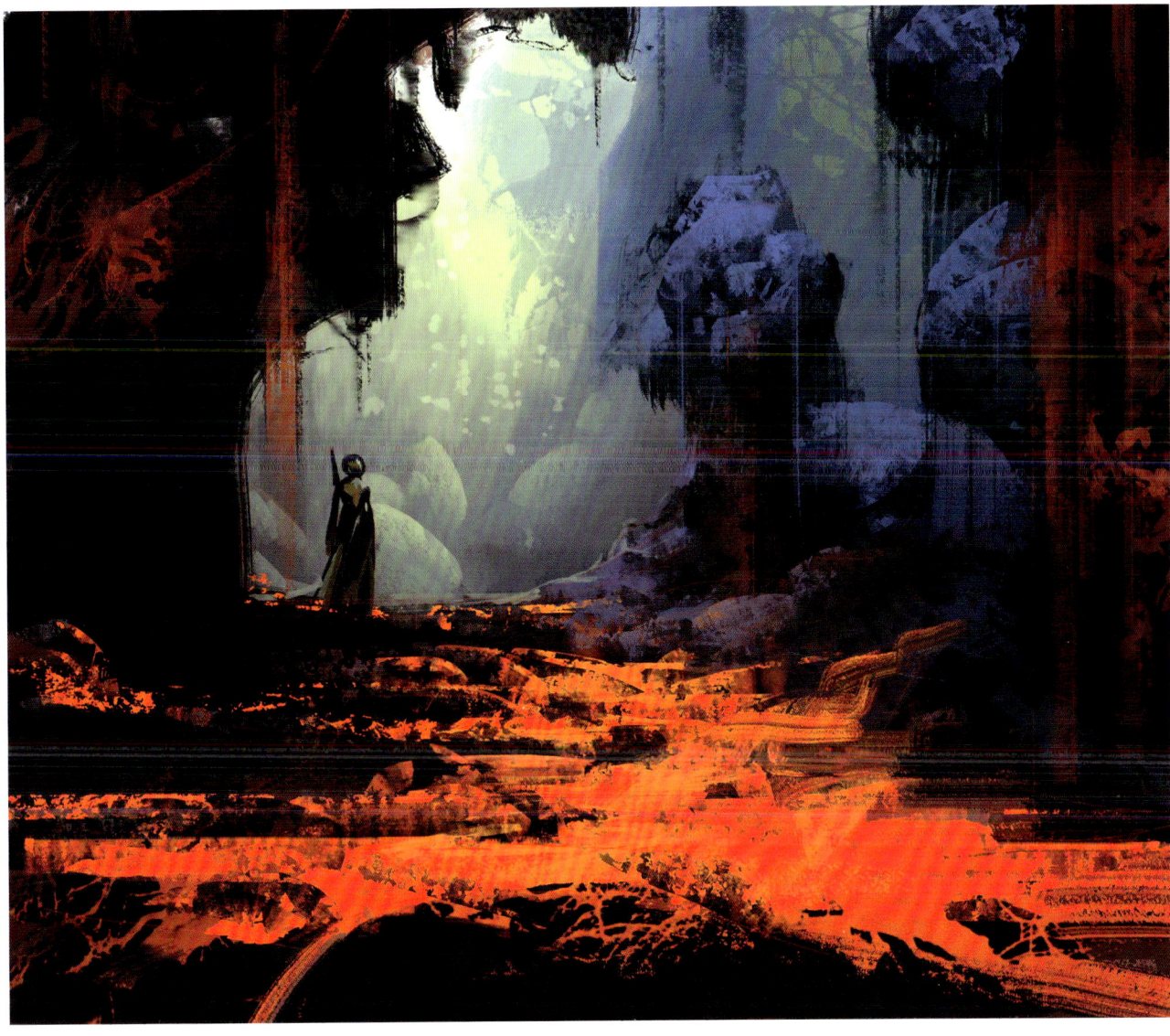

03. Fiery hot lighting gives this scene its intense, brooding drama

03. EXTREME TEMPERATURE

I've often discussed the importance of being willing to go to extremes to engage the interest of our viewers, so I thought I would wrap up our segment of warm and cool light with a fantasy of extreme light.

CROSSING THE BRIDGE

A big part of our job is finding interesting ways to relate the parts of our environment to the whole. There's a particular lighting idea that I think does this well, and I call it 'bridging'.

Notice how the light temperatures in the right painting gradually shift in hue and temperature as they move from foreground to background. This is a very intentional method of using light to move the audience through the environment in an interesting way. In the graphic version below you can see the stepping stones moving from warm light through gradations of cool light and back to warm again.

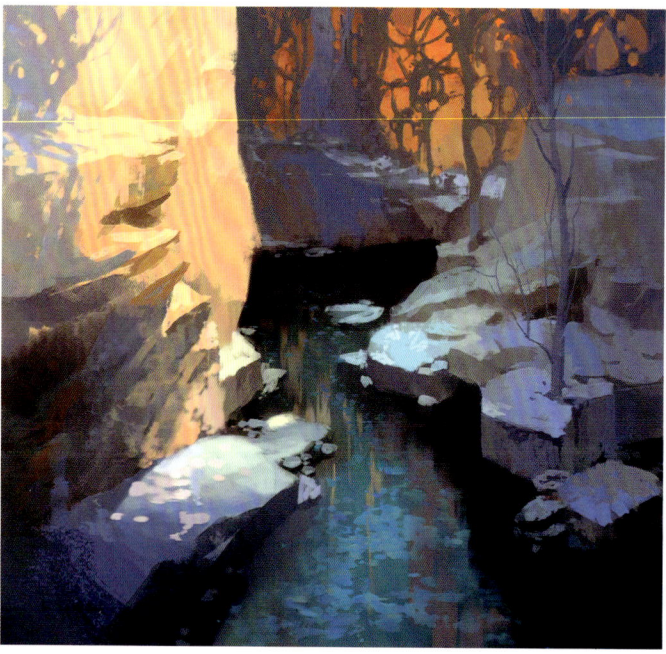

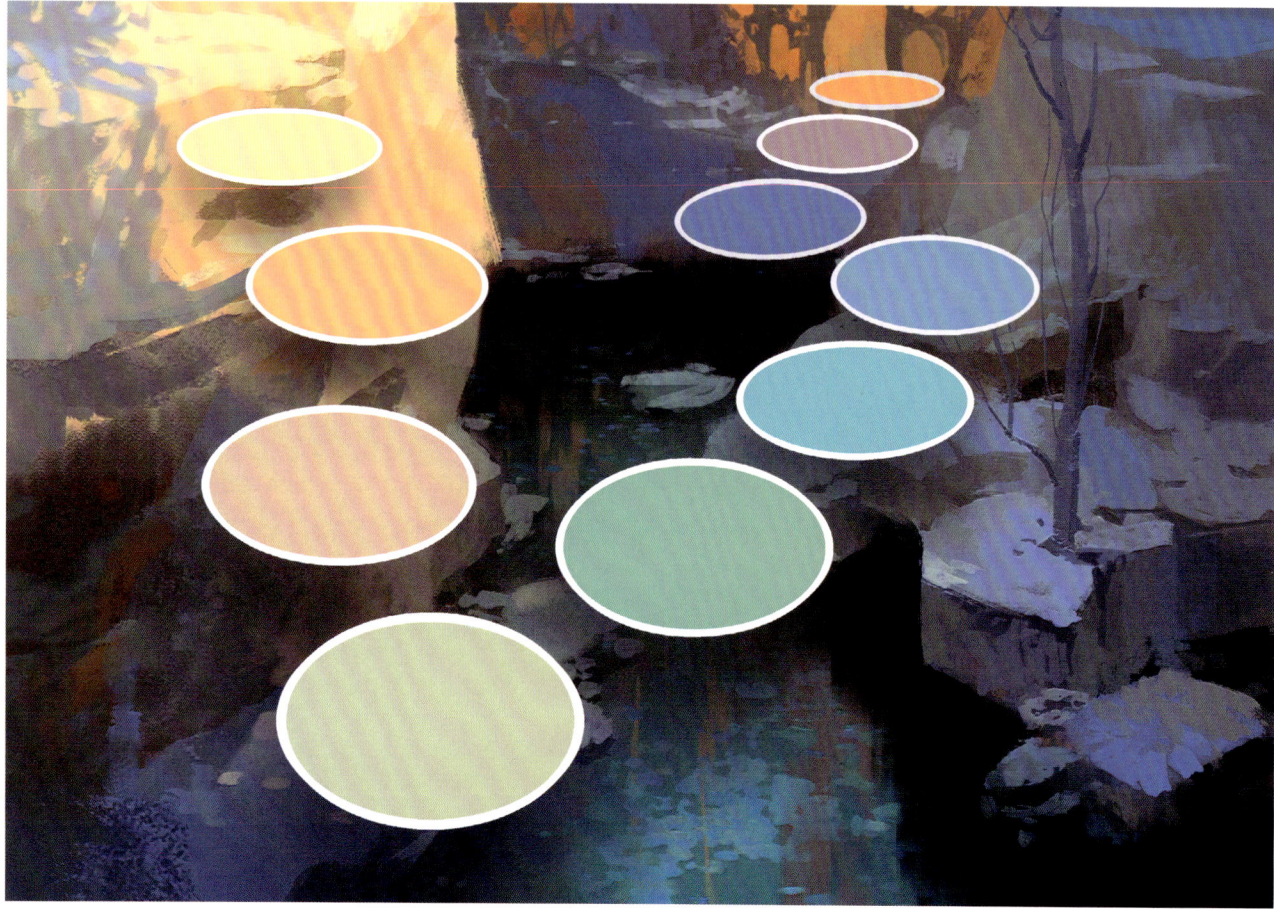

△ The stepping stones show the hue gradient in this example of bridging

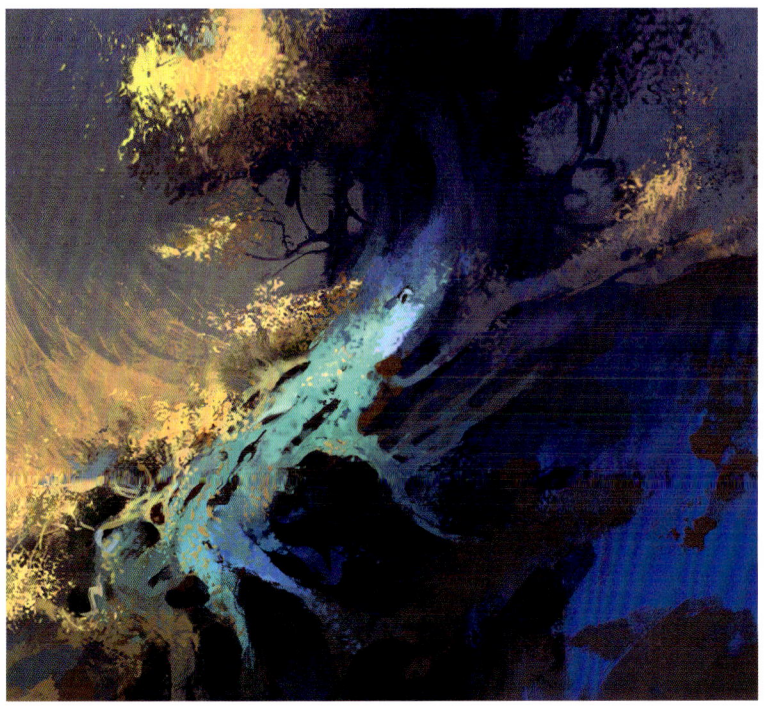

01. This image relies on some dramatic contrasts of lighting and color

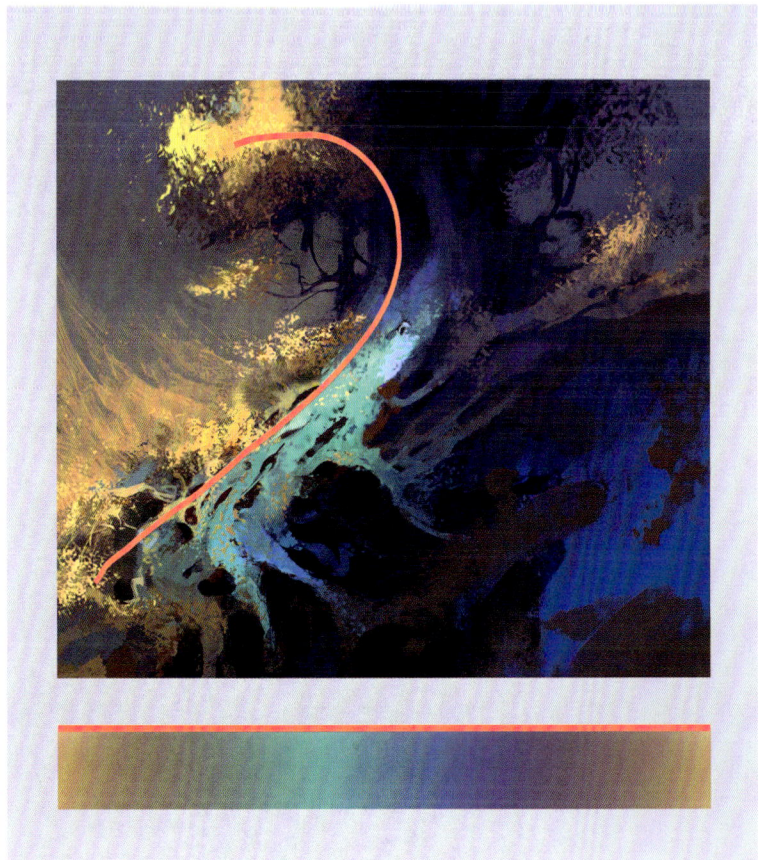

02. The hue gradient throughout this bridging example

01. ANOTHER EXAMPLE

Here I've created another image that uses the same idea for a different purpose. This is not an image about depth – it's about bringing an exciting color contrast to an otherwise bland, brown environment. For visual interest I exaggerated cool atmospheric lights shining on a bleached-white root system, giving life to an otherwise sickly color palette.

02. BRIDGING BREAKDOWN

The difficulty is getting such an extreme contrast to feel like it belongs rather than just being artificially tacked on. I solved this challenge through color bridging. On the lower left I started with warm foliage, which gradually transitions through neutrals until it arrives at full-strength cyan. Then, as the lighting transitions up to the right, it goes from cyan to cool gray, to warm gray-purple, to warm brown, then back again to the yellows that fill the environment. It's a way to get our audience to accept and even luxuriate in extremes of lighting-color contrast.

DAPPLED LIGHT

Dappled light is the broken quality of light that has passed through layers of foliage. It's an amazing way to create a sprinkle of visual interest, especially since it can be positioned strategically to give emphasis where you want it. It's also useful in describing the form and perspective of the surfaces it's falling across, as displayed here in these perspective grids.

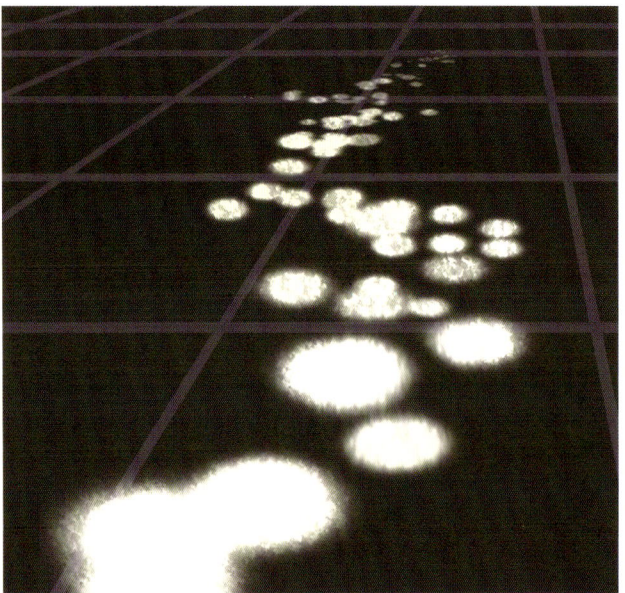 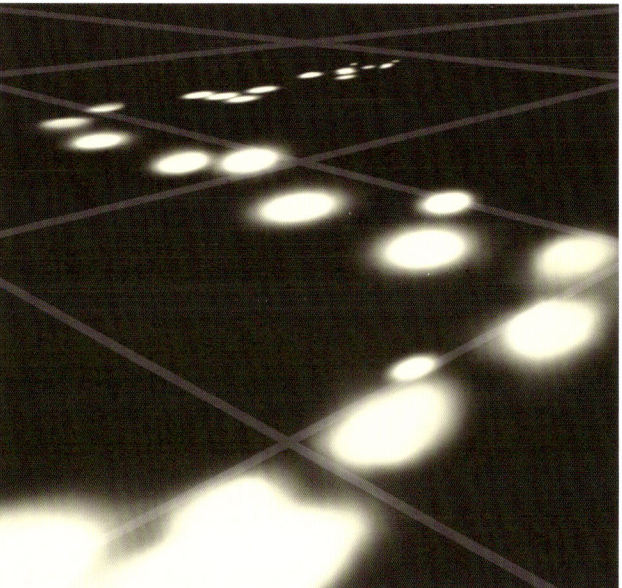

△ Spots of dappled light can be used to show perspective in your scene

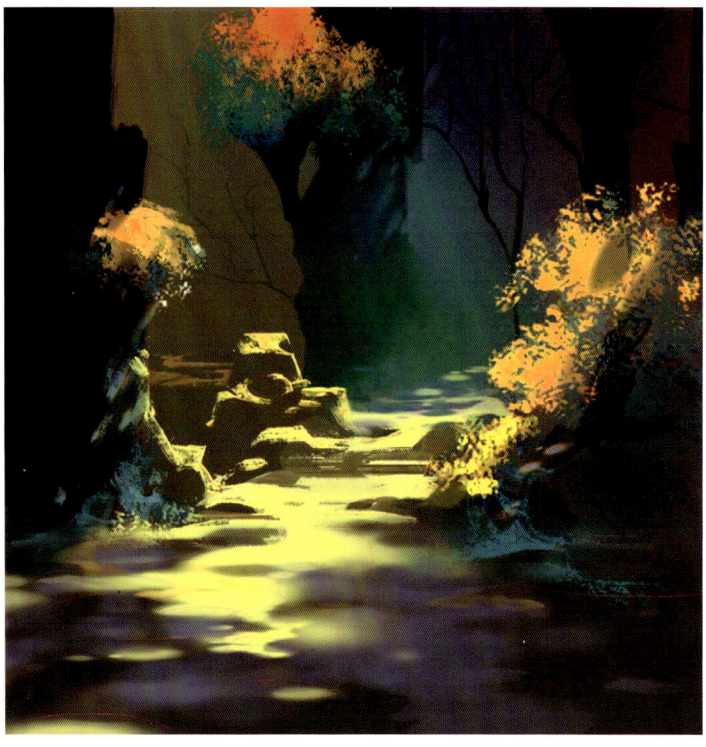

01. Dappled sunlight entices the viewer down this forest path

01. FOREST FLOOR

Here's a forest environment where I wanted to create the feeling of an entrance, as if you're on a pathway heading into its depths. Dappled light allows me to focus attention in a way that draws the viewer into the environment. Remember, our number one goal is to create purpose, and now we have a new way of achieving it.

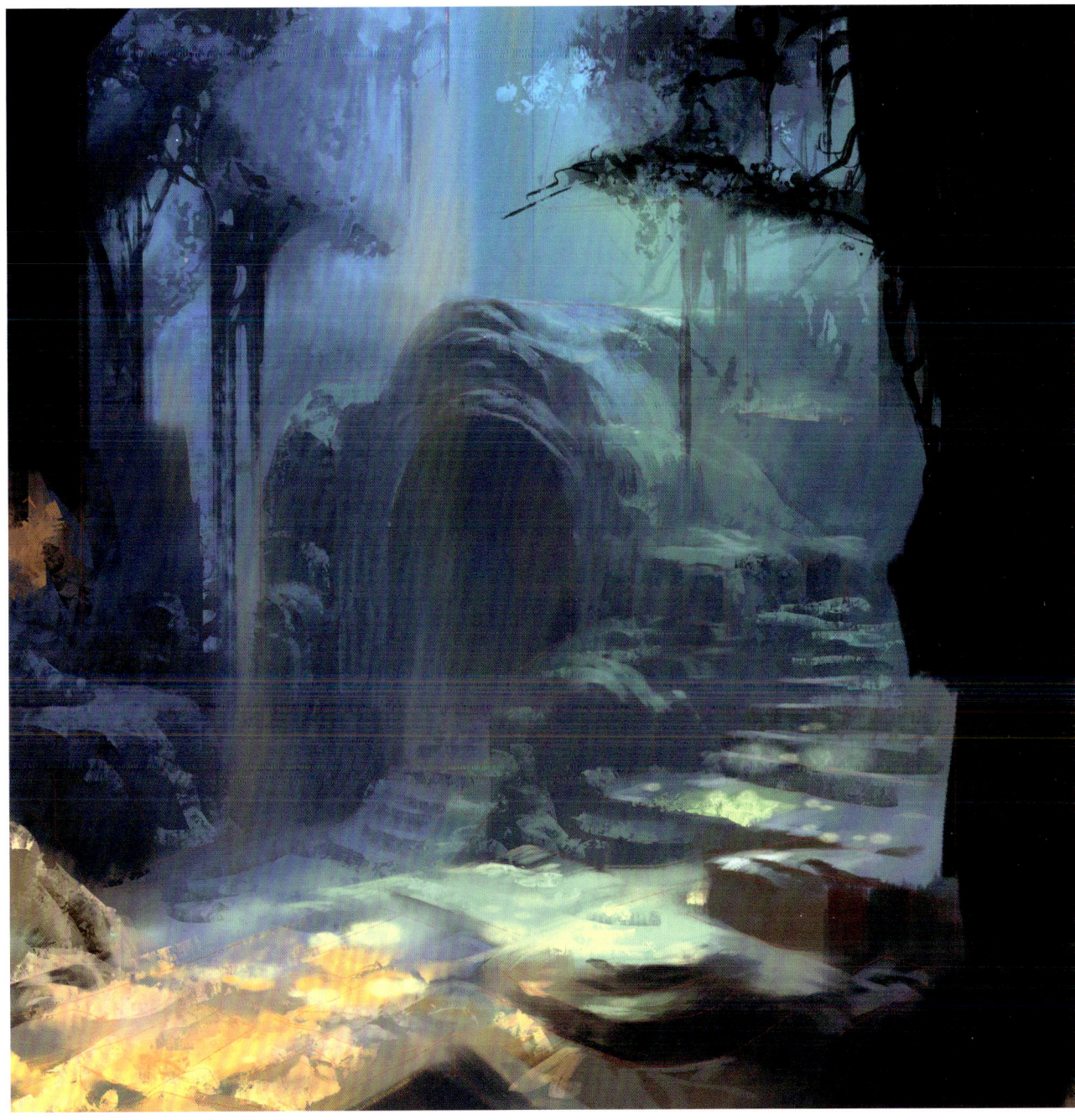

02. This image uses dapples of warm sunlight and cool skylight

02. LIGHT CONTRAST

For this image my goal was to evoke the magical quality that's promised by a sprinkle of dappled light, with warm sunlight in the foreground and cool skylight in the background, filtering down through the forest canopy. Dappled skylight tends to be much softer and dappled sunlight much stronger, so I lead with the warm sun to guide you into this mysterious and mystical place.

PATHWAYS

I often talk about creating the feeling that a painting is taking the viewer somewhere. It's an engaging concept because it appeals to a basic human desire: **we always have to know what's over the next hill.** This image is quite literally a pathway – the whole composition is based on it and I use lighting to emphasize it. If the entire purpose of the image is the pathway and the people walking there, then lighting is one of our most powerful tools to reinforce that quality of purpose.

01. SUNSET HILLS

I grew up hiking the hills of my native California and these old abandoned roads were irresistible. I had to find out where they led! So the lighting here is no coincidence – I specifically focused it there for the painting. It's about the feeling that the road is screaming for our attention, insisting that we have to go up and see what's on the other side of the hill.

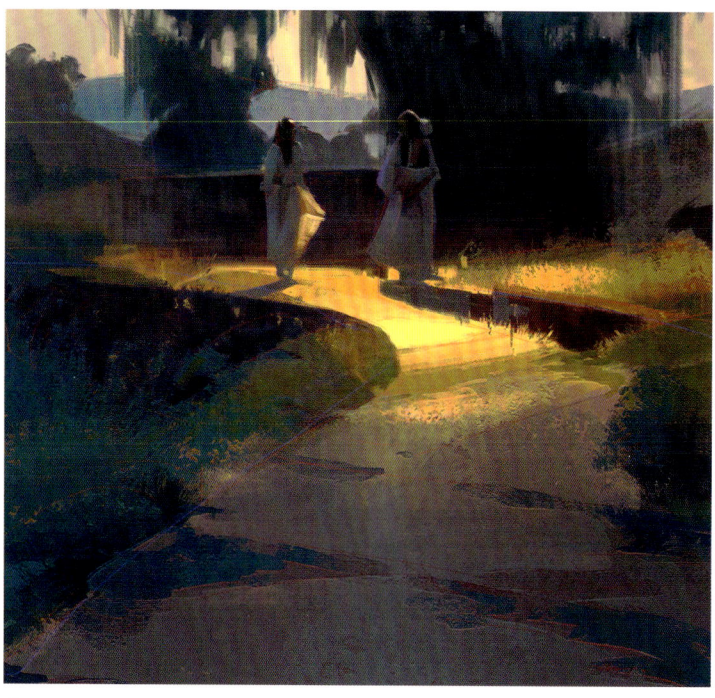

△ Our instinct is to follow paths – we can use this to our advantage in environment design

Pathways create the feeling that the painting is taking us somewhere because they engage a basic human desire: we always have to know what's over the next hill.

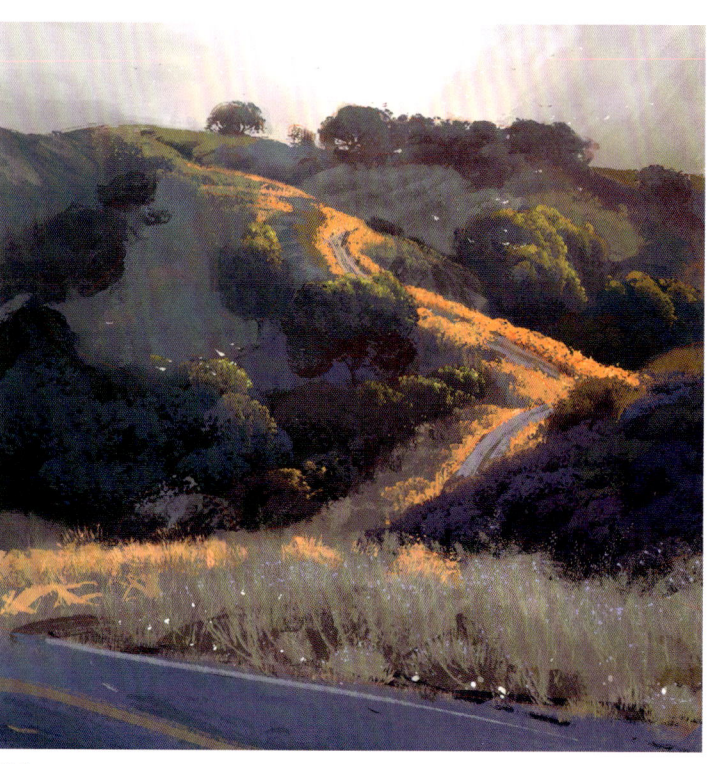

01. The sun catches the path up the hills in a way that naturally appeals to us

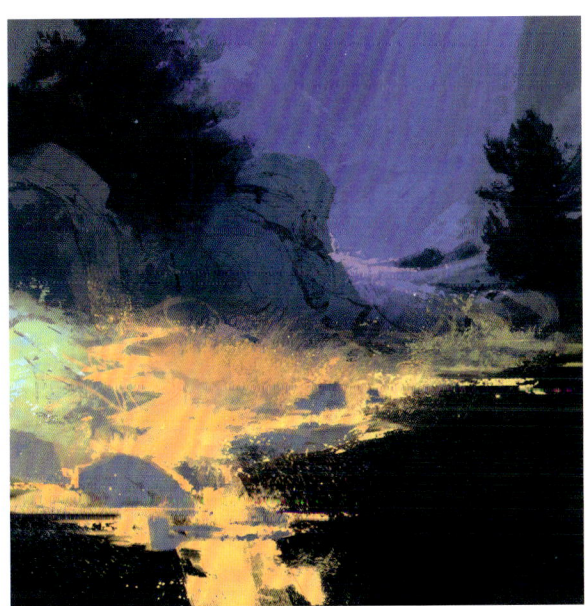

02. AN IMPLIED PATH

The painting on the left has no literal road or pathway, but the lighting design creates one for us. It all comes down to our viewers being so engaged by this place that they want to know more. What's behind those rocks? What are those distant moonlit mountains all about? The illuminated pathway reinforces these desires in our audience.

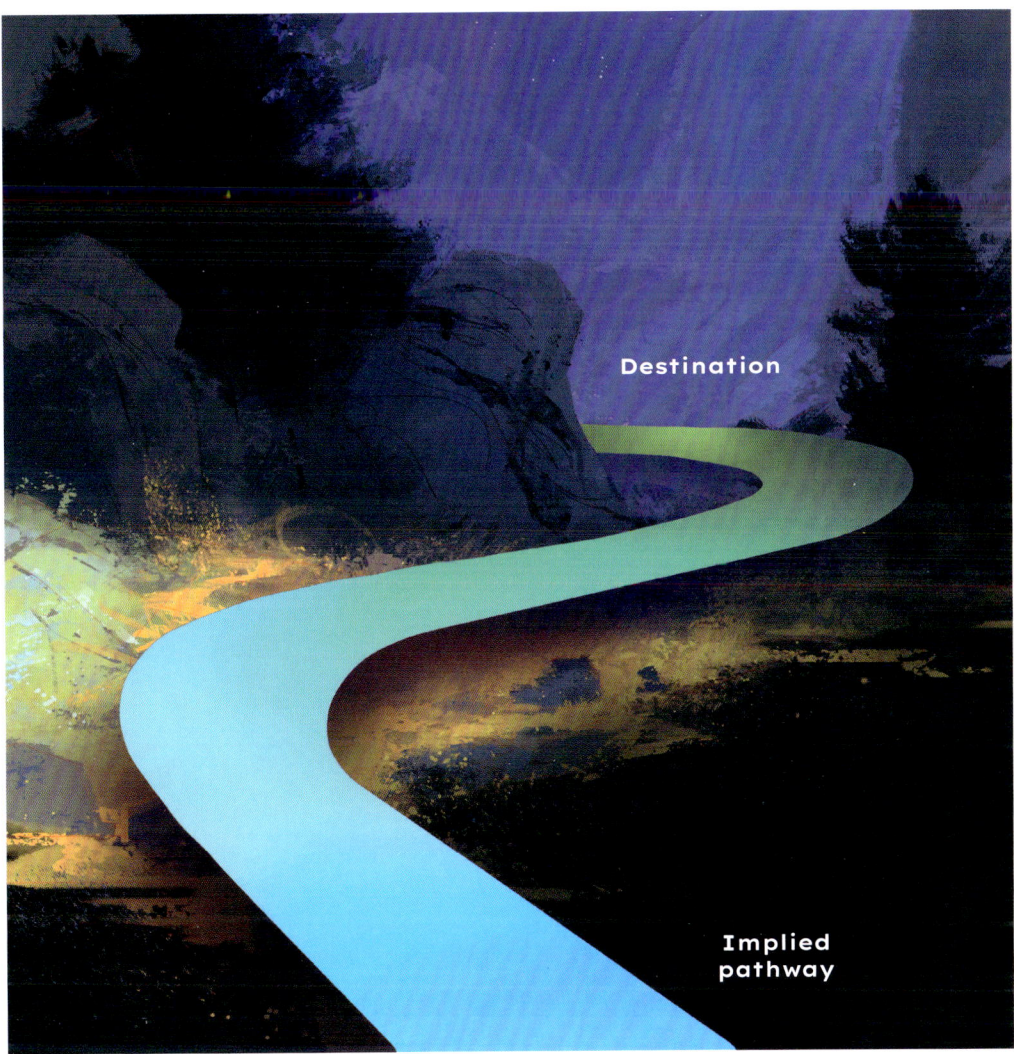

Destination

Implied
pathway

02. There isn't an actual path here but the composition creates one

03. DON'T FORGET THE SKY!

A cloudscape is a landscape in and of itself, and pathways of light can be woven through them as well. This Arabian palace is clearly an important destination that needs reinforcement – note the pathway created by light weaving across the ground plane to take us there, but don't miss that same quality woven into the cloudscape.

> Don't forget the sky – pathways of light and pattern can be designed into the sky just as on the land.

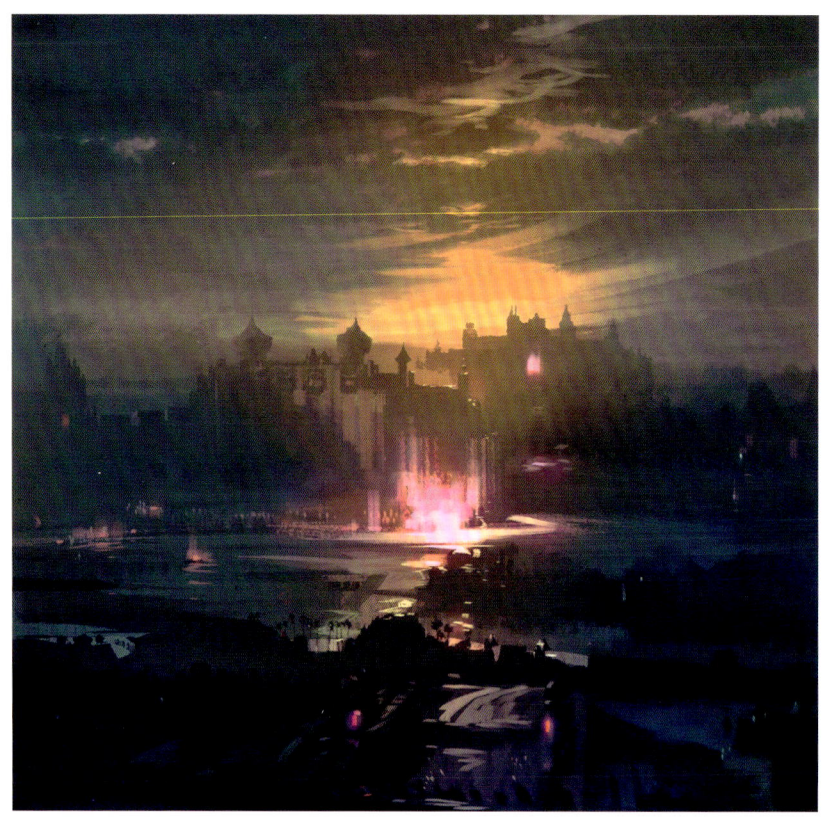

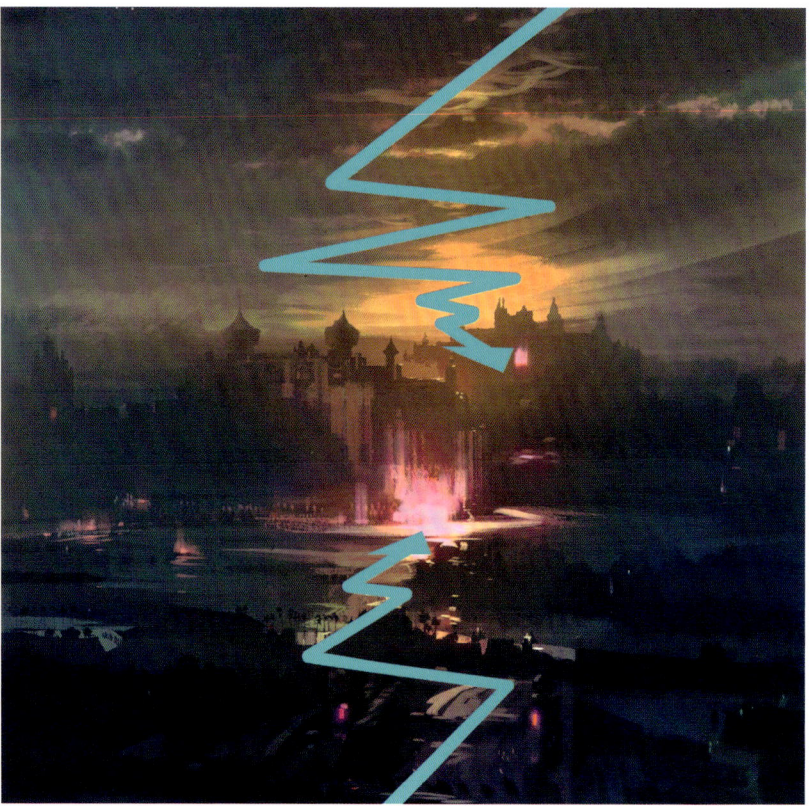

03. A pathway doesn't have to be limited to the ground

LIGHTING DESIGN

We've been pushing lighting design toward every extreme purpose we can think of because it's an amazing problem-solving tool, but patterns of light and shadow are beautiful for their own sake. So let's look at lighting design in terms of aesthetics, for no purpose other than it's attractive to look at.

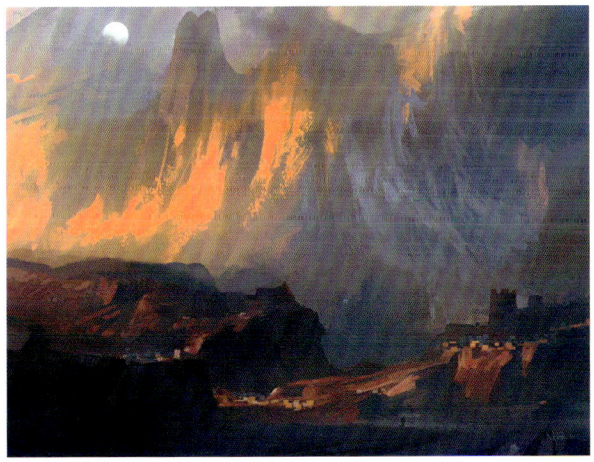

01. ACTIVE VS PASSIVE

When inventing this fantasy mountainscape, I simply wanted it to be an attractive and intriguing scene for my audience. My best judgment was that I could achieve this through passages of light. And how do you make light really special? We know that warm light can be nice to look at, but it's so much nicer if it's contrasted with cool shadow. So I carefully placed active passages of light adjacent to passive areas of shadow on the basis that something feels more special if it's surrounded by its opposite.

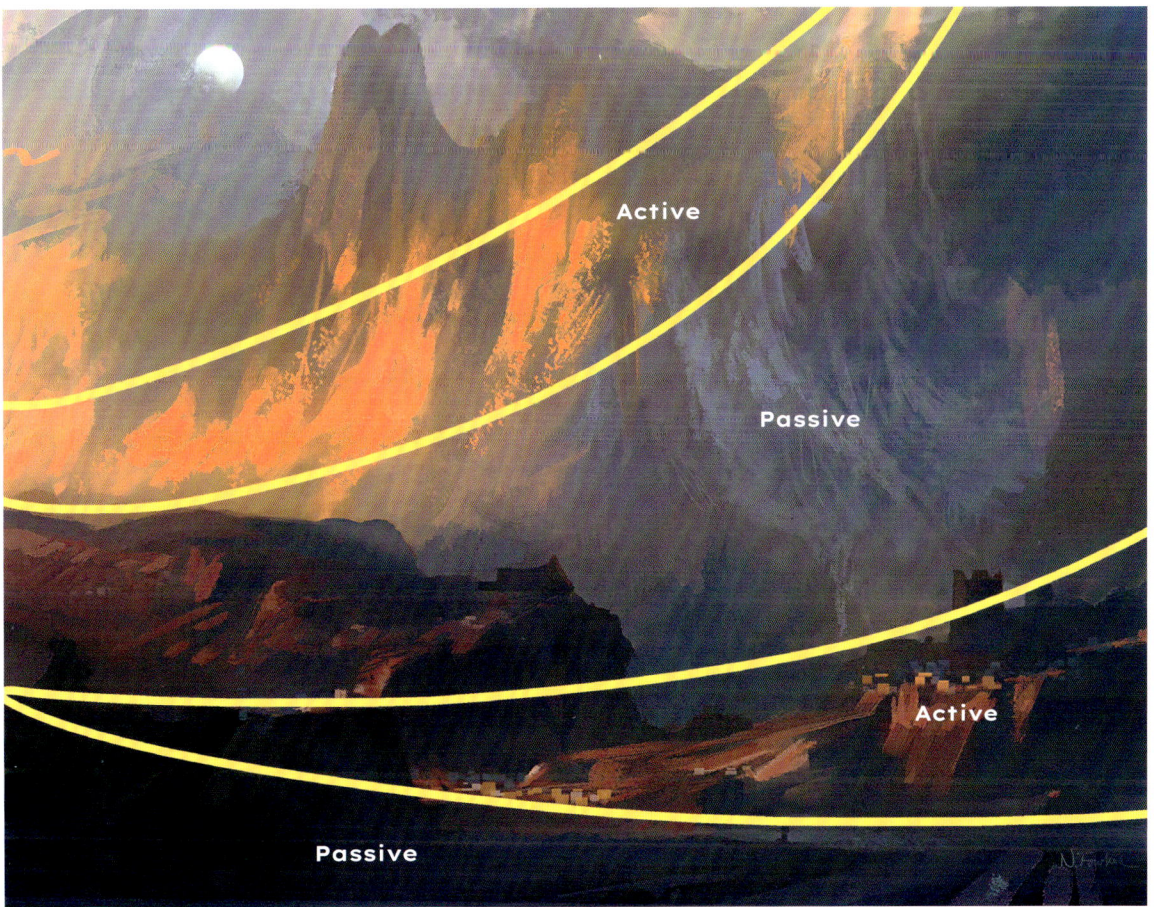

01. This scene alternates active, warm, bright areas with cool, passive, shadowy ones

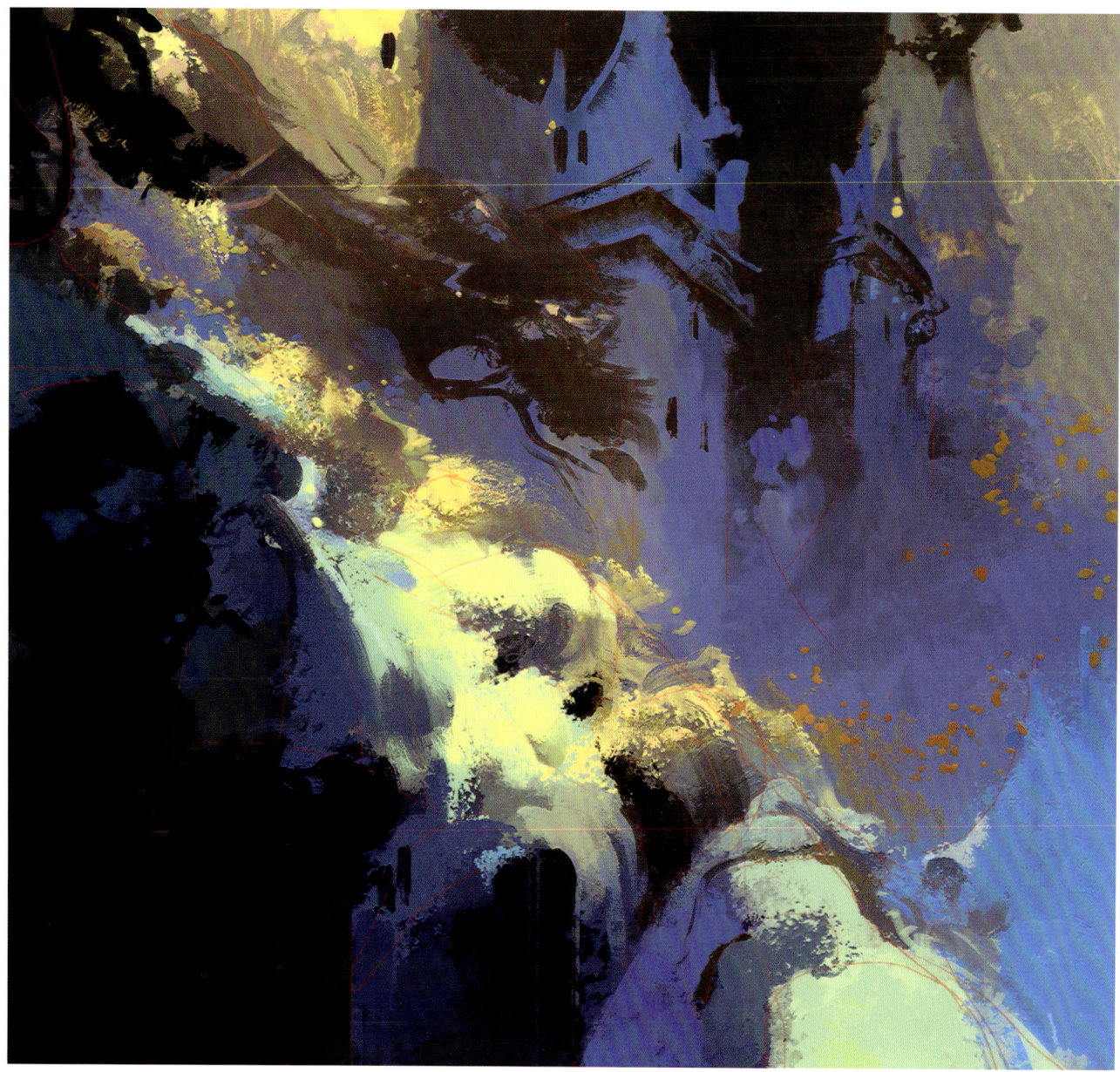

02. Staging light against shadow to create visual engagement

02. LIGHT VS SHADOW

What do you think? Does this diagonal slash of
vivid light make this mountainside palace more
engaging? Personally, I couldn't get this scene
to work without staging it with these passages
of light and shadow.

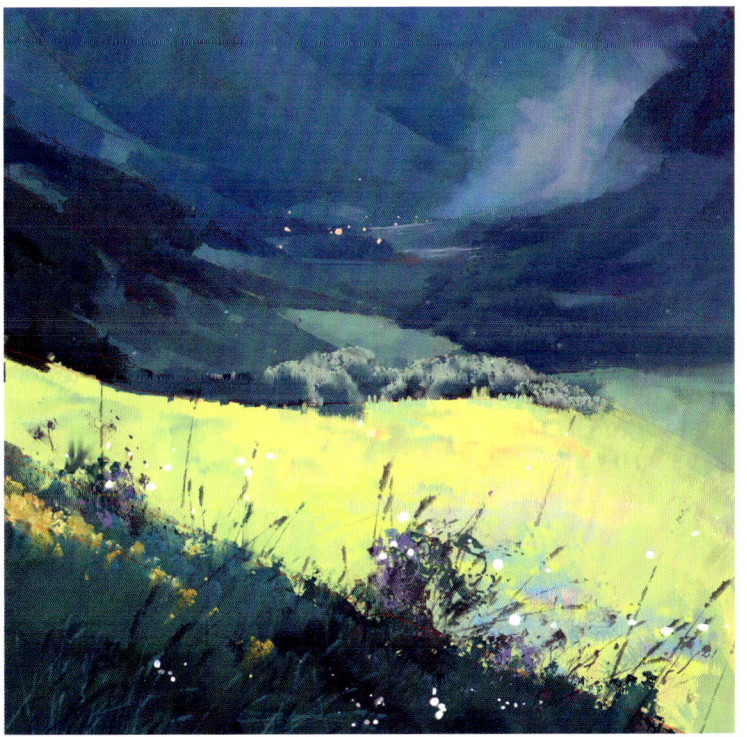

03. The bright area here is compositionally important but contains very little information

03. EMPTINESS VS DETAIL

The shadows in this mountain valley mean so much more with the presence of this open passage of light. We often feel that light must be the area that holds the important subject material, so I'm actively going against that idea in this study. The field of light is completely empty but it serves as a wonderful backdrop for the active splash of foliage in the foreground. But more important than that, there's a little town nestled in the shadow. It's not rendered in any way other than dots of light that tell us that people and their activities abound.

04. APPEALING ABSTRACTION

And this final image is inspired by a recent trip I took to Japan. The experience got me fascinated by the abstract qualities of light and shadow in landscape, and how they can flow from one subject to another. That's exactly what I'm going for here: aesthetically pleasing passages of light and shadow weaving through a landscape.

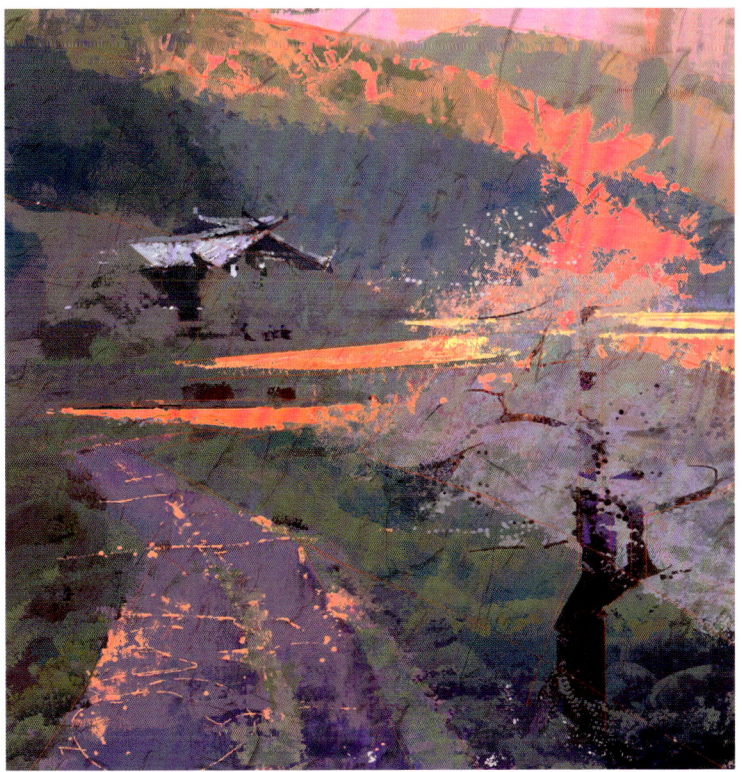

04. Strong light design can give your landscapes powerful aesthetic appeal

LOST & FOUND

Creating a *hierarchy of importance* in our environments is so important that I often restate it as we introduce new principles. The subject of 'lost and found' is no exception. Lost and found is when we let less-important elements disappear into adjacent areas, so that other elements take on a greater importance. Let's review some examples together.

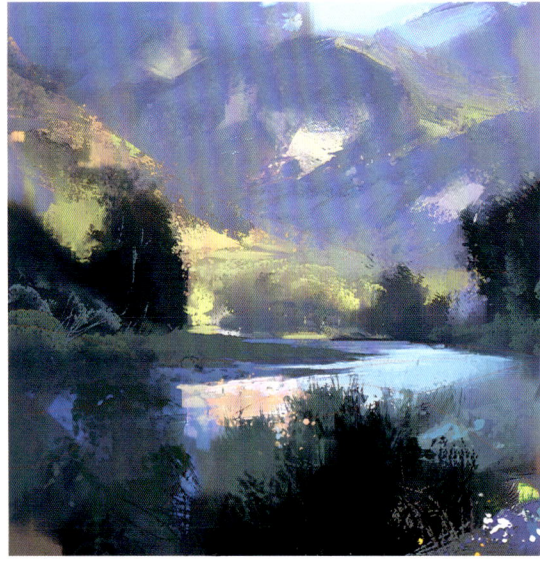

Great landscape painters ask themselves this very important question: 'What is it about this place that made me want to stop and paint it?' Then they make sure that every stroke serves that purpose.

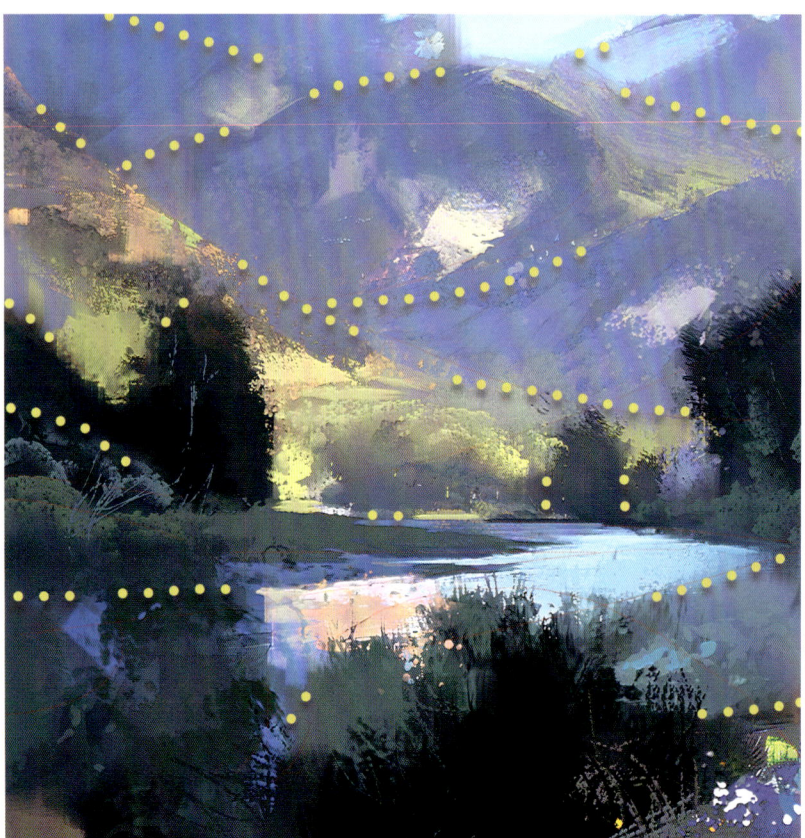

01. The dots indicate where edges and details were intentionally left out

01. EDITING OUT

This environment is based on a real place that I visited in Utah. This book is not a landscape-painting manual, but we can learn a great deal from that discipline. In this situation I did the thing that I believe strong landscape painters must often do: I asked myself the question, 'What is it about this place that made me want to stop and paint it?' The process after that is to make sure every stroke emphasizes that quality of purpose. If I force myself to stick to that, I have a shot at making art. If I drift off into the mindless painting of details, then there is no hope of a strong painting.

What I loved about this location were the passages of light contrasted with the strong darks in the mid-ground – so I 'found' those areas, so to speak, and let everything else become 'lost' in shadow.

I created a graphic for you to show all the areas where defined edges clearly existed, which I could see, but that I actively chose to *edit out*. I had decided what this image was going to be about and, by gosh, I fought the impulse to define every edge that I could see in favor of a more purposeful environment!

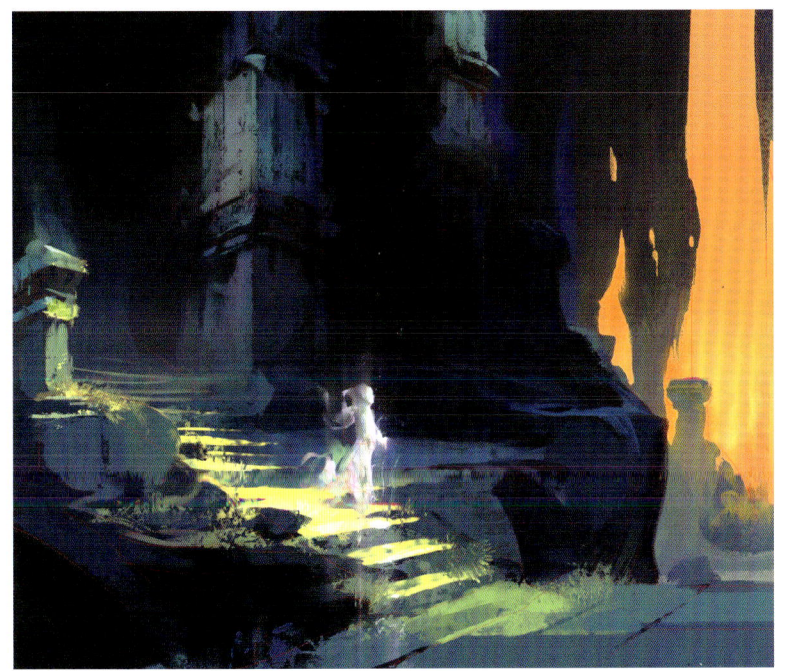

02. LOSING IN SHADOW

Let's switch to a mysterious and murky fantasy-scape to illustrate the principle of lost and found. Here we have some kind of ruin haunted by this spirit. The environment demands a sense of mystery! And you can't have mystery if you show everything to the audience. Let them become a participant in your environment. Create your images in such a way that you don't have to paint every detail, but rather your audience fills in the details for you with their imagination.

The graphic below shows the edges that I've allowed to completely disappear into adjacent shadows. We seem to perceive the standing columns as complete, even though much of their information has been 'lost'.

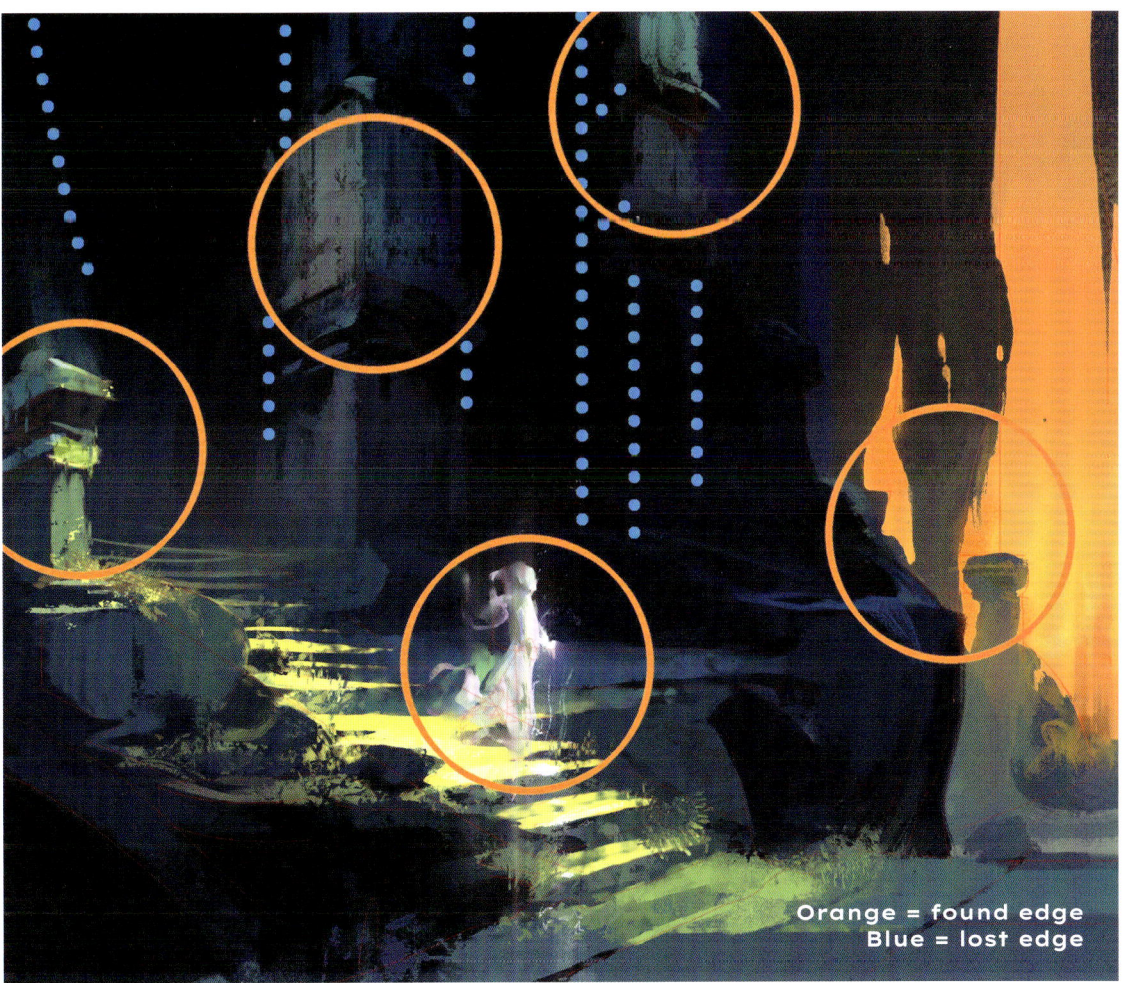

Orange = found edge
Blue = lost edge

02. We get a 'complete' impression of the pillars, but they're mostly hidden in shadow

03. LIGHT & SHADOW

I'm the type of person who's tempted to overuse the same solutions all the time, and I'm so horrified by this potential flaw that I go way out of my way to be sure I have a full range of solutions for visual problems. I can't rely on 'lost and found' in only dark shadows and distant hills in every case. So I've painted this scene for you, which is luminous in light *and* shadow, and I've carefully chosen what is lost and what is found in both. When we studied architecture earlier, I mentioned that when we need extreme simplification of detail on a building, we can often simply rely on windows. For this image I've 'found' the central character, the windows, and the important bits of jungle foliage, and 'lost' most everything else.

04. SIMPLE STATEMENTS

Have you ever had the experience of roughing out an idea and really liking the result, but when you brought it to a finish it lost its guts? Do you know why that happened? I do. It's because the comp didn't try and put information everywhere – it simply emphasized the more important elements of the scene and let everything else go. But when you undertook rendering it to a finish, you started 'finding' elements that weren't a part of the comp. The painting started becoming too much about elements that weren't important to the purpose, and so the whole thing fell apart. It lost its purpose. So I really enjoy doing loose paintings like this, because they remind me of the value of a simple statement, and one of the things that makes that statement so simple is the idea of lost and found.

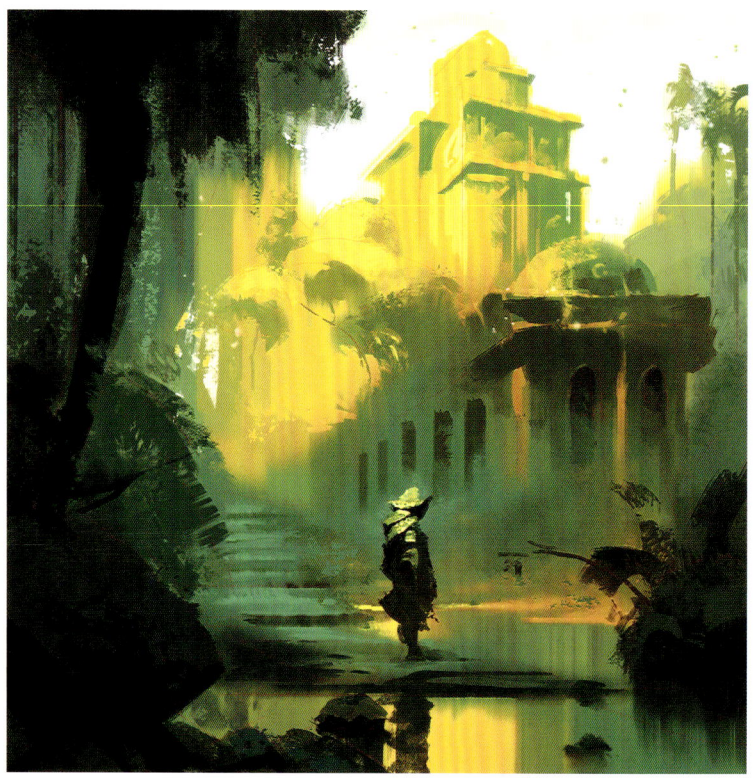

03. In this scene, details and edges disappear in light areas, too

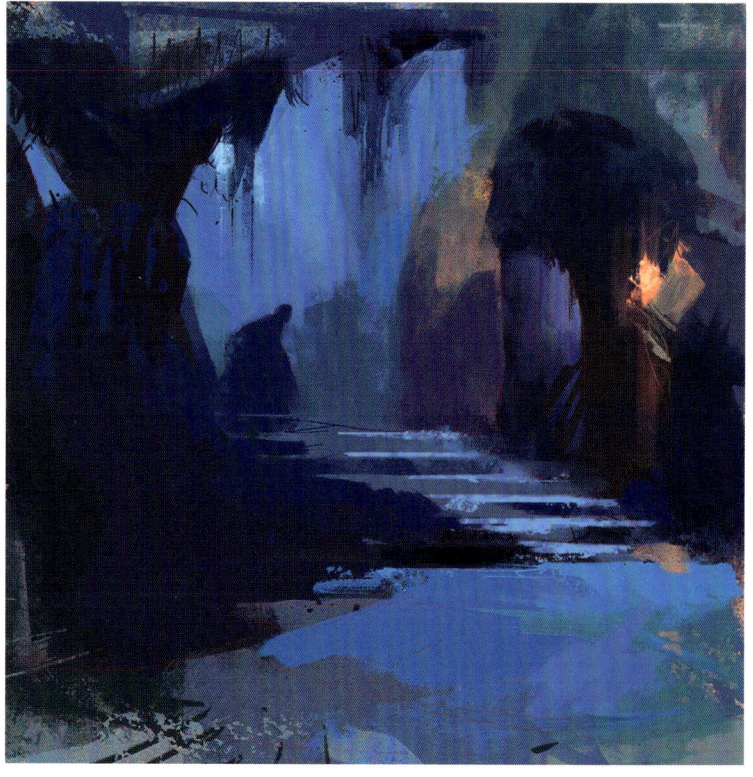

04. Practice making simple paintings with strong, simple goals in their lighting design

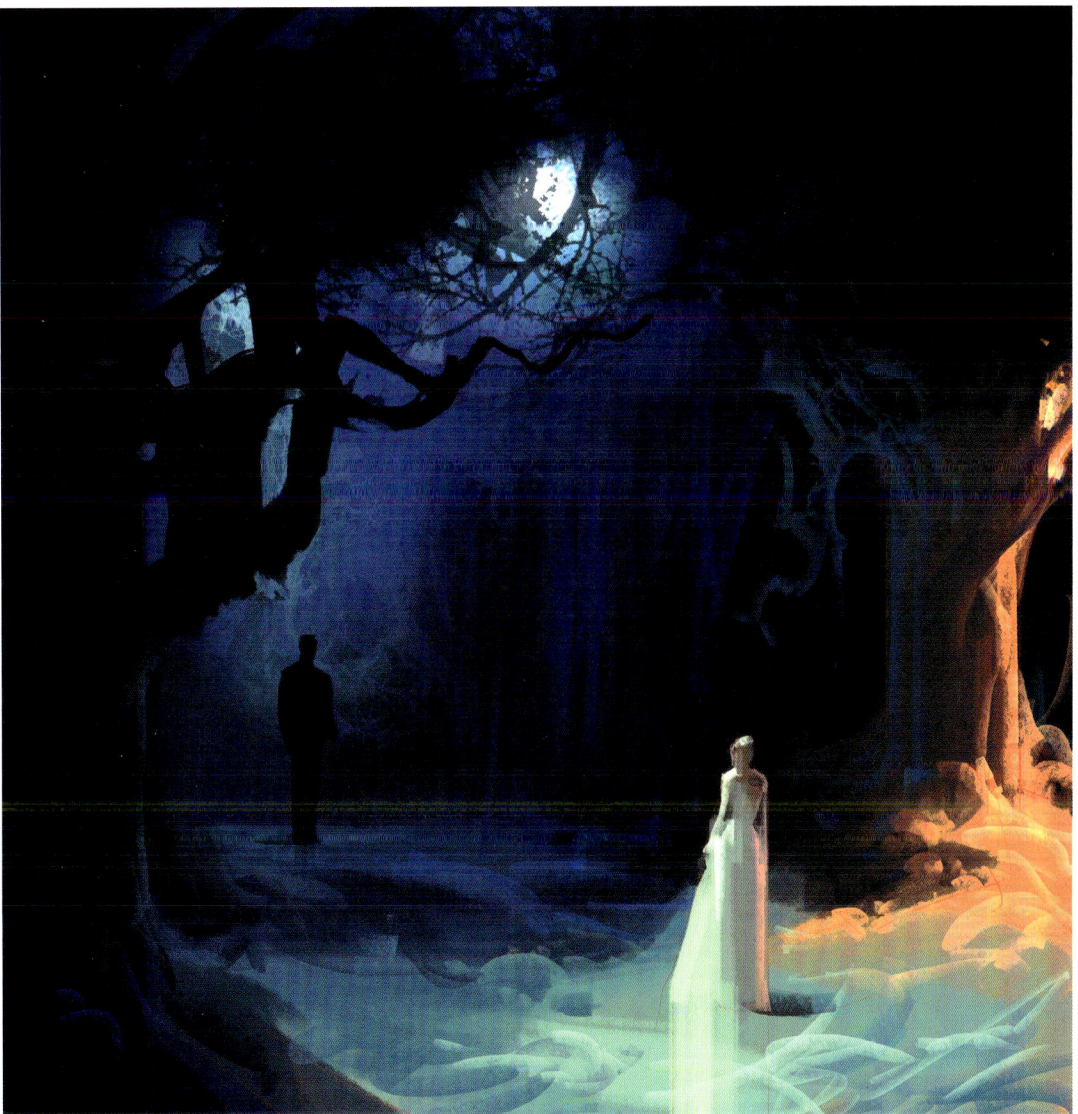

05. Here the focus is purely on emphasizing a narrative moment through lighting

05. SERVE THE MOMENT

For a proof of concept, let's look at a painting that is more definitive and finished than the previous one. Notice that I'm fighting to emphasize its purpose and let go of everything else! I believe the moment here is self-explanatory, and I'd like you to notice how the 'found' aspects of the environment are strategically placed and designed to serve that moment, and how almost everything else is 'lost'.

The concept of lost and found is profoundly important because our audience becomes a participant in the scene, with their own imagination filling in the gaps. If we over-render an image, it loses this quality – it's essentially talking down to the audience.

LIGHTING UP THE NIGHT

We've looked at this daytime cityscape before, but how would we handle it as a nighttime scene? We'll see shortly that there are many possible ways to design lighting at night, so we must design toward the purpose of the image. What's the purpose here? We have a massive freeway system leading us to a jam-packed metropolis that culminates in tall, iconic towers. We need to hold on to that idea but in a way that is new and different from the side-lit daytime version.

I decide to use the under-lighting that's typical of an active city at night, but then let the towers rise up into powerful silhouettes. I reinforce the silhouettes of the buildings by placing an exaggerated moon behind them, and for additional drama I set a bank of clouds between the two. The moon gives a sparkle of rim light to the city as well as illuminating the freeway system below.

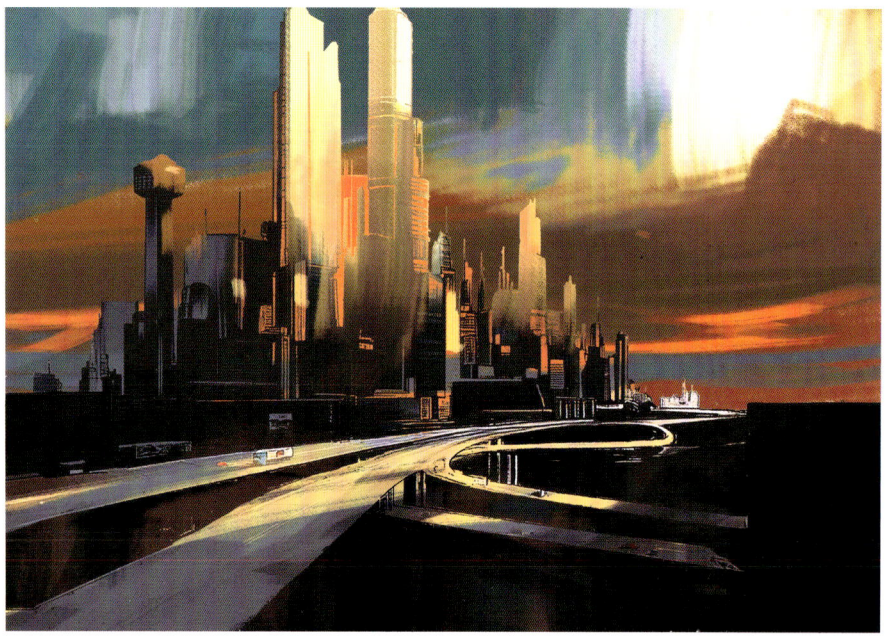

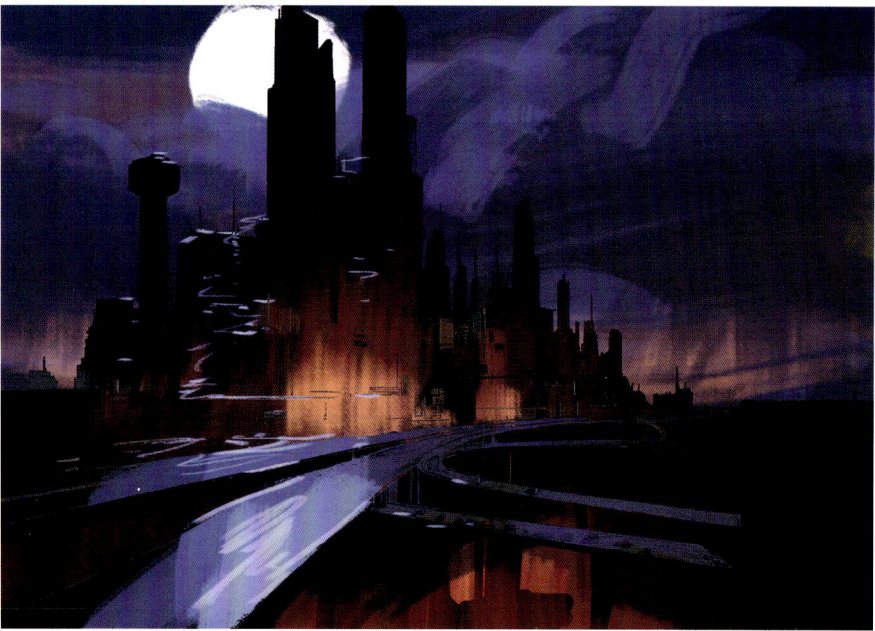

△ Nighttime encourages us to get creative with our illumination

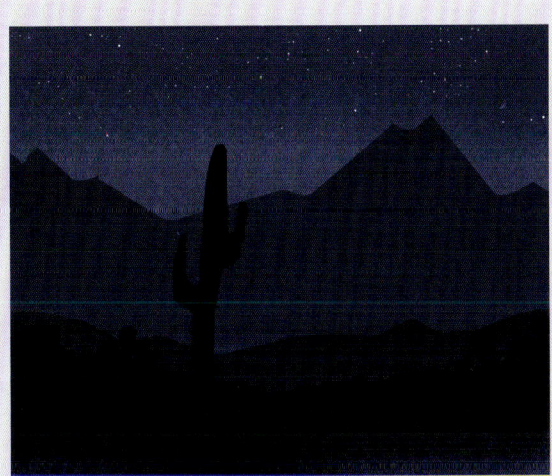

What a typical nighttime scene actually looks like. The sky is still a light source and is lighter than the landscape unless other light sources are present.

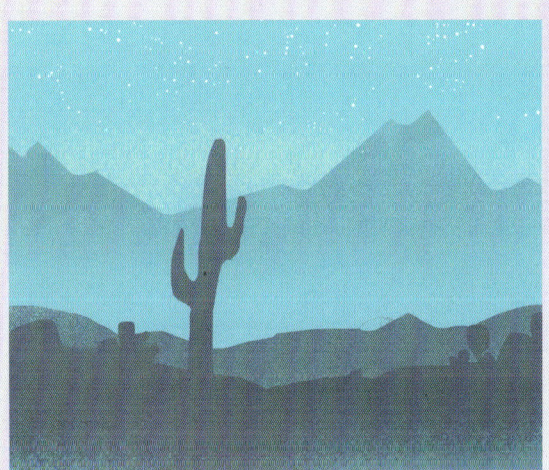

Night scenes can be hugely exaggerated depending on story needs. This is vastly brighter than the previous version but still feels like night – the key is stars and a cool or neutral color palette.

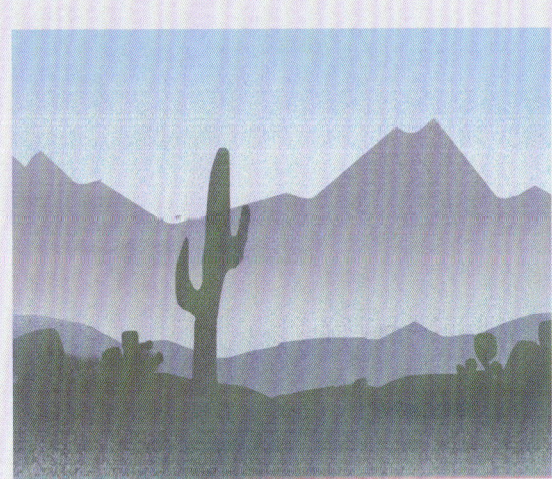

To prove the point, this scene has the same value structure as the previous but most viewers will not perceive it as night. It's more like a hazy dusk.

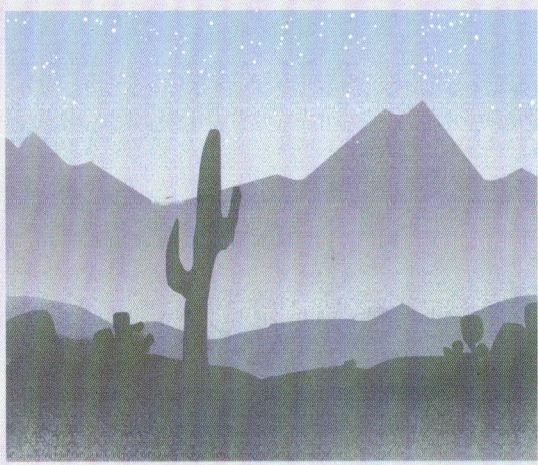

But if we simply add stars again, day turns to night! Night environments have a huge range of possibilities.

01. We can make night scenes that are light and colorful but still feel nocturnal

01. DAY FOR NIGHT

Let's get down to basics here. This batch of images begins with what we see under ordinary nighttime conditions, then compares the differences and similarities of nighttime and daytime conditions.

One useful idea is the cinematic process of 'day for night', as it's called in the movie business. We've all watched movies where nighttime scenes were filmed during the day and simply color-graded to feel like night. It's just too technically challenging and expensive to film with natural nighttime lighting in most situations. This was especially true in Western films during the 1960s, where moonlit scenes were filmed in full sun and a blue darkening filter was placed over the camera lens. So we've been primed to accept nighttime environments that have some of the qualities of day.

02. EMOTIONAL EXAGGERATION

Here are two versions of a painting inspired by a place where I camped with my family in the moonlight. It was a unique place and a unique moment, and I believed it deserved a painting. For me a painting is almost always a depiction of an emotional experience rather than a literal depiction of the place. To give you an idea of the level of emotional exaggeration, I altered the image to match my recollection of what the lighting was actually like. This is shown in the smaller image to the right. Some might prefer the darker, brooding quality of this image, and I like it too, but that wasn't the point I wanted to make on this occasion. That's the luxury of nighttime lighting – it can be altered, pushed, and exaggerated to fit our needs.

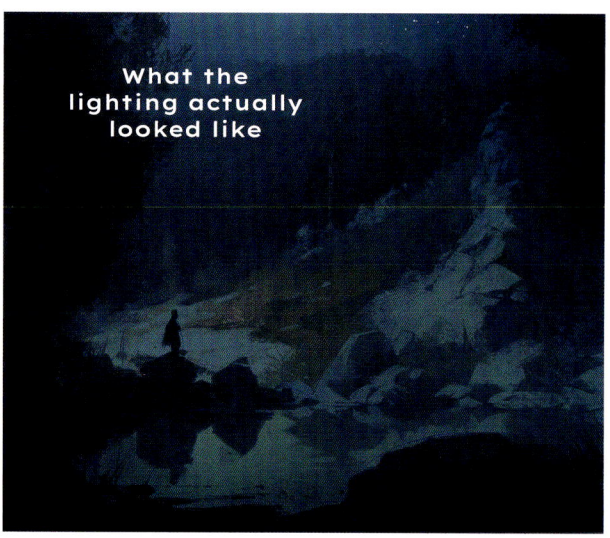

What the lighting actually looked like

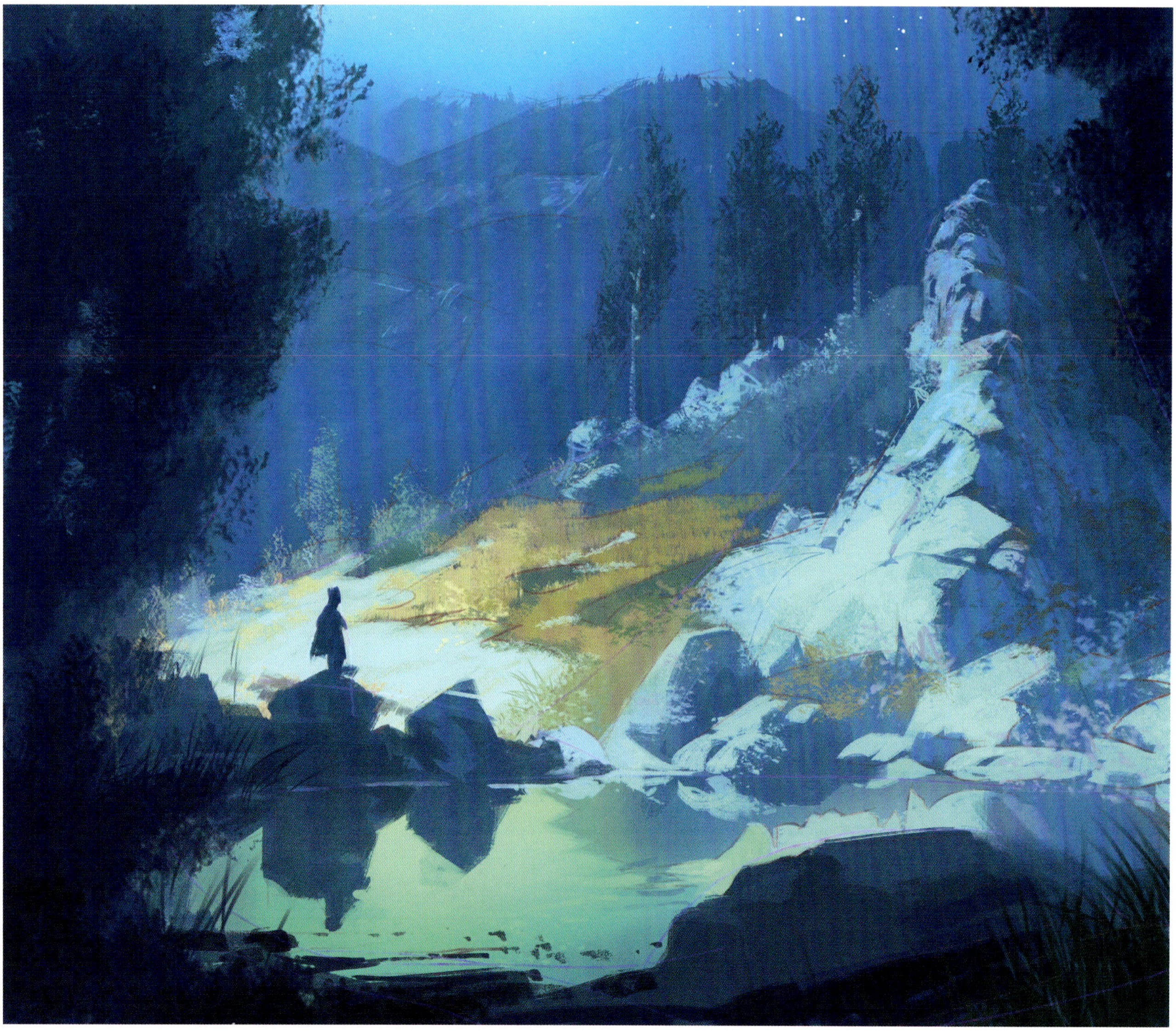

02. The final painting targets an emotional quality of luminosity, peacefulness, and mystery

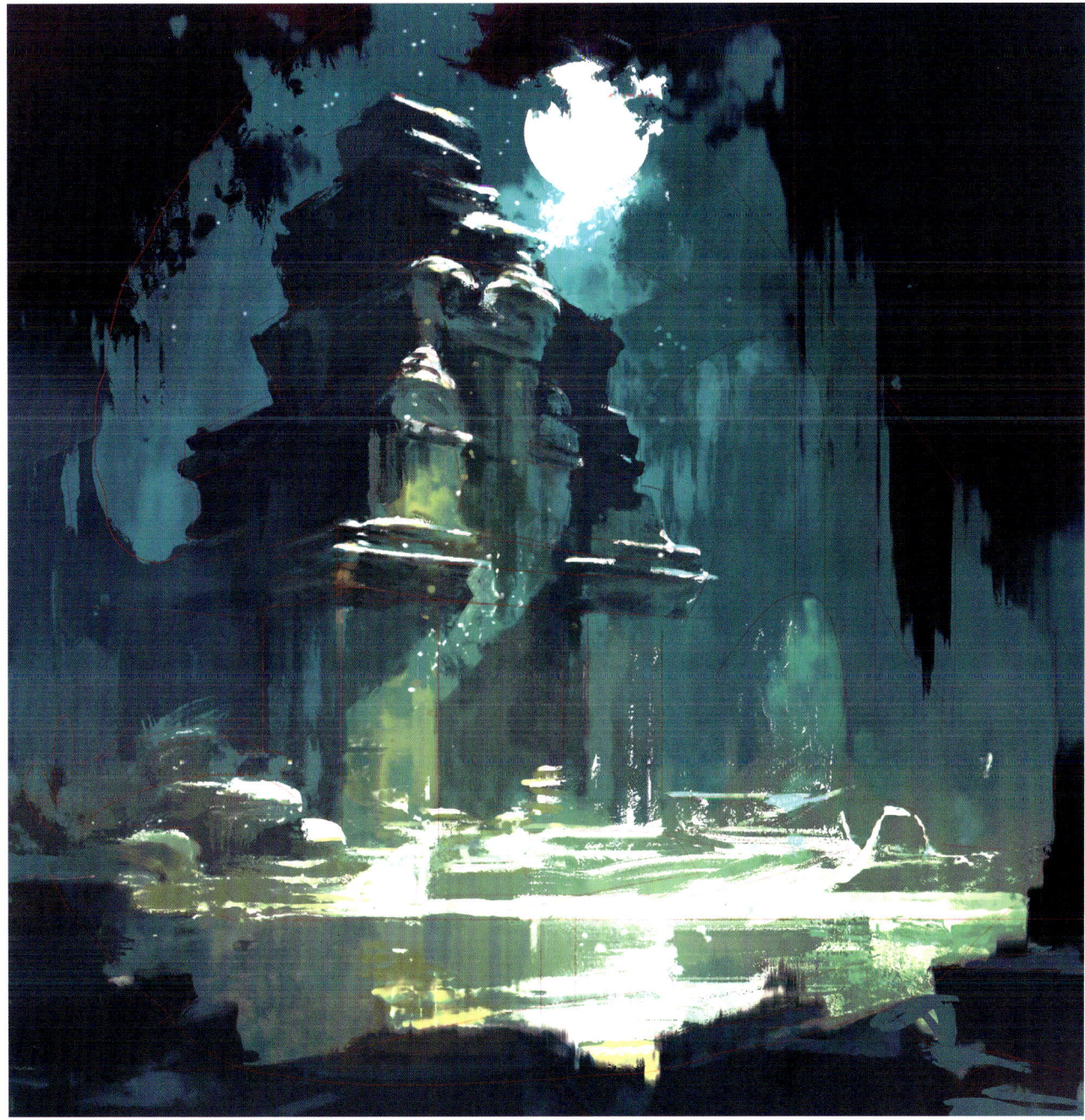

03. A cool, monochromatic night scene doesn't have to feel dim or muted

03. VIBRANT PALETTES

With the right context clues, you can get away with just about anything and call it a night. As we saw in the previous images, the basics for nighttime are cool or neutral temperatures and a starry sky. That's it – sometimes that's all it takes to convince our audience that it's night. And of course we can throw in the moon, as I've done in this image.

Local colors can be seen under moonlight but are hugely diminished, so I make this image lean toward a more monochromatic cyan color palette. I let some mossy greens creep into the ruins and brought a touch of magenta into the foreground elements for a little color contrast. The saturated cyan backdrop is an exaggeration, of course – we do whatever it takes to give our environment the quality of purpose and emotion that we need!

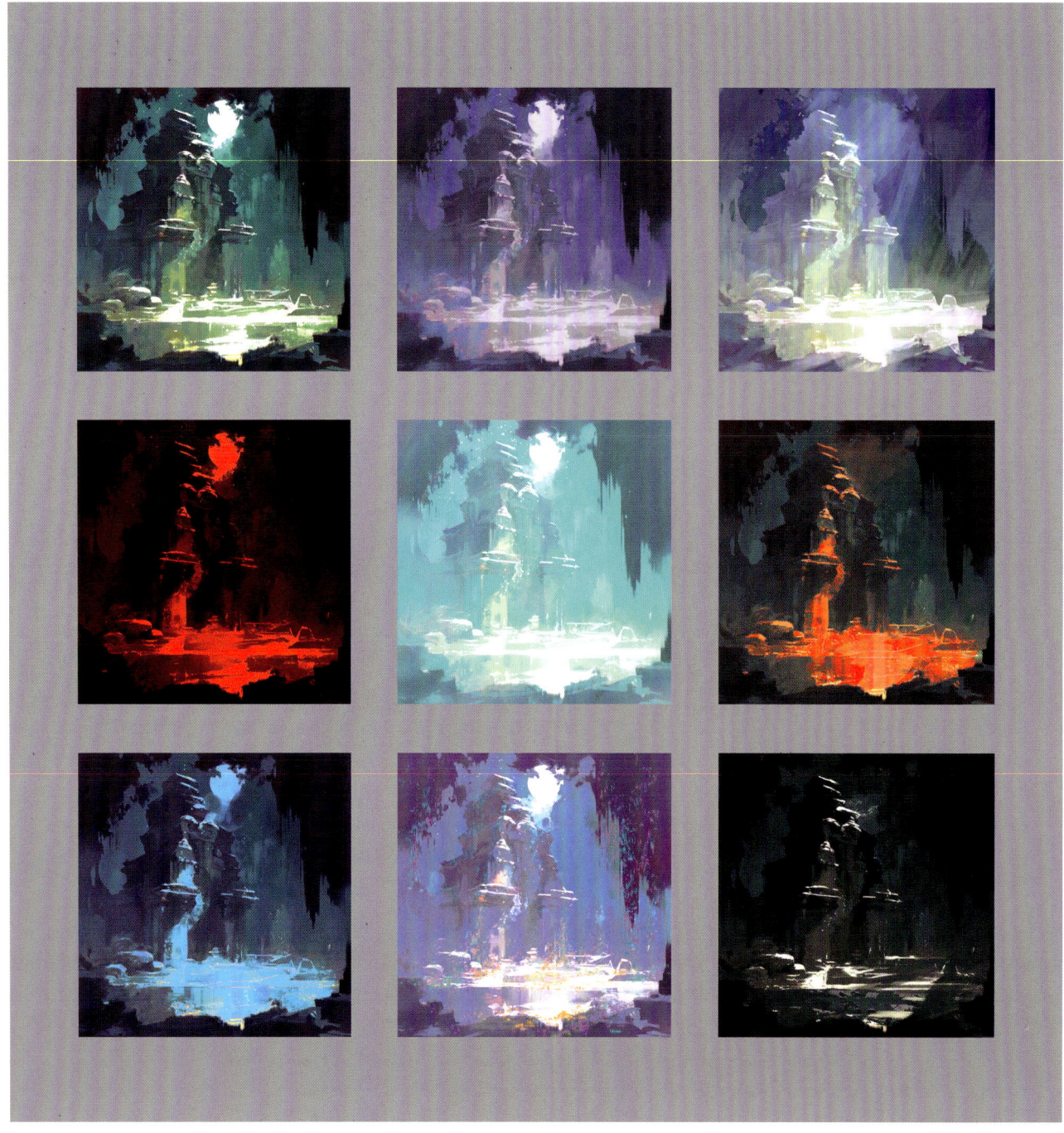

04. There are so many potential approaches to a nighttime scene!

04. ANYTHING GOES AT NIGHT

As a proof of concept, I've taken the previous image and exaggerated it about as far as I can to illustrate the idea of pushing nocturnal scenes to an extreme. There's no reason your nighttime scenes must always go to extremes – sometimes simple reality is called for – but don't hold back when it's time to get emotional.

Sometimes all it takes to bring night to our environments is a cool or neutral color palette and a starry sky.

05. A luminous green sky can give a nighttime scene warmth and contrast

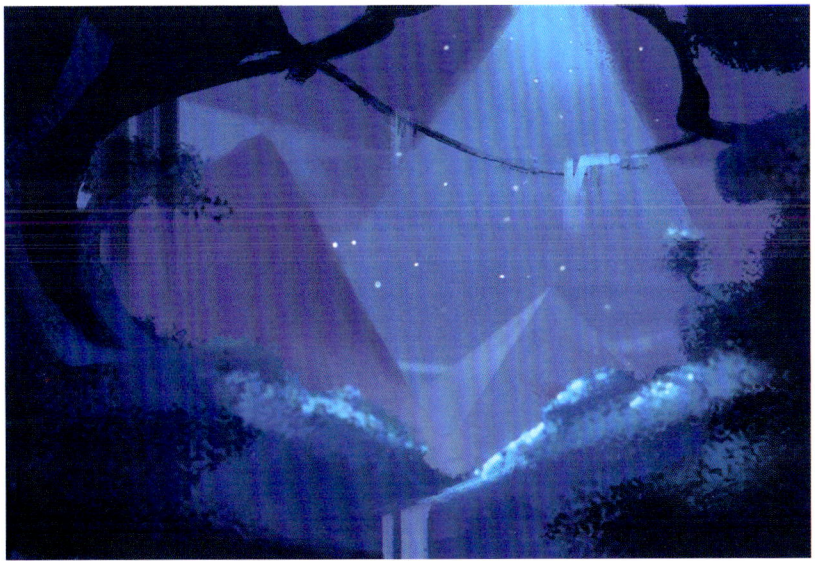

06. Don't limit your options to blues and greens. How about a purple sky?

05. GREEN NIGHT

There's a history of nighttime paintings that shift toward green – you've likely seen many. I can't speak for those artists, but I suspect their reasoning was the same as mine: the environment is more visually lush and interesting when it has a color versus the neutral hues of true night. We often use blue as the color solution, but shifting that color toward green gives a warmer, luminous, and surreal presence to the nighttime atmosphere. It's as if the spectral luminosity is a character playing their role in our environment. And there's a very simple and practical reason as well: nighttime firelight is usually red-orange, so when we lend an atmospheric green to the environment, we gain the rich contrast of a red/green color combination.

06. PURPLE NIGHT

I put together this image that intentionally has an altogether different style and lighting palette. I've moved away from spectral greens into fun but mysterious purples in this nighttime scene of purple pyramids and funky foliage. Green skies are fun but we have to be versatile.

295

07. INDOOR NIGHTS

We've been exclusively focusing on the outdoors – that's what we think of when we think 'environment' – but indoor locations need our attention too. Let's let ourselves into a spooky gothic mansion that has moonlight streaming through the windows. I've reached for green again in the lighting. Why? To contrast with the red carpet, of course! And there are similar constraints we can follow to help the quality of 'moonlight': the neutral local colors are depicted as cool in temperature and the deep shadows have little to no detail.

08. DAY OR NIGHT?

Is this scene of rocky monoliths day or night? It certainly could be presented as day with a heavy overcast, but I've decided that this is to be another luminous night, and it's the stars in the upper-right corner that make the difference.

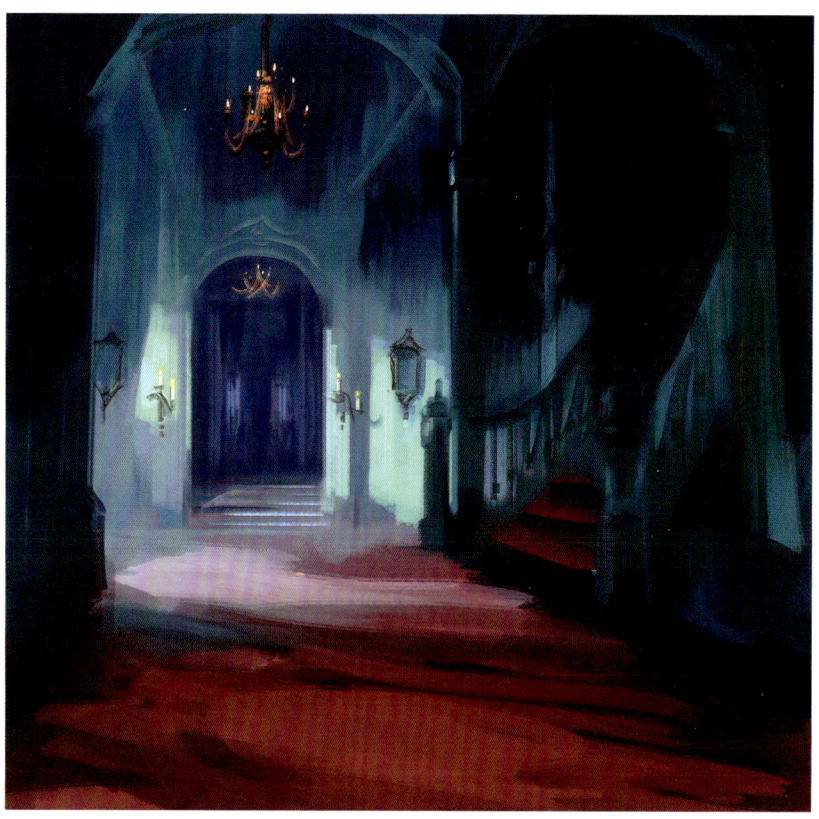

07. Sometimes we need to convey a nocturnal quality even when indoors

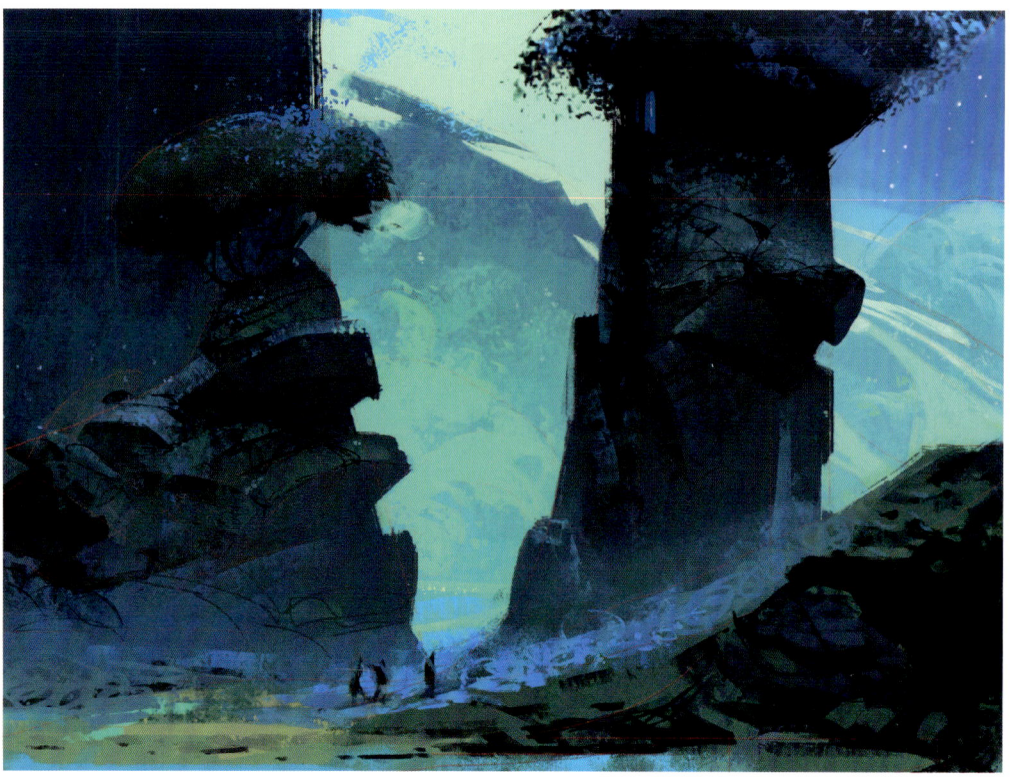

08. The use of stars makes the difference between daytime and stylized night

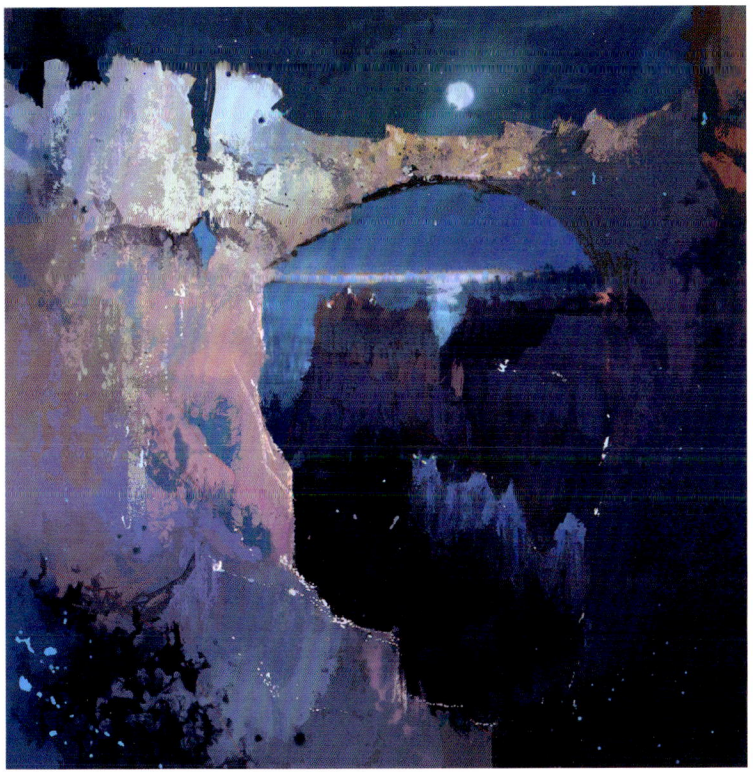

09. A stylized mix of day and night lighting is a legitimate cheat if it serves your artistic purpose

09. RED ROCK ARCH

Now let's really ask the question of whether this scene is day or night. Well, I like to mix and match! Everything about this says 'night', but I'm allowing the last rays of sunset to hold on a couple hours too long to light up that foreground arch. This environment is inspired by Utah's red-rock canyons, and cool ambient light and a little warm sunset light on such a local color is something really special. So the lighting here is a cheat, and one that I'm proud of.

10. SUN OR MOON?

Let's go to an even further extreme with this one. Is that the sun in the background or is it the moon? It doesn't matter. This is art, baby – we can do anything we want! And we should. As always, our environments are meant to create a unique experience for our audience. If taking them to an ethereal twilight fits the story we're telling, then that's what we must do.

10. If it looks good it is good, even if it might be technically wrong!

Is that the moon or the sun? It doesn't matter. We're creating a unique experience for our audience, and taking them to an ethereal twilight fits the story, so that's what we must do.

STAGING WITH LIGHT

Here we are in another fantasy nighttime scene, but from this point forward we'll jump around to whatever time of day and quality of light is appropriate for our environment. There's a bit of a story behind this image. My wife and I went to a Broadway play, which was something about somebody stealing some bread – I don't really remember because all I could focus on the whole time was the staging created by the lighting design. It was really well done!

I've always loved stage lighting, and this play made me realize my style of environment design can and should include treating the environment as if it's a stage. In fact, in animation it almost always is. The environment is a place where a story moment unfolds through character action, just like a play on a stage.

I came home from the play and made this image to explore this idea. You might note that the previous image was also very staged in lighting, but the difference here is that I'm going for something more intimate: a place that's not pulling you into vast distances or monolithic canyons, but a closed-off stage where a focused story can unfold.

So here we have the effect of cold backlighting, warm side-lights, and a spotlight on our central character. It's a strong affectation, but under the right circumstances it works.

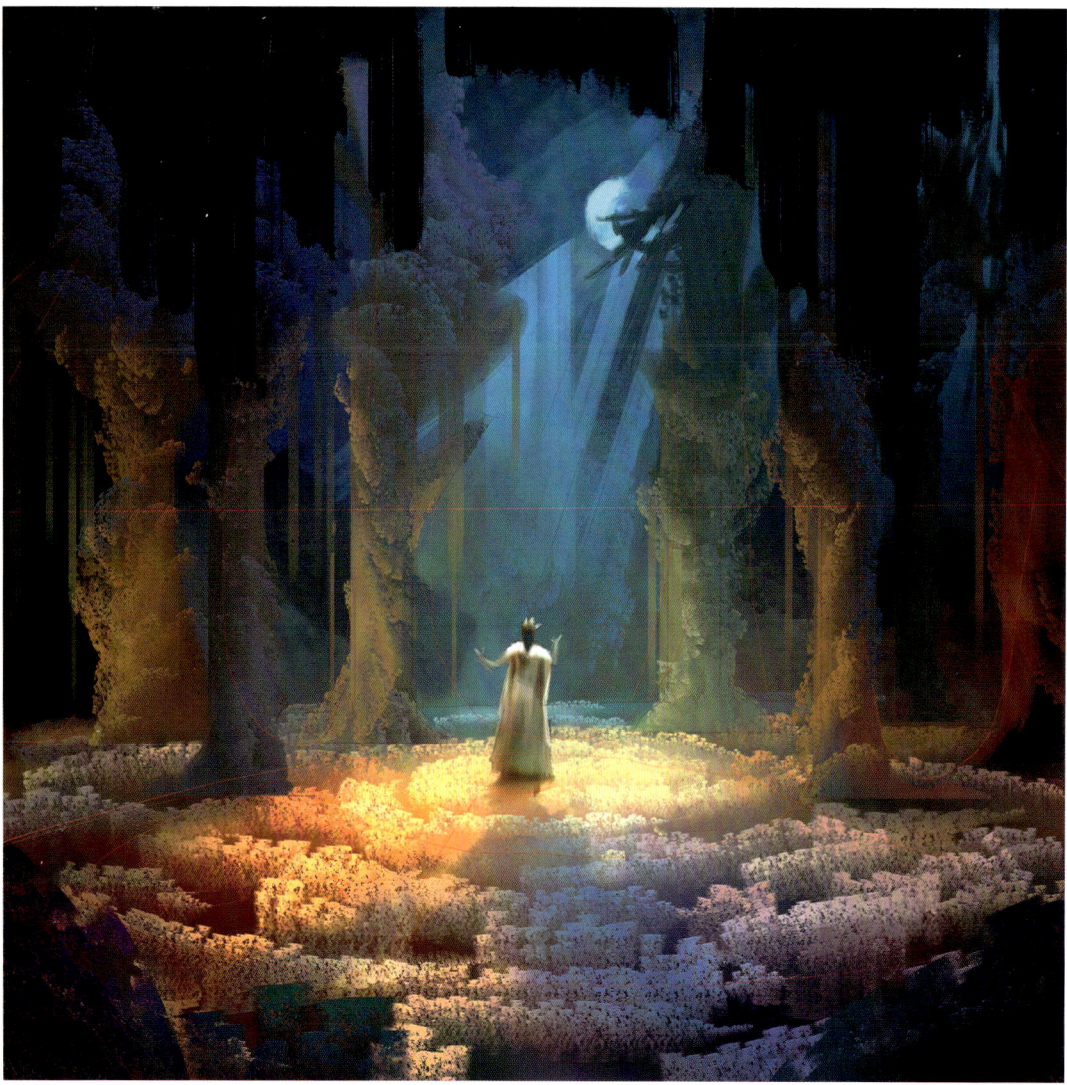

△ This carefully staged lighting was inspired by the lighting design of a play

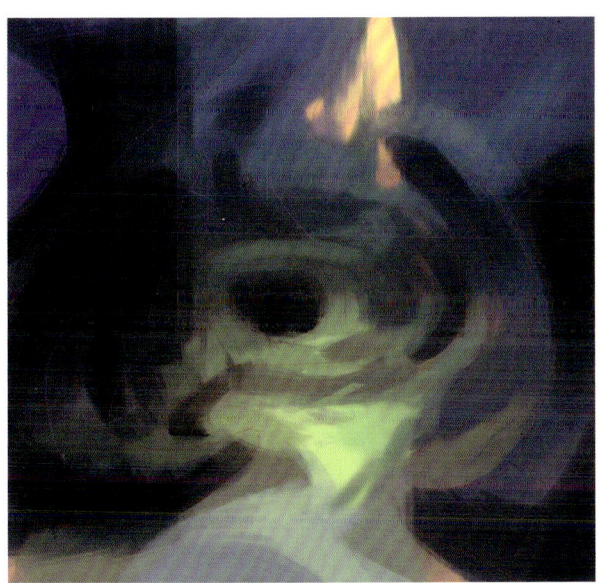

01. WOODLAND SCENE

Now let's bring the idea of staging to a more organic environment. I've included the rough lay-in on the left, so you can see how the environment is carefully designed to wrap around the center 'stage' area. For the spotlighting effect I'm using green to really get us into the forest vibe, as well as cool purples filtering down into the background. I don't want the area to feel completely closed off, so there is an opening in the background to suggest we're seeing through a thicket of trees to a distant sunset sky. You can see how effective the results are below. Now we're all set for something to unfold in this carefully crafted environment!

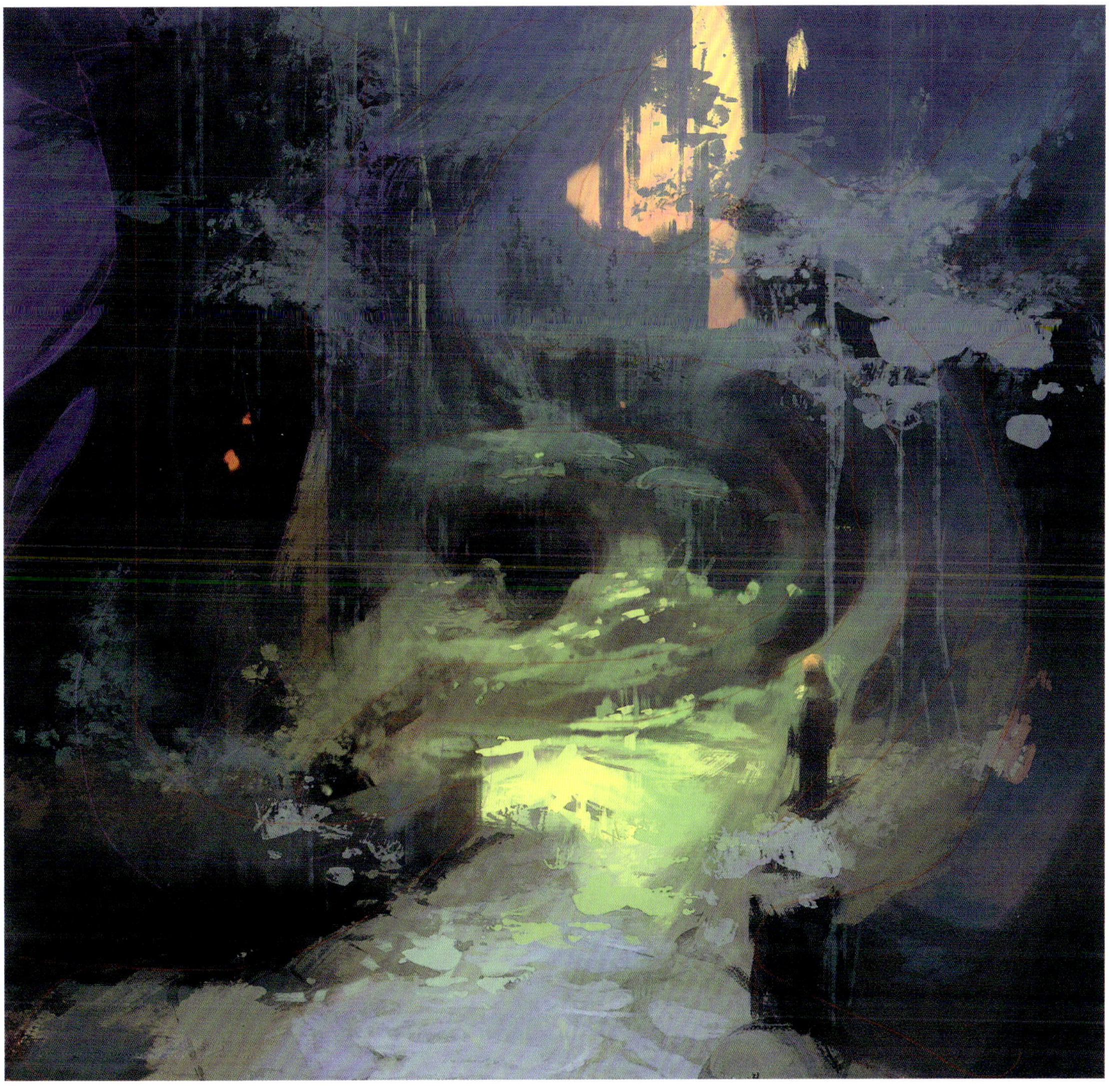

01. The location and lighting are all shaped around the 'stage' where the story happens

02. TWO TREES

This is a painting about a light tree and a dark tree interacting with each other. I want to lead you to their bases then lift you up into the shadowy canopy. The layout and composition is organized to do this, but the frosting on the cake is the lighting – it's carefully staged to achieve the purpose of the image.

03. CENTER-STAGE SAPLING

Staged images often aren't meant to look completely natural – they're meant to be intensely focused on a purpose. That's the nature of a fantasy image: we immediately know that it's molded to a purpose. So what's the molding in the case below? Well, we have a little sapling that is clearly the focus of all the fantasy styling. It must be important. It must have some sort of value, magic, or intrigue. That's what the picture is telling us, because everything about it is staging the grand entrance of this little sapling.

To make this clearer, I've also broken down the scene for you into the layers and groupings that are staged to achieve this goal.

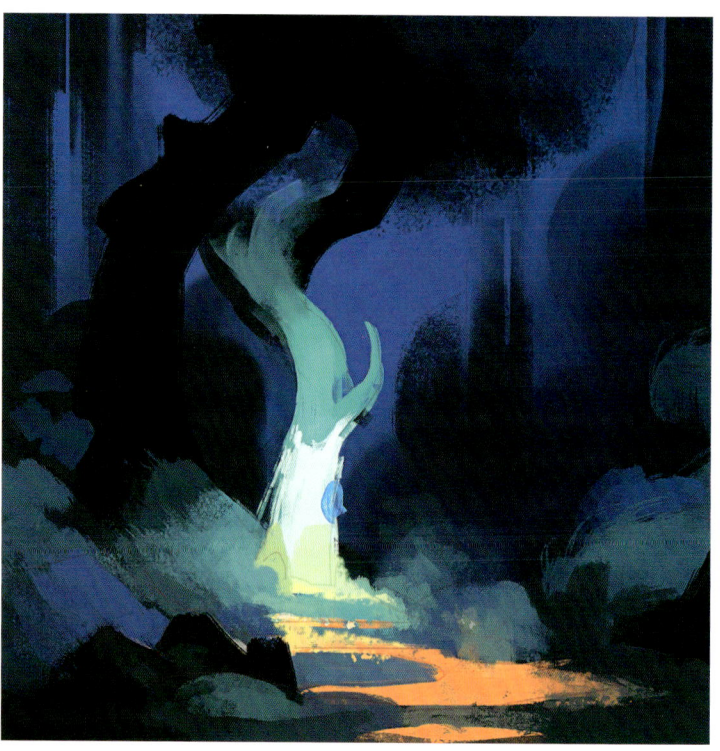

02. Note how the lighting guides the viewer along the trees from bottom to top

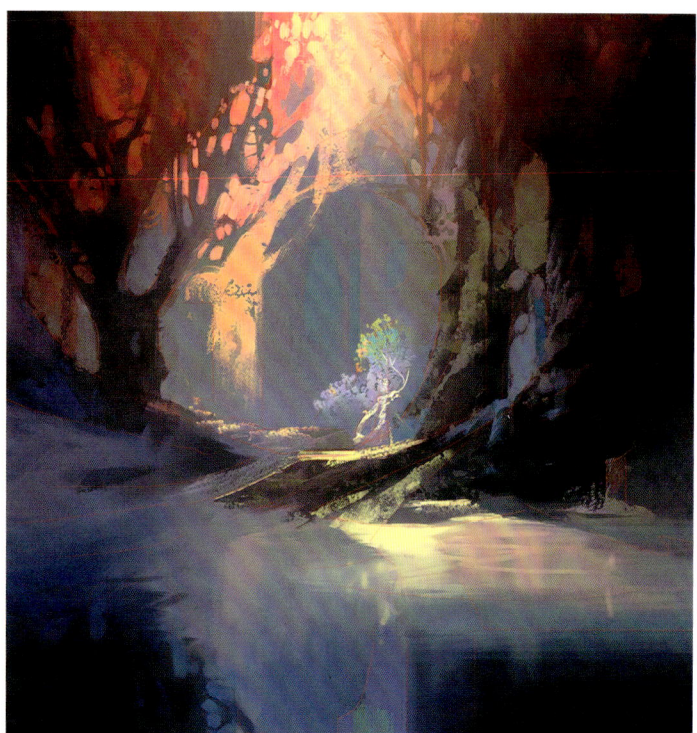

Why is staging a useful idea? Because everything on and around the stage is carefully arranged to serve an intensely focused purpose.

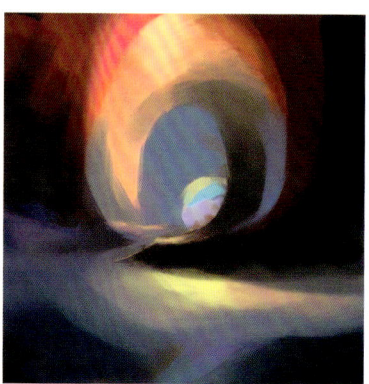

03. The tiny tree is clearly the centerpiece of this scene, with everything molded around it

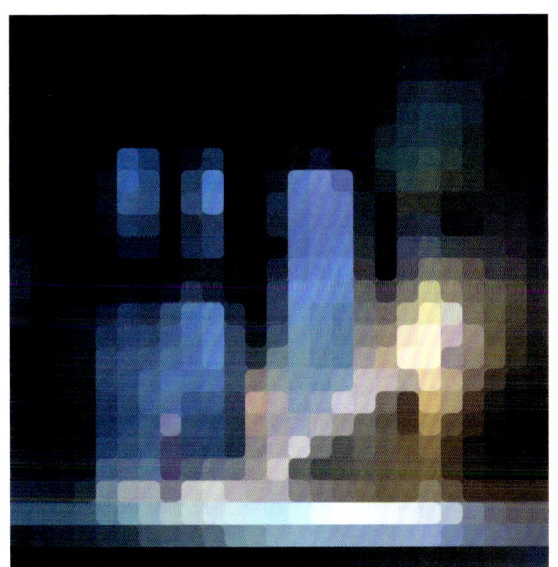

04. A THEATRICAL SCENE

Because I love operatic staging so much, I've put together this study that is actually meant to look like an opera stage in full set-dressing and lighting. Is this an image about grand architecture? Nope. It's about the timeless story of a young man and a young woman making a connection. Everything is carefully framed, staged, and illuminated toward that one purpose. I've also made a tile version of the image to help you see the simple arrangement of the color palette and lighting.

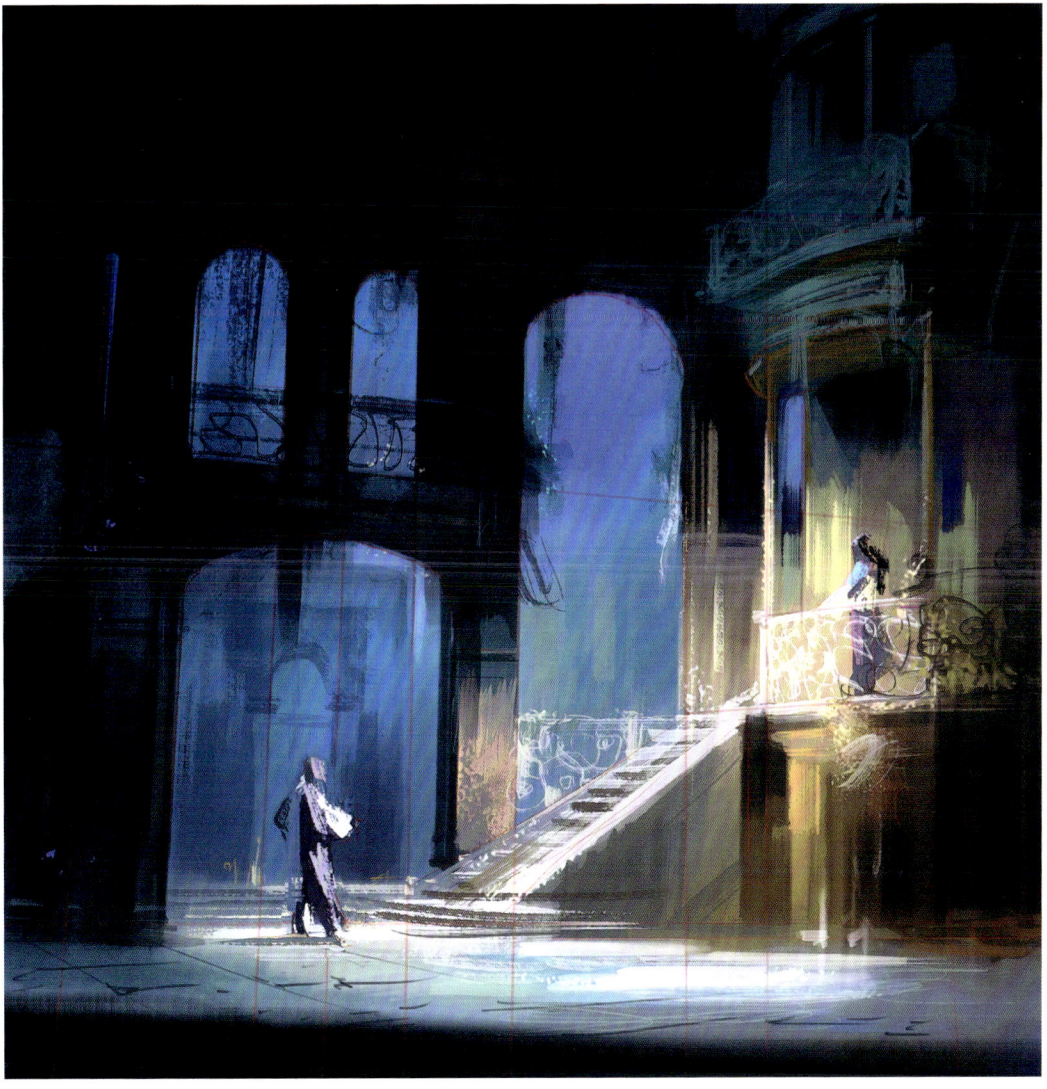

04. This image stages a clear narrative and even resembles a theater stage

DON'T OVERUSE SPOTLIGHTING!

I have spent the last several images telling you to use spotlighting, but that was just one tiny section in this massive book. Spotlighting is so immediately effective that up-and-coming artists have a tendency to throw a spotlight into every image, but doing so is *really, really bad*. It becomes a formula that makes every environment feel the same. Yes, use spotlighting when it's time for powerful staging, but look for other solutions. For instance, remember the 'color surprise' from the last chapter? When you find yourself tempted to overuse spotlighting, try a brilliant color hue contrast instead.

For this reason I've made the antidote image below. It's a careful study in lighting design to create a quality of purpose, but it doesn't just throw a spotlight on the subject. It's my attempt at greater subtlety. The road grabs us and leads us to the destination and, to reward the viewer, the road ends in a rich contrast of color hue and temperature. I've taken advantage of the Japanese cherry blossom trees that are fully in shadow but loaded with cool skylight. Then I've given them a backdrop of deep, warm sunset light that is nearly the same value as the cool light on the tree. This gives us a richness of color-hue contrast, without overusing blown-out lighting contrast.

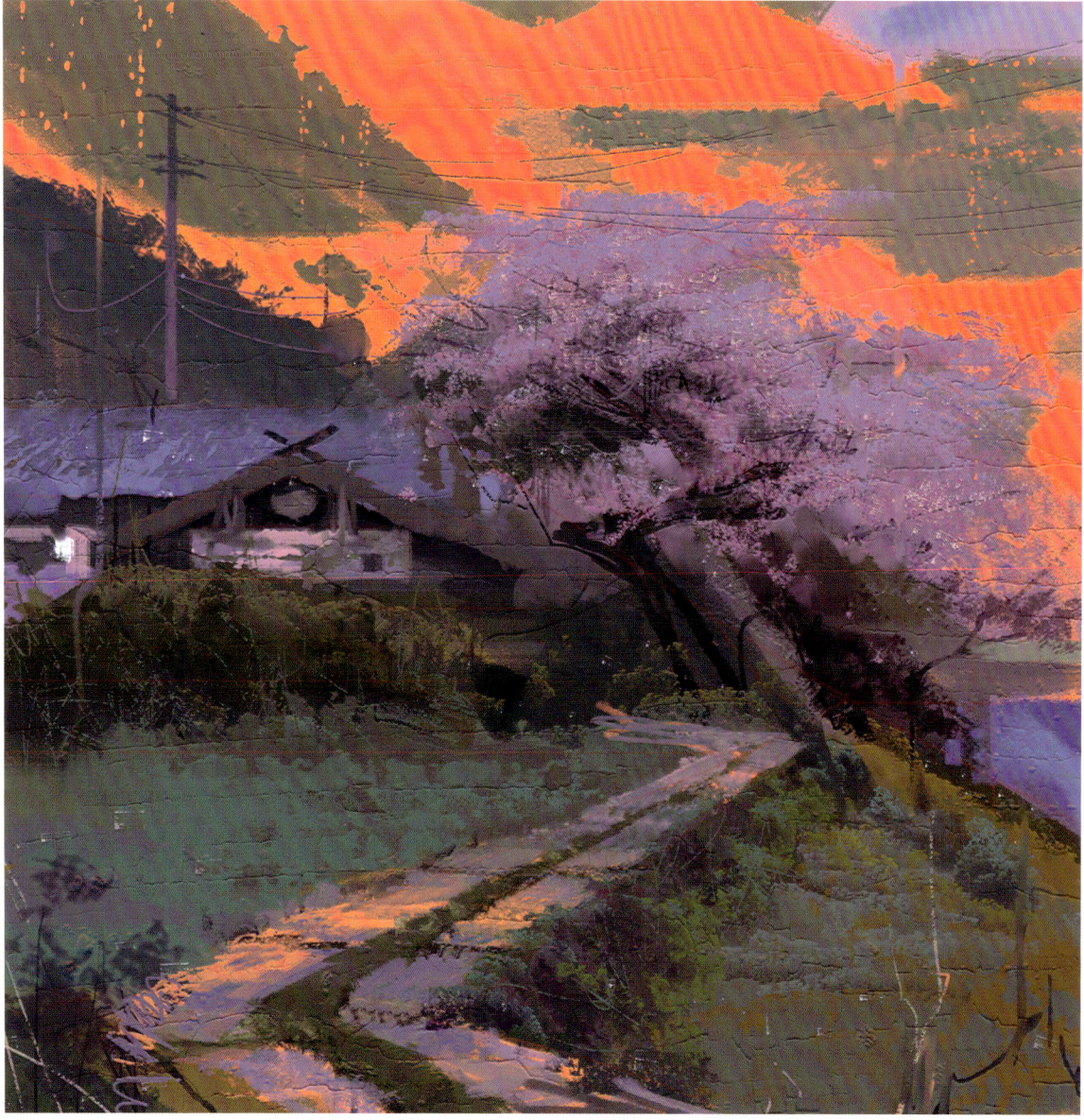

△ This image's composition is striking and purposeful without leaning on spotlighting

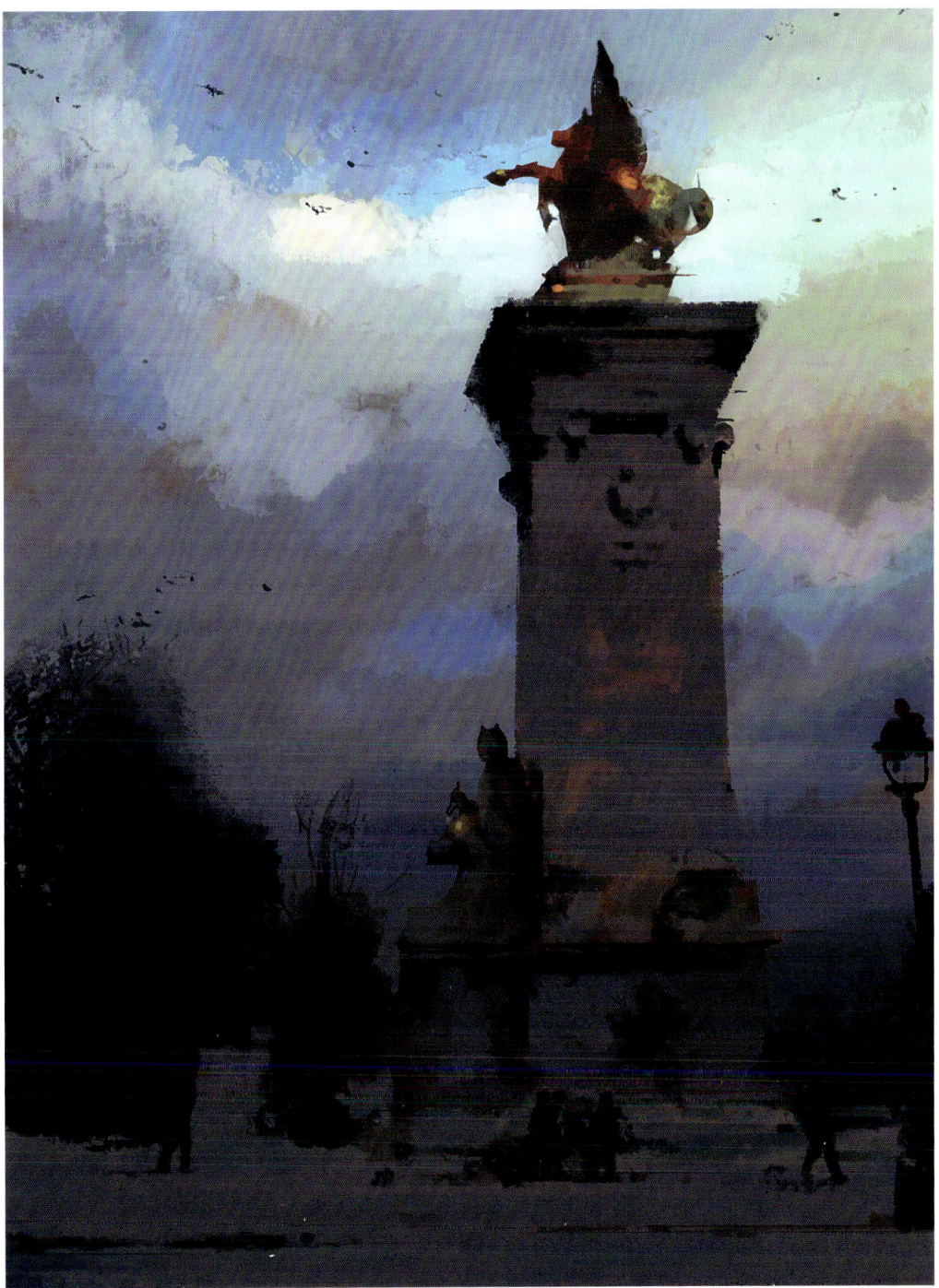

01. A dark object against light is a classic way to approach silhouette

01. SILHOUETTING WITH LIGHT

This is a place that you may recognize if you've traveled to Paris – it's a spot on the Pont Alexandre III. I was visiting the bridge and was inspired by the monument and *had* to do a painting. It's a monument of grandeur and authority, and thus needed to be depicted in a way that conveyed this sense of purpose. I chose to show it rising up and culminating in a bold silhouette. I kept the values fairly grouped on the subject and used the illuminated sky to give the winged horse at the crest the most contrast. I've used lighting design to create a purposeful silhouette of my subject.

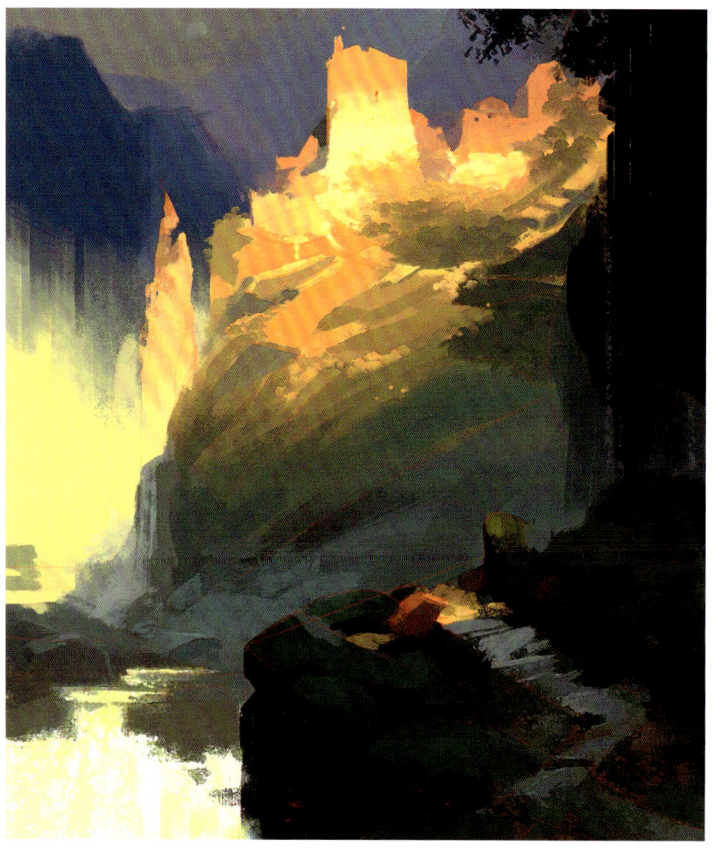

02. You can also set a light shape against a dark backdrop

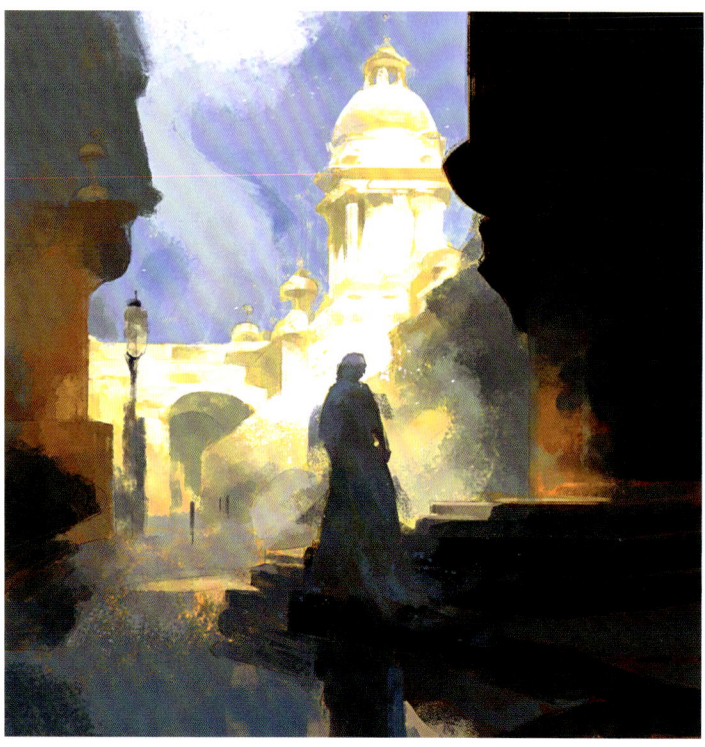

03. This image uses both dark and light silhouettes

02. LIGHT AGAINST DARK

The previous image was a case of silhouetting the subject by setting up dark values against light, but this image does the opposite. Here I've used illumination to create a light silhouette against a darker backdrop. Sometimes we make the destination in an environment special by adding detail and lots of contrast, but that wouldn't work well in an image such as this. Although in ruin, this castle still needs to command authority and convey grandeur as it sits atop the rise in this fantasy environment. To achieve this, I've silhouetted it in the light of dusk against a darkened sky.

03. MIXING DARK & LIGHT

I'm setting up an intentional progression for you. We've looked at dark against light and light against dark, so how about we do both now? This image takes the idea even further.

I had a lot of fun with this one – I call it *The Ghost of Berlin*. It's set against the Gendarmenmarkt square and background cathedral; the cathedral is made of light marble, and in full sunlight it silhouettes beautifully against a deep-blue sky. To contrast that I have the 'ghost' silhouetted as dark in the foreground. Note that the ghost still has a fairly light local color compared to the surrounding stone – it's simply in deep shadow.

Setting these two vertical elements against each other is the central theme of this composition. I've roughed out a simple black-and-white graphic to show you the core of the silhouetted relationships I was targeting in this image.

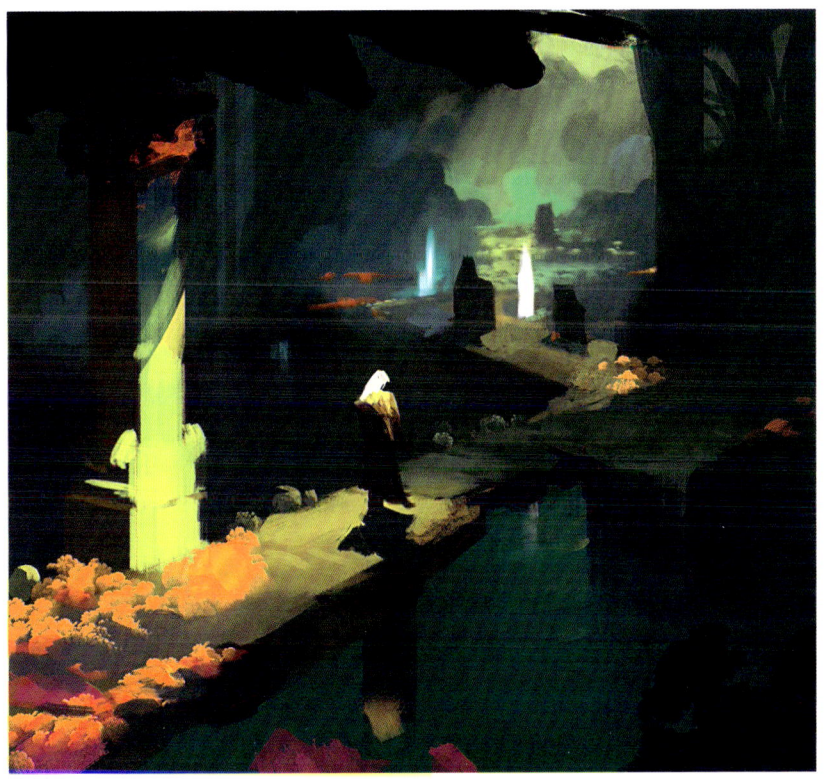

04. THE TRAVELER

I have a white-haired character that I like to sketch from time to time passing through strange fantasy and sci-fi environments. I call him 'the traveler'. (Maybe you and I can get together someday and make a video game about him!) He has white hair because it always silhouettes beautifully against various environmental elements.

My goal for this environment is to convince the audience that our traveler will be passing through great distances in this fantasy-scape. How do we achieve that? There's already been a whole chapter on the subject of space, but I've got a tidbit to add for you here. In this image I'm flip-flopping silhouettes as we go from front to back: I'm going to light, then dark, then light, then dark again, and so forth into the far recess of the mountains. Do you see it? The simplified black-and-white graphic helps show my idea more clearly.

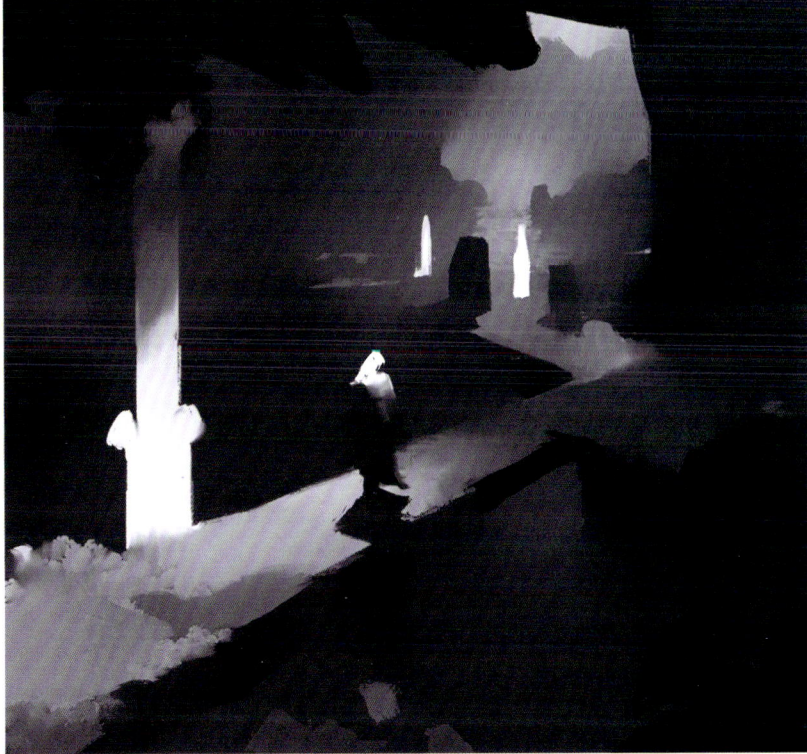

04. This fantasy scene uses light and dark silhouettes to add layers of distance

DEMONSTRATION: STAGING A COMPLEX NIGHT SCENE WITH LIGHT

Here's the final image we'll be looking at for our step-by-step demonstration. Let's take a moment to state the purpose and the emotion of the image. We have a speaker garbed in white addressing a mysterious crowd of forest people up on the ridge behind the tree.

My goal is for the scene to have operatic staging but also a depth of environment that goes beyond what's possible on a stage. The emotional tone is meant to be ancient, shadowy, and enchanting, as if it's a place that's hiding secrets. I've also created a simplified version of the image so you can see the basic organization that we'll be targeting.

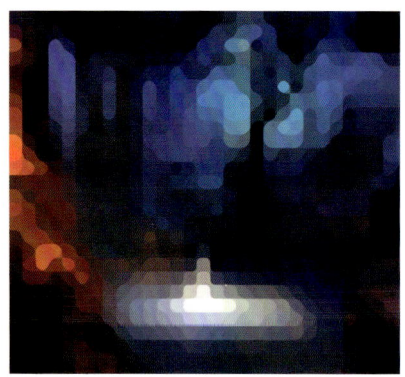

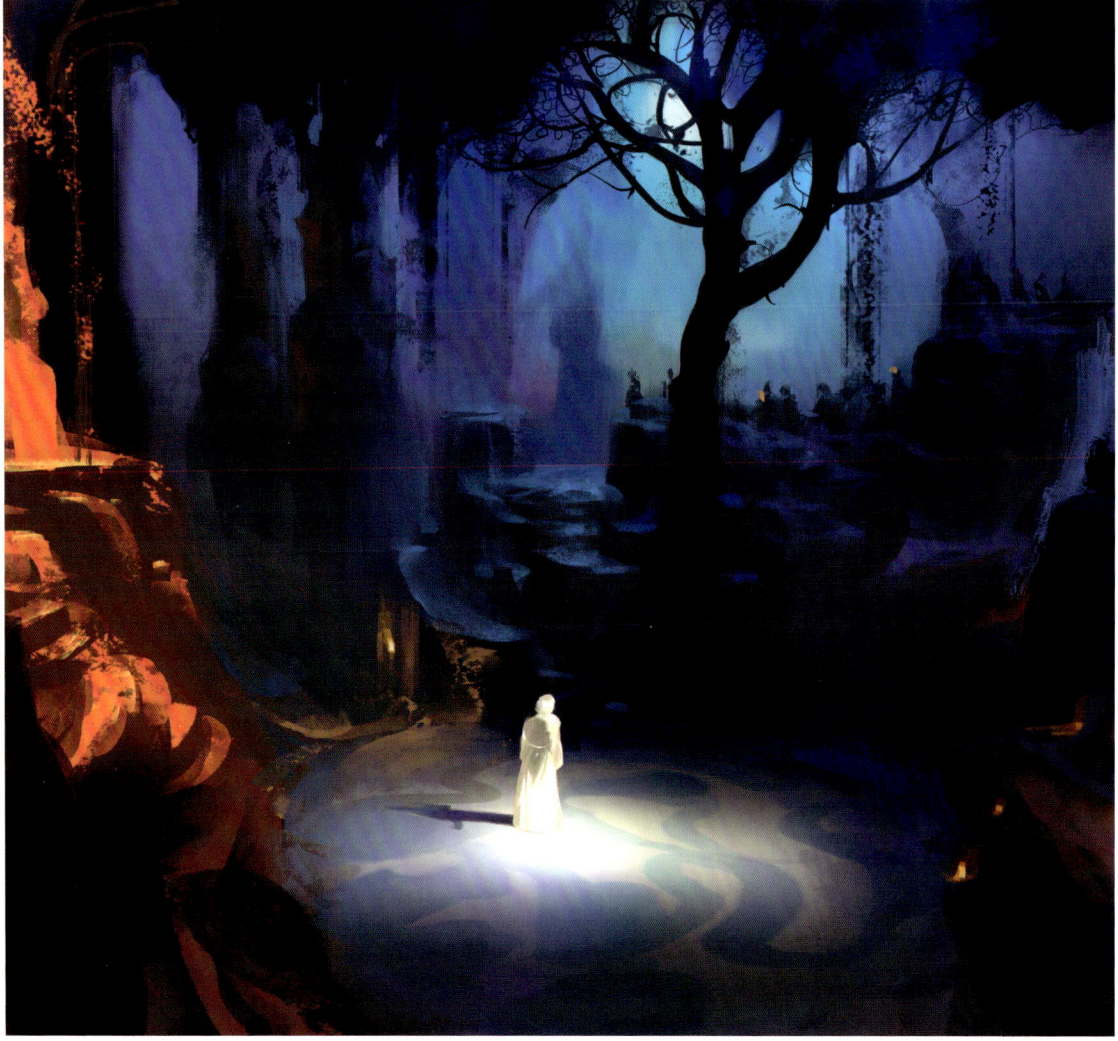

△ This scene feels commanding and mysterious, with quite theatrical staging

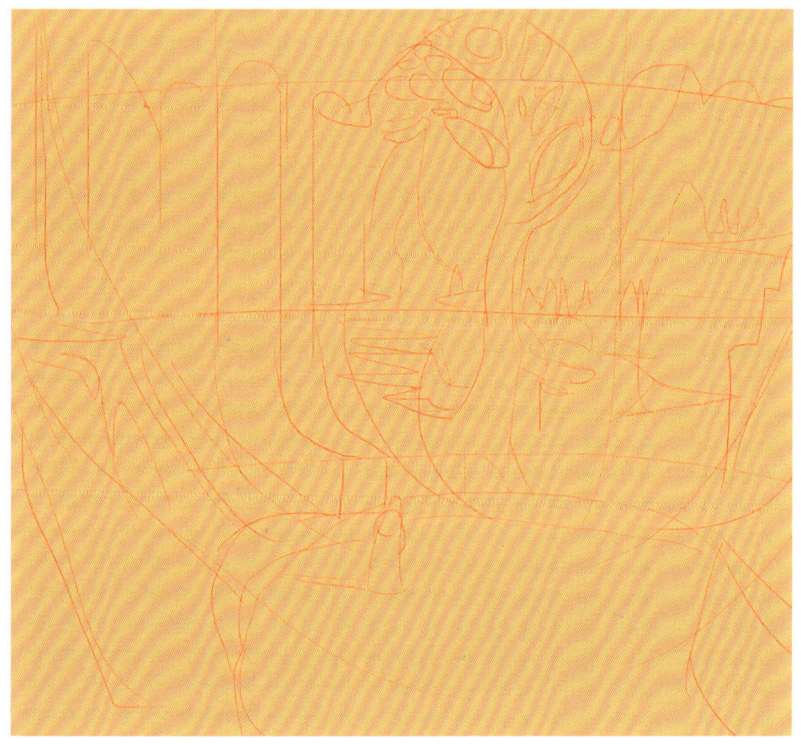

01. An orange base and construction lines tipping downward toward the character

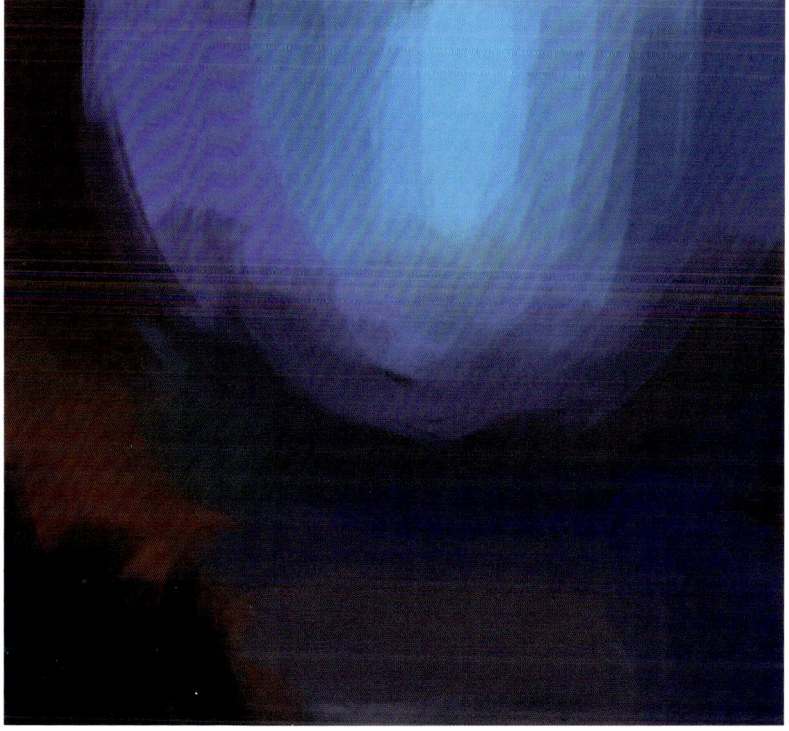

02. These early groups of shapes establish color temperature and composition

01. WARM UNDERTONE

This environment will be made of mostly warm materials, like stone and tree trunks, so I begin with a warm undertone. The drawing serves to rough out the basic organization. Note how my lines flow from top to bottom and curve in toward the main character – this is an important aspect of the composition, so I lay it out up front.

02. ROUGH SHAPES

Next I dive into the undercarriage of the environment. This is characterized by cool moonlight in the distance, gradually revealing the warmer local colors in the foreground. Notice how the shapes are very simple and organized, and how they follow the idea of lines curving downward from above, as established in the previous image.

03. BUILDING UP

The next step is to develop the moonlight in the background, then build up mid-ground shapes to create some layering. I continue to add the suggestion of depth by indicating trees, using their canopy as a framing element. I also establish the spotlight area in the foreground. This is still underpainting but it's meant to have all the right colors and values, so I can lay final lighting and textures over it when I'm ready.

04. THE TREE

Next I add in the central tree, which is a critical element in the scene. It's a powerful bridge between the moon and our main foreground character, and it also helps give the composition a very centralized quality that lends formality to the image.

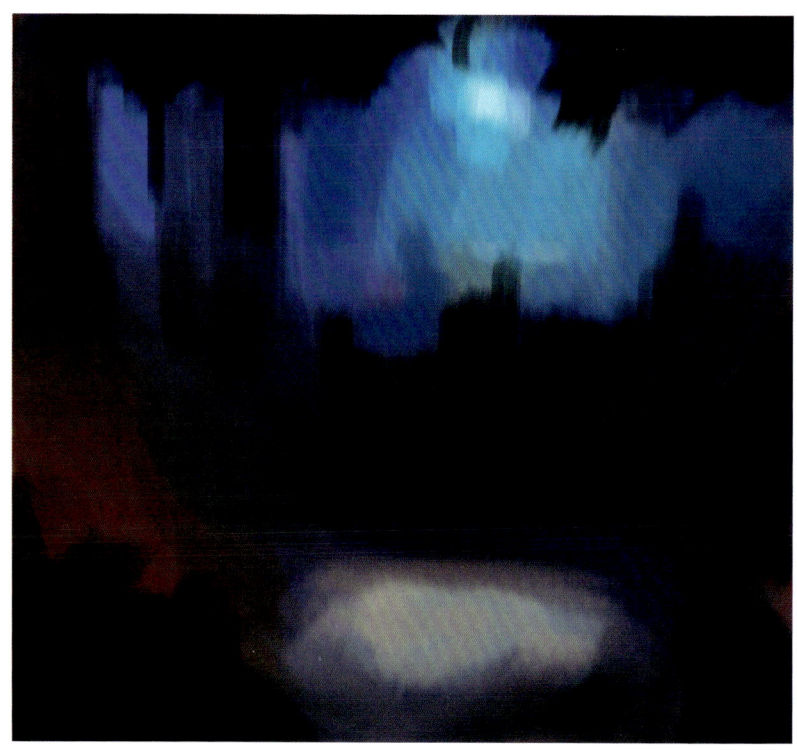

03. The scenery is starting to take shape and have depth

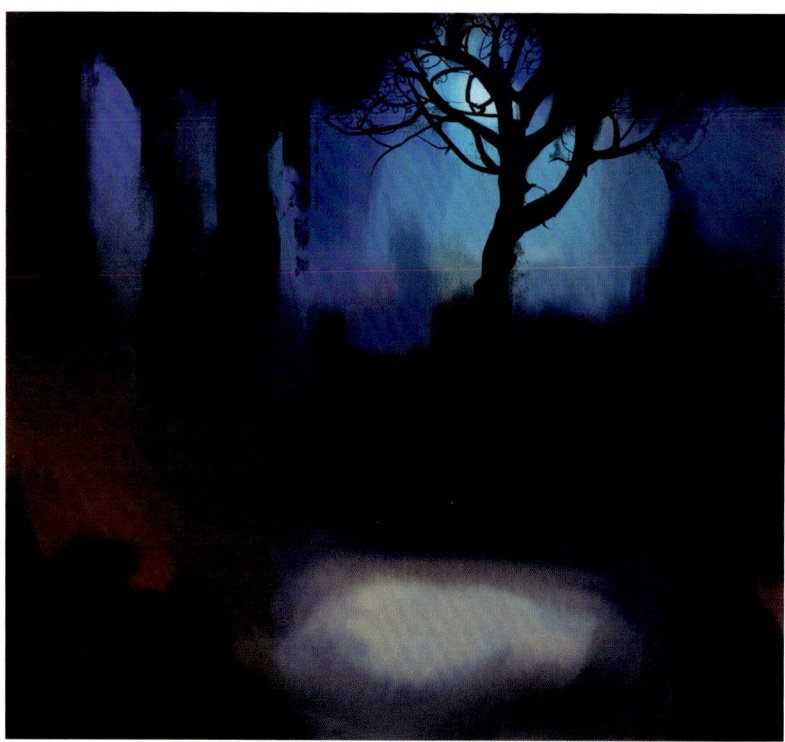

04. Adding the essential element of the tree

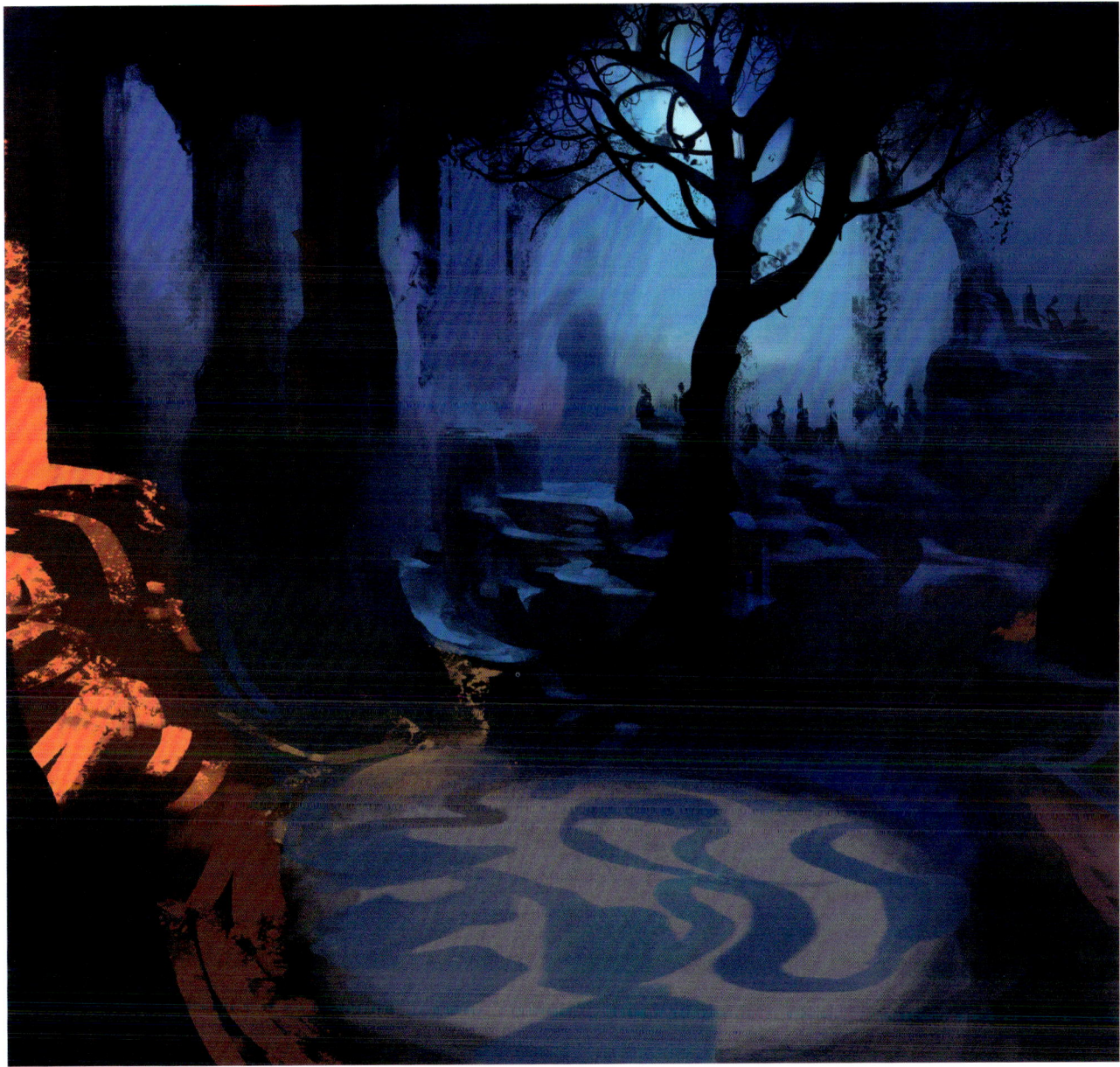

05. Tying the scene together with lighting and environmental details

05. LIGHTING

I'm ready to add lighting on surfaces at this stage. I begin with cool moonlight falling across the top planes of the rocky surfaces behind the tree; I intentionally have them flowing downward on the left side, leading down to where our main figure will be. I use warm lighting in the foreground for contrast and depth, weaving it down the rocky surfaces on the far left. Notice how the lighting stops right at the height of our main character. We're not rendering form, per se – we're designing a composition with light.

The main character will have a distant audience along the ridgeline, so it's time to suggest them now. Our minds are so primed to see character that all we need to do is indicate silhouettes that are about the right size and shape, and our viewers will fill in the gaps. I also work out the surface of the floor of this amphitheater-style area – it has flowing patterns that have a similar character to the rest of the image, but it's polished and smooth.

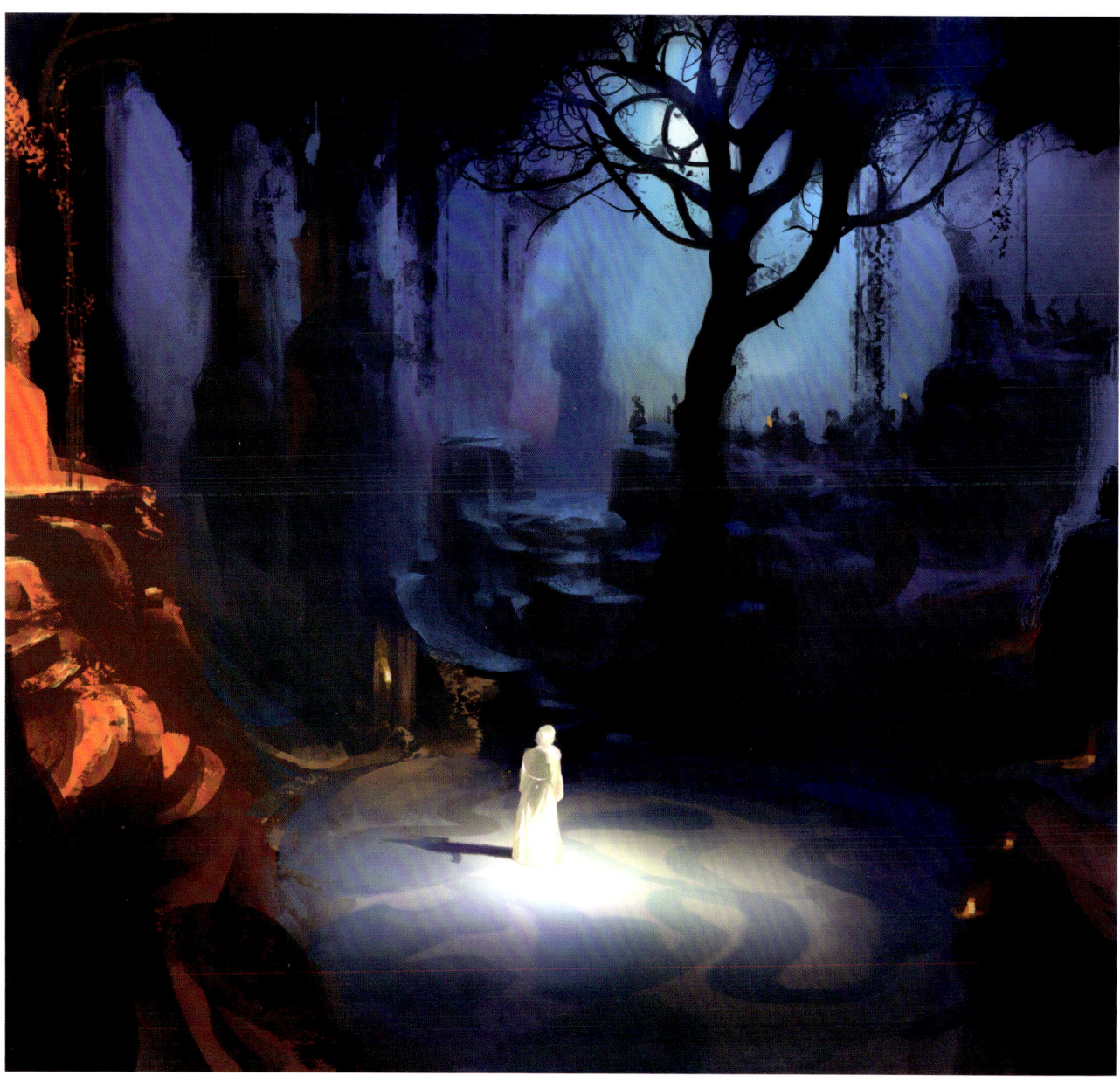

06. Does this image achieve the goals of being theatrical, ancient, and mysterious?

06. FINAL STEP!

There's a little touch-up to do in the environment, but this stage is primarily about working out our main character and associated lighting. I have him in flowing white robes with white hair to suggest age and wisdom. And it's time to turn the spotlight on! Again, this is a major cheat, an affectation, but it's one that serves our purposes and I think our audience has a context for it. I add a few torches for visual interest here and there: one near the character and a few in the far-right foreground. There's also a suggestion of a few torches being held by the characters back along the ridgeline.

And let me restate our goal for this image: 'Operatic staging but also a depth of environment that goes beyond what's possible on a stage. The emotional tone is meant to be ancient, shadowy, and enchanting, as if it's a place that's hiding secrets.' What do you think? Did I achieve my goal?

RECOMMENDED EXERCISE:
VARIETIES OF LIGHTING

This chapter has been all about using light in many ways to solve problems, so that will be your exercise. I want you to sketch out a very simple environment with a main subject – it can be a person, a building, a tree, anything you want. Then rework the image nine times, applying each of the lighting scenarios that I'm showing you here. That may sound like a lot of work, but if you keep your starting environment simple enough, it'll be pure fun to apply new lighting to each variation of your scene.

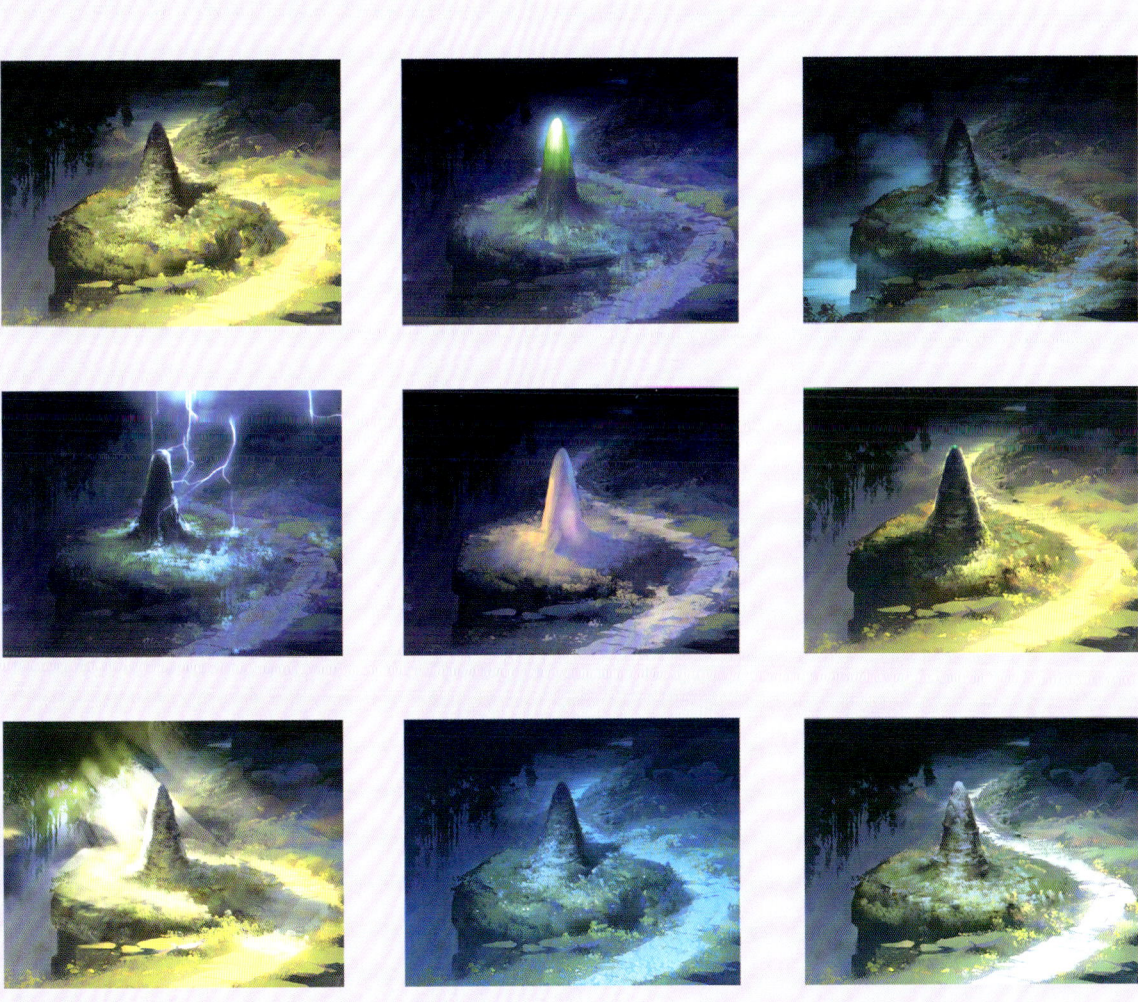

△ Test out these lighting scenarios on a simple scene of your own making

WEATHER & ATMOSPHERE

When we're creating an environment, we're doing so on a flat, passive surface such as a screen or canvas. It's boring until we make it otherwise.

AN INSIGHTFUL CONVERSATION

I once had a conversation with the great film illustrator Iain McCaig about how weather and atmosphere are used in concept art. I was opining to him that weather and atmosphere are not utilized enough in the field of concept art. He responded by saying, 'You know why that is, don't you?' and my response was pure genius. It was, 'Uhhh...' He said, 'It's because concept art mostly comes out of Los Angeles and you guys don't have any weather down there. It's not present to you like it is in most other places in the world.'

It made sense and I think he's right, so in this chapter we are going to right that wrong. We're going to thoroughly explore the use of weather and atmosphere for the design of environments.

Let's begin with a quick reminder of a central idea of environment design. Immediately after the introduction of this book, we dove into the power and authority of environment. And what drives that awesome quality? In most cases it's extremes of weather and atmosphere, and this image was my send-off example.

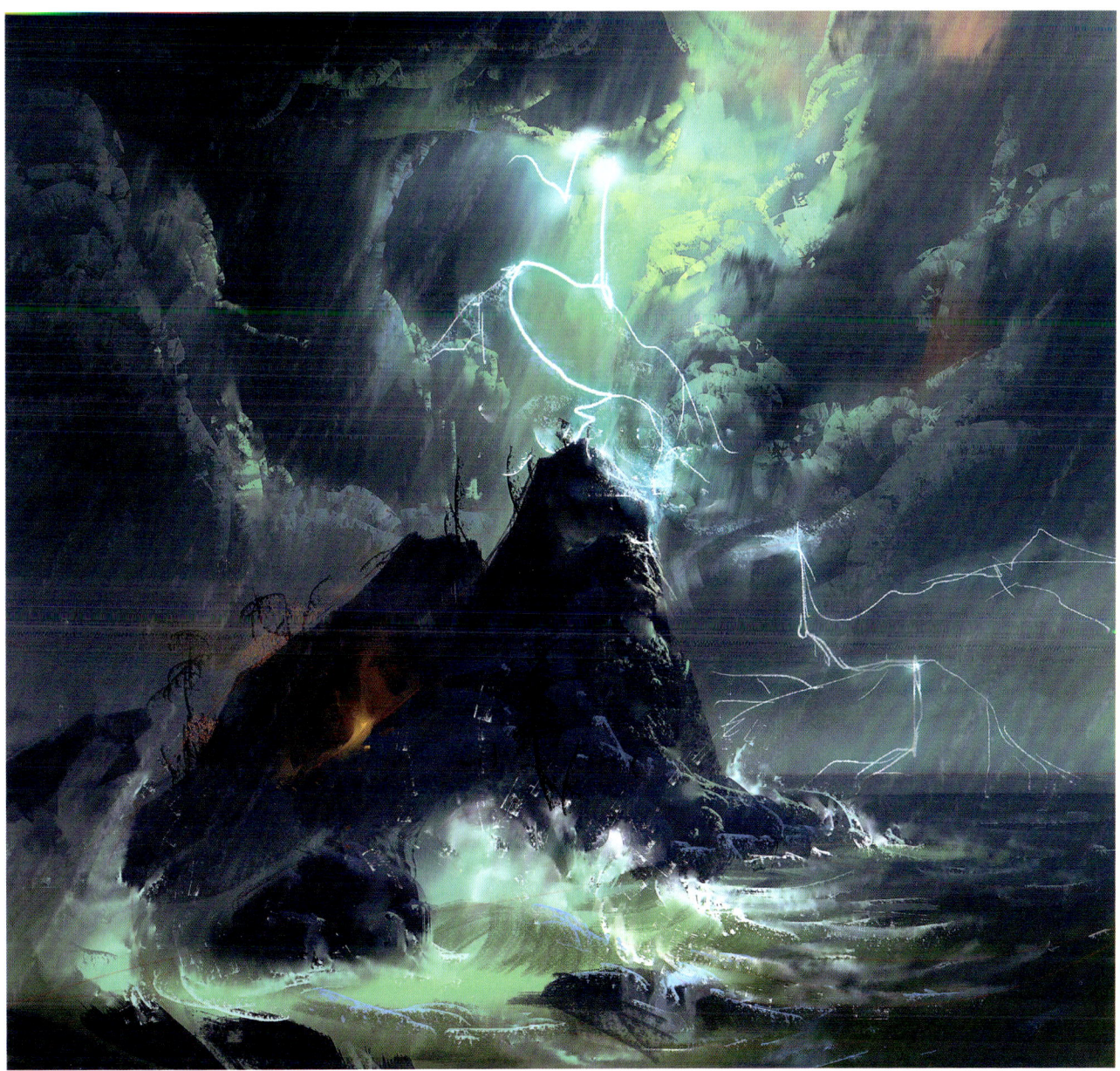

△ Effects of weather are some of the most powerful elements we can use in environment design

THE AUTHORITY OF WEATHER

I live in Los Angeles where there's a lack of extreme weather, but I did live and work in the San Francisco Bay Area for a time, where I made a point to get outside and sketch, as is my habit. Here's a sketch inspired by the San Francisco Bay on a stormy day. I decided I was going to push away from what was really there and exaggerate the stormy elements, to the point where the sketch was more about the emotion than a literal depiction of the place. The result was instructive for me because it's a much more engaging and powerful painting than had I mindlessly copied the immediate location.

01. FIERY MOUNTAIN

Let's move on to an invented scene, a mountainscape with an explosive sky. Is it a volcano? Is it an extreme of backlighting? I never decided and I don't think it matters. It's just meant to have the 'kaboom of doom' – nature is not kidding around here! For my hard-hitting scenes of extreme weather, I tend to overlap several different ideas. In this one I have:

- A monochromatic hot environment

- An epic range of mountains moving into the distance and disappearing into the atmosphere

- Vast flowing cloudscapes

- Explosive backlighting

- Foreground water to intensify the presence of the weather through reflection

- Dark contrast in the foreground

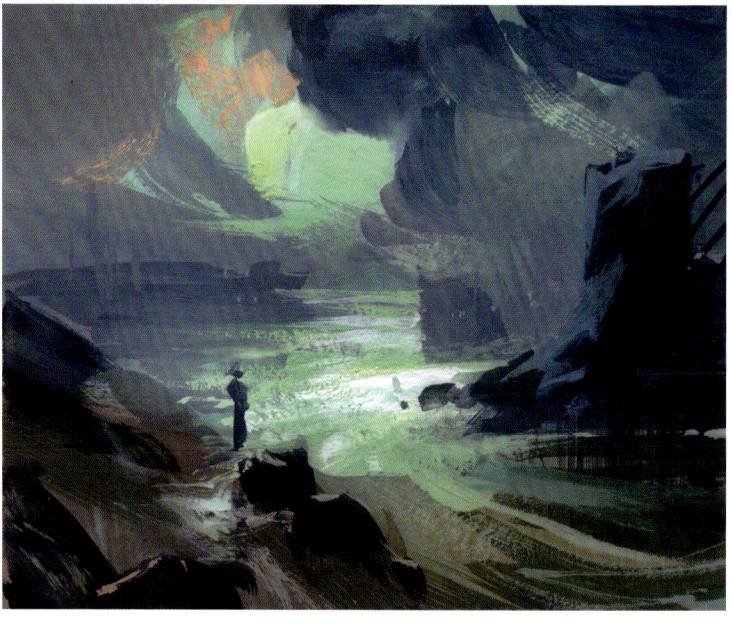

△ A stormy scene inspired by San Francisco Bay

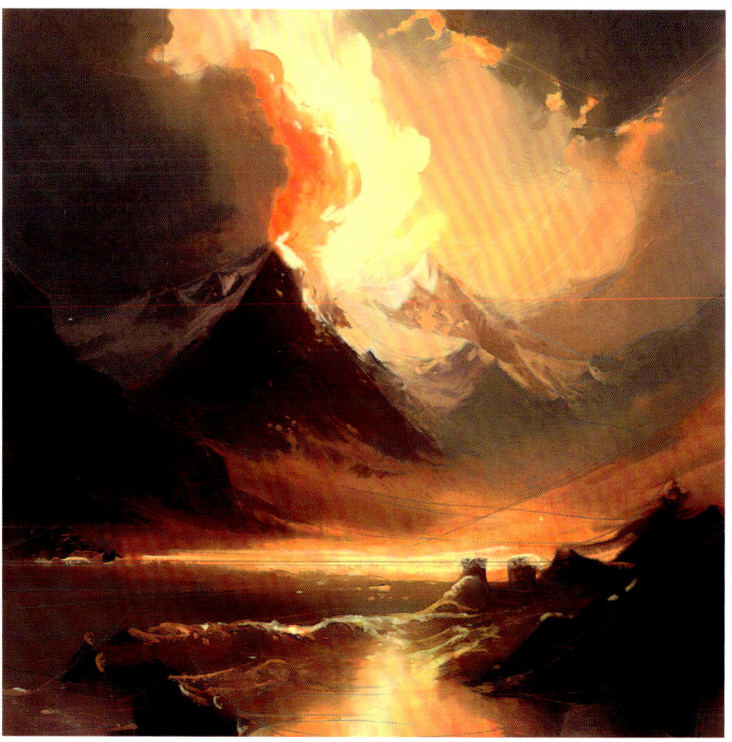

01. Multiple elements combine to make this landscape explosively striking

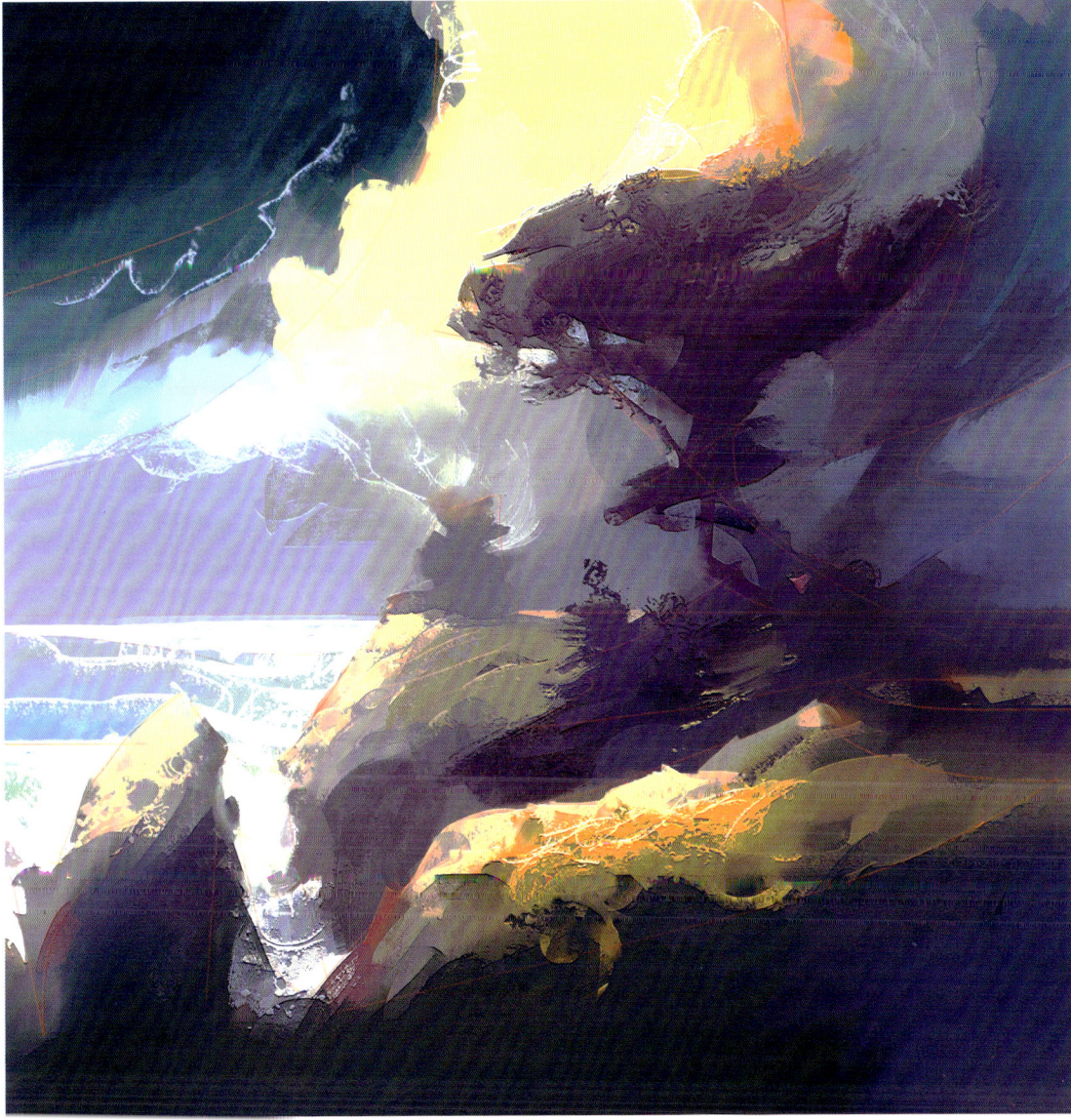

A windswept tree and sweeping clouds give this scene emotional impact

02. CENTRAL COAST

I love traveling up the Central Coast of California where you get the craggy shorelines and the windswept cypress trees. It's so emotional! Here's another environment where I took that inspiration and threw everything I could think of at it for another explosive experience of weather. This time I used:

- A cypress tree moving with the wind

- Sunlit cloudscape flowing with the wind direction

- Whitecap waves hitting the rock line

- A flash of electric-blue lightning

- Distant mountains

- Accents of spotlighting from sun rays

- High-contrast textures and edges

- A full range of contrasting colors, especially warm and cool

DESIGNING WIND

I'd like to cover the two kinds of weather that specifically involve movement and speed: wind and rain. Let's begin with wind. Think of a windy day – not a breeze and not a hurricane, but a forceful wind. Note that such a day feels emotionally different than an ordinary one: it's a day when the environment announces itself to everyone with real authority. When we visually render weather, it must carry the same authority.

Our work is done on a flat, passive surface such as a screen or canvas, and it's boring until we make it otherwise. We have to fight like crazy to create convincing visual effects of weather, such as a forceful wind. Let's look at some successful examples.

01. WIND INDICATORS

Environment design is pretty hard and pretty complicated. It's always a relief when there's a quick tip that can make a big difference, and I have one for you: tip the verticals in the direction of the wind. Just doing that one thing adds a powerful drama and dynamic to your scene. Here's a scene where I did just that. I've set up sequential examples so you can see the immediate difference.

You can see that there are other strong indicators of wind in this scene, too. Try the following next time you need a real shock of wind, and I'll show a unique example of each of these ideas next.

- Tip the direction of the perspective or the verticals in the direction of the wind.

- Design all foliage to be moving with the direction of the wind.

- Fill the air with a volume of moving debris and apply a motion blur in the direction of the wind.

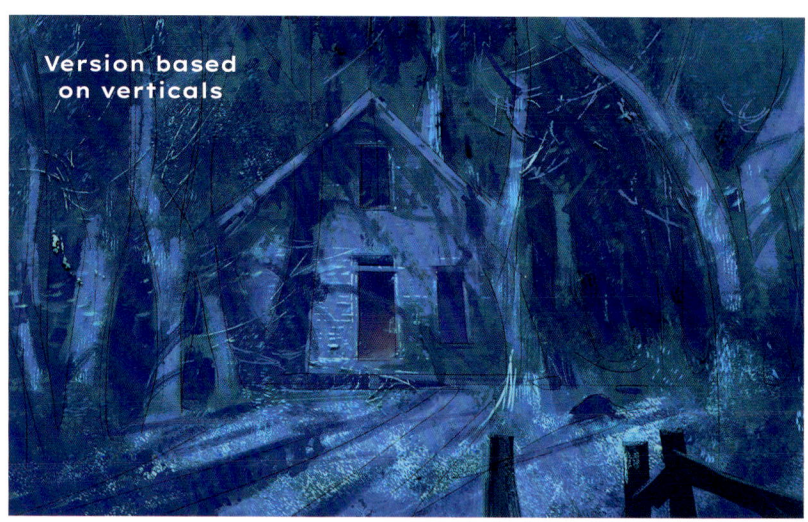

Version based on verticals

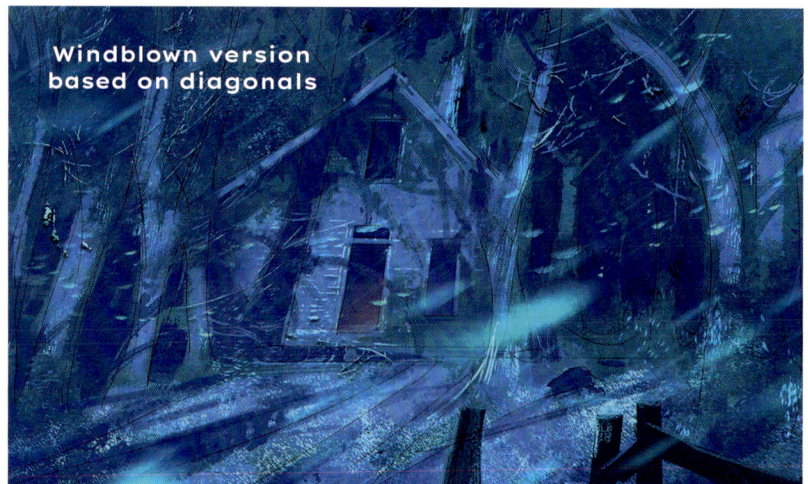

Windblown version based on diagonals

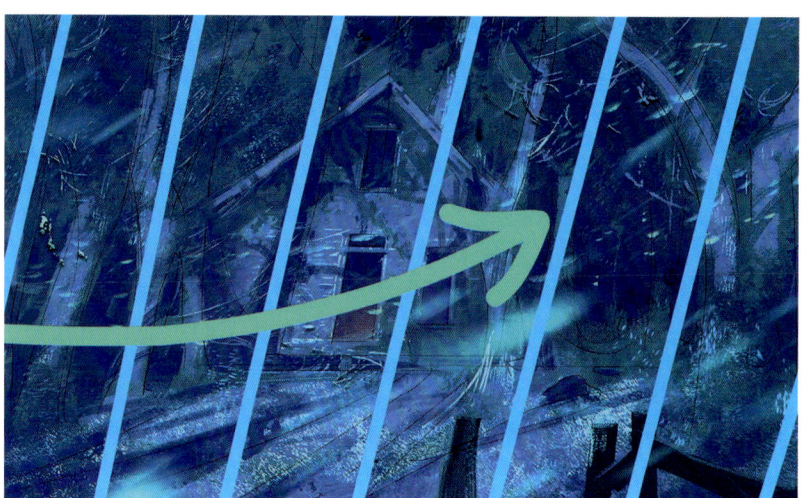

01. Diagonals and blurry debris are some quick tricks we can use to create a windy scene

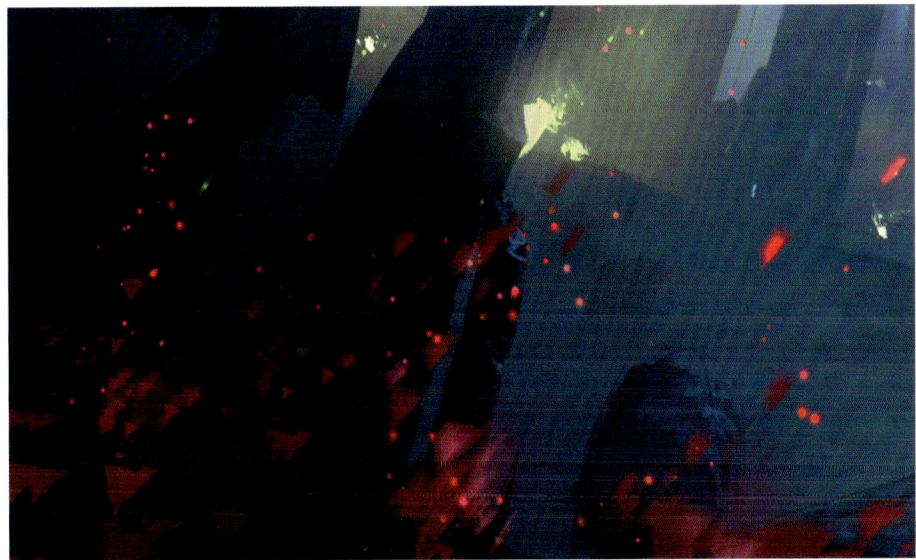

If it looks right it is right, and if it feels right it's even more right.

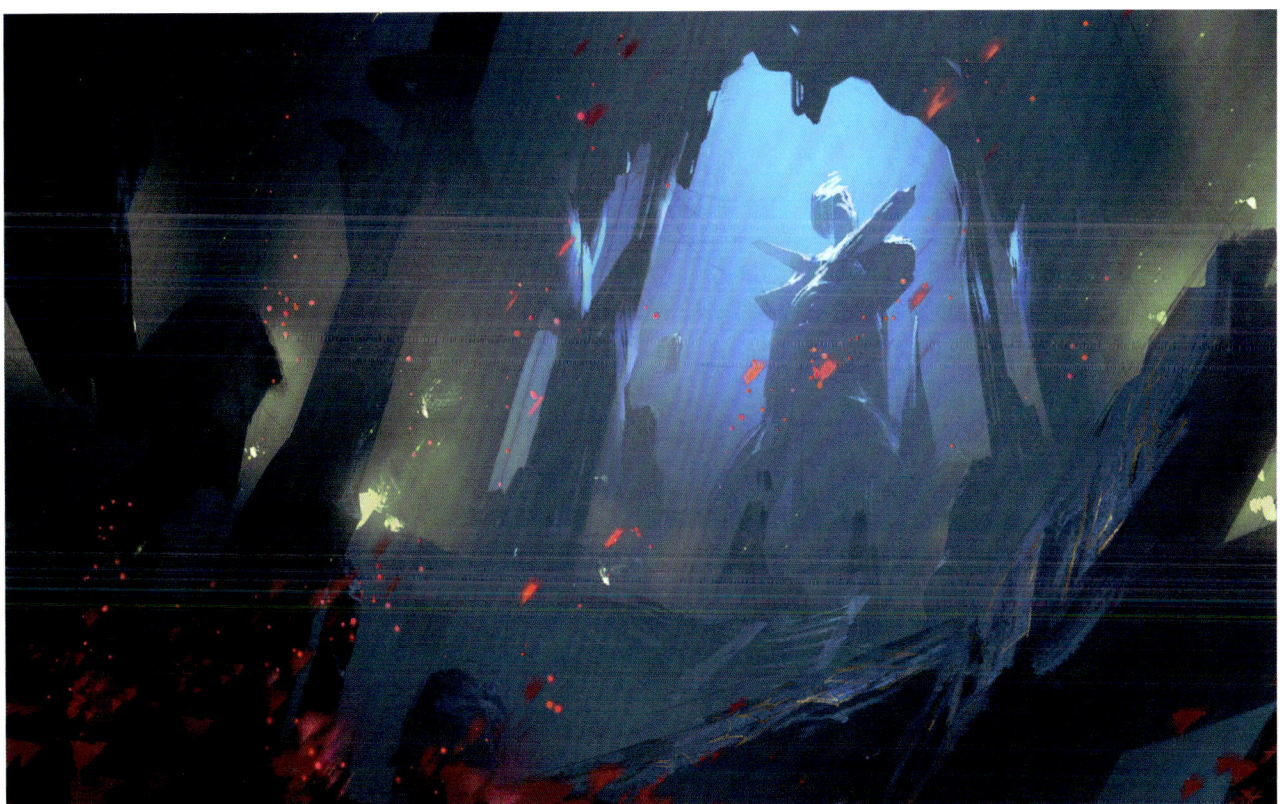

02. The exact nature of those red bits doesn't matter – they achieve what I set out to do

02. WINDSWEPT CAVE

Here's an image I was roughing out as a monochromatic cave scenario, but it needed some real vibrancy. The solution wasn't just adding color – it was also adding wind! What's that red stuff breezing through the environment? I don't know. Who cares? If it looks right it is right, and if it feels right it's even more right – that's what I always say. So I have that red fluff blowing through the cave with a little bit of motion blur, and it gives the scene just what it needs to have some life and excitement. And look, I'm also tipping the perspective with the direction of the wind!

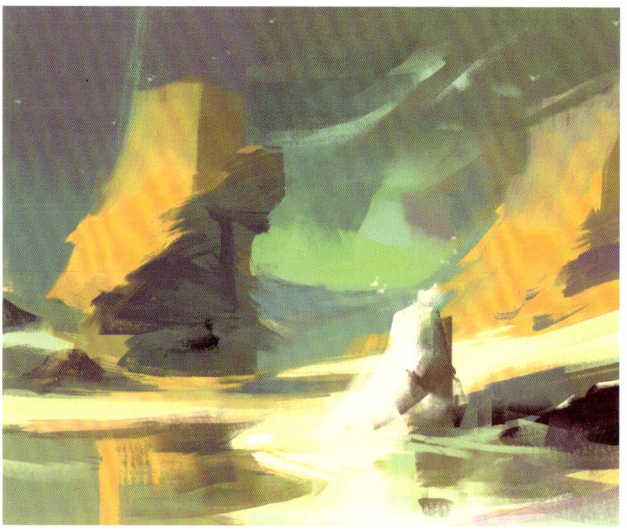 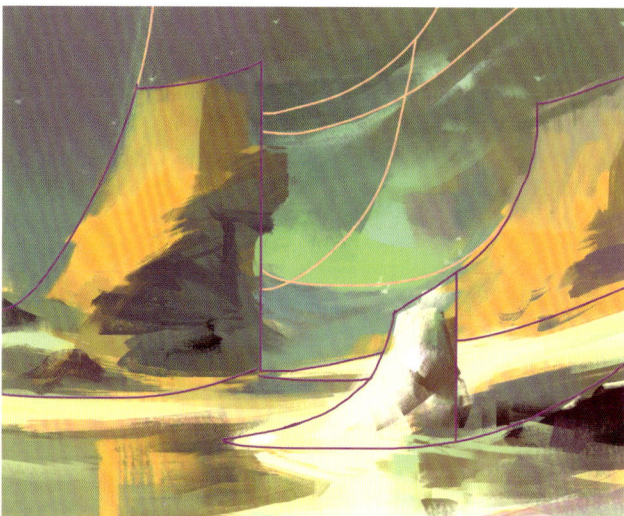

03. Here the landscape is exaggerated to match the powerful wind

Inspired design includes a serious consideration of the weather.

03. DRAMATIC BEACH

This beach environment is inspired by a real place but I wanted to give it an extreme dramatization. I exaggerated the color design, the lighting design, and the value relationships. The one thing I didn't exaggerate was the wind – it was a really windy day at the shoreline! So to create that visual impression, I gave a sweeping tip to all the rocks, and followed up with the same type of movement in the sky. Inspired design includes a serious consideration of the weather.

04. OUTER BANKS

This last image is inspired by real trees on the Outer Banks of North Carolina. The constant wind has forced these trees into a windblown state, whether wind is present or not. They appear so emotional when you're sitting there sketching them on a completely calm day. And in this book we always target the creation of emotion.

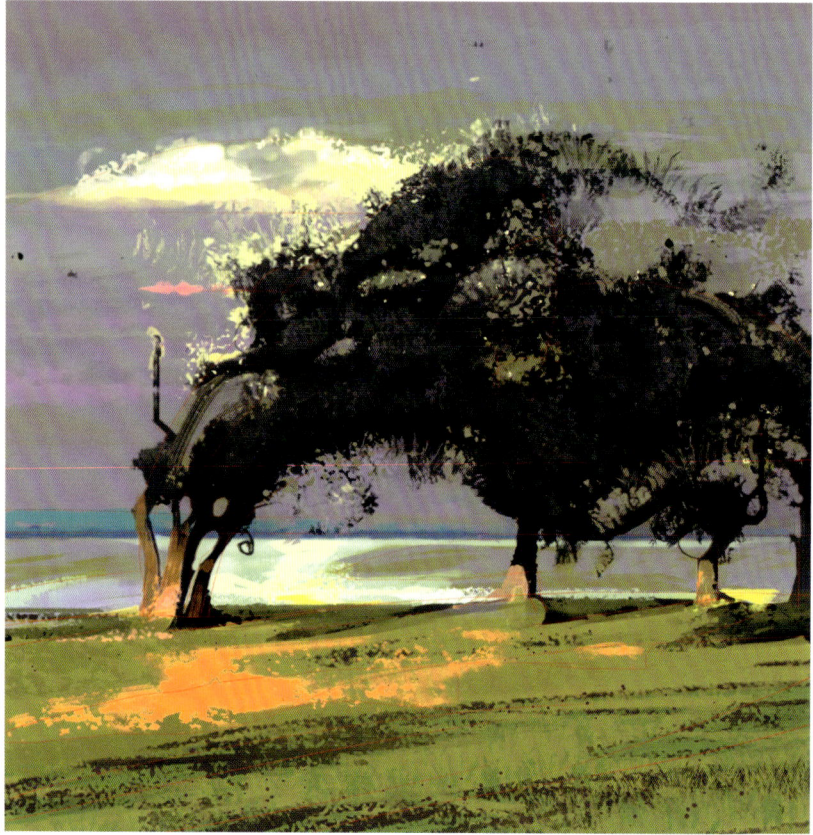

04. Strong sea winds have left these trees permanently bent

DESIGNING RAIN

In this windswept environment on the Oregon coast, the diagonal movement of rain is the main event. My very last step was adding the rain itself over the top of the painting. However, during most of the painting process I angled my brush so that each mark would have the same angle as the rain. If something is important in an environment, then we do whatever we can to emphasize that thing – it gives our environment a powerful quality of purpose. See what I did there? I brought this idea of weather right back around to the central idea of this book: purposeful, emotional environments. Our purpose here is capturing the rain and the mood it creates.

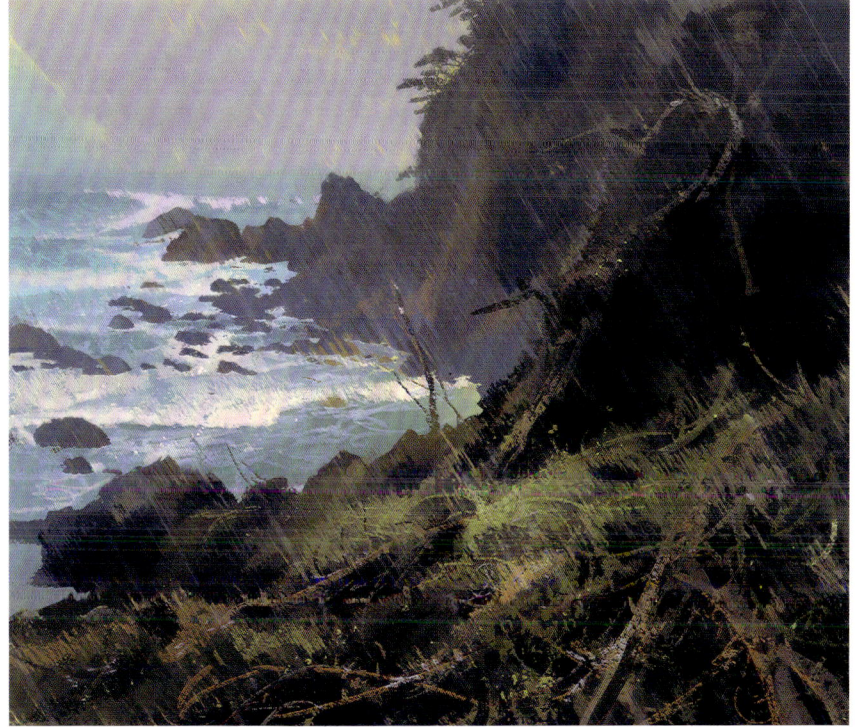

If something is important in an environment, then we do whatever we can to emphasize that thing – it gives our environment a powerful quality of purpose.

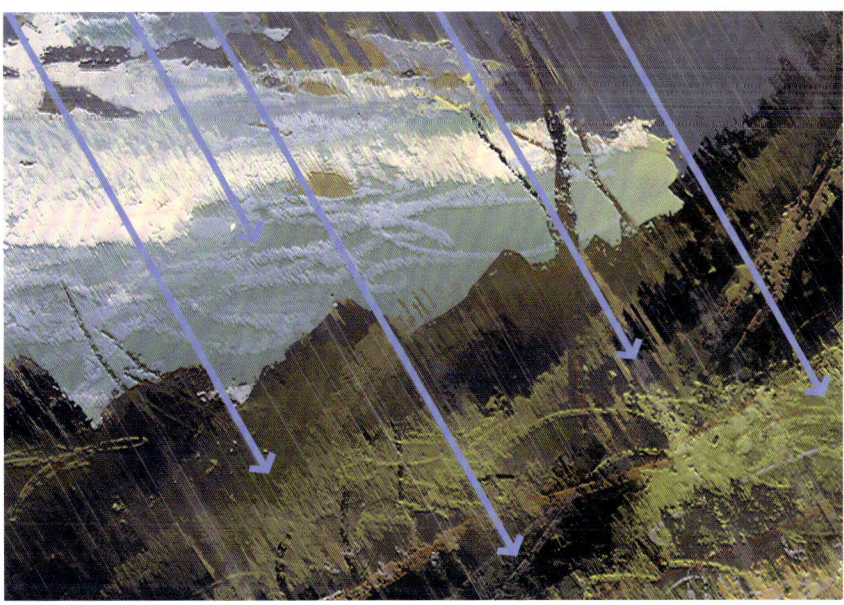

△ The brushstrokes in this landscape are geared toward emphasizing the rain

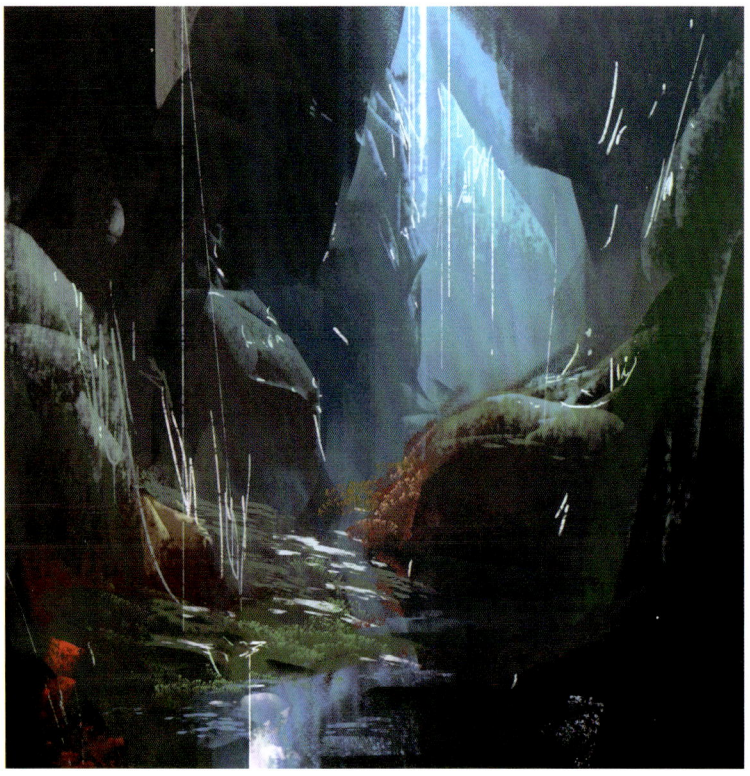

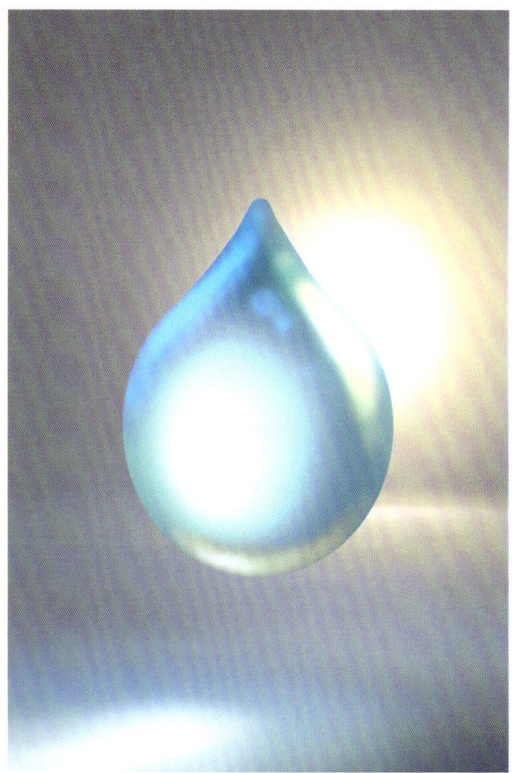

01. Backlighting and rim lights glint off the raindrops and wet surfaces here

01. WETNESS & WATER

I did this study of 'wetness' for you, and there's one thing happening here that emphasizes the wet quality in a special way. It's backlighting. When you have rain or dripping water in a scene, backlighting will bring the rain and the wet surfaces to life by giving them a glistening quality. On the top right you can see the effect of light passing through a droplet of water. In the scene I've played the glowing drops of water against the shadowy areas of the environment for contrast, and I've given all of the surfaces a rim-lit specular quality. The result is a scene that is really, really wet!

02. WET TERRAIN

Along with sodden rain and wet surfaces, don't forget the effect water will have on the environment itself. You're gonna get your shoes really muddy if you stomp through this environment!

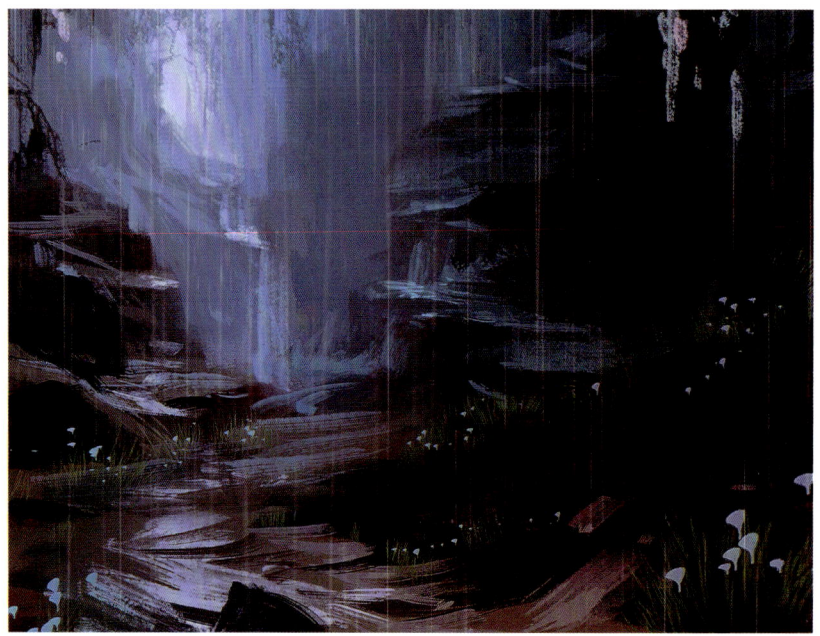

02. Water can physically alter the terrain beyond just lighting and reflections

DESIGNING DISTANCE WITH ATMOSPHERE

Our environments often need to portray vast distances. This brings us back to our basic technical challenge: our work is always seen on a flat, two-dimensional screen. It has no physical depth whatsoever. Three-dimensional images are an optical illusion created by us, so we have to really know what we're doing. There are three primary considerations when creating distance through atmosphere:

- Diminishing of detail into the distance

- Diminishing of value contrast into the distance

- Temperature changing from warmer to cooler into the distance

Let's look at a couple of examples.

01. MOUNTAIN RANGE

The top-right image is a craggy textural mountain range that's meant to have a grand scale and convey a great sense of distance. Observe that all forms of contrast, especially value and texture, are reducing into the distance. I've included a simplified graphic on the right for you.

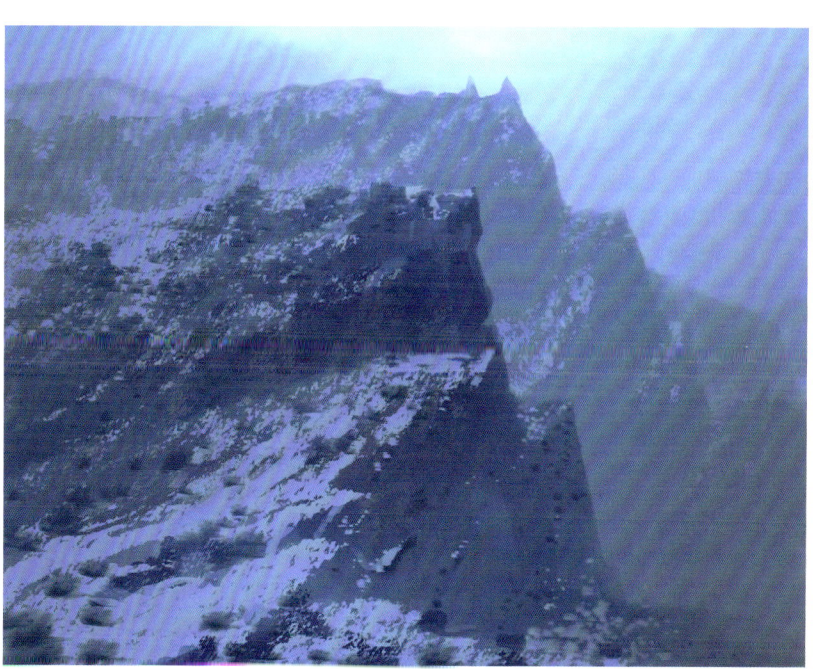

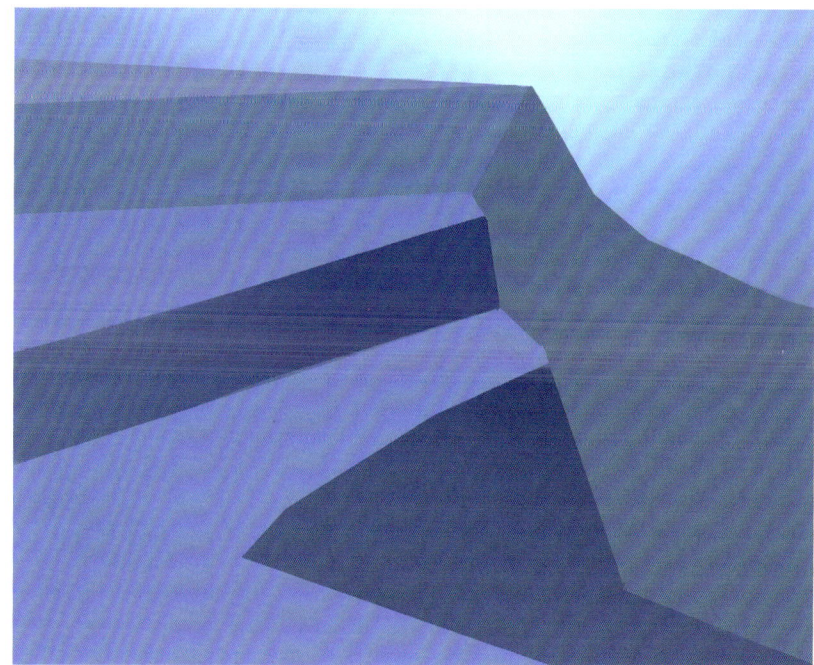

01. Note how different types of contrast help to give these mountains depth

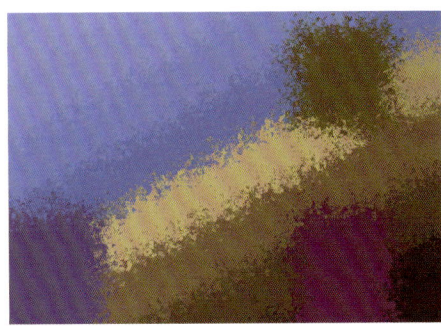

02. JUNGLE LANDSCAPE

Here are some jungle mountainsides where I needed to convey vast distance despite heavy texture throughout. My solution was to take the natural effects of atmospheric temperatures and exaggerate them. I began with warm local colors in the foreground, especially the strong reds and magentas, and then in the distance I shifted to cool atmospheric temperatures.

No doubt you're aware of this, but just in case you aren't: the blue or gray light from the sky is reflected and refracted through the volume of atmosphere, then reflected back to our eyes, so the greater the distance, the more 'cool' temperatures are infused into the environment.

03. CLOSE RANGE

Atmospheric depth doesn't have to happen only over long distances – it can also happen over very short distances. This environment features a clump of trees in which I wanted to make the foreground tree much more important. I let its trunk and especially its right-facing limbs emerge into the foreground, giving the tree a quality of depth, scale, and importance. I'm achieving it through heavy atmosphere and backlighting, and with shadows; the shadows weave toward us, describing the distance of the ground plane. (And by the way, calling a primary element in an image 'important' is just another way of stating the *purpose* of the image.)

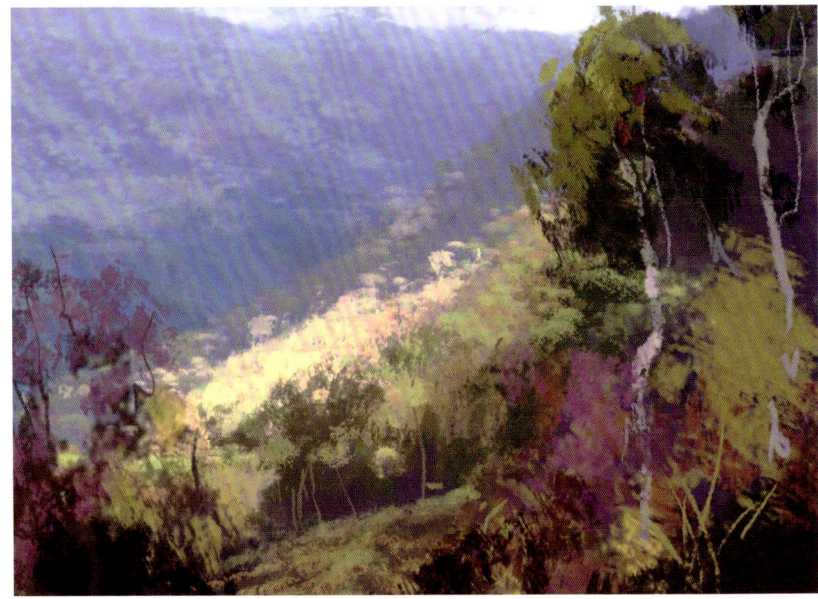

02. This environment uses local color and atmosphere to create vast distance

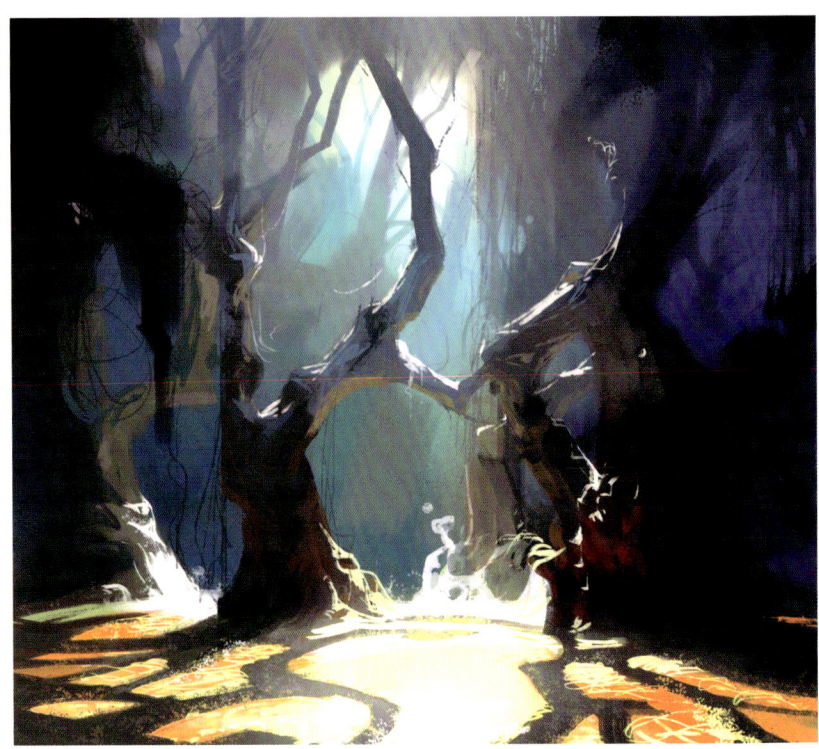

03. Atmospheric depth can be applied over short distances, too

04. ANCIENT RUINS

Now let's put it all together in this scene of ancient South American ruins. What's our goal here? What's our purpose? I want an engaging environment of epic ruins that's exciting to look at. One of the most immediate ways to achieve that goal is to give the architecture a strong presence and a grand scale, so I set the eye-level line lower in the picture plane – we're looking up at the buildings to give them grandeur. I add an especially strong atmosphere to give a sense of distance and scale, and this atmosphere accentuates the visual contrast, giving us vibrant warm buildings in the foreground that graduate to cooler atmospheric temperatures in the background. There are other uses of weather and atmosphere going on here, as shown in the graphic.

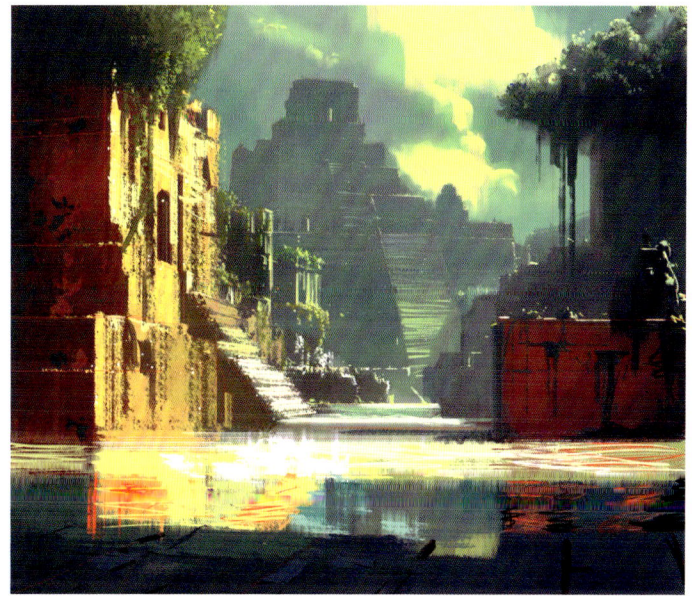

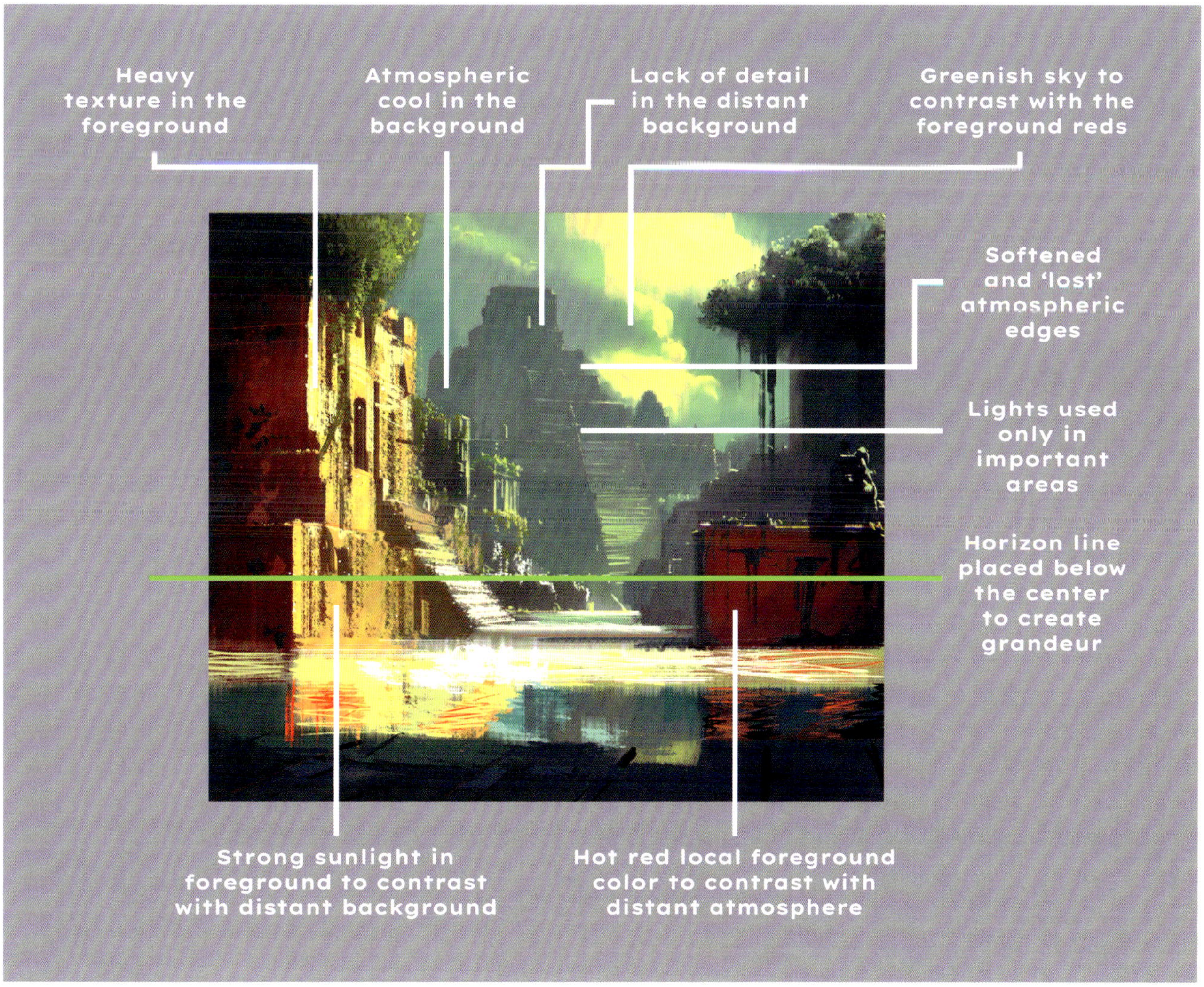

Heavy texture in the foreground

Atmospheric cool in the background

Lack of detail in the distant background

Greenish sky to contrast with the foreground reds

Softened and 'lost' atmospheric edges

Lights used only in important areas

Horizon line placed below the center to create grandeur

Strong sunlight in foreground to contrast with distant background

Hot red local foreground color to contrast with distant atmosphere

04. This scene combines multiple techniques for creating scale and grandeur

05. TEMPERATURE

Now let's try what is, to me, a fascinating experiment. I've mentioned temperature several times now and I want to see how far we can go with that idea. It's human nature to reach for value contrast when we want to dramatize something, and there's nothing wrong with that. But we also need the ability to be much more subtle at times. This temple scene certainly has value contrast, but I've diminished it as far as possible to rely on temperature relationships for depth rather than value. The chart here shows a mild value change from the mass of the foreground to the mass of the mid-ground, and an aggressive temperature change between the two areas. This is my way of getting an image that feels different from expectation. It's good for us to have some surprises up our sleeve.

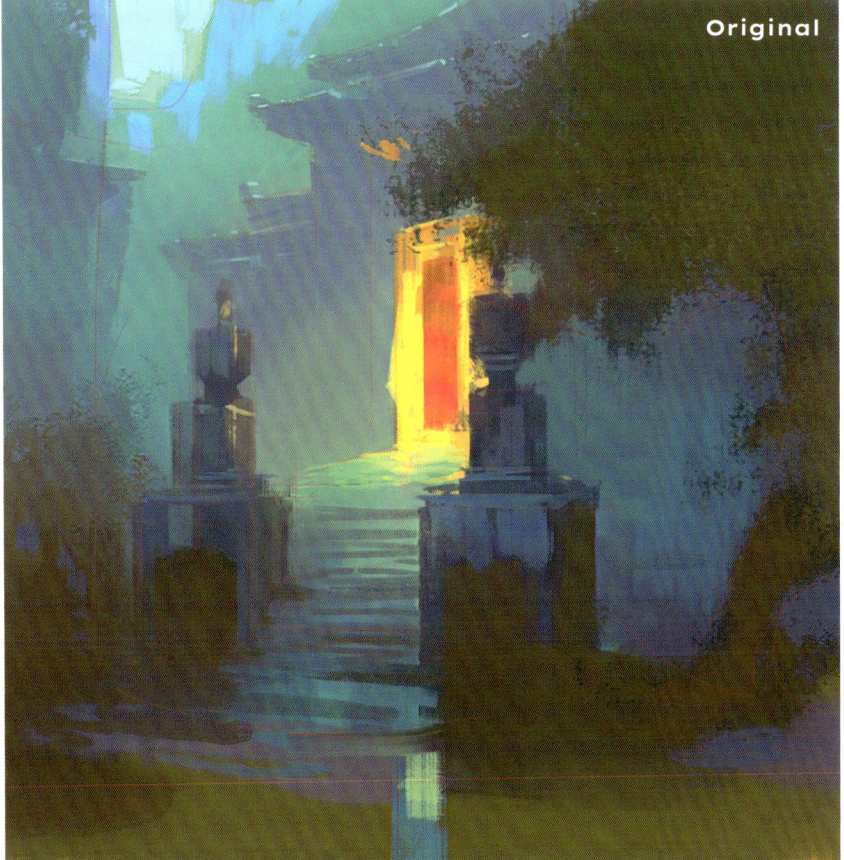

Original

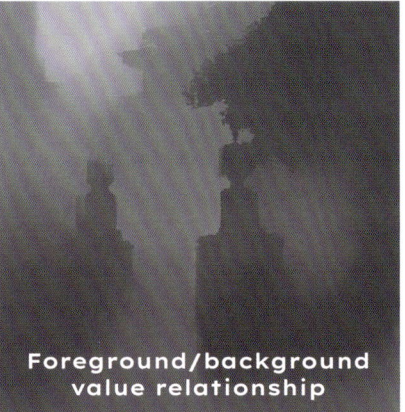

Foreground/background value relationship

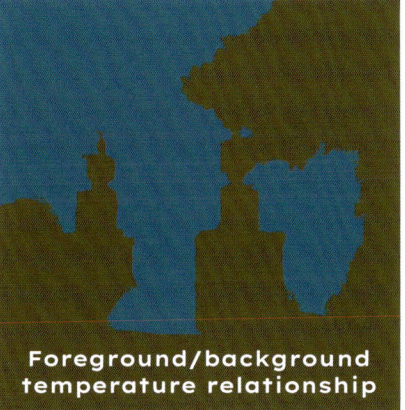

Foreground/background temperature relationship

05. The extreme contrast is achieved with surprisingly little change in value

It's human nature to reach for value contrast when we want to dramatize something, but we need the ability to be much more subtle at times. Try using temperature relationships for depth rather than value.

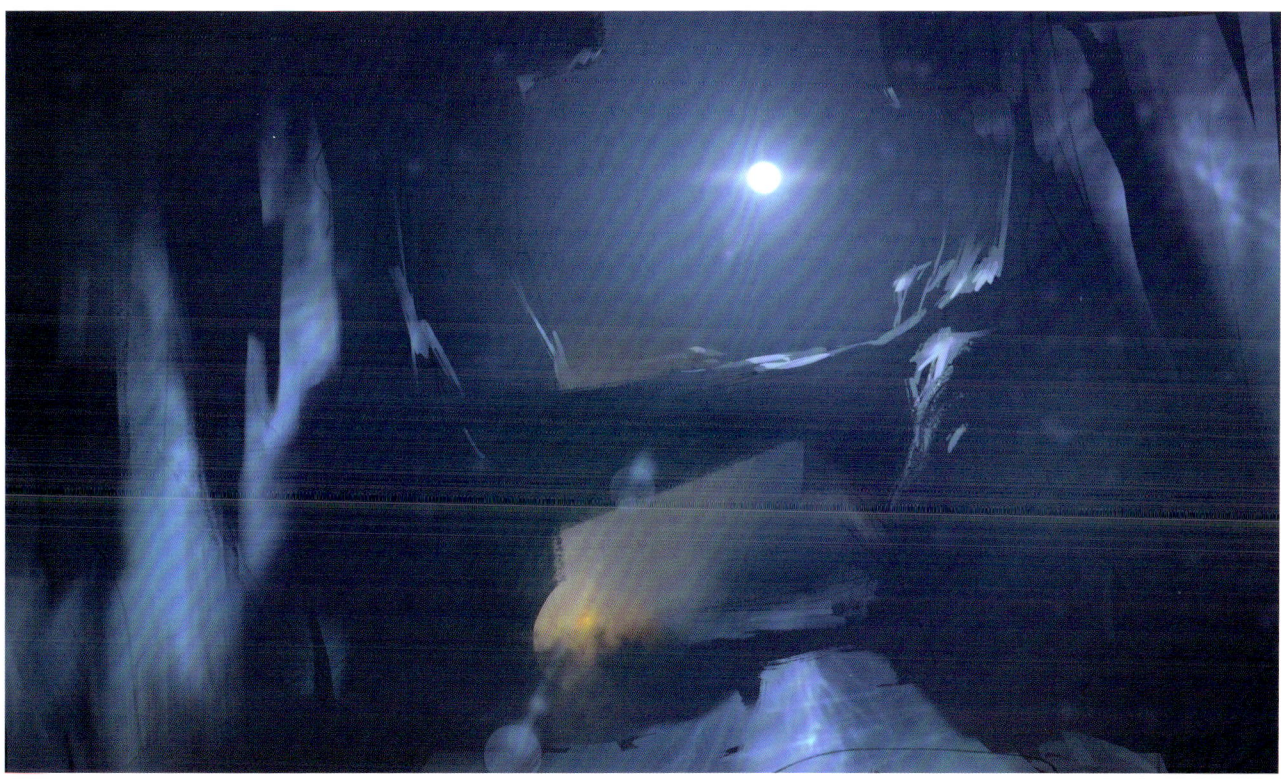

06. A lens flare changes the scale of this scene from unclear to vast and cavernous

06. LENS FLARES

A lens flare? Really? Aren't those considered to be a tacky and cheap effect when it comes to concept art? Maybe. I definitely believe it's an effect that can be overused, but let me tell you a little story. Way back in the nineties there was a sci-fi TV show called *Babylon 5* that used brand-new computer-generated effects. They look simple and quaint now but they were pretty good for their time. I remember watching this show and looking at the lens flare effects that would frequently happen as backlit spaceships traversed the depths of space. In deep space there's no scale reference, no way to judge depth and distance, but ... enter the lens flare. A lens flare has the feeling of crossing space all the way from the distant light source to our eyes. It's a sparkle of excitement and, more importantly, it conveys depth in a place that otherwise lacks depth cues. I put that idea in my pocket and use it on rare occasions.

I had a lot of fun working out this sci-fi environment in Photoshop but I absolutely did not use the Photoshop lens flare tool. I painted the lens flare mark by mark and circle by circle, as I needed it to follow my own requirements for the scene rather than using a random artificially generated effect. This is not a scene of deep space, but it is a scene with very little scale reference. The lens flare traverses from the distant light source, through the mid-ground, and right up to our point of view in the foreground.

C.I.A.

During the many years I spent at DreamWorks Animation, we had a quasi-official term for those motes of dust you'll often see softly floating through the air in a close-up scene. That term was 'C.I.A.'. This effect is a very useful quality of local atmosphere because it brings a realism and an immediacy to the spaces that fill our environments. So what does C.I.A. mean? Crap-In-Air.

01. DUST MOTES

I have a couple of sketches here to illustrate the use of C.I.A. for you. First is this scene of random jungle vines and roots where I want a feeling of humidity and dampness to give the atmosphere a volumetric presence. To get that feeling into the sketch, I have a shaft of light streaming in and a sprinkle of illuminated dust motes throughout. There are different layers of them – most are right in the beam of light, but some are nearer and have a focal blur to help with the quality of space and intimacy.

02. BACKLIT PARTICLES

It's not just in streams of light where C.I.A. readily appear. They're also very present in backlit scenes. I backlit this magical environment with vivid blue light and filled the atmosphere with layers of C.I.A. As the motes of dust get closer to us, I once again mimic a focal blur. This helps the audience feel that they're in a real place with a depth of volume, and it's up close and personal.

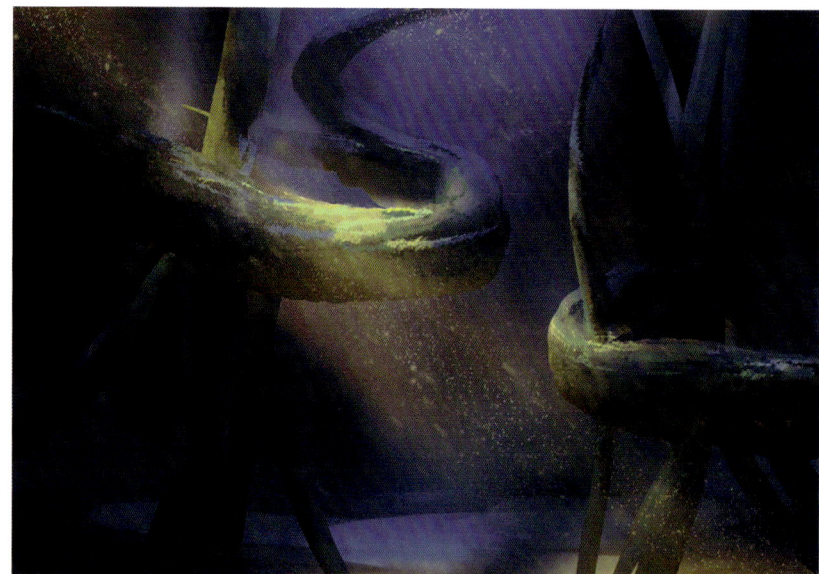

01. Floating particles give the atmosphere volume in this scene

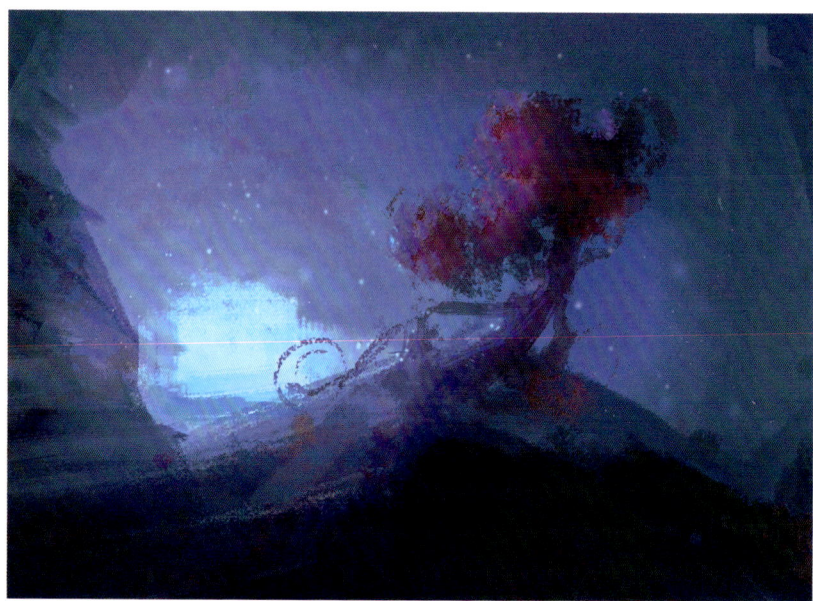

02. In this more open and airy scene, blurred layers of dust float close to the viewer

USING ATMOSPHERE

Atmosphere can be designed to create oh-so-many different qualities of environment, so I'd like to show a gallery of work now and discuss how atmosphere is used in each image.

01. ATMOSPHERIC LUMINOSITY

Here I've created three different images to show you varying levels of realism. The first one is a real place, a nearby street that had a particular luminosity one morning. I used the idea of simultaneous contrast of color (as discussed on page 242) to heighten the quality of luminosity. This is a way of exaggerating the atmospheric lighting of a place to reproduce the luminous experience of being there.

The second image is also based on a real place. The environment wasn't just luminous – it had wind blowing and a distant marine layer of haze glowing with light. It was quite spectacular! To create the feeling of the place I had to wildly exaggerate the atmospheric luminosity with simultaneous contrast, using moving, flowing brushstrokes.

The third environment is completely invented. With the experience of the previous two under my belt, I was able to give it a heightened, luminous, and even magical quality.

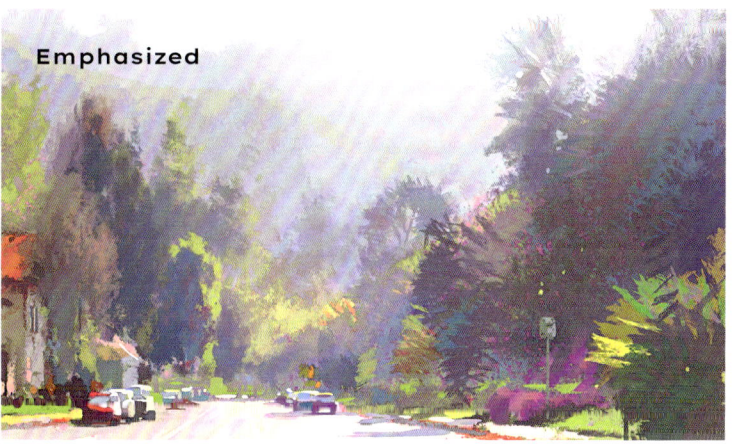

Emphasized

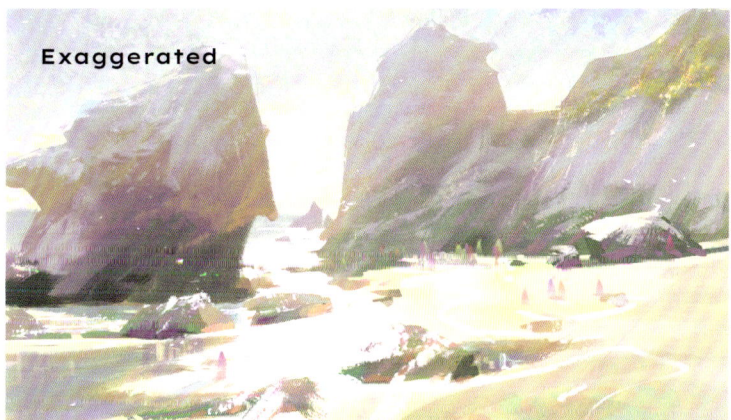

Exaggerated

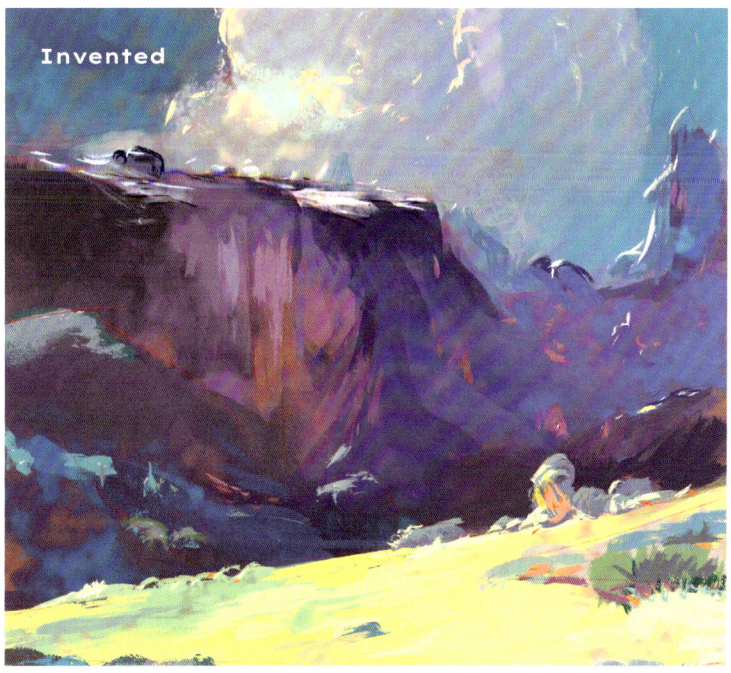

Invented

01. Comparing different approaches to atmospheric luminosity

Atmosphere can be used to drastically reduce the amount of detail in a scene, so that it does not distract from the primary purpose of the image.

02. REDUCING DETAIL

Let's go with a humid, atmospheric environment for another scene of South American temple ruins. Many years ago I worked on the DreamWorks movie *The Road to El Dorado*, set in 1500s South America. I painted dozens of scenes that appear in the movie and fell in love with the subject of ancient American temple ruins.

In this scene I use atmosphere to drastically reduce the amount of detail, so the image becomes about the discovery of an entrance to an ancient temple. I definitely don't want it to be about a complex textural scene, so sunlight streaming through the volume of atmosphere helps to adjust the contrast. Note how I use it to feature the entrance above all else.

03. BACKLIT HAZE

Here's a similar concept to the previous one, where I use atmosphere to reduce detail, this time with the point of view pulled out to show a vast distance. There could have been a huge amount of detail here, but the backlit atmosphere reduces it considerably, and what I'm left with are useful silhouettes. This scene is primarily about the obelisk in the distant background and the silhouetted reflections that come all the way into the foreground. The outside edges of the scene are lost to atmosphere.

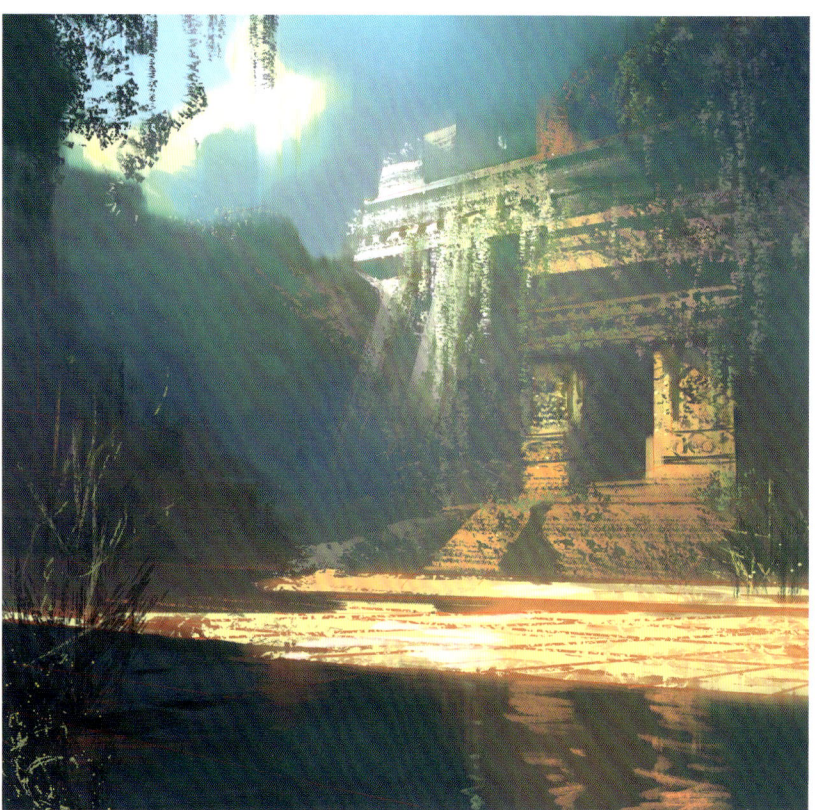

02. Sunbeams cut through the atmosphere to highlight the most important subject

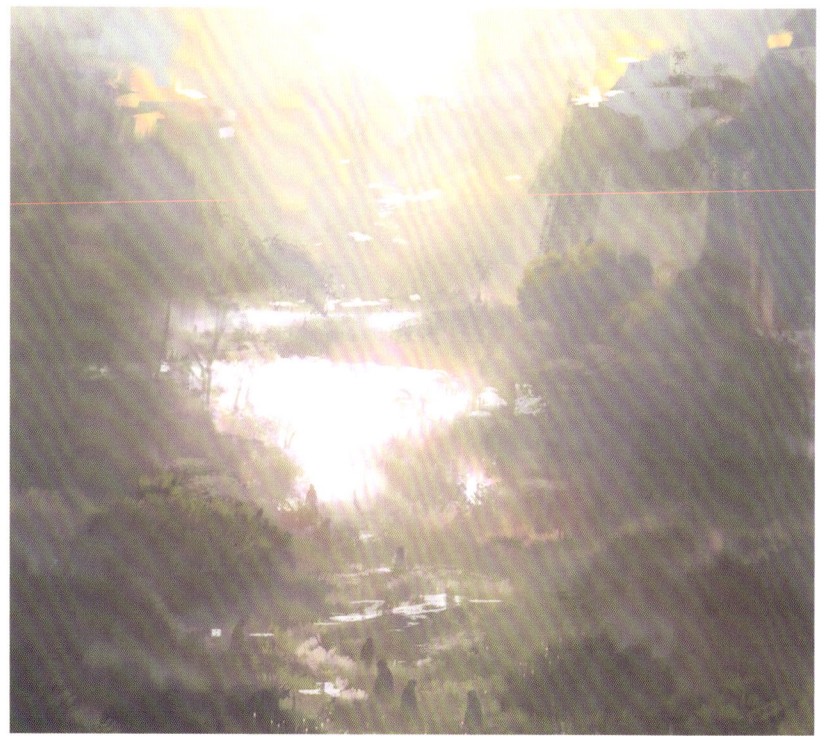

03. The less-important areas of this scene are deliberately lost in the hazy atmospheric glare

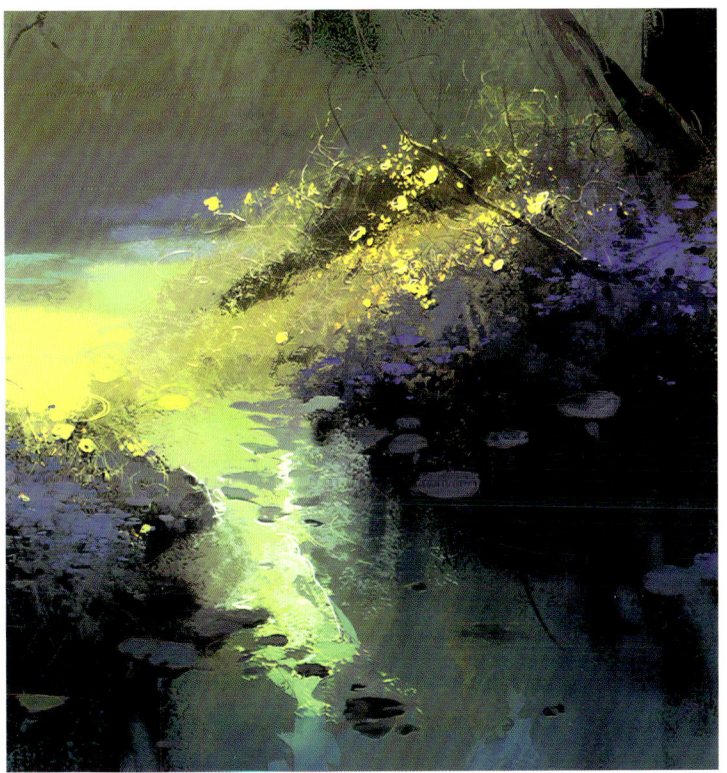

04. Note how little detail appears in the murky distance compared to the clear, vibrant focal area

04. FOCUSING THE SCENE

Let's continue using atmosphere to emphasize the important elements of an environment and reduce the less-important ones. This scene is all about the texture in the mid-ground where the cool violet light transitions into the sparkling yellow light. How special would this area seem if the background were also filled with glittery textural foliage? Not very. The humid atmosphere of the bayou helps us focus.

05. ATMOSPHERIC SHAPES

This swampy environment uses atmosphere to serve a completely new purpose. I wanted to avoid using atmosphere to mask elements in the environment, but instead use it to feature them. A jungle is filled with amazing organic shapes and it can be a brilliant, luminous experience. So here I have layers of jungle shapes with golden sunshine influencing the environment, set against distant cool atmosphere.

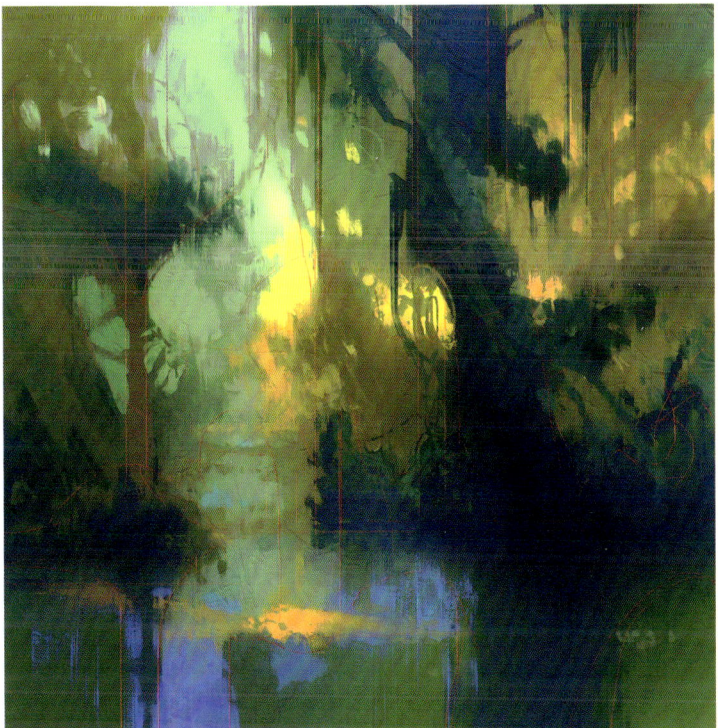

05. The atmosphere here has shapes and layers of its own, rather than simply obscuring

06. USING MIST

Here's a painting only about a jungle tree – that's the whole purpose. But a jungle is a visually competitive environment, filled with all sorts of crazy stuff to demand our attention. How do I fulfill the purpose of the image? You can and should go back through the chapters and freshen up on many different ways to design contrast. A jungle is a wet, humid, misty environment by its own nature, so let's use that! I've filled the environment with mist that captures both sunlight and atmospheric light in a way that makes the tree feel action-packed. Nothing is competing with it!

07. LOW VALUE CONTRAST

Let's wrap up this section with a very low-contrast atmospheric image. This is not an image about a contrasting tree, a silhouetted jungle, or textural foliage – it's about maintaining rich color relationships with low value contrasts. This kind of spooky and beautiful quality happens when both warm and cool light are streaming through an atmospheric environment that's primarily in shadow. We have a shaft of sunset light making its way into an abandoned alleyway with cooler atmospheric light in the background. As both temperatures combine in the distance, we get a nicely contrasting purple. The foreground is mostly warm but the rivulets of water reflect the cyan sky to give a special variety of temperature to this area.

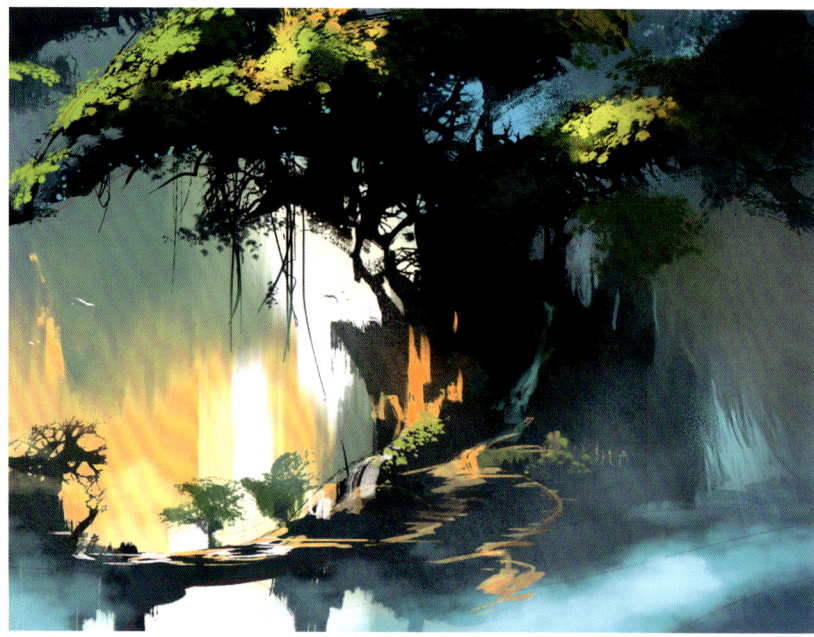

06. Humid jungle mist helps to hide unimportant areas, making the tree feel action-packed

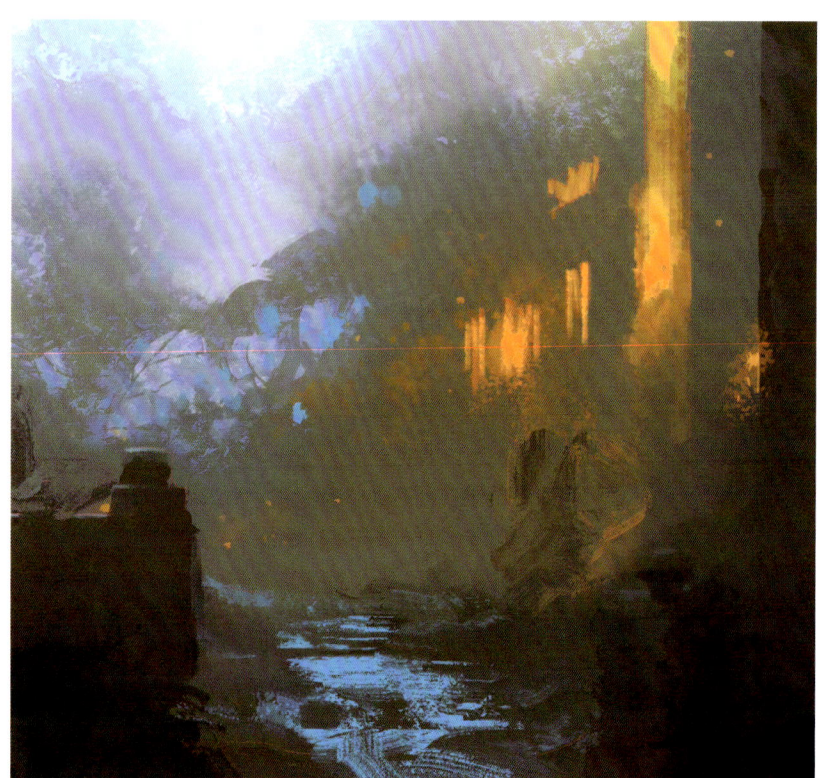

07. An atmospheric image with low contrast can still have rich, appealing color

INTERIOR ATMOSPHERE

We've all seen behind-the-scenes footage of live-action movie-making where a fog machine is used to give an atmospheric quality to an interior. The filmmakers are not creating fog, but simply volumizing the atmosphere. This is yet another way of using atmosphere to zero in on a quality of purpose. The light haze diminishes the contrast of the environment and allows the characters to be silhouetted with a clear quality of importance. Let's try out that idea in the next couple of images.

01. EMPHASIZING CHARACTERS

What's this study about? It's certainly not about columns and stairs – it's about two characters having an interaction. Passages of light and exaggerated interior atmosphere give this scene the clear statement and drama that I'm seeking.

02. FEAR OF THE UNKNOWN

I can't resist going back to the kind of Gothic mansion interiors you've seen in previous chapters. They're so spooky! You know what else is spooky? The things that we cannot see. I often refer to the idea that our eyes and our minds are likely to fill a void with a negative – something that might be even scarier than whatever our artistic capabilities could create. How about this silhouette? There are plenty of villains who are designed to have creepy expressions, but not being able to see who they are at all might be even scarier.

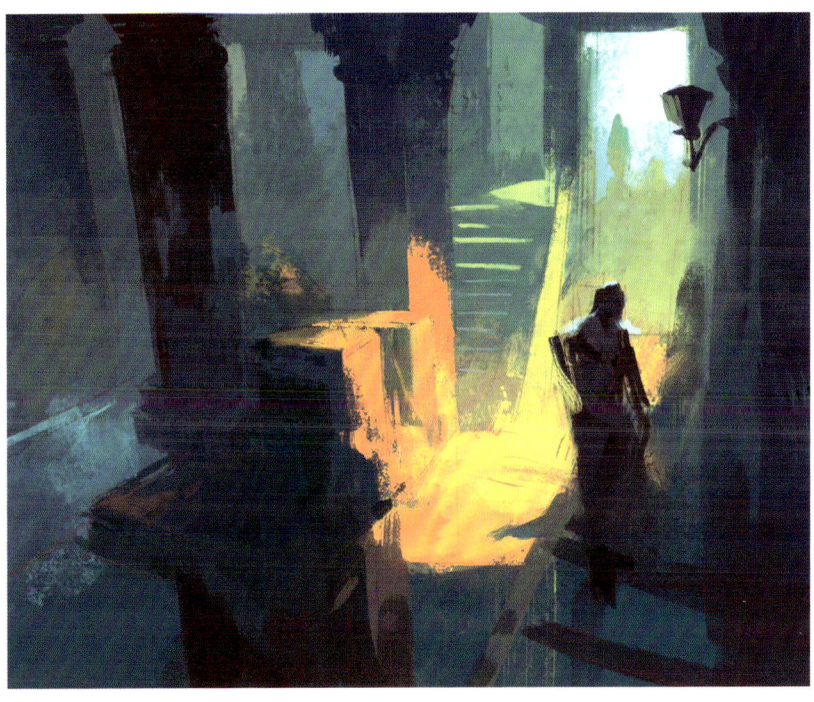

01. Even in an indoor setting, we can use the same concepts of atmosphere to create emphasis

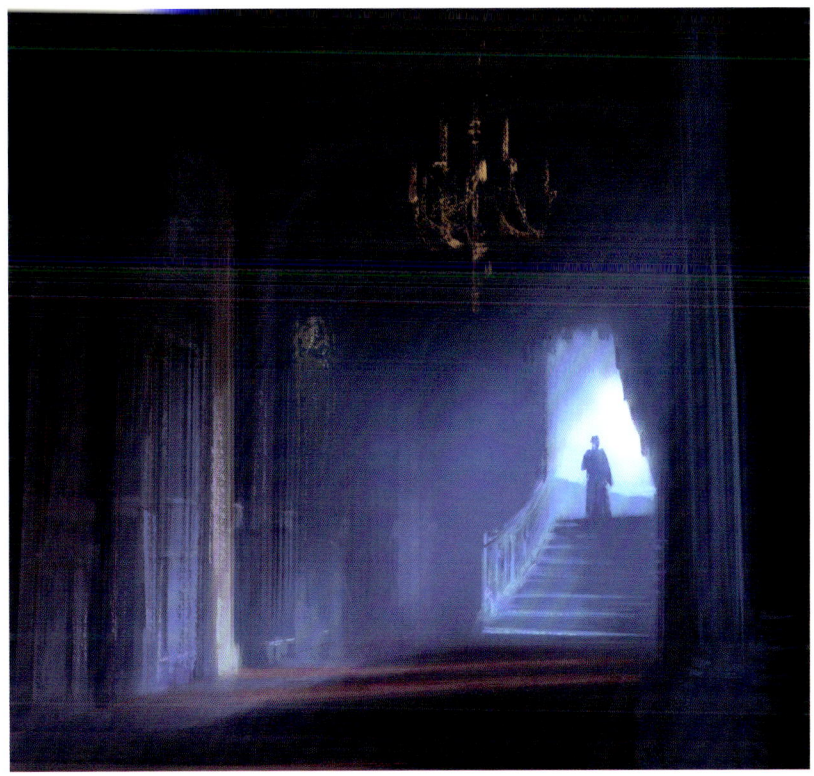

02. Use atmosphere to create silhouettes and shroud a scene with mystery

SUNRISE, SUNSET

Have you ever wondered if there's a difference between the light and atmosphere of sunrise versus sunset? There most certainly is, and it's a valuable bit of knowledge since we are called on to convey any and every possible time of day in the work we do.

Early in my career I was working on one of the *Shrek* projects and I was called on to do a montage scene that transitioned from evening into night, then early morning into day. The sunset scene had to feel different than sunrise, and I'm embarrassed to admit that at that time I didn't know how to do it. There was no Google and little internet. Luckily I had enough time to study up on the subject and work out the solution. I didn't have this book available, but you do, so we're guaranteeing that you'll never run into the same problem.

On the right page is a dramatic windswept scene at *sunrise*. I'll use it to chart out for you the differences in atmospheric qualities at the beginning and end of day. The chart below will give you the key points, but here's the main idea to be aware of: mist and fog tend to form after sunset as the earth and atmosphere cool and water droplets condense out of the air. As the sun rises the next morning, it can brilliantly illuminate these layers of fog and atmosphere until the warming air reabsorbs the water. This is the time-of-day effect you can take advantage of to convey morning versus evening.

The other thing to note is that in the morning *before sunrise*, pre-dawn light is scattered through the atmosphere, primarily the blue wavelengths, filling the environment with subdued ambient coolness. This is a highly useful time-of-day atmospheric effect, too.

Sunset

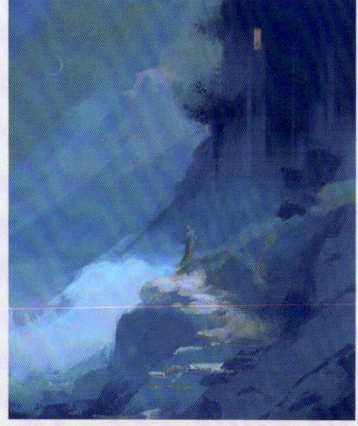

- Red-orange direct light
- Overall warmth
- Lack of low-lying fog

Pre-dawn, before sunrise

- Ambient blue light
- Low contrast
- Low-lying fog

Dawn, early sunrise

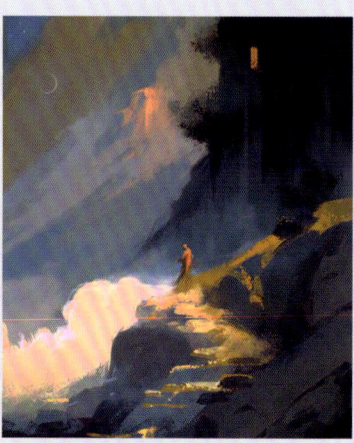

- Red morning light with ambient cool light
- Low-lying fog persists but will dissipate

△ The differences between the atmosphere and light quality at sunrise and sunset may surprise you

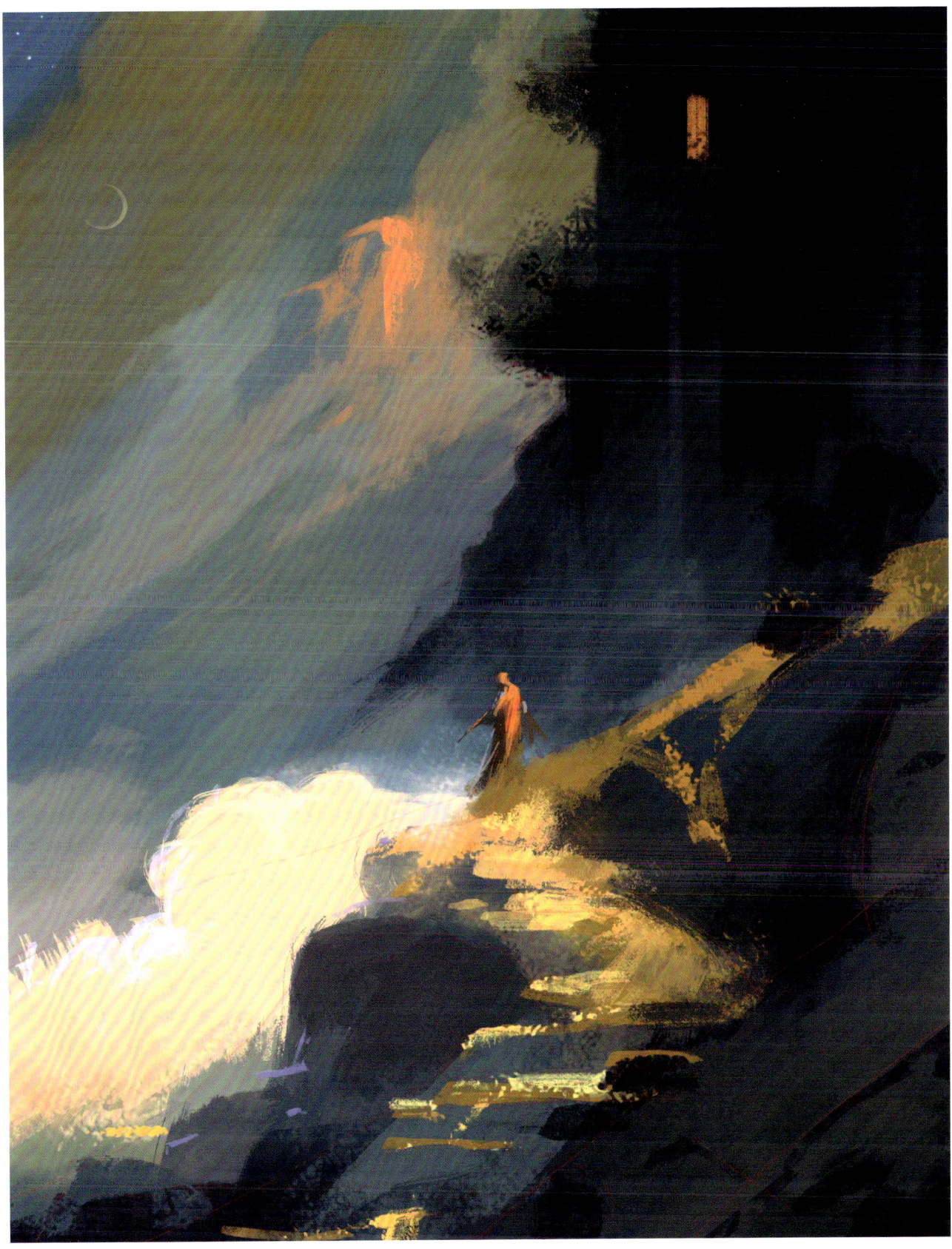

△ This early sunrise scene features both warm and cool light, and fog that will clear as the day warms up

LOST & FOUND, AGAIN

I had the opportunity to work in China for a time and took every opportunity to go sketching and sightseeing. A highlight was visiting Beijing's Forbidden City. For a Westerner, such architecture can seem mysterious and awe-striking, so back in the studio I wanted to create an image that captured that quality.

I'll repeat something that I've said before: too much information is like talking down to your audience, but carefully crafted 'lost and found' invites your audience to become a participant in the experience.

For this scene on the right, I've used heavy atmosphere to obscure architectural detail and rim light to emphasize the distinctive silhouettes. Less-important details are completely 'lost' and the important silhouettes are 'found'. I hope you enjoy the result.

01. WINTER LANDSCAPE

Let's jump from China to Poland. I accepted an invitation to do a workshop there, and luckily it was an indoor animation workshop, because the trip was during the dead of winter! For a Southern Californian, the winter environment was surreal and spectacular. When I got home, I made this scene inspired by a location visited on the trip. It's about a path leading through an atmospheric winterscape to a mysterious destination – a destination that the viewer can apply their own imagination to because the information here is 'lost and found'.

> A path leading to a mysterious destination lacking in visual information is a chance for the viewer to apply their own imagination. The information in the painting is 'lost and found'.

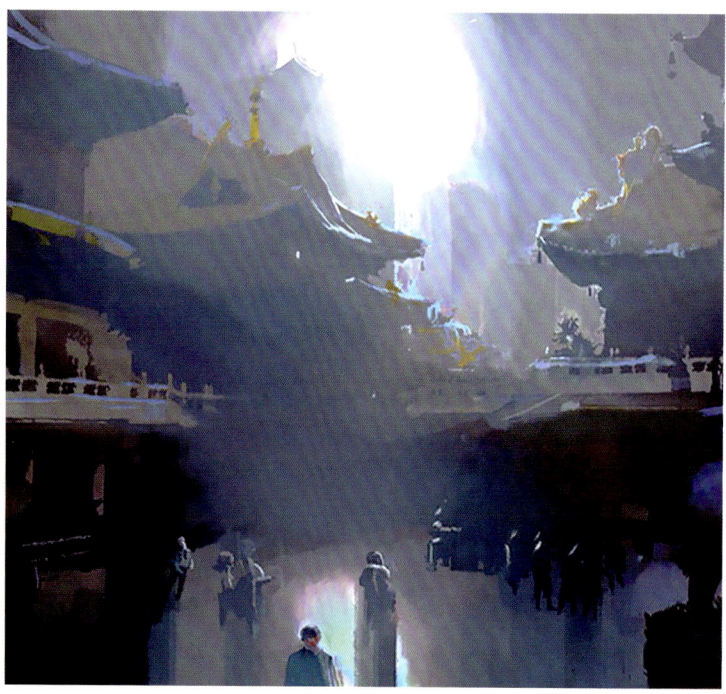

△ The use of 'lost' and 'found' details and edges give this scene its quality of purpose

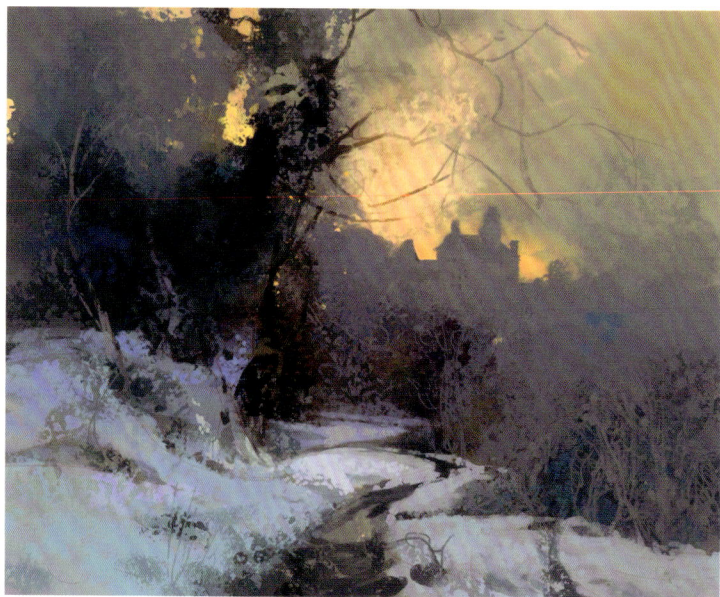

01. Here 'lost and found' adds to the stillness and mystery of the snowy landscape

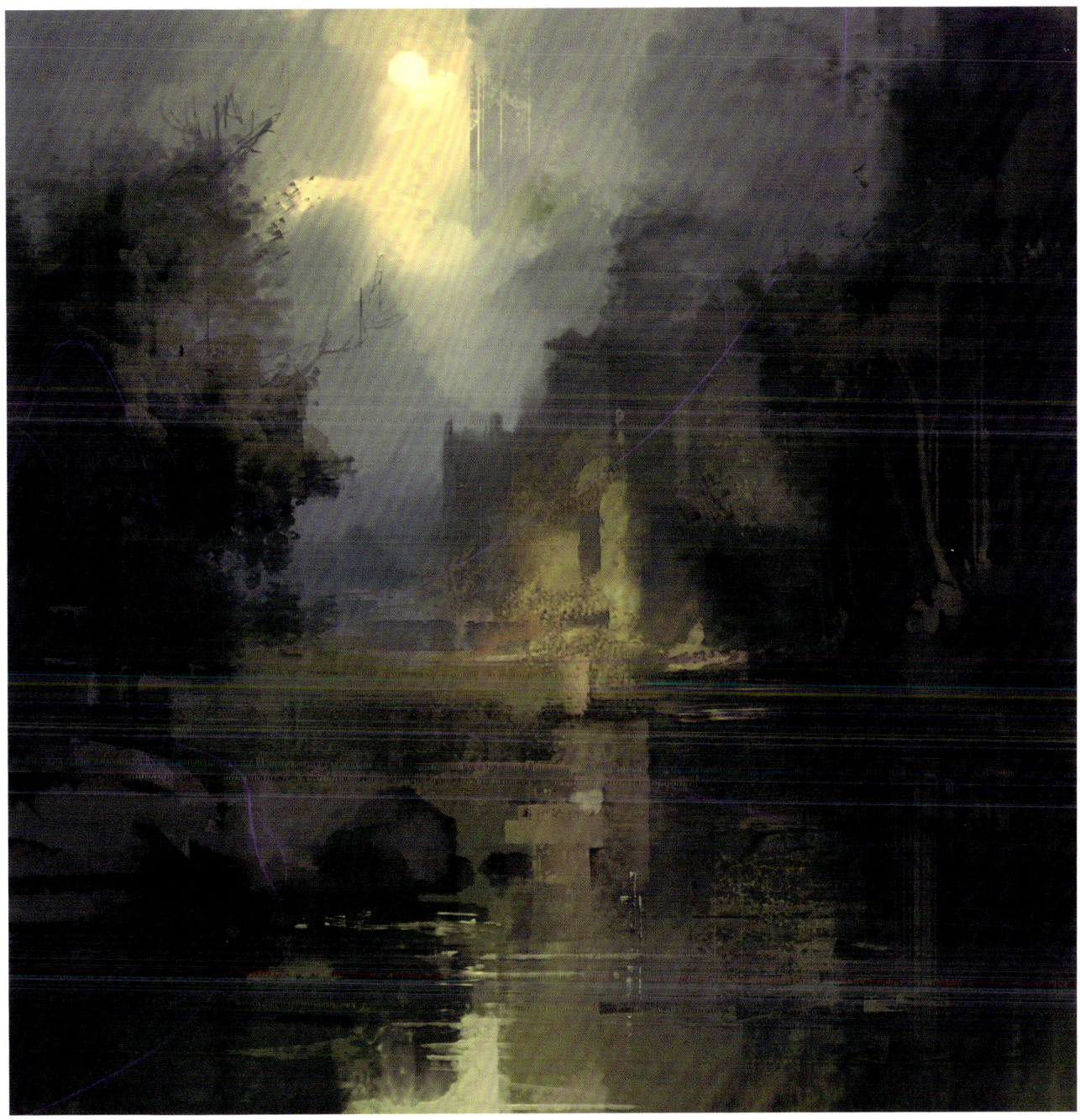

02. The edges of this scene are lost in dark atmosphere, emphasizing the brighter focal areas

02. MYSTERIOUS RUINS

Here's our final atmospheric 'lost and found' image. This is definitely not a place I ever visited – it's completely imagined. I was greatly inspired by the subject of mysterious ruins that painters in the late nineteenth century were enamored with. At that time photography was making artists aware of distant places that they couldn't otherwise access. They used these new references to paint ethereal atmospheric images that combined passages of light with areas of atmospheric mystery to great effect. I love those images and I wanted to do one too! So I worked out this scene where we are led through a reflecting lake to a distant ruin – a ruin shrouded in atmospheric mystery, but with a passage of light that helps us 'find' its entrance. The areas outside of this center of focus become more and more 'lost' in the atmosphere.

ATMOSPHERIC STYLING

You and I are visual storytellers, and we use any and every idea possible to achieve our narrative goals. So let's review additional ideas on how weather and atmosphere can be crafted to serve whatever environment and story moment is at hand.

01. MONOCHROME WINTER

Here's a little cartoon scene of icy wintertime to bring us back to the idea of the monochrome color palette. In our chapter on color (page 234), we discussed how a monochrome palette can have a singular intensity because it's only one thing, like when we experience powerful emotions. So consider using a monochrome palette when conveying emotionally powerful weather and atmosphere.

02. JUNGLE TWILIGHT

We're continuing here with a monochromatic atmospheric palette but for different reasons than the previous. This is not an icy cold environment – it's a secluded shack out in the humid jungles of South America in the pre-dawn hours. The monochromatic palette here is designed to do one thing: to accentuate the single illuminated window. Who would we meet if we ventured to this dwelling and knocked on the door?

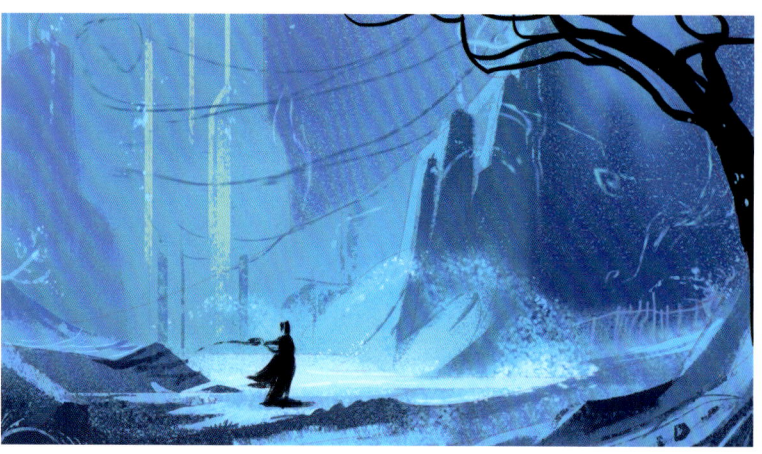

01. The all-blue palette gives this scene a highly stylized ice-cold look

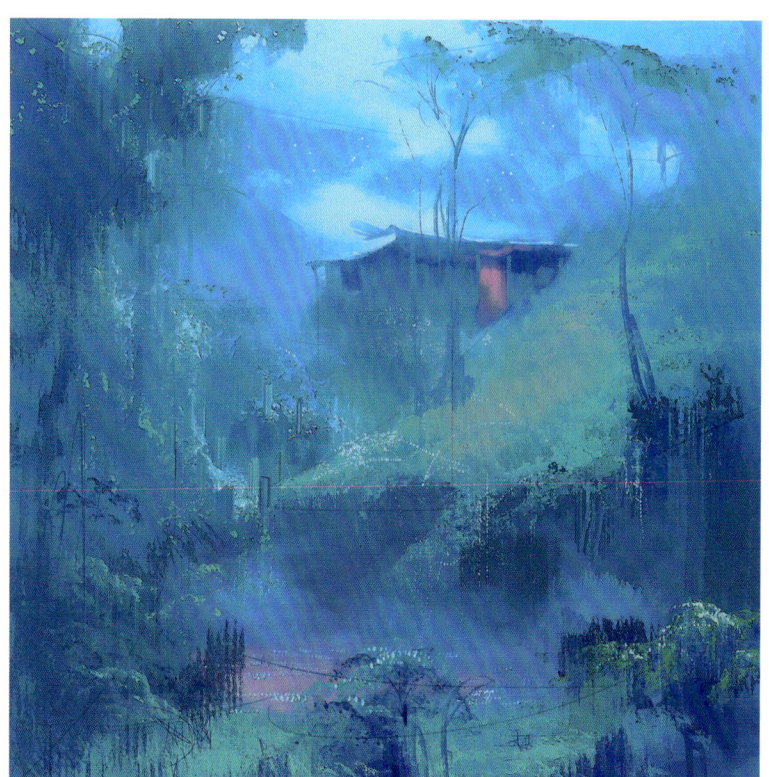

02. The cool surroundings place a strong narrative focus on the light from the hut

When we use atmosphere to make everything in an image monochromatic except for one element, that element becomes unique and special. It's a powerful way to create purpose.

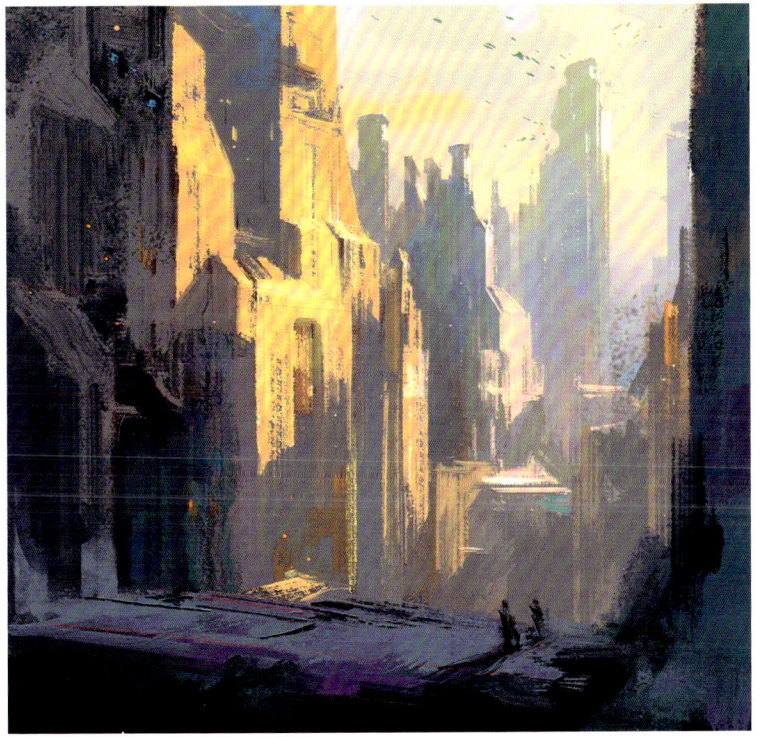

03. Monochrome local colors can appear varied and vibrant with the use of colored atmosphere

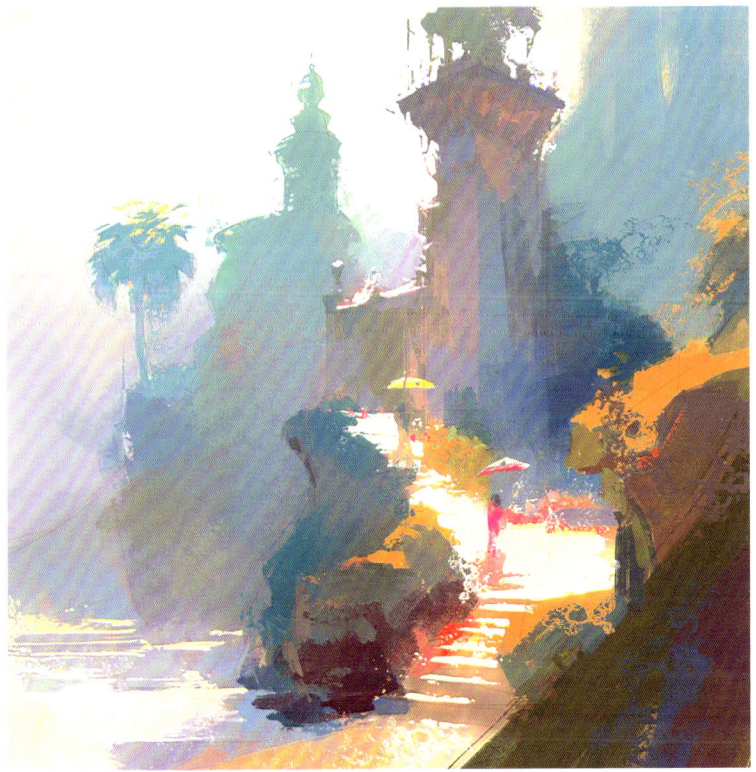

04. The colors progress from local warm tones to heightened atmospheric cools in the distance

03. WARM & COOL CITYSCAPE

Let's keep to the idea of a monochromatic palette in this sci-fi cityscape. But it's so colorful, why would I call it monochromatic? Because the local colors are monochromatic – everything is made of the same neutral substance. The part that's definitely not monochromatic is the atmospheric lighting. I'm carefully playing warm and cool in contrast to each other, with warm sunset light cascading into the city and cool atmospheric light filtering into the shadows and the distance. The key to this image is the exaggerated cool temperatures in various shadow areas. Notice how I sprinkle accents of cool green, cyan, and purple into selected areas of shadow and distance. These contrasting warms and cools give real life to a monochromatic location.

04. CLIFFTOP TOWER

Let's push harder! This image has mostly monochromatic local colors, except for accents in the foreground, and a particular emphasis on bounce light. Notice how we're progressing step by step in this section of the book: we began with a single atmospheric color, then we added a single light, then we added warm and cool contrast, and now we're adding a touch of local color and warm bounce light. These are elements that must be considered in each environment we create.

This scene gives us a special quality of depth as we're led up the stairway to this palatial tower. The orange highlights of local color hold their own in the foreground, the warm bounce light features the central tower, and the atmospheric light drops the background architecture into cool silhouettes against the glowing, luminous sky. We're making real progress in environmental expression here!

05. LOCAL LOST & FOUND

Let's now combine the idea of lost and found with the local color and atmospheric qualities discussed in the previous image. The result is something that's really good news for you and me: we don't have to spend forever rendering! We can meet challenging deadlines with expressive, engaging images! I painted this image very fast and it was well received when I posted it online; people seem to enjoy the engaging quality of atmospheric warms and cools leading us into a fantasy environment.

06. FANTASTICAL PURPLE

I keep saying to push further, so let's do it now – let's go for some purple! Remember, our job is to give our audience an experience that they don't get in their ordinary lives, an experience they can only get by coming to us.

We have here an atmospheric fantasy environment that moves from a yellow-ocher foreground to wildly exaggerated purple and magenta in the background. Why purple and magenta? First of all, they're an immediate indication of fantasy – we're now outside of the real world. Second, there's also a logic to them, because the background purples enliven the neutral ochers in the foreground. Most of all we have another shack here with a glowing green window. What strange magic is afoot in this place? And isn't it neat how the purples and magentas contrast with and enliven that glowing green?

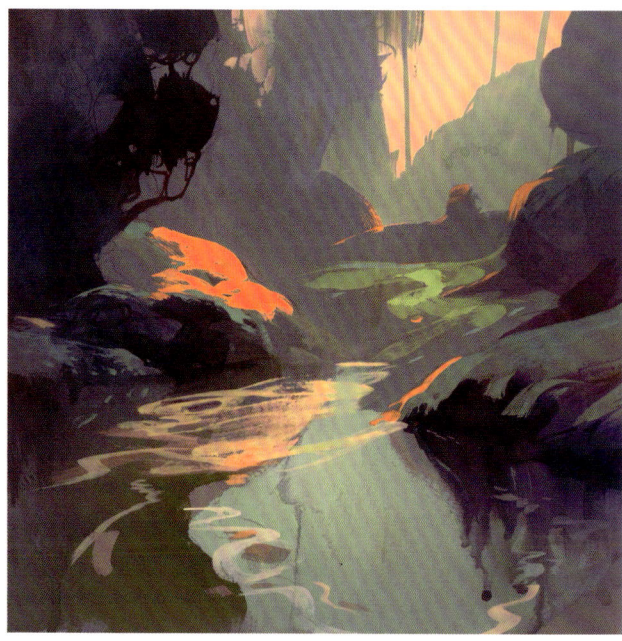

05. A 'lost-and-found' approach gives this meandering river a mysterious atmospheric depth

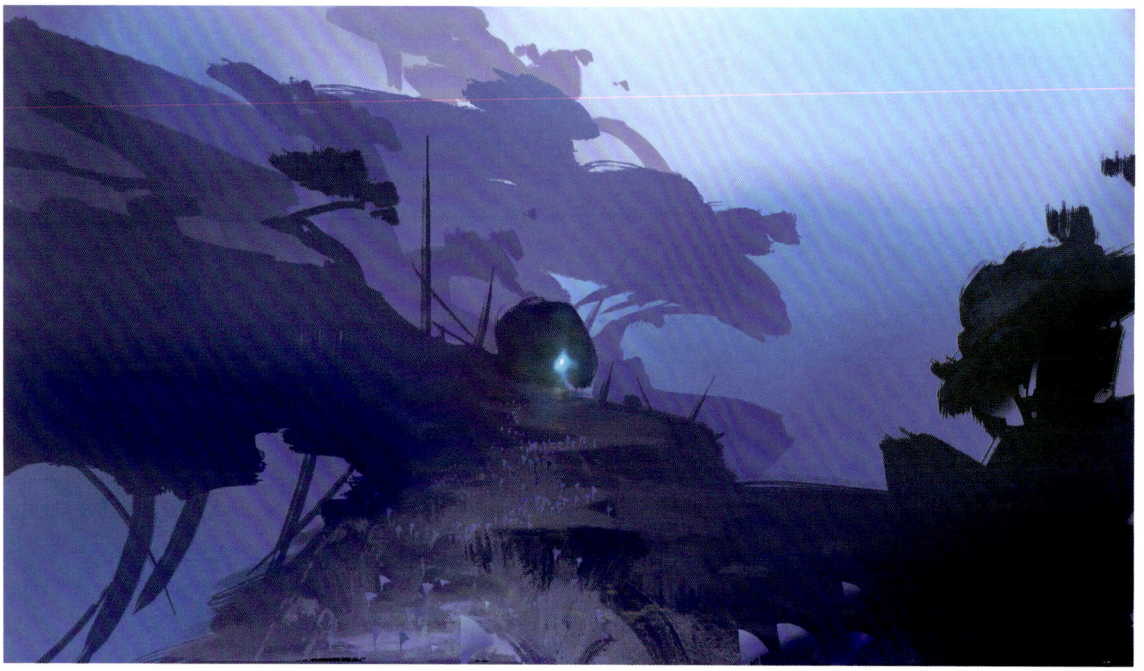

06. Purple hues immediately give a landscape an otherworldly, magical feeling

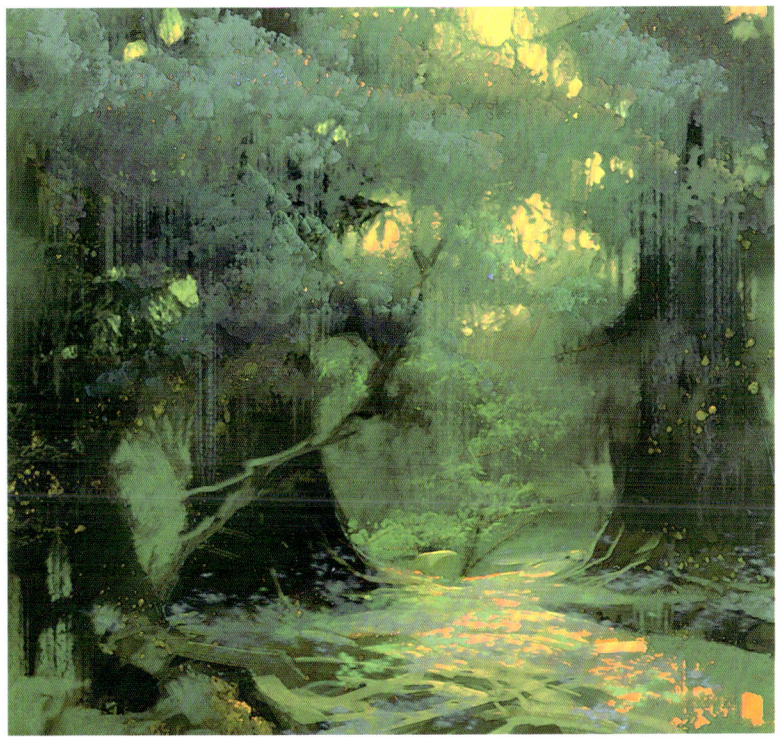

07. Natural colors such as green and yellow can appear mysterious and strange when stylized this way

When an environment has an intentionally unnatural quality of light, it tells us that the place has a mystery to be solved. This is the quality that draws in our audience, and anything that favors the attention of our audience is valuable to us.

07. DUOCHROME FOREST

OK, let's put the brakes on now. We're back to monochrome or nearly so. Let's call this a duochrome environment – it's just two colors. The two colors come from sunlight softened by the atmosphere and cool skylight throughout. I artificially pushed the atmospheric light toward green for the same reason I used purple in the previous scene. Something is different here – something is not completely natural. There's a story to be told about a forest that is not quite like any forest you've ever visited.

08. THE TICKET SELLER

For the last scene in this section, I've put together all the ideas we've been developing so far. I call this study *The Ticket Seller*. It's a scene dominated by cool atmospheric light with carefully placed accents of warm artificial light. There is some local color but only in key areas, those being the woman and child awaiting the vehicle that will take them to places unknown.

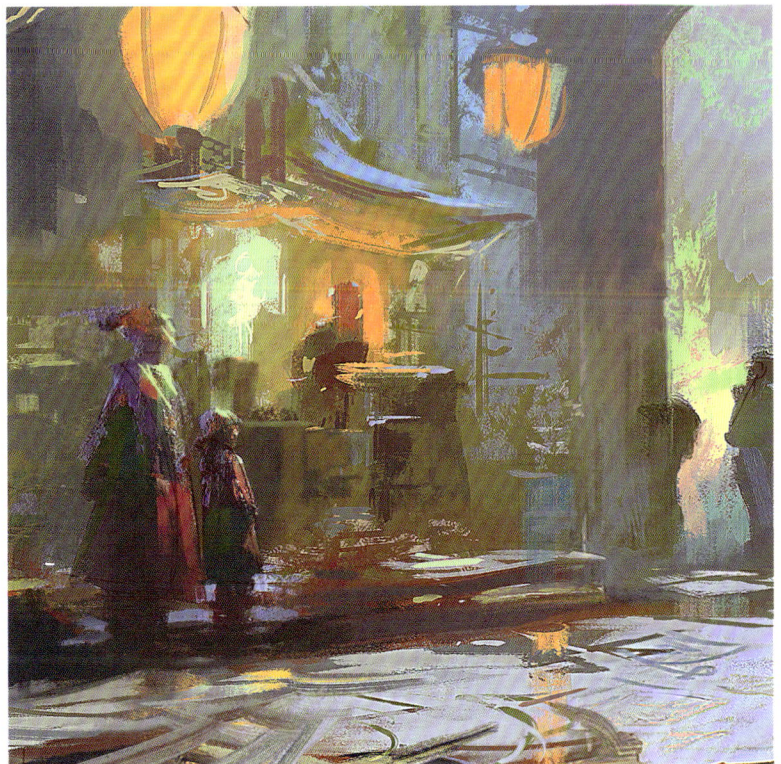

08. There is very little specific local color here, but the lighting and atmosphere are rich and colorful

FLIPPING THE SCRIPT

You might have noticed that a few of the scenes I've shown don't have the cool atmospheric background we often use to convey depth. Instead they have the opposite: a warm sunlit sky at dusk or dawn and cooler foreground. Such moments are a fantastic opportunity to feature cold atmospheric lights. I'm 'flipping the script' from the typical expectation of warmer foreground and cooler background. Let's take a look at how this effect can be used to our advantage in environment design.

01. SUNSET SKY

Next time you're looking out at an amazing sunset, take a moment to look straight up, and then look the opposite direction from the sunset. The distant horizon surrounding the sunset can be crazily warm, but the sky straight above and behind is often still intensely blue. That's the lighting I used in this scene, rather than the usual warm foreground and cool background. It flips the script in a way that gives a real magic to my subject, yet is completely natural.

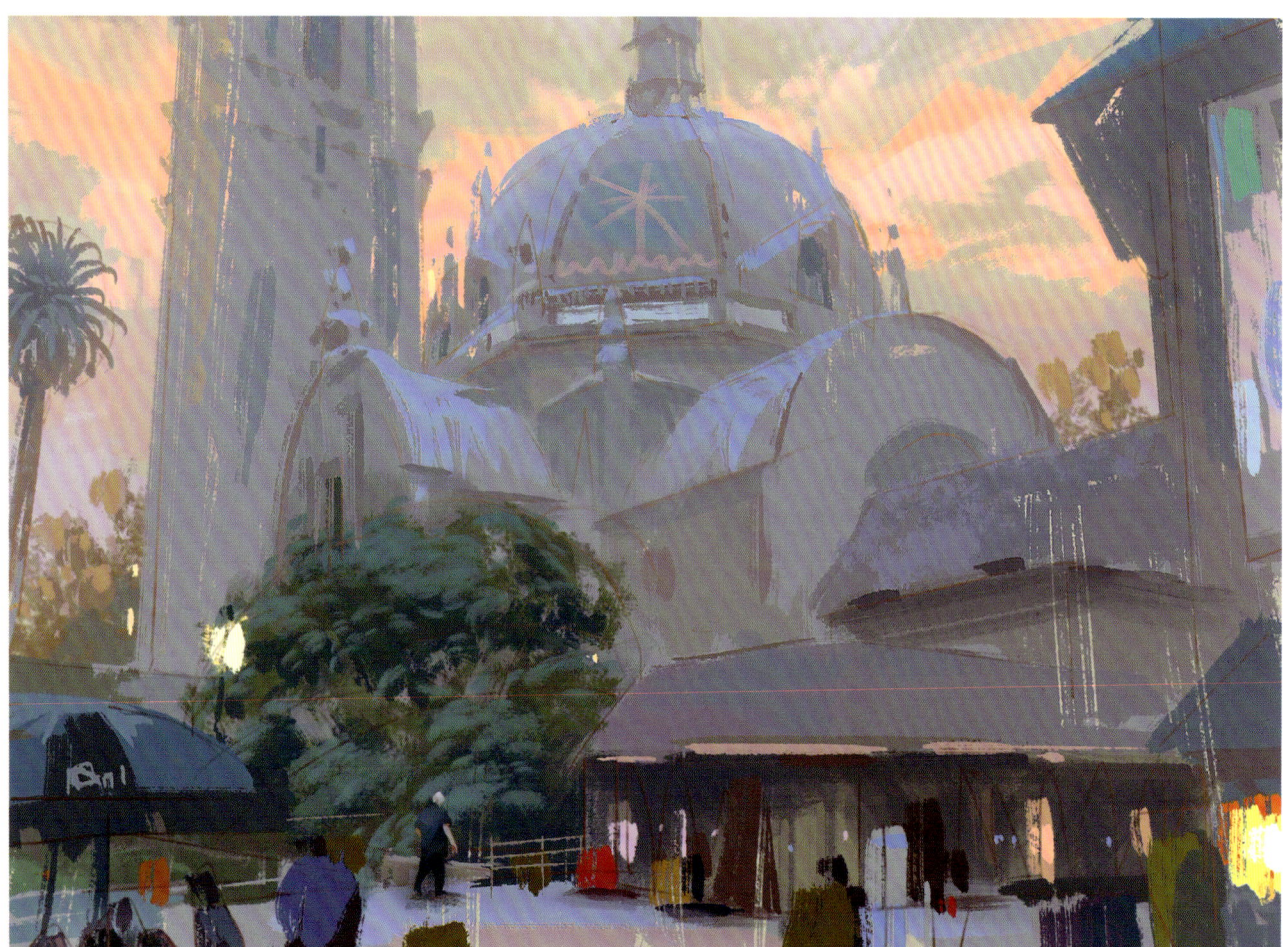

01. Blue atmospheric light on the building gives it an unexpected contrast against the warmth of the background sunset

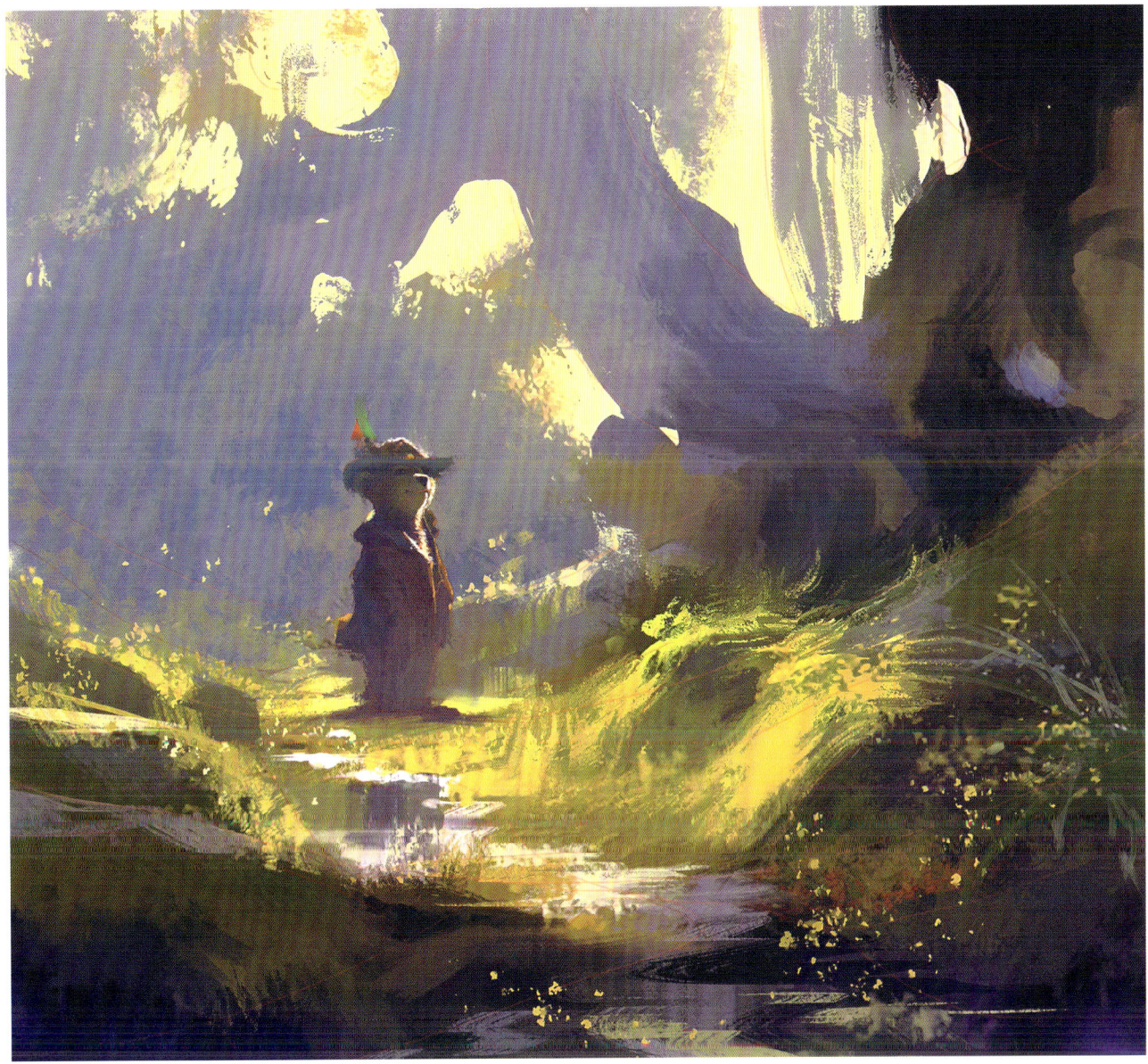

02. Cool atmospheric light makes this scene feel pleasantly warm rather than uncomfortably hot

02. WOODLAND WALK

Next up is a scene typical of my animation concept art. I call this *A Fine Day for a Stroll*. Here I wanted a glowing background atmosphere with lots of warmth, but still pleasant – too much warmth ends up feeling hot and sweaty. Once again, I used cool atmospheric lights, not so much on the subject this time but on the deep shadows in the foreground and especially the forest immediately behind the main character. I have all the warmth I need, but with enough cool contrast to feel like this is indeed a fine day for a stroll.

People tend to enjoy very warm environments, but an environment that is entirely warm starts to feel hot and sweaty rather than pleasant. Cool atmospheric light in the shadows and in key accents gives a warm environment a delightful comfort.

03. FORBIDDEN CITY

Here's another scene inspired by China's Forbidden City. It should be clear by now how I'm 'flipping the script' to give a mysterious and dramatic emphasis to the palace.

04. WARM, COOL, WARM, COOL

Here's our final image for this section. This nutty scene is what happens when you let me loose with Photoshop and no client to tell me 'no'! There's heat in the background, atmospheric cool in the mid-ground, a passage of hot direct sunlight in the front, and cool atmospheric light in the immediate foreground. Flip, flop, flip, flop – that's my formula here.

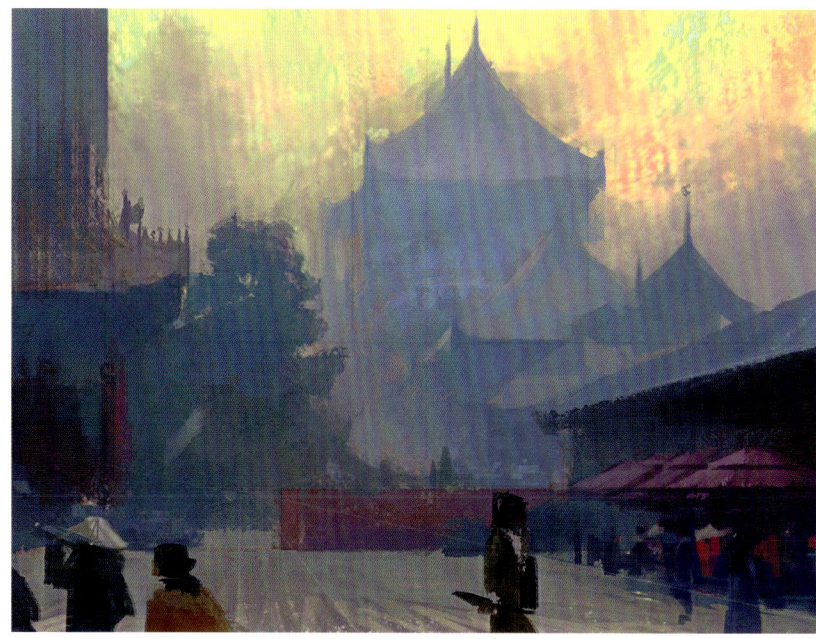

03. The cool blue buildings have a striking contrast against the warm-hued sky

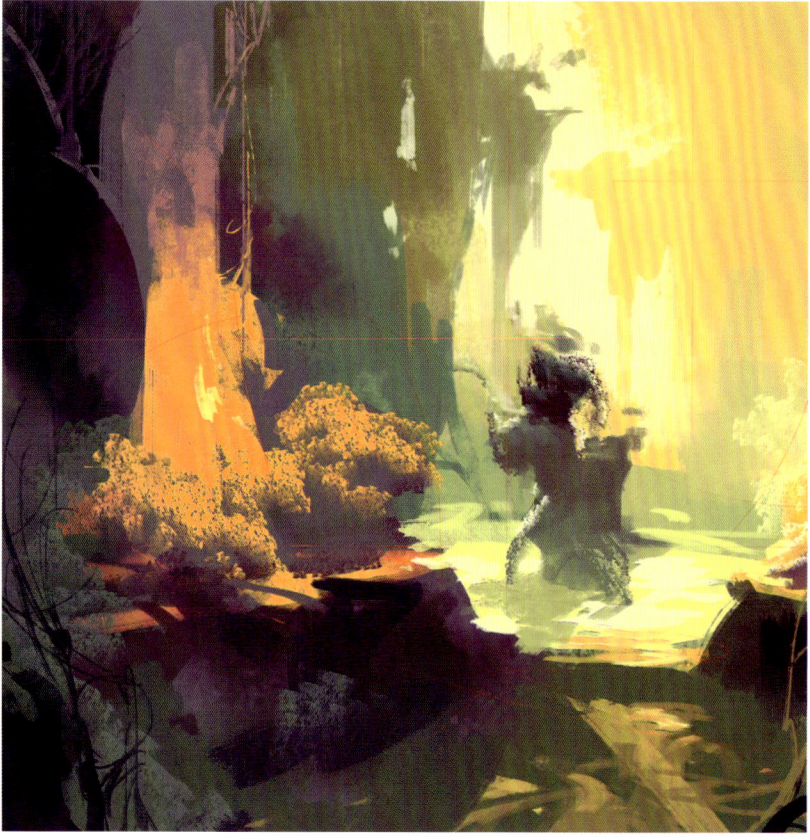

04. Can you see the alternating temperatures in this scene?

THE DESIGN OF SKIES

When designing an environment, we feel like our job is to design and light all the physical objects in the landscape, but doing that sometimes makes us forget the importance of designing the sky.

Here's a scene inspired by California's San Joaquin Valley, near where I was born and raised. It's not an area known for extreme weather but on occasion we'd get these extraordinary layers of clouds, sitting on a warm layer of air and slowly rolling through the sky. At dusk, when the sun would catch this uncommon feature of weather, the warm and cool contrasts were quite spectacular! This is not a painting about the land. It's not a landscape – it's a *skyscape*.

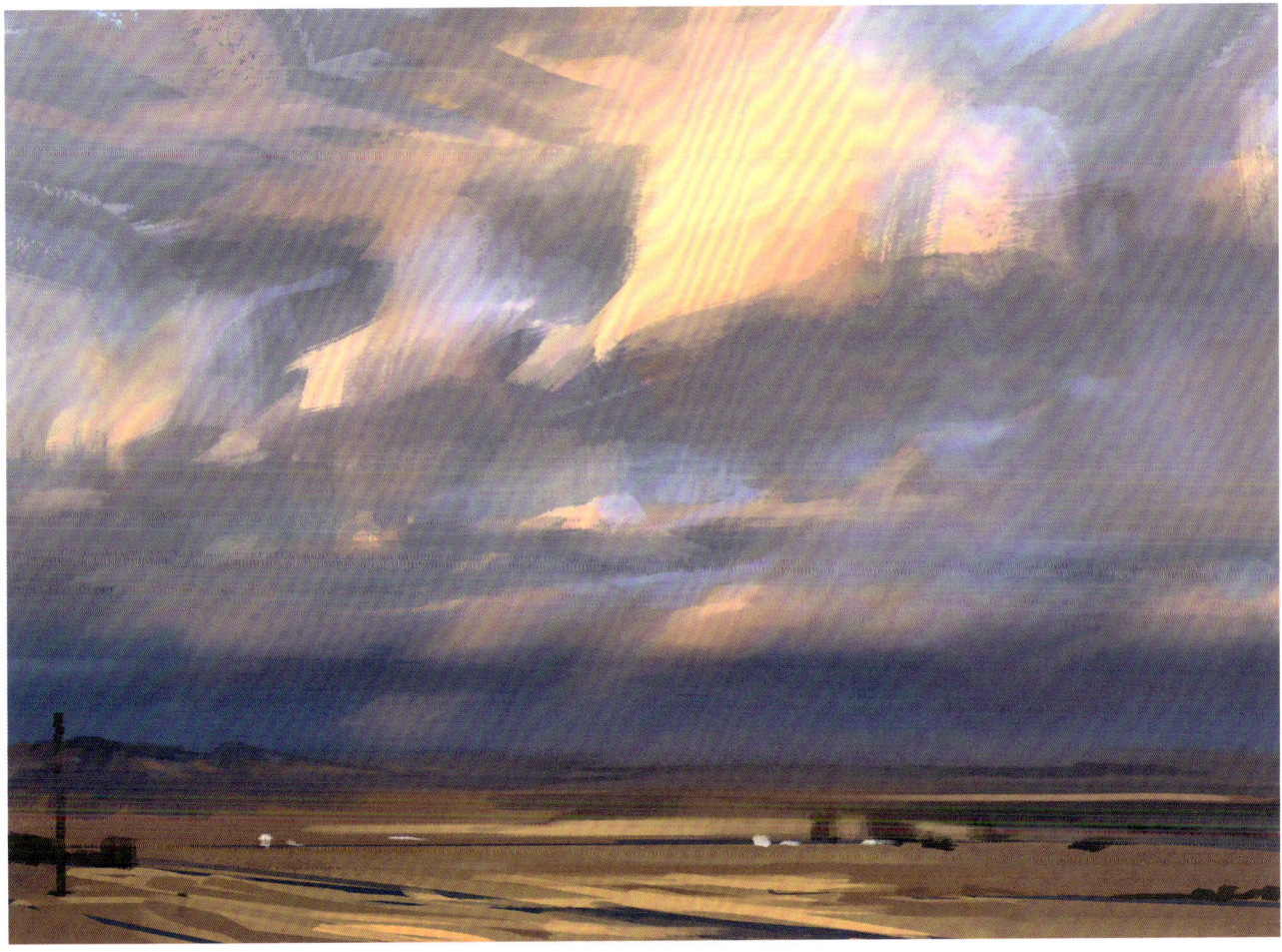

△ The design of clouds and skies can be as powerful as any landscape!

01. PARTS OF A SKYSCAPE

Let's take a moment to study the technical aspects of what's happening in the sky, because technical excellence is a rock-solid foundation that we can build artistry upon. First, clouds are subject to the laws of perspective just like anything else. I'm carefully following perspective here to give the sky the quality of a massive canopy that hangs over our heads.

Next, as fluffy and ephemeral as clouds are, they still have three-dimensional form. That quality can be emphasized to give them a substantive presence.

Finally, in this scene there's a flow of wind slowly pushing the clouds across the environment. All the clouds in the mid-ground and background have the same tipping quality to indicate that they are all affected by wind in the same way.

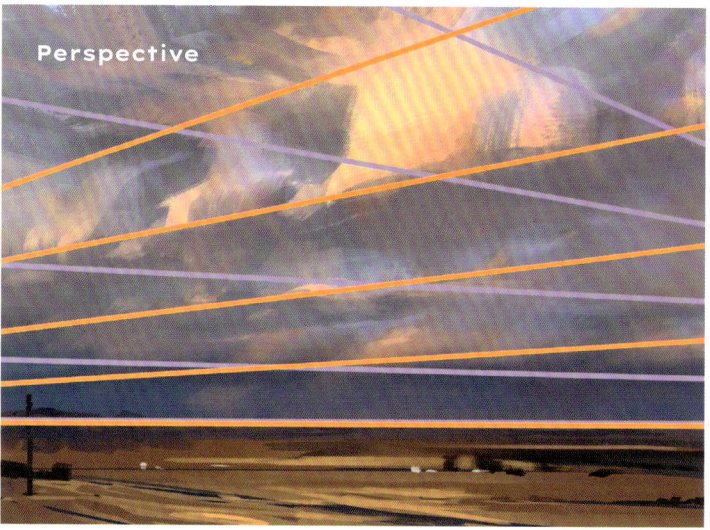

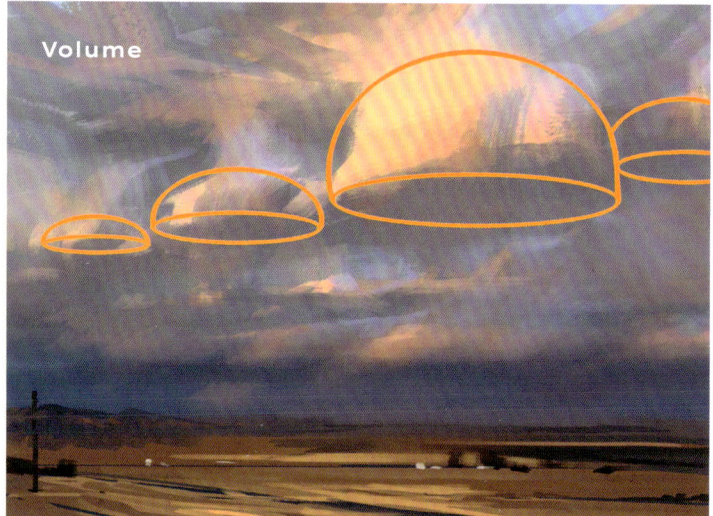

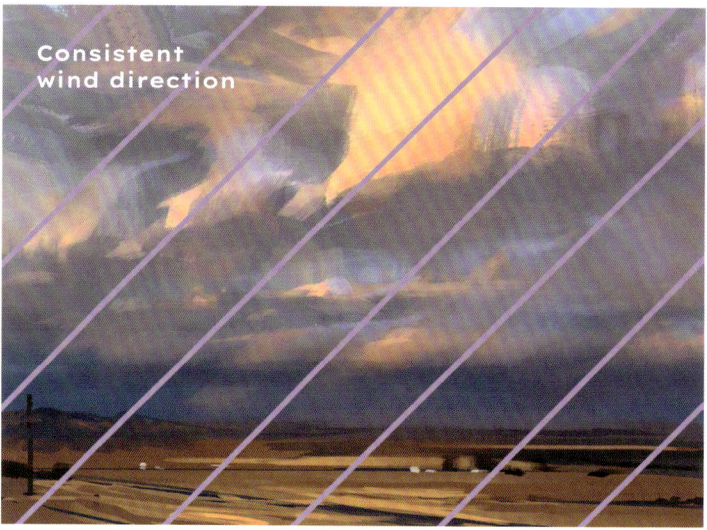

01. Keep these essentials in mind when painting skies and clouds

02. DRAMATIC CLOUDS

And since we're on the subject of clouds, let's really go for it here. If you've spent any time in the tropics, you've seen the awe-inspiring clouds and thunderheads that form there. The scale of the skies in a place like this is incredible, so I've made this painting about that idea: *scale*. The horizon line is very low in the frame so that we're looking up into the cloudscape. The tiny indications of people are a scale reference as well.

03. INTENSIFYING COLOR

Here's a moody painting inspired by the Gendarmenmarkt square in Berlin. I really wanted to do something tricky in this image: I wanted to feature the coppery accents of the dome and sculptures atop the Konzerthaus in a different way than one might expect. I'm sure you're familiar with the cyan-and-greenish patina that forms when copper is exposed to weather – many rooftop architectures have been made of copper throughout history, and the primary ingredient of bronze sculptures is also copper.

When we're contrasting a color, our instinct is to go to its 'opposite' – for example, a red hue to contrast with a green hue. But you've seen me use that idea many times already, so let's try something different! Let's intensify the importance of a color by repeating it. In the sky directly above the Konzerthaus sculptures I've indicated the crackling ozone of an electric storm. The cyans created by this effect give a unified importance to this particular area of the environment. This is careful design of a sky.

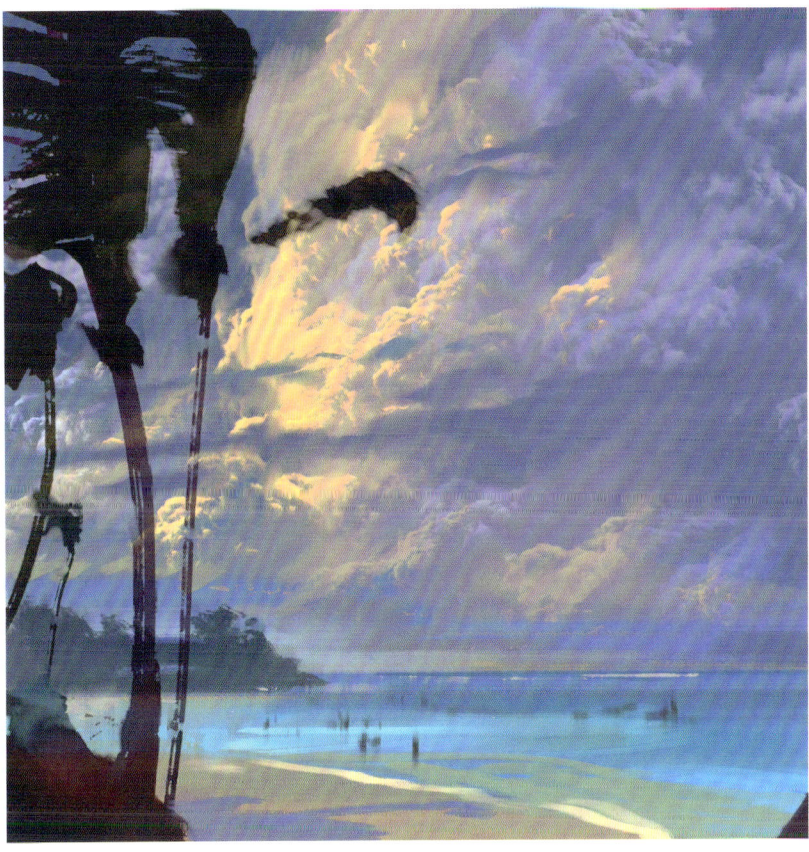

02. This scene is focused on emphasizing the vast scale of this tropical thunderhead

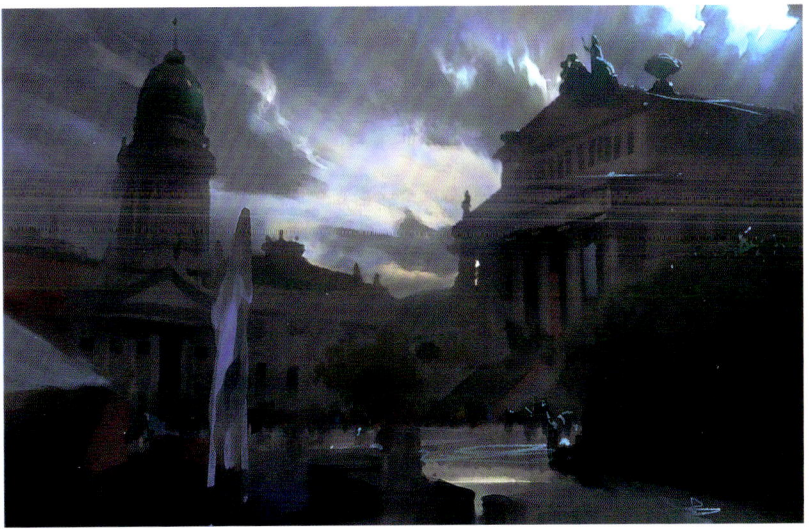

03. Here I use the cyans of an electrical storm to harmonize with the green oxidized copper on the rooftops

04. OPPOSITE COLORS

Green- and cyan-colored skies are really fun, right? So let's see if we can do it again. The Northern Lights are a great way to give real magic to a sky, and in this case I'm doing exactly the thing I was avoiding in the previous image. I've put a magical magenta in the mid-ground as a contrast to the cyan green of the distant sky.

05. HEAVY STORM

And let's wrap up sky design with one last hit of epic weather. We've all seen the oversized twisters that can form in the stormy skies over the American Midwest. These storms are so destructive that nothing can be done other than hiding yourself away in a specially designed storm cellar that will keep you from being carried away, never to be seen again. But in that cellar, you still hear and feel the rolling boom of thunder above. You can hide from the wind and rain but you can't hide from thunder. That's the feeling that I'm trying to evoke in this study of extreme weather.

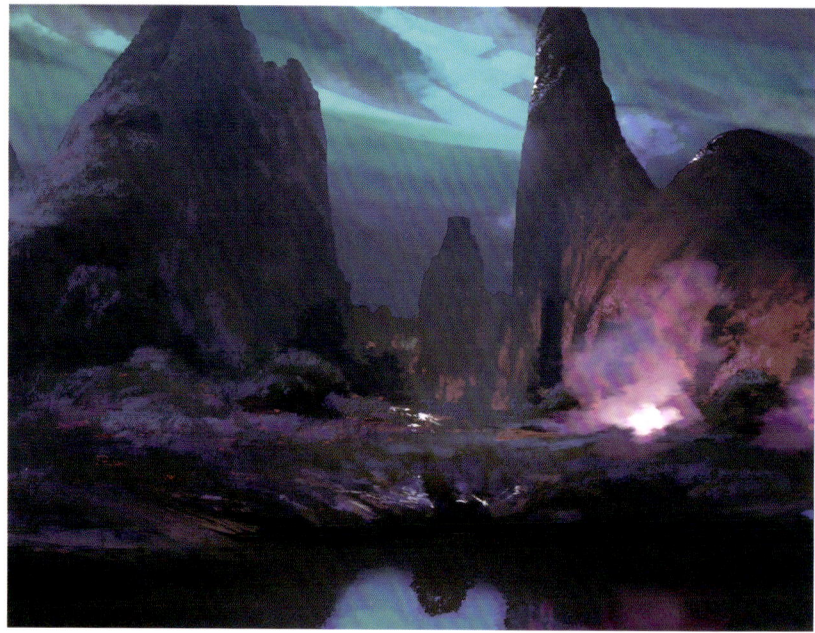

04. This time 'opposite' hues of magenta and red are used for contrast with the cool sky colors

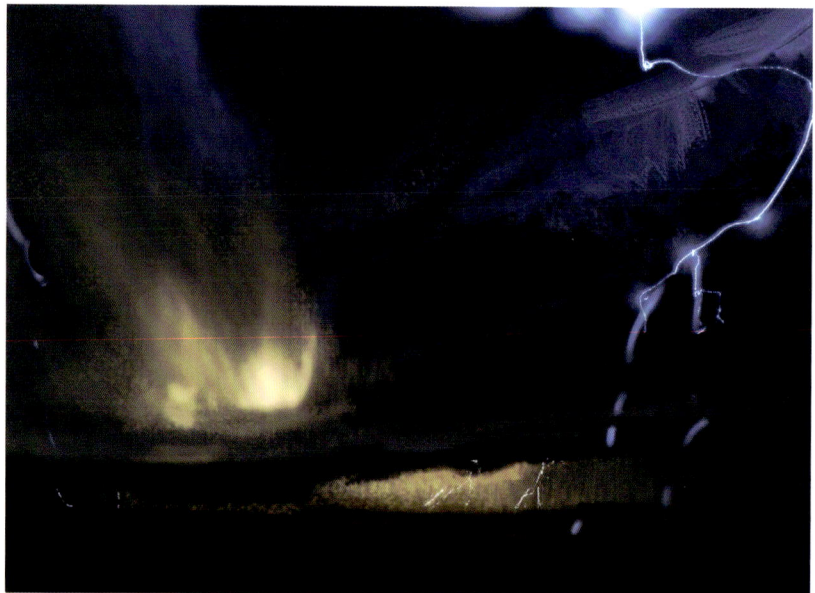

05. This skyscape is oppressively dark and inescapable

OH, THE EMOTION!

By now you're familiar with my pattern for every single chapter of this book: we go over a series of ideas and principles, and then we bring them all back to emotion. Nobody cares about our work if it doesn't evoke emotion in some way.

Let's continue with the design of skies here in this little seaside village, but now with an eye toward visually creating emotion. I'm changing up the sky each time with that goal in mind. Let's repeat one of my mantras: *you must have the technical and artistic ability to evoke any and every human emotion through visual design*. And, of course, weather and atmosphere are potent ways to achieve this.

Have a close look at each of the images below and observe how the sky has changed to evoke a new emotion each time. My favorite of these four images is the third, with the emotion of oppressiveness. Don't get me wrong, I don't like oppressive skies in the real world, but there's something so evocative about a low-hanging black canopy of clouds. It's almost claustrophobic in the way it bears down on you – I like this idea because it's so intensely emotional.

This section will go through a series of images where I'm attempting to have the totality of the environment evoke a singular emotion.

You must have the technical and artistic ability to evoke any and every human emotion through visual design, and weather and atmosphere are potent ways to achieve this.

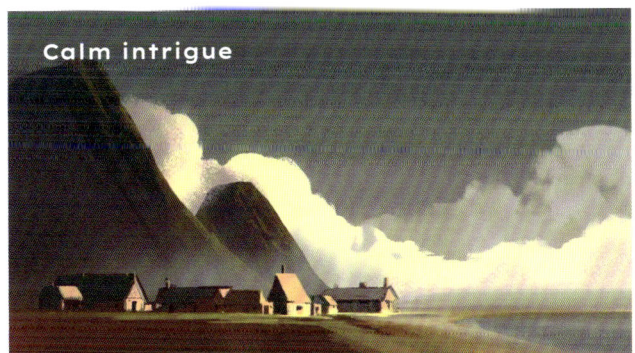

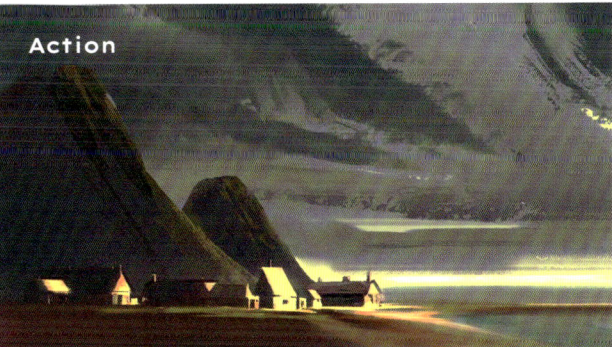

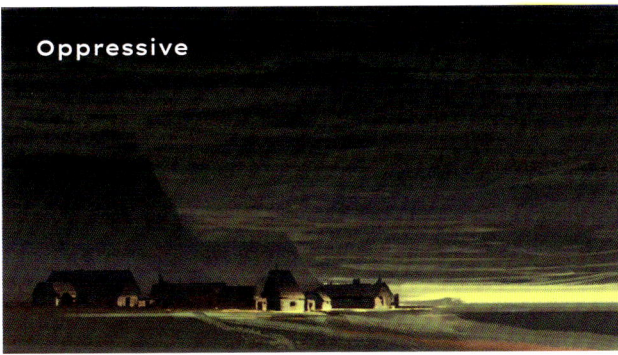

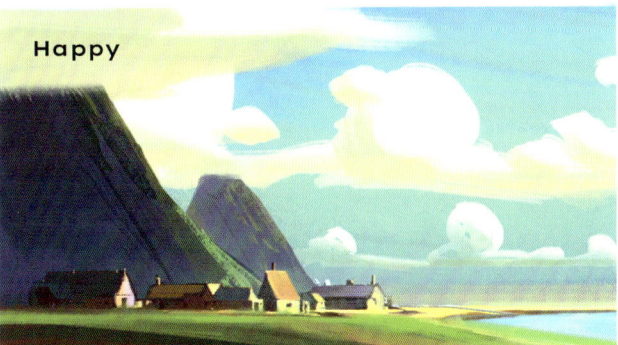

△ Changing the sky design alters our emotional perception of this seaside village

347

01. LIMINAL

At the time of writing this book, there's been a term going around that was new to me but that I've really fallen for: 'liminal space'. It's the idea or feeling of being at the edge of an event: something is happening, some new experience is coming, but we don't yet know what it is or what it will be. It's the uncertain feeling of being between places, literally or metaphorically.

Can such an abstract concept be conveyed visually in one image? I think it can, and here's my shot at it. In this environment, the oppressive marine layer hanging overhead contrasts with the electric green in the distance and creates that transitional effect that a change is coming. The overhang has the oppressive effect we looked at previously, and the electric green is a color that's almost supernatural. It's filled with possibilities and maybe even opportunities.

02. TRAGIC

This approach is no doubt familiar because it's so effective: monochromatic cool-gray lighting, a steady drizzle of rain, and sodden ground that's turned to mud, all combining to suggest a tragic sense of loss.

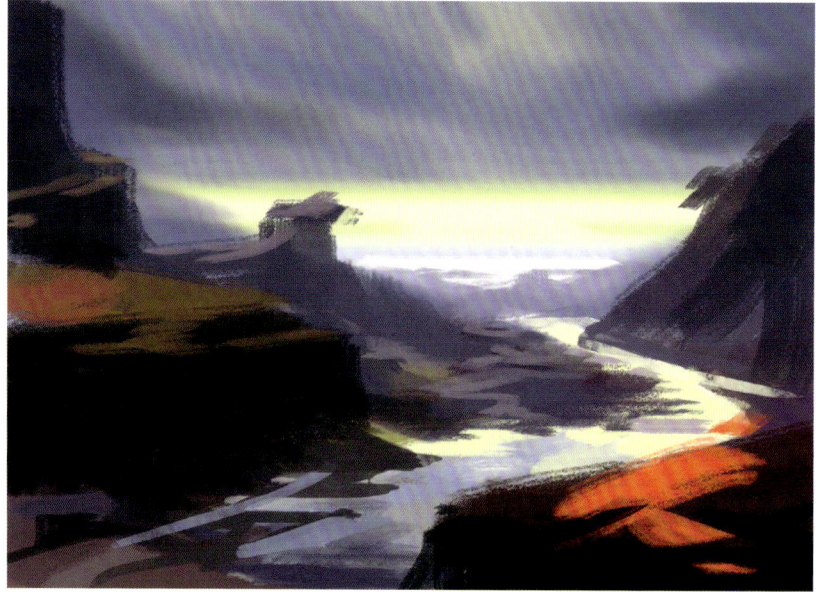

01. This scene aims for an uncertain, in-between feeling that something's about to happen

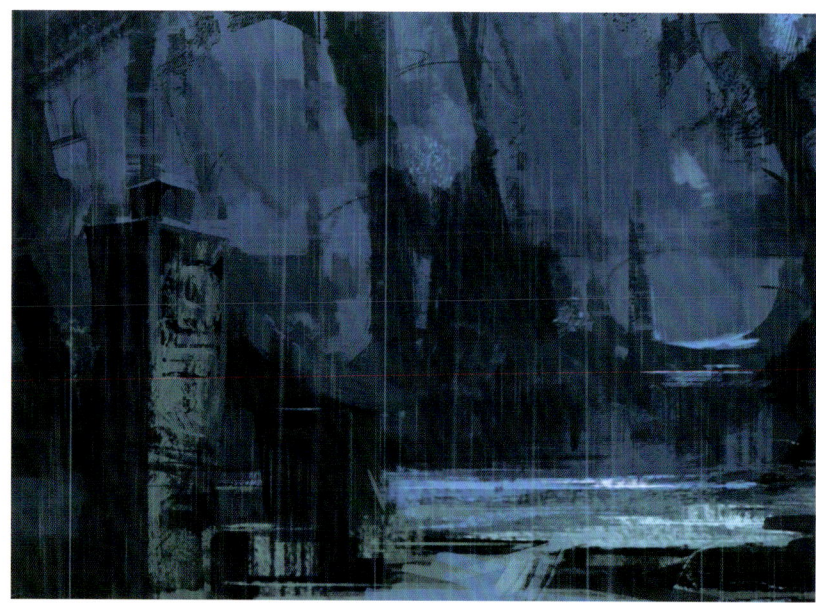

02. Dark, wet, and murky – this image projects a feeling of misery and tragedy

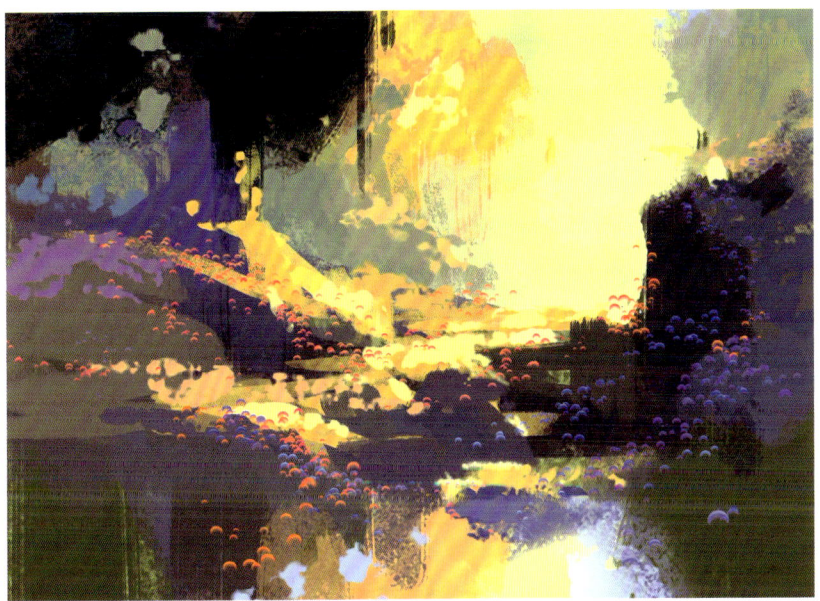

03. Sunny yellows and rich purples combine to make a cheerful, vibrant scene

03. JOYFUL

Enough of the moody depression – let's get back to the joy we all hope for. This warm environment is contrasted with some atmospheric cools and the local color accents of attractive magenta flowers. These all combine for a positive, uplifting quality.

04. DRAMATIC

When the sun cuts through a volume of clouds, extraordinary things can happen. The sun's rays can go wild as they radiate outward, and massive passages of light and shadow can be cast across the land. To intensify this dramatic effect I went back to the idea of a potent monochromatic color palette. I made everything red – a color filled with drama.

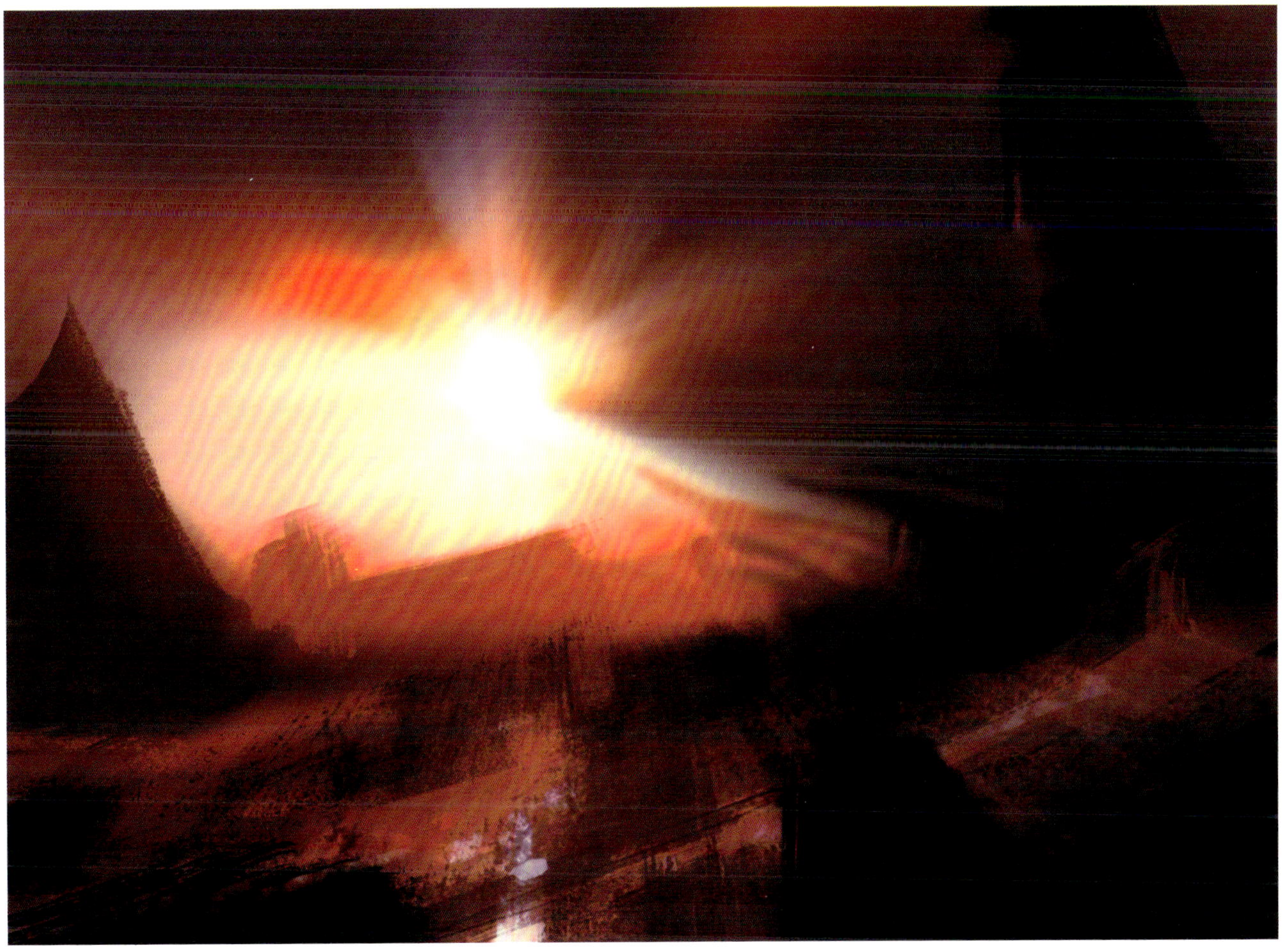

04. A red palette and striking rays of light make this image dramatic and powerful

05. SPOOKY

These two images are driven by their subject matter for their creepiness – dead trees, craggy rocks, and moldy local colors – but they both rely on atmosphere to clinch the effect. The first uses surreal greens for the atmospheric lighting, contrasted by rusty reds in the trees, to give it a sour, unnatural effect. The second uses the familiar trope of a full moon shrouded in clouds, backlighting a spooky house where bats undoubtedly dwell in the attic.

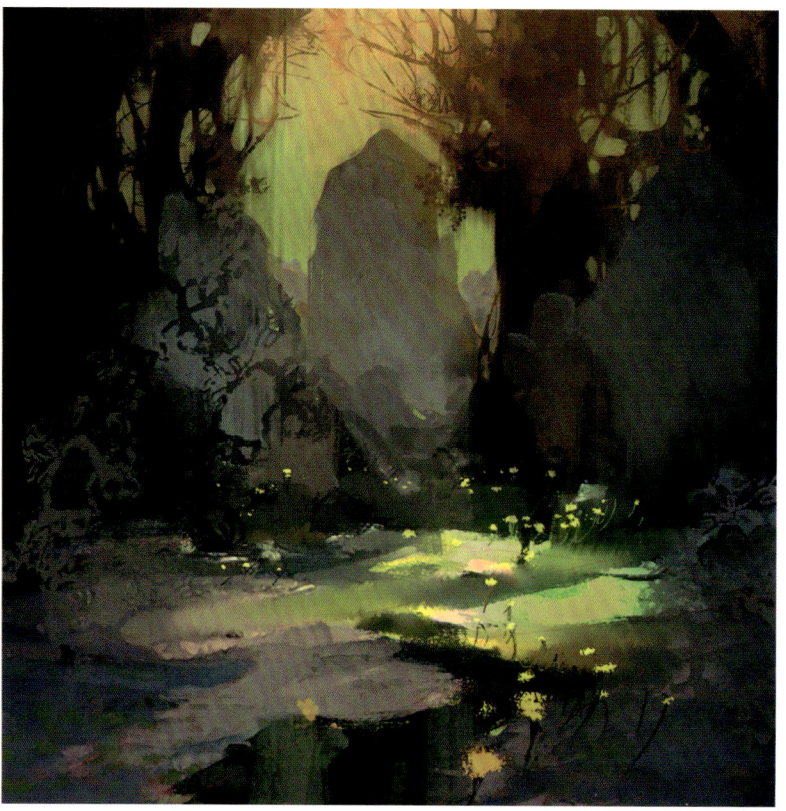

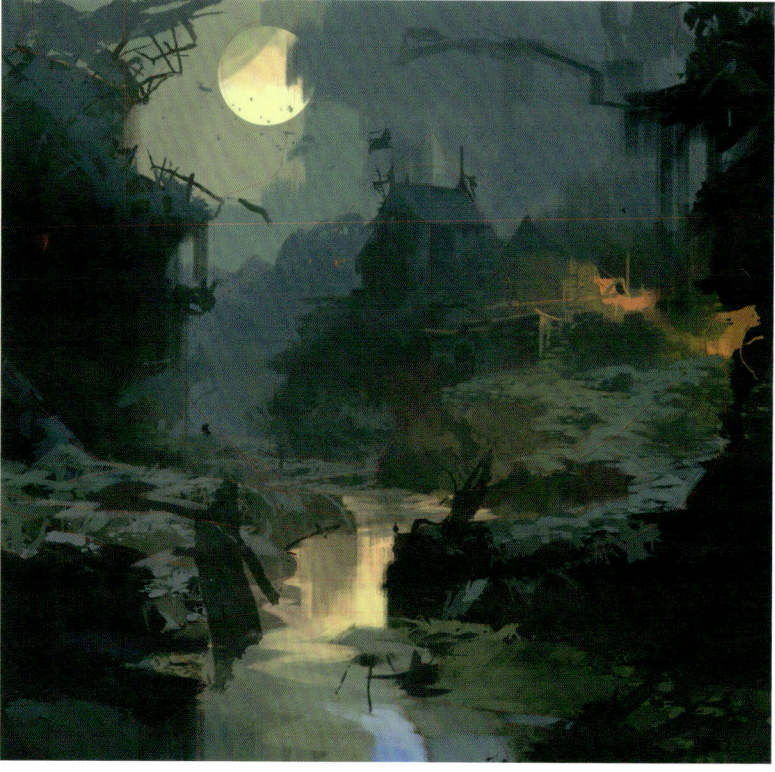

05. Spindly branches, craggy terrain, and sickly greens make these environments intriguingly creepy

06. REALLY, REALLY SPOOKY

I'm going for broke now! This ominous image combines dramatic triangular shape language with a wildly exaggerated tipping perspective. Add to that the stormy but eerily green illuminated sky and fierce rainfall, and we have something that's really, really spooky.

07. HOPELESS

This one was tricky for me to render. Everything in the distance needed to be misty and blurred by rain, but the scene also has a shallow depth of field, which would put a focal blur on everything in the near foreground. It was hard for me to find the right spots to bring into focus, but I worked at it until I felt good about the hard/soft balance. Of course, the character is important too, dragging his way through a sodden marsh in the pouring rain. I really hope he makes it!

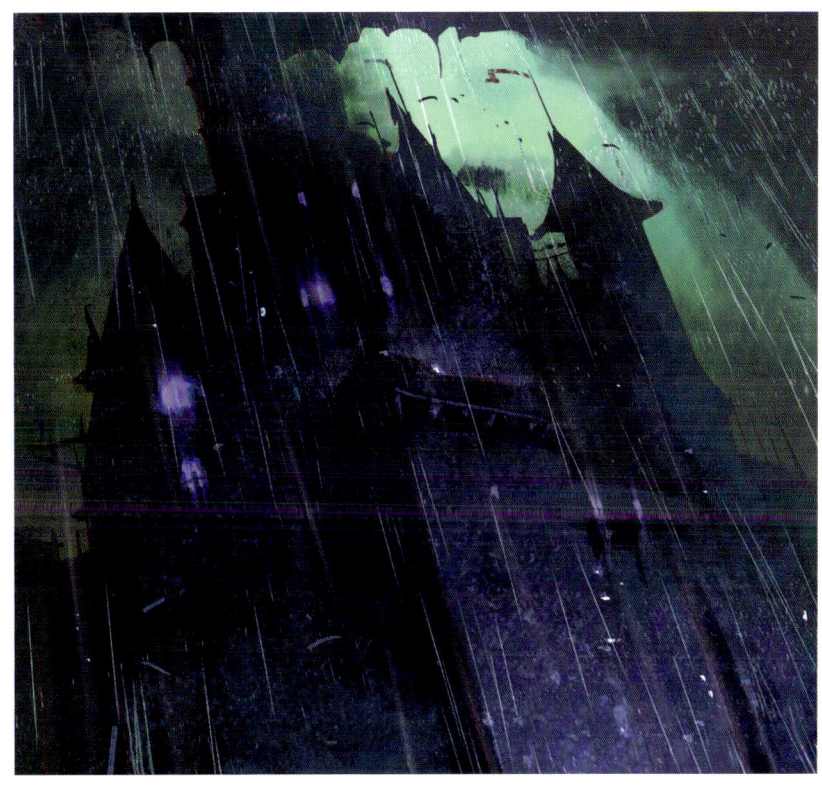

06. Sharp shapes, dramatic perspective, and eerie colors make this image darkly menacing

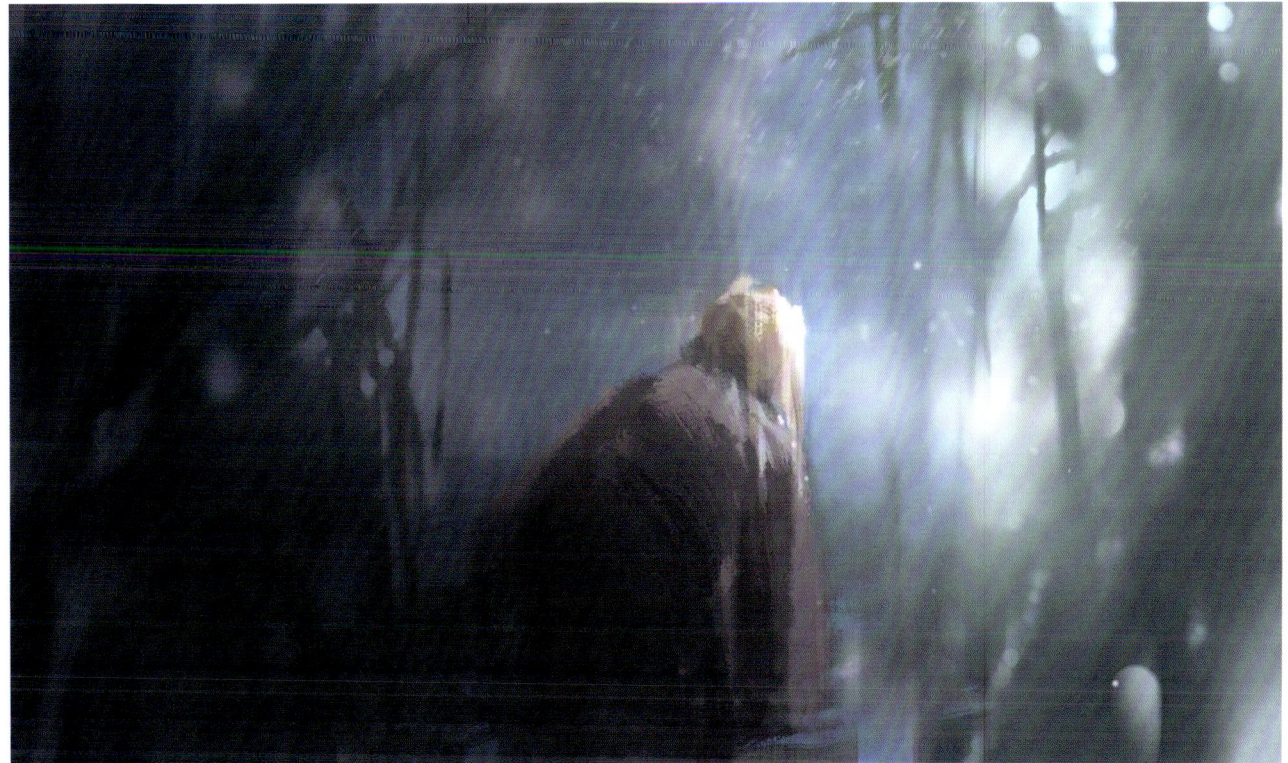

07. The feeling of despair comes through in the hazy gray wetness of this scene

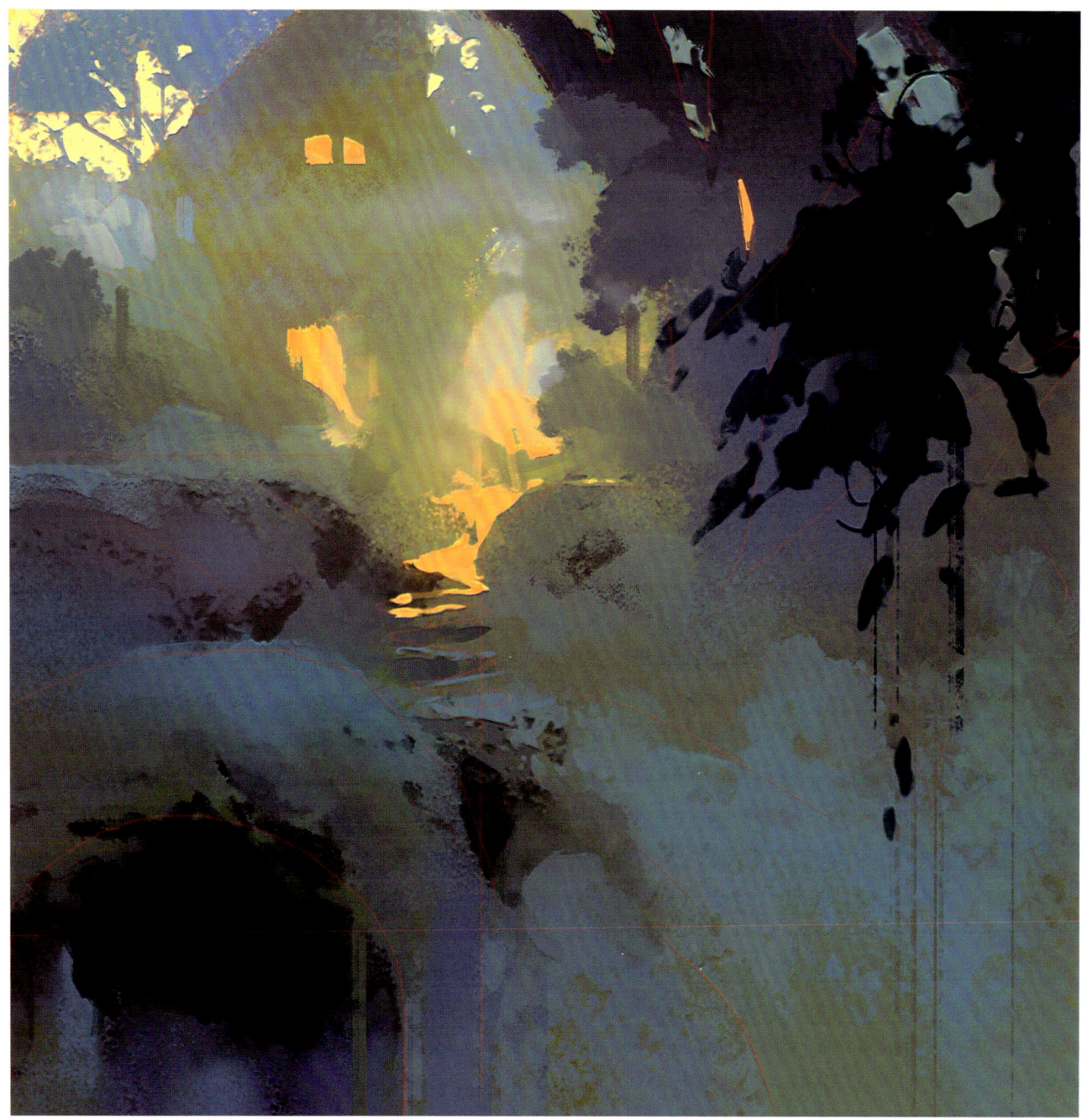

08. The distant mist glows with hot yellow light to intrigue the viewer

08. MYSTERIOUS

If you've been faithfully reading this chapter up to this point, you'll see all my tricks with atmosphere in this image: temperature, lost and found, cool elements in the distance, and so forth. The fun experiment with this one was putting in a hot shaft of light right in front of the house. It lights up the mist in that area and creates a lost-and-found effect that partially masks the mysterious house. It's a new way to create a little extra mystery.

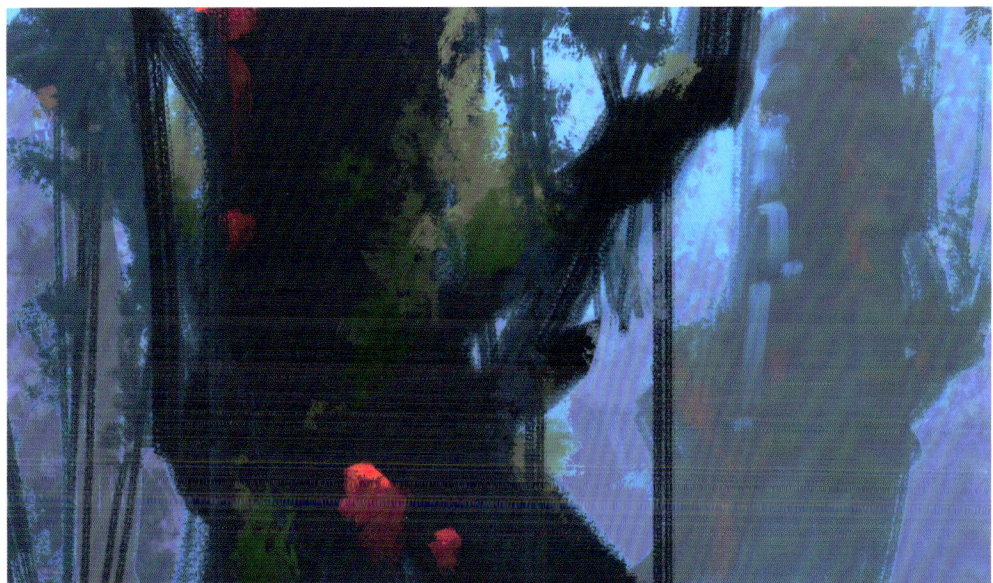

Try adding mystery with uncertain or unknown elements in a contrasting color

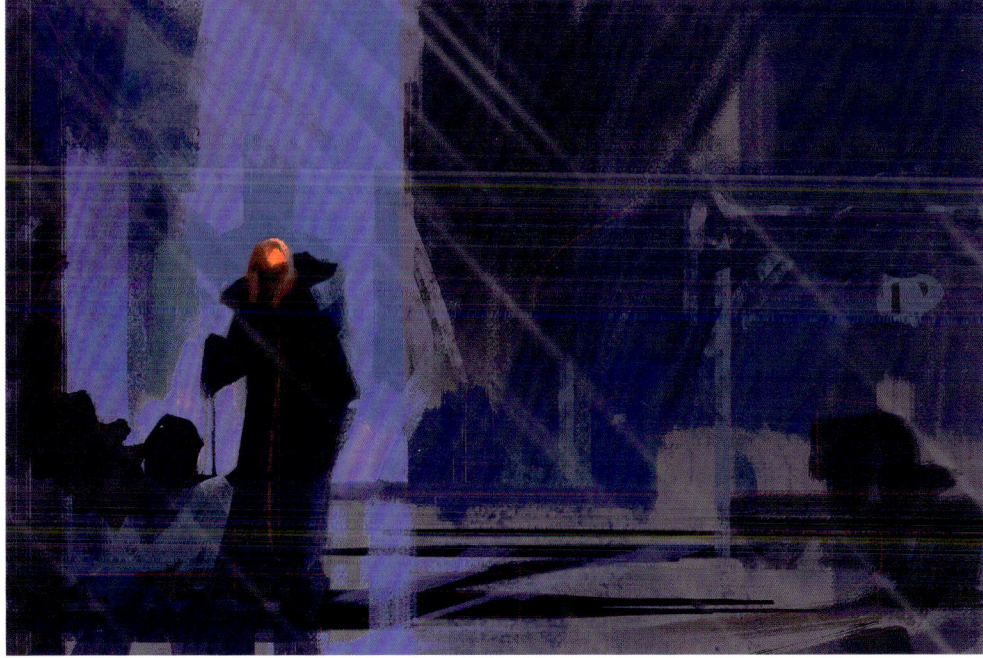

10. The contrasting character and driving rain create a feeling of ominous tension

09. MORE MYSTERIOUS!

Another thing you might notice about my process with these images is that I'll do a version that relies on light and atmosphere to get a particular emotion, and then I'll change it up and attempt to use local color to achieve the same kind of mood. It's about versatility – we must have a lot of arrows in our quiver to hit a moving target. These red patches of fungi, or sci-fi lichens, or whatever they are, create a special sense of mystery. Here we are in a forest shrouded in electric-blue swamp light and … wait a minute, what are those red things?! It's a mystery.

10. SOMETHING'S GONNA HAPPEN

Now I'm taking the idea of those weird red things from the previous image and doing the same with this character. Heck, maybe this guy was wandering through that forest and one of those things took over his brain or something, and now we have to be fearful because no one knows what this dude is going to do. The diagonal slashes of rain tell us that there's action afoot – something's gonna happen!

11. HOPEFUL

My proportion of positive images to negative or moody ones isn't good so far, so let's bring some positive hopeful emotions in. You saw this environment a little earlier when I was showing the spooky Northern Lights with the strange magic in the foreground, but I thought I would rework it to give it a completely new emotion. With the warm and natural local colors and vivid sunshine streaming down through what looks to be a stormy sky in the distance, it feels like blue skies are on their way!

12. EERIE & MAGICAL

Here's a strange, secluded village shrouded in mist, where the roofs are stretched upward into sharp pointy triangles, where bats fly freely, and the clouds form a circle around a magical swirl that may or may not be the moon. We just hit every single piece of visual language to tell the audience that this is a place of spooky magic!

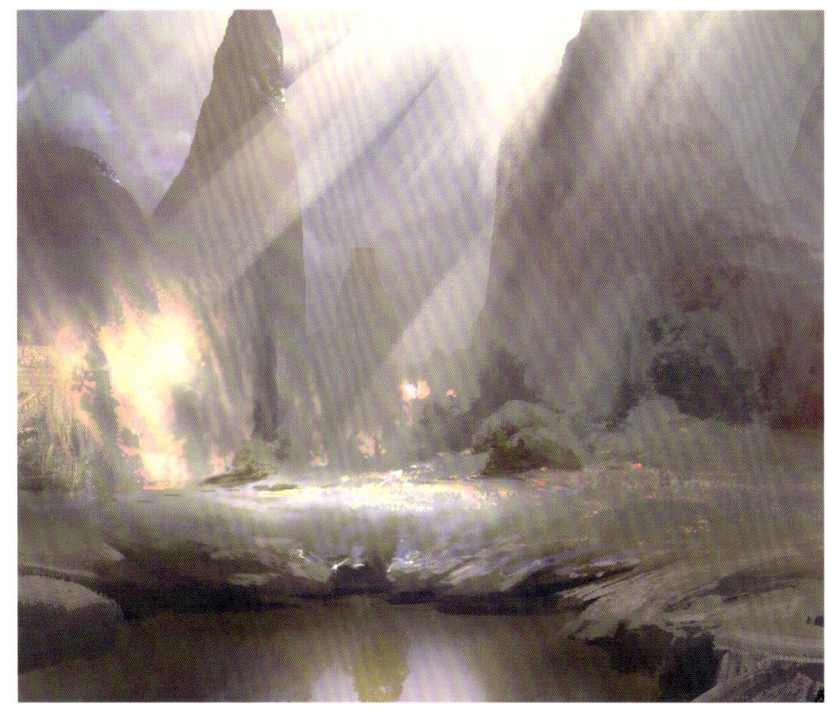

11. This is the same location as shown on page 346, but see how different it feels!

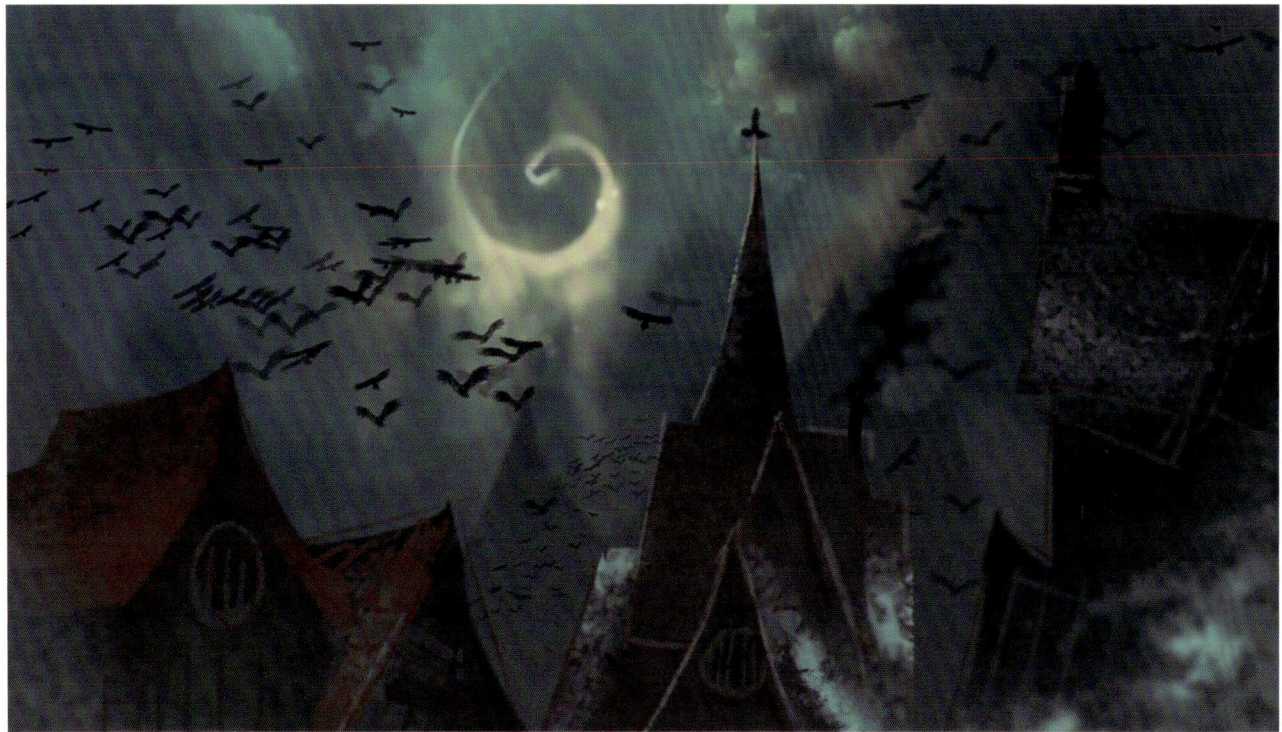

12. Shape language, combined with atmosphere, gives this spooky scene an appealing eccentricity

DEMONSTRATION: ACTIVE SHORELINE

Demonstration time! This is the image that we'll go through step by step. Let me point out a few things you can look for as we go. We'll be creating the feeling of light and a hard wind blowing in from the right. To counter that effect, the rocks will be tipping in perspective, leaning inward from the left to give the feeling of standing tall and firm against the ravages of weather. Balance and counterbalance can be a potent thing when we're expressing the forces of nature.

01. YELLOW BASE

Even though this will be a scene of dramatic storminess, the atmosphere is still meant to have an overall luminous glow, so I begin with a strong yellow as the under-painted color. The linework represents the basic shapes and overall movements of the environment; the center tower is meant to be most dominant, and the diagonal shapes at the far left and far right are especially important for the movement of the environment.

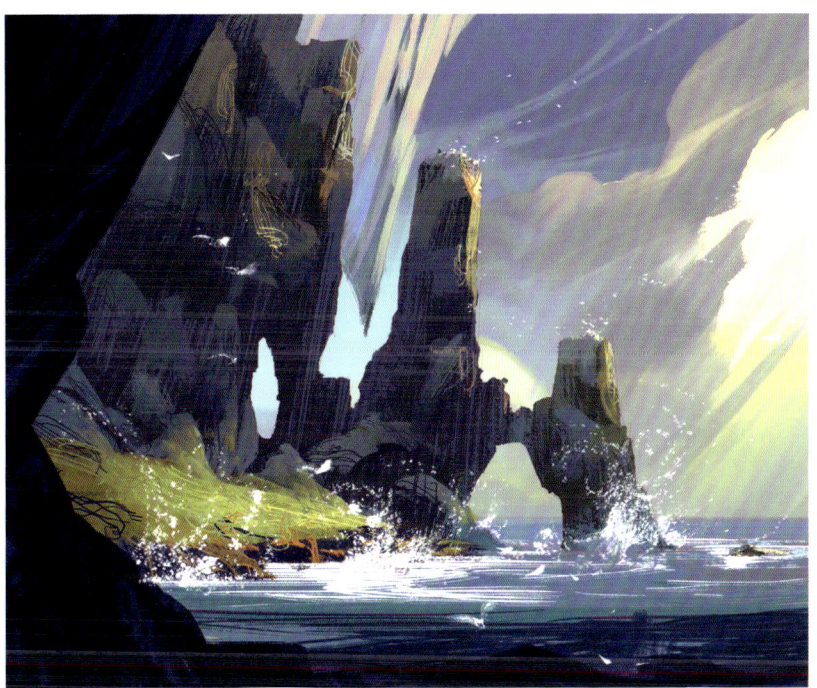

△ Note how the directions of the rocks and weather counterbalance each other

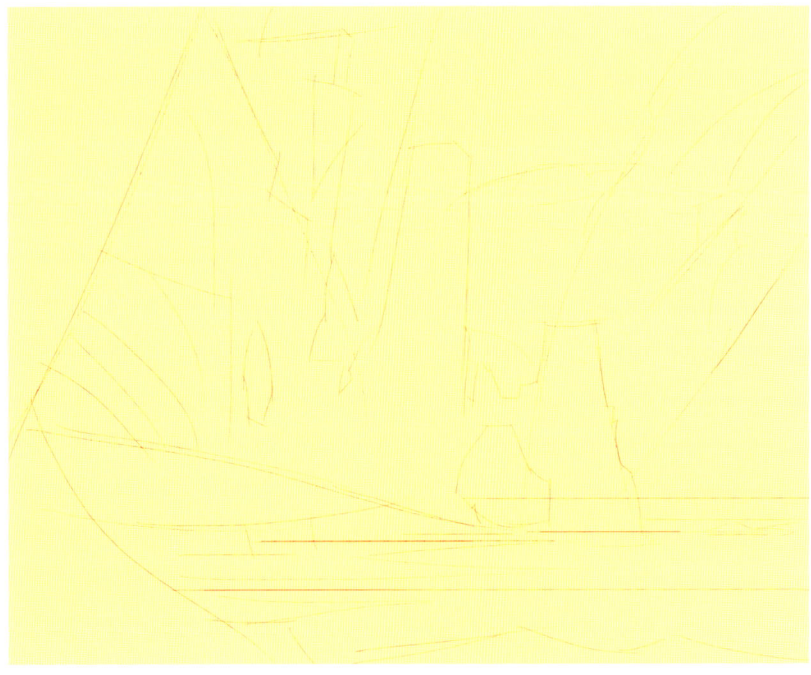

01. Start out with a yellow base color and loose drawing

02. ROUGH COLOR

We're ready to start the real painting now. I need to get the stormy grays just dark enough on the upper right, so the illuminated areas really contrast. I'm also careful to indicate the diagonal sweep of the sunshine radiating down from the right. Finally, I add a plane of gray water at the bottom – it's gray because it's reflecting the stormy clouds above.

03. SILHOUETTES

This is probably my favorite stage of this type of painting, because you can block in the silhouettes quickly and immediately know if the image is working or not. I lighten the rocky silhouettes at the top, since I don't want too much contrast right up against the top of the painting. I also add a cyan light coming up from under the water – this is caustic lighting, the kind of light that shines back up out of the water and illuminates adjacent objects. My last move here is to add a strong dark to the foreground, which is meant to push us into the more active central area.

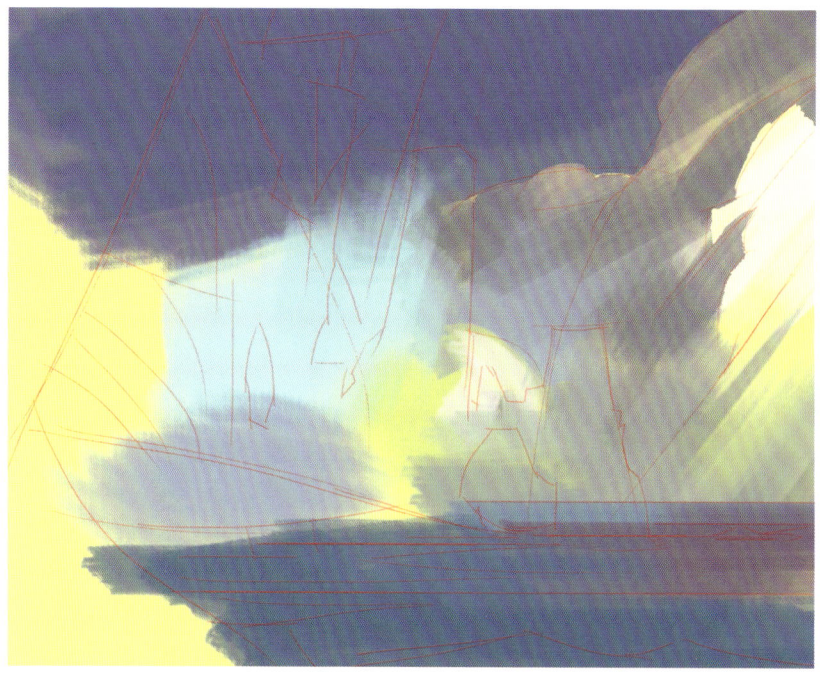

02. The water plane reflects the grayish color of the heavy clouds

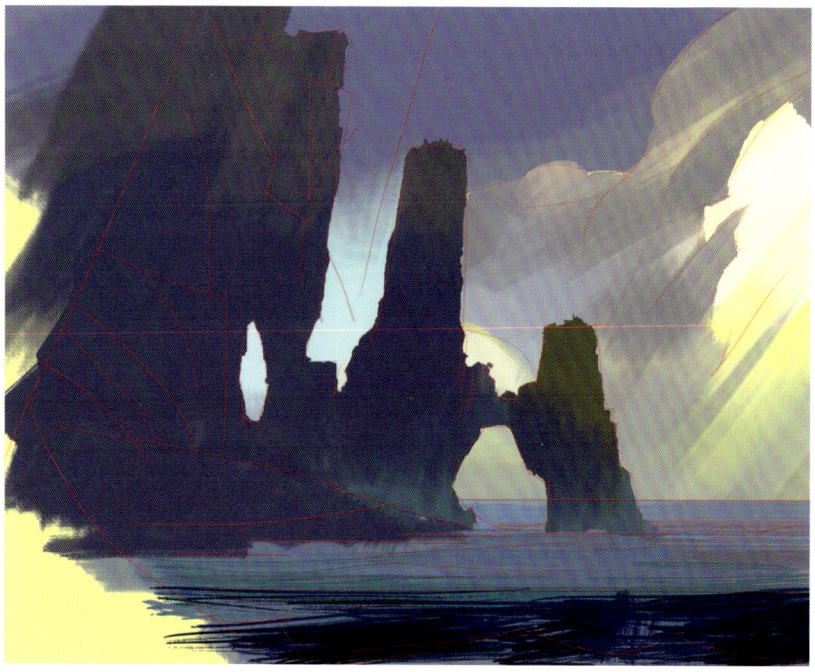

03. Add in the silhouettes of the rock formations and some caustic lighting to the water

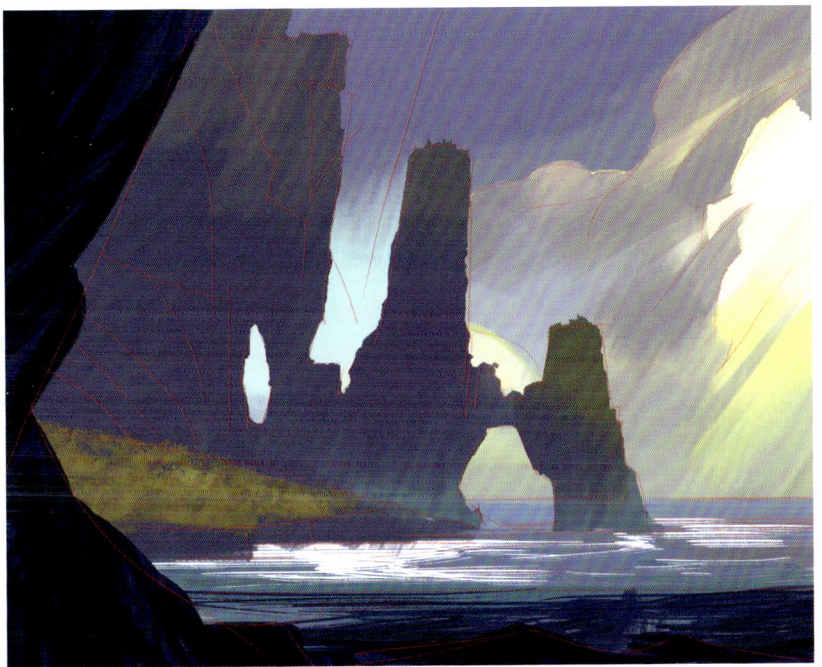

04. Dark rocks in the foreground help to frame the distant rocks and water

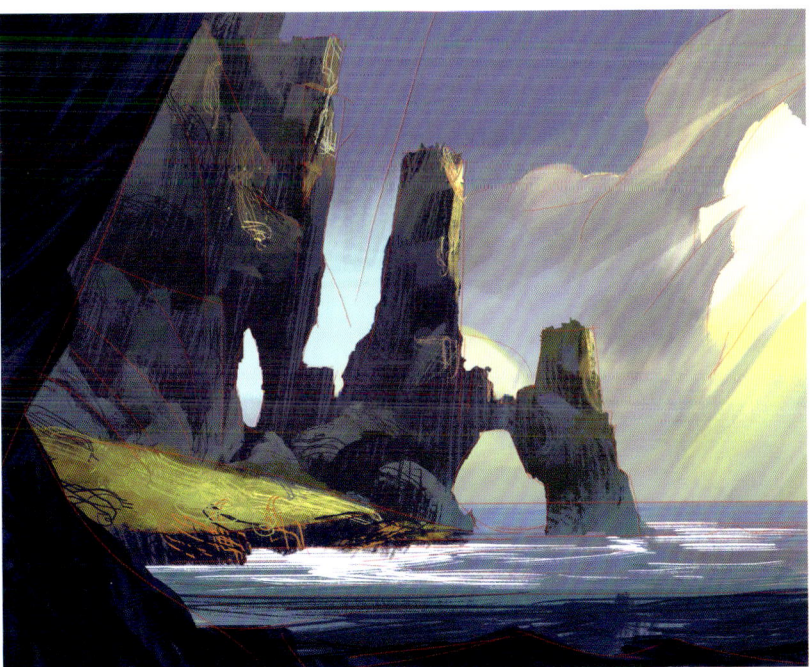

05. A streaky brush reinforces the rock formations with directional texture

04. FOREGROUND

My primary move in this step is to add the dark foreground to the left and bottom of the scene. These monolithic pillars have a dark local color, as if they're made of basaltic volcanic stone. The dark foreground serves the purpose of focusing us into the central area, where I also begin to add contrast. There will be lots of splashing and white-water activity in the final image, but right now I need to describe the flat surface of the water and make sure it works first. I also add a yellow-green local color to the middle-left slope.

05. RENDERING

Everything is now in place for me to really go for it with the rocks. I have a specific technique to support the monolithic quality of the vertical pillars, where I use a brush with a distinctive streaking effect and carefully follow the vertical direction of the stones. It's like adding vertical rebar to a cement structure – it reinforces and stabilizes. I also indicate that there are shapes within the pillars, which are darker underneath and cooler above as they catch skylight. Finally, I add a touch of direct light – I don't want to overdo this – that's just enough to ignite the pillar-tops.

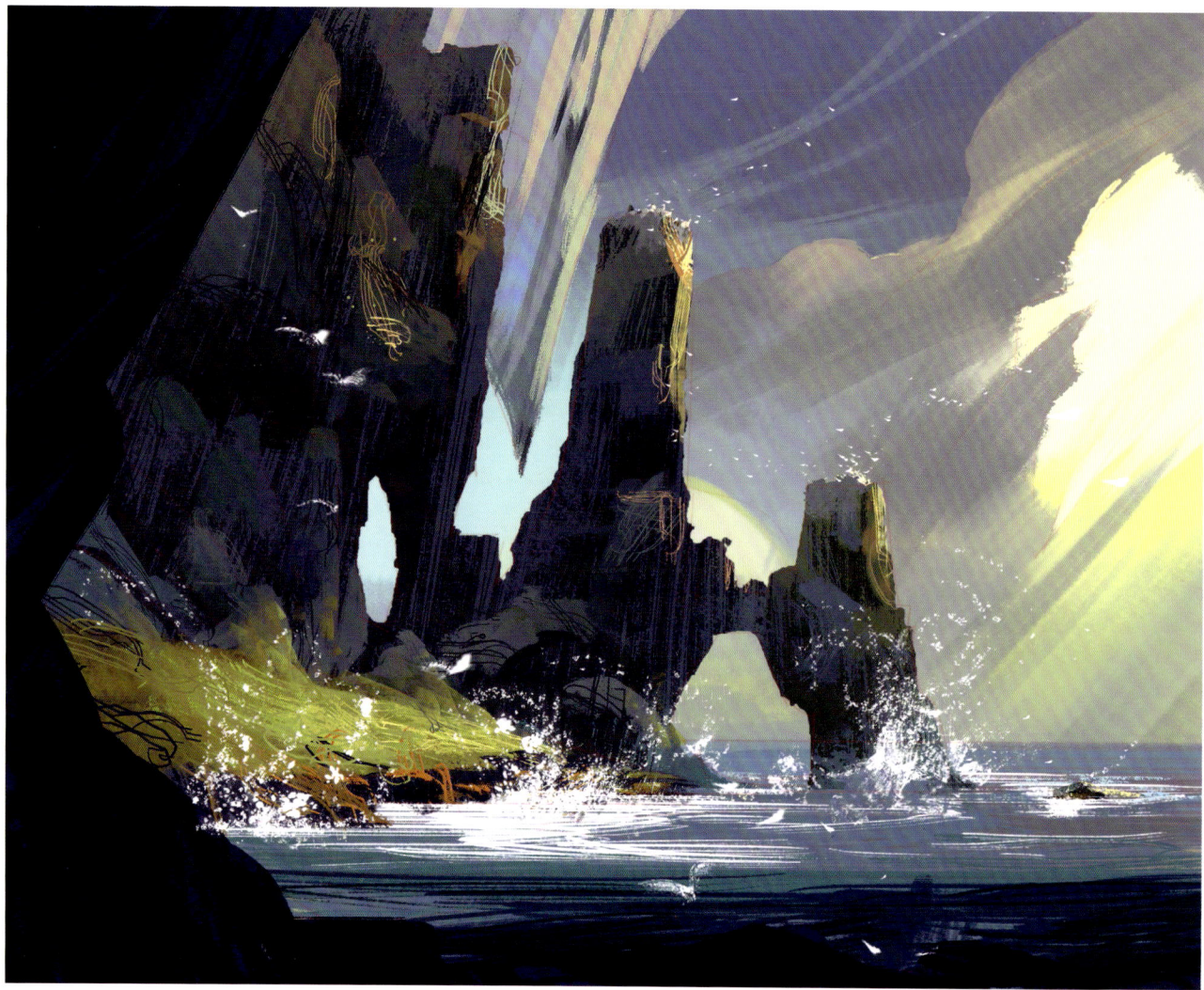

06. Crashing waves and strong winds complete the feeling of a shore battered by the elements

06. DYNAMIC ACTION

To take us to the finish line, we need some real visual activity. I rely on the whitewater splash of the waves against the island and the flapping wings of all the white seabirds that inhabit a place like this. For drama and environmental variety I add a luminous glacial shape to the center top – we've got to throw everything at this cataclysmic moment! Finally, some lines flowing through the upper background support the idea of wind. This is where wind, waves, stone, and ice all crash together to cry out for our emotional attention.

RECOMMENDED EXERCISE:
SKY DESIGN

We often get so caught up in designing and rendering the landscape that our sky design goes unattended. This is your opportunity to rectify that.

Here's a simple line drawing from the emotionally driven sky designs shown earlier in the chapter (page 347). I want you to take this linework and rough in as many different kinds of skies and clouds that you can think of. Scan this linework or sketch it out from scratch, however you want to approach it. Just remember that a fully skilled environment designer is also a skilled sky designer.

I've added the previously shown images here for your reference as well. How many new versions can you make? Happy painting!

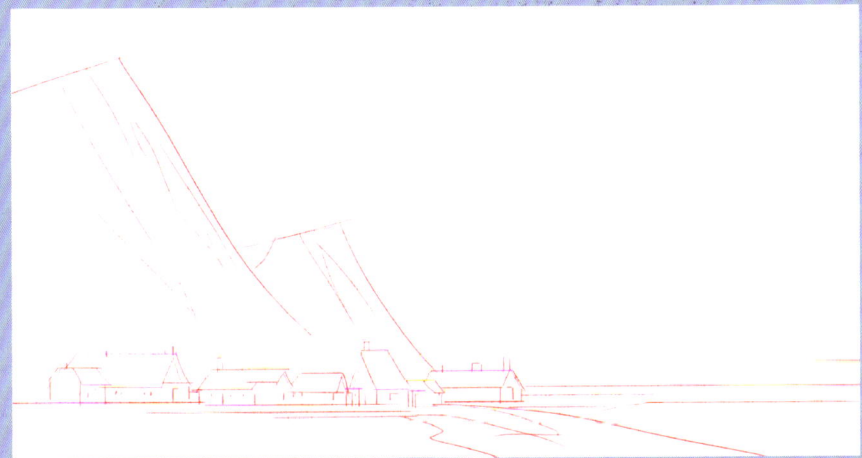

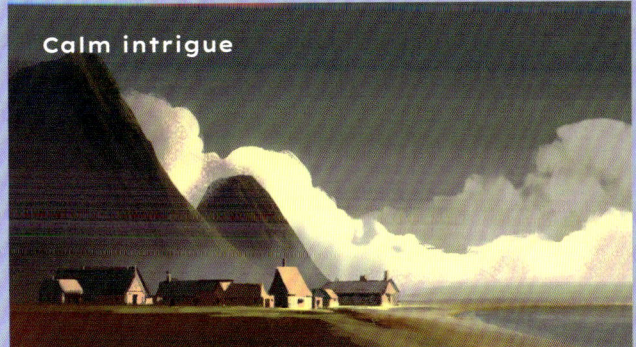

Calm intrigue

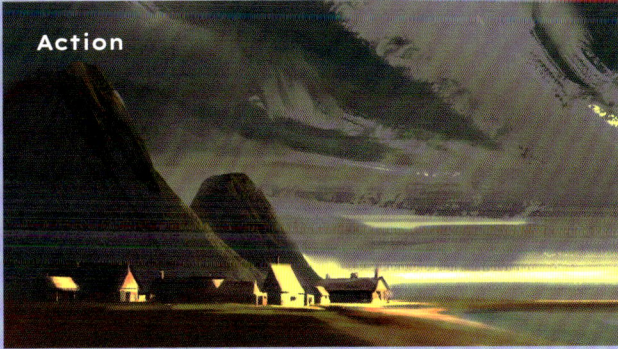

Action

Oppressive

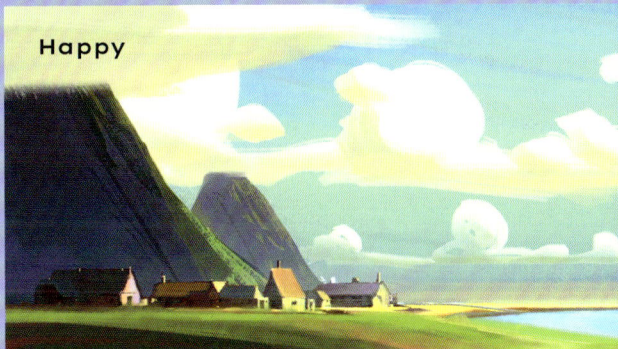

Happy

△ Replicate this sketch and use it as a base to explore your own emotional sky designs

ACHIEVING THE WOW FACTOR

Your career as an artist will be a search for how to give something of real value to your audience, and this is how you do it.

A HORRIFYING FIRE

You've likely heard about the devastating wildfires that Southern California suffers. Let me tell you about the time I found myself, my home, and my family right in the middle of one.

One afternoon while I was happily painting away, my wife called me at my office at DreamWorks in a panic. She said that there were police cars circling the neighborhood with loudspeakers, warning everyone to immediately evacuate. There was a fire and it was headed our way. I raced home, paying no attention to posted speed limits, and by the time I got there the fire was coming up the ridge behind our house.

Fire season in Southern California doesn't happen because there are more fires at a certain time of year. It's not even because of the seasonal dry brush that acts as fuel. It's because of the wind.

The Los Angeles area is not known for its wind, but we get a heavy dose of it for a short time in the fall. As temperatures change in the desert regions east of us, there's a pressure shift, and suddenly dry desert air begins rushing from the east, through the Los Angeles Basin and out to the ocean. These are called the Santa Ana winds. It's true that all the greenery from spring and summer spends months drying out in the heat, making perfect wildfire fuel but, nevertheless, fires would be controllable and containable if they didn't spread so fast and so far in these winds. Fire control simply cannot keep up.

This is the situation we found ourselves in. If you look at the photo below of our backyard area, you can see in the trees how hard the wind was blowing. The fire was coming from behind that ridge in our direction, so fast that should you find yourself caught in front of it, you could not outrun it, and you would be overcome.

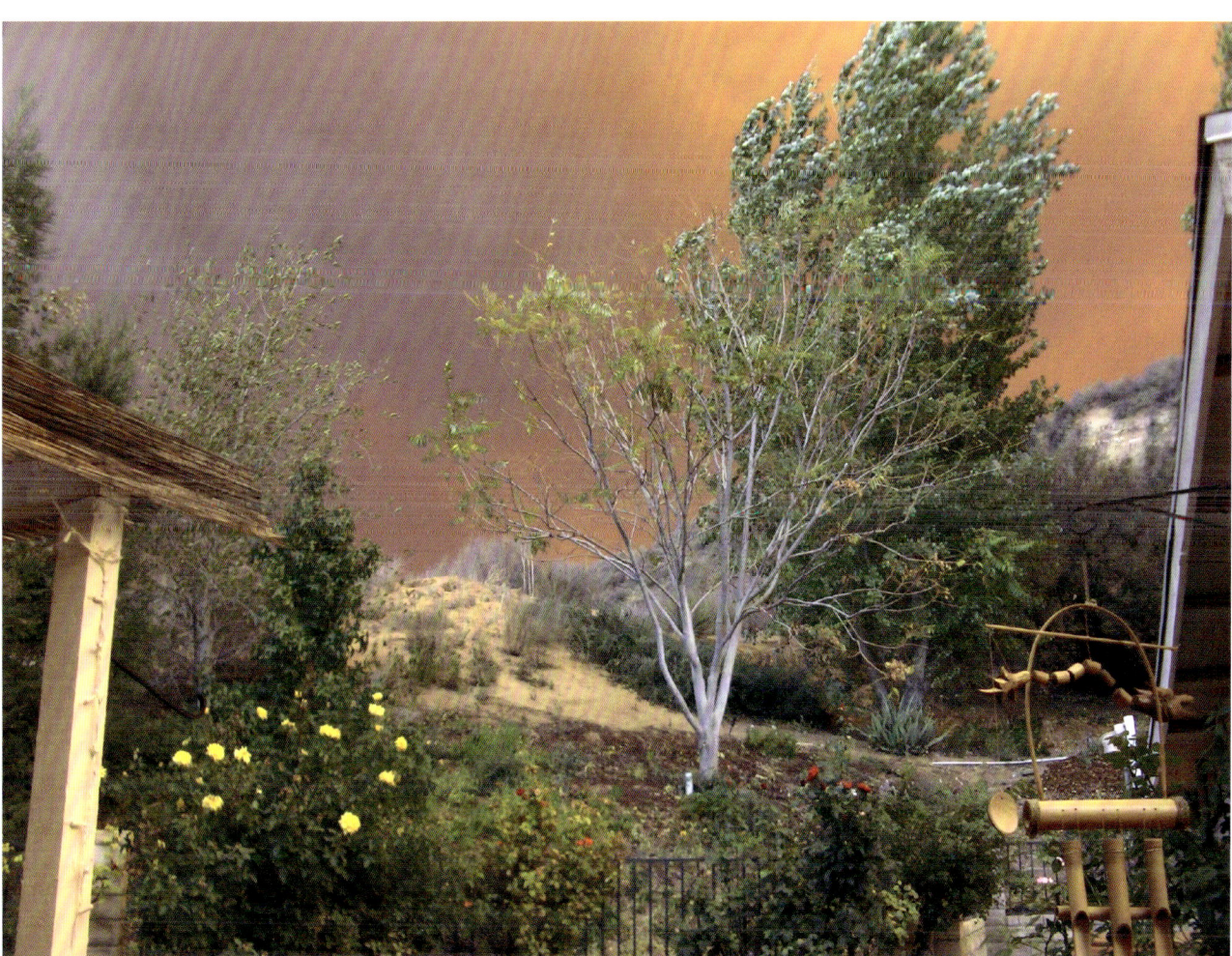

△ The view from our backyard as the wildfire approached

So we grabbed what keepsakes we could (and some sketchbooks and paintings out of my studio). As we prepared to leave, I went out back one last time and the fire was already coming up over the ridge. Let me tell you something here that I wouldn't normally admit, because I don't like to show weakness, but we're all friends here and we're all in this together, so I'll tell you – as I stood there realizing what was about to happen to us, my knees started to shake and I could not make them stop.

At that particular time, my wife and I had just gotten married; we had just purchased this new home and we were starting our brand-new lives together. I had set up my new studio, we'd furnished our home just the way we wanted, and now this.

Here are a few more photos I took as we drove around and observed the situation from a safe distance. One has to find a silver lining, and I thought to myself, 'Well, my house might be about to burn down, but these photos are great reference!'

And in fact they were. A short time later I switched to Blue Sky Studios to work on the movie *Rio 2*. One of the first scenes I was asked to conceptualize was the moment when the Amazonian blue macaws looked out from their beautiful jungle home to see a horrifying fire encroaching on them. It was exactly the same moment I had personally experienced. That painting has been published, so if you ever stumble across it, you'll see that I did in fact use exactly the reference you see here to help me create the concept. I knew how to create that environment and evoke that emotion.

So as we wrap up the last chapter in the book, this is one last example of the overwhelming and devastating power of the environment. It's also a reminder to travel far and wide with your camera and your sketchbook, so you'll be technically and emotionally prepared to give your audience what they came for. What did they come for? Exactly the same experience I had when I was so overwhelmed with emotion that I could not stop my knees from shaking. As our audience sits in the movie theater, we must bring to them such an extraordinary emotion that their knees shake right on the spot. That's the very definition of our job. My hope is that this book is a valuable part of that preparation for you.

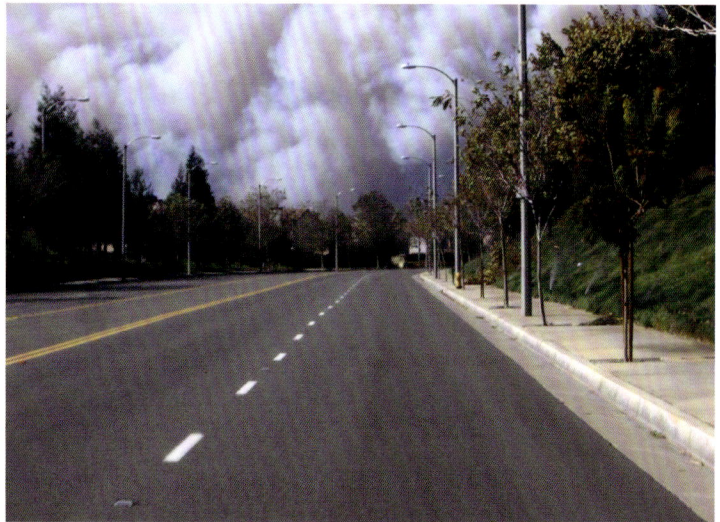

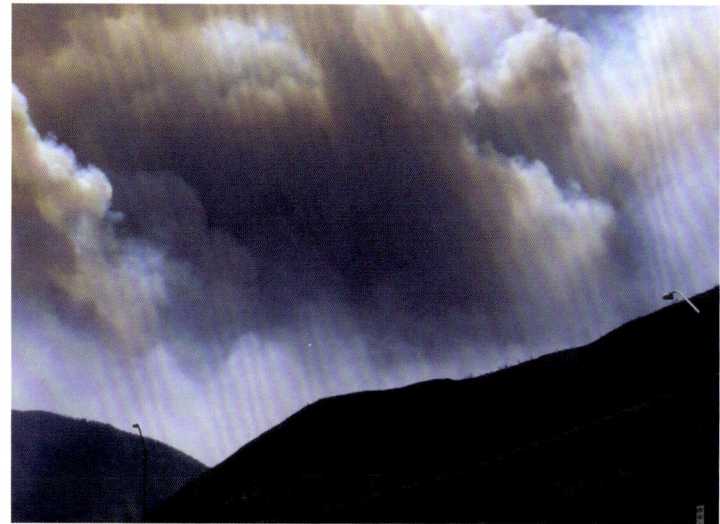

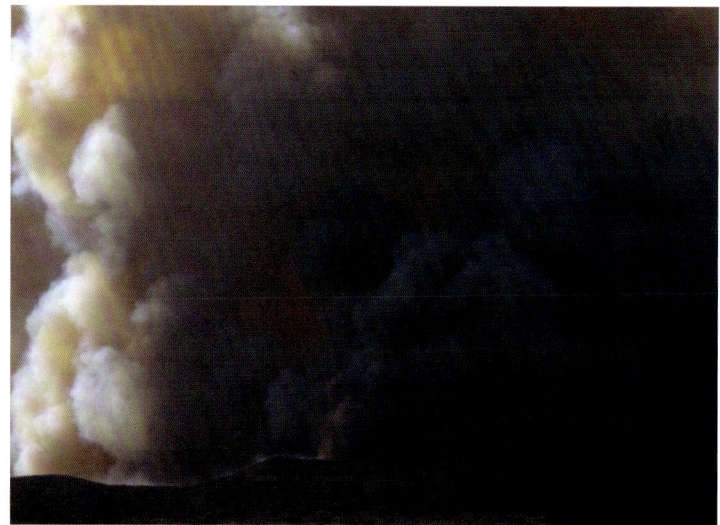

△ More views of the approaching wildfire as we evacuated the area

THE WHOLE ENCHILADA

The previous chapters have been expansive with principles, thoughts, and ideas, followed by a demonstration at the end, but I'd like our final chapter to be straight to the point. The body of the chapter itself will be the demonstration. We're going to put the primary principles of this book into practice. We certainly won't review every tip and idea, but we'll get right down the main thrust of the book.

I'm going to demonstrate the step-by-step process of a grand palace in its environment, and then give it a series of completely different emotions through our primary principles of environment design. Let's begin.

01. PURPOSE

My purpose for this image is to create an environment that has a grand, epic quality, something with such a presence that it captures our attention. Here's the tricky part, though: the style needs to be neutral enough that I can turn it toward any and every emotion that I want. I go for a big blocky palace framed by dark foliage; the entryway will be the main focus but the bridge leading there will be featured as well.

I'm using two-point perspective and setting our point of view (eye-level line) very low to get an upward view that emphasizes the massive scale of the architecture. The bridge will be huge in this view – an extension of the palace that forcefully reaches out into the foreground.

I try to get my linework as technically correct as I can, but with the understanding that I'll 'rough things up' as I go to avoid a modernistic-looking location with an artificially machined quality.

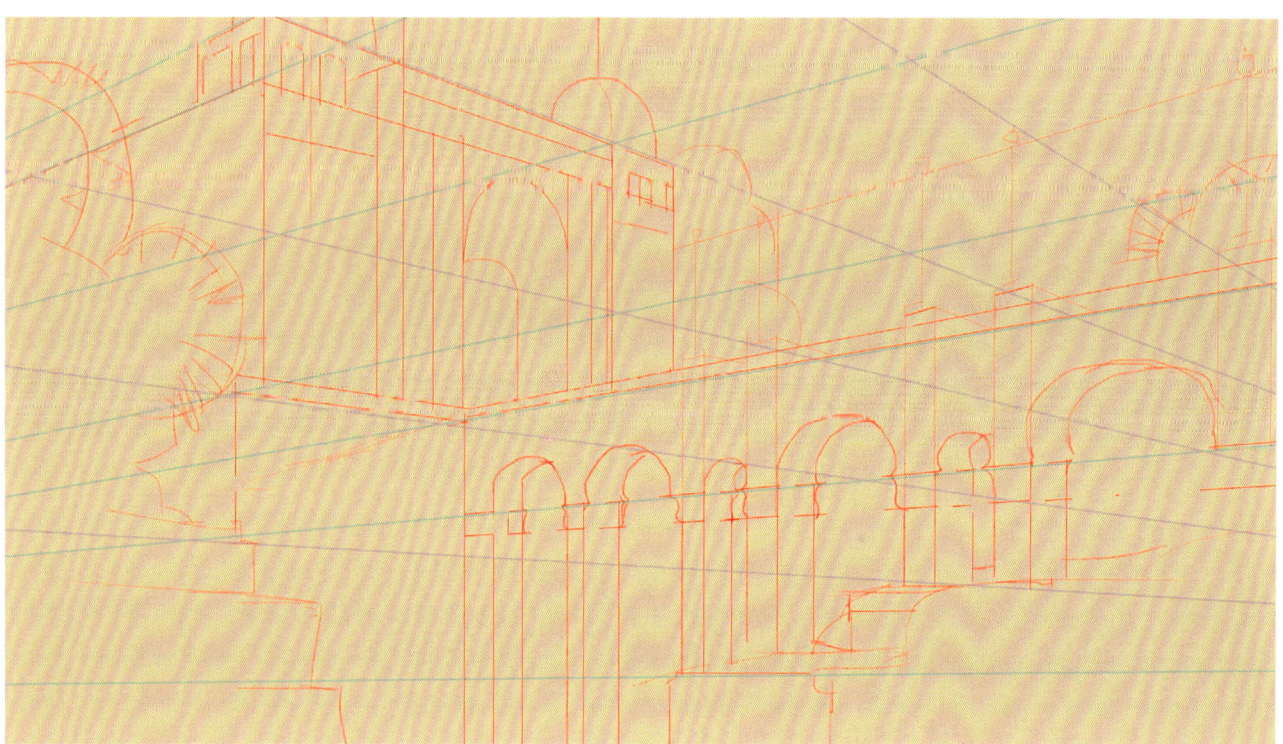

01. Establishing a warm base and fairly clean drawing of the environment

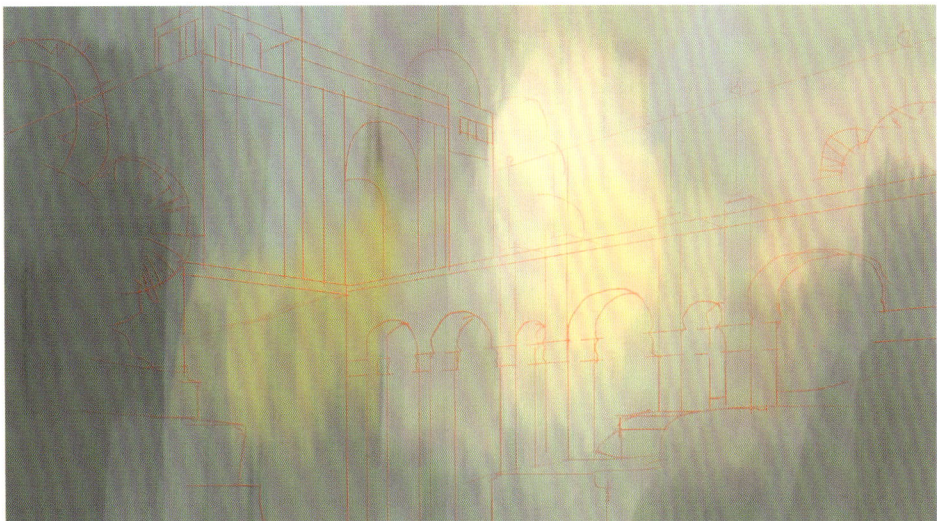

02. Rough background colors set the mood for the sky and atmosphere

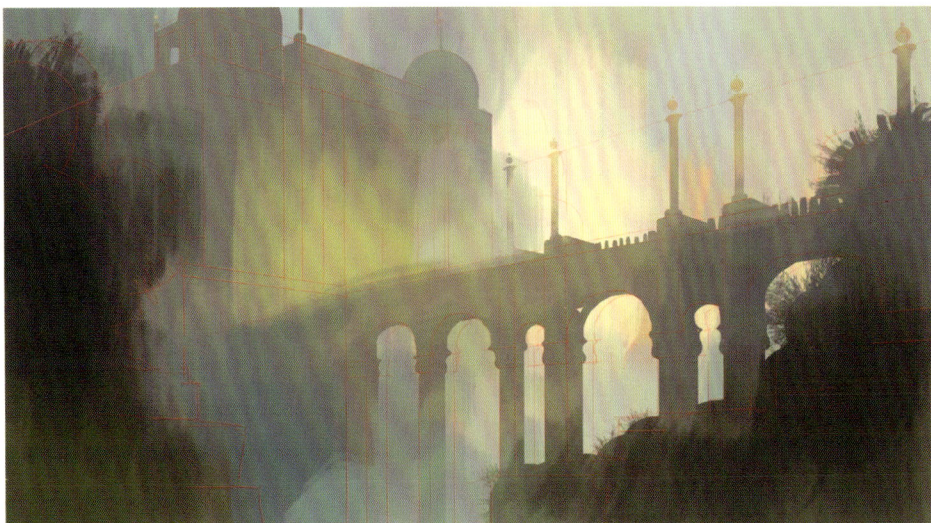

03. The imposing silhouettes of the palace and bridge start to take shape

02. BACKGROUND

I get things going in the background with mostly cool temperatures for the sky, but I'm careful to let some of the underlying warms bleed through, especially to the right. This is because the sunlight is glowing through the atmosphere from that direction and I want the sky to hold a warm luminous quality.

I'd like the silhouette of the palace to be featured; I also want the center of the bridge to come into high contrast. A glowing light cloud in the center should do the trick so I indicate that as well.

03. MAJOR SHAPES

Now it's time to really go for it and see if my big shapes are working. To do this efficiently I create masks of the palace and the bridge – it's simply a matter of using Photoshop's Lasso tool to outline the shapes, then saving that selection. This way I can quickly block in the big masses of the architecture and get the overall value structure of the scene in place.

I give some consideration to temperature here. For instance, I'm planning a strong passage of sunlight hitting around the doorway, so I add a warm glow in that area that will represent bounce light as I move forward. As important as that warm area is, it also creates a problem: I want that area to recede in space, but the warmth will do the opposite. So, just below, I create a strong passage of cool cyan that will do two things for me: it gives me an interesting warm/cool contrast, and it helps that area recede in space.

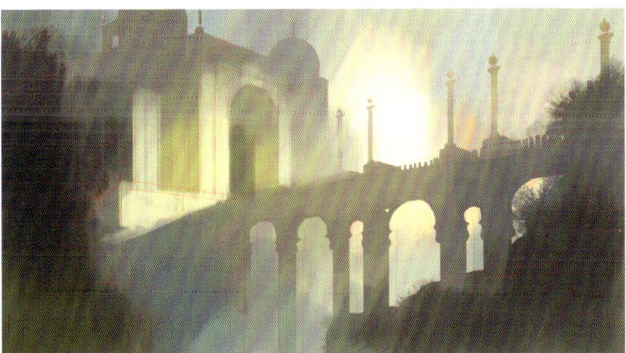

O4. Sunlight hits the front of the building and gives shape to its architecture

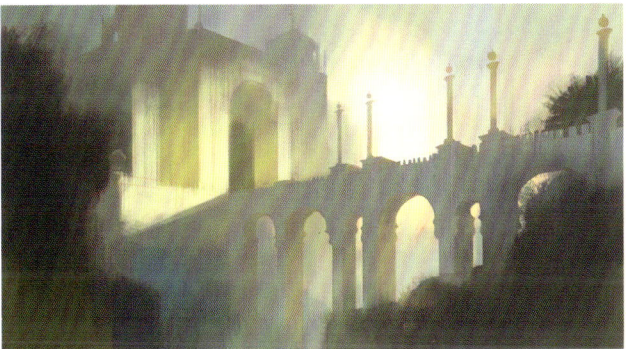

O5. Skylight and bounce light make a big difference to the architecture and atmosphere

O4. SUNLIGHT

Time for some direct sunlight! I want the sun to hit the palace in just the right way – 'the right way' always being the way that directly serves the purpose of the image. I previously mentioned that the silhouette and scale of the palace are important, but the most important part is the entrance. Can I handle the lighting in such a way as to address all three of these considerations? Hey, I'm a professional, I can do it – and so can you.

I achieve my goals here by simply spotlighting sunshine around the entryway and have it quickly fade into the shadows. Here's what is achieved by this:

- Limited lighting on the palace preserves its darker overall silhouette.

- The light transitioning to shadow across the palace suggests that it has a vast scale.

- Sunlight gives a strong contrast to the entryway, the most important area of the painting.

- The illuminated area of the palace allows the shadowy bridge to gain importance by its value contrast.

O5. REVISIONS

'This looks about the same as the last one. What changed?' The changes here are very subtle but very important. They mostly have to do with lighting temperatures, but first I have to fix the 'Mickey Mouse ear' problem. I initially thought that two dome shapes atop the palace would give it grandeur and a visual interest. Instead, the silhouette turned into something that looks like Mickey Mouse! I change those shapes into something blockier and feel like that works better.

The temperature changes come from three types of lighting: direct sunlight, cool atmospheric light, and warm bounce light. The side plane of the bridge faces away from the warm sunlight, so its source of illumination is cool skylight. This is ideal because it's both realistic and gives us an attractive warm/cool contrast. And to top it off, we have another wonderful source of contrast in the bounce light. Sunlight is hitting the low areas on the far side of the bridge, out of our view, and that light bounces up into the underside of the bridge. These subtle lighting and temperature changes are critical to the success of this image.

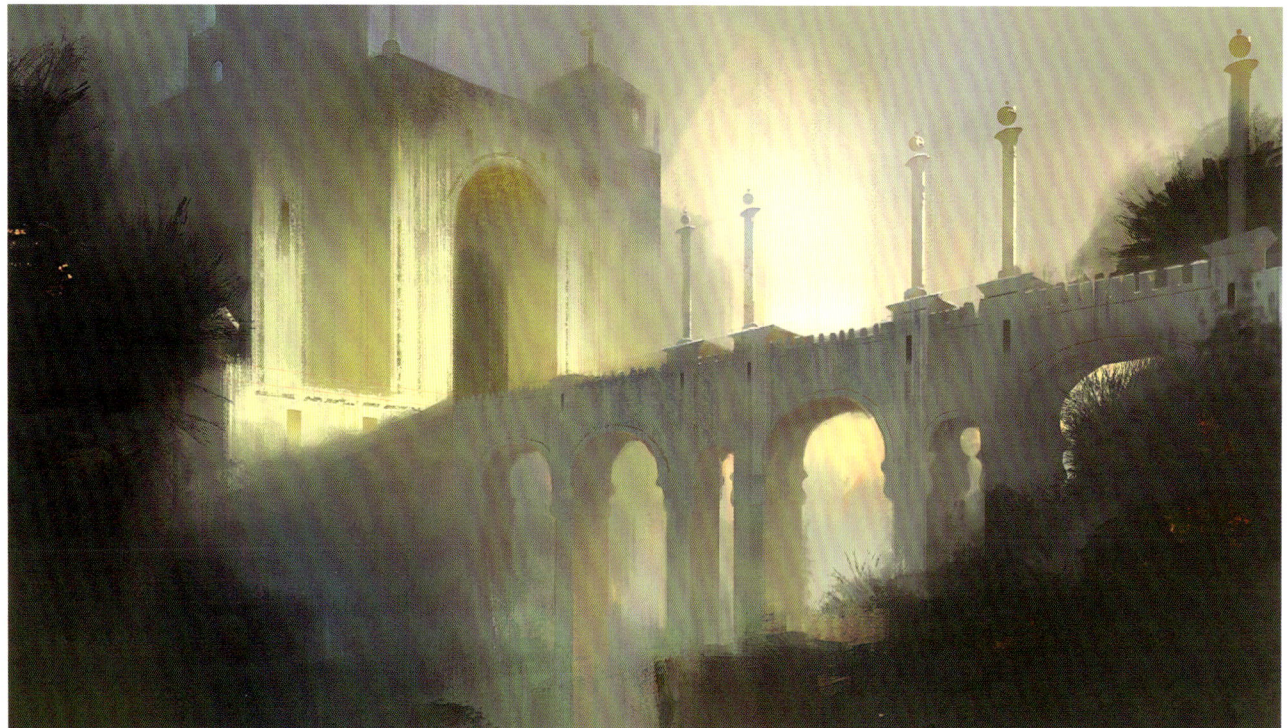

06. Windows, textures, and other small environmental details complete the scene

06. DETAILING

This is not meant to be a highly polished and detailed image – it's a foundation for the numerous versions that will follow. Nevertheless, I want it to feel finished without tons of rendering and detail, so here's my plan:

- **Windows.** These help with scale and visual interest – I keep them tiny to represent the vast scale of the palace.

- **Ornamentation.** I add linework carving around the arches of the architecture. It's not much but it helps the sense of completion.

- **Weathering.** This palace is very old and has seen many seasons, so I add streaking and watermarks to show the aging, especially below the windows.

- **Foliage.** I add just a touch of lost-and-found information along the silhouettes of the foliage – spiky shapes that curve with the mass of the greenery. I also add a few random dots and dashes for visual interest and to help this area come into the foreground.

- **Rim lighting.** The strength of sunlight will also be hitting along the edges of the bridge and its decorative columns. This gives the bridge realism and a strong contrast that helps it move into the foreground.

These subtle additions combine to bring our environment to a finish, but read on – this is just the beginning!

07. THE BIG IDEAS

We saw a version of this list toward the beginning of this book (page 40), and now it's adjusted to include big ideas from the last couple of chapters. These are the primary considerations I'll be looking at as I create variations of this environment. This is a 'big idea' list and lots of little things will also happen as we go. Keep an eye out for the recommended exercise at the end, which will push you toward a complete list of environment-design considerations.

08. PURPOSE & EMOTION: MYSTERIOUS TRANQUILITY

Tranquility means low contrast, no harsh winds or icy rain, no booming stereo-speakers to annoy you, no harsh light and shadow, no sunburns. Everything is low contrast.

To create this idea I'm relying on a layer of mist in the environment. The sun is still shining, but much of its light is diffused, which combines beautifully with the diffuse cool skylight. Soft edges abound but there's still plenty of contrast in the two areas I've identified as most important: the palace entrance and the center of the bridge. These primary elements themselves are mysterious, so it's the additions I've just listed that bring the whole to an emotion of mysterious tranquility.

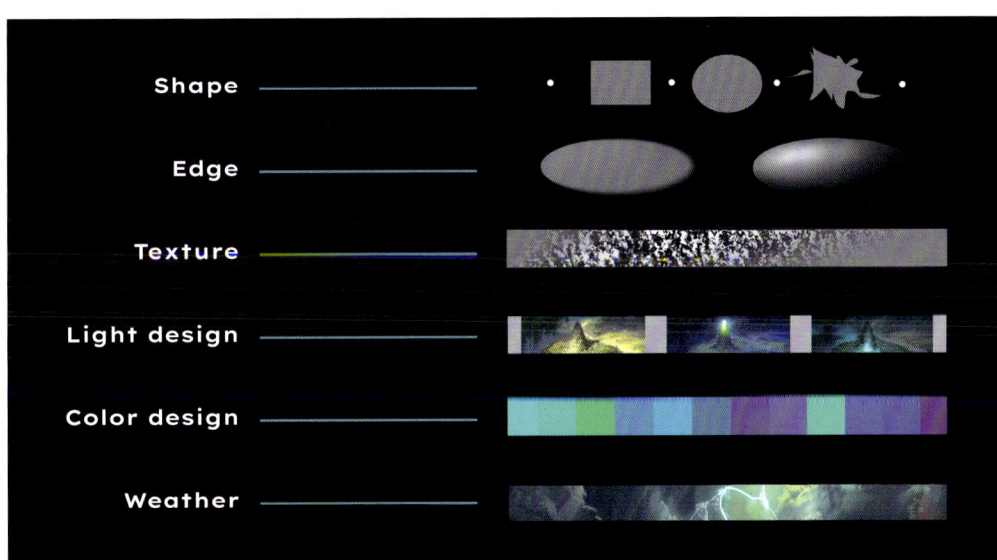

07. These are the primary factors I'll keep in mind as I move forward

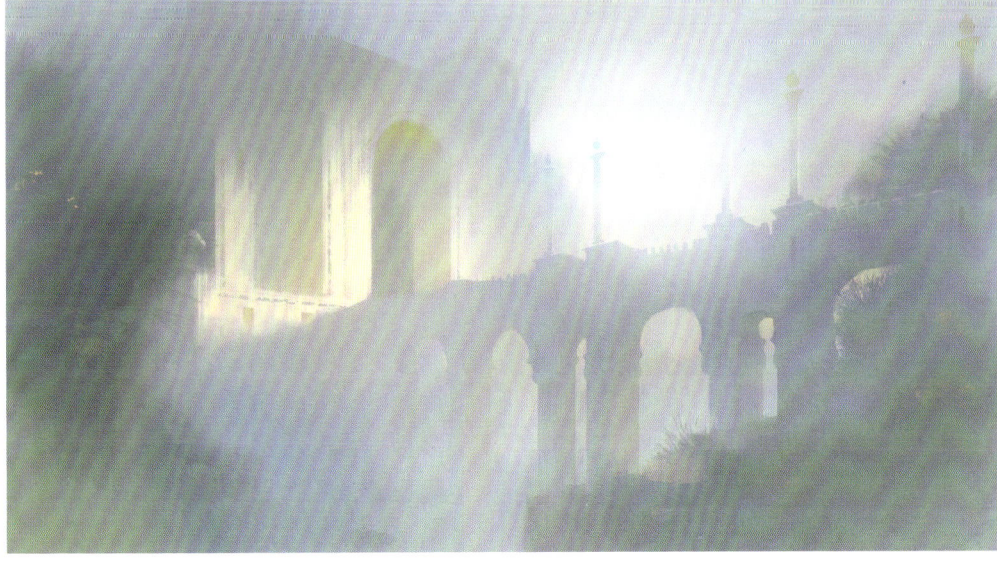

08. A soft mist gives the palace a feeling of quiet intrigue

09. PURPOSE & EMOTION: CONSUMED BY FIRE!

This chapter began with a raging fire, something I have direct knowledge of, so let's make use of it. Here are the elements I'm employing to depict the drama and emotion of the moment:

- Fire placed in key areas of the foreground. Random patches of fire follow the curve of the foreground foliage and assist with the depth of the scene.

- A back-glow of warmth throughout the sky. This conveys the ambient heat of the fire raging throughout the area.

- Lots of smoke! This place is being completely consumed, as indicated by the smoke filling up the sky. To give an extraordinary presence to the smoke, I light it up with cool skylight from above, but have an ambient heat of back-glow shining through the shadows. Refer back to the photos presented at the beginning of the chapter and you'll see my reference for this.

- A hard wind blowing in the same direction as the angle of the bridge. This convergence of directions gives the image force. The wind is indicated by the direction of the smoke and especially by the flecks of debris conveyed in a directional motion blur.

- Finally, the addition of birds. Here are flocks of blackbirds escaping the carnage, giving additional life and action to the moment.

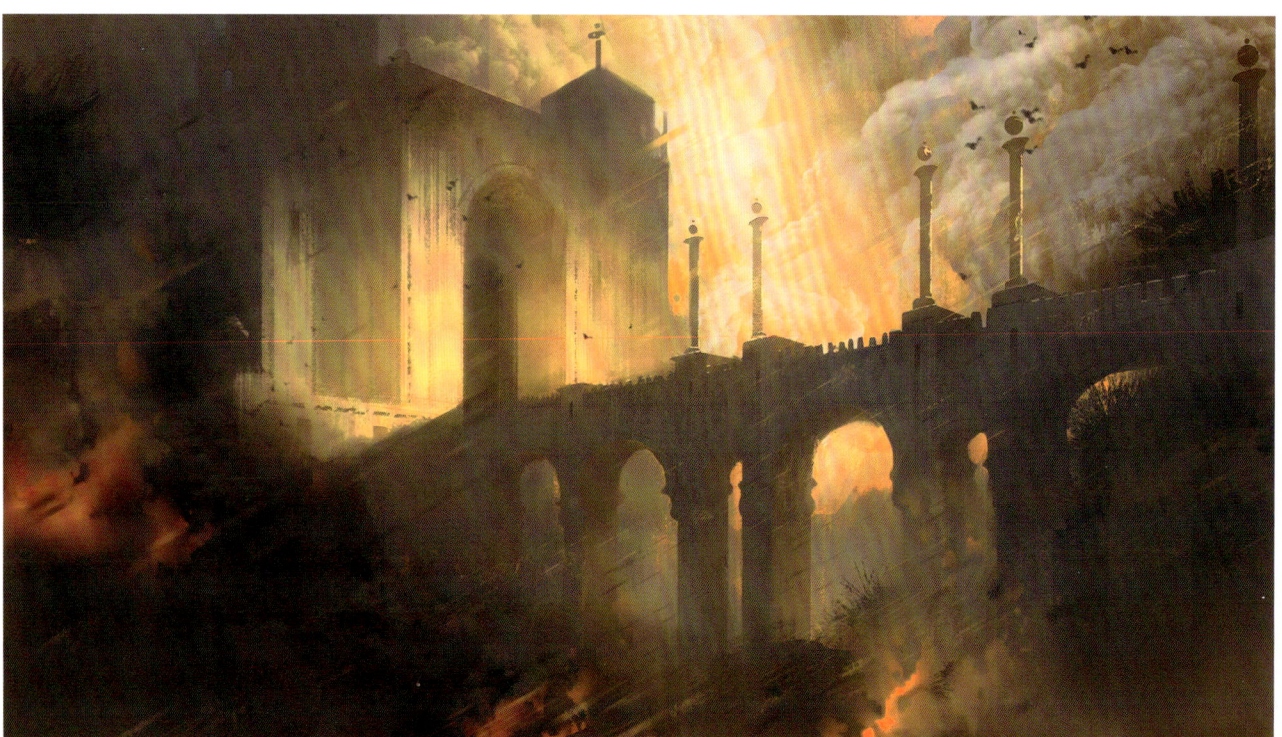

09. Raging flames, smoke, debris, and fleeing wildlife completely transform the scene!

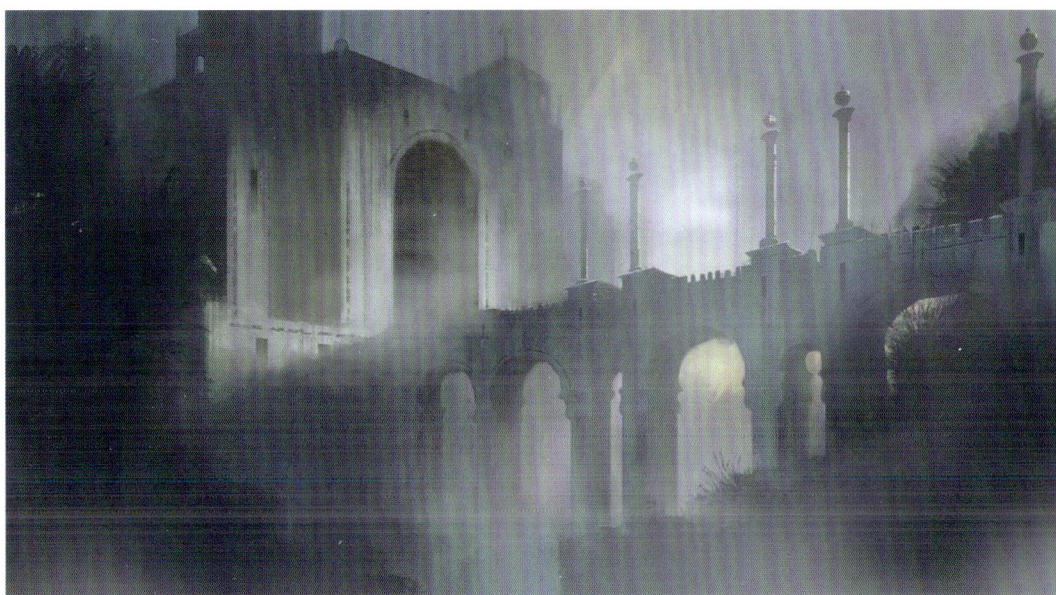

10. This version is moody and muted, but still has some subtle color variations

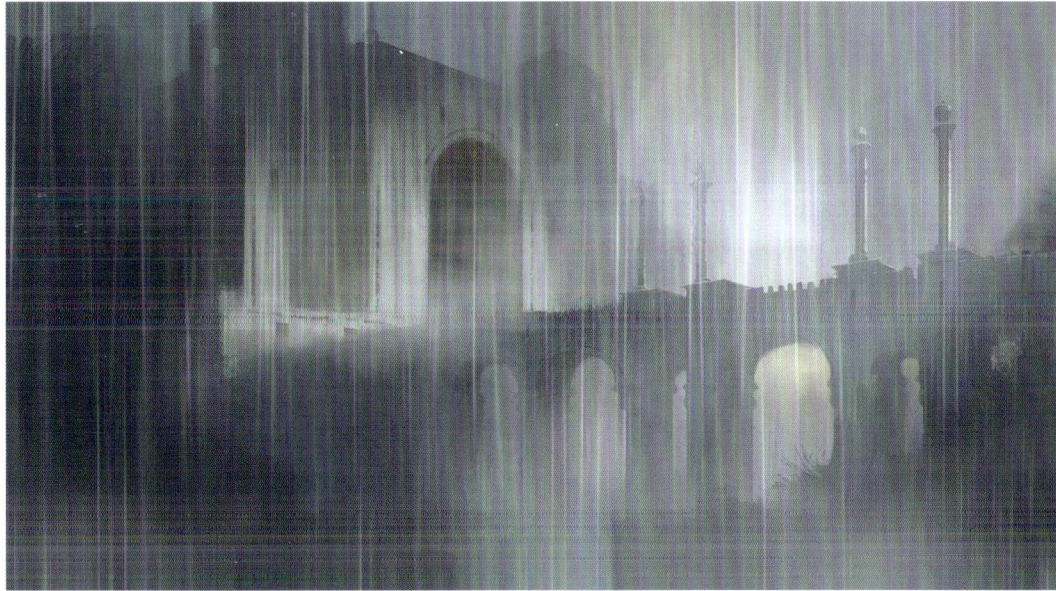

11. With a few additions and tweaks, the palace now feels flat, miserable, and run down

10. PURPOSE & EMOTION: MOODY, OVERCAST

It's time to get away from the theme of warm light and heat, so let's move to a silvery-gray overcast light. This version uses only gray light coming down from an overcast sky, and is filled with layers of mist to complete the moody quality. Note that I've maintained a slight difference in the local color temperature versus the light – the areas not exposed to the skylight or the mist have a little more warmth in the stone's local color. This helps the image hold on to a lifelike quality rather than looking like an artificial monochromatic overlay. This is a valuable emotional moment on its own, but it's also setup for the next few images.

11. PURPOSE & EMOTION: SODDEN, DEPRESSING RAIN

This is no longer a proud and dynamic palace – it's a sad architectural relic that has seen better days. At a glance, I've just taken the previous image and added rain to it, but look closer and you'll see that I've also done something subtle but critically important. To get the depressed emotion across, I've minimized diagonals and flattened and lengthened the image itself. The palace no longer stands tall and proud, and the bridge no longer reaches forcefully up and out into its environment. There's no movement of wind – the rain just comes straight down, soaking any travelers to the skin and depressing their spirits.

12. PURPOSE & EMOTION: FORCEFUL WIND

Let's restore the might of the environment by bringing in a powerful wind. We're still working with our moody gray image and an overwhelming rainfall, but now we're introducing the force of wind. I've restored the proportions and diagonals of the palace and bridge, and I've used a trick that I think you'll really like. I've stretched the palace into three-point perspective so the bridge tips further and further with the direction of the wind and rain. This is the same kind of forceful convergence that I mentioned in the fire image – when very different elements are unified, they become a thing of singular power. I've included a simple refresher on three-point perspective for you here.

13. PURPOSE & EMOTION: OMINOUS

The previous scene was physically forceful in a way that would drive travelers away. How can we change it to an environment that's so ominous that it will drive them away *emotionally*? Here's my solution:

• Add contrast and blacken the darkest parts of the image.

• Stretch the image to give it an exaggerated vertical quality.

• Employ three-point perspective to increase the palace's sense of scale and to give it a looming quality.

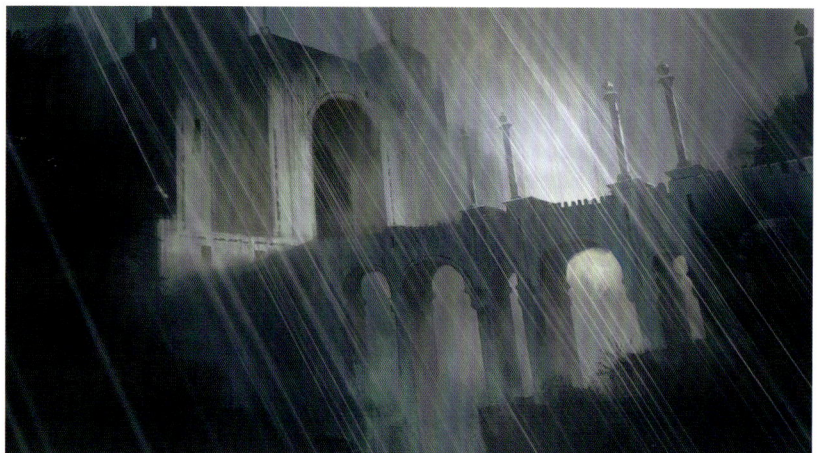

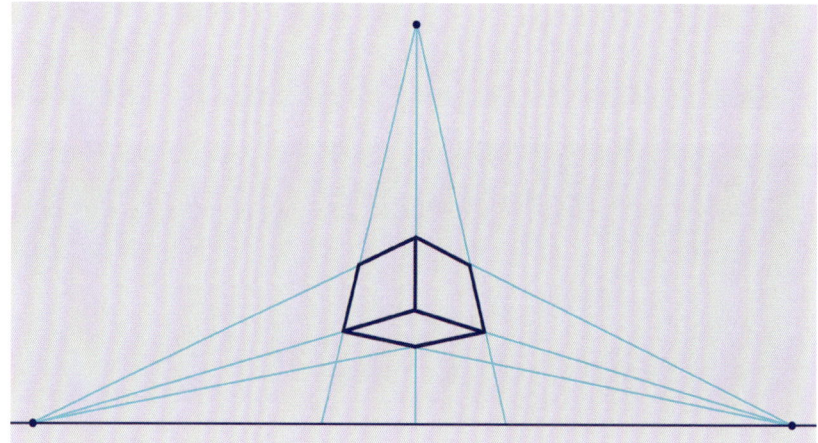

12. The rain's still pouring heavily, but a strong, dynamic wind and three-point perspective make a huge difference

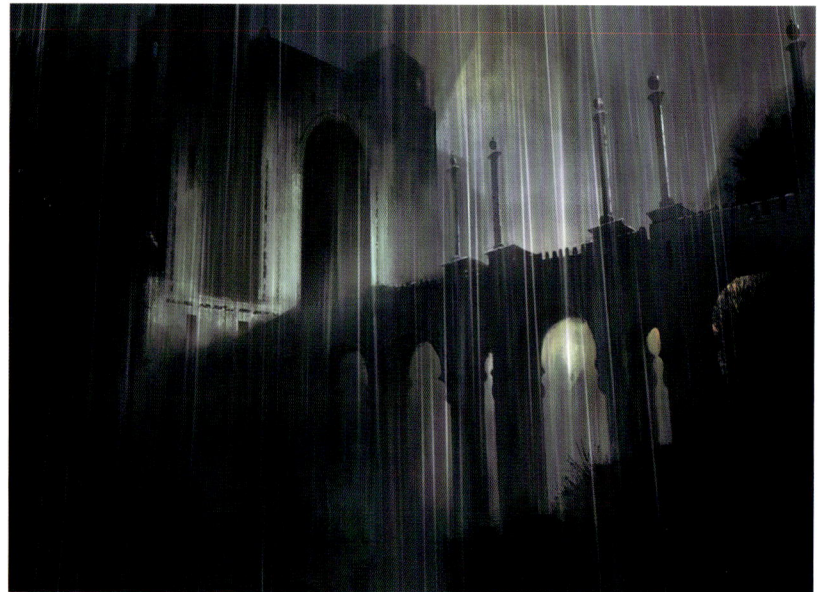

13. The image is heightened and darkened to give it an air of menace

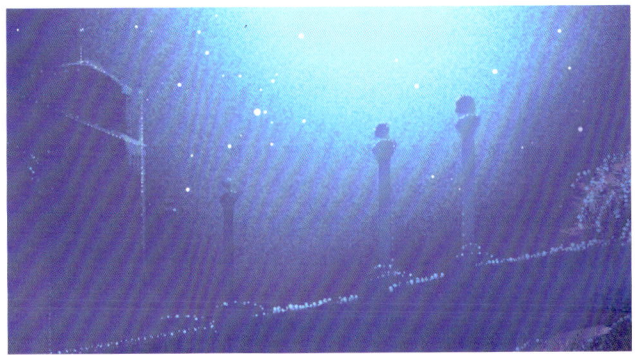

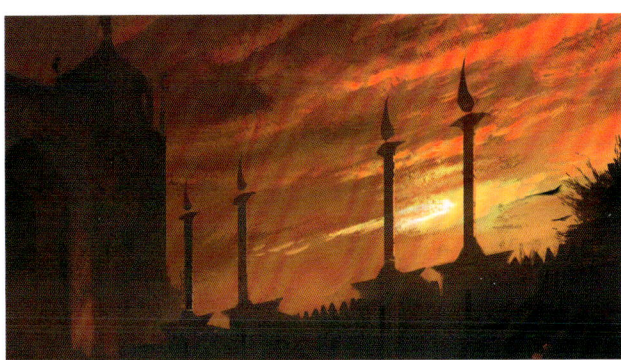

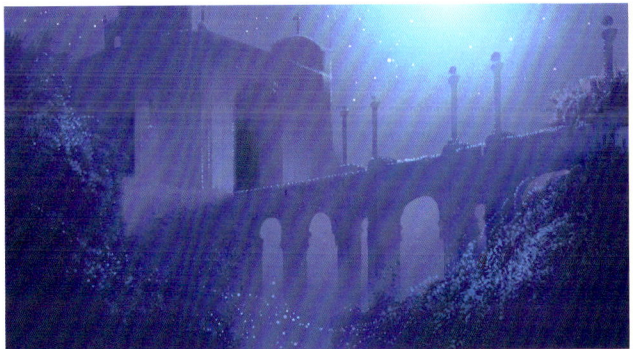

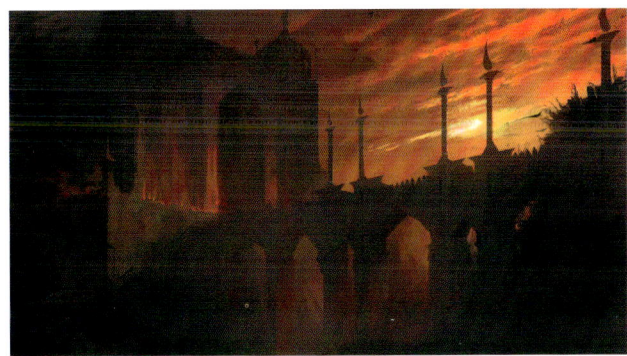

14. A complete change of mood – now the palace is tranquil, enchanting, and fairytale-like!

15. Ominous red lighting and sharp, threatening shapes will ward visitors away from this palace

14. PURPOSE & EMOTION: PRETTY, SERENE

To be honest, my real purpose here is to do something that feels completely different than any other version! I start off by making it a nighttime scene illuminated by moonlight, and to complete it I use the following:

- The soft atmospheric glow of cyan moonlight

- A rich purple quality of atmosphere in the environment

- Simplifying shapes for a toy-like, non-threatening quality

- Sparkly rim lighting

- Twinkling stars and a sparkle of moonlight on the foliage.

15. PURPOSE & EMOTION: THREAT, DANGER

This is the moment in a story where a young hero, who's been sent by a wizard to save a princess, obtain a ring, or whatever, says to himself, 'Maybe life on the pig farm wasn't so bad after all. I think I'll head back to that instead.'

The previous image was pleasantly mysterious with its stillness and purple calm. It was the kind of mystery that invites you to come and explore. This one is exactly the opposite. This one says, 'Fear ye who come here – a horrible death awaits you!'

Here are the specific elements I've employed to make this image very different than previous versions:

- Long diagonals in the sky that follow the diagonal perspective of the bridge

- Blood-red lighting with greenish shadows as a color contrast

- Everything is sharpened! Note that in all previous images the architecture itself had rounded arches and decorative elements. This version changes every one of those to a wickedly sharp point.

16. PURPOSE & EMOTION: CALM, POETIC, LUMINOUS, RICH WITH LIFE

Our variations so far have been misty, on fire, overcast, in the middle of a hurricane, vertically ominous, purple, and sharp as a knife, so let's wrap this up on a positive note. Here are the elements I've employed to achieve my purpose and emotion:

- Rounded, friendly shapes – even the Mickey Mouse ears!

- A luminous volume of atmosphere filled with glowing sunlight

- Lush with rounded shapes of foliage

- A lively stream of water moving through the environment

- White birds frolicking about.

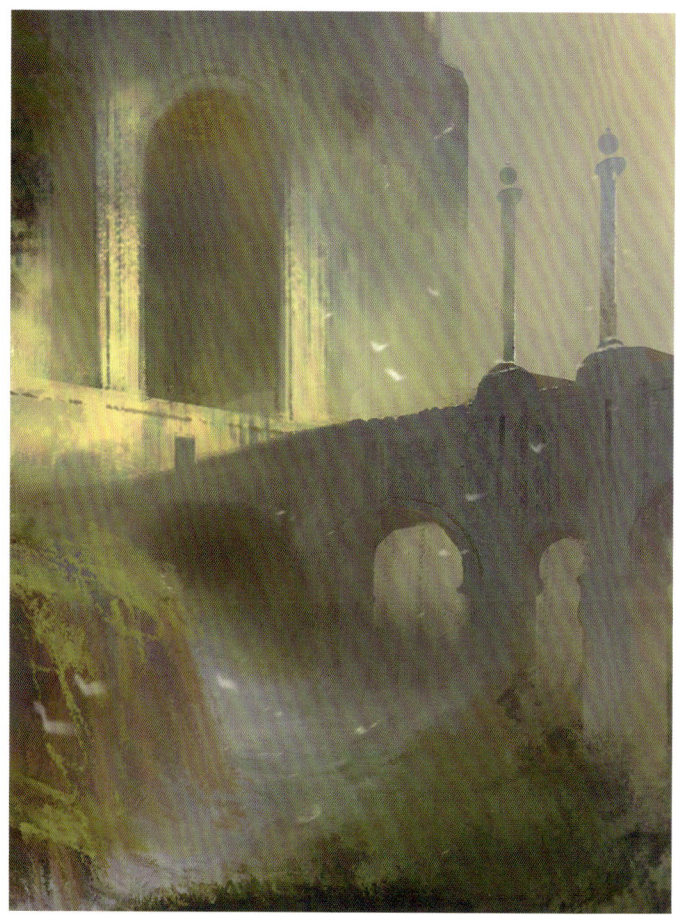

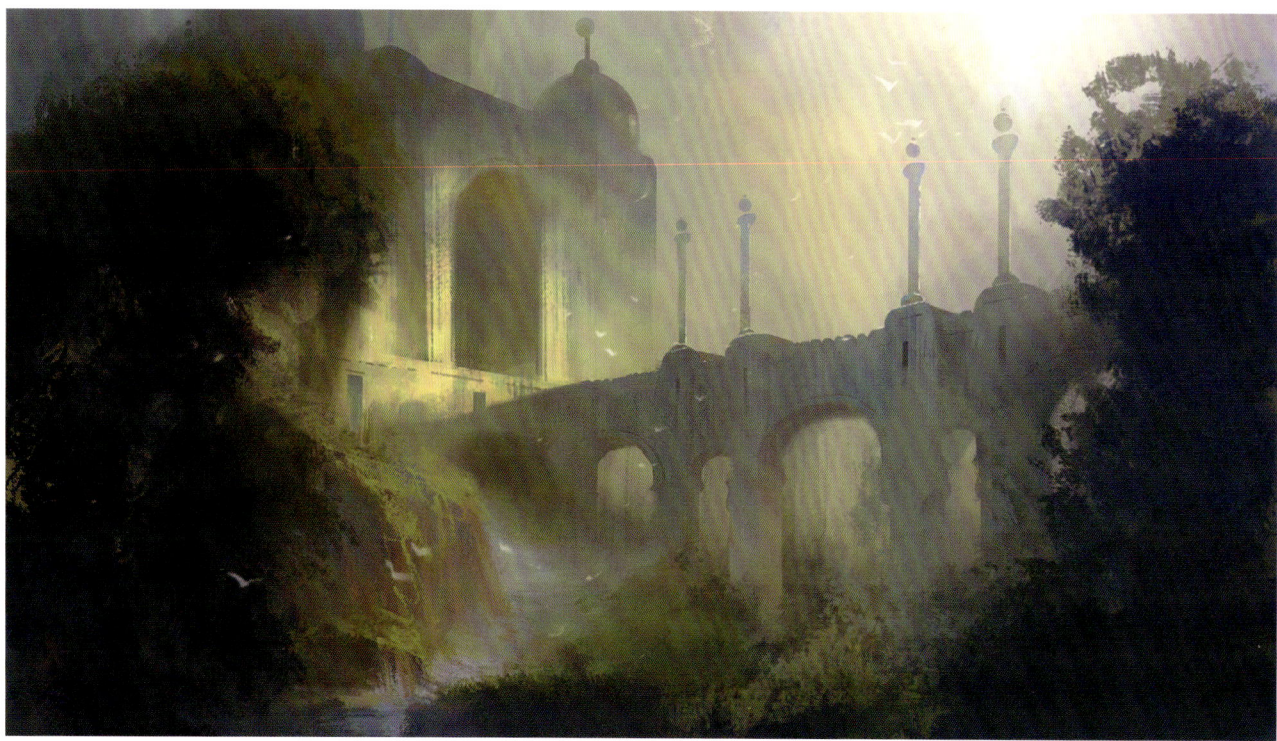

16. Finally, the palace becomes a lush, magical place that you'd want to visit

FINAL RECOMMENDED EXERCISE:
YOUR KEY PRINCIPLES

I am aware that many people buy art books that they never fully read. They may thumb through several times, they may skim the text, they may intend to read the whole thing, but life demands their attention elsewhere. This is true for all of us. Real life always gets in the way if we let it, so I want to give you my heartfelt appreciation for getting to the end of the book. I've tried my best to share with you principles that have led to the successes that my fellow artists and I have gained, and I invite you to take full advantage of it. Are you hoping to work for animation studios or in video games, or create inspirational places for whatever endeavor interests you?

I've worked at DreamWorks, Disney, Paramount, Netflix, Blue Sky Studios, and many others, not to mention numerous video-game companies. The principles of environment design and picture-making that have made these opportunities possible for me are the principles that fill the pages of this book.

The team at 3dtotal Publishing and I have very carefully designed this book to be of greatest benefit to you. We've given a clear headline in bold every time a new idea is introduced, and we've called out key ideas separate from the text for a special emphasis, not to mention all the callouts, diagrams, and explanations. I invite you to review this book from the beginning, underlining each principle that feels like it would be of value to you. **Create your own comprehensive outline of the key principles of environment design.** Pay special attention to the environment-design checklist in chapter 2 (page 18) and bring yourself all the way to our last chapter here.

In your career as an artist, you will be called on to work with any and every subject, create any possible lighting condition, with any and every kind of color palette, at any time of day (or night), and to convey any and every human emotion visually. It's very difficult, but let me offer you a moment of honesty: despite being on my high horse about how great my career has gone, I'm pretty average in most ways and even embarrass myself from time to time! Despite my shortcomings, the thing that has always served me is a determination and devotion to the dream of being an artist. So despite any inadequacies you feel you may have, if you take best advantage of the ideas in this book, you'll develop the ability to create environments that cry out to your audience, that grab them at that emotional level where art and storytelling live.

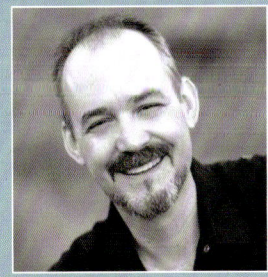

Your career as an artist will be a search for how to give something of real value to your audience, and this is how you do it: give them an emotional experience that they can't get anywhere else, that they can only gain by coming to you. When you can do that, your value as an artist is certain.

Happy painting and best wishes to you!

NATHAN FOWKES
Los Angeles, 2025

FOLLOW NATHAN...

nathanfowkes.com

instagram.com/nathanfowkesart

x.com/nathanfowkesart

youtube.com/@nfowkesart

GLOSSARY

AMBIENT LIGHT

A general non-direct light; the light source is the sky in most cases (but not direct sunlight).

ANALOGOUS COLORS

Colors that sit adjacent to each other on the color wheel and harmonize well. For example, yellow, orange, and red are analogous colors.

BIOME

A type of geographic region that has a distinct ecosystem and climate. Desert, tundra, and tropical rainforest are different biomes.

CAST SHADOWS

A hard-edged shadow created by an object blocking the light source from reaching another surface.

CAUSTIC LIGHTING

The distinctive lighting pattern created by light passing through a transparent material such as water.

COLOR KEY

Small, rough color sketches that are part of the preliminary design of an animated scene.

COMP

A concept sketch that is still rough but suitable for showing to clients. Derived from the now-obsolete term 'comprehensive sketch'.

COMPLEMENTARY COLORS

Colors that sit opposite each other on the color wheel and create striking contrast. Red and green are a classic complementary pairing.

CONTRAST

The quality of difference between elements, which can be used to create interest and focus in an image. For example, an area with strong difference between light and dark has high contrast that draws our attention.

GRAYSCALE

A palette consisting only of black, white, and gray tones, or an image using such a palette.

HUE

The general 'family' to which a color belongs. Sky blue and navy are different hues of blue.

LOCAL COLOR

The color of an object regardless of lighting. The local color of a blue shirt is blue; it may appear very different under red lighting, but its local color is still blue.

PERSPECTIVE

In drawing, this is the quality of three-dimensional space and depth in a two-dimensional image.

RIM LIGHT

The lit contour that appears around the edges of an object that has a light source behind it.

SATURATION

The concentration and purity of a color. A vivid orange is saturated and its desaturated version would be brown.

VALUE

The quality of a color's lightness or darkness. Black is a very dark value while white is a very bright, light value.

ARTISTS' MASTER SERIES

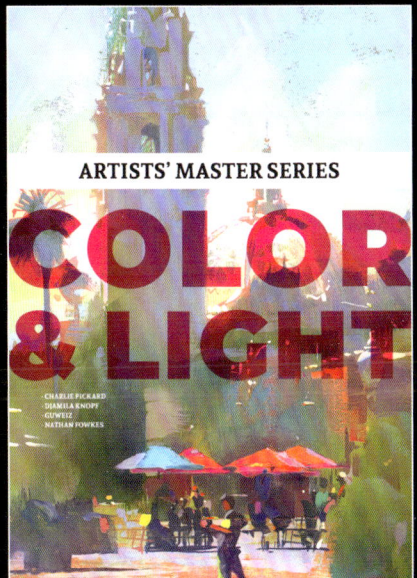

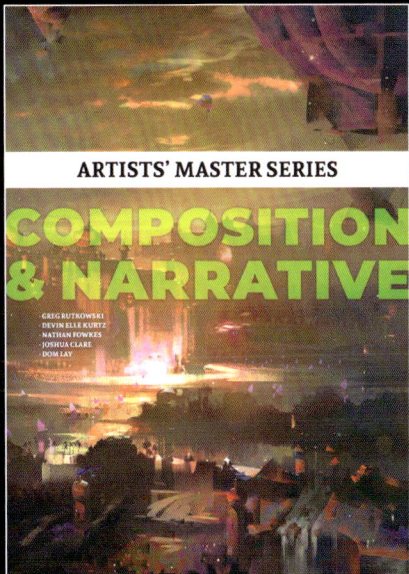

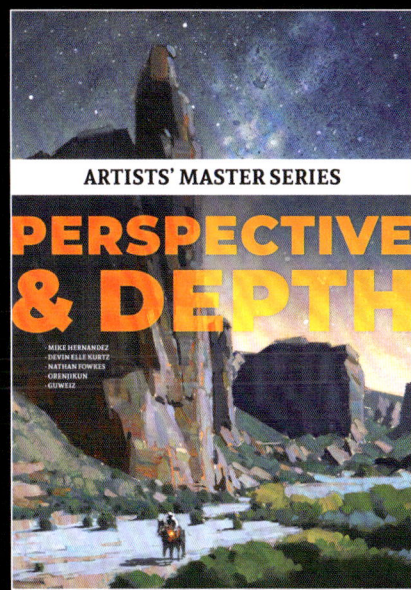

Learn from industry experts in the *Artists' Master Series*, which comprises three in-depth volumes packed with theory, tutorials, and inspiring art. Essential for artists of any skill level or medium, each book thoroughly unpacks art theory and practice, drawing on veteran artists' wealth of knowledge and experience.

The acclaimed first book, *Color & Light*, is a deep dive into these foundational subjects, presented in impressive detail by artists including Guweiz, Nathan Fowkes, and Djamila Knopf.

The second volume, *Composition & Narrative*, explores the mathematical rules and storytelling power of composition, featuring Greg Rutkowski, Devin Elle Kurtz, Joshua Clare, and more.

Perspective & Depth completes this impressive trilogy with insights from Mike Hernandez, Orenjikun, and more, making the *Artists' Master Series* a comprehensive, fully rounded education for any visual artist's shelf.

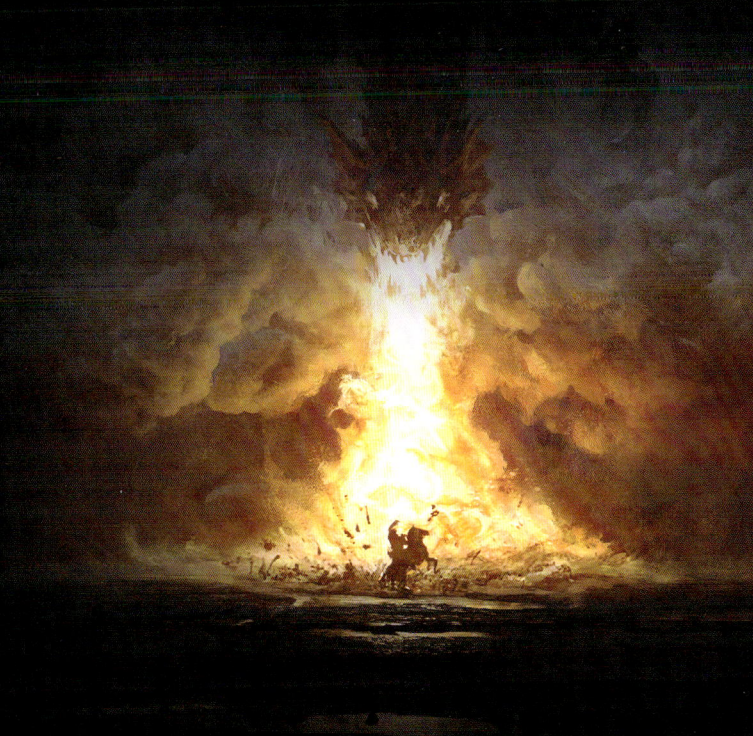

Image © Greg Rutkowski

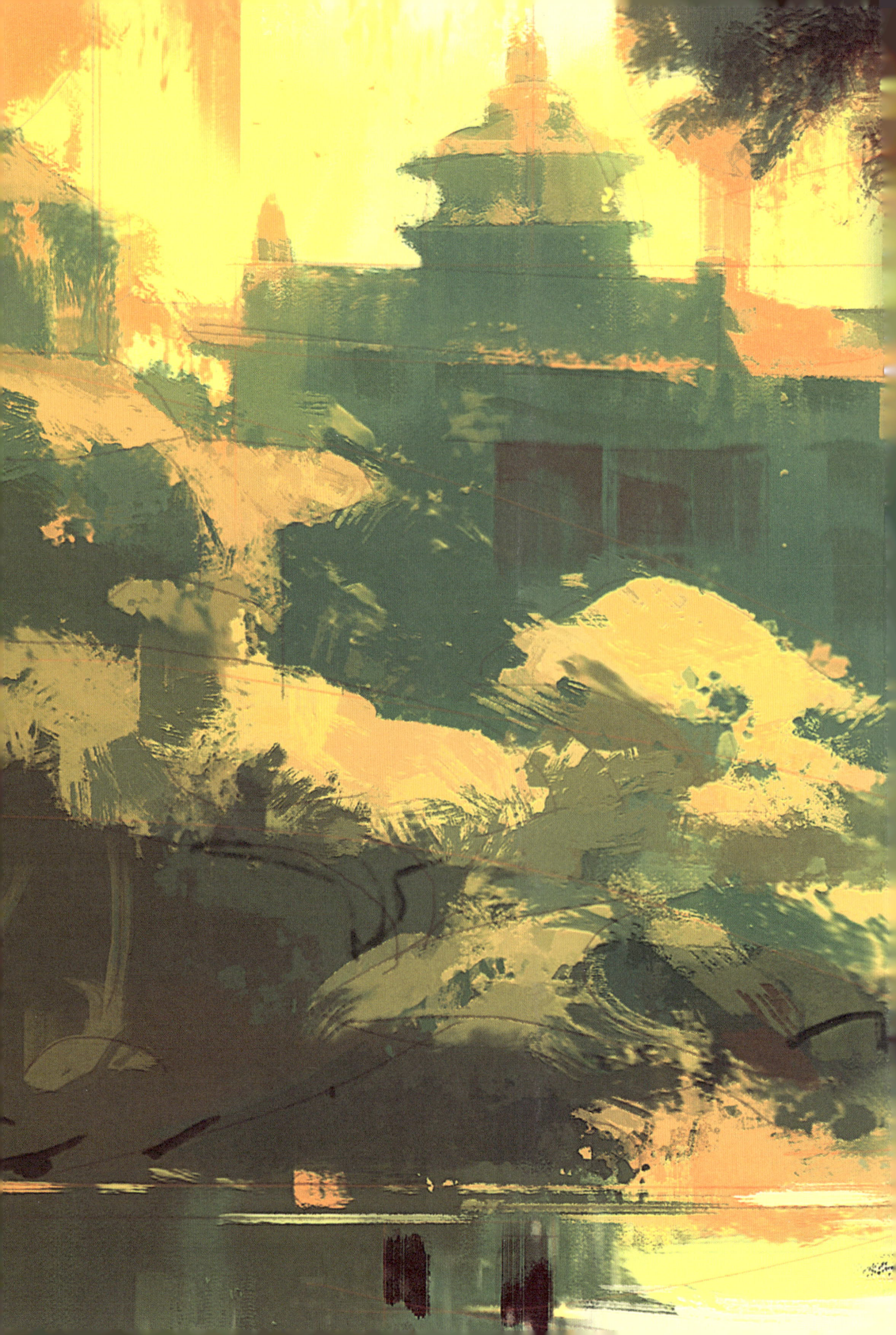